Latin American Women and Research Contributions to the IT Field

Adriana Peña Pérez Negrón
Universidad de Guadalajara, Mexico

Mirna Muñoz
CIMAT – Unidad Zacatecas, Mexico

A volume in the Advances in Human and Social
Aspects of Technology (AHSAT) Book Series

Published in the United States of America by
    IGI Global
    Engineering Science Reference (an imprint of IGI Global)
    701 E. Chocolate Avenue
    Hershey PA, USA 17033
    Tel: 717-533-8845
    Fax: 717-533-8661
    E-mail: cust@igi-global.com
    Web site: http://www.igi-global.com

Copyright © 2021 by IGI Global. All rights reserved. No part of this publication may be reproduced, stored or distributed in any form or by any means, electronic or mechanical, including photocopying, without written permission from the publisher. Product or company names used in this set are for identification purposes only. Inclusion of the names of the products or companies does not indicate a claim of ownership by IGI Global of the trademark or registered trademark.

Library of Congress Cataloging-in-Publication Data

Names: Peña Pérez Negrón, Adriana, 1961- editor. | Muñoz, Mirna, 1978-
  editor.
Title: Latin American women and research contributions to the IT field / Adriana Peña Pérez Negrón
  and Mirna Muñoz, editors.
Description: Hershey : Engineering Science Reference, 2021. | Includes
  bibliographical references and index. | Summary: "This book highlights
  the important role of Latin American women in IT by collecting and
  disseminating their frontier-research contributions"-- Provided by
  publisher.
Identifiers: LCCN 2020047956 (print) | LCCN 2020047957 (ebook) | ISBN
  9781799875529 (hardcover) | ISBN 9781799875536 (paperback) | ISBN
  9781799875543 (ebook)
Subjects: LCSH: Computer science. | Information technology. |
  Computer-assisted instruction. | Artificial intelligence--Industrial
  applications. | Women in computer science--Latin America. | Women
  computer scientists--Latin America--Influence.
Classification: LCC QA76.24 .I37 2021 (print) | LCC QA76.24 (ebook) | DDC
  004.082098--dc23
LC record available at https://lccn.loc.gov/2020047956
LC ebook record available at https://lccn.loc.gov/2020047957

This book is published in the IGI Global book series Advances in Human and Social Aspects of Technology (AHSAT) (ISSN: 2328-1316; eISSN: 2328-1324)

British Cataloguing in Publication Data
A Cataloguing in Publication record for this book is available from the British Library.

All work contributed to this book is new, previously-unpublished material. The views expressed in this book are those of the authors, but not necessarily of the publisher.

For electronic access to this publication, please contact: eresources@igi-global.com.

Advances in Human and Social Aspects of Technology (AHSAT) Book Series

Ashish Dwivedi
The University of Hull, UK

ISSN:2328-1316
EISSN:2328-1324

Mission

In recent years, the societal impact of technology has been noted as we become increasingly more connected and are presented with more digital tools and devices. With the popularity of digital devices such as cell phones and tablets, it is crucial to consider the implications of our digital dependence and the presence of technology in our everyday lives.

The **Advances in Human and Social Aspects of Technology (AHSAT) Book Series** seeks to explore the ways in which society and human beings have been affected by technology and how the technological revolution has changed the way we conduct our lives as well as our behavior. The AHSAT book series aims to publish the most cutting-edge research on human behavior and interaction with technology and the ways in which the digital age is changing society.

Coverage

- ICTs and human empowerment
- Technology Adoption
- Human-Computer Interaction
- Technoself
- Cyber Bullying
- Digital Identity
- Technology and Social Change
- Technology and Freedom of Speech
- Computer-Mediated Communication
- Human Rights and Digitization

IGI Global is currently accepting manuscripts for publication within this series. To submit a proposal for a volume in this series, please contact our Acquisition Editors at Acquisitions@igi-global.com or visit: http://www.igi-global.com/publish/.

The Advances in Human and Social Aspects of Technology (AHSAT) Book Series (ISSN 2328-1316) is published by IGI Global, 701 E. Chocolate Avenue, Hershey, PA 17033-1240, USA, www.igi-global.com. This series is composed of titles available for purchase individually; each title is edited to be contextually exclusive from any other title within the series. For pricing and ordering information please visit http://www.igi-global.com/book-series/advances-human-social-aspects-technology/37145. Postmaster: Send all address changes to above address. Copyright © 2021 IGI Global. All rights, including translation in other languages reserved by the publisher. No part of this series may be reproduced or used in any form or by any means – graphics, electronic, or mechanical, including photocopying, recording, taping, or information and retrieval systems – without written permission from the publisher, except for non commercial, educational use, including classroom teaching purposes. The views expressed in this series are those of the authors, but not necessarily of IGI Global.

Titles in this Series

For a list of additional titles in this series, please visit:
http://www.igi-global.com/book-series/advances-human-social-aspects-technology/37145

701 East Chocolate Avenue, Hershey, PA 17033, USA
Tel: 717-533-8845 x100 • Fax: 717-533-8661
E-Mail: cust@igi-global.com • www.igi-global.com

To my beloved grandmothers Luz María and Jovita, powerful, exemplary, and extraordinary women.
Adriana Peña Pérez Negrón
To Ari who has been the motor that move my live, Jez for being my better half on this path, and my family for all their love.
Mirna Muñoz

Editorial Advisory Board

Omar Salvador Gómez Gómez, *Escuela Superior Politecnica de Chimborazo, Ecuador*
Jezreel Mejía Miranda, *Centro de Investigación en Matemáticas, A.C. Unidad Zacatecas, Mexico*
Marco Antonio Pérez Cisneros, *Universidad de Guadalajara, CUCEI, Mexico*

Table of Contents

Detailed Table of Contents

Chapter 1

Alicia Mon, Universidad Nacional de La Matanza, Argentina

This chapter addresses the inclusion of women in the field of information technology from a perspective that promotes the creation of interdisciplinary spaces, making visible the knowledge inherent to the different professions capable of adding value to technological development. The model presented here was created to evaluate the level of technological development that will allow the determining of the components needed for the transformation towards Industry 4.0, from which you can determine the knowledge necessary for the development of products in their real context of use. Areas such as data science, virtual reality, or human-computer interaction design techniques, models, and/or tools for the construction of solutions that do not require strictly engineering-based knowledge. This chapter proposes a journey towards the development and adoption of technologies in the industry, which requires the inclusion of interdisciplinary knowledge, hence giving new meaning to the role of women in technological development.

Chapter 2

Vianca Vega-Zepeda, Universidad Católica del Norte, Chile

The chapter presents some experiences carried out in Computer Sciences Department of the Universidad Católica del Norte (Chile) related to the development of technological products at the service of people with disabilities. Since 2006, the author has been working with institutions made up of people with disabilities in co-creating solutions to problems that affect their independence and inclusion in different areas. Products have been created for the blind, deaf, and children belonging to autism spectrum disorder. The work teams of each project have been made up of the author of this chapter together with students from Computer Science and the Master's Program in Computer Engineering. Results have been satisfactory. The challenge is to achieve an effective universal design, which should include, from the early stages of each project, not only typical end users, but also those who present conditions that require special considerations to access the technology.

Chapter 3

Sandra Sanchez-Gordon, Escuela Politécnica Nacional, Ecuador

The purpose of this chapter is to present a seven-year journey to understand the barriers that people face when interacting with e-learning and e-health online platforms and to come up with software engineering solutions to make these platforms more inclusive. This chapter per the author presents a set of contributions intended to serve as steppingstones to future research efforts. These contributions include a literature review about accessibility of e-learning platforms; the accessibility audit of e-learning and e-health platforms; the identification of accessibility requirements; the design of architectures, process, and models to improve accessibility; and the definition of a life cycle for the management of accessible online courses. In this context, this chapter relate the evolution of the research process followed and summarize the results obtained so far.

Chapter 4

Lilia Esther Muñoz, Universidad Tecnológica de Panamá, Panama
Itza Morales, Universidad Tecnológica de Panamá, Panama

The different levels that comprise education seek to adapt techniques, practices, models, and strategies to complement teaching and learning generating knowledge in students; thus, in its different fields, it provides the basis for technology to develop software applications to assist with teaching and learning practices. Consequently, education undergoes rapid changes that influence improvement through the use of some of the tools such as robotics and augmented reality which contribute to improving learning scenarios in students, allowing them to develop their metacognitive skills using technological environments designed to educate and be a medium in the educational process. Therefore, this topic addresses the following study based in the completion of two projects aimed at elementary school students in fundamental subjects, allowing them to become familiar with technology as a means of learning.

Chapter 5

Janneth Chicaiza, Universidad Técnica Particular de Loja, Ecuador

In recent years, the processes of training, teaching, and online learning have become more widespread. In this context, open education has the role of empowering people to meet their learning goals. Aligned with this vision, educational institutions are offering open access to their educational resources. However, content is delivering from different platforms by making a challenging task for users to find accurate information. To face this issue, the academic community is adopting Semantic Web and Linked Data for publishing and sharing data. In this chapter, the author presents the main findings in this area. From a technological point of view, the contribution focuses on the main stages of the linked data publishing cycle. Also, from the perspective of the application domain, the author explains the research's contribution regarding three dimensions of Open Education. This chapter ends with some thoughts regarding the author's research path, her remaining tasks, and future trends.

Chapter 6

Carolina Zambrano-Matamala, Universidad de Concepción, Chile
Angélica Urrutia, Universidad Catolica del Maule, Chile

Currently, educational organizations have a large amount of local information from their academic processes, curricular management processes, diagnostic processes of university admission, among others. Also, educational organizations have access to large external databases with standardized test information that students have taken. In this sense, the data warehouse (DW) is presented as a technology that makes it possible to integrate educational information because it provides for the storage of large amounts of information that come from different sources, in a multidimensionally structured format for historical analysis. In this chapter, the authors present one example of DW applied to the field of education using fuzzy logic. A fuzzy DW will be defined as "a DW that allows storing and operating fuzzy measures, fuzzy relationships between levels and fuzzy levels." This chapter ends with a critical discussion of the advances and possibilities of technologies such as the DW applied to the field of education.

Chapter 7

Gloria Piedad Gasca-Hurtado, Universidad de Medellín, Colombia
María Clara Gómez-Álvarez, Universidad de Medellín, Colombia
Bell Manrique Losada, Universidad de Medellín, Colombia

The last decade has increased the demand of software products in several economy sectors; therefore, the need to train people in software engineering is growing. Software engineering, as a discipline, requires developing in engineers technical and social/soft competencies. For all the above, we have been working on the incorporation of new strategies in software engineering education, seeking that students build up software products aligned with organizations business processes. The core of most of such educational strategies is the 'game' constitutes a dynamic element that changes the ways of interaction and support in the learning processes. The authors present a set of approaches centered on innovation and creativity in which they have made significant contributions along the 10 last years, from the following work branches: 1) methodological, comprising methodologies, methods, techniques, and strategies; 2) application, presenting proposals oriented to games; and 3) support, including guidelines and instruments to evaluate and help in classroom practice.

Chapter 8

Beatriz Marín, Universidad Diego Portales, Chile & Universidad Politécnica de Valencia,
Spain

Software engineering courses traditionally mix theoretical aspects with practical ones that are later used in the development of projects. Teaching software engineering courses is not easy because in many cases the students lack motivation to exercise the topics prior to project development. This chapter presents the application of gamification on some topics of a software engineering course to engage students and increase their motivation. The authors argue that with the proper motivation, the students can better exercise the topics and obtain stronger knowledge. The authors have created five games to help in the learning process of the software engineering course. The games are related to risk management, BPMN modeling, Scrum process, design and inspection of class diagrams, and COSMIC functional size measurement.

Gamification has been applied during four years in the software engineering course, resulting in an improved learning experience for the students. Finally, lessons learned are presented and discussed.

Chapter 9

Software has become the core of organizations in different domains because the capacity of their products, systems, and services have an increasing dependence on software. This fact highlights the research challenges to be covered by computer science, especially in the software engineering (SE) area. On the one way, SE is in charge of covering all the aspects related to the software development process from the early stages of software development until its maintenance and therefore is closely related to the software quality. On the other hand, SE is in charge of providing engineers able to provide technological-base solutions to solve industrial problems. This chapter provides a research work path focused on helping software development organizations to change to a continuous software improvement culture impacting both their software development process highlighting the human factor training needs. Results show that the implementation of best practices could be easily implemented if adequate support is provided.

Chapter 10

What is software architecture? A clear and simple definition is that software architecture is about making important design decisions that you want to get right early in the development of a software system because, in the future, they are costly to change. Being a good software architect is not easy. It requires not only a deep technical competency from practicing software architecture design in industry, but also an excellent understanding of the theoretical foundations of software architecture are gained from doing software architecture research. This chapter describes some significant research, development, and education activities that the author has performed during her professional trajectory path to develop knowledge, skills, and experiences around this topic.

Chapter 11

Given the importance of team quality in the success of a project, this chapter presents a summary of the results obtained in 10 years of work, dedicated to the study and development of models and tools for the formation of project teams, from identifying the diversity of factors that can be taken into account in different contexts. The main characteristics of a model and versions of a configurable tool that support the model are described, which facilitates its application in different contexts and allows experimenting with different algorithms and solution methods to identify those that offer the best results.

Chapter 12

Software engineering (SE) is a human-intensive activity where human factors play a fundamental role. As such, SE is an inherently sociotechnical endeavor on which different social and technical aspects are involved. In fact, it is recognized that successful SE not only depends on technical or process issues, but also it is influenced by human factors. They have been proved to have impact on software process and their study is a growing research field. The summary presented in this chapter highlights the results obtained in a five-year effort research aiming at understanding the role that human factors play in SE. As a result, a holistic view of human factors on software process is given.

Nonverbal interaction includes most of what we do; the interaction resulted from other means than words or their meaning. In computer-mediated interaction, the richness of face-to-face interaction has not been completely achieved. However, multiuser virtual reality, a computer-generated environment that allows users to share virtual spaces and virtual objects through their graphic representation, is a highly visual technology in which nonverbal interaction is better supported when compared with other media. Still, like in any technology media, interaction is accomplished distinctively due to technical and design issues. In collaborative virtual reality, the analysis of nonverbal interaction represents a helpful mechanism to support feedback in teaching or training scenarios, to understand collaborative behavior, or to improve this technology. This chapter discussed the characteristics of nonverbal interaction in virtual reality, presenting advances in the automatic interpretation of the users' nonverbal interaction while a spatial task is collaboratively executed.

Chapter 14

Currently, virtual reality (VR) is a computer technology that is growing in terms of developments and discoveries. Virtual reality has been introduced in different areas due to the growing interest it has caused in people. The development of applications with virtual reality is increasingly varied, covering activities, tasks, or processes of everyday life in the fields of industry, education, medicine, tourism, art, entertainment, design, and modeling of objects, among others. This chapter will focus on describing the latest advances and developments in virtual reality within the scope of representing reality in the process of locating objects. With the support of virtual environments and intelligent virtual agents, the author has managed to develop a computational model that generates indications in natural language, for the location of objects considering spatial and cognitive aspects of the users.

Technology is currently a crucial benchmark in any application area. In general, society is immersed in the era of digitalization; therefore, incorporating digital technology in different application areas has been more accessible. Nowadays, claiming that adopting artificial intelligence systems in any area is already an emerging need. In this chapter, several artificial intelligence techniques are presented, as well as algorithms and tools that have been used to provide a variety of solutions such as artificial neural networks, convolutional neural networks architecture, AI models, machine learning, deep learning, and bio-inspired algorithms focused mainly on ant colony optimization, response threshold models, and stochastic learning automata. Likewise, the main applications that use AI techniques are described, and the main trends in this discipline are mentioned. This chapter ends with a critical discussion of artificial intelligence advances.

Chapter 16

Smart cities have been proposed as information technology strategies to generate solutions for the benefit of large cities to improve their quality of life, through phenomena identification tools that use artificial intelligence. Some work has been aimed at developing the infrastructure for monitoring events and the Internet of things, others merely on data analytics without an application system context. This work cites various investigations on data science processes of the smart cities and reports some of its works whose main topics are planning for the start of a smart city, the framework for the analysis of smart cities, and smart cities big data algorithms for sensors location. In these cases, the experiences in these cases are described as well as the trend towards a new process with the form of monitoring-analysis-evaluation-found pattern-driving object-decision-making and the future of smart cities is finally discussed.

This chapter is a case study of the dissemination of railway engineering research in Latin America developed by a railway engineering research group. The leader of the group is a female researcher. The authors aim to inspire to other women researchers in Latin American and Caribbean (LAC) countries who are trying to develop research in IT areas, many times facing serious difficulties, incomprehension, and great challenges. This chapter is divided in set sections like introduction, background, development of railway engineering research. This third section is divided into subsections like timetable planning and trains control, characterization of Panama metro line 1, dwelling times, fuzzy logic, artificial intelligence, social-economics railway externalities, and environmental railway externalities. The fourth section presents the results of the relationship between research activity and teaching of railway engineering obtained in this case study. Finally, the authors present a brief vision about future and emerging regional trends about railway engineering projects.

Foreword

Information Technology, in relatively few years, has changed the way of life of humanity. We communicate in a very varied and instantaneous way, we have almost unlimited access to information and with one click we enjoy endless services. This race does not end. We are promised vehicles that move alone, robots to take care of us, and even trips to the moon. This boom is being achieved thanks to the great investment in research and technology development of countries that seek their primacy in the world. Many technological developments, such as the Internet itself, which are widely used today, had their origins in man-made military projects. Perhaps this is one of the reasons why so few women have stood out as IT researchers or innovators.

In recent years a great worldwide movement has been born to invite women to study IT careers and postgraduate degrees. Its impact will be known in a few years. Women, by our nature, have a sensitivity to social problems and this should be reflected in future IT developments.

Meanwhile, I am very pleased to meet in this book the women researchers who are leading the way in Latin America and the Caribbean and they are confirming my hypothesis of worrying more about solving social problems.

The first important topic you will find in this book is the problem of inclusion. Starting with the women's inclusion in technological development from not strictly engineering areas like Data Science, Virtual Reality, or Human-Computer Interaction to increase interdisciplinary knowledge. Another major inclusion issue is the development of technological products for people with disabilities to help them regain their independence and inclusion in social life. People who do not have much experience in the use of technology can also have many problems in accessing, for example, educational or health online platforms. So investigating the barriers that people have can lead to proposing better software engineering solutions to make these platforms more inclusive.

The second important topic is education. No one has doubts about the importance of incorporating IT into the learning process. In this book, you will find women contributions to developing software applications, incorporating robotics, augmented reality, or games to assist the teaching and learning practices. An interesting Open Education proposal to empower people to meet their learning goals is presented as well as the Data Warehouse technology application to integrate educational information, using fuzzy logic, which can help to make managerial decisions in Education. Also, the application of gamification on some Software Engineering course topics to engage students and increase their motivation is discussed.

Software Engineering research topics also include some social elements. How human factor training needs can help software development organizations to change to a continuous software improvement culture. Another study of development models and tools is trying to identify the diversity of factors for the formation of project teams. Also, some significant research, development, and education activities to develop personal knowledge, skills, and experiences around the Software Architecture are reported, as well as the results obtained in five-year effort research aiming at understanding the role that human factors play in Software Engineering.

In this book, you will also find research summaries that include new trends in IT. For example, discussion about the characteristics of nonverbal interaction in virtual reality, presenting advances in the automatic interpretation of the users' nonverbal interaction while a spatial task is collaboratively executed. Also, you will find the latest advances and developments in Virtual Reality to develop a computational model that generates indications in natural language, for the location of objects considering spatial and cognitive aspects of the users.

As well as several artificial intelligence techniques focused mainly on ant colony optimization, response threshold models, and stochastic learning automata, or the framework for the analysis of Smart Cities and Smart Cities Big Data algorithms for sensors location. Finally, you will find a case study of the dissemination of railway engineering research in Latin America developed by a railway engineering research group leaded by a woman.

This book is an important testimonial to the IT research carried out in recent years by the women of the Latin American and Caribbean countries. New generations of women can learn not only about their research topics but also about the obstacles and challenges they had to face. It is a very interesting source of knowledge and inspiration for female researchers of the future. And for men too :)

Hanna Oktaba
Universidad Nacional Autónoma de México, Mexico

Hanna Oktaba *was born in Warsaw, Poland in 1951. Doctor in Computer Science from the University of Warsaw. She directed the MoProSoft project, which was published as the MNX-I-059-NYCE standard in 2005. Between 2006 and 2015, she was the representative of Mexico at WG 24 of ISO JTC1 / SC7 for the creation of the ISO / IEC 29110 standard for Very Small Entities based on MoProSoft. She is a full-time professor at the National Autonomous University of Mexico (UNAM), where she is the leader of the Kuali-Kaans research group.*

Preface

The role of women in society is constantly changing; day by day more women enter new different productive areas. However, the gap gender in Engineering and Science is a well-known and documented phenomenon (Samuel, George, & Samuel, 2018; Seron, et al.,2018; Ramachandran, Ramanathan, & Khabou, 2020). Unfortunately, the women underrepresentation in these areas conveys an adverse impact in the society, in cultural, academic, and industry fields. It has consequences such as the underutilization of human capital, the significant loss of diversity and variety of experiences, and different points of view vital for this fields (Ramachandran, Ramanathan, & Khabou, 2020; Samuel, George, & Samuel, 2018; Guzman et al., 2020).

Furthermore, women with STEM (Science, Technology, Engineering, and Mathematics) degrees are less likely to work in a STEM occupation (Ramachandran, Ramanathan, & Khabou, 2020), and they are more likely to be employed in engineering subfields more clearly integrating social skills, and they also earn significantly less (Cec, 2013). The women's participation in STEM fields decreases as the degree of specialization in academia or as the job level in the industry increases (Ramachandran, Ramanathan, & Khabou, 2020). Despite the wide acknowledgment about the vast benefits of incorporating women in the STEM fields, the gap persists (Samuel, George, & Samuel, 2018: Seron et al., 2018).

Some factors have been pointed out as closely related with the gender gap such as misconceptions of what is an engineer and what she does, fewer technical problem-solving opportunities for women than for men in the first student grades, and lack of confidence (Ramachandran, Ramanathan, & Khabou, 2020). It seems that what persons perceive about their own abilities is an important factor in the choice of certain behaviors or activities (Bandura, 1977). Also, the lack of awareness about certain careers, gender stereotyping, and less family-friendly support for them to study STEM fields, along with the lack of role models (Ramachandran, Ramanathan, & Khabou, 2020). On top, engineer women recognize and acknowledge their marginalization, but according to Seron et al., (2018) their main response is to adopt the norms and expectations, with the consequence of reducing their visibility contributing to maintain the status quo.

These facts apply in IT related majors such as computer science, computer engineering, and information systems (Guzman et al., 2020). The workforce demand in IT outpaces the offer, as a result increasing diversity in IT must be a priority (Smith & Gayles 2018).

In Latin America, even when women have almost half of the Ph.D. degrees and they are also almost half of the researchers, their contribution to science is not always as recognized as it should. Likewise, in the technology industry, the women participation is less than 20%, and it is concentrated in other areas and not in production or high management occupations (García-Holgado, Camacho Díaz, A., & García-Peñalvo, F. J., 2019).

With this book we want to do our bit, contributing to role models and visibility. This book highlights the important role of Latin American women in IT by collecting and disseminating their frontier-research contributions; their research work is expected to encourage other young women to get involved in the IT domain.

ORGANIZATION OF THE BOOK

Twenty-four female authors from eight Latin American and Caribbean countries (i.e. Argentina, Bolivia, Colombia, Chile, Ecuador, México, Panama, and Cuba) joined to present their research paths. Throughout the chapters, women provide a deep analysis of their trajectory path to high quality theoretical and applied relevant research in Computer Science and IT. A brief description of each of the chapters follows:

Chapter 1 addresses the inclusion of women in IT through interdisciplinary spaces.

Chapter 2 gives an experience perspective in the development of technological products for people with disabilities to a universal effective design.

Chapter 3 gives insight into the barriers in e-learning and e-health that people face toward accessibility.

Chapter 4 presents the basis to develop software applications to support teaching and learning practices.

Chapter 5 proposes Semantic Web and Linked Data for Open Education as standardization to share date.

Chapter 6 presents Data Warehouse to deal with a large amount of information in educational organizations.

Chapter 7 aims to incorporate new strategies for Software Engineering education including technical and social skills based on games.

Chapter 8 presents strategies to gamify Software Engineering education in the areas of risk management, BPMN modeling, Scrum process, design and inspection of class diagrams, and COSMIC functional size measurement.

Chapter 9 is regarding research in the application of Software Engineering in the software development industry highlighting the human factor training.

Chapter 10 establishes the foundations for software architecture and presents research in development and education on this topic.

Chapter 11 presents the study of developed models and tools for the formation of project teams in software development.

Chapter 12 presents research on the human factor in software development.

Chapter 13 deals with the automation of understanding nonverbal interaction in Virtual Reality

Chapter 14 presents the automatic generation of instruction for object location in Virtual Reality

Chapter 15 describes the application of Artificial Intelligence with a critical discussion on advances in this topic

Chapter 16 the important process to support Smart Cities is discussed in this chapter, to monitor and evaluate the Big Data generated from different sources, Data Science is used.

Chapter 17 research on railway control is described in this chapter and its dissemination in LA through a research group.

Adriana Peña Pérez Negrón
Universidad de Guadalajara, Mexico

Mirna Muñoz
CIMAT - Unidad Zacatecas, Mexico

REFERENCES

Bandura, A. (1977). Self-efficacy: Toward a unifying theory of behavioral change. *Psychological Review*, *84*(2), 191–215. doi:10.1037/0033-295X.84.2.191 PMID:847061

Cech, E. A. (2013). The (mis)framing of social justice: Why meritocracy and depoliticization hinder engineers' ability to think about social injustices. In J. Lucena (Ed.), *Engineering education for social justice: Critical explorations and opportunities* (pp. 67–84). Springer. doi:10.1007/978-94-007-6350-0_4

García-Holgado, A., Camacho Díaz, A., & García-Peñalvo, F. J. (2019). La brecha de género en el sector STEM en América Latina: Una propuesta europea. In M. L. Sein-Echaluce Lacleta, Á. Fidalgo-Blanco, & F. J. García-Peñalvo (Eds.), *Proceedings of the V Congreso Internacional sobre Aprendizaje, Innovación y Competitividad. CINAIC 2019, October, Madrid, Spain*, (pp. 704-709). Zaragoza, Spain: Servicio de Publicaciones Universidad de Zaragoza. doi:10.26754/CINAIC.2019.0143

Guzman, I., Berardi, R., Maciel, C., Cabero Tapia, P., Marin-Raventos, G., Rodriguez, N., & Rodriguez, M. (2020). Gender Gap in IT in Latin America. *Proceedings of the AMCIS 2020 Proceedings*. Available at https://aisel.aisnet.org/amcis2020/panels/panels/4

Ramachandran, B., Ramanathan C., & Khabou, M. (2020). *Advancement of Women in Engineering: Past, Present and Future*. American Society for Engineering Education, paper ID 31920.

Samuel, Y., George, J., & Samuel, J. (2018). Beyond STEM, How Can Women Engage Big Data, Analytics, Robotics and Artificial Intelligence? An Exploratory Analysis of Confidence and Educational Factors in the Emerging Technology Waves Influencing the Role of, and Impact Upon, Women. *2018 Annual Proceedings of Northeast Decision Sciences Institute (NEDSI) Conference*.

Seron, C., Silbey, S., Cech, E., & Rubineau, B. (2018). "I am Not a Feminist, but...": Hegemony of a Meritocratic Ideology and the Limits of Critique Among Women in Engineering. *Work and Occupations*, *45*(2), 131–167. doi:10.1177/0730888418759774

Smith, K. N., & Gayles, J. G. (2018). "Girl Power": Gendered academic and workplace experiences of college women in engineering. *Social Sciences*, *7*(1), 11. doi:10.3390ocsci7010011

Chapter 1
From Sociology to ICTs:
A Non–Random Path

Alicia Mon
Universidad Nacional de La Matanza, Argentina

ABSTRACT

This chapter addresses the inclusion of women in the field of information technology from a perspective that promotes the creation of interdisciplinary spaces, making visible the knowledge inherent to the different professions capable of adding value to technological development. The model presented here was created to evaluate the level of technological development that will allow the determining of the components needed for the transformation towards Industry 4.0, from which you can determine the knowledge necessary for the development of products in their real context of use. Areas such as data science, virtual reality, or human-computer interaction design techniques, models, and/or tools for the construction of solutions that do not require strictly engineering-based knowledge. This chapter proposes a journey towards the development and adoption of technologies in the industry, which requires the inclusion of interdisciplinary knowledge, hence giving new meaning to the role of women in technological development.

INTRODUCTION

Technological development requires engineering-based knowledge from hard sciences for the construction of correct and efficient solutions that solve increasingly complex problems. However, the understanding of the problem, the analysis of the users, the evaluation of each real context of use, as well as the knowledge of the specific domains, do not require a set of strictly engineering-based knowledge for the solution.

Techniques, methods or analysis models from the social or humanistic sciences, from various disciplinary fields, prove very useful when analyzing problems from the perspective of the domain and / or the real users of the solutions. In this way, engineering-based thinking can become a limitation of the understanding of the problem by constructing a correct technical solution that is detached from its context.

In this sense, women in Latin American countries, for various cultural reasons, are consolidated as professionals in soft disciplines aimed at the analysis and knowledge of a variety of problems in the

DOI: 10.4018/978-1-7998-7552-9.ch001

Copyright © 2021, IGI Global. Copying or distributing in print or electronic forms without written permission of IGI Global is prohibited.

real world. Multiple authors have addressed the analysis of cultural aspects that, from early childhood to undergraduate training, logical mathematical thinking and solving engineering problems outlines technical thinking, marking a deep division of genders (Dekhane, 2017).

On a world scale, the dominant technological development of recent years has generated an impact in all fields of the socio-productive life of different societies and cultures. Knowledge areas of multiple disciplines are traversed by technological advance in terms of digitalization, massive data generation, virtualization, robotization, artificial intelligence and the connection between objects.

The effect in all the socio-productive areas and sectors of today's societies generates changes in the forms of work and in the habits of life, imposing the cultural logic of technological development. The manufacturing industry is traversed by the insertion of these new technologies, modifying the productivity variables, as well as the generation of value, promoting what is known as the fourth industrial revolution, transforming companies into what is identified as "4.0 Industries" (Mon, 2019).

This concept arises in the second decade of the 2000s in which the production process that has been developed and expanded since then is based on the digital modeling of production processes and on the exchange of data generated in the manufacturing process itself between different machines or equipment.

However, when identifying the specific products that make up the new industry that is emerging, there are few works that explicitly identify the specific components that are developed; and that require characteristics, attributes and specific knowledge in their design, development and implementation in the real context of use, in order to generate the inevitable transformation.

In another sense, knowledge from humanistic disciplines such as sociology, communication sciences, anthropology, psychology or the areas of art and design, provide central knowledge for the development of these products that constitute the engines that drive the evolution of technologies.

In Latin American countries, the dominant cultural aspects exclude women from the possibilities of professional insertion in production areas. When the participation of women in the labor fields related to engineering that develop Information and Communication Technologies (ICTs) is analysed; the gap is even greater. This limitation is historically determined by the training of professionals with engineering-based thinking.

The discussion raised then, resides in that technological development requires a set of multidisciplinary knowledge for the detection of problems, definition of data, construction and analysis of information, among others, that come from different disciplines of knowledge; in the opposite way to classical engineering analysis. That is why the incorporation of knowledge from social disciplines, as well as the way that marks the great participation of women in them, seems to be an unavoidable path for technological development to be effective in each socio-productive environment.

By way of discussion, this chapter presents a model for evaluating ICTs in industry, which makes it possible to calculate an index of technological development and visualize the characteristics of the evolution of the sector towards Industry 4.0. From there, the specific products, the necessary knowledge for said transformation and the role of the professions in Latin America - chosen mainly by women - as the central axis for technological development are analyzed, establishing itself as the engine of development of the productive forces in the region.

BACKGROUND

The worldview of the engineering world is crossed by the dominant thinking of values and masculinity traits. The resolution of physical and material problems in Latin American countries is framed in cultural patterns that segment the production of knowledge and the generation of economic value, not only through the classic division of social classes, but also reinforced by the social segmentation of genders. That limits access to education, generating an effect on the possibilities of innovative jobs linked to technological development in the region. According to UNESCO, in the City of Buenos Aires, in a study carried out on girls between the ages of six and eight, nine out of ten (90%) link engineering with male skills (UNESCO, 2017).

In Argentina, by 2016 almost 2 million university students were registered, of which 57% are made up of women. Of this total number of students, 10% choose engineering careers, of which only 25% are made up of women, which indicates that of the million one hundred thousand female students, only 4% choose engineering careers (SPU, 2020) in a system that guarantees free study for all their careers in all regions of the country.

The compilation made in the publications of experiences of women in Engineering (Giordano, 2018; Giordano, 2020), allows to make visible the work of hundreds of Latin American women to study and practice the profession in various disciplinary fields of engineering. Although, the articles collected in both books denote a great personal effort of the authors, both in their personal lives and in academic or work; in many cases, they reproduce and strengthen the dominant cultural aspects in which the stereotypes of gender, associated with "values" such as strength or courage (Rathmann, 2020).

However, the overall development and the information technology industry has a different impact on the social fabric, resulting more permeable for the insertion of women in multiple areas, as well as in the world of professional practice. In this sense, engineering careers in the field of ICTs represent a slightly higher proportion, although it does not manage to modify the existing relationship in the gender disparity that the rest of the engineering programs manifest.

In Latin American countries, the technology industry is mainly concentrated in the software industry and scarcely in the construction of hardware or infrastructure and communications equipment. The teaching of programming remains the central node on which the strong development of the software industry is based. It is then that Computer Science Engineering, Systems, Computer Science or Electronics, are consolidated as the beginning foundations of an industry that has grown exponentially in recent decades.

Paradoxically, the mass use of technologies in all social spheres constantly requires the incorporation of knowledge from social disciplines that allow understanding users as recipients of products, selecting variables and indicators from the massive data that is analyzed, or manage work teams, among other knowledge. However, within the software industry, the areas of requirements analysis, data analysis, human-computer interaction analysis (HCI), product design, interface, or testing, are treated with the same logic and engineering knowledge requirements.

Understanding HCI as the discipline related to the design, evaluation and implementation of interactive systems for human use, it is possible to approach the body of techniques and methods that focus on people's abilities to use computers, the tasks that are performed with them, the communicative structure that is established and the functional and environmental elements that are part of programming and interface design (Bødker, 2015). HCI techniques can be separated into those focused on knowing and understanding the user to define their real needs and those focused on user feedback on the interface designs defined by the analyst. HCI then becomes the driving force behind technological transformation in the different domains of the real world to the extent that current makers are potential users of the systems that are being developed. The software industry generates products to be used by real human users (Mon, 2019).

Scientific references related to human-computer interaction usually mention, suggest and recommend the formation of development teams of software made up of people from various disciplines or multidisciplinary teams. Putting together teams with this knowledge structure is determinant in the development of software complimenting the role of the engineer or the programmer to develop software products that represent the needs of users and their context to offer more pleasant systems, that are efficient and easy to use (Granollers, 2005). However, as the author points out, *in the industrial field, it is observed that the development teams of the companies that are dedicated to advising on the usability in interactive systems are only made up of people from the field of programming and/or of graphic design. The belief of these professionals is evident, with foundations to carry out all of the work, without the need to incorporate the true experts in each area of knowledge, which shows a deficiency in the composition of the teams of multidisciplinary development* (Granollers, 2004).

Social disciplines, especially sociology and anthropology, provide conceptual tools for analysis on human behavior, on social behaviors, on the linguistic structures of interaction and communication between subjects and on individual practices and actions in a social group. In line with the dominant cultural patterns, engineering in the field of ICT is assumed to be dominant in the knowledge required by the different domains and in the representation of various real-world problems. It is paradigmatic to highlight Caballero's vision according to whom *the HCI techniques can be applied by the same developers and not necessarily by one skilled in HCI. The participation of end users when applying the techniques in an agile environment is not necessarily mandatory, however, their participation or that of representative users is valued* (Caballero, 2017).

Following this logic of thought, engineering rationality is imposed as knowledge for problem solving, but centrally as a discipline capable of addressing all types of domain, which includes the determining factors of humans in the performance of tasks, aspects related to accessibility and knowledge of the user experience, variables and sensitive data to be analyzed, down to the graphic details of the interfaces. It is unavoidable to highlight how this dominant logic of engineering thought displaces the introduction of knowledge from the social sciences.

This situation of the non-integration of multidisciplinary knowledge is strengthened as technological development is analyzed in different social spheres and even more so when focusing on the productive sectors of Latin American societies. In this sense, industrial transformation processes, with collaborative work strategies among workers in all productive organizations; constitute a necessary condition to improve productivity levels.

The impact generated by ICTs is manifested in production systems by linking the physical world through devices, materials, products, equipment, facilities and communications with the digital world, expressed through collaborative systems and interconnected software products with an infinity of devices to promote innovation in the industry (Uriarte, 2018). The different parts of the production process not only adopt intelligent functions, but also communicate autonomously between them, where knowledge management is part of the production systems. This transformation is what is identified as Industry 4.0, recognized as the fourth industrial revolution (Berger, 2016).

Although this transformation is oriented to the use of specific technologies, the combination of human capacity with the ease that allows the use of machines and in general of technological elements is inherent, requiring a plurality of skills from the professionals who contribute to the use of information, specialized machines, customer service and experience to generate immediate solutions in all aspects (Ningenia, 2016).

Industry 4.0 requires the horizontal integration of collaborative networks (Stezano, 2017) in which processes are directed by workers who are in communication with multiple areas of the plant, facilitating other processes such as routes, flows of goods, delivery and distribution, reducing costs while the complexity of products and processes increases driven by the set of technologies that are implemented (MINCyT 2015).

Dichotomously, Industry 4.0 requires professionals to respond with multiple and complex tasks to adapt to the needs of the industry, but also, according to Stezano, it opens the option to new professions that are framed in specific tasks as content creators, application creators or software specialists (Stezano, 2017).

In this opening, the professional profiles chosen mainly by Latin American women, constitute a channel to enable the incorporation of knowledge and know-how with a gender-focused and inclusive perspective, enabling a multidisciplinary vision that promotes the development of technology in the industry, focusing the analysis in the collective processes that are configured within a company and the needs of the real users that enhance the development of the productive forces as a whole.

In order to detect the central aspects of technological development towards Industry 4.0, the following section presents a model which was created to evaluate the level of insertion of ICTs, establish the level of technological development by company and branch of industrial activity, as well as for determining the necessary knowledge for the adoption of products that promote inclusive development with a strong predominance of women.

ICT´s EVALUATION FOR INDUSTRY 4.0

As technology designs new solutions, their application requires the implementation of products in a trilogy of the ICT taxonomy composed of software, hardware and infrastructure that accompany the benefits as a whole. An elementary factor resides in the adequate analysis of the interaction between human beings and the technologies that must operate.

Identifying the knowledge required for technological integration is necessary in order to be able to detect the set of concrete and specific products that are currently being developed and that provide various functionalities in multiple contexts. To this end, a model has been designed that allows detecting the technologies implemented within the manufacturing industry, in order to assess the degree of updating and calculate an index that determines the level of technological development for each industry and branch of activity in particular (Del Giorgio, 2019B).

The model has been developed based on a structure that divides ICTs into 3 types of products that must be implemented, interconnected and integrated with each other to consider them operational (Mon, 2019). The design and development of products in this trilogy requires increasingly broad and multidisciplinary knowledge that enables the operation of technical complexity with the capabilities of real human operators. Thus, Table 1 presents the first typology of ICTs that structures the model, from which the various products can be identified.

Software products constitute the intangible, the logical component of the computer. It refers to programs, information systems, applications, simulators, and operating systems, among other options.

Table 1. ICTs taxonomy

	Software
ICTs	Hardware / Equipment
	Communications / Infrastructure

Source: Author's own creation

Products that belong to the type of Hardware or Equipment refer to the physical part of a computer. It is composed of everything that can be touched, such as keyboards, monitors, printers, cables, electronic cards, hard drives, memories, robots, sensors, among others.

Products that are identified as Communications or Infrastructure type make up the set of elements on which the different services are based and can communicate with each other. It is made up of products such as cameras, application servers, and network elements such as Routers or Firewalls, among others.

According to this trilogy, the model proposes for each group different types and subtypes of specific products in their definitive application when fulfilling a precise function. Therefore, as new ICT products are developed that provide better benefits in any of the 3 types, the other components of the different typologies require the development of products that accompany the benefits.

The capabilities of each product can only be exploited in integration and interconnection with products of the other types and provide a higher level of technological development in the different attributes of functionality, efficiency, security, etc.

As the organizing axis of the functionality of ICT products, the structure of the model created crosses this typology with 7 basic functional areas of any manufacturing industry, within which each specific product fulfils particular functions linked to the area in which it is implemented and interconnected with others.

The generic functional areas identified are:

- **Logistics:** Includes logistic activities.
- **Production:** Includes operations activities.
- **Sales:** Includes marketing, sales and service activities.
- **Management:** Includes decision-making activities about the company in general and incorporates infrastructure support activities and human resource management.
- **Accounting and Finance:** Includes economic, accounting and financial management activities.
- **Engineering:** Includes product design, process design and technology development activities.
- **Purchases:** Includes purchasing and acquisitions activities.

The structure of the model links the ICT products with any of these seven functions in an industrial manufacturing organization type. That is to say, the products that are implemented in a company are created to meet a particular need.

The model contains an assessment of each technological product according to the time it has taken since its creation and is available in the market or by the degree of innovation generated by its implementation and application. The valuation of each product, according to the function it performs, makes it possible to calculate an index of technological development from the sum of the weighting of all the products that a company has implemented.

Table 2. Cross between products software and funcional areas

Funcional Areas® / ICTs⁻		Management	Finnance and Accounting	Engineering	Purchases	Logistics	Production	Sales
SOFTWARE	WEB Technologies - WEB page (External Site)	1						1
	WEB Technologies - WEB page (Internall Site)	1	1	1	1	1	1	1
	WEB Technologies - Extranet (Transactional)				5	5		5
	WEB Technologies - online Advertising	5						5
	Collaborative Systems - Video Conference	10		10				10
	Collaborative Systems - IP Telephony	5	5	5	5	5	5	5
	Collaborative Systems - Instant Messaging	1	1	1	1	1	1	1
	Collaborative Systems - Email	1	1	1	1	1	1	1
	Collaborative Systems - Social Networks	1						1
	Collaborative Systems - File Synchronization	5	5	5		5	5	5
	Collaborative Systems - Mobile Applications	5	5	5	5	5	5	5
	Office Tools - Word Processor	1	1	1	1	1	1	1
	Office Tools - Spreadsheet	1	1	1	1	1	1	1
	Office Tools - Presentations	1	1	1				1
	Office Tools - Database Manager		5	5	5	5	5	5
	Office Tools - Calendar and Email Manager	1	1	1	1	1	1	1
	Office Tools - PDF File Manager	5	5	5				5
	Office Tools - PDF File Reader	1	1	1	1	1	1	1
	Management Systems - Enterprise Resource Planning	5	5	5	5	5	5	5
	Management Systems - Customer Relationship Management	5	5					5
	Management Systems - Customer Claims Support							5
	Management Systems - Dashboard / Balance Score Card	10						10
	Management Systems - Business Intelligence	10	10	10	10	10	10	10
	Management Systems - Big Data	10	10	10	10	10	10	10
	Management Systems - Machine Learning	10		10			10	
	Management Systems - Energy Control Software			10			10	
	Management Systems - Logistics			5	5	5	5	
	Management Systems - Quality Management Systems	5	5	5	5	5	5	5
	Management Systems - HR Management	5	5					
	Production Control Systems - Programming and Planning			10			10	
	Production Control Systems - Product Data Management			10			10	
	Production Control Systems - Product Quality						5	
	Production Control Systems - Plant Engineering / Maintenance			5			5	
	Production Control Systems - Automation Control			10			10	
	Production Control Systems - SCADA Systems			10			10	
	Production Control Systems - Embedded Systems			10			10	
	Product and Process Desing - Computer Aided Desing			5				
	Product and Process Desing - Computer Aided Manufacturing						10	
	Product and Process Desing - Computer Aided Engineering			10				
	Product and Process Desing - Augmented Reatity			10			10	
	Product and Process Desing - Virtual Reality			10			10	
	Geolocation Systems - Distribution and Logistics					5		
	Geolocation Systems - Advertising							10
	Security Systems - Critical Infraestructure Security	5	5	5	5	5	5	5
	Security Systems - Critical Information Security	5	5	5	5	5	5	5

Source: (Del Giorgio & Mon, 2019)

Following these criteria, a scale with three values is defined. Value 1 (one) being the weighting of the technology that contributes the least in the update criteria, that is, those products that have been on the market the longest are valued with a 1. This weighting of products is called Basic. This is followed by a rating of 5 (five) to assign to each product that takes an average time to create and is available in the market and that does not settle for innovative products. This assessment is identified as Intermediate. Finally, with a weighting of 10 (ten), the most recent development products or those whose implementation has been available on the market for a short time are valued. This weight is identified as Advanced.

This scale according to the weighting for each ICT product results in the following categorization of technological development:

- **Basic:** With value 1
- **Average:** With value 5
- **Advanced:** With value 10

The model allows calculating the technological development index by evaluating each of the ICT

Table 3. Cross between products software and funcional areas

Funcional Areas® / ICTs⁻		Management	Finnance and Accounting	Engineering	Purchases	Logistics	Production	Sales
HARDWARE	Computers - Desktop PCs	1	1	1	1	1	1	1
	Computers - RISC Architectures			5			5	
	Computers - Notebooks	1	1	1	1	1	1	1
	Computers - Tablets	1		1		1	1	1
	Printers - Laser Printers	1	1	1	1	1	1	1
	Printers - 3D Printers			10			10	
	Printers – Scanners	5	5	5	5	5	5	5
	Printers – Plotters			10			10	
	Point of sale POS							5
	Share Disks	10	10	10	10	10	10	10
	Programmable Logic Controllers						5	
	Global Positioning Systems					5		
	RFID Device					5		
	Telephone exchanges - Traditional Telephone exchanges	1	1	1	1	1	1	1
	Telephone exchanges - IP Telephone exchanges	10	10	10	10	10	10	10
	Sensors						10	10
	Robots						10	10

Source: (Del Giorgio & Mon, 2019)

products that is implemented in a company, at its intersection with the areas to fulfil a certain function. For example, a web page as an external site has a rating of 1 (one) because it constitutes a technology

Table 4. Cross between products infrastructure and funcional areas

Funcional Areas® / ICTs⁻		Management	Finnance and Accounting	Engineering	Purchases	Logistics	Production	Sales
INFRASTRUCTURE	Wireles Convergent Networks - Mobile Telephony	1	1	1	1	1	1	1
	Wireles Convergent Networks - Wi-Fi Networks	1	1	1	1	1	1	1
	Wireles Convergent Networks - Bluetooth Networks	5	5	5	5	5	5	5
	Wireles Convergent Networks - Internet of Things Networks			10		10	10	
	Local Server	5	5	5	5	5	5	5
	Cloud Computing	5	5	5	5	5	5	5
	Wired Local Area Networks	1	1	1	1	1	1	1
	IT Security	5	5	5	5	5	5	5
	Internet Connection	1	1	1	1	1	1	1
	Closed Circuit Television					1	1	

Source: (Del Giorgio & Mon, 2019)

Table 5. Amount of totals and sums of values of each valuation

Valuation	Total amount of products	Sum of values	Cumulative sum
Basic (1)	120	120	120
Medium (5)	119	595	715
Advanced (10)	66	660	1375

Source: Author's own creation

that has been in use for a long time in the market, and at its intersection with the processes it fulfils functions for the Management and Sales areas, but not for the Production areas.

The Table 2, 3 and 4 shows the structure of the model that allows calculating the index, in which the ICT products are related to the functional areas. In the rows, each of the ICT products exposed in the first one is displayed, the Software, Hardware and Infrastructure taxonomy, and detailed by each subtype. The columns represent the productive processes of the functional areas in a typical organization dedicated to the production of manufactures in any of the branches, according to the taxonomy presented. Each box in the intersection contains the value assigned to the product (1, 5, or 10). In those crosses that do not contain values, it is given that there is no specific product to fulfil the function in the area of their intersection.

Starting from the weighting of each product in its specific function, the index is obtained with the sum of each of the values. This sum allows to determine a score for a specific company according to the products it has implemented, and a range within which each level of technology is determined.

Given that there are 120 ICT products identified at the intersection with the functional areas and the weighting of this category being 1, then the sum of these elements yields a result of 120 points for the Basic level.

Given that there are 119 ICT products identified at the intersection with the functional areas and the weighting of this category being 5, then the sum of these weighted elements yields a result of 595 points for the Medium level.

Given that there are 66 ICT products identified at the intersection with the functional areas and the weighting of this category being 10, then the sum of these elements yields a result of 660 points for the Advanced level.

The evaluations that arise from the sum of the weighting for the calculation of the index are shown in Table 5, where each level evaluation (Basic, Medium, Advanced) is represented in the column of total amount of products, the sum for each category it is represented in the sum of values column and the accumulated sum between one category and another of a lower level is represented in the cumulative sum column.

Table 6. Range and Level of Adoption of ICTs

Range	Level of Adoption of ICTs
Between 0 y 120	Basic
Between 121 y 715	Medium
Between 716 y 1375	Advanced

Source: Author's own creation

The results of the calculation of the index establish ranges according to the minimum and maximum values of the sums for each category. Thus, the Basic level category of ICTs is defined in a range from 0 to 120 points that represents the maximum value of the sum, the Medium level category of ICTs is defined in a range of 121 to 715 points that represents the maximum value of the accumulated sum, while the Advanced level of ICTs is defined in a range from 716 to 1375 points that represents the maximum value of the accumulated sum.

These results imply that it considers the sum of all the possible ICT products implemented in the different categories, which are not exclusive, or necessarily replaceable as technology evolves. In Table 6, these ranges are shown for each category where the rank column presents the maximum and minimum values of the sum of the weighted values for each category; while the ICT adoption level column shows the level of each category of ICTs.

This result of the model produces an evaluation index with 3 levels of ICT development. The Basic Level that identifies those technologies that have been in use for a long time in the market; the Medium Level that includes the technologies that have been on the market for an average time and the Advanced Level that identifies the latest solutions registered by the market within each of its types. Each of these products fulfils functions in one or more of the functional areas identified by the model. Thus, in the Advanced Level of the index, the specific software products are detected that, integrated with the equip-

Figure 1. ICT Products of Industry 4.0
Source: Author's own creation

ment and infrastructure, are found necessary to generate adequate innovation for the transformation of a manufacturing industry into Industry 4.0 (Mon, 2018).

The model allows calculating the ICT insertion index in a specific company, determining the level of technological development in a set of companies grouped by branch of activity, or in a specific region.

From the identification of the most advanced products, it is possible to determine that not all of them integrate the specific set of products of Industry 4.0. Some are not state-of-the-art, but they are essential for the integration and operation of the other products. Figure 1 shows the particular products that, in their integration, make up the subset of Advanced Level products, but which are identified as specific to industry 4.0, in its 3 typologies.

The development and implementation of this subset of ICT products that allow the transformation of the fourth industrial revolution, require a deep knowledge about the particular characteristics of users in industries, as well as the adoption process necessary for its correct and efficient application in its real context of use.

In the following section, the validation of the index is exposed and a field work carried out as a case study is presented to evaluate the level of technological development of the manufacturing industry in a region of Argentina.

INDEX APPLICATION - CASE STUDY

The exposed index has been validated through an investigative study with experts in technology and industrial organization that confirmed and expanded the types of products defined for the model and the functional areas in a typical industry (Mon et.al., 2018).

Likewise, it was applied as a case study to a group of companies of various branches and size, in an industrial district of the Province of Buenos Aires, in Argentina, and the levels of technological development found were determined.

The validation and the case study has been carried out by an interdisciplinary team, made up of experts in Industrial Engineering, Computer Science, Electronics and Sociology.

To carry out the survey, a set of methodological instruments from the social sciences were created to carry out the field study, evaluate the level of technological development and permanently carry out the systematic analysis on the insertion of ICTs in the industry:

Survey: A structured closed questionnaire was designed, with a set of questions conducive to accurately detecting the ICT products installed in each company and the function it fulfils according to the functional area in which it is used. It was digitalized to be able to do it both in person with a pollster or self-administered via the web.

Key Informant: The profile of the key informant who had to answer the survey was determined, so that within their knowledge they could answer about the products implemented in their company and the functions or detect the expert in the area involved.

Sample: A probabilistic sample was designed with a margin of error of 5%, to carry out the survey on a universe of 4,000 industries located in the district of La Matanza, located in the Buenos Aires suburbs, bordering the city of Buenos Aires.

Survey: A survey was carried out in 40 industries of various branches of branches and sizes, taking as a reference the international classification of economic activities (United Nations, 2012). The first part of the survey was carried out in person with an interviewer, contacting the key informant of each company. The second part was carried out in a self-administered way using digital means, contacting the referents of each company.

Software: Automatic evaluation software was developed, containing the ICT Index that allows calculating the level for each company. The application contains the self-administered Survey, generates the calculation and reports the result in a digital and private way to each user who completes the questionnaire with their company information. A database was created to process the surveys and record the calculation of the index.

Website: A web page was developed, hosted on the server of the University of the research group, from where you can access the index software and obtain the results of the evaluation individually and privately by each company, in addition to the index publications, information about the research group and an explanation and dissemination video (UNLaM, 2019).

Audio Visual: An audio visual video was filmed and edited as a persuasive and explanatory means of the index and evaluation in each company. The script has been written based on the potential users of the index, defined as entrepreneurs or technology managers of a manufacturing industry interested in knowing their level of technology insertion. Focus groups and interviews were carried out in the industries focused on the interest of the users. Likewise, the interviews were conducted by journalists and filmed in collaboration with the University's TV channel. The notes were broadcast on the channel's newscast and the images were used for video editing.

For the survey, all the instruments that were developed were applied.

From the analysis of the survey, it can be observed that 45% of the companies are Micro (up to 15 employees); 25% is made up of Small (up to 60 employees), while in the Medium category, section 1 and section 2 (up to 235 and 655 employees respectively), 25% are located between both categories

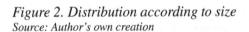

Figure 2. Distribution according to size
Source: Author's own creation

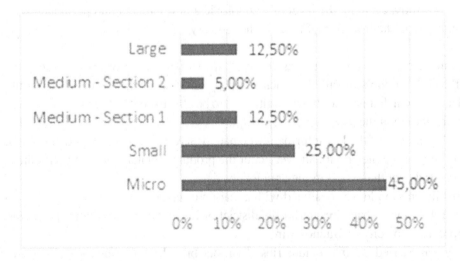

and only 12.5% are placed in the Large company category (more than 655 employees), as can be seen in the Figure 2.

Figure 3. Distribution by score
Source: Author's own creation

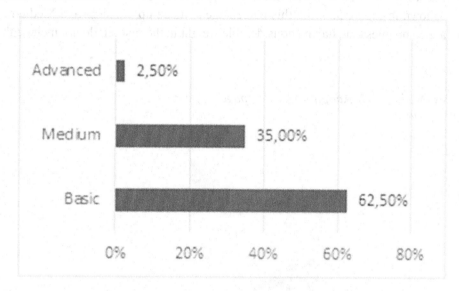

Figure 4. Industries (Basic ICT Adoption Level) by web page
Source: Author's own creation

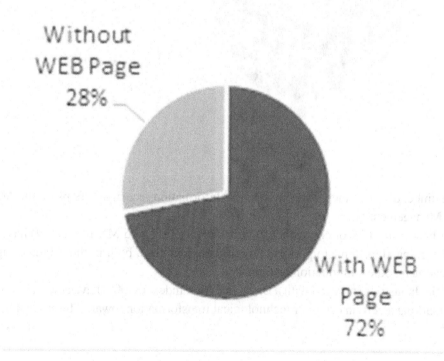

Regarding the application of the index, it can be observed that, of the 40 companies surveyed, 62.5% are in the Basic Level, 35% in the Medium Level and only 2.5% in the Advanced Level, such as shown in Figure 3.

Of the Industries surveyed with a Basic Insertion Index, a significant percentage of them, 28.00% do not have a WEB Page (External Site), as represented in Figure 4.

While, of the industries surveyed with a Medium Insertion index, 14.29% do not have a WEB Page (External Site), as shown in Figure 5, while this percentage is made up of Large and Medium, which implies that there are companies that, having considerable weight in the market, do not include this type of technology.

Figure 5. Industries (Medium ICT Adoption) by web page
Source: Author's own creation

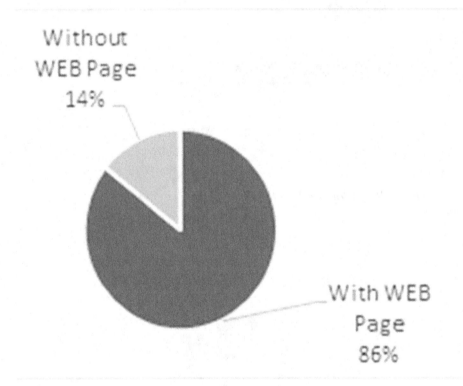

Of the total number of companies, 45% have critical Information security systems for the Accounting and Finance or Management areas.

On the other hand, only 15% of companies (1 Advanced Level and 5 Medium Level) have software with Machine Learning algorithms to perform any of their functions, both in the Engineering area, as well as in Management, Sales, Production or Finance.

However, of the Industries surveyed with a Basic Insertion Index, 60.00% have at least one Advanced Level product, marking a certain drive for technological transformation towards Industry 4.0.

These results represent a sample of the type of analysis that can be performed with the ICT index model created and the survey instruments, to evaluate the level of technological development of the industry in general, for a particular district, by size or branch of industry; as well as for a particular company.

The detection of specific products allows to establish the set of knowledge necessary for product design, for the definition of technology adoption processes, as well as the profiles required by users in the real context of industry use, from in such a way as to promote transformation in a multidisciplinary and coordinated path towards the 4th Industrial Revolution.

KNOWLEDGE NEEDED FOR INDUSTRY 4.0

The identification of specific products allows for the definition of the necessary knowledge for their development. Since the raw material for software development is knowledge, the construction of these products can be analyzed from 2 perspectives. One resides in the approach to the domain of the problem and the other from the formation of the work teams.

In the technological development of the manufacturing industry, the complexity of the domain requires the intersection with the analysis of the concrete and real users who operate the machine tools of production. ICTs replace, at an unprecedented speed, the manual work of operators with complex equipment and systems that increase productivity levels. Physical abilities are replaced by intellectual abilities.

From the perspective of the problem domain, software engineering has developed a set of tools that allow representing problems that are naturally foreign to development teams, but that need to know and analyze them in order to reproduce them in technological environments.

Knowledge profiles to cover problem analysis or user analysis activities require knowledge on each specific domain, but also require expert knowledge on how to interact and analyze human behavior.

This is how social anthropology provides tools and ethnographic techniques that allow an approach to users from the point of view of themselves. The analysis of tasks that involve both the logic of thought and the arrangement of bodies requires knowledge that allows a correct adduction.

The articulation of the language of the users, is possible to be approached from the knowledge of linguistics that they provide; in addition to sociology, anthropology, the sciences of social communication and where the subjects are analyzed in the real social contexts in which they communicate.

Whereas, the behavioral as well as psychological evaluation of users in the exercise of their daily tasks or of their interaction with other subjects; it is possible to be studied by the set of knowledge that psychology contributes in its different theoretical bodies on the behavior of individuals.

With regard to social behavior, sociology includes a series of theoretical and methodological tools that allow the study and analysis of users in their social environments in which they reproduce as social subjects, being able to detect both dominant and emerging processes. In another sense, sociology comprises a set of methodological and statistical knowledge that allows it to define the set of variables and indicators for the analysis of massive data in any domain in which it is applied.

Likewise, knowledge from disciplines such as graphic design, architecture and / or art define core capabilities when designing interfaces with specific users.

A determining area that may require knowledge unrelated to the specific technology is testing. Software products require a testing instance closer to the users or to the domain where knowledge of the problem and the attributes of the users is mandatory over the programming logic.

Usually, the role of the tester fulfils the tasks of verifying compliance with functional and non-functional requirements, analyzing and locating possible errors. The validity of automatic testing tools speed up the detection of errors in the code, leaving more space for functional validation. However, in the software industry, the role of the tester is usually covered by programmers who are subjectively closer to the code and not to the functional correctness of the application from the perspective of the real user.

Engineering-based thinking assumes as valid that it will be able to detect functional programming or design errors in the validation stage, minimizing the necessary contribution from other disciplines in the analysis of users to detect them in their various application possibilities.

Regarding the formation of work teams, the management of software projects requires knowledge and skills on team coordination, human resource management, administration elements, cost estimation and planning. Agile methodologies so deeply anchored in the management of development teams determine agility and good communication skills in management.

The skills are then focused on resource management capacities and coordination of activities, which form knowledge from soft disciplines. It is here as well, engineering-based thinking, assumes as valid that it will be able to conform agile teams with the necessary technological knowledge, minimizing the benefits of the contribution of other disciplines in the coordination and integration of different profiles to development teams.

These types of skills and knowledge are not engineering-based, on the contrary, they come from study areas in which knowledge is acquired in the analysis of the problems of technology users in their real context of use, as well as in the knowledge to the real and effective interaction that paves the way in solving problems. Engineering provides knowledge for the representation of problems and construction of solutions, however, it lacks training for the analysis of individuals, their actions and their social relationships.

From engineering, the analyst systematically evaluates the operation of the problem by examining the input, data processing and its subsequent production of information. In the technological products that the development of Industry 4.0 requires, the analysis of processes and data variables is highly demanding, allowing the products to be adapted to each specific domain and to the design focused on specific users. The implementation of technological solutions requires a deep knowledge of the subjects that operate them.

FUTURE TRENDS

The model presented allows for the determination of the level of technological development in the industry. By specifically detecting ICT products in their different levels of evolution and updating, it enables the identification of integration needs with the set of hardware and communications or infrastructure that allow an industry to start a transformation process towards Industry 4.0.

The adoption of such products requires the detailed analysis of both the massive data it reveals, the digitalization needs, the connection between objects and automation, the identification of indicators necessary to measure or to train a machine learning algorithm, as well as an in-depth analysis of users and their operations to represent it with virtual reality or augmented reality technologies.

These technological solutions put at the center of the debate the need to integrate multidisciplinary models and methodologies on problem domains that require the analysis of experts in social sciences. Thus, the roles of functional analyst, interaction analyst, data analyst, or tester, are constituted in profiles that require capacities to analyze individuals one-by-one as well as in their social relationships and in collective work actions.

The set of disciplines that address the different problems of human behavior are studied mostly by women in Ibero-American cultures. Women trained as professionals in the different social disciplines have the necessary background to assume a central role in determining variables, analyzing data, evaluating tasks or processes, as well as analyzing the interaction of real users, with capabilities to segment them according to the characteristics of each environment.

While the efforts to insert women into the world of industry in general and the development of technologies in particular are laudable, the paradigm of engineering thought continues to reproduce the cultural patterns that sustain it. The ICT industry needs the inclusion of interdisciplinary patterns of thought and knowledge, as well as gender diversity to analyze, design, develop and implement technologies.

As a line of research, the analysis of the characteristics, techniques and specific methodologies that allow the incorporation of this knowledge in a systematic way in the formation of multidisciplinary teams with gender diversity will be addressed in the future in such a way that they promote greater inclusion in technological development, adapted to the culture and knowledge that dominate current Latin American societies.

CONCLUSION

The imprint generated by the inevitable technological transformation puts the sources of engineering thought at the center of development with their capacities for practical problem solving. However, in said matrix of thought, limitations or biased features are observed when analyzing problems as they happen in the real world, as well as people who use technological products. The dynamics of global development prioritizes the speed in the construction of solutions over the adequacy of their functions, imposing the forms of social relations in a transversal way in the cultural framework of current Latin American societies.

This dynamic is doubly exclusive. On the one hand, it prevents users of technological products from defining how they want to use them and, on the other, it excludes professionals from social disciplines to analyze and define how they should be designed and operated.

The model presented in the chapter makes it possible to calculate an index of technological development and evaluate the aspects of the fourth industrial revolution. The validation of this model and the applied field study on a group of companies allowed to visualize the level of technological development in the context of an industrial district of Argentina.

The detection of specific products that make up Industry 4.0 enables the evaluation of the knowledge necessary for such developments, as well as the necessary capacities for their adoption. The creation of the index, the design of the methodology, the development of the survey instruments, as well as the validation field study, was carried out with an interdisciplinary team, made up of experts in technologies from various engineering and social disciplines, with parity of genre.

The research methodology, the collection and evaluation instruments were designed focused on the users of the model, made up of industry directors, company representatives, and process technicians.

Within the software industry, the construction of products has been analyzed from two different perspectives, both from the domain of the problem and the formation of work teams. In both senses, engineering borrows knowledge from social disciplines such as social anthropology, sociology, social communication, psychology, as well as resources and techniques from areas of knowledge such as design, architecture or art.

The development of applications with artificial intelligence algorithms, with large volumes of data, software that introduces virtual reality, applications with augmented reality, the definition of functional requirements, user analysis, interface design or the appropriate definition of testing cases in the various application domains require strong technological knowledge as well as deep knowledge about human behavior that must be taken as input for the development of these complex systems and their technological integration. Engineering problem solving is a part of development. The social analysis of the real context of use constitutes an indispensable requirement for its adoption.

It is significant then, that in the multiplicity of software that is produced, those who define the functional requirements, as well as the characteristics of the interaction, are usually not professionals from the social disciplines who work and know the usual management of users, nor do they usually perform usability evaluations with individuals in their real environment.

Although the effort to involve women in engineering has increased significantly in recent years, the strategies of the technology industry sector need to broaden the vision of strictly engineering thinking, which can include Latin American professional women from social and humanistic disciplines where they work.

That is why, it is seen with greater emphasis that the limitations of women to access greater social inclusion in the productive development of the manufacturing industry, as well as in technological development, is purely cultural and the structure of the matrix of dominant thought. The knowledge provided by social disciplines is the key to developing ICTs that are appropriate to the needs of real users.

These humanistic disciplines constitute the professions chosen mostly by Latin American women who access higher education. Their inclusion as professionals in the technology industry favors the promotion of a production that inevitably requires that the subjects use, apply and consume those technologies.

Waiting for the cultural transformation that encourages women to train and join the engineering logic can be a limitation for inclusion in current technological development. If it continues to be disjointed from the creators and end users, it only generates greater exclusion with fewer possibilities of social and labor insertion.

Therefore, the path from sociology to technology constitutes a non-random journey, but a search for broad solutions in interdisciplinary and inclusive contexts of gender diversity, which are very much required for there to be innovation in today's world.

ACKNOWLEDGMENT

This research has been supported by the National University of La Matanza, Argentina [PROINCE C209], the Ministry of Science, Technology and Productive Innovation, Argentina [PICTO 092-2013]; Ministry of Education, Secretariat of University Policies, Argentina [Vincular 2019].

REFERENCES

Berger, R. (2016). *España 4.0 El reto de la transformación digital de la economía*. Observatorio de la Industria 4.0. Recuperado de https://observatorioindustria.org/informes/

Bødker, S. (2015). Third-Wave HCI, 10 Years Later, Participation and Sharing. Magazines Interaction, 22(5).

Caballero Chi, L. O. (2017). *Incorporación de técnicas de HCI en un proceso ágil mediante patrones (Tesis Doctoral)*. Escuela Técnica Superior de Ingenieros Informáticos, Universidad Politécnica de Madrid.

Dekhane, S. & Napier, N. (2017) Impact of participation vs non: participation in a programming boot camp (PBC) on women in computing. *Journal of Computing Sciences in Colleges, 33*(2).

Del Giorgio, H., & Mon, A. (2019A). *Las TICs en las Industrias*. Editorial Universidad Nacional de La Matanza.

Del Giorgio, H. R., & Mon, A. (2019B). Niveles de productos software en la industria 4.0. *International Journal of Information Systems and Software Engineering for Big Companies*, 5(2), 53–62.

Giordano Lerena, R., & Páez Pino, A. (Eds.). (2018). Matilda y las mujeres en ingeniería en américa latina. Consejo Federal de Decanos de Ingeniería de Argentina CONFEDI. Latin American and Caribbean Consortium of Engineering Institutions.

Giordano Lerena, R., & Páez Pino, A. (Eds.). (2020). Matilda y las mujeres en ingeniería en américa latina II. Consejo Federal de Decanos de Ingeniería de Argentina CONFEDI. Latin American and Caribbean Consortium of Engineering Institutions.

Granollers, T. (2004). *Una metodología que integra la ingeniería del software, la interacción persona ordenador y la accesibilidad en el contexto de equipos de desarrollo multidisciplinares (Tesis Doctoral)*. Departament de Llenguatges i Sistemes Informàtics Universitat de Lleida.

Granollers, T., Lorés, J., & Cañas, J. J. (2005). Diseño de Sistemas Interactivos Centrados en el Usuario. Academic Press.

MINCyT. (2015). Industria 4.0: Escenarios e impactos para la formulación de políticas tecnológicas en los umbrales de la Cuarta Revolución Industrial (M. de Ciencia & P. Tecnología e Innovación, Eds.). Academic Press.

Mon, De María, Querel, & Figuerola. (2018). Evaluation of technological development for the definition of Industries 4.0. In *Proceedings of 2018 Congreso Argentino de Ciencias de la Informática y Desarrollos de Investigación* (pp. 523-530). Universidad Nacional de San Martín, IEEE Explore.

Mon, A., & Del Giorgio, H. (2018). Análisis de las tecnologías de la información y la comunicación y su innovación en la industria. In *Proceedings of XXIV Congreso Argentino de Ciencias de la Computación*, (pp. 1020-1029). Universidad Nacional del centro de la Provincia de Buenos Aires: Sedici Press.

Mon, A., & Del Giorgio, H. R. (2019). Usability in ICTs for Industry 4.0. In *Human-Computer Interaction 5th Iberoamerican Workshop, HCI-Collab*. Puebla, México: Springer.

Ningenia, L. (2016). *Qué es la Industria 4.0*. Recuperado de http://www.ningenia.com/2016/05/31/que-es-la-industria-4-0

Rathmann, L. (2020). Mujeres fuertes, valientes y comprometidas. Mujeres al fin…. In Matilda y las mujeres en ingeniería en américa latina II. Consejo Federal de Decanos de Ingeniería de Argentina CONFEDI. Latin American and Caribbean Consortium of Engineering Institutions.

SPU. (2020). *Estadísticas Universitarias, Secretaría de Políticas Universitarias, Ministerio de Educación, Argentina*. Recuperado de http://estadisticasuniversitarias.me.gov.ar/#/home

Stezano, F. (2017). The Role of Technology Center as Intermediary Organizations Facilitating Links for Innovation: Four Cases of Deferal Technology Centers in Mexico. *The Review of Policy Research*, *1*, 45–67.

UNESCO. (2017). *E2030: educación y habilidades para el siglo XXI. Informe, Naciones Unidas para la Educación, Oficina Nacional de Educación en América Latina y el Caribe. Santiago*. Recuperado de https://unesdoc.unesco.org/

United Nations. (2012). *Clasificación Industrial Internacional Uniforme, CIIU Rev.4*. United Nations Statistics Division. Recuperado de http://unstats.un.org/unsd/cr/registry/isic-4.asp

UNLaM. (2019). *Indice de TICs, Universidad Nacional de La Matanza*. Disponible en https://indicetics. unlam.edu.ar/it/

Uriarte, L. M., & Acevedo, M. (2018). Sociedad Red y transformación digital: Hacia una evolución de la consciencia de las organizaciones. *Revue d'Economie Industrielle*, *407*(1), 35–49.

KEY TERMS AND DEFINITIONS

HCI: Area within the software engineering that studies the interaction human-computers do.
ICTs: Set of information and communication technologies.
Industry 4.0: Fourth industrial revolution that is generated from the incorporation of new technologies since the second decade of the 21st century.

Chapter 2
Technological Development for the Inclusion of People With Disabilities:
Some Experiences at the Universidad Católica del Norte, Chile

Vianca Vega-Zepeda

iD https://orcid.org/0000-0002-2932-1639

Universidad Católica del Norte, Chile

ABSTRACT

The chapter presents some experiences carried out in Computer Sciences Department of the Universidad Católica del Norte (Chile) related to the development of technological products at the service of people with disabilities. Since 2006, the author has been working with institutions made up of people with disabilities in co-creating solutions to problems that affect their independence and inclusion in different areas. Products have been created for the blind, deaf, and children belonging to autism spectrum disorder. The work teams of each project have been made up of the author of this chapter together with students from Computer Science and the Master's Program in Computer Engineering. Results have been satisfactory. The challenge is to achieve an effective universal design, which should include, from the early stages of each project, not only typical end users, but also those who present conditions that require special considerations to access the technology.

INTRODUCTION

This chapter shows the experiences in the field of technological development for the inclusion of people with disabilities, developed in Computer Science Department of the Universidad Católica del Norte, located in the city of Antofagasta, in Chile. This line of applied research and technological development, called "Inclusive Computing" arises at the end of 2016, and has remained constant over time since then,

DOI: 10.4018/978-1-7998-7552-9.ch002

Copyright © 2021, IGI Global. Copying or distributing in print or electronic forms without written permission of IGI Global is prohibited.

covering inclusion issues from different perspectives. The projects and works described below have been led by the author of the chapter and developed with the participation of different students from the Computer Science and Magister in Computer Engineering programs at the Institution.

The topics and work that are described in the chapter are the following:

1. Usability and universal design. Usability is considered as one of the most important quality attributes, being a fundamental aspect in all software products. It is even more crucial in those systems that are designed for a wide variety of users, called by different authors as inclusive products. The target of this research topic is to provide a broad perspective on different factors influencing usability identified in several investigations focused on software products for users with sensory disability.
2. A first approach to the structure of a proposal for the elicitation of software requirements for inclusive systems, with an emphasis on the attribute of usability. This work is still in development, so only the phases that are being considered as part of the guide are indicated.
3. Experiences in mobile and web application development for people with disabilities. Specifically, they present a mobile application that allows the autonomous movement of blind or visually impaired people in closed spaces; a platform (web and mobile) for audiobooks; a mobile application to support language development in ASD children; a web page with a user interface based on Chilean Sign Language; and a mobile application to configure Smartag NFC for the blind and visually impaired.

The objective of this chapter is to share the experiences developed in the field of creating software products for people with disabilities. In doing this, the author seeks two results: firstly, to encourage other researchers and developers to create more technological products that reduce the inequalities that affect people with disabilities. Secondly, to show how universities can make a concrete contribution to the community's social problems. The two indicated results result in a win-win relationship between social organizations and institutions of higher education. Social organizations obtain solutions to their problems, while universities improve the teaching-learning process by solving real problems, with real clients and users.

BACKGROUND

According to the World Report on Disability of the World Health Organization (Banco Mundial & Organización Mundial de la Salud, 2011), around 15% of the world's population has some type of disability. The same report, declares that the number of people with disabilities is increasing, this mainly due to the aging of the population.

According to the World Health Organization, the concept of disability is defined as an umbrella term covering impairments, activity limitations, and participation restrictions, being a complex phenomenon that reflects the interaction between the characteristics of the body of a person and the characteristics of the society in which the person lives (Banco Mundial & Organización Mundial de la Salud, 2011). Hence, disability is a consequence of the functional impairments of a person that prevent them from successfully interacting with a product or service in a given context.

When talking about people with disabilities, a large part of the population associates it with a person who uses a wheelchair, a blind person with a cane or a deaf person. However, these disabilities are only part of a larger set of conditions, which are sometimes known as "invisible disabilities", because they are not visible to the naked eye. Among these are Autism Spectrum Disorder, visual decline, severe depression, speech difficulties, among others.

Disability is a barrier or limitation that is not found in the person who has a particular condition, but is located in the environment in which these people are inserted, that is, it is society who is not prepared to allow people with disabilities develop their potential for their own well-being and as a contribution to society.

The World Report on Disability (Banco Mundial & Organización Mundial de la Salud, 2011) lists a series of environmental obstacles that can facilitate or restrict the participation of people with disabilities. Among these, there is insufficient provision of services, in particular, as an important factor is the lack of accessibility, which indicates in a textual way: *Many built environments (including public accommodations), transport systems and information are not accessible to all...... Little information is available in accessible formats, and many communication needs of people with disabilities are unmet...... People with disabilities have significantly lower rates of information and communication technology use than non-disabled people, and in some cases they may be unable to access even basic products and services such as telephones, television, and the Internet.*

The aforementioned, highlights the importance of technological development to facilitate the inclusion of people with disabilities. While it is true, the ultimate goal is to ensure that all technological products are developed under the concepts of universal design, it is also necessary to have products specially designed for some type of disability. This is especially true, when, for example, the language to communicate requires to be some particular, such as the use of pictograms, sign language or the use of voice.

Through the years, multiple investigations and technological solutions for people with disabilities have been reported. For example in (Adya, Samant, Scherer, Killeen, & Morris, 2012) presents a review of assistive technology services models; in (Aleksandrova, 2019) assistive technology is analyzed as a factor that makes it possible to enhance the work of people with disabilities, emphasizing the accessibility of the urban environment, companies and workplaces in Russia; (Alves, Carvalho, Aguilar, Brito, & Bastos, 2020) carry out a systematic review of the literature to identify what types of technological tools have been used for the treatment of Autism Spectrum Disorder; in (Heck, 2009) A set of applications such as smart sensors, robotics and virtual reality applications are described at the service of people with disabilities. (Warnicke, 2019) analyzes different alternatives to be able to manage calls to emergency services by deaf people. Situations such as those described in this study require technological development focused on the distinctive characteristics of users, to allow solutions to such relevant problems as emergency calls.

In addition to applications such as those mentioned previously, there are recommendation guides that are important to know and apply in order to allow efficient access and use by anyone, regardless of their physical or sensory characteristics. Such is the case of Web Content Accessibility Guidelines (WCAG) 2.1 covers a wide range of recommendations for making Web content more accessible.

Below are the experiences of the Computer Science Department of the Universidad Católica del Norte, in research and technological development of products for people with disabilities.

DEVELOPED PROJECTS

The main projects developed are described below. All the works described here have arisen from needs expressed by organizations made up of people with disabilities and their families.

Elicitation of Requirements, Usability and Universal Design

As part of the development of a thesis in the computer engineering master's program at the Universidad Católica del Norte, we have investigated the concepts associated with Usability and Universal Design. Specifically, the objective of this research is to determine how the software requirements elicitation techniques are adapted to achieve inclusive systems that meet the universal design criteria.

There is research that has applied usability as a fundamental aspect to evaluate quality. However, it has been detected that a large part of the software products are not aimed at meeting the needs of people with disabilities, mainly of the sensory type (vision and hearing). Given the above, it remains one of the great challenges of software engineering, integrating users with disabilities from the early stages of a software product.

Assistive Technologies (AT) is a generic term that corresponds to devices created for people with motor and sensory impairments that are used for help, adaptation and rehabilitation (Bauer, Elsaesser, & Arthanat, 2011). This type of technology promotes greater independence by allowing people with disabilities to carry out tasks that previously presented great difficulties (Mesiti et al., 2011). Assistive Technologies are commonly created for a specific number of users based on a specific type of disability. However, there are products and services that are designed to meet the needs of a broader audience. These are inclusive designs (Department of Trade and Industry. Consumer Affairs Directorate, 2000). Keates (Simeon Keates, 2007) defines the concept of "universal access" or "inclusive design" as those environments, services and interfaces that work for people of all ages and abilities. According to the British Standards Institution, it is defined as the design of conventional products or services accessible and usable by as many people as is reasonably possible, without the need for special adaptation or specialized design (Simeon Keates, 2004). For us, inclusive software is a product that must be accessible and usable for all people (disabled or not), which must be taken into account from the specification of requirements to the validation of such products.

Accessibility and usability are two topics that are commonly discussed separately. Other research indicates that the accessibility and usability of software are properly integrated (Aizpurua, Harper, & Vigo, 2016; Petrie & Kheir, 2007). Usability is related to how software allows a group of users to achieve specified objectives in a specific use context. Accessibility describes the degree to which a product, device, or service can actually be used by all people (Mesiti et al., 2011). In inclusive software, usability is considered a critical attribute, because there are problems with different factors that prevent the product from being fully usable.

Pribeanu (Pribeanu, Fogarassy-Neszly, & Patru, 2014) identifies that the majority of usability problems in software products for people with disabilities are related to the grouping of structures and headers, flexibility / efficiency of using direct links and user compatibility. Minor usability issues are related to information density and readability.

Inclusive design or universal design contemplates the design of products and services that are accessible and usable by all, regardless of their disability status, cultural background, age, among other characteristics (Beyene, 2016).

The principles of universal design (Connell et al., 1997) are sustained by seven fundamental principles. Each principle is accompanied by a set of suggested guides.

1. **Equitable Use**. The design is useful and marketable to people with diverse abilities.
   a. Provide the same means of use for all users: identical whenever possible; equivalent when not.
   b. Avoid segregating or stigmatizing any users.
   c. Provisions for privacy, security, and safety should be equally available to all users.
   d. Make the design appealing to all users.
2. **Flexibility in Use**. The design accommodates a wide range of individual preferences and abilities.
   a. Provide choice in methods of use.
   b. Accommodate right- or left-handed access and use.
   c. Facilitate the user's accuracy and precision.
   d. Provide adaptability to the user's pace.
3. **Simple and Intuitive Use**. Use of the design is easy to understand, regardless of the user's experience, knowledge, language skills, or current concentration level.
   a. Eliminate unnecessary complexity.
   b. Be consistent with user expectations and intuition.
   c. Accommodate a wide range of literacy and language skills.
   d. Arrange information consistent with its importance.
   e. Provide effective prompting and feedback during and after task completion.
4. **Perceptible Information**. The design communicates necessary information effectively to the user, regardless of ambient conditions or the user's sensory abilities.
   a. Use different modes (pictorial, verbal, tactile) for redundant presentation of essential information.
   b. Provide adequate contrast between essential information and its surroundings.
   c. Maximize "legibility" of essential information.
   d. Differentiate elements in ways that can be described (i.e., make it easy to give instructions or directions).
   e. Provide compatibility with a variety of techniques or devices used by people with sensory limitations.
5. **Tolerance for Error**. The design minimizes hazards and the adverse consequences of accidental or unintended actions.
   a. Arrange elements to minimize hazards and errors: most used elements, most accessible; hazardous elements eliminated, isolated, or shielded.
   b. Provide warnings of hazards and errors.
   c. Provide fail safe features.
   d. Discourage unconscious action in tasks that require vigilance.
6. **Low Physical Effort**. The design can be used efficiently and comfortably and with a minimum of fatigue.
   a. Allow user to maintain a neutral body position.
   b. Use reasonable operating forces.
   c. Minimize repetitive actions.
   d. Minimize sustained physical effort.

7. **Size and Space for Approach and Use**. Appropriate size and space is provided for approach, reach, manipulation, and use regardless of user's body size, posture, or mobility.
   a. Provide a clear line of sight to important elements for any seated or standing user.
   b. Make reach to all components comfortable for any seated or standing user.
   c. Accommodate variations in hand and grip size.
   d. Provide adequate space for the use of assistive devices or personal assistance.

Digital inclusion has been a concept used as a framework to ensure that people have access to, and the skills to use, digital technologies (Real, Carlo, & Jaeger, 2014).

Elicitation Techniques of Requirements vs Type of Disability

In order to make software products inclusive, the needs determined by a disability condition must be considered from the requirements elicitation stage. For this reason, as part of this research, a traceability matrix was carried out between different requirements elicitation techniques, and their adaptation to users with visual or hearing disabilities. Traceability was developed based on a bibliographic review. Reports of inclusive product development experiences were reviewed, indicating the elicitation technique applied, in addition to other articles that recommended some technique for some type of disability.

Table 1 shows the traceability matrix.

Frameworks to Evaluate the Usability of Inclusive Systems

As part of the research carried out, two frameworks were identified that propose some criteria to assess whether a software product is inclusive. The detailed can be found in (Guerrero & Vega, 2018).

These models are being used as the basis for the generation of a practical guide that allows an easy evaluation of any product and a set of recommendations that improves the detected weaknesses.

The first framework is QUIM, proposed by Seffah (Seffah, Donyaee, Kline, & Padda, 2006). This raises eleven representative factors selected from different standards and models reported in the literature. The proposal adapts these factors and expresses them in the form of criteria and then relates the criteria to specific metrics. The eleven factors are:

1. Efficiency
2. Effectiveness
3. Productivity
4. Satisfaction
5. Learning capacity
6. Security
7. Reliability
8. Accessibility
9. Universality
10. Utility
11. Acceptability

These factors are influenced by a specific category of user, tasks or environments.

Table 1. Traceability matrix between elicitation techniques and types of disability

Techniques	Visually impaired users	Hearing impaired users
Interviews	X	X
Questionnaires / Surveys	X	X
Introspection	X	
Observation	X	X
Apprenticeship		X
Protocol analysis		X
Brainstorm	X	X
Focus Group	X	X
Requirements workshop	X	X
Team work		X
Domain analysis		X
Card sorting	X	X
Laddering	X	
Prototyped	X	X
Task analysis	X	X
Scenarios	X	X

Second model corresponds to the proposed Technological Acceptance Model for Inclusive Education (TAM 4 IE) proposed by Silva (Silva & Leite, 2015). This model considers five factors to evaluate usability. The factors are: subjective perception, perceived usability, perceived utility, future expectations, and enabling conditions. The perceived usability factor is subdivided into the sub factors: learning ability, memorability, accessibility and aesthetics. Satisfaction is considered as a subjective perception.

Proposals for the Creation of Inclusive Systems

As mentioned at the beginning of the section, this general project aims to determine how the software requirements elicitation techniques are adapted to achieve inclusive systems that meet the universal design criteria. The expected end result is a guide to eliciting requirements for creating inclusive software products.

To achieve this objective, an analysis of the state of the art was carried out, in relation to other proposals associated with the implementation of inclusive software products. Table 2 taken from (Guerrero & Vega, 2018) shows a summary of said analysis, incorporating the advantages and disadvantages of each proposal.

This research is still in progress. A guide for the elicitation of requirements for inclusive systems is being prepared, with emphasis on the usability characteristic. Below is the preliminary version of the guide that is in development. Below is the preliminary version of the guide that is in development, which is organized into five stages, each of which is broken down into specific tasks to be carried out.

Table 2. Comparative table of proposals for inclusive systems

Proposals	Advantages	Disadvantages
Keates and Clarkson Framework (S Keates, Clarkson, & Street, 2003)	Identify the wishes and aspirations of users. Subsequently determines the needs of users	It does not provide metrics to validate whether the product is truly inclusive. Requirements not related to usability
CEN / CENELEC Guide (*Guide for addressing accessibility in standards*, 2014)	It allows considering the needs of users based on different clauses, addressing usability and accessibility problems.	The guide does not offer mechanisms to relate the usability factors in a quantitative way.
HAAT model (Cook & Polga, 2015)	It relates the needs of the users with the activities they carry out daily.	It does not formalize the information capture process from the early stages of the model. Does not include metrics.
CAT model (Hersh, 2008)	Categorize user requirements in order to analyze information	It does not consider usability factors in the context of the model.
USERfit model (Abascal, Arrue, Garay, & Tomás, 2002)	In the user analysis phase, it allows considering functional implications and necessary actions to counteract the impediments generated by the disability. It allows integrating the characteristics with existing norms in the literature.	Does not include metrics in user analysis. It does not delve into the usability factors.
Goodman Model (Goodman, Langdon, & Clarkson, 2006)	Define the problem and then detail the user requirements. Integrates elicitation techniques in the analysis and data collection process.	Does not consider metrics. It does not relate the requirements to aspects of software quality.
Inclusive software development model (Bonacin, Rodrigues, & Antônio, 2009)	The tasks and attributes of each user are identified	Metrics are not proposed in the model development cycle. It does not incorporate usability in the decomposition phase of tasks. It is only integrated in the evaluation of the model.

Stage I: Understand the application domain. Include determine the objective and scope of the software project; know the type of disability of the people to whom the software is directed; Inquire about the usability limitations of people with disabilities; and investigate technological support tools in inclusive systems.

Stage II: Identification of sources of requirements. Include selection and identification of project stakeholders and categorization of project stakeholders.

Stage III: Selection of elicitation techniques. Include select at least three effective elicitation techniques, according to the type of disability of the users.

Stage IV: Elicit the requirements. Include apply elicitation technique in users with disabilities.

The tasks that are pending in the investigation are to adjust the stages and activities, generate the assets that facilitate the application of the guide and carry out the validations by executing some case studies.

Experiences in Mobile and Web Application Development

This section presents some products developed for people with disabilities. All were developed based on a co-creation process with the end users.

The presentation of each of the products developed includes the problem it seeks to solve, the purpose of the product, the characteristics of the users, a description and the results obtained.

Voice Talk Beacons

Problem: Blind and visually impaired people learn to move autonomously in spaces that are familiar and recurrent in their daily lives. For example, they can memorize the arrangement of furniture within their home, allowing for fluid movement without requiring assistance from someone to guide them. However, they face difficulties in their autonomous movement in closed spaces that are not usual for them, for example, when they must attend a health center or a shopping center.

Purpose: To allow the autonomous movement of blind and visually impaired people in an unknown closed environment

Users: The main users of this product are the members of the Association of the Blind and Visually Impaired of Antofagasta. This group is made up of about 30 people, whose ages vary between 12 to 70 years approximately. The process of co-creation and validation of the product was developed in conjunction with this group.

Description:

The team working on this project was made up of three Computer Science students together with the author of this chapter. The participants were: Miss Estefanía Flores, Mr. Arturo Espinosa and Mr. Eduardo Carvajal.

As mentioned previously, this application was developed in conjunction with the *Agrupación de Ciegos y Disminuidos Visuales de Antofagasta* (Grouping of the Blind and Visually Impaired of Antofagasta, ACA, by its Spanish name) and with the financing of the *Servicio Nacional de la Discapacidad* (National Disability Service – Chile), a government entity whose purpose is to promote the right to equal opportunities for people with disabilities, in order to obtain their social inclusion, contributing to the full enjoyment of their rights and eliminating any form of discrimination based on disability, through the coordination of State actions, the execution of policies and programs, within the framework of inclusive local development strategies.

Its development was carried out in the context of a larger project, which had the following objectives:

1. Promote inclusion and respect for people with disabilities.
2. Train visually impaired people to use software for the use of computers and in cell phone applications.
3. Provide computer tools that can promote the autonomy and use of new technologies to people in situations of visual impairment.

The problem posed by ACA is related to the difficulties faced by blind people, in order to move independently in public spaces where they must occasionally attend.

To resolve this situation, different technological alternatives were analyzed, including geolocation, Bluetooth devices, NFC technology and the use of QR codes. These technologies were compared based on different criteria, which included acquisition costs, ease of use for blind people and location accuracy (considering that the travel spaces considered are public buildings), among others.

The selected technology was the use of Bluetooth devices called Beacons. They were selected because they are more accurate in displaying a travel route, do not require an internet connection and facilitate usability for blind people.

The Figure 1 shows a scheme of the application's operation. With Bluetooth devices, paths are modeled from a starting point to different points of interest. The mobile application detects the different devices, and based on said identification, recognizes the user's location and determines the route to continue.

Figure 1. Scheme Voice Talk Beacons Operation

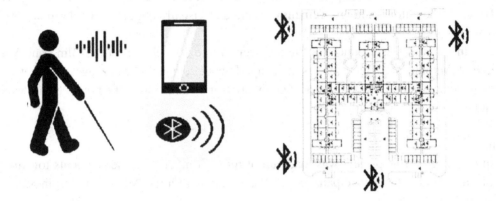

The implementation of the application was carried out at the hospital in the capital of the second region of Chile of the city of Antofagasta. However, it can be implemented in any other public or private building that wants to strengthen access and autonomous movement for blind people.

Results: As a result of this project, two of the students who participated in the development of the application formed a Start Up called *Inclunova*. Among the services and products offered by this company, is the installation and configuration of a new improved version of Voice Talk Beacon, called *Pasos*.

IncluBooks

Problem: Access for Blind and Visually Impaired people to literature in general requires the use of formats other than traditional printed or even digital ones. Although it is true, there are books written in Braille, not all blind people know this language. This is especially true for those who lose their vision as adults. It is necessary that the content of the books is available orally, so that they can be heard through some type of sound player.

Purpose: Make available to blind and visually impaired people in Chile, a tool that allows them to access audiobooks, with audios that incorporate the idioms and language of the area. In addition, the incorporation of complementary reading texts that the Ministry of Education includes in the study programs of basic and secondary education was especially considered.

Users: The main users of this product are the members of the Association of the Blind and Visually Impaired of Antofagasta. This group is made up of about 30 people, whose ages vary between 12 to 70 years approximately. The process of co-creation and validation of the product was developed in conjunction with this group.

Description:

IncluBooks is a platform for audiobooks, which was developed as a final project of Computing Science degree for four students, guided by the author of this chapter. The students were: Mr. Arturo Espinosa, Ms. Estefanía Flores, Mr. Christian Fuenzalida and Mr. Yilmar Muñoz. In this project, we had the participation with the participation of the *Agrupación de Ciegos y Disminuidos Visuales de Antofagasta* (ACA).

Chile has little preparation to include people with disabilities, since many factors are not considered in the different activities that the country has. Among these activities is reading, whether for cultural, educational or entertainment topics. People with visual disabilities have different methods or tools to carry out this activity, among which are the following:

- **Books in Braille**. These are books written with a tactile reading and writing system based on cells and points with reliefs. The problem that people with visual disabilities have when using books in Braille, is that not all have learned the system, since many are not blind from birth and did not have the need to learn it. In addition, access to these is not easy, since they are expensive and at the same time as they are very large, they are uncomfortable to load.
- **AudioBooks**. These are books described in audio, which relate the content of the books specifying each detail, taking the reader to the context of the situation. Its advantage is that they are free for blind people, since there is a treaty called the Marrakesh Treaty[1] which indicates that all audiobooks must be freely accessible and their commercialization is prohibited.

The problem that people with visual disabilities have when using audiobooks is that there is no easy access to them and those that can be found have idioms from other countries which makes understanding difficult.

While you could use a screen reader like Cortana or Jaws to listen to books in Word or pdf format, this also presents some problems like the absence of virtual bookmarks. Since, if a person uses this alternative and needs to turn off or restart the device, they will not be able to save where part of the book was and so the next time read from that point.

As a result of this, many platforms have been created that store and reproduce audiobooks. However, these platforms are limited in access, since most of them require a paid subscription. In addition, these platforms do not have an inclusive design; therefore, they hinder the use of these platforms.

Figure 2 shows a schematic of the Inclubooks structure.

The details of the implementation of this platform are available at (Espinosa, Flores, Fuenzalida, Muñoz, & Vega, 2016).

Results: This project culminated in the training of members of the group for the blind and visually impaired on the use of the platform. In addition, a call was made for volunteers willing to record the readings of the books. On the part of the University, the result was the degree of four students.

PictoLomi

Problem: Children belonging to Autism Spectrum Disorder have difficulties in language development. A widely used strategy to facilitate communication is pictograms. A pictogram is a drawing or graphic symbol that represents some concept.

Figure 2. Inclubooks Scheme

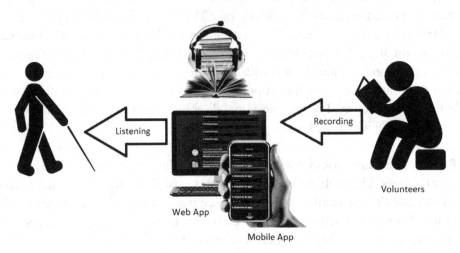

When a therapist or family member of an ASD child wishes to communicate through the use of pictograms, they need to have a large number of them printed. It is not convenient to move and organize the pictograms for quick use.

Purpose: Create a tool that supports therapies for language development in ASD children, based on the use of pictograms. To make the tool attractive to children, it was designed in a game format.

Users: The users of this application are children belonging to the Autism Spectrum Disorder. The co-creation process was supported by a therapist from the OID. Pictolomi validation was carried out with the participation of the therapist and her patients.

Description:

PictoLomi is an application for language development, based on the use of pictograms for children with Autism Spectrum Disorder. This application was implemented with the collaboration and guidance of the *Oficina de Integración para Personas en Situación de Discapacidad* (Integration Office for People with Disabilities, OID by its name in Spanish) of the Municipality of Antofagasta. This project was funded by the Chilean Ministry of Education. The participants in this project were four Computer Science students together with the author of this chapter, as a tutor. The students were: Mr. Kevin Araya, Mr. Víctor Araya, Mr. Germán Rojo and Mr. Diego Saavedra.

OID specializes in working with children, youth, and adults with ASD. The speech therapists of this organization carry out different activities that include therapies to enhance and develop cognitive skills in order to improve language and communication in people with this disorder.

One of the most developed activities is to have patients describe different actions shown through images morphosyntactics, and patients should indicate what they are trying to do through the use of drawings or icons that figuratively represent a real object, or a meaning called pictograms.

In order to improve the accessibility to these therapeutic activities developed on paper, we sought to develop a software or application that can carry out these activities, but in a digital way and thus reach more people and children with ASD.

Since the end users of this application are children, it was designed as a game. The development of this application was carried out based on the SUM development methodology (Coppes, Mesa, Viera, Fern, & Vallespir, 2009). This is a methodology that adapts the structure and roles of Scrum, providing flexibility to define the life cycle and can be easily combined with other methodologies to adapt to different realities. It primarily seeks to achieve high productivity from the quality development team in time and cost.

Table 3 shows the summary of the game definition.

Table 3. Pictolomi definition

Element	Description
Game Vision	PictoLomi is a puzzle game focused on children with ASD. This game is about solving the syntax of a sentence whose difficulty is increasing and constant progressdue to illness, work, family or other commitments.
Gender	It is considered as a puzzle-puzzle, but originally PictoLomi is based on a methodological activity carried out by a speech-language pathologist looking for an improvement in children's language.
Game Mechanics	As a starting point there is a main menu in which you can make some settings if necessary, in addition to being able to access the game. There are two game modes: • Challenge Mode: Solve sentences that increase their difficulty by dragging pictograms. • Creative Mode: Provides all the video game material to be used as a tool for communication.

In addition, a statistics session called *My Advance* is included, which shows the data obtained from the game modalities.

PictoLomi is characterized by the following aspects:

- Variety of game modes.
- Lomi, is the name of the pet which is a dog. You will be a guide and a pleasant company during the experience.
- Simple design, seeks for the user to focus on the activity that enhances language development.
- Simple sentences with as few words as possible, so that the child's interest is not lost.
- Audiovisual stimuli for each level check, achievements and input / output of the application.
- Creative mode mainly seeks for the child to apply what has been learned in challenge mode.
- Difficulty progresses slowly to make it step-by-step learning.
- The My Advance mode is mainly focused on the responsible adult or therapist in charge.
- An amount of 20 levels is considered per difficulty.
- The difficulties are in the form of "worlds" where each one has its own setting.

PictoLomi implements the functional requirements mentioned below. For each requirement, the defined criteria are indicated to assess compliance.

1. **Challenge Mode**. An image showing an action or situation is presented along with the pictograms associated with the image. The main objective is to drag the pictograms to the correct positions, such that a sentence is established with a valid syntax.

In addition, this mode consists of three levels of difficulty, which are the following:

- Easy: Three word sentence
- Medium: Four word sentence
- Difficult: Five word sentence

In the medium and difficult levels a distracting pictogram will be included in order to increase the degree of difficulty more simply and not so overwhelmingly.

Evaluation criteria: Display of pictograms according to the image to be analyzed, animations, effects and corresponding sounds, progress between levels in the normal way.

2. **Creative Mode.** Similar to the previous mode. This function seeks that the child sees PictoLomi as a support tool. Mainly leaving the pictogram resources fully available to facilitate communication and needs.

Evaluation criteria: Prayer to be formed according to the valid structure.

3. **My Progress**. Section where all the statistics of which a user's progress can be demonstrated, such as stages completed, words formed, errors, efficiency of attempts, will be recorded.

Evaluation criteria: Stored data is true.

4. **About**. Description of the developer team and contributions from institutions, explained by Lomi.

Evaluation criteria: Informative for certain parents and therapists.

In addition, the main characteristics that the graphical user interface must meet were defined as the main non-functional requirement.

5. Attractive and easy to use GUI

Evaluation criteria: that the child is not distracted visually and understands in the shortest possible time how to navigate the application.

Figure 3 shows how Pictolomi is structured. There are two modes of interaction: Player and Parents. The player can access 60 levels in three degrees of difficulty. Parents or guardians have three features available: Level Selection allows you to select a specific level to play; creative mode lets you create new sentences of any difficulty; and Advance by Level show progress statistics for each available level.

Results: Pictolomi is available for download in Play Store for mobile phones with Android operating system

Web System Based on the Use of Sign Language

Figure 3. Pictolomi Scheme

Problem: Deaf people have difficulties in the development of reading / writing. Since their primary language is Sign Language, they have difficulty following written instructions. Web systems usually do not consider this feature, and present all their menus in writing.

Purpose: Implement a web system whose interface is based on the Chilean Sign Language, thus facilitating the interaction of deaf users.

Users: The users of this web system and those who participated in the process of co-creation and validation of the product are the members of the Fundación Sordos Iguales.

Description

Table 4. Work team

Group	Students
Group 1	Denis Miranda Jauregui Javiera Muñoz Melo Cristina Pérez Quiroga Nicole Pérez Quiroga Felipe Varas Jara
Group 2	Ignacio Carrasco Martínez Camila Núñez Paez Cristian Nuñez Rojas Juan Quispe Ticona David Rivera Godoy
Group 3	Julio Díaz Meléndez Pablo Julio Vitalic Juan Maury Rojas Manuel Zuleta Bernal
Group 4	Gerardo Díaz Villena Bárbara Hormazábal Piñones Sebastián Villarroel García

Another project developed was the implementation of a web page based on the use of Sign Language for the Fundación Sordos Iguales (Deaf Equals Foundation) in the city of Antofagasta. This project was developed through the application of the *Learning + Service* methodology in a subject of Computing Science degree at the Universidad Católica del Norte. The team was made up of seventeen Computer Science students, organized into four groups. The list of students is shown in the Table 4.

The main feature of this web system is the use of a user interface that incorporates videos in Chilean Sign Language, to facilitate interaction with deaf people.

This web system is made up of a public and a private part. In relation to the public part, the objective is to serve as a point of contact for the entire community with the Fundación Sordos Iguales. It is used for the promotion and dissemination of activities carried out by the Foundation.

The private part, available only to authorized Foundation members, allows the administration of the information that is available to the general public and the registration of students and grades associated with the Sign Language courses offered by the Foundation.

An extra element that was incorporated into the web system was the implementation of an interface, very easy to use for users with little or no knowledge of web development, which allows them to create new sections for the public part of the system.

Figure 4 shows a schematic of the Web System. A public user can access the presentation of the organization, the services it offers, news and a contact form. While the administrators access the administration of public information through login and password, in addition to the management of the

Figure 4. Web system scheme
Results: The web system is available and in use at the address http://sordosiguales.cl/

Chilean Sign Language courses.

Mobile App to Configure "SMARTAGS NFC" for Blind and Visually Disabled People

Problem: Not all blind or visually impaired people know how to operate some of the more advanced functions of mobile phones. When they need to perform a lesser-known task, they may face complications that go against their autonomy because of how complex it can be.

Purpose: Facilitate the interaction of a blind or visually impaired person with a mobile phone, allowing the activation of a set of functions, through the use of NFC chips.

Users: The main users of this product are the members of the Association of the Blind and Visually Impaired of Antofagasta. This group is made up of about 30 people, whose ages vary between 12

to 70 years approximately. The process of co-creation and validation of the product was developed in conjunction with this group.

Description

The creation of this application was developed as a final year project by Computer Science student Mr. Bryan Echeverría, mentored by the author of this chapter.

Currently there are several software products for mobile devices, which seek to help people with visual disabilities. Speech recognition is the point at which these applications focus. However, there are certain aspects in which these technologies do not deliver the expected result when performing actions on the cell phone, either due to ambient noise or the level of voice recognition.

In order to overcome these obstacles, the NFC technology of cell phones was used. The objective of this work was to automate simple tasks on mobile devices, and perform tasks with the simple action of bringing a "Smart Tag" or NFC chip closer to the mobile phone.

For example, a visually impaired person, before going to sleep, could send a message to a loved one, set an alarm and silence their mobile phone, just by approaching an NFC chip programmed to perform all these functions automatically, without need to access or unlock the device.

To carry out this task, the minimum viable product of a mobile application was developed, which will allow blind people to program these NFC chips with the most used functions of their mobile phone. In this way tasks are automated and the use of mobile phones is made more efficient.

Figure 5. NFC app scheme

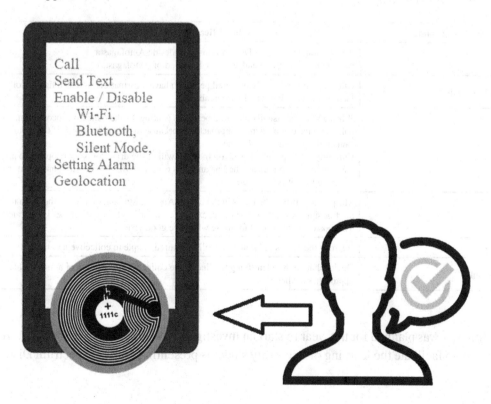

Most of the options are managed by a menu, which can be navigated via finger swipes and voice recognition. The system responds with voice and vibration reproductions.

Figure 5 shows NFC App schematic. The user, using the NFC chip, can make calls, send text messages, enable / disable Wi-Fi, Bluetooth, silent mode, in addition to setting alarms and using geolocation.

All the technical details of the implementation of the NFC application is available at (Brayan Echeverría & Vega, 2016)

FUTURE TRENDS AND CURRENT CHALLENGES

Nowadays, the line of technological development for people with disabilities from the Department of Computer Sciences of the Universidad Católica del Norte continues to generate new projects. More Academics and students have joined. In addition, the type of solutions under development has expanded.

At the moment, the Support Program for the generation of Entrepreneurship in the Internet of Things, Smart Cities & Smart Industries is being executed. This is a project financed by CORFO. CORFO is the Chilean economic development agency that works daily to improve the competitiveness and the productive diversification of the country by encouraging investment, innovation and entrepreneurship. This program has posed six challenges to its participants, which require IoT-based solutions. Among these challenges, there are two that seek to solve problems that affect people with disabilities. Tables 5 and 6 describe each of the indicated challenges.

Table 5. Description challenge 1

Challenge name	Identification of collective locomotion
Provider	Agrupación de Ciegos y Disminuidos Visuales de Antofagasta (Grouping of the Blind and Visually Impaired of Antofagasta)
Challenge Description	Allow a blind or visually impaired person to have information on which line of collective locomotion is arriving at the whereabouts.
Context	When a blind or visually impaired person is waiting for the collective locomotion, they are able to notice that a micro is approaching (because they hear the noise of the motor) but cannot distinguish what the line is. Currently, these people depend on the goodwill of the driver or other people who are in the whereabouts, who indicate the line and thus can make the decision to request that the bus stop or continue waiting for another line.
The problem	The problem is that the buses in the city of Antofagasta (and in most of them) do not have any alert or signal to identify their line, except for the sign where the number is indicated. This poster is only useful for those who have good vision.
Challenge Goal	Improve the access of blind or visually impaired people to collective locomotion
Expected result	Device that allows identifying the line of the collective locomotion of a mobile that approaches a whereabouts

In addition, it was planned for this year to start an investigation whose objective is to analyze the use of technology to facilitate the learning of university students presenting Autism Spectrum Disorder. It is hoped to obtain as a result a platform that can be applied in the Faculty of Engineering and Geological Sciences that supports the academic performance of students with this condition.

Unfortunately, this project had to delay its start, due to the pandemic generated by COVID-19.

CONCLUSION

As main conclusions, it can be mentioned that the experience in technological development has been successful thanks to the participation and commitment of end users. In each case, a process of co-creation of the products has been developed; in which people with disabilities participate with the support of health professionals.

There are many other needs that have been identified and raised by organizations made up of people with disabilities. These technological development opportunities are waiting to obtain resources for their implementation.

The greatest difficulties faced have been the mechanisms of interaction with people with disabilities. For example, the work with *Fundación Sordos Iguales* required the participation of a Sign Language Interpreter, or the validation of PictoLomi should have the support of psychologists and speech therapists that facilitate contact with ASD children without causing decompensation in them.

The work developed with people with disabilities has been an enriching experience that has allowed us to learn a lot to those who make up the work teams. It has also demanded a preparation that goes be-

Table 6. Description challenge 2

Challenge name	Locating and monitoring children with ASD
Provider	Escuela Raíces
Challenge Description	Design some low-cost device that can be placed in the clothing or body of ASD children, in such a way that it generates an alert to their guardians (parents, teachers or temporary caregivers) when they are moving away from a pre-defined physical space (For example: a classroom)
Context	"ASD is a disorder of neurobiological origin that affects the configuration of the nervous system and brain function, leading to difficulties in two main areas: communication and social interaction and flexibility of thought and behavior."[2] The current situation is that surveillance and control is carried out by one or more people. In particular, in a classroom, one or two people should supervise several children. This can cause that while the caregivers are attending to some, others may move away and flee from the space destined for the activity they are carrying out. There is a device on the market that, based on GPS and mobile devices, identifies children's geolocation and generates messages for a tutor. These devices cost from US$ 60 upwards, which does not allow low-income families and establishments to access them. It is for this reason that a low-cost solution is required, which is not invasive for the user (children), which makes it possible to monitor that the user remains within a predetermined physical space, and in case he / she moves away from this place, issue some kind of alert to whoever is in charge of their surveillance.
The problem	An ASD child can escape from a confined space without his or her guardian noticing
Challenge Goal	Facilitate the work of caregivers in charge of ASD children who are in a certain closed physical space
Expected result	Low cost device that generates an alert when the child moves away from a pre-defined physical space

yond technological knowledge. It has been a win-win relationship to improve student learning in Systems Engineering and Computer Science Department. The projects developed have allowed students to face real problems that affect many members of the social environment and provide concrete solutions to the inclusion of people with disabilities by eliminating some of the barriers present in society.

Until now, there has been the commitment and active participation of students who have accepted the challenge of working on inclusive projects. The strategy that is being applied as an institution, to maintain this type of work, and to ensure that more students and professionals continue to participate, is the formalization of the application of Learning + Service in more subjects of the study programs. The foregoing considers training the teachers in charge of the subjects, and the accompaniment of a unit specialized in methodological innovation for university teaching. On the part of the students, to maintain their commitment, the Department is including inclusion issues in all the projects and activities that are developed. Experience has shown that when young people participate and work face-to-face with people with disabilities, there is a long-term change in attitude.

An important pending challenge is to achieve widespread use of the products developed, through their availability to other organizations with similar characteristics to those that have participated in the co-creation processes. To achieve this, it is necessary to formalize a Technological Development Laboratory and to establish relationships through agreements with organizations that can finance the dissemination and distribution of the products created.

I hope that the experiences reported in this chapter will inspire more researchers, especially women, to work for the inclusion of people with disabilities. The potential for creating inclusive technology is almost infinite with the continuous advancement of the computing power of machines and new devices to process and display information. The needs of the disabled community are ongoing, but not always evident. The call is to contribute from our position as researchers to the construction of a more just and inclusive society, where we can all develop our potential, without contextual barriers associated with the diversity of conditions that a person may present.

ACKNOWLEDGMENT

The author thanks all the students who have accepted the challenge of working for the inclusion of people with disabilities, making their time and knowledge available in the projects described.

In addition, she especially thanks all the organizations that have trusted in the work that is carried out in the department of computer science, allowing strengthening the line of technological development for the inclusion of people with disabilities.

REFERENCES

Abascal, J., Arrue, M., Garay, N., & Tomás, J. (2002). USERfit Tool. A Tool to Facilitate Design for All. In *Universal Access Theoretical Perspectives* (pp. 141–152). Practice, and Experience.

Adya, M., Samant, D., Scherer, M. J., Killeen, M., & Morris, M. W. (2012). Assistive / rehabilitation technology, disability, and service delivery models. *Cognitive Processing*, *13*(S1), 75–78. doi:10.100710339-012-0466-8 PMID:22820864

Aizpurua, A., Harper, S., & Vigo, M. (2016). Exploring the relationship between web accessibility and user experience. *International Journal of Human-Computer Studies, 91*, 13–23. doi:10.1016/j.ijhcs.2016.03.008

Aleksandrova, O. (2019). Accessibility of Assistive Technologies as a Factor in the Successful Realization of the Labor Potential of Persons with Disabilities : Russia ' s Experience. *Societies (Basel, Switzerland), 9*(70).

Alves, F. J., Carvalho, E. A. D. E., Aguilar, J., Brito, L. L. D. E., & Bastos, G. S. (2020). Applied Behavior Analysis for the Treatment of Autism : A Systematic Review of Assistive Technologies. *IEEE Access, 8*(1968).

Banco Mundial, & Organización Mundial de la Salud. (2011). *Informe mundial la discapacidad.* Author.

Bauer, S. M., Elsaesser, L.-J., & Arthanat, S. (2011). Assistive products for persons with disabilities – classification and terminology. In *Disability and Rehabilitation* (pp. 243–259). Assistive Technology.

Beyene, W. M. (2016). Realizing inclusive digital library environments: opportunities and challenges. In *20th International Conference on Theory and Practice of Digital Libraries* (pp. 3–14). 10.1007/978-3-319-43997-6_1

Bonacin, R., Rodrigues, M. C. C. B., & Antônio, M. (2009). An Agile Process Model for Inclusive Software Development. In *Enterprise Information Systems* (pp. 807–818). Springer. doi:10.1007/978-3-642-01347-8_67

Connell, B. R., Jones, M., Mace, R., Mueller, J., Mullick, A., Ostroff, E., … Vanderheiden, G. (1997). *The principles of universal design.* Retrieved from https://projects.ncsu.edu/design/cud/about_ud/ud-principlestext.htm

Cook, A. M., & Polga, J. M. (2015). *Assistive Technologies Principles and Practice* (4th ed.). Elsevier.

Coppes, A., Mesa, G., Viera, A., Fern, E., & Vallespir, D. (2009). *Una Metodolog´ıa para Desarrollo de Videojuegos. In 38°.* JAIIO - Simposio Argentino de Ingeniería de Software.

Department of Trade and Industry, Consumer Affairs Directorate. (2000). *A Study of the Difficulties Disabled People Have when Using Everyday Consumer Products.* Author.

Echeverría, & Vega. (2016). *Creación de prototipo funcional de aplicación móvil para configurar "smartags nfc" para personas ciegas y disminuidas visuales.* Universidad Católica del Norte.

Espinosa, A., Flores, E., Fuenzalida, C., Muñoz, Y., & Vega, V. (2016). *Creación de un Prototipo de una plataforma tecnológica para acceso inclusivo a audiolibros para personas ciegas y disminuidas visuales.* Universidad Católica del Norte.

Goodman, J., Langdon, P. M., & Clarkson, P. J. (2006). Providing Strategic User Information for Designers: Methods and Initial Findings. In J. Clarkson, P. Langdon, & P. Robinson (Eds.), Designing Accessible Technology (pp. 41–51). Springer Link.

Guerrero, H., & Vega, V. (2018). Usability analysis : Is our software inclusive? Guide for addressing accessibility in standards.

Heck, H. (2009). Assistive technologies. In *Technology Guide* (pp. 226–229). Springer., doi:10.1007/978-3-540-88546-7_44

Hersh, M. (2008). Disability and Assistive Technology Systems. In M. Hersh & M. A. Johnson (Eds.), *Assistive Technology for Visually Impaired and Blind People* (pp. 1–50). Springer-Verlag. doi:10.1007/978-1-84628-867-8_1

Keates, S. (2004). Developing BS7000 Part 6 – Guide to Managing Inclusive Design. In *User-Centered Interaction Paradigms for Universal Access in the Information Society* (pp. 332–339). Springer. doi:10.1007/978-3-540-30111-0_29

Keates, S. (2007). Designing for Accessibility: A Business Guide to Countering Design Exclusion. Lawrence Erlbaum Associates.

Keates, S., Clarkson, P. J., & Street, T. (2003). Countering design exclusion : Bridging the gap between usability and accessibility. *Universal Access in the Information Society*, *2*(2), 215–225. doi:10.100710209-003-0059-5

Mesiti, M., Ribaudo, M., Valtolina, S., Barricelli, B. R., Boccacci, P., & Dini, S. (2011). Collaborative Environments: Accessibility and Usability for Users with Special Needs. In Community-Built Databases (pp. 319–340). Springer.

Petrie, H., & Kheir, O. (2007). The Relationship between Accessibility and Usability of Websites. In *Proceedings of the SIGCHI Conference on Human Factors in Computing Systems* (pp. 397–406). 10.1145/1240624.1240688

Pribeanu, C., Fogarassy-Neszly, P., & Patru, A. (2014). Municipal web sites accessibility and usability for blind users : Preliminary results from a pilot study. *Universal Access in the Information Society*, *13*(3), 339–349. doi:10.100710209-013-0315-2

Real, B., Carlo, J., & Jaeger, P. T. (2014). Rural Public Libraries and Digital Inclusion : Issues and Challenges. *ITAL Information Technology and Libraries*, *33*(March), 6–24. doi:10.6017/ital.v33i1.5141

Seffah, A., Donyaee, M., Kline, R. B., & Padda, H. K. (2006). Usability measurement and metrics : A consolidated model. *Software Quality Journal*, *14*(2), 159–178. doi:10.100711219-006-7600-8

Silva, S., & Leite, L. (2015). Technology Acceptance Evaluation by Deaf Students Considering the Inclusive Education Context. In *Human-Computer Interaction* (pp. 20–37). INTERACT.

Warnicke, C. (2019). Equal Access to Make Emergency Calls : A Case for Equal Rights for Deaf Citizens in Norway and Sweden. *Social Inclusion*, *7*(1), 173–179. doi:10.17645i.v7i1.1594

KEY TERMS AND DEFINITIONS

Chilean Sign Language: Language used by the deaf community. It is based on the description of signs using the hands and facial and body expression.

Disability: Barriers to the environment that make it difficult for people with any special physical, social or mental condition to participate in different social, academic or other fields.

Inclubooks: Technological platform made up of web and mobile applications, developed for blind people to have access to audiobooks in the cultural context of Chile.

Inclunova: Start up that arises from the first inclusive project developed by the Department of Computer Sciences of the Universidad Católica del Norte. This company is dedicated to the development of inclusive technologies.

Near Field Communication (NFC): Technology that enables wireless communication and data exchange between two nearby devices.

Pasos: Mobile application marketed by the company Inclunova. This application is responsible for guiding the movement of a blind person in a closed environment, such as inside a building.

PictoLomi: Mobile application that implements a video game that, based on the use of pictograms, seeks to support the language development of children with the ASD condition.

Universal Design: Principles of design that seek that any product be created for the use of all people, regardless of the conditions it presents, in such a way that redesign is not required to adapt its use to any particular group of users.

Usability: Characteristic of a product that describes how easy it is to use it in a given context.

Voice Talk Beacon: Mobile application developed by the Department of Computer Sciences of the Universidad Católica del Norte, installed in the Hospital of the city of Antofagasta (Chile). Its objective is to guide the movement of blind people who need to attend a service in said area.

ENDNOTES

[1]   http://www.wipo.int/treaties/en/ip/marrakesh/
[2]   http://www.autismo.org.es/sobre-los-TEA

Chapter 3
Striving for Inclusion in E–Learning and E–Health

Sandra Sanchez-Gordon
https://orcid.org/0000-0002-2940-7010
Escuela Politécnica Nacional, Ecuador

ABSTRACT

The purpose of this chapter is to present a seven-year journey to understand the barriers that people face when interacting with e-learning and e-health online platforms and to come up with software engineering solutions to make these platforms more inclusive. This chapter per the author presents a set of contributions intended to serve as steppingstones to future research efforts. These contributions include a literature review about accessibility of e-learning platforms; the accessibility audit of e-learning and e-health platforms; the identification of accessibility requirements; the design of architectures, process, and models to improve accessibility; and the definition of a life cycle for the management of accessible online courses. In this context, this chapter relate the evolution of the research process followed and summarize the results obtained so far.

INTRODUCTION

I have no legs,

But I still have feelings,

I cannot see,

But I think all the time,

Although I'm deaf,

I still want to communicate,

DOI: 10.4018/978-1-7998-7552-9.ch003

Copyright © 2021, IGI Global. Copying or distributing in print or electronic forms without written permission of IGI Global is prohibited.

Why do people see me as useless, thoughtless, talkless,

When I am as capable as any,

For thoughts about our world.

Coralie Severs, 14 years old, United Kingdom. (UNICEF, 2009)

The Universal Declaration of Human Rights was adopted by the United Nations in 1948 to identify and promote the observance of rights and freedoms to which all human beings are entitled regardless any condition (Gordon, 2018).

Article 25 of the Universal Declaration of Human Rights establishes the right to medical care:

(1) Everyone has the right to a standard of living adequate for the health and well-being of himself and of his family, including food, clothing, housing and medical care and necessary social services, and the right to security in the event of unemployment, sickness, disability, widowhood, old age or other lack of livelihood in circumstances beyond his control.

(2) Motherhood and childhood are entitled to special care and assistance. All children, whether born in or out of wedlock, shall enjoy the same social protection. (United Nations, 1948)

In addition, Article 26 establishes the right to education:

(1) Everyone has the right to education. Education shall be free, at least in the elementary and fundamental stages. Elementary education shall be compulsory. Technical and professional education shall be made generally available and higher education shall be equally accessible to all on the basis of merit.

(2) Education shall be directed to the full development of the human personality and to the strengthening of respect for human rights and fundamental freedoms. It shall promote understanding, tolerance and friendship among all nations, racial or religious groups, and shall further the activities of the United Nations for the maintenance of peace.

(3) Parents have a prior right to choose the kind of education that shall be given to their children. (United Nations, 1948)

In 2006, the United Nations adopted the Convention on the Rights of Persons with Disabilities (CRPD) with the support of 159 signatories and 151 ratifications. The CRPD proposes a new approach to human rights monitoring and enforcement, shifting the responsibility for disability from individuals and caretakers to society and government (United Nations, 2006). Kanter (2015) reflects on the importance of the CRPD envisioning a world where persons with disabilities are recognized as right holders entitled to full and equal citizenship, as well as social participation and inclusion.

The CRPD establishes that States Parties must take appropriate measures to ensure that persons with disabilities have access to the physical environment, to transportation, to information and communications technology, and to other facilities and services open or provided to the general public (Kanter, 2015) (United Nations, 2008).

The CRPD recognizes in Article 24 that persons with disabilities have the right to education without discrimination and based on equal opportunity:

(1) States Parties recognize the right of persons with disabilities to education. With a view to realizing this right without discrimination and on the basis of equal opportunity, States Parties shall ensure an inclusive education system at all levels and lifelong learning directed to: a. The full development of human potential and sense of dignity and self-worth, and the strengthening of respect for human rights, fundamental freedoms and human diversity; b. The development by persons with disabilities of their personality, talents and creativity, as well as their mental and physical abilities, to their fullest potential; c. Enabling persons with disabilities to participate effectively in a free society.

(2) In realizing this right, States Parties shall ensure that: a) Persons with disabilities are not excluded from the general education system on the basis of disability, and that children with disabilities are not excluded from free and compulsory primary education, or from secondary education, on the basis of disability; b) Persons with disabilities can access an inclusive, quality and free primary education and secondary education on an equal basis with others in the communities in which they live; c) Reasonable accommodation of the individual's requirements is provided; d) Persons with disabilities receive the support required, within the general education system, to facilitate their effective education; e) Effective individualized support measures are provided in environments that maximize academic and social development, consistent with the goal of full inclusion.

(3) States Parties shall enable persons with disabilities to learn life and social development skills to facilitate their full and equal participation in education and as members of the community. To this end, States Parties shall take appropriate measures, including: a) Facilitating the learning of Braille, alternative script, augmentative and alternative modes, means and formats of communication and orientation and mobility skills, and facilitating peer support and mentoring; b) Facilitating the learning of sign language and the promotion of the linguistic identity of the deaf community; c) Ensuring that the education of persons, and in particular children, who are blind, deaf or deafblind, is delivered in the most appropriate languages and modes and means of communication for the individual, and in environments which maximize academic and social development.

(4) In order to help ensure the realization of this right, States Parties shall take appropriate measures to employ teachers, including teachers with disabilities, who are qualified in sign language and/or Braille, and to train professionals and staff who work at all levels of education. Such training shall incorporate disability awareness and the use of appropriate augmentative and alternative modes, means and formats of communication, educational techniques and materials to support persons with disabilities.

(5) States Parties shall ensure that persons with disabilities are able to access general tertiary education, vocational training, adult education and lifelong learning without discrimination and on an equal basis with others. To this end, States Parties shall ensure that reasonable accommodation is provided to persons with disabilities. (United Nations, 2006)

Similarly, Article 25 states the right to health without discrimination on the basis of disability:

States Parties recognize that persons with disabilities have the right to the enjoyment of the highest attainable standard of health without discrimination on the basis of disability. States Parties shall take all appropriate measures to ensure access for persons with disabilities to health services that are gender-sensitive, including health-related rehabilitation. In particular, States Parties shall: a) Provide persons with disabilities with the same range, quality and standard of free or affordable health care and programmes as provided to other persons, including in the area of sexual and reproductive health and population-based public health programmes; b) Provide those health services needed by persons with disabilities specifically because of their disabilities, including early identification and intervention as appropriate, and services designed to minimize and prevent further disabilities, including among children and older persons; c) Provide these health services as close as possible to people's own communities, including in rural areas; d) Require health professionals to provide care of the same quality to persons with disabilities as to others, including on the basis of free and informed consent by, inter alia, raising awareness of the human rights, dignity, autonomy and needs of persons with disabilities through training and the promulgation of ethical standards for public and private health care; e) Prohibit discrimination against persons with disabilities in the provision of health insurance, and life insurance where such insurance is permitted by national law, which shall be provided in a fair and reasonable manner; f) Prevent discriminatory denial of health care or health services or food and fluids on the basis of disability. (United Nations, 2006)

According to the World Report on Disability of the World Health Organization more than one billion people live with some form of disability. This is around 15% of the world's population (World Health Organization, 2011). Disabilities can be analyzed from two perspectives.

First, personal disabilities which are those related to body or mental impairments of the human being that can be of birth or acquired via illnesses or accidents at any point in a person's life and can be permanent or temporary, e.g. vision, hearing, speech, motor, cognitive, and psychosocial (World Wide Web Consortium, 2019).

Second, environmental disabilities which are those related to situations surrounding the human being that can occur at any point in a person's life and are usually temporary, e.g. cognitive issues due to lack of language proficiency and environmental conditions (Sanchez-Gordon & Luján-Mora, 2014). With this second perspective, the number of persons that experience some form of disability increases appreciably.

In 2013, the author was preparing to start her doctoral research project knowing she wanted to contribute to solve education and health issues that affect underserved populations such as persons with disabilities, elderly people and foreign citizens. The author figured it would be a good idea to start reading and learning about how other people have come up with ideas to solve humankind problems creatively throughout history. Giving that the research project involved web accessibility, she realized that the problem at hand was not lack of accessibility but lack of inclusivity. The author began to ponder that accessible environments increase usability, remove barriers, diminish disability and enable inclusion. In virtual settings, those environments are not physical but online platforms instead.

Hence, the research problem is how to increase the level of inclusiveness in e-learning and e-health platforms. In this context, the purpose of this chapter is to present contributions to improve the inclusion of four types of users: students with disabilities, elderly students, foreign students and tele rehabilitation patients.

The rest of this chapter is organized as follows. First, a theoretical background is presented. Then, there is a section that explains the research problem, goal, beneficiaries, contributions, technologies, and trends for each of the four types of users. A brief discussion about inclusion in times of pandemic is included. Then, there is a section about research impact and visibility of the studies by the author. The chapter ends with a conclusion section.

BACKGROUND

This section presents the main conceptualizations and fields of application of this research effort. The key terms defined are disability, usability, accessibility, adaptability, inclusion, e-Learning, MOOC, WCAG, e-Health and tele-rehabilitation.

Disability

The definition of disability adopted in this research has a social approach as explained by Scope, a London-based disability equality charity organization, cited by Iniesto (2020):

Disability is caused by the way society is organized, rather than by a person's impairment or difference (including age, cultural environment and economic difficulties). It looks at ways of removing barriers that restrict life choices for disabled people. When barriers are removed, disabled people can be independent and equal in society, with choice and control over their own lives. (Scope)

Disability, for this research purpose, is mainly explained by the person himself through self-identification and profiling of his accessibility needs and preferences according to his current life situation.

Usability

The International Organization for Standardization (2018), in the standard ISO 9241-11:2018 Ergonomics of human-system interaction - Part 11: Usability: Definitions and concepts, defines usability as the "extent to which a product can be used by specified users to achieve specified goals effectively, efficiently and with satisfaction in a specified context of use". According to Yonaitis (2002), usability focuses on designing a product or service to meet users' expectations and adapting it to their needs with efficiency and ease such that it enables optimal use by the target users.

Usability and accessibility are closely related as less accessibility implies low usability. Petrie & Bevan (2009) explain that non-accessible features are not usable; however, usable features may not necessarily be accessible.

Accessibility

The International Organization for Standardization (2008a), in the standard ISO 9241-171:2008 Ergonomics of human-system interaction - Part 171 Guidance on software accessibility, defines accessibility as the "usability of a product, service, environment or facility by people with the widest range of capabilities". In this sense, accessibility is the ability to access and make use of things to reach a goal regardless of the conditions of the user and the environment.

The Global Learning Consortium (2020) states that accessible systems adjust its user interface, locate needed resources and adjust the properties of such resources to match the needs and preferences of the user. Doing so decreases exclusion and increases usability.

Adaptability

The International Organization for Standardization (2008b), in the Standard ISO/IEC 24751-1: 2008 Information technology – Individualized adaptability and accessibility in e-learning, education and training, defines adaptability as the "capacity of a digital resource of a system of provision to adjust the presentation, the methods of control, the structure, the way of access and the support to the user, in its presentation".

Hence, the accessibility is the ability of an environment to adjust or adapt to the needs of all users. Adaptability is determined by the flexibility of the environment and the availability of adequate alternative-but-equivalent content and features.

Inclusion

As explained in Coughlan et al. (2019), inclusiveness implies understanding the needs of groups of people to facilitate their equitable access to a service or product. Accessibility is a key feature to promote inclusive education and health services in virtual and distributed environments where there is a great diversity in the accessibility needs and preferences of users (Sanchez-Gordon & Luján-Mora, 2018a).

e-Learning

e-Learning is a type of distance learning that relies on electronic mechanisms to mediate the learning experience. An e-Learning platform host online courses that can be delivered asynchronously. That is, learners and instructors does not need to meet at the same time. This enables education for learners who cannot attend in person to an educational institution and lower cost of the educational service (Sanchez-Gordon & Luján-Mora, 2018c).

MOOC

The acronym MOOC was coined in 2012 and stands for Massive Open Online Courses. MOOC differ from traditional online courses hosted in e-Learning platforms in that MOOC can have a great number of participants since generally they do not have enrollment requirements and can be taken for free or optionally paying small fees for official certificates or extra services, such as instructor feedback. The accessibility of MOOC and the educational resources contained in them must be guaranteed, since the probability that students with different types of disabilities participate in a MOOC is much greater than in traditional online courses (Otón et al., 2020).

WCAG

The World Wide Web Consortium (W3C), organization in charge of developing web standards, created the Web Accessibility Initiative (WAI) to develop guidelines for universal access (World Wide Web

Consortium, 1997). In 1999, WAI published the Web Content Accessibility Guidelines (WCAG) 1.0. In 2008, accessibility experts and users with disabilities made corrections and extensions that led to WCAG 2.0 (World Wide Web Consortium, 2008). In 2012, ISO recognized WCAG 2.0 as an international standard, named ISO/IEC 40500:2012. In 2018, WCAG 2.1 was released as a W3C recommendation (World Wide Web Consortium, 2018). In 2020, W3C published the first working draft of WCAG 2.2 (World Wide Web Consortium, 2020). Several countries around the world reference WCAG 2.0 in their accessibility laws.

WCAG 2.0 establishes four principles that give the foundation of web accessibility (World Wide Web Consortium, 2008): Perceivable, Operable, Understandable, and Robust, known as POUR. The perceivable principle states that users must be able to perceive with their able senses both the content and the user interface. The operable principle states that users must be able to operate the interface through interaction that the users can perform. The understandable principle states that users must be able to understand the content as well as the operation of the user interface. The robust principle states that users must be able to access the content as technologies advance.

In the new versions, WCAG 2.1 (World Wide Web Consortium, 2018) and WCAG 2.2 (World Wide Web Consortium, 2020), one new guideline and 18 new success criteria has been added to improve accessibility guidance for three major groups: users with cognitive or learning disabilities, users with low vision, and users with disabilities on mobile devices. Currently, under the four principles, there are 13 guidelines and 79 success criteria. The guidelines are not testable but provide the framework and overall objectives to help developers understand the testable success criteria. To meet the needs of different groups of users and different situations, three levels of conformance defined are A (lowest), AA, and AAA (highest).

e-Health

e-Health is the provision of health care using electronic mechanisms to deliver and enhance the services and information provided to the patients. In a broader sense, the term characterizes not only a technical development or the confluence of Internet and Medicine, but also a commitment to improve health care locally, regionally, and worldwide by using information and communication technology (Eysenbach, 2001).

Tele-rehabilitation

Tele-rehabilitation is the application of telecommunication technologies to provide support, advice, and intervention remotely to patients in need of physical rehabilitation (Pilco et al., 2019b). Tele-rehabilitation platforms are used for the treatment of several conditions such as neurological, cardiopulmonary, musculoskeletal, and orthopedic conditions (Pérez Medina et al., 2019).

INCLUSION OF STUDENTS WITH DISABILITIES

Problem

There are two historical events that illustrate the problem of exclusion of students with disabilities in e-learning platforms. They happened when two important organizations confronted disability law in United States.

In 2015, the MOOC platform provider edX Inc. had to reach a settlement with the United States Department of Justice to include accessible content on its platform. As a result, edX Inc. changed its policies as follows:

MOOCs have the potential to increase access to high-quality education for people facing income, distance, and other barriers, but only if they are truly open to everyone. This landmark agreement is far-reaching in ensuring that individuals with disabilities will have an equal opportunity to independently and conveniently access quality higher education online. (US Department of Justice, 2015)

A year later, University of Berkeley decided to take a different position to the same problem. University of Berkeley opted to remove more than 20,000 audio and video files from its online open-access platforms instead of investing in making that content accessible (Jaschik, 2016).

Although some online courses have reached enrollments as massive as 370,000 students, for instance "Circuits and Electronics" offered by edX in 2012, the completion rates range from 0.7% to 52.1% according to Jordan (2015). Hence, a concern often raised about MOOC is that although thousands enroll, usually only a small proportion of students complete the courses.

Goal

The goal of this research effort is to propose engineering solutions to increase the completion rates of learners with disabilities in e-Learning courses.

Beneficiaries

In 2019, there was a total of 110 million students enrolled in more than 13500 online courses worldwide (Shah, 2019). From them, approximately 16.5 million are expected to experience some type of disability while studying (World Health Organization, 2011). Those are the potential beneficiaries of the solutions proposed in this section.

Contributions

The first step was to perform a systematic literature review to identify the corpus related to accessibility and e-learning. This systematic literature review covered publications from 2012 to 2016 and identified 40 relevant studies. The stages of the method followed is presented in Figure 1 and was based in (Kitchenham, 2007).

Table 1 shows the results of the systematic literature review. A total of 40 relevant studies were identified. A total of four studies from the year 2012 to the year 2013. Followed by 9 studies per each year

Figure 1. Stages of the systematic literature review method (Sanchez-Gordon & Luján-Mora, 2018a)

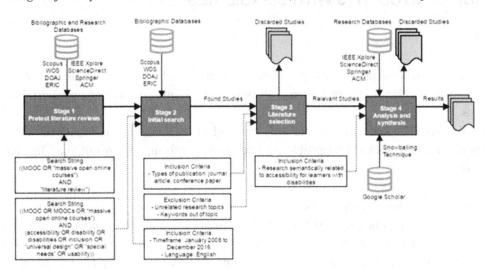

2014 and 2015. The number of studies duplicated in the year 2016. The sources were: Scopus, Web of Science (WOS), Directory of Open Access Journals (DOAJ), Education Resources Information Center (ERIC) and Google Scholar (GS).

Table 1. Relevant studies per year and sources.

Sources	2012	2013	2014	2015	2016	2012-2016
Scopus	1	2	6	6	10	25
WOS	1	3	7	6	8	25
DOAJ	0	0	0	1	0	1
ERIC	0	0	0	1	0	1
Total (with duplications)	2	5	13	14	18	52
Total (without duplications)	1	3	7	7	11	29
GS (additional studies)	0	0	2	2	7	11
Total	**1**	**3**	**9**	**9**	**18**	**40**

As a result, eight research dimensions were identified: problem characterization; needs identification; use of industry guidelines, specifications, and standards; accessibility requirements specification; architectures; design strategies; verification of accessibility requirements compliance; and validation of user needs satisfaction. These dimensions were refined in 58 sub dimensions and the publications were mapped to them. Figure 2 shows the distribution of the studies per year and research dimension. The less researched dimensions were architecture, design, and requirements.

The next step was to establish a disabilities classification to take in account when identifying accessibility requirements for e-Learning platforms and courses. Figure 3 illustrates the eight types of disabilities proposed in this research: vision, hearing, speech, motor, cognitive, psychosocial, language and cultural.

Figure 2. Distribution of studies per research dimension (Sanchez-Gordon & Luján-Mora, 2018a)

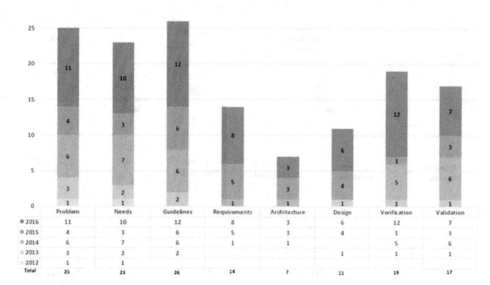

	Problem	Needs	Guidelines	Requirements	Architecture	Design	Verification	Validation
▪ 2016	11	10	12	8	3	6	12	7
▪ 2015	4	3	6	5	3	4	1	3
▪ 2014	6	7	6	1	1		5	6
▪ 2013	3	2	2			1	1	1
▪ 2012	1	1						
Total	25	23	26	14	7	11	19	17

The integration of the POUR accessibility principles of WCAG sets up the accessibility requirements specification model for MOOCs proposed in this study. Figure 4 presents a partial view of the associated UML Use Case Model. The actor Learner can specialize in Blind, Low Vision, Dyslexia, and so on. The actor Learner performs the use case MOOC Platform Tasks including the use case Manage Profile, which has a use case extension Manage Accessibility Preferences. When the actor Learner performs the use case Navigate MOOC content, the appropriate use case extensions are executed. The alternative

Figure 3. Classification of disabilities (Sanchez-Gordon & Luján-Mora, 2014)

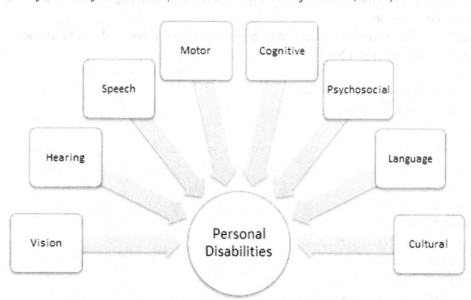

Figure 4. Accessibility requirements UML use case model (Sanchez-Gordon & Luján-Mora, 2016b)

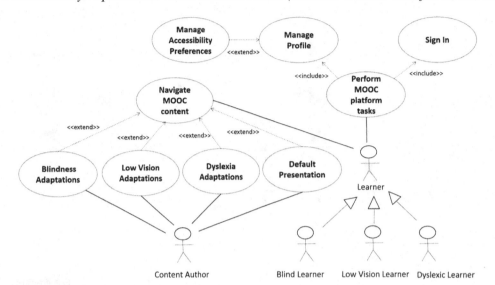

accessible interfaces are created by the actor Platform Developer. The alternative accessible content formats are created by the actor Content Author.

The proposal to manage the profile information is that the learner with disabilities accesses a user interface where he or she can select accessibility preferences. Figure 5 presents a prototype of such interface.

Based on the profile, the e-Learning platform performs the necessary adaptions in the user interface controls and in the content. The goal is to apply adaptive techniques based on rules according to the accessibility needs stated in the user profile. Figure 6 shows a sample page of an online course adapted for a user with a profile of two combined disabilities: low vision and dyslexia. Dyslexia is a neurological condition that impairs a person's ability to read, recognize words, spell correctly and decode written information (Kalyvioti & Mikropoulos, 2013). Dyslexia is a common cognitive disability since 10% of the global population has it.

Below an extract of the ruleset sequence to be executed to resolve dyslexia based on the research developed by De Santana et al. (2012).

```
<!—Adaptive Content Rule Set -->
<ruleset name="Adaptation Content Rule Set">
<description>
This rule set defines rules to adapt content according to the related
disability
</description>
<!-- Dyslexia -->
<rule name="dyslexia">
<text-font>Verdana</text-font>
<text-font>Arial</text-font>
<text-font>Calibri</text-font>
<text-font>Sans serif</text-font>
```

Figure 5. User interface to select accessibility preferences (Sanchez-Gordon & Luján-Mora, 2016b)

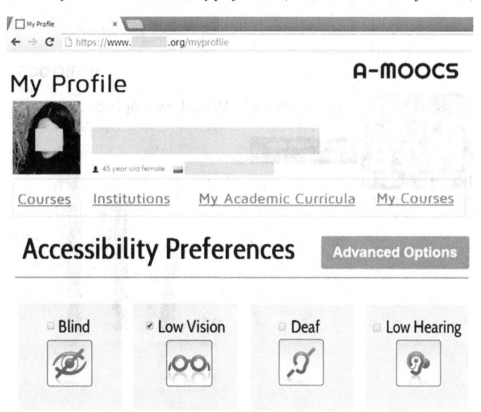

```
<text-size>12</text-size>
<line-spacing>2</line-spacing>
<text-justification>unjustified</text-justification>
</rule>
</ruleset>
```

It is necessary to define a lifecycle for the development and management of the courses hosted in e-Learning platforms that allows educators to focus on teaching, interaction with their students and other elements indispensable for the success of the learning experience. The lifecycle covers both the online course development process as well as its management, considering both pedagogy and software engineering. The lifecycle includes three stages: development, management, and improvement of the online course, as depicted in Figure 7.

Table 2 lists the research publications and summarizes the main contributions to the inclusion of learners with disabilities in e-learning platforms and courses.

Technologies and Trends

The main technologies involved in the field of inclusion of learners with disabilities in e-Learning environments are:

Figure 6. Low vision and dyslexia adaptation (Sanchez-Gordon & Luján-Mora, 2016b)

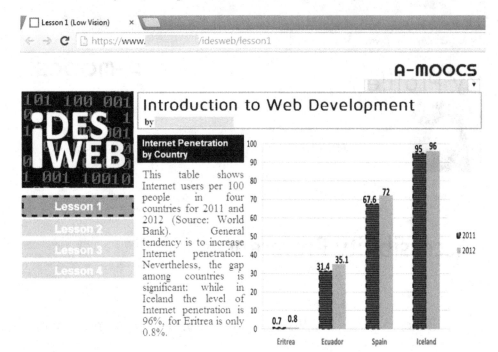

Figure 7. Lifecycle for online courses development and management (Sanchez-Gordon & Luján-Mora, 2018b)

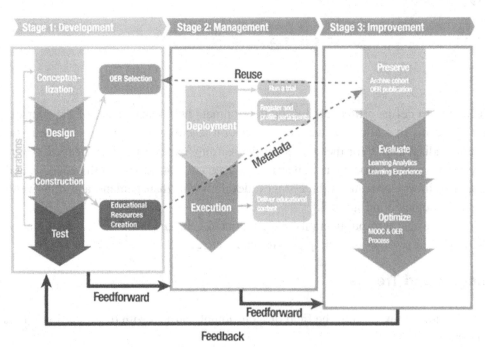

Table 2. Research publications and their contributions to the inclusion of students with disabilities

Publication	Contributions
Web Accessibility Evaluation of Massive Open Online Courses on Geographical Information Systems (Calle-Jimenez et al., 2014).	· Describes some of the challenges that exist to make accessible MOOC on Geographical Information Systems. · Presents results of the evaluation of a MOOC called "Maps and the Geospatial Revolution" using three tools: Chrome Developer Tools – Accessibility Audit, eXaminator and WAVE.
Web accessibility requirements for massive open online courses (Sanchez-Gordon & Luján-Mora, 2014).	· Proposes two categories of accessibility requirements: for personal and for non-personal disabilities. · Each category is characterized and a preliminary list of web accessibility requirements for each one is presented.
Adaptive content presentation extension for open edX. Enhancing MOOCs accessibility for users with disabilities (Sanchez-Gordon & Luján-Mora, 2015a).	· With the proposed extension, the particular situation of a person with disabilities may go unnoticed for both instructors and peer students, so the person with disabilities can be treated truly equally, hence assuring real inclusiveness.
An ecosystem for corporate training with accessible MOOCs and OERs (Sanchez-Gordon & Luján-Mora, 2015b).	· Presents approaches to use MOOC in the context of corporate training where the goal is to facilitate employees´ learning of job-related competencies within their company culture and goals. · Proposes an ecosystem to enable accessible MOOCs and Open Educational Resources (OERs) deployment in corporate training contexts. The proposed ecosystem includes three stages: develop, publish, and improve.
How Could MOOCs Become Accessible? The Case of edX and the Future of Inclusive Online Learning (Sanchez-Gordon & Luján-Mora, 2016a).	· edX Studio does not comply with Authoring Tool Accessibility Guidelines (ATAG) 2.0. · Design proposal to improve the accessibility of courses created and hosted in edX platform.
Design, implementation, and evaluation of MOOCs to improve inclusion of diverse learners (Sanchez-Gordon & Luján-Mora, 2016b).	· Presents accessibility requirements that need to be considered in the design, implementation, and evaluation of MOOC to ensure they are inclusive · Explains how to design and implement accessible MOOC. · Explains how to evaluate the level of accessibility of MOOC.
Editor for accessible images in e-learning platforms (Sanchez-Gordon et al., 2016c)	· Presents a set of twenty features for managing accessible images when generating educational content. · Assess a sample of eight e-Learning platforms regarding image accessibility. · Presents a visual text editor for accessible images designed to be a base component across e-learning platforms.
Research challenges in accessible MOOCs: A systematic literature review 2008-2016. Universal Access in the Information Society (Sanchez-Gordon & Luján-Mora, 2018a).	· This systematic literature review identified 40 relevant studies in the field of accessible MOOC published between 2012 and 2016. · Eight research dimensions and 58 sub dimensions were identified, and the studies were mapped to them.
Lifecycle for MOOC development and management (Sanchez-Gordon & Luján-Mora, 2018b).	· Proposes a lifecycle is based on the Plan-Do-Check-Act cycle and the standard ISO/IEC 29110-5-1-2: 2011 Lifecycle profiles for Very Small Entities (VSEs) - Part 5-1-2: Management and Engineering guide.
Implementing Accessibility in Massive Open Online Courses' Platforms for Teaching, Learning and Collaborating at Large Scale (Sanchez-Gordon & Luján-Mora, 2019).	· Presents manual evaluations of a Coursera sample using three test procedures. In test cases 1 and 2, 100% of the sample failed to comply. In test case 3, 75% failed to comply. · Authors test-drove features of edX Studio by re-creating a real scenario where an instructor creates a course, add images, videos, text content and quizzes. Open edX Studio does not comply with level A of the Authoring Tool Accessibility Guidelines (ATAG) 2.0 since the content created with it does not comply with level A of the WCAG 2.0.
Building hybrid interfaces to increase interaction with young children and children with special needs (Jadán-Guerrero et al., 2020a).	· Uses Design Thinking methodology to create hybrid interfaces. · Educational Board Games where augmented reality markers give an extra information to the players. · Tangible educational resources, which integrate Makey-Makey device and Scratch with fruit, clay, aluminum foil or water to build a laboratory.
Interactive storytelling books for fostering inclusion of children with special needs (Jadán-Guerrero et al., 2020b).	· Varying the types of materials available to children is another way to make the classroom more inclusive. · The interactivity of traditional tale books was increased by incorporating QR codes, NFC tags and augmented reality.
Implementation of controls for insertion of accessible images in open online editors based on WCAG guidelines. Case studies: TinyMCE and Summernote (Sanchez-Gordon et al., 2020a).	· The ATAG 2.0 compliance of TinyMCE was improved by adding entry fields for the type of image to be inserted, long description and title. TinyMCE is used in content management systems such as WordPress, Joomla, and Drupal. · Similarly, in Summernote entry fields were added for the type of image to be inserted, alternative text, long description, and title. Summernote is an open online editor. · In both cases, controls were implemented to validate mandatory and optional fields according to the type of image.
Evolution of Accessibility Metadata in Educational Resources (Otón et al., 2020).	· Presents the evolution of accessibility metadata in educational resources. In the area of e-learning environments and digital educational resources, the use of accessibility metadata is still incipient.
Model for Generation of Profiles for Persons with Disabilities in e-Learning Environments (Sanchez-Gordon et al., 2020b).	· Proposes a model for the generation of profiles for persons with disabilities in e-Learning environments. The model allows registering accessibility needs and preferences regarding the use of different sensory modes for the perception and understanding of information depending on the current life situation. The model is based on the specification IMS Access for All 3.0 PNP.

- Accessibility guidelines, such as WCAG and ATAG.
- Assistive technologies, such as screen readers and speech-to-text software.
- Automated usability and accessibility evaluation tools.

The future trends in this field are:

- Profiling.
- Natural user interfaces (NUIs).
- Adaptive learning engines with artificial intelligence (AI).
- Recommender systems with AI.

INCLUSION OF ELDERLY STUDENTS

Problem

Worldwide there is an ever-increasing number of elderly people that develops combined disabilities due to natural aging and have the right to education lifelong learning (Sanchez-Gordon & Luján-Mora, 2013a). E-learning is an opportunity to help older people become integrated with the rest of society and to fight feelings of loneliness and lack of life purpose. E-learning brings great opportunities to enhance the quality of life of elderly people by enabling learning experiences and the inclusion in learning communities. Unfortunately, the problem is that older people face several challenges when using e-Learning platforms and courses due to diminishing capacities, such as vision decline, hearing loss, decremented motor skills and cognition issues.

Goal

The goal of this research effort is to propose engineering solutions to increase the participation of elderly people in e-Learning courses.

Beneficiaries

The increase of life expectancy is provoking a global demographic change consisting of an increase in the fraction of elderly people. The number of older persons is projected to reach nearly 2.1 billion by 2050 (United Nations, 2017). Globally, the number of persons aged 80 years or over is projected to increase more than threefold between 2017 and 2050, rising from 137 million to 425 million (United Nations, 2017). The learners' range in age reported by main e-Learning platforms are Udacity: 13 to 80 years old, Coursera: 16 to 88 years old, and EdX: 7 to 96 years old (EdX, 2018). Solutions in education and life-long learning opportunities for older persons allow them to acquire skills they might need to remain active in the labor market and to maintain cognitive function, as well as physical and mental health.

Contributions

Based on the findings by the Web Accessibility Initiate WAI-AGE Project, the author proposed a categorization of thirty-eight accessibility requirements that reflect the different needs of elderly students in e-Learning platforms and courses. First category relates to text size. Older users need large text due to declining vision. This includes not only body text but also text included in form fields and other types of interface controls. Here is the requirement correspondent to success criterion 1.4.4 of WCAG. Second category relates to text style and text layout. Text style and its visual presentation impacts how hard or easy it is for older students to read the text, taken in account their declining vision. Here are eleven requirements corresponding to the success criteria 1.4.5, 1.4.8, 1.4.9, 2.4.1, 2.4.2, 2.4.4, 2.4.6, 2.4.7, 2.4.9 and 2.4.10, plus six additional non-WCAG requirements: avoid bold body-text, avoid underlined text other than links, ensure links change color after visit, clearly separate links, make search results visible and make sure the user notices small page changes/updates. Third category relates to color and contrast. Most older people's color perception changes even become color blindness. Older people also lose contrast sensitivity. Here are three requirements corresponding to the success criteria 1.4.1, 1.4.3 and 1.4.6 plus one additional non-WCAG requirement: avoid the use of fluorescent colors. Fourth category is related to multimedia. Many older people need transcripts, captions, and low background sound due to declining vision and hearing. Here are 10 requirements corresponding to the success criteria 1.1.1, 1.2.1, 1.2.2, 1.2.3, 1.2.4, 1.2.5, 1.2.7, 1.2.8, 1.2.9, 1.3.1, 1.3.2, 1.3.3, 1.4.7, 3.1.1, 3.3.2, 4.1.1 and 4.1.2.

Table 3 lists the research publications and summarizes their main contributions to the inclusion of elderly students in e-learning platforms and courses.

Table 3. Research publications and contributions to the inclusion of elderly students

Publication	Contributions
Web accessibility of MOOCs for elderly students (Sanchez-Gordon & Luján-Mora, 2013a).	· Raise awareness towards a better understanding of the accessibility challenges that elderly users face. · Five courses hosted in the Coursera platform from different world regions were analyzed. The analysis included: announcements, video lectures, quizzes, and discussion forums. · Twenty-nine accessibility requirements for older users were identified where twenty-two were mapped to the correspondent success criteria from WCAG 2.0. · The e-Learning platform and courses analyzed in this preliminary study have accessibility issues that need to be addressed.
E-government accessibility in Ecuador: A preliminary evaluation (Sanchez-Gordon et al., 2020c).	· Presents the results of a preliminary evaluation carried out with a sample of the five most visited Ecuadorian e-Government websites that provide online services to senior citizens and general citizens alike. · Two automated web accessibility evaluation tools were used: WAVE and Cynthia Says. The results reveal that all the evaluated websites have accessibility issues that put barriers for citizens failing to comply with the Ecuadorian regulations regarding WCAG 2.0 AA.

Technologies and Trends

The main technologies involved in the field of inclusion of elderly students in e-Learning environments are the same as those for students with disabilities since they can be considered as users with a combination of disabilities in different degrees.

Taken in account that elderly students are adults, future trends in this field – additional to the ones listed in the previous section - are:

- Flexible learning.
- Behavioral analytics.
- Curation.
- Content aggregators with AI.

INCLUSION OF FOREIGN STUDENTS

Problem

Many online courses are offered only in English. A quick review of edX as of July 2020 shows that of 3,264 courses, 2,619 are offered in English, representing 80.2% of the offer; Spanish is the second language with the most courses offered, 384, but it only represents 11.8%. The other 8% is shared by 261 courses in 18 different languages: French, Chinese – Mandarin, Italian, Russian, Simplified Chinese, German, Japanese, Arabic, Dutch, Portuguese, Korean, Turkish, Hindi, Traditional Chinese, Hungarian, Tibetan, Urdu and Vietnamese.

Students with different native languages might have difficulties related to their proficiency in English and their cultural background that lead to cognitive overload. Language and cultural barriers discourage many potential learners, especially from developing countries.

Goal

The goal of this research effort is to propose engineering solutions to increase the participation and completion rates of foreign students in e-Learning courses.

Beneficiaries

The potential beneficiaries are all the students around the world that take online courses offered in a language different than their mother tongue. In Coursera, 76% of the students are from outside United States (Smith, 2020). An exploratory study of MOOC´s learners' demographics showed that for the case study offered in English only 19.8% of the students were from United States, followed by 25.2% from China and other 81 different countries from all the continents (Bayeck, 2016). Taken in account that in 2019, there was a total of 110 million students enrolled in more than 13500 online courses worldwide (Shah, 2019), it can be estimated that at least 80 million were foreign students.

Contributions

The model proposed in this research effort involves three actors: the non-native speaker, the local instructor, and the online course author. The non-native speakers (NNS) register as learners in the learning experience. They participate both in the local study group and the learning management system. They are responsible for managing their personal user profile. The local instructors guide and motivate students through their learning experience. They also elaborate and grade face-to-face examinations. Local instructors should receive previous training in the model and the use of the e-learning platform. Authors are responsible for creating and managing learning materials including several alternative formats. They also manage the course profile. Figure 8 shows the general architecture that includes three e-learning platform components: a learning management system, a content management system, and an adaptive content engine.

Figure 8. e-Learning model for non-native speakers (Sanchez-Gordon & Luján-Mora, 2015c).

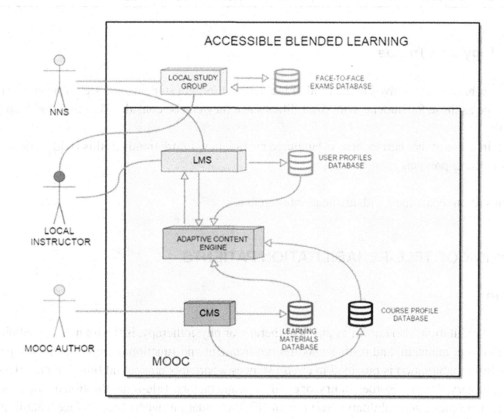

Table 4 lists the research publications and summarizes its main contributions to the inclusion of foreign students in e-learning platforms and courses.

Table 4. Research publications and contributions to the inclusion of foreign students

Publication	Contributions
Accessibility considerations of Massive Online Open Courses as creditable courses in Engineering Programs (Sanchez-Gordon & Luján-Mora, 2013b).	· Presents a list of five general requirements and 28 accessibility requirements for non-native speakers when using MOOC. · Establishes criteria for selection of MOOC as creditable courses in engineering programs.
Accessible blended learning for non-native speakers using MOOCs (Sanchez-Gordon & Luján-Mora, 2015c).	· Elicits requirements from WCAG 2.0, ISO/IEC 24751:2008 Individualized adaptability and accessibility in e-learning, education and training, published results of related research, non-native speakers that have participated in MOOCs in English, and authors´ own experience as instructors and students of MOOC. · Proposes a design for enabling accessible blended learning experiences for non-native speakers using MOOC. The architecture involves three actors: non-native speakers, local instructors, and MOOC authors; one non-virtual component (a local study group), and three platform components: a learning management system, a content management system and an adaptive content engine.
Barriers and strategies for using MOOCs in the context of Higher Education in Ibero-America (Sanchez-Gordon & Luján-Mora, 2016d).	· Identifies five groups of barriers for the use of MOOC: Internet access, cost, language, accessibility, and pedagogy. · Presents a FODA analysis and 18 strategies.

Technology and Trends

The main technologies involved in the field of inclusion of foreign students in e-Learning environments are the same as those for students with disabilities since they can be considered as users with cognitive disabilities.

Taken in account that barrier here is language proficiency, future trends in this field – additional to the ones listed in previous sections - are:

● Translation technology with artificial intelligence.

INCLUSION OF TELE-REHABILITATION PATIENTS

Problem

Physical rehabilitation, also known as physical therapy or physiotherapy, is the branch of medicine that aims to develop, maintain, and restore maximum movement and functional ability through a person's life. Physical rehabilitation is provided in circumstances where movement and function are affected by age, pain, surgery, illness, disorder, injury, or environmental factors. Tele-rehabilitation provides new opportunities to implement rehabilitation services in different situations where face-to-face rehabilitation is complicated or practically impossible. Unfortunately, the potential benefits of tele-rehabilitation to improve healthcare is partially dependent on its ease of use (Sousa & Lopez, 2017). Currently, tele-rehabilitation platforms are not designed with usability and accessibility in mind. Thus, rehabilitation patients with diminished mobility during their recovery process, elderly patients or patients with permanent disabilities face barriers to use the services and get the information provided by tele-rehabilitation platforms.

Goal

The goal of this research effort is to propose engineering solutions to improve the usability and accessibility of tele-rehabilitation platforms for patients.

Beneficiaries

Online platforms for tele-rehabilitation are of interest not only for patients who cannot go to a rehabilitation center and their families, but also for public health since the use of technology saves infrastructure and mobilization costs. A home program of physical rehabilitation is very convenient for these patients. The program should be one that patients can do easily and safely in their homes without direct supervision from their therapist or doctor. Tele-rehabilitation provides new opportunities to implement rehabilitation services in different situations where face-to-face rehabilitation is complicated or not possible.

Contributions

Figure 9 depicts a proposed process to improve the usability and accessibility of tele-rehabilitation platforms. The method included three inputs, three processes and one final output. The inputs are the tele-rehabilitation platform, a set of usability and accessibility requirements prioritized by level of severity and a testing procedure. These three inputs fed the first process, which is an analysis using automated tools, heuristics evaluations, cognitive walkthroughs, and NASA TLX assessments. The output of the first process is a report of barriers that presents the tele-rehabilitation platform at that point. This report serves as input for the second process, the user interface refactoring using agile methods. In this way, the evolution of the level of usability and accessibility of the tele-rehabilitation platform and the results obtained from the analysis allows the developers to measure the utility of the improvement process through several iterations while keeping a record of the changes made. The refactorized user interfaces are re-tested to verify the improvements. These phases iterate until the tele-rehabilitation platform reaches the desired level of usability and accessibility.

Figure 9. Process for improvement of tele-rehabilitation platforms (Calle-Jimenez et al., 2019).

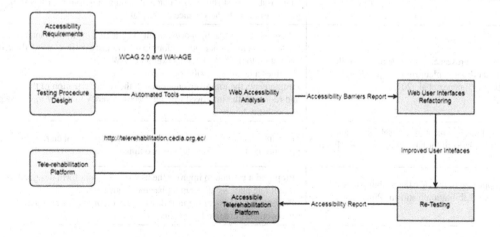

Figure 10 shows a comparative of errors reported by the evaluation tools for a tele-rehabilitation platform mapped to WCAG criteria, before and after the improvements. As can be seen, the re-testing results show a significant improvement with respect to the initial testing. In this example, it is still necessary to fine-tune the implementation to reach conformance with success criteria 1.3.1 and 3.2.2 and comply fully with WCAG.

Figure 10. Comparative of errors before and after usability improvement (Calle-Jimenez et al., 2019).

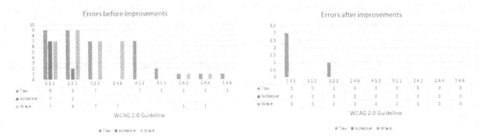

Table 5 lists the research publications and summarizes their main contributions to the inclusion of patients in tele-rehabilitation platforms.

Technology and Trends

The main technologies involved in the field of inclusion of patients in tele-Rehabilitation environments are:

Table 5. Research publications and contributions to the inclusion of tele-rehabilitation patients

Publication	Contributions
Usability study of a web-based platform for home motor rehabilitation (Pérez Medina et al., 2019).	· Reports the empirical results based on the subjective usability perception and self-reported feedback based on the IBM Computer System Usability Questionnaire. · The usability test shows that a lack of or an ambiguous user feedback can be a great barrier in the acceptance of the platform.
Analysis and improvement of the web accessibility of a tele-rehabilitation platform for hip arthroplasty patients (Calle-Jimenez et al., 2019).	· Presents the results of an accessibility evaluation of the web interfaces of the tele-rehabilitation platform for hip arthroplasty patients using three the evaluation tools: WAVE, AChecker and TAW. · Defines a list of accessibility improvements. · Implements the improvements through the re-factorization of the existing code and re-testing the improved web interfaces to verify that they meet acceptable accessibility levels.
Analysis and improvement of the usability of a tele-rehabilitation platform for hip surgery patients (Pilco et al., 2019a).	· Presents a set of heuristics relating to navigation, visual clarity, coherence, prevention of errors, user guidance, online help and user control.
An agile approach to improve the usability of a physical tele rehabilitation platform (Pilco et al., 2019b).	· Proposed a method to improve the usability of a platform designed to rehabilitate patients after hip replacement surgery. · Presents the results of the usability evaluation organized as a list of improvements ordered by severity.

- Accessibility guidelines, such as WCAG and ATAG.
- Assistive technologies, such as screen readers and speech-to-text software.
- Automated usability and accessibility evaluation tools.
- NASA TLX.

The future trends in this field are:

- Natural user interfaces (NUIs).
- Behavioral analytics.
- Translation technology with artificial intelligence.

INCLUSION IN TIMES OF PANDEMIC

In 2020, humanity faces the Covid-19 pandemic. Confinement, social distancing, and bio-security measures are imposed to avoid massive contagions in the population worldwide. Nevertheless, both public and private health and education services must keep going. Those are basic rights of all human beings. However, both have had to be reinvented to adjust to the new circumstances. In this context, Internet takes over to offer solutions based in tele-education and tele-medicine.

However, real inclusion will only occur to the extent that the services and information offered by means of online platforms are usable and accessible to all people regardless of their capacities and environmental conditions. Current solutions must be audited to determine their level of usability and accessibility, and then be redesigned to meet desired levels of usability and accessibility. In the same manner, new solutions must be conceived, architected, developed, tested, and deployed with usability and accessibility requirements in mind.

RESEARCH IMPACT AND VISIBILITY

From 2013 to 2020, the author has kept writing scientific publications to maximize the reach and usage of the research results in three dimensions: visibility, to enable researchers worldwide to reach and interact with the content of the publications; impact, to contribute within the scientific community; and connectivity, to assist other researchers around the world to further develop their own projects. The research results have been published in eight articles in scientific journals with JCR impact, thirty-five

Table 6. Visibility metrics in four scientific repositories.

	Publications	Citations	H-Index
Scopus	43	192	8
Web of Science	27	126	8
Google Scholar	62	614	14
ResearchGate	74	431	11

articles in scientific congresses and seven book chapters. So far, the author has obtained the outcomes detailed in Table 6.

According to Scopus, a total of 192 citations was reached in the month of September 2020. The most cited research publication is "Web accessibility of MOOCs for elderly students" with 32 cites in Scopus, 20 cites in Web of Science, 76 cites in Google Scholar and 68 cites in ResearchGate. The author ResearchGate's score is 23.82, higher that 80% of all ResearchGate members´ scores. Another important metric is the number of peer reviewed scientific publications. So far, 86 verified reviews are registered in Publons. In 2018, the author was granted a peer review award for being in the top 1% of reviewers in Computer Science who performed the most verified pre-publication peer reviews on Publons.

Promoting the visibility of the scientific production is important as it helps to increase the impact of the results in the research community and the recognition of the researcher's contribution. Figure 11 shows a summary of the publications and citations trends by author as presented by Scopus.

Figure 11. Publications and citations trends by author as presented by Scopus.

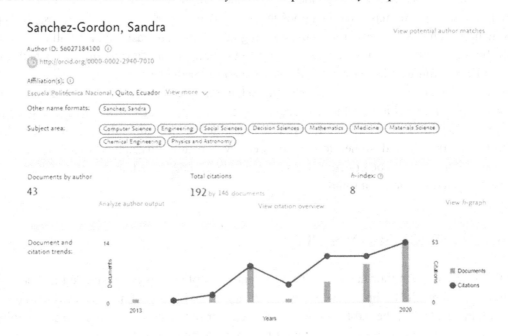

Finally, the author presents a set of guidelines directed to young researchers that from her experience can be useful to improve the visibility and impact of their research results:

- Create and manage online research profiles, such as ORCID, ResearchGate, Google Scholar with their institutional affiliation.
- Create and manage a repository of their research publications in their institutional web portal.
- Actively participate in research conferences and academic events with international reach.
- Create and manage a blog for scientific dissemination for the public.
- Participate in international research networks.
- Participate in international research projects.

- Participate in forums and interviews to explain about their research work.
- Apply for international research funds.
- Do not stop teaching and involving students in research-based instructional strategies.
- Volunteer in organizations that offer underserved population opportunities to learn about their research work.

CONCLUSION

Software solutions must adapt to users, not the other way around. This is the best cost-effective way to design a solution, especially in scenarios where large numbers of diverse users are expected to access and use a service, as is the case in e-learning and e-health. Global population in general can potentially benefit of inclusive e-learning and e-health environments that enable users with and without disabilities to receive health and education services and information in an equal fashion. This chapter per the author hope to have contributed to raise awareness and join the efforts to improve inclusiveness for the benefit of all people.

ACKNOWLEDGMENT

The author wants to thank all past, present, and future fellow researchers that strive for inclusion in e-learning and e-health.

REFERENCES

Bayeck, R. (2016). Exploratory study of MOOC learners' demographics and motivation: The case of students involved in groups. *Open Praxis.*, *8*(3), 223–233. doi:10.5944/openpraxis.8.3.282

Calle-Jimenez, T., Sanchez-Gordon, S., & Luján-Mora, S. (2014). Web accessibility evaluation of massive open online courses on geographical information systems, In *Proceedings of the Global Engineering Education Conference (EDUCON)* (pp. 680-686). 10.1109/EDUCON.2014.6826167

Calle-Jimenez, T., Sanchez-Gordon, S., Rybarczyk, Y., Jadán, J., Villarreal, S., Esparza, W., Acosta-Vargas, P., Guevara, C., & Nunes, I. L. (2019). Analysis and improvement of the web accessibility of a tele-rehabilitation platform for hip arthroplasty patients. In Advances in Human Factors and Systems Interaction. Advances in Intelligent Systems and Computing (pp. 233-245). Cham, Switzerland: Springer. doi:10.1007/978-3-319-94334-3_24

Coughlan, T., Lister, K., Seale, J., Scanlon, E., & Weller, M. (2019). Accessible inclusive learning: Foundations. In REducational visions: Lessons from 40 years of innovation (pp. 51–73). Ubiquity Press.

De Santana, V. F., De Oliveira, R., Almeida, L. D. A., & Baranauskas, M. C. C. (2012). Web accessibility and people with dyslexia: a survey on techniques and guidelines. In *Proceedings of the International Cross-Disciplinary Conference on Web Accessibility* (pp. 1-9). 10.1145/2207016.2207047

EdX. (2018). *Age Demographics*. Retrieved from https://edx.readthedocs.io/projects/edx-insights/en/latest/enrollment/Demographics_Age.html

Eysenbach, G. (2001). What is e-Health. *Journal of Medical Internet Research*, *3*(2), e20. doi:10.2196/jmir.3.2.e20 PMID:11720962

Global Learning Consortium. (2020). *Accessibility*. Retrieved from https://www.imsglobal.org/activity/accessibility

Gordon, M. (2018). In search of a universal human rights metaphor: Moral conversations across differences. *Educational Philosophy and Theory*, *50*(1), 83–94. doi:10.1080/00131857.2017.1336920

Iniesto, F. (2020). *An investigation into the accessibility of Massive Open Online Courses (MOOCs)* (PhD thesis). The Open University, London, UK.

International Organization for Standardization. (2008a). Standard ISO 9241-171:2008 Ergonomics of human-system interaction – Part 171 Guidance on software accessibility.

International Organization for Standardization. (2008b). Standard ISO/IEC 24751-1:2008 Information technology – Individualized adaptability and accessibility in e-learning, education and training.

International Organization for Standardization. (2018). Standard ISO 9241-11:2018 Ergonomics of human-system interaction — Part 11: Usability: Definitions and concepts.

Jadán-Guerrero, J., Guevara, C., Lara-Alvarez, P., Sanchez-Gordon, S., Calle-Jimenez, T., Salvador-Ullauri, L., Acosta-Vargas, P., & Bonilla-Jurado, D. (2020a). Building hybrid interfaces to increase interaction with young children and children with special needs. In Advances in Human Factors and Systems Interaction. Advances in Intelligent Systems and Computing (pp. 306-314). Cham, Switzerland: Springer. doi:10.1007/978-3-030-20040-4_28

Jadán-Guerrero, J., Sanchez-Gordon, S., Acosta-Vargas, P., Alvites-Huamaní, C. G., & Nunes, I. L. (2020b). Interactive storytelling books for fostering inclusion of children with special needs. In Advances in Human Factors and Systems Interaction. Advances in Intelligent Systems and Computing (pp. 222-228). Cham, Switzerland: Springer. doi:10.1007/978-3-030-51369-6_30

Jaschik, S. (2016). *University may remove online content to avoid disability law*. Retrieved from https://www.insidehighered.com/news/2016/09/20/berkeley-may-remove-free-onlinecontent-rather-complying-disability-law

Jordan, K. (2015). *MOOC Completion Rates: The Data*. Retrieved from http://www.katyjordan.com/MOOCproject.html

Kalyvioti, K., & Mikropoulos, T. (2013). A Virtual Reality Test for the Identification of Memory Strengths of Dyslexic Students in Higher Education. *J. UCS*, *19*(18), 2698–2721.

Kanter, A. S. (2015). *The development of disability rights under international law: From charity to human rights*. Routledge.

Kitchenham, B. (2007). *Guidelines for performing systematic literature reviews in software engineering*. EBSE Technical Report.

Otón, S., Ingavélez-Guerra, P., Sanchez-Gordon, S., & Sánchez-Gordón, M. (2020). Evolution of Accessibility Metadata in Educational Resources. In R. Mendoza-González, H. Luna-García, & A. Mendoza-González (Eds.), *UXD and UCD Approaches for Accessible Education* (pp. 1–20). IGI Global. doi:10.4018/978-1-7998-2325-4.ch001

Pérez Medina, J. L., González Rodríguez, M. S., Pilco, H., Jimenes, K., Acosta-Vargas, P., Sanchez-Gordon, S., Calle-Jimenez, T., Esparza, W., & Rybarczyk, Y. (2019). Usability study of a web-based platform for home motor rehabilitation. *IEEE Access Journal, 7*, 7932–7947. doi:10.1109/ACCESS.2018.2889257

Petrie, H., & Bevan, N. (2009). The evaluation of accessibility, usability and user experience. *The Universal Access Handbook*, 299–315.

Pilco, H., Sanchez-Gordon, S., Calle-Jimenez, T., Pérez-Medina, J. L., Rybarczyk, Y., Jadán, J., Guevara, C., & Nunes, I. L. (2019b). An agile approach to improve the usability of a physical tele rehabilitation platform. *Journal of Applied Sciences (Faisalabad), 9*(3), 480.

Pilco, H., Sanchez-Gordon, S., Calle-Jimenez, T., Rybarczyk, Y., Jadán, J., Villarreal, S., Esparza, W., Acosta-Vargas, P., Guevara, C., & Nunes, I. L. (2019a). Analysis and improvement of the usability of a tele-rehabilitation platform for hip surgery patients. In Advances in Human Factors and Systems Interaction. Advances in Intelligent Systems and Computing (pp. 197-209). Cham, Switzerland: Springer. doi:10.1007/978-3-319-94334-3_21

Sanchez-Gordon, S., Calle-Jimenez, T., Villarroel-Ramos, J., Jadán-Guerrero, J., Guevara, C., Lara-Alvarez, P., Acosta-Vargas, P., & Salvador-Ullauri, L. (2020a). Implementation of controls for insertion of accessible images in open online editors based on WCAG guidelines. Case studies: TinyMCE and Summernote. In Advances in Human Factors and Systems Interaction. AHFE 2019. Advances in Intelligent Systems and Computing, 959 (pp. 315-326). Cham, Switzerland: Springer.

Sanchez-Gordon, S., Estevez, J., & Luján-Mora, S. (2016c) Editor for accessible images in e-learning platforms. In *Proceedings of the 13th Web for All Conference* (pp. 1-2). 10.1145/2899475.2899513

Sanchez-Gordon, S., Jadán-Guerrero, J., Arias-Flores, H., & Nunes, I. L. (2020b). Model for Generation of Profiles for Persons with Disabilities in e-Learning Environments. In I. L. Nunes (Ed.), *Advances in Human Factors and Systems Interaction. AHFE 2020. Advances in Intelligent Systems and Computing, 1207* (pp. 242–249). Springer.

Sanchez-Gordon, S., & Luján-Mora, S. (2013a). Web accessibility of MOOCs for elderly students. In *Proceedings of the 11th International Conference on Information Technology Based Higher Education and Training* (pp.1-6). 10.1109/ITHET.2013.6671024

Sanchez-Gordon, S., & Luján-Mora, S. (2013b). Accessibility considerations of Massive Online Open Courses as creditable courses in Engineering Programs. In *Proceedings of International Conference of Education, Research and Innovation* (pp. 5853-5862). Academic Press.

Sanchez-Gordon, S., & Luján-Mora, S. (2014). Web accessibility requirements for massive open online courses. In *Proceedings of the V International Conference on Quality and Accessibility of Virtual Learning* (pp. 530-535). Academic Press.

Sanchez-Gordon, S., & Luján-Mora, S. (2015a). Adaptive content presentation extension for open edX. Enhancing MOOCs accessibility for users with disabilities. In *Proceedings of the 8th International Conference on Advances in Computer-Human Interaction* (pp.181-183). Academic Press.

Sanchez-Gordon, S., & Luján-Mora, S. (2015b). An ecosystem for corporate training with accessible MOOCs and OERs. In *Proceedings of the IEEE International Conference on MOOCs, Innovation and Technology in Education* (pp. 123-128). 10.1109/MITE.2015.7375301

Sanchez-Gordon, S., & Luján-Mora, S. (2015c). Accessible blended learning for non-native speakers using MOOCs. In *Proceedings of the IEEE International Conference on Interactive Collaborative and Blended Learning* (pp. 19-24). 10.1109/ICBL.2015.7387645

Sanchez-Gordon, S., & Luján-Mora, S. (2016a). How could MOOCs become accessible? The case of edX and the future of inclusive online learning. *Journal of Universal Computer Science (J.UCS)*, 22(1), 55-81.

Sanchez-Gordon, S., & Luján-Mora, S. (2016b). Design, implementation and evaluation of MOOCs to improve inclusion of diverse learners. In R. Mendoza-Gonzalez (Ed.), *User-Centered Design Strategies for Massive Open Online Courses* (pp. 115–141). IGI Global. doi:10.4018/978-1-4666-9743-0.ch008

Sanchez-Gordon, S., & Luján-Mora, S. (2016d). Barriers and strategies for using MOOCs in the context of Higher Education in Ibero-America. In P. Gómez Hernández, A. García Barrera, & C. Monge López (Eds.), *The culture of MOOCs* (pp. 141–160). Editorial Síntesis.

Sanchez-Gordon, S., & Luján-Mora, S. (2018a). Research challenges in accessible MOOCs: A systematic literature review 2008-2016. *Universal Access in the Information Society*, 17(4), 775–789. doi:10.100710209-017-0531-2

Sanchez-Gordon, S., & Luján-Mora, S. (2018b). Lifecycle for MOOC development and management. In R. Queirós (Ed.), *Emerging Trends, Techniques, and Tools for Massive Open Online Course (MOOC) Management* (pp. 24–48). IGI Global. doi:10.4018/978-1-5225-5011-2.ch002

Sanchez-Gordon, S., & Luján-Mora, S. (2018c). Technological Innovations in Large-Scale Teaching: Five Roots of MOOCS. *Journal of Educational Computing Research*, 56(5), 623–644. doi:10.1177/0735633117727597

Sanchez-Gordon, S., & Luján-Mora, S. (2019). Implementing Accessibility in Massive Open Online Courses' Platforms for Teaching, Learning and Collaborating at Large Scale. In A. Meier & C. Terán (Eds.), *eDemocracy & eGoverment. Stages of a Democratic Knowledge Society* (pp. 151–160). Springer.

Sanchez-Gordon, S., Luján-Mora, S., & Sánchez-Gordón, M. (2020c). E-government accessibility in Ecuador: A preliminary evaluation. In *Proceeding of the Seventh International Conference on eDemocracy & eGovernment* (pp. 50-57). Academic Press.

Shah, D. (2019). *By the numbers: MOOCs in 2019*. Retrieved from https://www.classcentral.com/report/mooc-stats-2019

Smith, C. (2020). *Coursera Statistics and Facts*. Retrieved from https://expandedramblings.com/index.php/coursera-facts-statistics/

Sousa, V. E. C., & Lopez, K. D. (2017). Towards usable e-health. A systematic review of usability question-naires. *Applied Clinical Informatics*, *8*(2), 470–490. doi:10.4338/ACI-2016-10-R-0170 PMID:28487932

UNICEF. (2009). *It's about ability. Learning guide on the convention on the rights of persons with disabilities.* Retrieved from http://www.unicef.org/publications/files/Its_About_Ability_Learning_Guide_EN.pdf

United Nations. (1948). *Universal declaration of human rights.* Retrieved from http://wwda.org.au/wp-content/uploads/2013/12/undechr1.pdf

United Nations. (2006). *Convention on the rights of persons with disabilities.* Retrieved from https://www.un.org/disabilities/documents/convention/convention_accessible_pdf.pdf

United Nations. (2008). *Convention on the rights of persons with disabilities and optional protocol.* Retrieved from https://www.un.org/development/desa/disabilities/convention-on-the-rights-of-persons-with-disabilities.html

United Nations. (2017). *World population ageing.* Retrieved from https://www.un.org/en/development/desa/population/publications/pdf/ageing/WPA2017_Highlights.pdf

US Department of Justice. (2015). *Justice Department reaches settlement with edX Inc.* Retrieved from http://www.justice.gov/usao-ma/pr/united-states-reaches-settlement-provider-massiveopen-online-courses-make-its-content

VandenBos, G., Knapp, S., & Doe, J. (2001). *Role of reference elements in the selection of resources by psychology undergraduates.* Retrieved from http://jbr.org/articles.html

World Health Organization. (2011). *World Report on Disability.* Retrieved from https://www.who.int/disabilities/world_report/2011/en/

World Wide Web Consortium. (1997). *World Wide Web Consortium launches international program office for Web Accessibility Initiative.* Retrieved from https:// www.w3.org/Press/IPO-announce

World Wide Web Consortium. (2008). *Web content accessibility guidelines (WCAG) 2.0.* Retrieved from https://www.w3.org/TR/WCAG20/

World Wide Web Consortium. (2018). *Web content accessibility guidelines (WCAG) 2.2.* Retrieved from https://www.w3.org/TR/WCAG21/

World Wide Web Consortium. (2019). *Introduction to Web Accessibility.* Retrieved from https://www.w3.org/WAI/fundamentals/accessibility-intro/

World Wide Web Consortium. (2020). *Web content accessibility guidelines (WCAG) 2.2.* Retrieved from https://www.w3.org/TR/WCAG22/

Yonaitis, R. B. (2002). *Understanding accessibility: A guide to achieving compliance on web sites and intranets.* HiSoftware.

KEY TERMS AND DEFINITIONS

Accessibility: Extend to which a person can access and use an object, reach a place, or obtain a service.

ATAG: A set of guidelines to maximize the accessibility of authoring tools used to produce web content.

Disability: A consequence of environmental barriers that limits a person's activities or participation in a permanent or temporal fashion.

Inclusion: The act or practice of including and accommodating people who have historically been excluded (as because of their race, gender, sexuality, or ability).

MOOC: A type of online course that can accept massive number of students without prerequisites.

OER: Open educational resources are teaching and learning materials that may be freely used and reused.

Usability: The quality or state of being usable, ease of use.

WAI: An initiative of the World Wide Web Consortium to promote the accessibility of the web.

WCAG: A set of guidelines to maximize the accessibility of web content.

Chapter 4
Development of Teaching– Learning Strategies Through Technology

Lilia Esther Muñoz
Universidad Tecnológica de Panamá, Panama

Itza Morales
Universidad Tecnológica de Panamá, Panama

ABSTRACT

The different levels that comprise education seek to adapt techniques, practices, models, and strategies to complement teaching and learning generating knowledge in students; thus, in its different fields, it provides the basis for technology to develop software applications to assist with teaching and learning practices. Consequently, education undergoes rapid changes that influence improvement through the use of some of the tools such as robotics and augmented reality which contribute to improving learning scenarios in students, allowing them to develop their metacognitive skills using technological environments designed to educate and be a medium in the educational process. Therefore, this topic addresses the following study based in the completion of two projects aimed at elementary school students in fundamental subjects, allowing them to become familiar with technology as a means of learning.

INTRODUCTION

Education is one of the most effective instruments to reduce poverty, inequality, and crime and lays the foundations for sustained economic growth, because it allows for development of learning strategies to that promote an environment of competence and cooperation among individuals with the objective of achieving multidisciplinary knowledge (Chen et al., 2020). In fact, human capital together with technology and knowledge are considered as the main engines of growth (Anonymous, 2013). Likewise, education is considered the catalyst to minimize sustainability problems in organizations and institutions, due to the economic impact of having trained personnel to carry out different functions and achieve success

DOI: 10.4018/978-1-7998-7552-9.ch004

Copyright © 2021, IGI Global. Copying or distributing in print or electronic forms without written permission of IGI Global is prohibited.

(Singh & Segatto, 2020). This involves evaluating adequate training, because they follow educational standards promoting the development of skills (Alessa D. Gonzales, 2020) that supports learning through the use of open models in cognitive and metacognitive development, which improve performance and analytical skills of individuals for problem solving and driving innovation in best teaching practices (Hooshyar et al., 2020).

The world education environment is registering accelerated changes and transformations with consequences in the demographic, economic, social, cultural, political, and technological order. To these constant elements of the human environment, the focus is added at the level of the competitiveness of knowledge, which due to its inherent dynamism behaves, in the same way as we mentioned before, it is a consequence in the being and work of humanity. Likewise, the conditioning in the fields of action has scopes that are in the process of being assimilated. Inevitably leading us to the development of novel phases of reflection, inventiveness and action.

On the other hand, Information and Communication Technologies (ICT) have become fundamentally significant resources for the development of all spheres in our lives. Therefore, it is difficult to dismiss the core role that ICTs have currently had in education (Pellón, Miranda, Gonzalez, & Reynal, 2017). Analyzing the different perceptions that ICTs offer in the formation of educational needs implies adapting them to the teaching-learning process (Palomino, 2017; Serin et al., 2009), allowing the use of technological tools to increase the development of best practices in education.

The emergence of new roles in teachers and students, as well as the creation of new teaching-learning materials are the changes that have most influenced ICT in the educational field. In that way, it allows to minimize ambiguities regarding the importance generated by the adoption of technology tools as a means for facilitating the best mechanisms in the formation of human capital.

BACKGROUND

Structure of Education in Panama

The Panamanian educational system is divided into three (3) levels: The General Basic Education, High School Education and Higher Education. The General Basic Education includes: Pre-school (Pre-kindergarten and Kindergarten, one year each) for children between 4 and 5 years, Elementary school lasts six (6) years and Middle or Junior High School lasts three (3) years. The second level is High School Education which lasts three (3) years and the last level is Higher Education. The third rung consists of 3 years and it is more diversified because it prepares young people to get an occupation or to continue higher education. It has an academic structure according to Education Law 34: Regular subsystem, which are the aforementioned levels, and the Non-Regular Subsystem, which includes: Basic Literacy Education, Early Childhood Education II 2 and 3 years, Early Childhood III 4 and 5 years; Middle Education and Supplementary Education.

Panama provides free and compulsory Elementary education until the ninth grade and there is also a special system for students with disabilities. On the other hand, education in Panama has had important advances in recent decades, especially in access and coverage at all levels of education; preschool, primary, pre-middle and middle education. Despite this, Panama is among the top five countries with the highest growth in Latin America. An educational landscape that has enables us to invest more in the education sector. Consequently, the educational system also has it's weaknesses, without a doubt, this investment must have guarantees of execution.

Technologies in the Teaching-Learning Process

We will approach this topic in two contexts: Augmented Reality and Educational Robotics, although there are many other aspects from the point of view of Technology.

Augmented Reality

In recent years, technology has evolved, generating new tools to be developed and adapted to facilitate better interaction with users. Consequently, within the technologies that have emerged as a solution to multidisciplinary problems, it involves the rise of Augmented Reality (AR) to move the user to a more realistic environment about experiences because it offers great possibilities for its attractiveness and ability to insert objects virtual in a real space, where it is applied to different scenarios at the level of education, medicine, military, agribusiness, cinematography and video games, among other applications (Aebersold et al., 2020; Lohre et al., 2020; Nishizawa et al., 2013; Pranoto & Panggabean, 2019). Based on this context, within the field of education, the project developed by (Marín, Muñoz, & Vega, 2016) is presented as an example, which use AR to bring natural science learning to the smallest of the system educational, through El Volcán, an application that allows students to know how and why earthquakes occur.

In addition, one of the most recurrent experiences has been based on the metaphor of the augmented book, used above all in applications related to educational environments. Thus, from a bookmark printed on one of the pages it is possible to access additional information through 3D graphics that show virtual figures on the pages of the book and are visualized through the screen of a simple computer with a webcam. One of the first tests was developed by the Human Interface Technology Laboratory of the University of Washington when it presented the so-called "MagicBook", which evidenced the didactic value of this technology and the great appeal that it represents in educational contexts (Pertejo-López, 2017).

For their part, (Alvarez, Delgado, Gimeno, & Marín, 2017), present the Educational Arenero project that uses AR to implement a resource in the teaching of mathematics and natural sciences, its application uses an infrared camera to read the three-dimensional surface of the sand and then draw on it contour lines and bodies of water that it is transformed when the user interacts with the sand. In another context, (Sáez, Cózar, & Dominguez, 2018) implemented a didactic unit in three phases using Iberian art models through AR as an educational resource. It should be noted that significant improvements in the recognition of artistic contents are highlighted when fully manipulating objects with the developed application.

Otherwise, in Panama, AR has been manifested and incorporated in some areas. For instance, in 2013, "AR in the coastal belt" was developed which it is a project that consisted of offering an "interactive totem" that allowed Users select and view different parts of the coastal strip in 3D (Innovae, 2013). Another of the projects in 2015 was "The Panama Canal in 3D and AR" (Redacción, 2015) focused on the third set of locks on the Panama Canal. This project provides an interactive brochure that it is activated with the Aurasma application, which can be installed on tablets and smartphones by connecting and combining physical with virtual reality. The brochure shows videos on the most relevant aspects of the world's largest civil engineering work and animated 3D with the enormous magnitudes of the project (dredging, excavation, concrete and steel). There is also a 360° 3D function that allows you to zoom in, zoom out and turn among other functions. However, despite all this development, it has achieved little in the educational field in Panama.

Educational Robotics

Robotics in education has been implemented in different countries of Europe and America as mentioned in (Aris & Orcos, 2019), (Chen, y otros, 2017), (Monsalvez, 2011), (Orcas & Aris, 2019) among others, making the use of educational robotics more and more popular inside and outside the curricula of different educational centers around the world. Through the educational robots, students can access to this new technological world, and in addition, they are one of the best didactic tools for the teaching of academic disciplines STEM (Science, Technology, Engineering and Mathematics). In this sense, different researchers have shown that the interaction of students with programmable educational robots, as is the case of the Bee-Bot in appropriate educational contexts, have promoted the acquisition of mathematical and geometric concepts in a significant way (Moreno, Muñoz, & Serracin, 2012), (Ramírez & Sosa, 2013), (Benavides, Otegui, Aguirre, & Andrade, 2013). As well as obtaining several achievements acquired by students through experimentation with the Bee-Bot, and the application of different strategies to discover their functions and characteristics (Taborda & Medina, 2012), (Misirli & Komis, 2014), (Caballero & Muñoz-Repiso, 2017).

The work of (Angeli & Valanides, 2019) presented an interesting study conclusion of the teaching and learning effects using the Bee-Bot on young boys' and girls' computational thinking within the context of two scaffolding techniques. The study statistically reports significant learning gains between the initial and final assessment of children's computational thinking skills. According to the findings, while both boys and girls benefited from the scaffolding techniques, a statistically significant interaction effect was detected between gender and scaffolding strategy showing that boys benefited more from the individualistic, kinesthetic, spatially-oriented, and manipulative-based activity with the cards, while in contrast girls benefited more from the collaborative writing activity.

In addition, (Greenberg, Thiruvathukal, & Greenberg, 2020) shows how students can be guided to integrate elementary mathematical analyses with motion planning for typical educational robots. Instead of using calculus as in comprehensive works on motion planning, its show students can achieve interesting results using just simple linear regression tools and trigonometric analyses. Experiments with one robotics platform show that use of these tools can lead to passable navigation through dead reckoning even if students have limited experience with use of sensors, programming, and mathematics. Another interesting work is the one developed by (Estivill-Castro, 2019), the author have developed three lessons supported by the principles of Inquiry-Based Learning (IBL) and Problem-Based Learning (PBL) in educational robotics with the aim of steering and emphasizing the mathematics aspects of the curriculum and the role of mathematics in STEM, at the same time touching on the social context and impact of STEM.

The learning of mathematics supposes, together with reading and writing, one of the fundamental learnings of elementary education, given the instrumental nature of these contents. Therefore, understanding the difficulties in learning mathematics has become a manifest concern of many of the professionals dedicated to the world of education, especially if we consider the high percentage of failure in these contents presented by students who complete the compulsory schooling. In this scenario, the learning of this subject involves complex processes that require a great diversity of methodologies to achieve the maximum possible efficiency. The use of ICT and educational robotics is especially well suited to this issue such as the use of images, graphs, and spreadsheets among others in calculators and computers; it allows us to advance very quickly and, most importantly, to understand and retain the necessary information. In addition, these tools open the possibility of creating new learning environments and, therefore, of developing new methodologies and exploit the resources available the most.

Below, are the results of projects that we have been working on in recent years. These projects are focused on education in different contexts, applying the use of ICT.

AUGMENTED REALITY IN THE SCIENCE TEACHING-LEARNING PROCESS

Purpose of the Project

The ICT boom worldwide is constantly growing and taking advantage of its benefits in education, integrating them in different ways and in diverse subjects. Nowadays, the way in which knowledge is transmitted within classrooms is changed even more; however, AR-based technological solutions are not provided for the educational field in Panama and much less aimed at schools located in rural areas. Moreover, the purpose of teaching natural sciences at school is to promote the scientific literacy of citizens from early schooling, seeking to understand concepts, practice procedures and develop attitudes that allow them to participate in an analytical culture and criticism of emerging information.

In this context, the province of Chiriqui, located west of the capital of the Republic of Panama, has a great variety of flora and fauna due to the amount of natural sites it has, but as the years go by some of these sites are mainly affected by various human activities and as a consequence generates great damages to the environment. Although there are sites that still remain protected that benefit their conservation, they do not escape this reality. People should take care these resources to avoid damages in the future. For the development of this project, some sites of the province have been visited. For instance the Chico River, which has been damaged by human activities as well as the Gualaca Buckets, a river, which remains a highly valued tourist site.

However, an aspect important for this project, is considered the pollution is a detrimental change in the physical, chemical or biological characteristics of the air, land and even water, which can adversely affect human life or other species, the living conditions of human beings and deteriorate the renewable natural resources (González & González, 2010). Pollution is an alarming factor within society, the application of AR, that is sought to be developed and implemented, focuses on the conservation of natural sites due to the level of contamination and deterioration of natural resources that is causing great damage in Panama; as well as in the rest of the world. These damages are due to the destruction of forests which has led to the extinction of plants and animals. In this perspective, preserving the environment of natural sites through the use of AR, allows students and teachers to incorporate the use of technology in the teaching process on the importance of natural resources and to preserve the image of the place. Through an interactive medium, where the student can participate and receive positive feedback regarding the information about the Gualaca buckets, their flora and fauna, geographical position and importance in the tourist field. Therefore, the proposal and the results of the project are described in the following sub-points.

Proposal

The general objective of this project was to develop an application for mobile devices to make children aware of the conservation of the environment at an early stage. For this, AR was used, since it is a technology that provides the interactive aspect, in addition to supporting the teaching-learning process in the subject of natural sciences.

The results obtained were the following:

- A platform for mobile devices that contains the virtual information of the selected natural sites and their conservation.
- Didactic sheets that illustrate each chosen site, their information and steps to follow, in order to keep these sites preserved.
- A satisfactory virtual interaction of the user when view the sheet that is delivered together with the developed AR application.
- A culture of conservation in the students who use the platform, contributing within their learning process in the subject of natural sciences and technological resources.

Additionally, the results of the application developed for the Gualaca Buckets scenario are included.

Results

As part of the results of this project, a mobile application has been developed. The architecture of the application can be seen in figure 1.

Some of the components of the application architecture that was developed with the Vuforia tool were:

- Camera. It ensures that each frame captured by the camera is efficiently transferred to the tracker.
- Tracker. It contains the different computational vision algorithms that allow detecting and tracking each of the objects in the captured frames. Based on the image taken by the camera, different algorithms are responsible for detecting the reference images.
- State of objects. It is where the results obtained by the tracker are stored to be used by the video processor.
- Video processor. It processes the captured image that is stored in the object state. Video rendering performance varies depending on the device.
- Image converter. The pixel format converter converts the format the camera works with to a format suitable for rendering and tracking.
- It involves a subsampling whose purpose is to obtain the image captured by the camera in different resolutions, available in the converted frame stack.

Sheets

The sheets that were produced in the project contain selected images of the sites that were chosen and visited. Within the general structure of the plates, the shown name of the site in each one must be highlighted. Figure 2 shows the sheet of the Gualaca Buckets, located in Gualaca district.

Figure 1. Application architecture
Source: Own elaboration

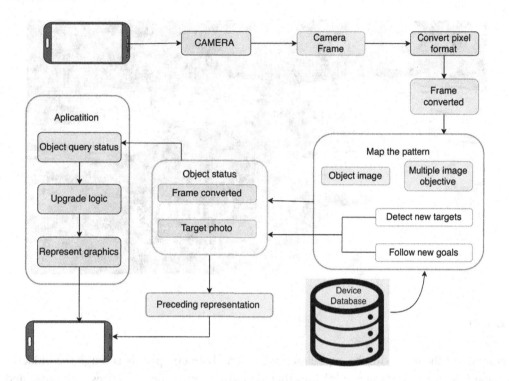

The user will be able to obtain sheet's information from each site, as well as the conservation practices that must be carried out in order to keep them preserved. These aspects are also included on affectations that can occur due to human activities.

As the user focuses the camera of their device on the didactic sheet, they can interact in real time with the AR content that the application will provide, with the purpose of technologically supporting the teaching of natural sciences and care for the environment.

Interface

The AR application interface is a simple screen that allows the user to choose, start or exit the app and get information about AR.

Once the user decides to start the session, the input of images shown through the camera can be seen on the mobile screen, so that at the moment of detecting a pattern stored in the database, the corresponding animation is displayed, allowing the user to interact and learn. The "Exit" option allows you to exit the application, and the "About AR" option allows you to view the purpose for which the application was created and provides a brief description of what AR is. Figure 3 shows the interface of the application.

Figure 2. Sheet of the Gualaca Buckets
Source: Own elaboration

Interaction

The interaction of the user with the application was carried out completely through the didactic sheets, which contain the images of the natural sites that were used for the project. These are presented before the camera of the mobile device, to obtain all the AR content that is associated within the application.

In order to obtain the 3D animations correctly, the user keeps the sheet in front of the camera - they should avoid covering it with any object - so that the pattern to be recognized remains visible whenever it is in use. In case the user no longer wants the displayed animation, just need to stop focusing the film with the camera, or if you want to interact with another site you only must move the device and focus on

Figure 3. Main application screen
Source: Own elaboration

another film. Figure 4 shows one of the students using the application and interacting due to it transports you to the natural scene of the place referring to the field of study of social sciences.

The application of AR is intended to facilitate user interaction with virtual content and pictures at all times in order to avoid confusion about their use and to provide them with an interactive, attractive and easy handling tool around teaching natural science about conservation.

Figure 4. Student using the application
Source: Own elaboration

Further, for the evaluation of the developed application authorization was requested from the school management School Lassonde Neighborhood School. The address us assigned the teacher who taught third grade. It was explained to her what the project consisted of, you were instructed in the use of the application; she was responsible for selecting 20 students whose ages ranged from eight to nine years of age. The purpose of this stage was to validate the operation of the application. The students used the app and they answered questions about of functionality, design, and content.

The app evaluation determined that the students adapted in a good way to the use of the application. It was not excellent since the organization of information in Sheets in the first instance was not adequate.

When the sheets were developed, they were placed three images of the site in each, but only the image larger master was activating of 3d content; the other two were like reference to different views of the site to show, what which - we consider - confused the student, so changes were made to the sheets and left only one image per sheet.

As for the ease of navigation, the user understanding and satisfaction, results were excellent, allowing us to demonstrate that the developed application allows simple way to teach the student concepts and visualize what the natural sites of a more real way. In figure 5 you can see the results obtained in the evaluation.

Figure 5. App evaluation
Source: Own elaboration

Discussion

Today, the demands regarding the use of ICT have increased to such an extent that new strategies must be constantly applied, even more in the educational field, in order to improve the way of attracting the attention of students and obtaining thus a better performance (Horra, 2017). This is possible with the help of flexible platforms that have the correct visuality, so an adequate synthesis of all the information be transmitted is carried out. For this reason, AR becomes an important tool to be used no matter the content to be displayed.

Currently, the development of projects in AR environments is carried out in almost all fields of knowledge. The educational environment does not escape this reality. There is a significant improvement in learning processes thanks to AR due to the motivation of students is increased by incorporating 3D content in teaching materials. This technology enhances the educational effect by offering entertainment activities and at the same time it is a great tool that motivates students. By obtaining the aforementioned benefits, this project serves to improve the traditional way in which classes are taught in school classrooms applied to the area of natural sciences, so that they become more attractive through the implementation of a new technology. Therefore, little by little, it is becoming a useful instrument of great importance for teaching and it helps us to instill in the students that knowledge that they often do not know about the natural sites that surround them. Similarly, it discloses in early stages the appropriate practices for the conservation of the nature.

The project implemented in primary education for children in the province of Chiriquí, is closely related to comprehensive education, where each student must understand the importance of using ICT to improve the teaching process and through AR in the educational context of the social and natural sciences, the project is developed for schools in rural areas and the main limitation found was the lack of applications with which students could interact.

In parallel, the main objective of the presented work is to provide a tool that facilitates the effective teaching-learning process in the natural sciences, particularly in the conservation of the environment. The tool allows you to interact with each of the elements in an attractive three-dimensional plane using sheets which provide relevant information about natural sites and the instructions for their care.

The benefits and contributions that this research can generate important challenges that require:

1. Bring students in early stages to the care and protection of the environment,
2. Recognize that AR motivates the student and allows their learning to be more effective, and
3. Promote the use of AR for the development of applications in other educational settings related to Mathematics, Spanish, etc.

The project sought to reinforce the importance of incorporating into the educational curriculum the use of AR as a teaching-learning medium for primary-level students, by introducing them to technology to convert traditional education into continuous participation, reinforcing the appropriate use of AR in educational environments and provide students with, explore and manipulate technological tools that allow them not only to know about the academic content, but also to understand part of the knowledge generated by the correct use of this tool, since it is applicable at teaching levels, as well as for the development of video games, movies or three-dimensional scenarios; Therefore, it allows children to show that they too can be participants and in the future develop applications that help other children who do not have the appropriate technology to learn areas of knowledge such as natural or social sciences from an interactive perspective.

MATHEMATICS IN INITIAL STAGES THROUGH EDUCATIONAL ROBOTICS

Purpose of the Project

The initial stages in children between the age of 4 to 7 years, represent the stage in which they should be involved in activities for the understanding of the teaching-learning contents, because they are prone to more easily receive the knowledge that is provided to them through educational tools. Therefore, it is necessary to include in the educational system the use of technology as a means for teaching mathematical content, from the early stages of schooling, and reduce the information gap that is generated in students due to ignorance of the different applicabilities that technology has in the educational context. Through this, in one of its lines of application, is educational robotics, which allows students to physically interact with a device and in turn, allows them to learn about a certain academic subject. In this context, educational robotics incorporates different implementation scenarios, focused both on children in the initial stages and in the professional and scientific field; Therefore, it is one of the best means to provide students with the information and importance of this for the curricular content and the benefits generated by its correct approach. In fact, the second project on the use of educational robotics for the teaching of mathematics in initial stages is aimed at children between 5 and 7 years of age, and through coordination between education professionals they were facilitated use of the robot "Bee-Bot" for the mathematical contents of this school stage. Likewise, the robot allows children to develop their meta-cognitive and motor skills and their mathematical analysis, because it is designed to capture the child's attention and its operation is practical and easy to use. In addition, Bee-Bot together with other didactic materials were developed to provide students and teachers with learning-teaching guides, visual sheets according to the level of study and materials to make conventional mathematics activities within the classroom where each student interacts with the robot and learns the mathematical contents visually, develops their cognitive thinking and mathematical analysis from their first stage of learning.

Previously, the importance of robotics in educational contexts focused on initial stages of learning in children has been exposed, for this purpose, the implementation of the second project was developed in the province of Chiriquí, selecting 3 primary schools, where a minimum percentage of students presented learning deficiencies and disabilities, therefore, it was necessary to adapt the materials in order that all students received mathematics instruction through the technological tool. From this point of view, the following sub-points explain the proposal and the results of the project.

Proposal

The general objective of this project was to design, develop and implement innovative resources to improve the teaching process of mathematics. Aimed at both primary school students and teachers, using programmable educational robots as a low-cost robotic element. First grade and preschool students were taken as a point of reference, integrating educational activities that will allow, on the one hand, the achievement of curricular objectives in the area of mathematics, as well as the development of digital skills and competences described above, including tools in the process technology-oriented programming of educational robots. For this, three public schools in the province of Chiriquí, Republic of Panama have been selected. One of the schools is a rural area multi grade school and the other two belong to the urban area.

Consequently, the number of students per school varied and the way the content was taught to the children was tailored according to their learning abilities in order to comply with the established planning of academic information. In addition, through the use of the "Bee-Bot" robot, the students then participate and learn to work as a team in order to develop the activities designed for mathematics. The project seeks to allow students to interact with technological tools through "Bee-Bot", and learn basic programming principles, introducing them in a simple way how to build instructions for a device to execute them; This is how they learn not only mathematical concepts, but also initial programming knowledge. This means that the project has a greater scope due to the use of robotics and the positive impact generated by its correct implementation.

Methods and Materials

This section, deals with the materials and methods used in the project, it was developed a set of innovative resources for teachers and students of first grade and preschool level in public primary schools, to improve the teaching-learning process of mathematics, using programmable educational robots as a low-cost robotic element. The methods and materials that will be used are described below.

Methods

The project includes two stages, the first with a theoretical basis, which contemplates a systematic review of the literature of the subject under study. In addition, a set of recreational activities organized in didactic guides for teachers and students was developed in this stage. These will be accompanied by a set of rubrics, checklists and questionnaires that will allow the resulting data to be collected. The second stage is of an experimental type through training sessions for teachers and students who participate, based on the area of mathematics; all this with the support of programming tools and educational robotics appropriate to the educational level. Both stages of the project led to the analysis of the learning capacity of the students with respect to the use of robotics in mathematical content plans and to identify on a scale through the analysis the way in which they perceive the information and its relationship with the use of the robot and whether or not they showed learning progress in the period in which the project was developed, an aspect that is discussed in the results analysis section.

Materials

As a tool for programmable educational robotics activities, the Bee-bot Kit (Caballero & Muñoz-Repiso, 2017) was used, which is an educational material designed to develop the elementary skills in programming and computational thinking, such as: spatial location and cognition, motor skills and perception, logic and strategy. These robots perform movements at 90° angles and must be programmed to follow a coherent sequence on each mat. So, with proper programming, the robot bee will be able to find the answers to an addition to give an example, each time it stops in a space, depending on the mat or sheet that is used with the Kit. In addition, computers were used for the design and development of activities (cards, mats, pictures); likewise, in the classroom, the use of mobile devices such as Tablets and Smartphones to carry out the evaluation tests on students.

Previously, for the development of the project, meetings were held with authorities and directors of the Ministry of Education (MEDUCA - for its initials in Spanish), with the purpose of presenting the project and at the same time obtaining the permits to entry the schools where the project will be executed.

Methodology

Currently, the project is in the development phase. However, some results have been obtained and mentioned below.

- The project has the approval of three (3) schools from different locations, two of them from urban areas and one from a rural area. One of the schools is multi-grade.

- There will be a population of 250 children of which 150 have been selected as sample for the development of the project.
- Work will be done with preschool and first grade children.
- A scheme has been developed for the execution of every activities; an example can be found in Table 1.

Table 1. Activity scheme

Activity Name: Learning Numbers from 1 to 10 with Bee-Bot	
Objectives	· Identify and memorize the numbers with the help of «Bee-Bot». · Match the number of objects with the number for better compression. · Speed up your logical capacity, so «Bee-Bot» travels to the number indicated by the teacher.
Materials Needed	· Mat or Number template 　-Dimension: 80x80 cm · Bee-Bot Kit
Recommended Age	4 – 6 years
Period	15 – 30 minutes
Competencies worked	· Development of logical thinking, communication and collaboration. · Maths · Learning to learn · Basic concept of displacement or trajectory and proximity of the number to be found. · Spatial relations (right, left, forward, back).
Development of Activity	1. Form groups of 3 students to develop collaboration and communication skills. 2. Place the mat or templates on the floor and explain how they should perform the activity of the route with the numbers as well as the relationship between the number of objects. 3. Give the «Bee-Bot» to the students, so that they begin the journey; each time it reaches its final position, explain to the student the relation between object and number; this way they will easily memorize the numbers of 0 to 10. 4. At the end of the activity, the «Bee-Bot» must return to their origin/start point or to the cell of the flower with the honey according to the position closest to where the «Bee-Bot» is.
Complementary Activities	Make 2 teams of 5 students where they select 3 equal colors and make the fastest route, mentioning at the end of the ascending order of the numbers with the selected color.

- The equipment that will be used in schools has been acquired, as it can be seen in Figure 6.

- Some mats have been produced to develop the first activities. It can be seen in figure 6, one which it is sought to familiarize preschool children with numbers from one to twelve; for this purpose, images that can attract the attention of children have been used.

The training of the children was given within the activities of the project.

Figure 8 shows the application of some of the activities in a group by each level (Kindergarten and first grade) for each of the 3 schools: Lassonde, La Pita and Leopoldina Field, developed during the second stage of the project in the that the students carried out the challenges that were indicated to them,

Figure 6. Kit for the development of the project

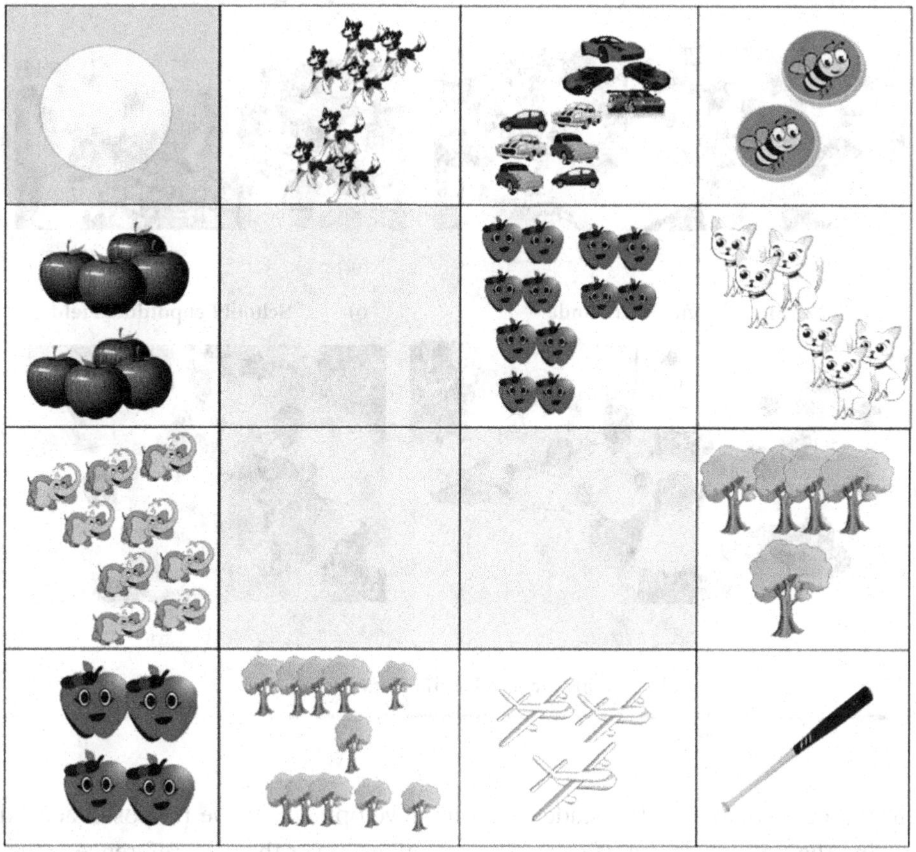

working as a team and understanding better the sequence of programming with which they had to give the instructions to the Bee-Bot.

Statistical Analysis

This section refers to the statistical analysis on the general evaluation obtained by each student from the three schools involved in the project, with respect to Kindergarten and first grade students respectively.

Kindergarden

The analysis of the results of the kindergarten groups of three schools in the province of Chiriquí was carried out based on a t-student test for two related samples, in this sense, the pre-test and post-test results were taken. For its part, Table 2 presents the descriptive statistics generated from the data collected in both tests. The total values are observed, where the mean calculated for the data collected in the post-test is higher than the pre-test mean of the kindergarten groups of the 3 schools.

In perspective, Table 3 shows the results of applying the statistical t-student test for samples related to the pre-test and post-test data. The results indicate significant differences in the calculated values

Figure 7. Mat to learn to count directed toward children at preschool level. Own elaboration

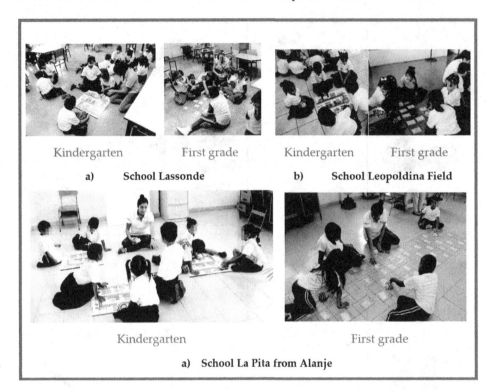

that represent the performance of the students in the development of the proposed activities. As can be seen regarding the asymptotic significance (Sig.), Values lower than the reference value of p <0.05 were obtained.

On the other hand, the effect size was calculated using Cohen's d, the value obtained was d = 0.517. According to the theory (Cohen, 2013), for this type of tests they are classified with the scale: small = 0.20; medium = 0.50; large = 0.80. In this case the effect is medium according to the results obtained. According to the data obtained, it can be affirmed that better results were obtained in the post-test evaluations.

First Grade

In parallel, the analysis carried out on the kindergarten groups in the pre-test and post-test tests, as well as the t-student, the same analysis was used for the first grade groups, with the difference that the amount of student population is superior to preschool groups. As a result, Table 4 presents the descriptive statistics generated from the data collected in both tests and the calculated mean for the data collected in the post-test is greater than the pre-test means.

In contrast, Table 5 shows the results of applying the statistical t-student test for samples related to the pre-test and post-test data. The results indicate significant differences in the calculated values that represent the performance of the students in the development of the proposed activities. As can be seen regarding the asymptotic significance (Sig.), Values lower than the reference value of p <0.05 were obtained. On the other hand, the effect size was calculated using Cohen's d, the value obtained was d

Figure 8. Practical workshop on the use of Bee Bot with students. Own elaboration

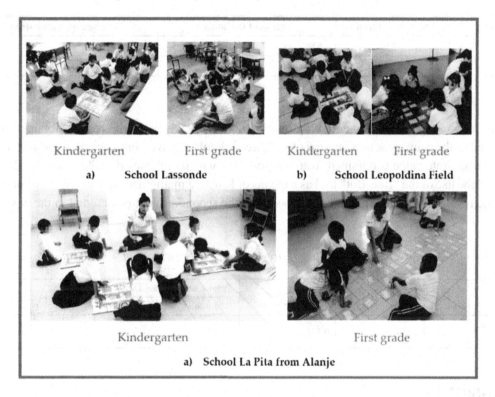

= 0.595. According to the theory (Cohen, 2013), for this type of tests they are classified with the scale: small = 0.20; medium = 0.50; large = 0.80. In this case the effect is medium according to the results obtained. According to the data obtained, it can be affirmed that better results were obtained in the post-test evaluations.

Table 2. Descriptive statistics for the pre-test and post-test values in Kindergarten

	N	Mean	Standard Deviation	Standard Error Mean
Pre-Test	96	3.177	1.8732	.1912
Post-Test	96	4.167	2.4192	.2469

Table 3. T-student test for related samples of pre-test and post-test data in Kindergarden

	Mean	Standard Deviation	Standard Error Mean	95% Confidence Interval of the Difference		t	gl	Sig.
				Lower	Upper			
Pre-Test Post-Test	– 0.9896	2.0026	0.2044	−1.3953	−0.5838	−4.842	95	0.000

Table 4. Descriptive statistics for the pre-test and post-test values in First Garde

	N	Mean	Standard Deviation	Standard Error Mean
Pre-Test	144	3.92	1.533	0.128
Post-Test	144	4.48	2.062	0.172

In this section we have commented and emphasized the analysis of the results obtained from the tests applied to the primary school groups of the three schools involved in the project and it is identified that a more accurate value is obtained from the post-test, which indicates that the students adapted and understood the use of the "Bee-Bot" tool as a means of learning mathematics. This aspect offers an overview of the results of the study, and the discussion of the second project is included in the next section.

Table 5. T-student test for related samples of pre-test and post-test data in First Grade

	Mean	Standard Deviation	Standard Error Mean	95% Confidence Interval of the Difference		t	gl	Sig.
				Lower	Upper			
Pre-Test Post-Test	−0.556	1.577	0.131	−0.815	−0.296	−4.228	143	0.000

DISCUSSION

This section deals with the synthesis of the analysis carried out on the results obtained in the course of the project of teaching mathematics in kindergarten and first grade schools, because their level of capturing the information was lower than the other students, therefore that, the data shown in a general way in the previously described sub-point, indicates that two tests were applied (pre-test and post-test) to identify the first approximation of the use of the tool in mathematics and later the final evaluation to know the children's learning curve regarding mathematical content.

In fact, the use of educational robotics in initial teaching contexts in public schools in the province of Chiriquí in Panama, highlights the importance of developing projects like this, because it allows students to become more familiar and understand the basic functioning of a robot. and its use in academic content.

Additionally, the benefits generated by both students and teachers is the use of low-cost technological tools and that, therefore, shows them that Mathematics can be taught and learned with a robot, and not necessarily in the traditional way. Meaning that the teacher develops the curricular contents, but allows the student to reason, analyze, learn to program by means of instructions to a robot to execute and indicate the answer to a mathematical operation, as well as the visuospatial and cognitive development in preschool children. It should be noted that there is still work to be done, because it seeks to include a greater number of students and know how they adapt to the use of the "Beet-Bot" robot. Along with if the students level of learning improves or is maintained, to know the effect both Positive as well as negative generated by the implementation of this within the study plan of elementary students.

FUTURE TRENDS

Following the guidelines on the field of technologies as a teaching-learning process in the area of augmented reality and educational robotics with the use of Bee-Bot, it is significant to explore other scenarios with different subjects of the Panamanian educational system where the student interacts with the tool and complements your knowledge. In this sense, it can be applied to subjects such as English, Spanish and art; Likewise, it may be aimed at children with learning disabilities, who find it more difficult to understand the information simultaneously like the rest of the students. In the same way, a detailed analysis can be carried out and those students who present learning deficiencies in mathematics or in the form of writing can be carried out, if they present imperative behavior in the classroom or there is little communication between their classmates. Each of these aspects can be evaluated as future work, in order to use technology to identify educational deficiencies in students and include different academic content in the tools implemented in both educational projects. In addition, it seeks to implement both projects in other educational centers in the province of Chiriquí, and evaluate the scope and learning curve that general use of AR and educational robotics in elementary school children; in contrast, with the results that are traditionally obtained with the methods that are implemented in schools.

Likewise, it is important to involve more teachers in the use of technologies such as playful didactic strategies in the classroom.

CONCLUSION

In summary, the integration of ICT in education provides tools and methods that promote learning and motivation on students thereby achieving the development of better educational settings. Besides, it allows to incorporate content curriculum in an interactive and dynamic in the use of technologies as well as learn the importance to complement teaching with the appropriate tool in the classroom. In fact, through the design and development of scenarios for teaching and conserving natural sites through AR, it has been possible to recreate animations that allow students to effectively assimilate information from the sites, thus reinforcing their learning through interactive content that generate a greater motivation to learn. In this way, the creation of the different didactic sheets was necessary whereas it allows them to live that experience of interacting with various virtual contents. Thanks to its use, it is possible to optimize learning processes and increase students' interest and participation.

Parallel, educational robotics generates many benefits in the learning of the smallest kids for this reason it is important to continue investing in new technologies for their early development. Indeed, it is a resource that allows them to acquire knowledge while playing. The development of the play and programming experience with the Bee-Bot® robots was effective and useful to strengthen the design, structure and evaluation mechanisms of planned activities.

Therefore, AR and educational robotics represent two of the technological tools used in the teaching of students in order to reinforce, motivate, teach and develop cognitive, spatial, motor and analytical skills in students. In turn, they are shown the benefits generated by its effective implementation and the motivation to learn new academic content in a more interactive and appropriate way to the content plan that the teacher develops. Both objectives of the projects were met, and the advantages for those involved (teachers and students) was the use and interaction through the application of AR and the robot "Bee-Bot", offering them a basic knowledge of programming and three-dimensional objects such as complement to the learning of the academic contents that included mathematics, natural sciences and social sciences. In summary, with the results obtained from both projects, it allows reducing the knowledge gap in the use of technology in schools with educational vulnerabilities and a shortage of technological equipment that reinforces teaching at different levels of schooling; and, therefore, provide students with a new vision of technological tools and their participation during the teaching process.

ACKNOWLEDGMENT

This research was supported by the Secretaria Nacional de Ciencia, Tecnología e Innovación (SENACYT)

REFERENCES

Aebersold, M., Rasmussen, J., & Mulrenin, T. (2020). Virtual Everest: Immersive Virtual Reality Can Improve the Simulation Experience. *Clinical Simulation in Nursing, 38*, 1–4. doi:10.1016/j.ecns.2019.09.004

Alessa, D., & Gonzales, K. S. (2020, April 14). Perceptions of service learning in pharmacy education: A systematic review. *Currents in Pharmacy Teaching and Learning, 8*. Advance online publication. doi:10.1016/j.cptl.2020.04.005 PMID:32624146

Angeli, C., & Valanides, N. (2019). Developing Young children's computational thinking with educational robotics: An interaction effect between gender and scaffolding strategy. *Computers in Human Behavior, 105*. Advance online publication. doi:10.1016/j.chb.2019.03.018

Aris, N., & Orcos, L. (2019). Educational robotics in the stage of secondary education: Empirical study on motivation and STEM skills. *Education in Science, 9*(2), 73. doi:10.3390/educsci9020073

Benavides, F., Otegui, X., Aguirre, A., & Andrade, F. (2013). Robótica educativa en Uruguay: de la mano del robot butiá. *XV Congreso Internacional de Informática en la Educación.*

Caballero, Y. A., & Muñoz-Repiso, A. G.-V. (2017). Development of computational thinking and collaborative learning in kindergarten using programmable educational robots. *Proceedings of the 5th International Conference on Technological Ecosystems for Enhancing Multiculturality*, 1-6. Obtenido de https://dl.acm.org/doi/abs/10.1145/3144826.3145353

Chen, G., Shen, J., Barth-Cohen, L., Jiang, S., Huang, X., & Eltoukhy, M. (2017). Assessing elementary students' computational thinking in everyday reasoning and robotics programming. *Computers & Education, 109*, 162–175. doi:10.1016/j.compedu.2017.03.001

Chen, X., Zou, D., Cheng, G., & Xie, H. (2020). Detecting latent topics and trends in educational technologies over four decades using structural topic modeling: A retrospective of all volumes of Computers & Education. *Computers & Education, 151*(February), 103855. doi:10.1016/j.compedu.2020.103855

Estivill-Castro, V. (2019). Inviting teachers to use educational robotics to foster mathematical problem-solving. *Advances in Intelligent Systems and Computing, 1023.*

Greenberg, R. I., Thiruvathukal, G. K., & Greenberg, S. T. (2020). Integrating Mathematics and Educational Robotics: Simple Motion Planning. *Advances in Intelligent Systems and Computing*, 262-269.

Hooshyar, D., Pedaste, M., Saks, K., Leijen, Ä., Bardone, E., & Wang, M. (2020). Open learner models in supporting self-regulated learning in higher education: A systematic literature review. *Computers & Education*, *103878*. Advance online publication. doi:10.1016/j.compedu.2020.103878

Lohre, R., Warner, J. J. P., Athwal, G. S., & Goel, D. P. (2020). The evolution of virtual reality in shoulder and elbow surgery. JSES International, 1–9. doi:10.1016/j.jseint.2020.02.005

Misirli, A., & Komis, V. (2014). Robotics and Programming Concepts in Early Childhood Education: A Conceptual Framework for Designing Educational Scenarios. *Educational Software Use in Kindergarten*, 99-118.

Moreno, I., Muñoz, L., & Serracin, J. (2012). La robótica educativa, una herramienta para la enseñanza-aprendizaje de las ciencias y las tecnologías. *Teoría la Educación: Educación y Cultura en la Sociedad la Infinformación*, *13*(2), 74–90.

Nishizawa, H., Shimada, K., Ohno, W., & Yoshioka, T. (2013). Increasing reality and educational merits of a virtual game. *Procedia Computer Science*, *25*, 32–40. doi:10.1016/j.procs.2013.11.005

Orcas, L., & Aris, N. (2019). Perceptions of secondary education teachers in educational robotics as a teaching resource in the STEM approach. *Opción*, *35*(90), 810–843.

Palomino, M. del C. P. (2017). Teacher Training in the Use of ICT for Inclusion: Differences between Early Childhood and Primary Education. *Procedia: Social and Behavioral Sciences*, *237*(June), 144–149. doi:10.1016/j.sbspro.2017.02.055

Pellón, R. T., Miranda, D. R., Gonzalez, S. B., & Reyna, I. C. H. (2017). Las tecnologías de la información y la comunicación en la enseñanza de inglés en Ciencias Médicas. *Educación Médica Superior*, *31*(2).

Pranoto, H., & Panggabean, F. M. (2019). Increase the interest in learning by implementing augmented reality: Case studies studying rail transportation. *Procedia Computer Science*, *157*, 506–513. doi:10.1016/j.procs.2019.09.007

Ramírez, P. A., & Sosa, H. A. (2013). Aprendizaje con robótica, algunas experiencias. *Review of Education*, *37*(1), 43–63.

Serin, O., Serin, N. B., & Saygili, G. (2009). The effect of educational technologies and material supported science and technology teaching on the problem solving skills of 5 th grade primary school student. *Procedia: Social and Behavioral Sciences*, *1*(1), 665–670. doi:10.1016/j.sbspro.2009.01.116

Singh, A. S., & Segatto, A. P. (2020). When relational capabilities walk in education for sustainability scenario. *Journal of Cleaner Production*, *263*, 121478. Advance online publication. doi:10.1016/j.jclepro.2020.121478

Taborda, H., & Medina, D. (2012). *Programación de Computadores y Desarrollo de Habilidades de Pensamiento En Niños Escolares: Fase Exploratoria. Cali.* Universidad ICESI. Obtenido de http://eduteka.icesi.edu.co/pdfdir/Icesi_Investigacion_Scratch_FaseI.pdf

KEY TERMS AND DEFINITIONS

Augmented Reality: Is an interactive experience of a real-world environment where the objects that reside in the real world are enhanced by computer-generated perceptual information, sometimes across multiple sensory modalities, including visual, auditory, haptic, somatosensory, and olfactory.

Education: Is the process of facilitating learning, or the acquisition of knowledge, skills, values, belief and habits.

Educational Robotics: Teaches the design, analysis, application, and operation of robots. Robots include articulated robots, mobile robots, or autonomous vehicles.

Environment Conservation: Is basically the practice of us humans to save the environment from collapsing, such as loss of species, ecosystems due to pollution and human activities.

Information Technology: Is the use of computers to store, retrieve, transmit, and manipulate data or information. IT is typically used within the context of business operations as opposed to personal or entertainment technologies.

Natural Sciences: Is a branch of science concerned with the description, prediction, and understanding of natural phenomena, based on empirical evidence from observation and experimentation.

Robotics: Is an interdisciplinary research area at the interface of science and engineering.

Chapter 5
Leveraging Linked Data in Open Education

Janneth Chicaiza

https://orcid.org/0000-0003-3439-3618

Universidad Técnica Particular de Loja, Ecuador

ABSTRACT

In recent years, the processes of training, teaching, and online learning have become more widespread. In this context, open education has the role of empowering people to meet their learning goals. Aligned with this vision, educational institutions are offering open access to their educational resources. However, content is delivering from different platforms by making a challenging task for users to find accurate information. To face this issue, the academic community is adopting Semantic Web and Linked Data for publishing and sharing data. In this chapter, the author presents the main findings in this area. From a technological point of view, the contribution focuses on the main stages of the linked data publishing cycle. Also, from the perspective of the application domain, the author explains the research's contribution regarding three dimensions of Open Education. This chapter ends with some thoughts regarding the author's research path, her remaining tasks, and future trends.

INTRODUCTION

In recent years, the processes of training, teaching and learning online have become more widespread through the web. Thus, the World Wide Web has become the most popular platform for creating, sharing and accessing educational services and resources. An open and extensible platform like the web facilitates the creation, publication and exchange of a wide variety of resources for learning and the generation of new knowledge (Chicaiza, Piedra, Lopez, & Tovar-Caro, 2015). Yet, in this environment, information overload and heterogeneous content make it difficult to find valuable content (Chicaiza, Piedra, Lopez, & Tovar-Caro, 2017), and reduce the possibilities of sharing and exchanging information (Piedra, Chicaiza, Lopez, Martinez, & Tovar-Caro, 2010). To reduce the problems of discovery, interoperability, and reuse of web data stored in heterogeneous systems (Tapia-Leon, Aveiga, Chicaiza, & Suárez-Figueroa, 2019), the academic community is adopting the use of Semantic Web (SW) and Linked Data (LD) technologies.

DOI: 10.4018/978-1-7998-7552-9.ch005

Copyright © 2021, IGI Global. Copying or distributing in print or electronic forms without written permission of IGI Global is prohibited.

As a result of this convergence, the web is becoming an ecosystem of structured and interconnected data that facilitates the automatic integration and consumption of information. In this chapter, the author explains the motivations behind her research on LD approaches, and based on her experience, presents the main contributions of her researcher activities.

Since teaching and learning processes have become popular on the web, many things have shifting. Nowadays, the process of creating and publishing educational content is not exclusive to teachers or educational institutions. Every day, a set of courses and educational resources are published through different platforms and services. In addition, the creation of educational material has become a horizontal process, and the role of creating knowledge is not exclusive to teachers. Different initiatives that have emerged in recent years are aligned with the philosophy of Open Education (OE). Today, an increasing number of learners want to have the freedom to choose when and where to learn, and how and what they want to learn. Through this vision, educational institutions and service providers can meet these demands (Gorissen, 2013).

One of the most recognized movements that emerged is the Open Educational Resources (OERs). OER includes a wide range of materials that make it the most significant icon that has emerged within the open educational content movement (Chicaiza, Piedra, Lopez, & Tovar-Caro, 2015). One of the main objectives of the OER movement is to enable people to access the resources they need for learning. The first step for users to start this process is to find information and resources according to their training needs (Chicaiza, Piedra, Lopez, & Tovar-Caro, 2014). But given the vast amount of information on the web, the teaching community and learners may require some support in discovering the most appropriate resources to incorporate into their teaching and learning processes (Chicaiza et al., 2017).

In distributed and heterogeneous information repositories, the formal languages of the SW allow us to create structured and machine-readable data, thus improving the processes of information exchange, aggregation and search. Similarly, Linked Open Data (LOD) is a powerful approach to linking different web data sets. Today, several higher education institutions have been publishing their data using the SW + LD approach, thus facilitating the reuse of data to create valuable services for their students. This objective is aligned with the original vision of the SW, to create intelligent agents that can cooperate to perform tasks for users (Zamazal, 2020).

In this chapter, the author will try to highlight how Latin American women, through research and IT, can contribute to improving their environment. Specifically, the author will explain her role and the impact of the research she has carried out in relation to the application of semantic technologies in the OE field. In the following section, after presenting the theoretical foundations, the author will explain the framework she applied to highlight her work in relation to the creation and use of LD for enhancing certain educational tasks. The chapter ends with some thoughts of the author regarding her research path, pending tasks and future trends.

BACKGROUND

In this section, the author describes the two areas on which she has focused her research. On the one hand, open education constitutes the application domain, and on the other hand, the SW and LD define the technological framework used to address different problems in the domain.

From Open Educational Resources to Open Education

One of the most important services of the web is providing access to learning material for self-learners, practitioners, and the entire academic community. Several initiatives, under the umbrella of the Open Access (OA) movement, have contributed to populating the web with open educational materials. The first initiative, called "OpenCourseWare[1]", was promoted by the Massachusetts Institute of Technology (MIT). In 2001, MIT offered, for the first time, open courses. From this year onwards, more institutions have joined this movement. Organizations such as UNESCO and the Open Education Consortium promote projects and support people and institutions that produce, use, adapt and share these types of resources.

Educational materials that are published in open form are called OER. The "open" dimension of an educational resource implies that the resource *has been released under an open license that permits no-cost access, use, adaptation and redistribution by others with no or limited restrictions* (Open Education, n.d.). Thus, in the field of online learning, OERs offer potential benefits such as (1) providing access to a diverse set of quality resources (Caswell, Henson, Jensen, & Wiley, 2008); (2) promoting the universal right to education, i.e., people use open resources free of charge and any time; (3) encouraging people to get competencies that boost their development; and (4) fostering openness, sharing and creation of new knowledge.

Institutions that facilitate access to open academic material from anywhere in the world and at any time, contribute to opening up education. However, this is not the unique requirement for ensuring OE. In addition to open content, open education is defined as open instructions, open tools, open control for customization and personalization (Chih-Hsiung, Cherng-Jyh, Sujo-Montes, & Sealander, 2018).

OE is a vision and philosophy to encourage learners to drive their learning, i.e. to become self-learners (Chih-Hsiung et al., 2018). Likewise, OE implies the promotion of cultural diversity, and assuring access to high-quality educational experiences and resources for everyone, i.e. open education is inclusive. Thus, OE attempts to eliminate educational barriers that include high monetary costs, outdated or obsolete materials, and legal mechanisms that prevent collaboration among learners and faculty (Deepak, 2015). Therefore, OE has the potential of increasing equity, promoting the creation of distributed and decentralized content and knowledge. Finally, OE also has to ensure that learners receive the most pertinent resources, services, and information according to their preferences and context. In this sense, this vision also means personalization of learning.

As such, in order to ensure that OERs are enablers of OE, and to ensure that the education community has access to the most relevant resources, the material must meet certain characteristics that make them more accessible and adaptable to the needs of users. Semantic technologies can help meet this purpose.

Semantic Web and Linked Data

Berners-Lee, Hendler & Lassila (2001) introduced the term semantic web to refer to *an extension of the current web, where information has a well-defined meaning, better-enabling computers and people to work in cooperation*. Figure 1 shows the main features of the SW; these features try to face two of the main challenges of the traditional web: information overload and automatic interchange of data.

1.   Structured data. The semantic content is structured, making it easier to query information units as in a global database.

Figure 1. Main features of the semantic web and goals

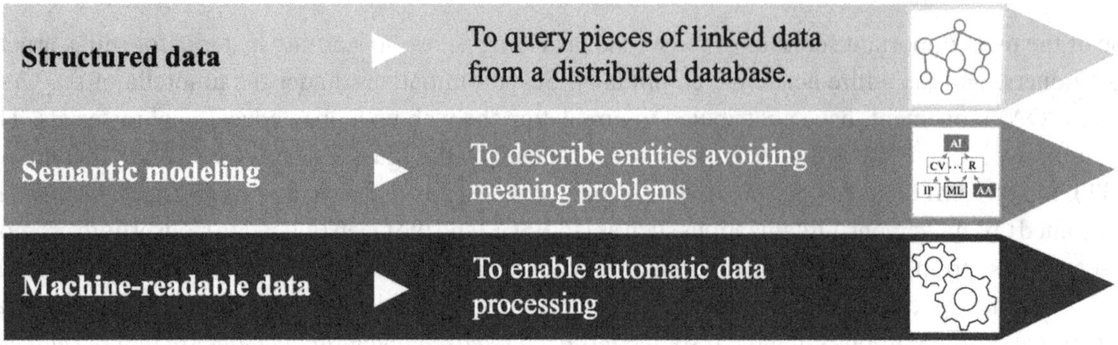

Structured data	▷	To query pieces of linked data from a distributed database.	
Semantic modeling	▷	To describe entities avoiding meaning problems	
Machine-readable data	▷	To enable automatic data processing	

2. Semantic modeling. In the SW, real-world entities are described and connected through consensus models, which easy the common understanding of the terms of a domain and allow the explicit definition of the meaning of the information.
3. Machine-readable data. This format enables the processing of data at a large scale.

All these features try to solve some data meaning issues and to improve interoperability, accessibility, and reuse of resources and information on the web. Figure 2 illustrates the paradigm shift in browsing and data consumption.

Figure 2. Browsing and data consumption of educational content

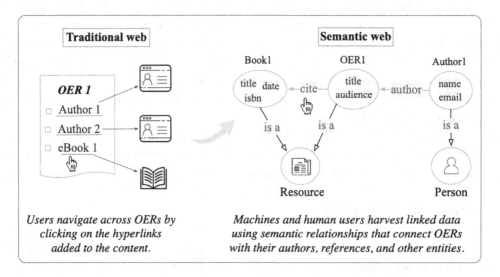

As mentioned, the SW adds structure and meaning to the web of documents, so it is easy processing by machine agents. But, considering that much of the web content is unstructured, it is complex to convert the existing content massively and automatically. Therefore, one of the first efforts of the SW was populating the web with LD. Web of Data corresponds to the web vision in which data has to be linked to other external datasets to create a single global data space (Bizer et al., 2009).

To publish interoperable data on the web of data, Tim Berners-Lee proposed in 2006 the LD design issues. The term *linked data* refers to a set of best practices for publishing and connecting structured data on the web (Bizer et al., 2009). These criteria provide guidelines on how to use SW technologies to publish and connect data on the web. These technologies and LD publishing practices ease the web-wide data sharing and reuse (Dietze, Drachsler, & Giordano, 2013).

To define the structure and how data are connected and queried, the SW provides a stack of technologies. The core technology used for describing and interchanging data is the Resource Description Framework (RDF). Next, ontologies and vocabularies allow the creation of open and consensual models; these technologies are the reference for describing real-world entities and resources. Finally, SPARQL is the query language that retrieves RDF data to build several valuable applications.

Linked Data application in Open Education

Semantic web technologies and linked data provide interoperability among repositories of educational data and resources. The ability to share and connect data has encouraged many institutions to begin a movement to use these technologies in education (Pereira et al., 2018).

Several studies highlight the adoption of SW + LD criteria for publishing educational data in a machine-readable format. Next, the author groups research in three categories: semantic modeling, description and publishing, and data leveraging.

Semantic Modeling

In the web of data two types of models are popular for describing resources and entities of interest, linked open vocabularies (Vega-Gorgojo et al., 2015), and ontologies (Allemang, Hendler, & Gandon, 2020). In OE, two goals drive the use of these models. (1) To describe the different resources and entities of the academic domain using a common vocabulary that facilitates communication between different institutions, educational systems, content providers, and users. (2) In massive learning environments, semantic models support the automation of tasks involving the management of large volumes of data, such as early detection and follow-up to students who demonstrate patterns related to drop-out or unsuccessful completion of the course.

So far, for describing entities of scholarly and educational domains, there are some models. In (Mikroyannidi, Liu, & Lee, 2016) the authors describe the Curriculum Ontology to organize learning resources and allow users to discover content via the UK curricula. This model was incorporated in the architecture of the BBC Knowledge & Learning Beta Online Pages. Vasiliev, Kozlov, Mouromtsev, Stafeev, & Parkhimovich (2016) identify other semantic models to describe the educational context.

Description and Publishing

Educational institutions are publishing linked data. According to the literature mapping made by Pereira et al. (2018), the provenance of data is diverse: statistical data, organizational data, educational resources such as videos, presentations, lectures, books, and games.

One of the data publishing projects to be highlighted is LD from the Open University[2]. The RDF data describe OERs, scientific production, organization, research projects, documentation, and social media. Another 21 educational RDF datasets are identified in (Taibi, Fulantelli, Dietze & Fetahu, 2016) and in the Linked Open Data (LOD) Cloud site[3].

Maybe, digital libraries are one of the most popular areas chosen for educational institutions for exposing their data in a machine-readable format. Two of the active projects are Linked Data for Physical and Digital Collections at the University of Washington[4] and Mannheim University Library[5].

Leveraging

Consumption and integration of LD from heterogeneous systems, in a simple and automatic way, promote the creation of different educational services. According to Pereira et al. (2018), recommendation (and customization) of educational content, and expansion of search terms most popular application.

Regarding the research carried out in universities, Ortiz-Vivar, Segarra, Villazón-Terrazas, & Saquicela, 2020 propose REDI (Semantic Repository of Researchers of Ecuador). REDI is a Linked Data-powered framework for academic knowledge management and research networking. In the web portal[6], users search and visualize papers, authors, institutions, and collaboration networks.

To end this section, a use case illustrates the potential use of semantic technologies. Figure 3 shows how users could learn by using online content. At left, there is a text based OER, the traditional format for delivering content. Also, Figure 3 shows semantic annotations (highlighted text) that are recognized by the classification service available on the Computer Science Ontology (CSO) portal[7]. Semantic annotations imply to add metadata to the data (Konstantinou & Spanos, 2015a), therefore, they provide users with information about each topic. At right, from semantic annotations and the CSO structure (Salatino et al., 2018), a network of topics is built. Here, users can navigate through this visual representation to understand the new topic they need to learn.

FRAMEWORK

In this section, the author describes the framework designed to explain her research's development from two points of view: technological, and applicative domains.

Figure 4 shows the framework used to classify the author's research contribution. From the technological point of view, the figure highlights the three stages of LD publishing cycle: semantic modeling, description and publishing, and data leveraging. Also, from the perspective of the application domain, the figure highlights three dimensions of open education: personalized learning, self-learning, and inclusive learning.

Research by Linked Data Stage

The publication of LD involves the execution of a set of tasks organized in stages. The author has organized research according to three main stages: semantic modeling, description and publishing, and data leveraging. The following section describes, for each stage, (1) its purpose; (2) potential benefits of designing a solution based on SW technologies; and (3) the contribution of the main publications in the area, as well as the impact they have created based on citations and readings.

Figure 3. Enhancing learning using semantic annotations and topic networks

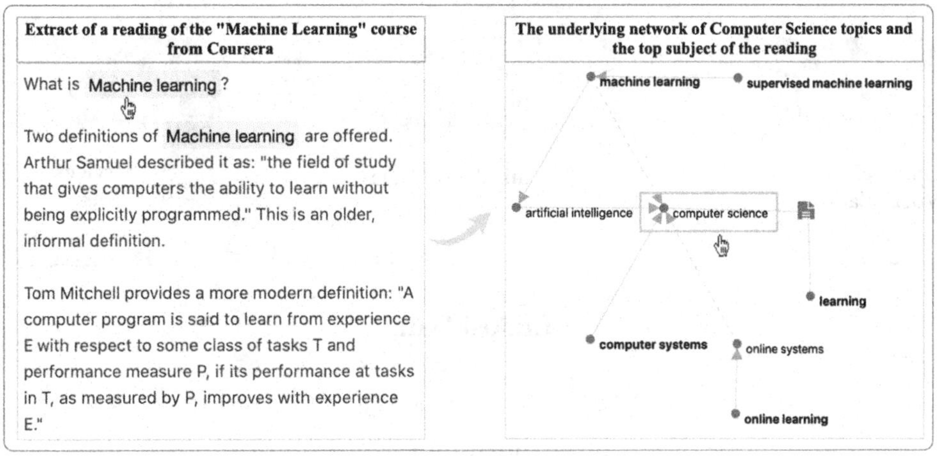

To determine the research impact of the selected documents, the author has used a five-star scale (see Table 1). The data to classify each publication has been obtained from Scopus and ResearchGate (R^G).

The author recognizes that the capacity of a researcher cannot be measured solely by the number of publications, citations or readings; nevertheless, it is the strategy selected in this chapter because it is the most direct and popular form used in scholarly communication.

Finally, for each stage of the cycle of LD, the author will explain her contribution based on three of her most representative publications, which do not necessarily correspond to those with the highest impact. The author made the publishing selection by assessing her role and contribution to each research.

Contribution on Open Education Dimensions

To determine the contribution of previous research in OE, the author has identified three fundamental dimensions of the application domain:

1. *Personalized learning.* The web is the perfect technological environment for personalized learning (Dagiene, Gudoniene, & Burbaite, 2015). Teachers, for example, can reuse external resources in their courses and adapt them according to the particular needs of their class. The process of adaptation or reuse could also be automated thanks to semantic technologies (Nahhas et al., 2018; Piedra, Chicaiza, Lopez, & Tovar-Caro, 2014).
2. *Self-learning.* Today, people have less time for learning using traditional methods (Chicaiza et al., 2015), therefore, self-learning is an important skill in the 21st century. In formal education, learning is structured according to a curriculum and is geared towards obtaining specific accreditation. In contrast, in informal education, learning is more flexible, diverse, and learner-centered; in this case, the learners are responsible for their own learning itinerary and time. Finally, in a non-formal system, which occurs in organizations, people must develop new skills to adapt to emerging occupational contexts and thus contribute to the development of their environment. Therefore, under the OE paradigm, education institutions should promote practices and offer services that allow students to acquire and strengthen their self-management skills (Chicaiza et al., 2015).

Figure 4. Framework for classifying the research contribution

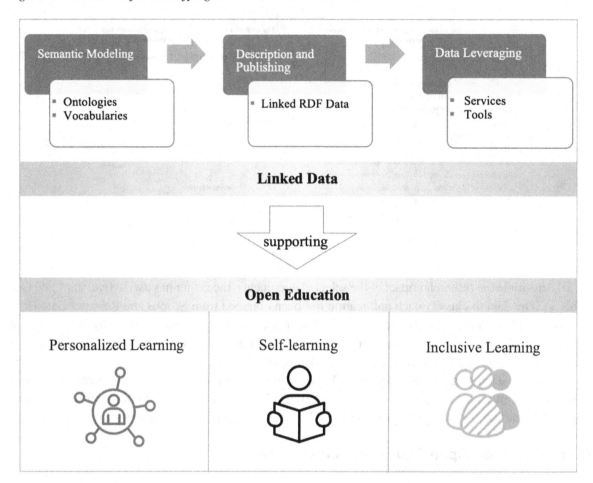

3. *Inclusive learning.* The internet is the primary channel for accessing and creating educational content. In this regard, it is essential that academic institutions promoting web-based learning, ensure that their resources and services are accessible to all. However, there are certain technical and infrastructural barriers that prevent or hinder access and participation of vulnerable sectors of

Table 1. Scale for measuring the impact of main research documents

Citations (c)		Readings (r)	
Range	**Research impact**	**Range**	**Research impact**
c <=10	*	r <= 50	*
10 < c <=20	**	50 < r <= 150	**
20 < c <= 30	***	150 < r <= 300	***
30 < c <= 40	****	300 < r <= 500	****
c > 40	*****	r > 500	*****

the population. In the current web, content is in a human-readable format, which makes it difficult to perform certain tasks, such as adapting content.

In the following section, for each dimension, the author will explain how LD publication processes can change or positively influence the improvement of educational services received by learners and academic community.

AREA RESEARCH AND CONTRIBUTION IN OPEN EDUCATION

Outcomes and Impact by Semantic Stage

For each of the stages of LD publishing cycle described in the methodology, this section provides information related to the main results achieved by the author in these areas.

Semantic Modeling

In formal education, there are some metadata schemas for describing users and learning objects. But, to use these models in open educational environments is not a scalable solution (Piedra et al., 2010; Chicaiza et al., 2015; Tapia-Leon et al., 2019). Here, the author highlights the use of open vocabularies and ontologies to improve interoperability, sharing, and reuse of data in OE.

With the objective of summarizing the author's work in the creation of semantic models for education, Table 2 identifies the most relevant publications in the area and the impact in the field of OE and research. The work carried out in this area has been performed following well-known creation and validation processes in the field of ontological engineering. In addition, formal technology and recognized metadata standards have been used in each domain.

With regard to the semantic description of digital resources, the author has participated with other researchers and domain experts in the definition of some semantic models. In order to create each proposal, the researchers carried out systematic research to obtain the most representative terms of each domain. In addition, the authors based the design considering existing ontological and non-ontological resources, with the aim of optimizing the time and costs associated with the creation of a new semantic model.

Table 2 describes the three papers selected by the author that describe the work done in this area: (1) ontology to describe OERs, (2) vocabulary to describe profiles of OER's users, and (3) ontology to represent syllabuses. From the research point of view, of the three publications, the oldest work is that which has achieved the greatest impact, according to the citations received in Scopus and ResearchGate, and the number of readers of the R[G] platform. The last paper corresponds to one of the last works done by the author, a model to describe syllabuses. Tapia-Leon et al. (2019) describe the work that has achieved the least impact, nevertheless, it is also the most complete and the best documented through technical reports available on the web[8].

Description and Publishing

When a team plans to execute a LD publication project, in addition to considering the publication guidelines defined by Berners-Lee, it must define a systematic process based on a set of tasks. The breakdown

Table 2. Main publications and contribution related to semantic modeling

No.	Paper	Year	Contribution	Research impact		
				Scopus cites	R^G cites	R^G readings
1	An Approach for Description of Open Educational Resources based on Semantic Technologies (Piedra et al., 2010).	2010	The ontology to represent OERs facilitates the implementation of rules to identify inconsistencies between the permissions enabled and the way learning materials are used	**	**	****
2	A User Profile Definition in Context of Recommendation of Open Educational Resources. An Approach based on Linked Open Vocabularies (Chicaiza et al., 2015).	2015	The vocabulary proposed for OER users is extensible and flexible. In other words, vocabulary makes it easy to add new attributes and also allows users to describe aspects that in the medium term may reflect their interests. However, it is not highly recommended due to the dynamicity of the web	*	*	**
3	Ontological Model for the Semantic Description of Syllabuses (Tapia-Leon et al., 2019).	2019	The creation of the ontological model to describe syllabus was based on the analysis of documents published by renowned Latin American institutions. As a result, a consensus model was created that can support different structures and terminology used in each region.	*	*	*

and effort required to perform each task depends on the source, structure and quality of the data, along with the scope and goals of the project. In general, three steps are fundamental:

1. *Extraction of data from selected sources and refinement of their quality.* There are variety of institutional repositories and open sources, whose data can be published on the web in machine-readable format. However, before making the decision to publish it, determining the quality of the data and the impact of its exposure is essential.
2. *Transformation of data into machine-readable formats (RDF) according to the defined semantic models.* Efforts to publish LD can be decreased if educational providers use tools or software to programmatically manipulated data. Konstantinou & Spanos (2015b) describe different categories of tools for preparing the data sources and managing LD. Thanks to these tools, several of them are open and free, the academic community can convert large volumes of data to RDF format.
3. *Publication and storing RDF data, and creation of data links with external sources made available in the cloud.* The goal here is to share the data on the web and make it easily searchable via query languages or APIs. In addition, links between entities from different sources make it possible to conduct data integration and enrichment tasks using data available from third-party sources.

The process described above has been applied in different LD-based projects where the author has participated. The results related to the development of the projects were disseminated in some scientific communications. Table 3 identifies the three publications selected by the author representing her work in three domains: (1) OpenCourseWare (OCW) courses, (2) digital libraries, and (3) OERs.

Table 3. Main publications and contribution related to description and publishing

No.	Paper	Year	Contribution	Research impact		
				Scopus cites	R^G cites	R^G readings
1	Consuming and producing Linked Open Data: The Case of OpenCourseWare (Piedra, Tovar-Caro, Colomo-Palacios, Lopez, & Chicaiza, 2014).	2014	Enrichment of open learning content and improvement of the search for OCW courses created by the member universities of the UNIVERSIA network.	*****	*****	*****
2	Framework for the Integration of Digital Resources based-on a Semantic Web Approach (Piedra, Chicaiza, Quichimbo, et al., 2015).	2015	The publication process was conducted in the bibliographic domain. Digital materials of certain educational institutions of Ecuador were transformed.	**	**	***
3	Integrating OER in the Design of Educational Material: Blended Learning and Linked-Open Educational Resources Data Approach (Piedra, Chicaiza, Lopez, & Tovar-Caro, 2016).	2016	The designed architecture improves the reuse of OERs in blended learning. The reuse of OERs, at a personal or institutional level, has a creative and economic positive impact in open education environments.	*	**	*****

The first work (Piedra et al., 2014) corresponds to the publication of OCW courses' data of the Universia consortium. Universia is a network that currently has over 1400 member universities in 20 countries. In 2014, thanks to the support of the OCW Consortium (now called The Open Education Consortium) and OCW-Universia, the project team formed by researchers from the Universidad Técnica Particular de Loja and the Technical University of Madrid managed to publish, as linked data, thousands of metadata from the OCW courses. In (Piedra et al., 2014), the authors describe the publication cycle and demonstrate how OCW course data from different educational institutions can be connected and integrated.

Of the three publications presented in Table 3, the first one is the most important in which the author has participated because it is, so far, the most cited in her entire career. It has more than 40 citations in Scopus, more than 50 citations in R^G, and more than 800 readings in RG. This paper demonstrated the importance of publishing the OER data in open format, not solely the contents. (Piedra et al., 2014) shown that OER repositories had become information silos. Information silos make it difficult to exchange information, in the context of OERs, they make it difficult to find and reuse materials, therefore the user is the most affected.

The second paper focuses on the publication of bibliographic resource data. This work was developed thanks to the development of several projects financed by the National Network of Ecuadorian Research and Education (CEDIA). Piedra, Chicaiza, Quichimbo, et al., (2015) present a framework for the publication of bibliographic data extracted from digital repositories using OAI-PMH. Between 2015 and 2017, the author participated in the conversion of different digital library collections of CEDIA member universities.

Finally, Table 2 highlights (Piedra et al., 2016) because it has been of interest to the community that accesses R^G, in fact, it is one of the author's most read publications on this platform. In this research, OER data are utilized to enable teachers to locate the most appropriate materials for incorporation into their classes, thus reducing the efforts and costs associated with the creation of new material.

Leveraging

Figure 5 presents some services and applications that can be created from LD datasets, and the potential benefits derived from the use of semantic technologies.

Figure 5. Applications and benefits of linked data

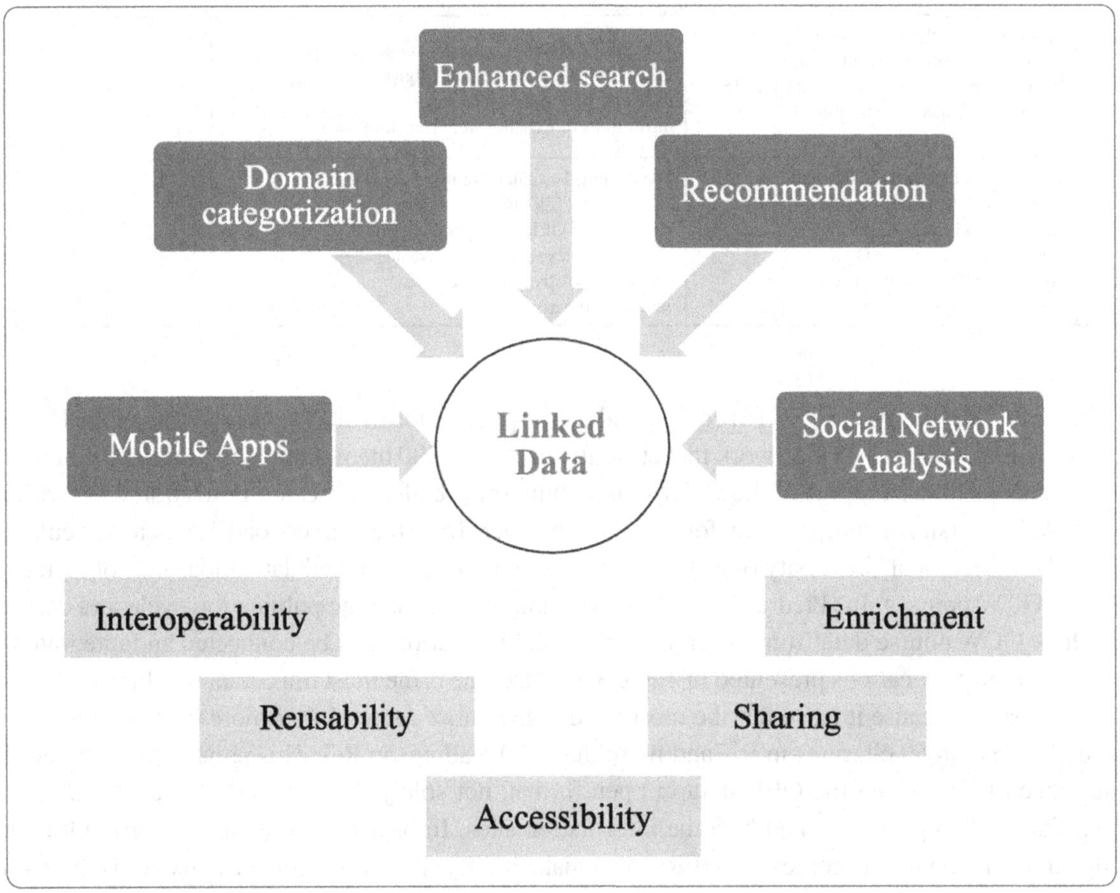

Before explaining some of the LD applications that the author has worked on, she explains the potential benefits locate at the bottom of Figure 5.

- *Interoperability*. The LD approach offers significant advantages over traditional data publishing practices based on raw data exchange. In the web of data, resources and their metadata are identified through URIs, so the data is no longer the basic unit of data exchange. When a resource is accessed through its URI it is possible to retrieve useful information about the resource without giving rise to problems related to the meaning of the information.

- *Enrichment.* LD available in various data sources can be used to complement or enrich the semantic description of the resources of interest (Nahhas et al., 2018). By adding these descriptions to current data, it is possible to create services of value to users.
- *Reusability and sharing.* RDF data catalogs are reusable and easily shared because, (1) they are available on the web and can be accessed through query languages and other services available from the provider; and (2) they are published along with metadata describing them such as license, title, creators, publication date, etc., this information facilitates data reuse because contributors can be made aware of the legal terms and permissions under which the provider made the data set available.
- *Accessibility.* LD provides a standardized and uniform way of consuming data regardless of content or location, thus ensuring data accessibility (Vega-Gorgojo et al., 2015). On the other hand, accessibility can also be interpreted as the ease of using user models to create services and resources adapted to their needs.

The five potential benefits associated with LD allow the construction of some applications such as those shown in the upper part of Figure 5. Now, Table 4 highlights research related to the LD-driven apps shown in Figure 5.

Table 4. Main publications and contribution related to data leveraging

No.	Paper	Year	Contribution	Research impact		
				Scopus cites	R^G cites	R^G readings
1	Domain Categorization of Open Educational resources based on Linked Data (Chicaiza, Piedra, Lopez, & Tovar-Caro, 2014).	2014	It facilitates the thematic classification of digital resources according to the topics of a thesaurus. Thus, users can find resources more efficiently.	**	***	***
2	Seeking Open Educational Resources to Compose Massive Open Online Courses in Engineering Education an Approach Based on Linked Open Data (Piedra, Chicaiza, Lopez, & Tovar-Caro, 2015).	2015	The proposed architecture allows for the optimization of the process of creating massive online courses through the reuse of existing materials.	***	***	****
3	Recommendation of Open Educational Resources. An Approach based on Linked Open Data (Chicaiza, Piedra, Lopez, & Tovar-Caro, 2017).	2017	The recommendation framework is capable of providing answers to diverse users, whether they are linked to a formal education system or not. It therefore promotes equity in education.	*	*	*

- *Mobile apps.* In Lopez, Tovar-Caro, & Martínez (2012), the authors present a framework for designing services that combine the benefits of LD and mobile devices. One of the mobile applications analyzed within of OpenCourseWare domain is the OCW POIs-Mobile. This app renders a map indicating nearby OCW content locations based on the current GPS position of a mobile device.

- *Domain categorization*. The first research in Table 4 deals with the thematic classification of digital resources. Classification is a common task of document systems and is usually done manually. In (Chicaiza et al., 2014) the authors present a process for supporting the semi-automatic classification of OER extracted from OCW sites. To conduct this task, characteristics of the LD such as data enrichment and inference were exploited. From the research impact point of view, this publication is the second highest impact of the selected works.

- *Enhanced search*. The research impact of (Piedra, Chicaiza, Lopez, et al., 2015) has been important considering the number of readings in R^G, and the number of citations in Scopus and in R^G. In this paper authors propose an architecture to promote the reuse of open materials in massive online courses. The central element of the architecture is an information filtering engine based on SPARQL. The engine uses data from DBPEDIA to enrich the OER data extracted from OCW (Piedra et al., 2014). The enriched data increases the recall of the system by expanding its search capability. In addition, semantic technologies facilitate the construction of intuitive navigation mechanisms. Thus, the user will be able to find and understand key concepts and relationships in a knowledge domain.

- *Recommendation*. Chicaiza et al. (2017) address the challenge of finding valuable information in large volume data collections, while trying to overcome the problem of providing recommendations to anonymous users. Classical recommendation approaches require processing historical information about users and their preferences, and this does not fit into the context of open education where there may be sporadic users or users with very little information profiles. Therefore, the authors apply a knowledge filtering approach that is flexible enough to meet the needs of heterogeneous users. The complexity of identifying resources that match a user's interests is reduced by a simple filtering mechanism that takes advantage of the large amount of linked data available on the web. Third-party data serves to enrich user profiles and the representation of educational resources.

- *Social Network Analysis* (SNA). In (Piedra et al., 2015), the authors propose a component based on SNA to discover influential users of a given topic. This component uses LD to expand the terms used to extract tweets from Twitter. Likewise, the authors use linked data for contextual enrichment of entities found in tweets. As a result, users receive a list of related hashtags and influential users in a given topic.

Contributions and Impact on Open Education

In open education, LD and SW offer a set of revolutionary practices and technologies (d'Aquin, 2012). Likewise, OERs are a representative symbol of OE, therefore, all the efforts that contribute to improving their use are positive. Next, the author identifies some aspects related to the impact of LD and SW in each of the three dimensions of OE defined in the methodology.

Personalized Learning

There are different ways to personalize learning. In this chapter, the personalization route consists of providing the learning contents according to the specific requirements of each user.

In this dimension, the author participated in the design and construction of the personalized search (Chicaiza et al., 2015; Piedra, Chicaiza, Lopez, et al., 2015; Piedra, Chicaiza, Lopez, Tovar-Caro, &

Bonastre, 2011) and recommendation services (Chicaiza et al., 2017; Lopez, Piedra, Chicaiza, & Tovar-Caro, 2015) for OER. Here, the researchers' team addresses the challenge of finding the best resources to support self-learning and lifelong learning processes of heterogeneous users.

Another author's contribution is related to the definition of semantic models for the description of different entities and resources in the educational and academic fields. In addition to the mentioned models, the author has led the creation of ontologies aimed at describing theses, personal learning environments (PLET), accessibility frameworks, among others. To create some ontological models, the author played a special role by training and leading a female team. Now each team member can build and redesign other proposals to personalize the content, learning paths, activities, or educational services that learners receive.

To provide personalized learning experiences, institutions and teachers must make considerable efforts, for example, to create custom materials from scratch. Through the analysis of machine-readable data, resources to be reused to build complete courses are identified. This is another of the contributions of the author's papers (Piedra et al., 2016; Piedra, Chicaiza, Lopez, et al., 2015).

Self-Learning

To support self-learning, user's models are a crucial piece of this process. The learner model, defined by Chicaiza et al. (2015), describes user preferences according to the topics defined by knowledge organization systems. Exploring topics through hierarchical relationships allows users to refine their searches. Here, one of the most interesting contributions of the author was to propose an open and scalable model in which users decide what information to share with educational service providers. Likewise, the proposed vocabulary supports the definition of a varied set of characteristics of users such as learning objectives, previous skills, and required skills, resources of interest, among other aspects. From information provided by the user, different agents can share and exchange that information to offer the respective support to the user during their training process.

Here, another fundamental aspect is to guide users to direct their training process. Through knowledge map-based visualization services or faceted search services, users can have a better understanding of the domain and thus provide meaningful feedback for the system (Chicaiza et al., 2015). The ability to understand the users' requirements will depend on the information that the user provides. Therefore, to ease the exploration of knowledge domains is essential so that the users who are starting their study can better understand an area of interest.

Finally, the role of learning resources is essential to promote that independent, autonomous and self-directed learners can acquire the necessary skills to carry out their tasks (Dagiene et al., 2015). Through search engines and recommendation services, access from mobile devices, among other projects in which the author has participated, she tried to contribute in this area (Chicaiza et al., 2017; Piedra, Chicaiza, Lopez, Tovar-Caro, & Martínez, 2012).

Inclusive Learning

The semantic models mentioned in this chapter can be extended or mapped to third-party models to include metadata of the context and the particular accessibility requirements of the users. The semantic representation of the resources and the educational environment facilitates the adaptation of the content and the personalized deployment of the services to students with special access requirements. The barriers to accessing digital content and interaction are easier to overcome when machines are able to identify the characteristics of each user and react according to their needs.

Furthermore, the use of vocabularies and ontologies facilitates the reuse and sharing of data between applications and different educational systems. In this way, service providers can create valuable services that seek to integrate and maintain the student in less structured training processes. Through some works (Chicaiza et al., 2015; Chicaiza et al., 2015), the author has tried to contribute by improving access to education for all.

Inclusive education requires a multidisciplinary effort, so technology is not the only element that must be considered. Even more important is that the learning content is accessible, this implies that teachers must learn to create and evaluate accessible content (Amado-Salvatierra, Hilera, Tortosa, Rizzardini, & Piedra, 2016). In this context, in 2013, the author participated in a training program focused on improving accessible virtual teaching techniques for teachers. In (Chicaiza, Piedra, & Valencia, 2014), authors discuss the main results of the program applied to teachers from institutions in eight different countries in Latin America.

To end this section, it is important to note that each research cited here was supported by the author's vision, knowledge, and skills. Especially, the research and findings reached in her doctoral thesis (Chicaiza, 2016) were valuable in order to identify and try to close research gaps in LD, personalized search, and OERs.

RESEARCH PATH AND LEARNED LESSONS

Here, the author shares some data and lessons that she has acquired during her researcher career and that could encourage and foster collaboration with other researchers. On the other hand, the author makes a self-evaluation about the aspects that can be improved to achieve a greater contribution in her environment.

Production and Global Impact

One of the essential purposes of science is the communication of its findings. Common methods of scholarly communication include publishing peer-reviewed articles in academic journals, book' chapters, and conference papers. In this subsection, the author presents her annual production in terms of the number of documents published in scientific databases and the number of citations that the publications have received.

Annual Production

Figure 6 shows the annual evolution of the documents published by the author in two sources, Scopus and Microsoft (MS) Academy. The figure differentiates the documents indexed in the scientific database Scopus, versus the totality of documents in which the author has contributed as a co-author and which are consolidated in MS Academy.

As of mid-2020, the author has 3 different profiles in Scopus, with which she adds up 46 publications. On the other hand, there are 56 documents in MS Academy. This means that, out of every 6 scholarly publications, 5 are indexed in Scopus. Furthermore, considering the number of publications and her career length in Scopus (2009-2020), the author has an average production of 4 documents per year.

Figure 6. Annual production of scholarly publications

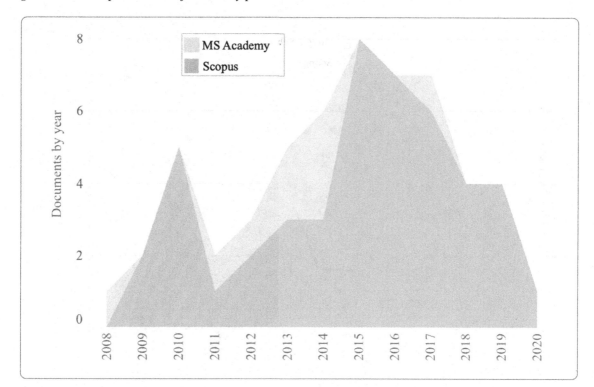

Citations Timeline

Figure 7 shows the citations timeline of the author's publications in two sources. In Scopus there are 310 accumulated citations with an h-index of 10, while in Google Scholar there are 642 citations and an h-index of 14.

The production accomplished by the author has been possible thanks to teamwork with researchers from different institutions, her 62 co-authors mainly coming from Ecuador, and Spain.

Participation in Projects

Most of the research presented here is the output of activities developed as part of research projects and networks. Table 5 identifies some projects and funding agencies (or host institutions) that aided the development of the author's research.

Also, all papers have been partially funded by the scholarship provided by the "Secretaría Nacional de Educación Superior, Ciencia y Tecnología" of Ecuador (SENESCYT), and the Universidad Técnica Particular de Loja (UTPL), Ecuador, institution where the researcher works.

Research Topics

Here is an overview of the topics on which the author has worked. Figure 8 presents a network of terms created from the abstracts of the papers, while Figure 9 shows a tag cloud created from the papers' titles.

Figure 7. Citations timeline of scholarly publications

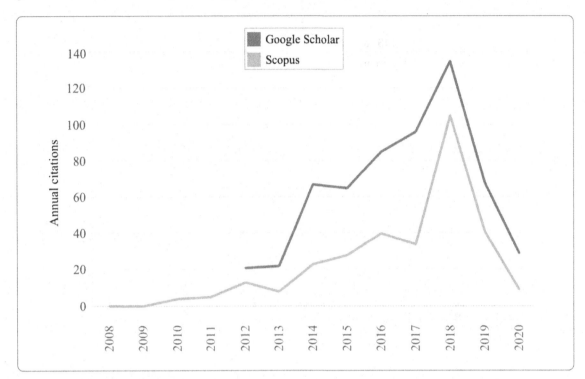

Table 5. Research projects

Projects	Funding agency / host institution	Country
Implementation of a Search Prototype for the Linked University Data Project.	Universidad Técnica Particular de Loja	Ecuador
A Semantic Web Platform for the Integration, Publication, and Integrated Query of Bibliographic Resources.	Ecuadorian Corporation for the Development of Research and Academia (CEDIA)	Ecuador
Design of an Ontological Model for the Semantic Description of Syllabuses.	University of Guayaquil	Ecuador
Startup Project (531206-LLP-2012-IT-KA3-KA3MP) http://startupproject.eu/	European Community, EC under the LLP KA3 ICT programme	European Union
ESVI-AL - Inclusive Virtual Higher Education - Latin America. http://www.esvial.org/	European Community, under the ALFA III programme	European Union
Application of Emerging Web technologies to Study the Impact of Spanish and Latin American OCW repositories on Higher Education. Searching OCW Framework by Applying Emerging Technologies from the Web and Mobile Devices.	Technical University of Madrid	Spain
eMadrid project (S2013/ICE-2715)	Regional Government of Madrid	Spain
RESET project (TIN2014-53199-C3-1-R)	Spanish Ministry of Economy and Competitiveness	Spain

The terms presented in the two figures highlight the technologies and application domains that have been discussed in the previous sections and confirm the consistency of the research conducted during the author's career.

Recently, the author has begun to explore other areas of interest in higher education, such as open science, scientific knowledge graphs, and the detection of publication patterns by gender in the computer science field.

Tools and Intellectual Property

The type of research performed by the author is applied research. For this reason, in addition to the prototypes and proofs-of-concept described in her publications, the author has also supported the creation of some functional tools and software products that are in operation.

To date, the author has two registration certificates (QUI-044958 and QUI050036) accredited by the development of two software systems that are used by Ecuadorian researchers for managing their curricula. The certificates were granted by the Ecuadorian Institute of Intellectual Property.

Finally, two LD-based search tools that the author has contributed to creating are highlighted. The first tool is Serendipity[9], a faceted search engine specialized in finding free educational material available on the web. The search engine is designed to take advantage of open knowledge sources, which have been described by semantic technologies. The second tool is ScienceQuest[10] (Chicaiza et al., 2018). In

Figure 8. Network of terms based-on papers' abstract

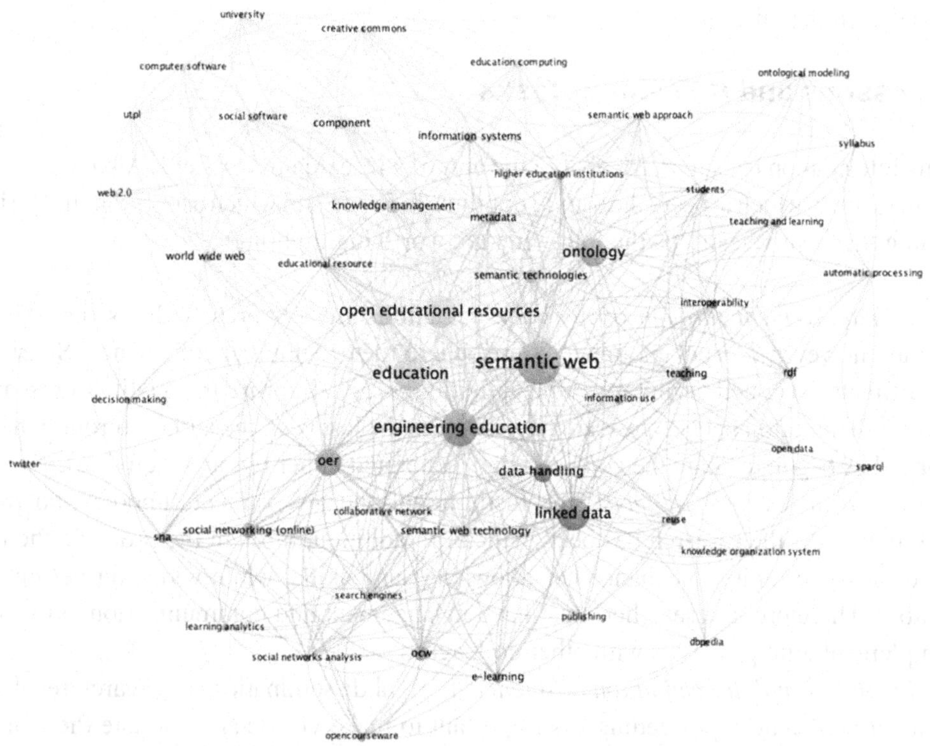

Figure 9. Tag cloud based-on papers' titles

this case, LD are used to help researchers find the most appropriate means of dissemination to publish their scholarly publications. The technological platform consolidates data from different sources such as CFP catalogs and scientific databases. ScienceQuest provides the user with different specialized and personalized search options.

Learned Lessons and Remaining Tasks

The previous information tries to make visible the author's research in her field. Also, this exercise has allowed her to identify which aspects she should continue to foster, and which aspects should be improved.

Concerning the positive aspects, the following are worth highlighting:

- *Research management through open practices.* Publishing research findings through papers is important, however, it is not enough to contribute to the development of science. Sharing the different artifacts generated during scientific activities helps to improve the quality of research and to promote collaboration between researchers. Thus, in the last year, the author, through the GitHub[11] platform, has begun to share the code and data generated in her research activities.
- *Participation in research projects.* The institutional and government support, and funding received to conduct the research has been critical. In addition, through the projects, the researcher has had the opportunity to enhance her knowledge and skills, while widening her circle of collaborators. Therefore, a researcher must have management and communication skills to develop and implement joint proposals with other colleagues.
- *Formal and informal dissemination of science.* Formal dissemination of research results, through journals or conferences proceedings, is important to make visible and validate the work done by

researchers and to get feedback from their academic peers. But, nowadays, it is also important to use less conventional means to make diffusion. For example, by communicating through social networks, researchers can communicate their findings to a more diverse audience and find potential partners for collaboration.

On the other hand, the aspects to be strengthened are:

- *Critical mass formation and participation in multidisciplinary research teams*. There is insufficient critical mass in Latin America to conduct research using SW technologies. In addition, designing solutions that are relevant to a community's problems and needs requires diversifying research groups, including experts from other areas of study. Therefore, it is a pending issue for the author to use the most appropriate strategies to build and become part of multidisciplinary groups of researchers.
- *Research impact*. Although some of the research conducted has generated functional and useful software for the academic community, one aspect that has not made so far is conducting evaluations with end users. The findings of the research impact on people are a crucial input to improve the proposals and to publish results in impact journals.
- *Enabling open education*. Enabling OE implies to empower all people to meet their learning goals. To know who is accessing online services, and what and how users learn is crucial to help them you achieve your learning goals. So far, the author's research has focus try three dimensions of OE: personalization, self-learning, and inclusive learning. But there is a gap related to monitoring the effectivity in the learning process cycle.

FUTURE TRENDS

Educational providers produce large volumes of data. Likewise, the OE domain is heterogeneous, i.e., there are a variety of educational systems and platforms, data sources, data, and users. Therefore, as d'Aquin states (2016), *education represents a perfect use case for Linked Open Data* (pp. 3).

Considering the three stages of the LD processing cycle, next, the author outlines some of the gaps and future trends regarding their development in OE.

1. *Semantic Modeling*. From a SW and LD vision, it is necessary to create an ecosystem of linked models using semantic relationships between equivalent concepts or properties; thus, there will be a greater possibility of interoperating data from different repositories.

In addition to improving the visibility and matching of existing proposals, it is necessary to create domain ontologies that enable communication between educational providers and that support learning in specific areas of study. In the analysis carried out by Taibi, Fulantelli, Dietze & Fetahu (2016) uncovered an inherent topic bias of educational resources represented in datasets. Computer Science and Life Sciences are more popular disciplines, while Social Sciences appear to be underrepresented.

Domain ontologies can play a critical role in automatically classifying educational resources (Salatino et al., 2018) according to a specific set of subject areas. Also, this type of ontology is useful for creating personalized learning resources and services. Personalized education is critical in current massive online learning scenarios, but it is also basic in informal or non-formal learning environments to self-learner engagement.

2.   *Description and Publishing.* Several educational linked data publishing initiatives have focused on gathering and processing structured or semi-structured data. As a result, the most common RDF datasets are those that describe metadata of educational, bibliographic, and research resources.

However, the web is massively populated with unstructured data. The exponential increase in unstructured data on the web makes it difficult efforts for publishing educational linked data. In this emerging area, there are some research gaps in which researchers are working. Mainly, they are focused on processing and mining text from unstructured content and transforming to RDF data. To aim this goal, technologies of Natural Language Processing, like embedding models, and Deep Learning are combined to process the big volume of educational information.

After providers generate RDF data, they must ensure the integration and reuse of their data. For this, the academic and scientific community must assume at least three challenges (Tandon, 2019):

- To create external links. Matching entities from two datasets is not a trivial task due to each provider can use different identifiers and manage different data of each entity. Therefore, to complete this task, entity disambiguation and resolution techniques and tools have to apply.
- Data availability and scaling: To make retrieval data at the large-scale, providers should provide varied mechanisms such as libraries, APIs, and query editors. Some open infrastructures to store and publish RDF data include a set of these services. Also, to overcome scaling are emerging solutions such as NoSQL databases and processing distributed of graphs like Apache Giraph.
- Data security and privacy. To try to preserve the data privacy of learners, institutions have to design a systematic solution that covers different goals and dimensions of data security (Chicaiza, Cabrera-Loayza, Elizalde, & Piedra, 2020). Legal, ethical, technological, methodological, and other dimensions must be integrated to provide valuable data while keeping in mind privacy and security concerns.
    3.   *Leveraging.* Through different initiatives, education is an emerging sector that can benefit from the adoption of data-driven technologies and applications. But, to handle the potential of educational linked data sources, educational services providers should unify efforts to provide useful services based-on quality data.

Regarding technological development, many tasks related to question answering, recommendation, and information retrieval are evolving to manage knowledge structures. Currently, thanks to Google, the term Knowledge Graph (KG) has become popular to refer to data models where there are relationships between entities of a domain. RDF knowledge graphs could be crucial for building smart applications such as question answering, recommendation, and information retrieval.

One of the application areas in which the author has focused on is the recommendation of OER. Here, a future trend is to use Graph Neural Networks (GNN) to extract entities' characteristics and relations from a KG. From this knowledge, deep learning algorithms are used to build recommender systems. According to Gao, Li, Lin, Gao, & Khan (2020), this approach would help to address practical recommendation issues such as scalability, cold-start, and data-efficient.

CONCLUSION

The web is the largest ecosystem of documents and data, but its open and distributed nature makes accessing and retrieving data in a uniform and automatic manner challenging. In this chapter, the author presented a compilation of her research focused on application of SW technologies and LD to overcome some of the problems associated with the discovery and reuse of open educational content. Although no new evidence or knowledge related to the subject is presented here, this chapter aims to inspire others, and especially women in Latin America, to adopt emerging web technologies, with the aim of fostering transformation and innovation in OE.

ACKNOWLEDGMENT

The author is deeply grateful to all her colleagues from the Advanced Web Technologies and Knowledge-Based Systems group at the Universidad Técnica Particular de Loja. In addition, she thanks all her co-authors, the higher education institutions and funding agencies that have provided the necessary support for the development of the research activities presented in this chapter.

REFERENCES

Allemang, D., Hendler, J., & Gandon, F. (2020). *Semantic Web for the Working Ontologist* (3rd ed.). ACM Books. doi:10.1145/3382097

Amado-Salvatierra, H. R., Hilera, J. R., Tortosa, S. O., Rizzardini, R. H., & Piedra, N. (2016). Towards a Semantic Definition of a Framework to Implement Accessible e-Learning Projects. []. IICM.]. *Journal of Universal Computer Science*, 22, 921–942.

Bizer, C., Heath, T., & Berners-Lee, T. (2009). Linked Data - The Story So Far. *International Journal on Semantic Web and Information Systems*, 5, 1–22.

Caswell, T., Henson, S., Jensen, M., & Wiley, D. (2008). Open Content and Open Educational Resources: Enabling Universal Education. *International Review of Research in Open and Distance Learning*, 9(1), 1–11. doi:10.19173/irrodl.v9i1.469

Chicaiza, J. (2016). Un enfoque basado en Linked Data para soportar la Búsqueda Personalizada de Recursos Educativos Abiertos (Thesis Doctoral). Technical University of Madrid (UPM) doi:10.20868/UPM.thesis.44387

Chicaiza, J., Cabrera-Loayza, M. C., Elizalde, R., & Piedra, N. (2020). Application of Data Anonymization in Learning Analytics. In *ACM International Conference Proceeding Series*, (vol.1, pp. 1–6). 10.1145/3378184.3378229

Chicaiza, J., Piedra, N., Lopez, J., & Tovar-Caro, E. (2014). Domain Categorization of Open Educational Resources based on Linked Data. *Communications in Computer and Information Science*, 468, 15–28. doi:10.1007/978-3-319-11716-4_2

Chicaiza, J., Piedra, N., Lopez, J., & Tovar-Caro, E. (2015). Promotion of self-learning by means of Open Educational Resources and semantic technologies. In *Proceedings of 2015 International Conference on Information Technology Based Higher Education and Training (ITHET)*, (pp. 1–6). 10.1109/ITHET.2015.7218024

Chicaiza, J., Piedra, N., Lopez, J., & Tovar-Caro, E. (2015). A User Profile Definition in context of recommendation of Open Educational Resources. In *Proceedings of 2015 Frontiers in Education Conference, (FIE) 2015* (pp. 1–7). 10.1109/FIE.2015.7344314

Chicaiza, J., Piedra, N., Lopez, J., & Tovar-Caro, E. (2017). Recommendation of Open Educational Resources. An Approach based on Linked Open Data. In *Proceedings of 2017 IEEE EDUCON Conference*. 10.1109/EDUCON.2017.7943018

Chicaiza, J., Piedra, N., & Valencia, M.-P. (2014). Consideraciones de accesibilidad en la producción y distribución de recursos educativos en formato PDF. Un caso de implementación para la formación Virtual Accesible en América Latina. *Proceedings of the V Congreso Internacional Sobre Calidad y Accesibilidad de La Formación Virtual (CAFVIR 2014)*.

Chih-Hsiung, T., Cherng-Jyh, Y., Sujo-Montes, L., & Sealander, K. (2018). Digital Lifelong-Learning Literacy. In R. Papa & S. Armfield (Eds.), *The Wiley Handbook of Educational Policy* (pp. 531–550). John Wiley & Sons.

d'Aquin, M. (2012). *Linked Data for Open and Distance Learning Prepared for the Commonwealth of Learning*. http://oasis.col.org/handle/11599/219

d'Aquin, M. (2016). On the Use of Linked Open Data in Education: Current and Future Practices. In D. Mouromtsev & M. d'Aquin (Eds.), Lecture Notes in Computer Science: Vol. 9500. *Open Data for Education* (pp. 3–15). Springer. doi:10.1007/978-3-319-30493-9_1

Dagiene, V., Gudoniene, D., & Burbaite, R. (2015). *Semantic Web Technologies for e-learning: Models and implementation* (Vol. 26). Informatica. doi:10.15388/Informatica.2015.46

Deepak, M. (2015). Open Educational Resources. In G. Thakur (Ed.), *Recent trends in ICT in education*. Laxmi Book Publication.

Dietze, S., Drachsler, H., & Giordano, D. (2013). A Survey on Linked Data and the Social Web as facilitators for TEL recommender systems. In N. Manouselis, H. Drachsler, K. Verbert, & O. C. Santos (Eds.), Recommender Systems for Technology Enhanced Learning: Research Trends and Applications. Academic Press.

Gao, Y., Li, Y.-F., Lin, Y., Gao, H., & Khan, L. (2020). *Deep Learning on Knowledge Graph for Recommender System: A Survey*. http://arxiv.org/abs/2004.00387

Gorissen, P. (2013). Open textbooks: trends and opportunities. In R. Jacobi, H. Jelgerhuis, & N. van der Woert (Eds.), Trend report: Open Educational Resources 2013 (pp. 1–114). Academic Press.

Konstantinou, N., & Spanos, D. E. (2015a). Technical Background. In *Materializing the Web of Linked Data* (pp. 17–49). Springer. doi:10.1007/978-3-319-16074-0_2

Konstantinou, N., & Spanos, D. E. (2015b). Deploying Linked Open Data: Methodologies and Software Tools. In *Materializing the Web of Linked Data*. Springer; doi:10.1007/978-3-319-16074-0_3

Lopez, J., Piedra, N., & Chicaiza, J. (2015). Recommendation of OERs shared in social media based-on social networks analysis approach. Proceedings of Frontiers in Education Conference, FIE. 10.1109/FIE.2014.7044454

Mikroyannidi, E., Liu, D., & Lee, R. (2016). Use of Semantic Web Technologies in the Architecture of the BBC Education Online Pages. In D. Mouromtsev & M. d'Aquin (Eds.), Lecture Notes in Computer Science: Vol. 9500. *Open Data for Education* (pp. 67–85)., doi:10.1007/978-3-319-30493-9_4

Nahhas, S., Bamasag, O., Khemakhem, M., & Bajnaid, N. (2018). *Added Values of Linked Data in Education: A Survey and Roadmap* (Vol. 7). Computers. doi:10.3390/computers7030045

Open Education. (n.d.). Retrieved from https://hewlett.org/strategy/open-education/

Ortiz-Vivar, J., Segarra, J., Villazón-Terrazas, B., & Saquicela, V. (2020). REDI: Towards knowledge graph-powered scholarly information management and research networking. *Journal of Information Science*. Advance online publication. doi:10.1177/0165551520944351

Pech, F., Martinez, A., Estrada, H., & Hernandez, Y. (2017). Semantic Annotation of Unstructured Documents Using Concepts Similarity. *Scientific Programming*. Retrieved from https://www.hindawi.com/journals/sp/2017/7831897/

Pereira, C. K., Siqueira, S. W. M., Nunes, B. P., & Dietze, S. (2018). Linked Data in Education: A Survey and a Synthesis of Actual Research and Future Challenges. *IEEE Transactions on Learning Technologies*, *11*, 400–412. doi:10.1109/TLT.2017.2787659

Piedra, N., Chicaiza, J., Lopez, J., Martinez, O., & Tovar-Caro, E. (2010). An approach for description of Open Educational Resources based on Semantic Technologies. In *Proceedings of IEEE EDUCON 2010 Conference*, (pp. 1111–1119). 10.1109/EDUCON.2010.5492453

Piedra, N., Chicaiza, J., Lopez, J., & Tovar-Caro, E. (2014). Supporting openness of MOOCs contents through of an OER and OCW Framework based on Linked Data Technologies. *Proceedings of IEEE Global Engineering Education Conference, EDUCON*. 10.1109/EDUCON.2014.6826249

Piedra, N., Chicaiza, J., Lopez, J., & Tovar-Caro, E. (2015). Seeking Open Educational Resources to Compose Massive Open Online Courses in Engineering Education an Approach based on Linked Open Data. *Journal of Universal Computer Science*, *21*, 679–711.

Piedra, N., Chicaiza, J., Lopez, J., Tovar-Caro, E., & Bonastre, O. M. (2011). Finding OERs with Social-Semantic Search. In *Proceedings of IEEE EDUCON Education Engineering 2011* (pp. 1–6). Amman: IEEE.

Piedra, N., Chicaiza, J., Lopez, J., Tovar-Caro, E., & Martínez, O. (2012). Combining Linked Data and Mobiles to Improve Access to OCW. In *Proceedings of Global Engineering Education Conference (EDUCON)*, 2012 (pp. 1–7). doi:10.1109/EDUCON.2012.6201202

Piedra, N., Chicaiza, J., Lopez, J., & Tovar-Caro, E. T. (2016). Integrating OER in the design of educational material: Blended Learning and Linked Open Educational Resources Data Approach. *Proceedings of IEEE EDUCON Conference*. 10.1109/EDUCON.2016.7474706

Piedra, N., Chicaiza, J., Quichimbo, P., Saquicela, V., Cadme, E., Lopez, J., & Tovar-Caro, E. (2015). *Framework for the Integration of Digital Resources based-on a Semantic Web Approach. Revista Iberica de Sistemas e Tecnologias de Informacao*. Associacao Iberica de Sistemas e Tecnologias de Informacao. doi:10.17013/risti.e3.55-70

Piedra, N., Tovar-Caro, E., Colomo-Palacios, R., Lopez, J., & Chicaiza, J. A. (2014). *Consuming and Producing Linked Open Data: The case of OpenCourseWare*. Program. doi:10.1108/PROG-07-2012-0045

Salatino, A., Thiviyan-Thanapalasingam, Andrea-Mannocci, A., Osborne, F., & Motta, E. (2018). The Computer Science Ontology: A Large-Scale Taxonomy of Research Areas. *Proceedings of International Semantic Web Conference 2018*. 10.1007/978-3-030-00668-6_12

Taibi, D., Fulantelli, G., Dietze, S., & Fetahu, B. (2016). Educational Linked Data on the Web - Exploring and Analysing the Scope and Coverage. In D. Mouromtsev & M. d'Aquin (Eds.), Lecture Notes in Computer Science: Vol. 9500. *Open Data for Education* (pp. 16–39). Springer. doi:10.1007/978-3-319-30493-9_2

Tandon, A. (2019). Reconciling Your Data and the World with Knowledge Graphs. *Towards Data Science*. https://towardsdatascience.com/reconciling-your-data-and-the-world-with-knowledge-graphs-bce66b377b14

Tapia-Leon, M., Aveiga, C. A., Chicaiza, J., & Suárez-Figueroa, M. C. (2019). Ontological Model for the Semantic Description of Syllabuses. In *Proceedings of 9th International Conference on Information Communication and Management* (pp. 175–180). 10.1145/3357419.3357442

Vasiliev, V., Kozlov, F., Mouromtsev, D., Stafeev, S., & Parkhimovich, O. (2016). ECOLE: An ontology-based open online course platform. In D. Mouromtsev & M. d'Aquin (Eds.), Lecture Notes in Computer Science: Vol. 9500. *Open Data for Education* (pp. 41–66). doi:10.1007/978-3-319-30493-9_3

Vega-Gorgojo, G., Asensio-Pérez, J. I., Gómez-Sánchez, E., Bote-Lorenzo, M. L., Munoz-Cristobal, J. A., & Ruiz-Calleja, A. (2015). A Review of Linked Data Proposals in the Learning Domain. *Journal of Universal Computer Science*, *21*, 326–364.

Zamazal, O. (2020). A Survey of Ontology Benchmarks for Semantic Web Ontology Tools. *International Journal on Semantic Web and Information Systems*, *16*, 47–68. doi:10.4018/IJSWIS.2020010103

KEY TERMS AND DEFINITIONS

DBPedia: It is the most popular project around linked data. DBPedia provides ontologies and RDF data of the infoboxes extracted from Wikipedia pages.

OWL: It is the acronym of Web Ontology Language, semantic web technology used to create an ontology computable model.

Semantic Annotation: It is a process that consists of finding text fragments that mention or name entities described in semantic repositories.

SPARQL: Query language used to access and retrieve RDF data distributed in different geographical locations.

URI: It is the acronym of uniform resource identifiers and it is used to identify resources on the semantic web.

Vocabulary: It is a data model that defines the terminology of a domain of interest.

ENDNOTES

[1]   https://ocw.mit.edu/about/

[2]   https://data.open.ac.uk

[3]   https://lod-cloud.net

[4]   https://www.lib.washington.edu/cams/ld

[5]   http://data.bib.uni-mannheim.de/

[6]   https://redi.cedia.edu.ec/

[7]   https://cso.kmi.open.ac.uk/classify/

[8]   The OntoSyllabus ontology achieved four-star according to the five-star scheme for linked open data vocabularies. Documentation and computable model are available at https://archive.org/services/purl/ontosyllabus/root

[9]   http://serendipity.utpl.edu.ec

[10]   http://sciencequest.cedia.org.ec

[11]   https://github.com/jachicaiza/

Chapter 6
Fuzzy Data Warehouse in the Field of Education

Carolina Zambrano-Matamala
Universidad de Concepción, Chile

Angélica Urrutia
Universidad Catolica del Maule, Chile

ABSTRACT

Currently, educational organizations have a large amount of local information from their academic processes, curricular management processes, diagnostic processes of university admission, among others. Also, educational organizations have access to large external databases with standardized test information that students have taken. In this sense, the data warehouse (DW) is presented as a technology that makes it possible to integrate educational information because it provides for the storage of large amounts of information that come from different sources, in a multidimensionally structured format for historical analysis. In this chapter, the authors present one example of DW applied to the field of education using fuzzy logic. A fuzzy DW will be defined as "a DW that allows storing and operating fuzzy measures, fuzzy relationships between levels and fuzzy levels." This chapter ends with a critical discussion of the advances and possibilities of technologies such as the DW applied to the field of education.

INTRODUCTION

Organizations have more information every day because their systems produce many daily operations that are generally stored in transactional databases. To analyze this historical information, an interesting alternative is to implement a Data Warehouse (DW). A traditional DW is a data collection oriented to a certain area (company, organization, etc.), integrated, non-volatile and variable in time, which is used to support decision-making in the entity in which it is used (Chaudhuri & Dayal, 2004; Malinowski & Zimanyi, 2008). The main elements of a traditional DW are dimensions, hierarchies, facts, and measures. A dimension is an abstract concept that shapes a context for analysis. Hierarchies can be defined on the dimensions, allowing access to the data at different levels or categories of detail (Chaudhuri &

DOI: 10.4018/978-1-7998-7552-9.ch006

Copyright © 2021, IGI Global. Copying or distributing in print or electronic forms without written permission of IGI Global is prohibited.

Dayal, 2004; Malinowski & Zimanyi, 2008). The facts represent a tuple of primary key, foreign key, and measures. The measurements are numerical values, therefore the type of analysis that can be performed is quantitative. However, in the decision-making process, qualitative analysis is also valued, especially in the educational field.

Qualitative analysis is aimed at analyzing characteristics of an object. The quantitative analysis is oriented to analyze quantities. In the context of quantitative analysis, DWs are used. Then, to extend a traditional DW to a Fuzzy Data Warehouse (FDW), fuzzy logic is used (Zadeh, 1965). An FDW includes qualitative aspects in data analysis. Then it is necessary to understand what the elements of a traditional DW that are extended to create an FDW. The first element to understand is a fuzzy attribute.

A classification of fuzzy information is presented in (Galindo et al., 2009) where fuzzy attributes are defined as type 1, type 2, and type 3 attributes. Fuzzy type 1 attributes are classic attributes that support imprecise treatment, where defined language labels will only be used in fuzzy query conditions (Galindo et al., 2009). Fuzzy type 2 attributes (Galindo et al., 2009) are attributes that support both classical (crisp) and fuzzy (imprecise) data, in the form of possibility distributions over an ordered underlying domain. Type 2 also allows the representation of incomplete information in the form of Unknown, Undefined and Null type data. Fuzzy attributes type 3 (Galindo et al., 2009) are attributes on discrete domain data on underlying domain not ordered by analogy. In these attributes you can define sets of labels with a relation of similarity or proximity defined on them. Also, in type 3, possibility distributions on the domain can be accepted.

Currently, most of the research and case studies that include data analysis using FDW are related to the impact or benefit of applying FDW to business contexts (Fasel, 2009; Molina et al., 2005). Without considering the contribution of the application of FDW to the educational field that allows qualitative analysis such as: the academic performance of students. In addition to considering the contextual scope of each educational organization, it is not the same to classify a student as good in an educational institution A than in an educational institution B. The above due to considerations such as: the university access score and performance academic in the career he is studying. This chapter has as objective presents the design of an FDW applied to the educational field. The FDW proposal includes three fuzzy elements that are: Fuzzy Relationship, Fuzzy Measures and Fuzzy Level that will be explained in the next section.

BACKGROUND

In this section of the chapter the elements of the FDW are described: Fuzzy Level, Fuzzy Measures, Fuzzy Relationship and Trapezoidal Membership Functions. Also, literature is reviewed.

Elements of the FDW

For a better understanding, Figure 1 schematizes an FDW with its elements: levels, relationships, fuzzy levels, fuzzy relationships, and fuzzy measures. The levels observed in Figure 1 are: Student, Advance Level, Graduated and City. Region_Distance is fuzzy level with the associated labels: near and far. The fuzzy relationship is represented by a dotted line between the Advance level and Student level. The fuzzy measure is Mark.

Fuzzy Level

For the case Fuzzy Level, a fuzzy concept is added that has associated membership functions that will contain the labels. For example, in the case of fuzzy level Region_Distance shown in Figure 1, the fuzzy concept is the location, the labels are represented by near and far (each with a degree of belonging depending on the distance to some place).

Figure 1. Scheme FDW.

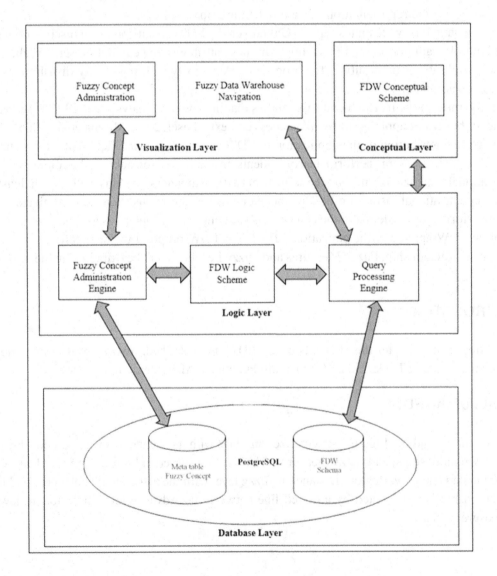

Fuzzy Measures

When a measure is fuzzy it is considered that it can be type 1 or type 2. If it is fuzzy type 1, only one label is added to the measure. If it is a type 2 fuzzy measure, it means that a fuzzy concept has been associated that has associated linguistic labels that are represented by membership functions (see figure 3).

Fuzzy Relationship

When a relationship between levels (from a multidimensional scheme) is fuzzy, each lower level instance will be associated with more than one higher level instance, generating a many-to-many relationship, between the parent level and the child level. This type of hierarchy is not strict (Hurtado & Gutierrez, 2007). Figure 1 shows an example of a fuzzy dimension scheme. The relationship between *Student* and *Advance Level* has been defined as fuzzy represented by a dotted line. That the relationship is fuzzy implies that there is a degree of belonging associated between the dimension instances that participate in said relationship.

For example, a Student may be associated with more than one Advance Level, this is very frequent because students fall behind due to failing subjects and thus remain at different levels (semesters) with subjects of different levels without being associated at one level. Then a degree of membership should be associated with the relationship as shown in Figure 2, where it is observed that student A1 is associated with level 1 (Lev1) in 0.7 degree of membership and associated with level 2 (Lev2) in 0.3 degree of membership. It is important to indicate that the degree of membership must be obtained from the data (Rojas et al., 2011) and to sum 1.

Trapezoidal Membership Functions

It is defined by a lower limit a, an upper limit d and the support limits b and c (lower and upper respectively). The definition of the trapezoidal function is seen in Figure 3.

For example, in Figure 4 *Mark* measure is fuzzy type 2 and its fuzzy concept is quality for which three labels are defined to classify the grade obtained as: bad, regular, or good.

LITERATURE REVIEW

Fuzzy Data Warehouse

Currently, there are few works related to FDW designs and / or implementations (Zambrano et al., 2012; Zambrano et al., 2017; among others), unlike traditional DW (Zambrano et al., 2011; Zambrano et al., 2018; among others). This could be associated with the fact that the implementation process requires a technical effort that takes considerable time.

Furthermore, the concept of FDW has recently been included by the academic field and there is no standard for its definition. In this area the following works apply FDW (Asanka & Perera, 2018; Asanka & Perera, 2019; Fasel, 2009; Fasel & Zumstein, 2009; Fasel, 2010; Fasel & Shahzad, 2010; Fasel & Shahzad, 2012; Molina et al., 2005; Sapir et al., 2008; Zambrano et al., 2012; Zambrano et al., 2017).

Figure 2. Extract of dimension instance for the fuzzy relationship between Student and Level.

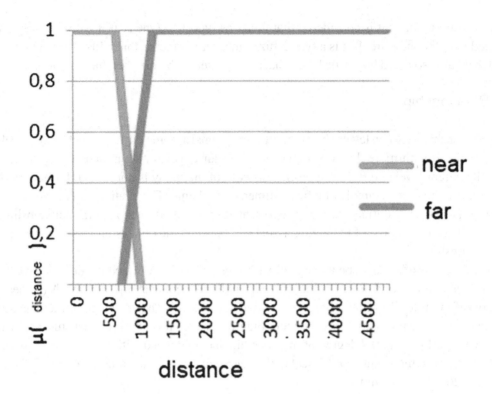

In data warehouse, different types of fuzzy membership functions can be introduced. Arbitrary, data driven, linguistic, derived, survey-based membership functions are introduced in (Asanka & Perera, 2018) for different cases in data warehouse. Then, the research of Asanka and Perera (2019) has utilized existing fuzzy membership functions to derive linguistic functions, for the purpose of using linguistic analysis in a data warehouse.

At work of (Fasel & Shahzad, 2012) the authors employ a fuzzy classification based on approach to data storage. To do this, they present a fuzzy data warehouse modeling approach, which allows for the integration of fuzzy concepts without affecting the core of a classic data warehouse. The sense of the approach is that a meta-table structure is added to relate non-numerical terms with numerical values. This allows the integration of fuzzy concepts in dimensions and facts, preserving the data warehouse time invariance.

In the research presented in (Fasel & Zumstein, 2009) shows the usefulness of using an FDW in the field of analysis of indicators and Web metrics such as pages visited by a user. In this context, the authors present an FDW schema that includes Meta tables that support fuzzy elements in dimensions and facts. In addition, they describe how to apply the Fuzzy Slicing and Fuzzy Dicing operation to get results. Then in Fasel (2009) the same author applies his FDW approach that uses fuzzy dimensions and fuzzy facts to customer data from an instrument factory, this work is based on the same structure shown in (Fasel & Zumstein, 2009).

The formalization of the FDW structure used in (Fasel, 2009; Fasel & Zumstein, 2009) is presented in the work of Fasel & Shahzad (2010) that explains how to incorporate fuzzy elements into a DW to

Figure 3. Definition of the trapezoidal function

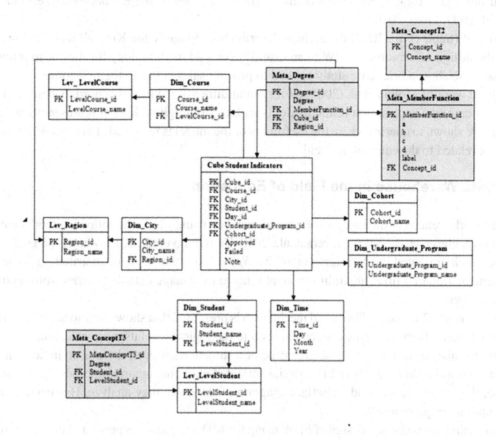

Figure 4. Trapezoidal membership functions for the mark quality concept. And bad, regular, and good linguistic labels defined on the mark attribute.

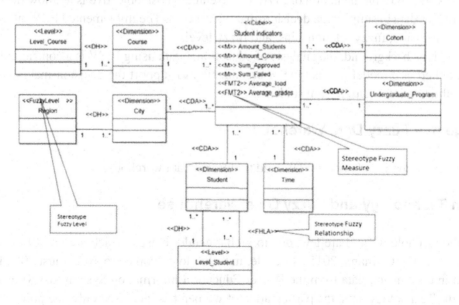

convert it into FDW using meta-table structures. However, none of these works analyzes educational data (Fasel, 2009; Fasel, 2010).

At work of (Sapir et al., 2008) the authors describe how to apply the Kimball methodology that is used for the design of a traditional DW to an extension of said methodology for the construction of an FDW. They also show a brief case study applied to product sales data and their customers.

Finally, at work of Molina et al. (2005) a fuzzy multidimensional model is used to analyze financial data. In this case, the explanation of the model is included through its logical representation and then the results are shown to queries where the usefulness of the model is reflected. This is an FDW use case, but it is not related to the educational field.

Fuzzy Data Warehouse in the Field of Education

Regarding works related to the analysis of educational data using FDW, the following works have been proposed (Appelgren et al., 2013; Carrera et al., 2010; Zambrano et al., 2012; Zambrano et al., 2017).

The research presented in (Appelgren et al., 2013) is a work whose main contribution is the design and implementation of a fuzzy multidimensional scheme to manage data that comes from repositories of learning objects.

In Carrera et al. (2010) an MDA-based mechanism is presented that shows how to transform a diffuse multidimensional scheme from the conceptual level to the logical level using as an example case study applied to the analysis of the average degree time of a student. However, there is no indication of how to implement queries because it is an FDW design-oriented work that incorporates only fuzzy measures. Therefore, they show the star and snowflake diagram of the cases they analyze. However, there is no implementation or query result.

Other research related to the design of FDW using the MDA approach is presented in Zambrano et al., (2012). In this work the FDW design is applied to a case study of educational data analysis. Nonetheless, the implementation of the FDW for the analysis of educational data is not carried out.

An investigation that includes fuzzy relationships between the data is presented in (Zambrano et al., 2017). In this work, an implementation of FDW is presented whose objective is to allow the qualitative analysis of student data to support the decision-making process. The implemented FDW allows operating with fuzzy measure, fuzzy relationships, and fuzzy levels.

For the previous background, the analysis of educational data using FDW is a contribution because it could be applied as a model in this type of organization to support the decision-making process by providing qualitative information from students.

Advantage of a Fuzzy Data Warehouse

Table 1 shows a comparison between FDW and traditional data warehouse.

Women in Technology and Fuzzy Data Warehouse

Women in the technology field are few, due to global gender biases, which are not different in Latin America (Razo, 2008; Ortmann, 2015). In Chile, in technology women represent just 20%. Regarding the variation in enrollment, data from the Higher Education Information System (SIES) reveal that in ten years in the Technology area, the participation of women has increased only one point.

Table 1. Comparison between Fuzzy Data Warehouse and Traditional Data Warehouse

Fuzzy Data Warehouse	Traditional Data Warehouse
It allows to include the classification of data depending on the context. That is, the labeling of the data will depend on the criteria defined by the organization. For this reason, classification can be done through membership functions.	It is not designed to allow for classification or labeling of student data.
The design and implementation of a fuzzy data warehouse allows qualitative analysis of student data.	Allows quantitative analysis.
Allows an instance to belong to more than one category because the aggregation function is extended to fuzzy aggregation. For example, if a student fails subjects and falls behind in his career, there is the option of associating him with all the levels (semesters and / or trimesters) in which he takes his subjects.	Allows associating a student to a category given a category instance.

One of the origins of research led by women in the field of fuzzy logic is the works developed by the Spanish researcher Amparo Vila (Marin et al., 2000; among others). In the case of FDW, there is also research that originates in Amparo Vila's group at the University of Granada, Spain. The following works are distinguished (Marin et al., 2000; Delgado et al., 2003; Molina et al., 2006; among others).

In Latin America, the field of research on fuzzy logic has been developed in various works carried out in Chile (Galindo et al., 2009; Urrutia et al., 2006). In particular, the case of the development of FDW by Latin American women is evidenced in works such as (Carrera et al., 2010; Zambrano et al., 2012; Zambrano et al., 2017).

Regarding FDW in the field of education, this chapter of the book Impact of Latin American Women in IT presents part of a master's thesis in computer science developed at the University of Concepción that proposes a model for the analysis of educational data using fuzzy elements.

METHODOLOGY

The multidimensional design of a DW can be implemented using supply-driven approaches, demand-driven approaches, and hybrid approaches (Cravero & Sepúlveda, 2012). The supply-driven approach is also known as the data-driven approach. In this case, the process begins with the modeling of the DW from a detailed analysis of the data sources to determine the elements of the DW such as facts and possible dimensions to consider with the data that is available.

The information considered in the facts represents measures for business processes and seeks to answer questions such as What is the subject most students fail in a certain career? From this point of view, the dimensions represent the framework for the analysis of these measures (Winter & Strauch, 2003). The demand-driven approach is also known as the requirements-driven or goal-driven approach. In this case the design process begins by determining the requirements from the needs of the users. Then the multi-dimensional design is created according to the selected objectives. The advantages of this approach are that it can support the process of restructuring business processes. This approach allows answering questions such as is it possible to meet the stated objective? (Romero & Abello, 2009).

Analysis of educational data using FDW was carried out using an MDA-based approach (Zambrano et al., 2012). This paradigm is data-oriented, that is, because of an exhaustive analysis of the data, the elements that were possible to design and implement in the FDW were determined. In addition, the usefulness of the results obtained in the educational context was validated with an education expert. The following tasks were included in the process:

1. **Analysis of the Data Sources:** At this stage the data sources were studied to determine the design of the FDW, that is, what dimensions could be implemented with the existing data, what measures and what relationships between the data could be fuzzy. Also, it was studied what levels and measures could be diffuse.
2. **Validation with an Education Specialist:** At this stage, the design of the FDW was validated with an education specialist who acted as a user specialist in the validation of the objectives of analysis, design, coherence, and utility.
3. **Conceptual Design of the FDW:** In this stage the design of the conceptual scheme was implemented.
4. **Logical Design of the FDW:** At this stage, the logical scheme was designed.
5. **Implementation:** At this stage, the ETL process was carried out to load the data in the cube and in the target tables that support the fuzzy elements of the FDW proposal.

The conceptual and logical scheme for the FDW Student Indicator Cube is shown below.

Student Indicator Cube

The Student Indicators Cube is made up of six analysis dimensions that are: Time, Student, City, Course, Cohort, Undergraduate_Program. For the implementation, the undergraduate data from a Chilean university were used. The purpose of implementing these indicators is to provide information on the average load of students and their average grades, allowing an analysis by Student, City, Course, Cohort, Undergraduate_Program. In this context, the following fuzzy elements were defined:

1. **Fuzzy Measures:** The Average Load and Average Notes were defined as fuzzy measures.
2. **Fuzzy Level:** The fuzzy level is associated with the region.
3. **Fuzzy Relationship:** The relationship between the Student and Student Level categories was defined as a fuzzy relationship.

The fuzzy relationship between Student and Student Level is fuzzy given that students are regularly not up to date in the progress of their curriculum, but, on the contrary, have subjects at different levels (semesters), which indicates that their degree of belonging to level of his career is fuzzy. In the case of the location dimension, it is observed that it has two levels that are city and region. The region level has been marked as fuzzy. This indicates that it can be labeled as a fuzzy attribute type 2.

The Figure 5 shows the Conceptual Scheme for the Student Indicator Cube. It is represented by an instance of the Fuzzy CWM OLAP meta model (Zambrano et al., 2012). In this figure, can see the stereotype <<FMT2>> that represents the fuzzy measure type 2, the stereotype <<FuzzyLevelT2>> that represents the fuzzy level type 2 and the stereotype <<FHLA>> that represents the fuzzy relationships in a hierarchy.

Then, they are identified: cubes, measures, dimensions, attributes of dimensions, levels, attributes of levels, association classes and the fuzzy attributes type 1, type 2 in measures, fuzzy levels type 2 and fuzzy relationships of the instance of the Fuzzy CWM OLAP meta model (Mazón & Trujillo, 2008;

Zambrano et al., 2012). Figure 6 shows the Logical Scheme for the Cube Students Indicators. Also, the structures to support the fuzzy elements are observed.

The results on the proposed FDW are presented below.

Figure 5. Conceptual Scheme for the Cube Student Indicator with fuzzy elements. Stereotyped <<FMT2>> for Fuzzy Measure, <<FuzzyLevel>> for Fuzzy Level, <<FHLA>> for Fuzzy Relationship

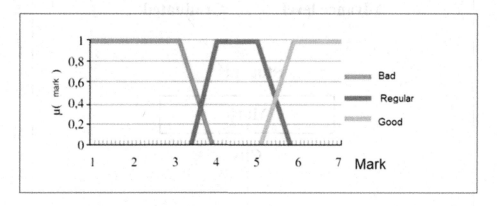

ARCHITECTURE

This section explains the architecture of the FDW composed of four layers that are: visualization layer, conceptual layer, logic layer and database layer. The four layers interact with each other. Visualization Layer interacts with Logic Layer. Conceptual Layer is the conceptual basis for the logical design represented in the Logic Layer. Likewise, Logic Layer interacts with Database Layer which contains the physical structure of the FDW. Figure 7 shows a diagram of the prototype of proposed architecture.

Figure 6. Logical scheme for the cube students indicators

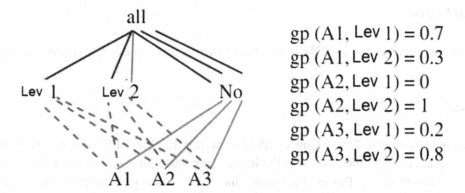

$$gp (A1, Lev 1) = 0.7$$
$$gp (A1, Lev 2) = 0.3$$
$$gp (A2, Lev 1) = 0$$
$$gp (A2, Lev 2) = 1$$
$$gp (A3, Lev 1) = 0.2$$
$$gp (A3, Lev 2) = 0.8$$

Figure 7. Overview of prototype architecture

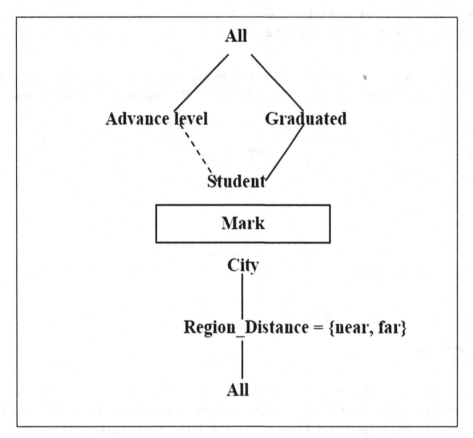

Visualization Layer

Visualization Layer is composed of Fuzzy Concept Administration and Fuzzy Data Warehouse Navigation. Fuzzy Concept Administration, this component allows to administer the fuzzy concepts for their entry and management. Fuzzy Data Warehouse Navigation, this component allows you to manage the results. That is, it allows to represent the visualization of the results.

Conceptual Layer

Conceptual Layer is composed of FDW Conceptual Scheme, representing the conceptual design of the FDW.

Logic Layer

Logic Layer is composed of Fuzzy Concept Administration Engine, FDW Logic Scheme and Query Processing Engine. FDW Logic Scheme is the logical representation *"the logical scheme"* that allows the management with Query Processing Engine and Fuzzy Concept Administration Engine. Query

Processing Engine is a component that contains Sql queries and Engine Fuzzy Concept Administration Engine allows the logical administration of the meta tables containing the fuzzy elements.

Database Layer

Database Layer is composed of Meta table Fuzzy Concept and FDW Schema. This layer contains the physical structure of tables stored in PostgreSQL according to the logical design.

RESULTS

The following queries were executed in the FDW in PostgreSQL DBMS to respond to the indicators sought. Fuzzy elements were loaded in the ETL stage (Malinowski & Zimanyi, 2008; Kimball & Ross, 2011) of the process. The queries refer to Analysis using Fuzzy Relationship, Analysis using Fuzzy Measures, Analysis using Fuzzy Level.

Analysis using Fuzzy Relationship

The hierarchical relationship between the Student level and the Level_Student level can be fuzzy (see stereotypical relationship <<FHLA>> in the conceptual diagram of Figure 4). In the implementation, the Average Grade for Level query is a query that gives the average of marks for each level and calculates the degree of possibility of each fact resulting from the aggregation because each student has a diffuse relationship with the levels.

Table 2. Results of the query for the indicator "Average of Notes by Level", using the parameters $\alpha = 0.3$, and the fuzzy relationship between Student and Level_Student

Student_Level	Avg_Note	α
101	3,71	0,30
102	4,06	0,30
201	3,96	0,30
202	3,82	0,30
301	4,29	0,30
302	4,53	0,32

Table 2 presents the results of the indicator "Average of Notes by Level". It is observed that only levels 101 to 302 are delivered as a result (the first three years), because there are no notes that have a degree of relationship between Student and Level_Student that exceeds the threshold $\alpha = 0.3$ used in the consultation.

Analysis Using Fuzzy Measures

The proposal gives the ability to label a measure of the facts using linguistic labels grouped into concepts. For the example, student indicators, the concept of "performance" has been defined, which groups the following linguistic labels: bad, fair and good, each with its trapezoidal belonging function for measures based on the note with a scale from 1 to 7. Figure 4 showed the functions defined for each label.

Fuzzy type 2 attributes in the proposed model may be associated with variables that make up measures in the set of facts. In this way it is possible to perform fuzzy selection operations on these attributes to select variable values in the facts according to the criteria defined in the linguistic labels. The fuzzy selection operators (Rundensteiner & Bic,1989) are used to perform this operation.

Result: Number of High Notes According to Score

Table 3 presents the results of the query "Number of High Notes per Income". It is observed that the income with the highest number of good grades is 2007 income with 416 notes with possibility 1 of being good. Another example is that for the 2013 income, only 22 good notes are observed with a 0.5 possibility (μ).

Table 3. Result of the query "Number of high notes per year of income"

μ vs count ()	2007	2008	2009	2010	2011	2012	2013
0,50	74	73	66	63	62	46	22
0,62	84	80	67	52	63	39	25
0,75	66	67	52	43	39	32	20
0,87	64	48	48	30	26	39	24
1,00	416	362	300	249	183	201	103

Analysis using Fuzzy Level

The proposal presented in this book chapter includes fuzzy levels. In the example, (see Figure 8), Region level has a distance attribute that is associated with the distance concept that has the near and far linguistic labels with their respective trapezoidal membership functions as shown below.

The labeling of levels allows the selection of level instances not only through their exact values or attributes, but also from their linguistic labels. The fuzzy levels allow a full level of detail and analysis when performing the operations, he says, but does not affect the roll-up or drill-down operation.

Result: Number of Students in Near and Far Regions

When levels are labeled as type 2 fuzzy attributes, they allow the operations OWA, in our specific case MAM and MOM operators (Delgado et al., 2004; Yager,1994).

Table 4 contains the results of a query that allows calculating the number of students per Region, considering only the regions that are far and near at the same time. In this way, the query deals with the

Figure 8. Trapezoidal membership functions for the distance concept and the near and far linguistic labels defined on the distance attribute of the Region level.

$$\mu(x; a, b, c, d) = \begin{cases} 0, & x \leq a \\ \dfrac{x-a}{b-a}, & a \leq x \leq b \\ 1, & b \leq x \leq c \\ \dfrac{d-x}{d-c}, & c \leq x \leq d \\ 0, & d \leq x \end{cases}$$

application of the MAM operation on the two membership functions described above. It can be seen from the results that only the instances from Tarapacá to Libertador Bernardo O'Higgings are considered in this category, except those that are totally close, such as the Atacama Region itself.

It is also observed that membership is quite low in all cases, this is due to the defined functions, which perhaps do not correctly define this concept, which has been done in a conscious way to demonstrate the importance that a good definition of membership functions.

Regarding the definition of the parameters of the membership functions, a manual definition can be used using the criteria of a user that is related to the analysis context or a proposal can be used for the parameterization of membership functions for FDW using multi-level thresholding (Rojas et al., 2011) and thus obtain the parameters of the membership function automatically from the data.

The above is very useful because it will allow obtaining parameters of the membership function according to the context that is validated by the data of the organization itself, since it is not the same to label a student as good in an A university, as in B university. Well, the above depends on various aspects, such as entrance score, motivation for the career, lack of learning strategies, etc.

Table 4. Result of the query "Number of students in near and far Regions"

Region	μ_{near} MAM μ_{far}	Cantidad
Region of Tarapacá	0,04	9
Region Metropolitana	0,12	62
Region of Valparaíso	0,01	31
Region of Libertador General Bernardo O Higgins	0,28	28

DISCUSSION

In modern data warehouses, linguistic analytics is an important aspect. However, in most of the data warehouse implementations, it is designed for crisp analysis. Therefore, the FDW that has been presented in this chapter represents a contribution to decision-making in the educational field from the perspective of intelligent data management (Di Martino & Sessa, 2020; Fasel & Shahzad, 2012; Hussain et al., 2020; Rojas et al., 2011; Zambrano et al., 2011; Zambrano et al., 2017; among others).

The implementation of the FDW for the analysis of educational data showed examples of analysis for the cases of fuzzy elements that have been proposed in this research, such as: fuzzy measurements, fuzzy relationships, and fuzzy levels. This implementation with fuzzy elements allows flexibility of information to the user (Galindo et al., 2009).

The parameters of the membership function depend on the context, that is, there is no universal parameterization, but rather depends on the context of the organization where the analysis is applied. Therefore, the ideal is to obtain the parameters of the membership function considering the organization's own data (Rojas et al., 2011) because each institution has its own reality based on its data.

The proposal represents a useful model for data mining on educational data (Romero & Ventura, 2010; Dutt et al., 2017). It can also be indicated that in the decision-making process it is natural to think about aspects of qualitative analysis, so the proposal shows through the results of the FDW a contribution to decision-making at the level of educational data in an organization. Finally, in the educational field, the diversity of student profiles can be represented using fuzzy logic and an implementation of FDW provides that advantage.

FUTURE TRENDS

Today, technology is a fundamental benchmark in any application area. In this context, the field of education is not exempt, quite to the contrary, the pandemic by covid 19 accelerated the virtual teaching-learning processes (Cabero, 2020; Cabero & Valencia, 2021). Therefore, digitization in the field of education will generate paradigm shifts towards the construction of new scenarios for learning, and with it, many data will be available for analysis. In this sense, it will be necessary to create new procedures, protocols and forms of teaching that will generate an enormous amount of data in the digital school.

So, questions arise such: how does the use of FDW influence in the field of education? And what consequences could have the use of educational data managed from DW? To give possible answers, it is necessary to understand that the main objective of a DW is the management of historical data to allow the monitoring of said information over time. Then, the influence of the use of FDW could allow an intelligent analysis of educational information considering that structures contain pre-processed data by classification algorithms that belong to the field of artificial intelligence (Di Martino & Sessa, 2020; Fasel & Shahzad, 2012; Hussain et al., 2020; Rojas et al., 2011; Zambrano et al., 2011; Zambrano et al., 2017; among others).

In this scenario, in addition to the advantages provided by the analysis of educational data for the monitoring of data over time, there are threats that must be considered to define ethical protocols, make visible and make aware that the record of the actions carried out carried out in the virtual learning-teaching processes could be used to control the progress of a student and / or the tasks that a teacher performs or not.

CONCLUSION

A proposal for the implementation of FDW for the analysis of educational data was presented. The proposal includes examples of analysis for the fuzzy elements: fuzzy measures, fuzzy relationships between levels, fuzzy levels, and fuzzy facts. Regarding the results, the adequate definition of the membership function parameters allowed obtaining adequate results for the consultations.

Therefore, the main conclusion regarding the definition of these parameters is that they depend on the context. Consequently, there is no universal parameterization, but depends on the context of the organization where the analysis is applied. In addition, it is ideal to obtain the membership function parameters using the available data. In this sense, knowledge is extracted from the data itself and, consequently, the analysis of educational data through the proposed FDW represents a process of analysis from the perspective of the data science analysis process.

In conclusion, the proposal represents a useful model for conducting educational data mining. Also, it can be indicated that in the decision-making process it is natural to think about aspects of qualitative analysis. Therefore, the proposal represents, through the results, a contribution to decision-making using educational data.

REFERENCES

Asanka, P. D., & Perera, A. S. (2018). Defining Fuzzy Membership Function for Fuzzy Data Warehouses. *4th International Conference for Convergence in Technology*, 1-5.

Asanka, P. D., & Perera, A. S. (2019). Linguistics Analytics in Data Warehouses Using Fuzzy Techniques. *IEEE International Research Conference on Smart Computing and Systems Engineering (SCSE)*, 165-171. 10.23919/SCSE.2019.8842764

Cabero, J., & Valencia, R. (2021). And COVID-19 transformed the educational system: Reflections and experiences to learn. *International Journal of Educational Research and Innovation*, *15*, 217–227. doi:10.46661/ijeri.5246

Carrera, S., Varas, M., & Urrutia, A. (2010). Transformación de esquemas multidimensionales difusos desde el nivel conceptual al nivel lógico. *Ingeniare. Revista Chilena de Ingeniería*, *18*(2), 165–175.

Cravero, A., & Sepúlveda, S. (2012). A chronological study of paradigms for data warehouse design. *Ingenieria e Investigacion*, *32*(2), 58–62.

Delgado, M., Molina, C., Sánchez, D., Ariza, L. R., & Vila, M. A. (2003). A flexible approach to the multidimensional model: The fuzzy datacube. In *Conference on Technology Transfer*, (pp. 26-36). Springer.

Delgado, M., Molina, C., Sánchez, D., Vila, A., & Rodriguez-Ariza, L. (2004). A fuzzy multidimensional model for supporting imprecision in OLAP. *IEEE International Conference on Fuzzy Systems*, *3*, 1331-1336. 10.1109/FUZZY.2004.1375362

Di Martino, F., & Sessa, S. (2020). Fuzzy Transform for Data Classification. In *Fuzzy Transforms for Image Processing and Data Analysis*. Springer. doi:10.1007/978-3-030-44613-0_11

Fasel, D. (2009). A fuzzy data warehouse approach for the customer performance measurement for a hearing instrument manufacturing company. *IEEE Sixth International Conference on Fuzzy Systems and Knowledge Discovery*, *7*, 285-289. 10.1109/FSKD.2009.266

Fasel, D., & Shahzad, K. (2010). A data warehouse model for integrating fuzzy concepts in meta table structures. *IEEE International Conference and Workshops on Engineering of Computer Based Systems*, 100-109. 10.1109/ECBS.2010.18

Fasel, D., & Shahzad, K. (2012). Fuzzy data warehouse for performance analysis. In *Fuzzy Methods for Customer Relationship Management and Marketing: Applications and Classifications* (pp. 217–251). IGI Global. doi:10.4018/978-1-4666-0095-9.ch010

Fasel, D., & Zumstein, D. (2009). A fuzzy data warehouse approach for web analytics. In World Summit on Knowledge Society, (pp. 276-285). Springer.

Galindo, J., Urrutia, A., & Piattini, M. (Eds.). (2009). *Fuzzy databases: Modeling, design, and implementation*. IGI Global.

Hurtado, C., & Gutierrez, C. (2007). *Data warehouses and OLAP: concepts, architectures and solutions. In Chapter Handling Structural Heterogeneity in OLAP*. Idea Group, Inc.

Inmon, W. H. (2005). *Building the data warehouse*. John Wiley & Sons.

Kimball, R., & Ross, M. (2011). *The data warehouse toolkit: the complete guide to dimensional modeling*. John Wiley & Sons.

Lara, G. A., Delgado, M., & Marín, N. (2013). Fuzzy multidimensional modelling for flexible querying of learning object repositories. In *International Conference on Flexible Query Answering Systems* (pp. 112-123). Springer. 10.1007/978-3-642-40769-7_10

Malinowski, E., & Zimanyi, E. (2008). *Advanced Data Warehouse Design: From Conventional to Spatial and Temporal Applications*. Springer.

Marin, N., Pons, O., & Vila, M. A. (2000). Fuzzy types: A new concept of type for managing vague structures. *International Journal of Intelligent Systems*, *15*(11), 1061–1085. doi:10.1002/1098-111X(200011)15:11<1061::AID-INT5>3.0.CO;2-A

Mazón, J. N., & Trujillo, J. (2008). An MDA approach for the development of data warehouses. *Decision Support Systems*, *45*(1), 41–58. doi:10.1016/j.dss.2006.12.003

Molina, C., Gómez, M. E., Torre, J. M., & Vila, M. A. (2005). Using Fuzzy Data Cube for Exploratory Analysis in Financial Economy. In *EUSFLAT Conf.* (pp. 424-429). Academic Press.

Molina, C., Rodriguez-Ariza, L., Sánchez, D., & Vila, M. A. (2006). A new fuzzy multidimensional model. *IEEE Transactions on Fuzzy Systems*, *14*(6), 897–912. doi:10.1109/TFUZZ.2006.879984

Ortmann, C. (2015). Mujeres, ciencia y tecnología en las universidades: ¿la excepción a la regla? *Revista del IICE*, (38), 95-108.

Pons, O., Calvet, M. D., Tura, M., & Muñoz, C. (2013). Análisis de la igualdad de oportunidades de género en la ciencia y la tecnología: Las carreras profesionales de las mujeres científicas y tecnóloga. *Intangible capital, 9*(1), 65-90.

Razo, M. L. (2008). La inserción de las mujeres en las carreras de ingeniería y tecnología. *Perfiles Educativos, 30*(121), 63–96.

Rojas, D., Zambrano, C., Varas, M., & Urrutia, A. (2011). A multi-level thresholding-based method to learn fuzzy membership functions from data warehouse. In *Iberoamerican Congress on Pattern Recognition* (pp. 664–674). Springer. doi:10.1007/978-3-642-25085-9_79

Romero, C., & Ventura, S. (2010). Educational data mining: A review of the state of the art. *IEEE Transactions on Systems, Man and Cybernetics. Part C, Applications and Reviews, 40*(6), 601–618. doi:10.1109/TSMCC.2010.2053532

Romero, O., & Abelló, A. (2009). A survey of multidimensional modeling methodologies. *International Journal of Data Warehousing and Mining, 5*(2), 1–23. doi:10.4018/jdwm.2009040101

Rundensteiner, E. A., & Bic, L. (1989). Aggregates in possibilistic databases. *Proc. Conf. Very Large Databases.*

Sapir, L., Shmilovici, A., & Rokach, L. (2008). A methodology for the design of a fuzzy data warehouse. In *4th International IEEE Conference Intelligent Systems* (Vol. 1, pp. 2-14). IEEE. 10.1109/IS.2008.4670400

Urrutia, A., Galindo, J., Jimenéz, L., & Piattini, M. (2006). Data Modeling Dealing with Uncertainty in Fuzzy Logic. *IFIP World Computer Congress, 8*, 201-217. 10.1007/978-0-387-34732-5_19

Winter, R., & Strauch, B. (2003). A method for demand-driven information requirements analysis in data warehousing projects. *36th Annual Hawaii International Conference on System Sciences, Proceedings of the IEEE.*

Yager, R. R. (1994). Aggregation operators and fuzzy systems modeling. *Fuzzy Sets and Systems, 67*(2), 129–145. doi:10.1016/0165-0114(94)90082-5

Zadeh, L. A. (1965). Fuzzy sets. *Information and Control, 8*(3), 338–353. doi:10.1016/S0019-9958(65)90241-X

Zambrano, C., Rojas, D., Carvajal, K., & Acuña, G. (2011). Análisis de rendimiento académico estudiantil usando data warehouse y redes neuronales. *Ingeniare. Revista Chilena de Ingeniería, 19*(3), 369–381. doi:10.4067/S0718-33052011000300007

Zambrano, C., Rojas, D., & Salcedo, P. (2018). Un método para analizar datos de pruebas educacionales estandarizadas usando almacén de datos y triangulación. *Formación Universitaria, 11*(4), 3–14. doi:10.4067/S0718-50062018000400003

Zambrano, C., Urrutia, A., & Varas, M. (2017). Análisis de rendimiento académico estudiantil usando Data Warehouse Difuso. *Ingeniare. Revista Chilena de Ingeniería, 25*(2), 242–254. doi:10.4067/S0718-33052017000200242

Zambrano, C., Varas, M., & Urrutia, A. (2012). Enfoque MDA para el diseño de un data warehouse difuso. *Ingeniare. Revista Chilena de Ingeniería, 20*(1), 99–113. doi:10.4067/S0718-33052012000100010

KEY TERMS AND DEFINITIONS

CWM OLAP Meta Model: CWM OLAP meta model is a standard for representing a multidimensional database.

DBMS: Data base management systems.

Fuzzy Attributes TYPE 1: Are classic attributes that support imprecise handling, where the defined linguistic labels will only be used in the fuzzy conditions of the queries.

Fuzzy Attributes TYPE 2: Are attributes that support both classical (crisp) and fuzzy (imprecise) data, in the form of possibility distributions over an ordered underlying domain.

Fuzzy Attributes TYPE 3: Are attributes on discrete domain data on underlying unordered domain with analogy.

MDA: Model-driven architecture.

Stereotype: A stereotype allows adding a new semantic meaning to the model element.

Chapter 7
Innovation and Creativity in Software Engineering Education

Gloria Piedad Gasca-Hurtado
Universidad de Medellín, Colombia

María Clara Gómez-Álvarez
Universidad de Medellín, Colombia

Bell Manrique Losada
Universidad de Medellín, Colombia

ABSTRACT

The last decade has increased the demand of software products in several economy sectors; therefore, the need to train people in software engineering is growing. Software engineering, as a discipline, requires developing in engineers technical and social/soft competencies. For all the above, we have been working on the incorporation of new strategies in software engineering education, seeking that students build up software products aligned with organizations business processes. The core of most of such educational strategies is the 'game' constitutes a dynamic element that changes the ways of interaction and support in the learning processes. The authors present a set of approaches centered on innovation and creativity in which they have made significant contributions along the 10 last years, from the following work branches: 1) methodological, comprising methodologies, methods, techniques, and strategies; 2) application, presenting proposals oriented to games; and 3) support, including guidelines and instruments to evaluate and help in classroom practice.

INTRODUCTION

Globally, Software industry has grown in the last decade and it is expected to continue growing at a very high rate (Bosch, 2017) whereby the major software companies have defined ambitious plans and growth targets for the future. However, in the last years Software industry has shown dissatisfaction in relation to the training level of recently graduated professionals (Portela *et al.*, 2017), identifying as its

DOI: 10.4018/978-1-7998-7552-9.ch007

Copyright © 2021, IGI Global. Copying or distributing in print or electronic forms without written permission of IGI Global is prohibited.

main cause the lack of proper Software Engineering (SE) education which may have severe consequences (Garg & Varma, 2008) and may negatively affect the industry growth targets.

SE education emerges as a way of contributing to this dynamic process, looking for a balance between theory and practice in the teaching-learning process (Balaban & Sturm, 2018), and provides students with the knowledge to move to mature companies with a defined structure (Devadiga, 2017). Such a process is oriented to answer mainly two questions: (i) *what* to teach and (ii) *how* to teach, for students to develop the competencies required by the software development industry in which solving complex problems and innovating based on creativity is crucial (Crawford *et al.*, 2012).

Faced with the first question, *what* to teach in SE, it requires developing technical competencies and social/soft skills for the students. Technical competencies, according to Bourque and Fairley (IEEE, 2014), are related to the proper application of techniques, methods, tools, criteria, principles, and values to create and manage software applications. Social skills are centered on the ability to make decisions and produce deliverables with responsibility (Garg & Varma, 2008), as well as communication skills, leadership, managing time, negotiating with the customer, making decisions, and achievement orientation (Matturro *et al.*, 2019). The curricular fundamentals used by Higher Education Institutions for defining what to teach are found in guidelines such as SWEBOK (IEEE, 2014) that presents a body of knowledge comprising the topics that a software engineer should know and the Software Engineering Curricula (Shackelford *et al.*, 2006), that contains the subjects and some guidelines for the design of syllabus.

Regarding to the second question, *how* to teach, software engineering courses and programs have been addressed using traditional teaching strategies like lecture classes, where the professor presents concepts and the student is a passive actor in the process (Casallas *et al.*, 2002), and, active teaching strategies like project-based learning, problem-based learning, and collaborative learning, where the students face a real software development project (Runeson, 2001; Groth & Robertson, 2001). Although these strategies have generated good results in terms of learning, there is a latent interest in developing critical competencies in today's engineer such as innovation and creativity during their professional training process. According to Sternberg (1997), creativity refers to the mental process of creation, and innovation refers to the materialization of the creative idea in a product. There can be no innovation without creativity, and as affirm Marina (2012), creativity is a capacity or skill that can be learned. Thus, the development of creativity is a function of education that must be present from the instructional design to the development of the teaching-learning process (Guerrero, 2009).

López-Díaz suggests link creativity with the teaching-learning processes, giving a central role. In this way, creative experiences help foster mental growth and develop creative thinking, which provides opportunities to try new ideas, try new ways of thinking, and solve problems (Ribes, 2011), main skills in the software engineering education. It is also necessary to rethink the teaching-learning process and practices with innovation and creativity strategies. Interesting approaches have found in the literature and it is have made proposals and applications in our close practice. This chapter is focused on such approaches mentioned.

In this sense, to improve the teaching-learning process, it is present the following work branches in innovation and creativity in the software engineering classroom in which it is have made significant contributions: 1) *Methodological branch*, comprising methodologies, methods, techniques, didactics, and strategies; 2) *Application branch*, presenting proposals oriented to games or applications implemented; and 3) *Support branch*, including guidelines, tools, and instruments to evaluate and help the classroom practice.

The remainder of this chapter is structured as follows. Section II presents the review of the background and relevant related work on innovation and creativity in education and its technological progress and evolution. Section III describes recent approaches in *Methodological branch* and the most relevant proposal from our work and experience. Section IV summarizes the approaches from the *Application branch* and *Support branch*. Section V shows the examine the expected impact of these work branches and some outcomes and expected future trends developments. Finally, Section VI describes some conclusions.

BACKGROUND

Nowadays, universities are teaching students whose main distinctive characteristic is the strong relationship they have with information and communication technology (ICT). They are the millennial generation who have a different learning style and who is most effective when doing multisensory activities. Higher education institutions face a big challenge in finding ways to improve the learning experience and academic performance of these and future students. Research has shown that ICTs used for educational purposes can help in meeting this challenge (Hernandez-de-Menendez *et al., 2019*). In this chapter, the study of methods, methodologies, frameworks, and games that can be applied to innovate in the educational field is undertaken.

The study of innovating in the educational field in software engineering necessarily requires approaching the nature of software engineering, to know the advances in SE education, and to identify creative and innovative elements incorporating strategies. The background shows technological advances about innovation and creativity in SE education and games as novel technologies involved in this field like strategies related to innovation and creativity.

The highly technical nature of software engineering requires people to have knowledge and experience in diverse software processes, methodologies, tools, and techniques (Matturro *et al.*, 2019). The above added to the skills of the human dimension, related to teamwork, the interaction between stakeholders, and problem-solving, offers many complexities and big opportunities for creativity and innovation.

SE education must help to train students with the knowledge to adequate transition to the software industry, closing the gap between the demand and supply (Garg & Varma, 2008). This training involves human and technical factors, risk, time-long processes, and uncertainty, which implies a dynamic and agile set of skills to identify, conceptualize, and deliver features as per market needs. Also, it requires the adoption of development trends in software processes, application of the newest engineering practices (*i.e.* DevOps), to form skills to manage agile projects (iterations, fast releases, prototyping), and the ability to take on multiple roles. It is found evidence in the literature of the last 5 years about how SE education has also been changing, with more agile and innovative elements, for featuring both in content and delivery style (Towey *et al.*, 2017); helping to give students exposure to more realistic software development experiences (Dawson, 2000; Buffardi, Robb & Rahn, 2017; Simpson & Storer, 2017); motivation in the classroom behind training environments (Towey, Ng & Wang, 2016; Su, 2016; Diniz *et al.*, 2017); forming interdisciplinary teams to create businesses based on software products (Buffardi, 2018; Nascimento *et al.*, 2019), among others.

There are many elements and components for considering the specification of teaching-learning strategies and techniques for engineering areas, most of them centered on principles of creativity (creative process to generate a software product or creative problem solving) and innovation (novelty and value of the product).

Creativity studies in technological context and software engineering have been developed by several years, among others it is important to remark: dimensions of the creative process in software projects (Plsek, 1997); methodological approach to integrate creativity in software engineering (Bobkowska, 2015); risk management of creativity in software projects (Bobkowska, 2019); application of creativity techniques in business analysis and requirements engineering (Lemos *et al.*, 2012); and creativity related to agile projects (Conboy *et al.*, 2009; Hollis & Maiden, 2013).

Innovations in teaching and learning have impacted the educational processes in software engineering. New technologies and approaches, including:

- More open and flexible technology-enhanced learning options such as massive open online courses (MOOCs) and other open educational resources (Towey & Walker, 2018), have led to advances in classroom practices. Because of increasing demands for innovations, there is a need for more creativity in software engineering (Bobkowska, 2019).
- Innovative pedagogy to conduct a learner-centered learning environment for SE courses, such as flipped classroom (Lin, 2019); blended learning (Slomanson, 2014); usage of design thinking in several stages of software development (Palacin-Silva et al., 2017); gamification approaches applied as an innovative learning context-focused in engaging and motivating learners to perform desired behaviors (Laskowski, 2015) and gamification of specific software engineering activities (Singer & Schneider, 2012; Galvao & Neto, 2012); active teaching strategies like project-based learning, problem-based learning, and collaborative learning, where the students face a real software development project (Runeson, 2001; Groth & Robertson, 2001).

Although these strategies have generated good results in terms of learning, there is a latent interest in developing critical competencies in today's engineers such as innovation and creativity during their professional training process. In this sense, it is necessary to rethink the teaching-learning process and practices with innovation and creativity strategies.

For all the above, we have been working on the incorporation of new strategies in software engineering education, seeking that students build up software products aligned with the organization's business processes creatively. The core of the most such educational strategies is the 'game' as a dynamic element that changes the interaction ways in the learning processes. Games have been used in the teaching-learning process because of allowing "learning-by-doing" and stimulate pairs-learning (Smart & Csapo, 2007), as well as, increase learning speed in students (Mahmoudi *et al.*, 2015). In general, games are an intrinsic feature of civilization and can be viewed from different perspectives, for this reason, researchers continually tried to harness the potential to several contexts, especially learning and education (Qian *et al.*, 2016). Among the sixteen learning principles, the principles of *interaction, well-ordered problems*, and *performance* before competence are significant examples linking back to the learning theories and show how games can be a valuable tool for learning and education (Paravizo *et al.*, 2018). In software engineering teaching, there are several experiences using games such as:

- Problems and programmers is a card game used to exemplify the software development process, emphasizing the implementation phase, where programmers face human and technical challenges, or changes in the initial scope of a project (Baker et al., 2003).

- Requirements game is a role-play game that guides the development of a small software application in the context of a project, to simulate aspects such as compliance with requirements, specialization of functions, completeness of documentation, teamwork, etc. (Zapata, 2007).
- Consistency Game is a puzzle game that seeks to show students the relationships among the different UML (Unified Modeling Language) models (Zapata & Duarte, 2008).
- Risk Management Game is a board game developed at Carnegie Mellon University to teach the basics of risk management in the software development process. This game is applied in different Software Engineering courses to strengthen decision-making regarding risk management in a software development project (Taran, 2007).

In conclusion, it is possible to affirm ICTs have led to the emergence of a variety of active and innovative teaching methods, above all associated in SE education. For example, role-playing, which consists of simulating a real-life situation, in the school context, in which the student takes on a certain role and interacts with other students in a fictitious situation. Framed in this scenario, the present study aims to show if the application of the role-playing method promotes the improvement of attitude variables and practical skills. To this end, the works presented in this chapter advocates the use of a quasi-experimental methodology, with a control and experimental group and the application of a post-test. The sample is composed of 138 students from the Master of Teachers of Compulsory Secondary Education in Ceuta (Spain). The results showed that the students positively valued the application of the method, obtaining better scores in the set of variables studied, especially in motivation, creativity, and collaboration. Therefore, the application of innovative methodologies through technology promotes the increase of multiple skills in the student body. Some studies present results related to the use of active methods for demonstrating an increase in students' skills, and that, therefore, is possible use sustainable pedagogies to promote a real innovation in the classrooms (Moreno-Guerrero, 2020).

Regarding approaches for incorporating educational games in SE teaching, there are working in several proposals, models, strategies, and methodologies to design pedagogic instrument. The most relevant results are presented in the following sections. These proposals have been addressed during the study of SE education, seeking to innovate in this area of knowledge.

METHODOLOGICAL BRANCH

Some strategies such as collaborative learning, game-based learning, role playing, skill operation, and remote live broadcasting prove that smart classroom has provided extensive and effective support for teaching innovation (Xie, 2018). However, the methods and methodologies to design these strategies are to be developed yet. Therefore, this chapter shows approaches related to methods, methodologies, and strategies to improve SE teaching.

In general, such approaches aim to increase student motivation and commitment in the classroom. For instance, Alexandre and Santos (2018) propose to incorporate Problem-Based Learning (PBL) through a tool consisting of a Canvas-PBL and a set of cards intended to guide the planning of teaching. Other authors use PBL in SE teaching including gamification as a motivation agent in the application of the agile Scrum methodology of software development (de Vasconselos *et al.*, 2018). In addition, Dorodchi *et al.* (2019) present a model to an undergraduate SE course of a computer science curriculum. Such a model includes students working with open source software to simulate working on an enterprise project and learn agile development. This proposal looks for students to face real project challenges and develop professional competencies. Finally, Kurkovsky *et al.* (2019) present the use of Lego to support designing hands-on case studies that mix studying SE concepts with the elements of team building and playful creativity. Specifically, the authors present software requirements teaching activities based on Lego obtaining student engagement in the course.

The next section presents proposals oriented to methods, methodologies, and didactics for promoting innovation and creativity in SE teaching.

Methods and Methodologies

Method to Design Teaching Strategies

Pre-service teachers frequently express negative prejudices towards science and the methodologies traditionally used during their training. Gamification is a booming technology based on combining the psychological aspects, mechanics, and dynamics of a game in non-ludic environments (López Carrillo *et al.,* 2019). The usage of gamification has shown good outcomes in terms of increasing students' motivation, creativity, and commitment to the sciences. A support strategy for teachers who intend to innovate in the classroom was developed as a method to facilitate the design of teaching strategies. Such a method is based on gamification principles, looking for increasing student motivation in their learning process. This method aims to guide the design of pedagogic instruments based on: 1) experience as a key factor to learning, and 2) gamification in an educational environment, as a strategy to stimulate the classroom work and increase the participant motivation.

The method has five components as shown in Figure 1 and are as follows (Gómez-Álvarez *et al.*, 2016):

1. Preparation: The purpose of this component is defining the pedagogic instrument learning goals
2. Design: In this component, the designers select the gamification components to be included in the instrument.
3. Pilotage: The goal of this component is to apply the instrument in a group to refine the rules, mechanics, and dynamics of such an instrument.
4. Scheduling: This component refers to defining the spaces and necessary resources for using the pedagogic instrument.
5. Assessment: This component allows to know the participants perception about the instrument and facilitator performance.

Such a method was evaluated through a pilot study case for teaching subjects related to software design in the context of PSP (Gómez-Álvarez *et al.*, 2016). After the game application, the participants

Figure 1. Method components

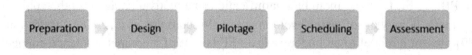

(20) filled out a questionnaire obtaining the following results: enjoyment level was assessed Good and Very good for the 85% of participants reinforcing the importance of gamified activities as learning motivators. In fact, activities designed with this method facilitate student's engagement to SE courses through methods and methodologies to innovate in the classroom.

Method to Learn to Code Creating Videogames

The main purpose of this method is to engage students in the introductory programming courses based on the development of video games, looking for engaging and motivating students during their learning. The proposal includes two active teaching strategies: PBL and Games-based learning for promoting active participation in the learning process. Figure 2 shows the phases of methodology:

Figure 2. Phases of method

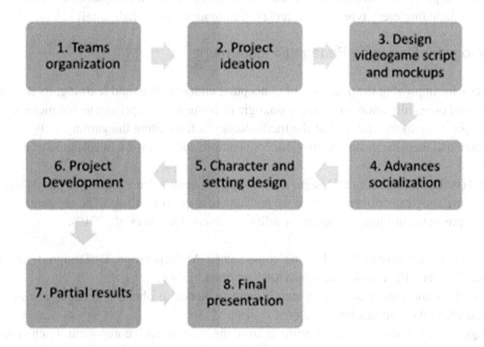

First, the professor uses different game activities related to teamwork in class to identify skills and conforms teams of three and four members. Then, each team must explore project ideas for a videogame, identifying needs and problems interesting by the team. This phase finishes with the presentation of project ideas in class (title, logo, problem or need, game goal, game scope, and potential users). In phase 3, the teams design the videogames mockups and scripts, including game gender, game script, game rules, and a storyboard for simulating game scenarios. Then, in phase 4, the students present their game prototypes and obtain feedback from their classmates and guest professors. Later, phases 5 and 6 are oriented to videogame development (including characters and setting design) adjusting the prototypes according to the feedback received. In such phases, Scrum roles (Scrum Master, Product Owner, and Team members) are very important for the product backlog, items definition, management, and prioritization. Finally, during videogame development, teams present partial results and advances and show their software product in a final demo session where the best project receives an award (Puerta & Gómez-Álvarez, 2018).

Additionally, some authors evidence that the present generation of students is growing up with innovative technologies that are embedded in their daily lives. These students can promote their daily activities using digital information, can be connected to each other and doing many cooperative tasks simultaneously. As in our proposal "Method to learn to code creating videogames" innovations and mobile-based technologies can provide wide-range opportunities to embed learning in authentic environments and thus can enhance students' motivation and learning process (Mivehchi *et al.,* 2020).

Such a method was proved in semester 01-2017 for eight weeks and 4 hours by week in a course of Introduction to Programming, with an experimental group and a control group. In this pilot, the students of the experimental group implemented a videogame achieving collaborative work which helped them to spend more time on course activities and promote creativity thanks to the videogame design process. Other positive aspects are continuous feedback and the students have the opportunity to design and create a product including every type of ideas (crazy, fun, innovative, or traditional).

Methodology for Designing Pedagogic Instruments

As a strategy for improving the processes of conceptual understanding and learning, its define a methodology, based on gamification, to design pedagogic instruments, comprising techniques and materials to teach a specific subject. The goal of the methodology is facilitating the gaming activities design in the classroom and then, increasing motivation, cooperation, and teamwork in participants in their learning process.

The PID (Pedagogic Instrument Design) methodology is designed as a sequential path where a trainer can obtain a pedagogic instrument to guide the teaching of a specific subject. The elements of the methodology are presented in Figure 3 and are as follows (Gasca-Hurtado *et al.*, 2019):

- Components. Comprises the following components: A) Preparation, B) Design, C) Pilotage, D) Scheduling, and E) Assessment, which are described in Table 1.
- Steps. Each component contains a step-by-step sequence to obtain a pedagogic instrument designed under the gamification strategy.
- Pedagogic instrument. Generated artifacts from the steps of each component. Each generated instrument comprises Participants (groups of students or professionals in training; Trainer or facilitator (professors, trainers, or facilitators of an activity conducted with an instrument), Materials (set of necessary resources for the application of the gamified pedagogic instrument.

The methodology was designed considering the following pedagogical principles: 1) Planning; 2) Gamification Environment; and 3) Experimentation.

One of the most important advantages of our proposal for designing pedagogic instruments is the assessment component. This proposal includes specifically an assessment component to change student assumptions regarding frightening evaluation activities that must be changed by packing them into an IT-based educational games (Juliantari *et al.*, 2018).

A pedagogic instrument for teaching software design under the PSP (Personal Software Process) for employees from a software company was designed using the methodology mentioned. The results

Figure 3. Elements of the PID methodology
Source: *(Gasca-Hurtado et al., 2019)*

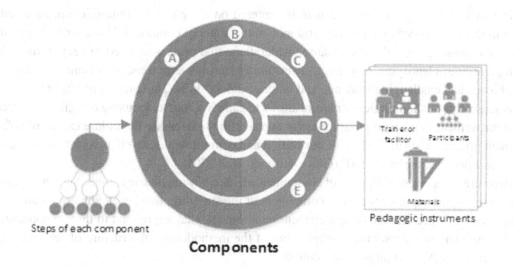

obtained from the survey support the conclusion that the didactic technique applied to the instrument is appropriate. In fact, 100% of participants say they would apply the concept of PSP in the area of SE, which they currently perform, showing that if other alternatives are sought to present the subjects, it is possible to obtain more receptivity of the public.

Despite the growing adoption and acceptance of gamification approaches among companies, the relationship between gamification and the early stages of innovation is confusing and deserves further attention to produce added-value exploratory knowledge. In the pilot study case of this proposal, the results of the application of a gamification proposal in a software development company are presented. Given that, these results are still preliminary, it is necessary to consider proposals such as the analytical framework that provides a consistent and organized picture of the use of gamification approaches for innovation purposes (Patrício *et al.*, 2018).

Table 1. Components of PID. Source: (Gasca-Hurtado et al., 2019)

Component				
A–Preparation	**B–design**	**C–Pilotage**	**D–scheduling**	**E–assessment**
Define goals to achieve with the instrument, based on the analysis of 1) competencies to be developed, 2) learning goals, 3) profile of the population, 4) particular interests and age of the population	Outline elements of gamification to include in the instrument. *i.e.* be reward, status, achievement, and competition. Also, the mechanics of the instrument is defined, *i.e.* the rules and processes	Test the instrument with a different audience to the target population (friends, family, and colleagues). Then adjusts of the game mechanics (rules, materials, or time for each activity) are executed.	Provide spaces, resources, and materials required for the application of the final instrument	Identify participants perception about the instrument and facilitator performance, by using the assessment proposal presented in [20].

Methodological Structure for Gamifying a Course

The main motivation for gamifying a course is centered on the game containing elements of education, both in terms of procedures and the substance of the material contained. However, although using IT-based educational games, there are four considerations that professors need to keep in mind when evaluating learning: identifying objectives, determining learning experiences, defining standards that can be achieved and challenging students, and honing student skills (Juliantari *et al.*, 2018).

In this sense, this methodological structure allows to gamify a course, focusing on agility for software process improvement. Such a proposal looks for contributing to decrease the failure causes of software development projects, such as the lack of motivation and commitment, as well as social and human factors that affect processes related to SE (Gasca-Hurtado *et al.*, 2018).

The structure is represented by a set of components denoted by geometric figures, shown in Figure 4. Each geometric figure represents a basic component of the structure; thus, each phase contains at least one component and specifies the design element requirements that are related to that component. The design of these elements allows the configuration of the methodological structure of the pedagogical experience. In this way, each phase is structured.

Figure 4. Methodological Structure
Source: (Gasca-Hurtado et al., 2018)

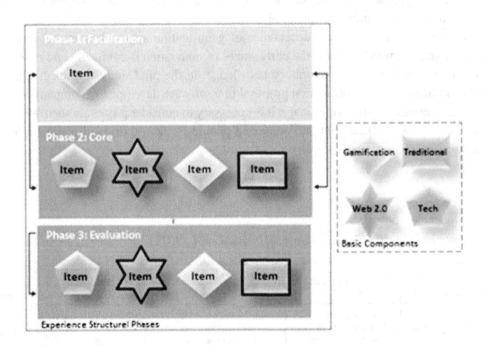

The *facilitation phase* indicates that any course should have a kickoff phase, wherein setting elements are established for both the student and the professor or facilitator to familiarize with the session and the subject matter that will be addressed in a given period time.

The *core phase* is the central phase of the structure, where the basic contents of the course will be developed. In this phase, the set of components that must be designed to establish a gamified strategy is proposed. The minimum components are 1) a gamification component as a strategy to make the classroom environment dynamic and 2) a technological component that may support the development of the elements designed in the gamification component. When a component is highlighted with a black border in the structure (refer to Figure 4), the component is deemed as an alternative component for that phase. In this phase, the traditional and Web 2.0 components are alternative components, which may be designed by the professor or facilitator to support the minimum components or to remove the components from the structure when necessary.

In the *evaluation phase*, the gamification component is proposed as the minimum component. This component must be articulated with the gamification elements designed in the core phase. It is recommended that there be at least one evaluation element associated with this component; therefore, the gamification component of the core phase must be associated with at least one gamification component in the evaluation phase. For example, if there is a traditional component in the core phase, then at least one traditional evaluation element must be designed.

Such a proposal was used for creating a gamification experience for the Organization and Information Systems course in the Computer Sciences Program at the Universidad de Medellín, Colombia. This course is taught in the 3rd semester and is the first class in the software engineering track of this undergraduate program. The three thematic units of the course syllabus are Systems General Theory, Organization and information systems, and Information Technology. In the first step, the subject matter selected is "Introduction to General Systems Theory."

For the facilitation phase, a new gamification component is created and defined as a Pictionary®-type activity. Likewise, for the core phase, a new component is created to present the video game strategy; all the characteristics of this component are recorded. In addition, as a technological component for this phase, Greenfoot, Android Studio, and MIT Inventor elements are selected and documented. In the evaluation phase, Elevator Pitch is selected as an alternative to evaluate competencies for this subject matter, supported by the Powtoon technology component.

In conclusion, this methodological approach allows us to incorporate creativity components for the different phases (facilitation, core, and evaluation) of the teaching process like games and ludic activities even for assess student learning decreasing the tension and stress levels of the students.

Theory for Software Engineering Teaching

This proposal consists of a general theory for software engineering teaching, called SETMAT (Software Engineering Teaching Methods And Theory). SETMAT comprises concepts and relations relevant to the software engineering teaching domain. Such concepts and relations—identified during the review of previous experiences—incorporate the competencies that students expect to acquire, according to different roles of a software development team (Gómez-Álvarez *et al.*, 2019).

SETMAT includes all elements of SEMAT kernel (OMG, 2015) like software engineering theory, and adds software engineering teaching process using the same language and Essence elements like alphas, activity spaces, competencies, activities, work products, and patterns. About software engineering teaching process, the following sub-alphas are added to the base elements of Essence: 1) for the alpha *team*, the *student* sub-alpha, 2) for the alpha *work*, the sub-alphas *course* and *subject*, and 3) for the alpha *way of work*, the sub-alphas *learning objectives*, *teaching strategy*, *learning activity*, *resources*, and *assessment method* (See Figure 5).

Besides, the sub-alpha deliverable is associated with the alpha requirements, since the different deliveries of a product, from the requirements specification to the test cases, are requirements implementation (See Figure 5). Also, the three activity spaces presented in Figure 6 cover the different activities of the software engineering teaching process.

In addition, a new set of competencies required in software engineers is proposed based on the proposal of Durango *et al.* (2018) considering the different roles within a software development team. The new competencies are "communication", "service orientation", "systemic thinking", "knowledge management", "change management", "collaborative work", and "achievement orientation".

By formulating this theory, it enables the representation of software engineering teaching practices and allows professors to define the minimal elements of any teaching strategy in this area. Moreover, it

Figure 5. SETMAT Subalphas. Source: (Gómez-Álvarez et al., 2019)

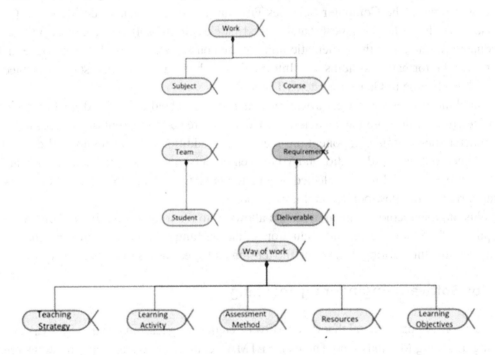

Figure 6. New SETMAT activity spaces
Source: (Gómez-Álvarez et al., 2019)

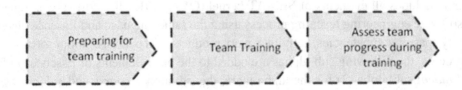

allows for comparing and transferring their strategies more effectively, understanding a teaching strategy as a set of teaching practices with a specific purpose.

This theory allows representing and transferring any type of software engineering teaching practice, including innovating elements such as game design, simulated professional teams using Scrum or XP, among others. A pilot was carried out with 24 software engineering professors from Colombia, Chile, and México. This pilot included the following activities: i) Participants presentation, ii) Apply a team's game for introducing SETMAT, iii) Conform teams of two members taking into account common interest in SE teaching, iv) Representing one SE teaching practice using SETMAT, and iv) Fill out a questionnaire individually.

In relation to the questionnaire questions:

- ¿Are there elements of the practice that were not able to be represented with SETMAT? ¿Which? The professors responded that some elements of the practices that they were not able to represent in SETMAT are the modalities of execution of the practice (virtual, face-to-face) and the prerequisites that students must meet to carry out the learning activities.
- Regarding the SETMAT easy of usage for representing SE teaching practices, 77.8% of teachers rated it as high and 22.2% as very high, which provides an initial idea about the potential of SETMAT to represent, transfer, and share software engineering teaching practices.
- ¿Would you recommend this theory to another colleague? Describe your reasons. 100% of the professors answered affirmatively, which shows the potential of SETMAT as a mechanism for representing practices, as well as the importance of using alternative strategies, such as games, to present a topic.

Didactics Approaches

The approaches presented in this section aim to energize the software engineering teaching process achieving more student commitment and participation in course activities. For example, Palacin-Silva *et al.* (2017) present the design of a human-centric SE capstone including design thinking techniques and agile practices in the software project life-cycle. Design thinking is a powerful mean of problem-solving and effectively supports SE education in bringing a more hands-on and minds-on, problem-based curriculum.

Concerning agile simulation in practical SE courses, Hof *et al.* (20017) describe the use of a multi-week Scrum Paper City simulation game for promoting the Agile principles and values such as openness, transparency, among others. As a result, the students like to experience the agile approach directly in a project for the enjoyment and collaboration between project team members.

Finally, the use of ideation techniques for the co-creation of products/services is a widely accepted SE teaching practice that seeks to develop creative and innovative products satisfying stakeholders' needs. Zhu *et al.* (2019) propose the use of co-design workshops with adolescents with autism for exchanging ideas and points of view. The proposal is identifying users' needs and software requirements for this population.

This section describes some of the innovative didactics practices that it is have applied in SE courses in recent years.

Design Thinking in Requirements Engineering.

A requirements engineering course incorporates Design Thinking –DT- for generating tangible prototypes, capturing and validating end-user needs, and envision new products and services. This didactic strategy is human-centered and leads to creativity and innovation. The application of this strategy integrates DT practices with agile methodologies to improve the quality of software products for the end-users and enable businesses to achieve creativity and innovation.

Such a master course includes DT practices like empathy map and brainstorming combining with agile SE techniques like product box and user stories, looking for visioning a product initial of their master theses, and interact with target stakeholders of such products.

Joint Project in Software Engineering

This didactic strategy raises the figure of "Joint Project" of the courses of the SE area in the undergraduate program of Computer Sciences at Universidad de Medellín (Manrique-Losada *et al.*, 2011). This project is supported by the other areas of the training curricular plan, articulating other disciplines with a realistic experience of software product development.

A joint project, as an articulated and organized process with a purpose (Rivas & Revelo, 2007), has a beginning at courses of 3rd level and an end at the last course of the SE area (8 levels later), covering some phases of a software product development for solving a real challenge/problem. This project has a medium scale of complexity and uses as knowledge variables the knowledge acquired in different topics and subjects during a specific period (one academic semester), integrating them incrementally to generate a unique software product. To do this, they use the conceptual bases, techniques, models, tools, languages, and platforms studied in the theoretical-practical classes and laboratories, covering the requirements, analysis, design, implementation, validation, verification, testing, and maintenance and training phases.

Agile Development Team Simulation

This didactic strategy is oriented to simulate the application of an agile framework in the course Software Engineering IV in the undergraduate program of Computer Sciences at Universidad de Medellín. Such a course goal is to acquire competencies in students associated with planning, estimation, organization, direction, control, and evaluation of software development projects. This strategy includes a simulation of software development teams in a software product implementation based on traditional and agile approaches. All this work is grounded in the "Joint Project" concept.

The course dynamics includes two phases:

- Phase 1 looks for implementing agile methodologies in project management based on Scrum framework. This phase incorporates a simulation including four sprints of one week. In each sprint, the teams apply Scrum meetings, roles, and deliverables like user stories, prioritization, and tasking techniques.
- Phase 2 is oriented to the implementation of traditional methodologies for project management, taking into account models like PMBOK and CMMI process areas. Such an implementation includes one iteration for implementing software product requirements.

In both phases, the best practices application (for agile and traditional approaches) in software development allows evidence of the acquisition of competencies related to project management in students.

Ideation of Software-Based Products/Services

This didactic strategy is designed to solve challenges executing the creative stages of a design process. The goal is the ideation for the solution of challenges from real companies/organizations, based on software. Several courses where is necessary to solve a problem and the visualization of a future software product incorporates creative idea generation techniques. Some of these techniques are the people-scenario technique, scenario design, storytelling, storyboard, MindMapping, and SCAMPER.

APPLICATION AND SUPPORT BRANCH

Other proposals are oriented specifically to games or videogames, which provide innovation and creativity to the classroom. Ahmad *et al* (2015) present an analysis of educational games design frameworks for SE. Such survey includes a frameworks comparison based on criteria for effective videogames such as motivational attributes, goals, and rules and narrative context, among others. Garcia *et al.* (2020) propose a serious game for teaching the fundamentals of ISO/IEC/IEEE 29148 systems and SE Lifecycle Processes –Requirements Engineering at undergraduate level. Such standard specifies the required process to be implemented by requirements engineering for software products and services. This game is called *Requengin*, his goal is to strengthen the comprehension and application of the main processes of the standard, and some related requirements engineering techniques. Also, Calderón *et al.* (2019) describe the use of a serious game to make students aware of the relevance of measuring to improve the quality of the processes and facilitate students contact with software process improvement initiatives.

The next section presents some games and videogames proposals for SE teaching as well as some approaches to supporting such process.

Games Proposals

Game to Defect Tracking

This game is oriented to the following learning goals (Gasca-Hurtado *et al.*, 2016):

1. Recognizing the roles of a software development team according to the PSP/TSP framework.
2. Identifying the responsibilities and goals to be achieved for each phase of a software development project.
3. Promoting social skills in teamwork that facilitate the interaction of its members such as negotiation, effective communication, teamwork, and creativity.
4. Identifying business requirements in each phase and verifying such requirements from the results obtained.
5. Understanding the basic formulas for measuring defects and their importance in controlling the product quality.

During the game, the participants assume three possible roles in the teams: Developer, who builds paper boats following the guidance and acceptance criteria, Leader, who coordinates the development team and, Tester, who verifies the quality of the finished product and takes measures. Regarding the game, the necessary materials are sheets of paper, pencils, and a sheet with origami instructions.

The game rules are as follows:

1. Conform teams of at least three members with the following roles: 1) leader, 2) developer, and 3) tester.

2. The facilitator defines and explains to the leader the acceptance criteria of paper boats. Such criteria refer to software quality requirements. In the game acceptance criteria relate to the folds, uniformity, wrinkles, false folds, brands, and paper breaks.

3. The facilitator gives the leader the material and the origami instruction sheet for building paper boats (Five units of paper of 32 cm by 25.5 cm are provided in each phase).

4. Participants should build paper boats in a process consisting of four phases. Each phase has an origami instruction sheet for each product to build. In phases 1 and 2 a paper boat of low complexity is built and in phases 3 and 4 participants build a paper boat of medium complexity.

5. The participant with the role of developer must build five paper boats per phase, considering: a) acceptance criteria defined and explained by the facilitator, and b) the duration of each phase. For phases 1 and 2 the duration is 5', while for phase 3 is 15' and for phase 4 is 20'.

6. Upon completion of construction time, developers deliver finished products to the tester for verification, without the intervention of other team members.

7. The tester and the leader record the verification and validation metrics for each phase. In the template, defects found are quantified according to acceptance criteria and the result of verification is recorded.

8. At the end of each phase, the tester shall submit to the team a report of the verification done and measures of injected and removed defects per phase. This game activity intends that participants recognize the performance achieved as a team and productivity improvements during different phases. In addition, this exercise helps to develop communication skills and teamwork between testers and developers.

9. At the end of the four phases, the facilitator should promote a space for reflection about issues such as learning achieved, the performed roles, the strategy to follow in the game to achieve the highest productivity, and learned lessons from teamwork.

This game reinforces the importance of the ongoing search of training strategies for software engineering where motivation, assimilation of concepts, and development of skills such as leadership, negotiation, and teamwork are achieved. These skills are essential for social interaction within development teams. The gamification proposal presented aims to achieve the development of social skills that emerge in teamwork, which are key to consolidating the high performance of software development teams. From the analysis of the gamification principles in the game components proposed, it is evident that the incorporation of elements like amusement factors, well-being and oriented knowledge promotes training related to defect management and performance improvement of software development teams.

Trouble Hunters

Trouble Hunters is a game where participants make up commissions of inquiry to analyze the failed cases of software development. In this way, participants must identify causes, consequences, missing competencies, and wrong decisions by engineers. Additionally, creativity is promoted with answers through cartoons, logos, or hieroglyphics (Gómez-Álvarez *et al.*, 2017).

As learning goals, at the end of the game, the participants must be able to:

1. Analyze a failed case of software or hardware product development (embedded system) and identify the following elements: 1) current situation, 2) consequences, 3) wrong decisions, 4) best practices, and 5) missing competencies in systems engineers in charge of such cases.
2. Represent such elements through alternatives schemes to the Spanish language such as acrostics, hieroglyphs, or logos, seeking to promote creativity, teamwork, and the establishment of the agreements.

The materials required by teams are instructions sheet with the question and representation scheme (See Table 2), and markers and paper sheet to elaborate on each phase representation.

Table 2. Trouble Hounters Instructions

Phase	Question	Representation Scheme
1	Current Situation	Hieroglyph
2	Consequences	Caricature
3	Engineers wrong decisions	Saying
4	How the trouble could have been avoided?	Acrostic
5	Missing competences in systems engineers	Free representation
6	Case Logo	Drawing

Source: (Gómez-Álvarez et al., 2017)

The game rules are the following:

1. The participants conform teams (investigation commissions) of 3 to 5 members.
2. The teams have 20 minutes to analyze the information available on the case, which they previously consult and bring to the classroom.
3. Each team selects an initial phase and must answer the question with the assigned representation.
4. Teams rotate clockwise and have 3.5 minutes to complete the assigned activity in each phase.
5. Once the team or commission returns to the phase in which it started, it has 5 minutes to review the representations made and choose an exhibitor of the case.
6. Each team has 3 minutes to present their case to the other participants in the activity.

Figure 7 shows some application evidence of the trouble hunters game in SE undergraduate courses.

Figure 7. Trouble hunters classroom participants

In 2015, this game was applied in three different initial courses of Systems Engineering Programs with the following results:

1. Facilitator Performance: At least 75% of participants assess positively the facilitator performance. This is a key factor because a good introduction and presentation of the game goals depend largely on the performance and attitude of the students towards the activity.
2. Game Feedback: At least 90% of participants of each group assess the enjoyment level as Good, Very good, or Excellent. This assessment shows that this type of activity, with a playful and creative component, is a motivating factor for students and can derive in significant learning.

Car Design

This proposal is a pedagogic instrument for teaching software design under PSP (Personal Software Process) using an analogy between 'car design' and 'software design' and elaborating the structural models of a final product (Gómez-Álvarez *et al.*, 2016).

According to the PID (pedagogic instrument design) methodology (Gasca-Hurtado *et al.*, 2019) a pedagogic instrument, called Car Design PSP, for teaching software design under PSP was designed. This instrument uses a checklist to evaluate the product quality, corresponding to the PSP premise: "measure before improve". The learning goals of the game are as follows:

1. Identifying software bugs in early stages caused by software design models of poor quality.
2. Emphasizing the importance of software design in the software engineering process, and encouraging the implementation of good practices described in the PSP framework for software design.

The game rules are the following:

1. Participants conform teams of five persons where a participant assumes the role of car-inspector and the other four will be experts from the automotive sector.
2. It has four quadrants corresponding to categories to generate checklists for car design: design, technical specifications, safety, technology, and comfort.

3. The inspector tells the team when starting to fill the quadrant (distributed by experts) identifying items and assigning them a priority for generating checklists.
4. The inspector assesses the expert performance in the team, and it has a satisfactory performance and delivers puzzle pieces to assemble a car.
5. The winning team is the one that makes the most detailed specifications of each category of car design and assembles the puzzle in the shortest possible time.

The materials for the game are: 1) checklist for the var-inspector to register the mechanical, design, and technology elements for the car; 2) colored paper; 3) puzzle; 4) template of the 4+1 architectural view model (Manrique-Losada *et al.*, 2015), and 5) chronometer. The roles for Car Design PSP are 1) Car inspector who checks if the the 4+1 architectural view model is consistent with the car elements, 2) Expert who works in a team and assembles the puzzle, and 3) Facilitator who helps to teams in achieving the game objectives.

Car Design PSP was evaluated in a case study, applied to 20 people (professionals from a software company at Medellín-Colombia, and systems engineering students at the Universidad of Medellín). The results obtained from the survey support the conclusion that the didactic technique applied to the instrument is appropriate. In fact, 100% of participants say they would apply the concept of PSP in the area of SE, which they currently perform, showing that if other alternatives are sought to present the subjects, it is possible to obtain more receptivity of the public. In relation to the level of learning achieved by the participants, they recognize the importance of PSP (50%), to a lesser extent the importance of software design (10%), and the use and prioritization of checklists (10%). This means that at the level of competencies of the participants, was achieved to emphasize the importance of software design and the use of PSP framework in this phase of software development.

Videogames Proposals

The use of videogames to improve learning has been widely studied in different software engineering subjects (Baker *et al.*, 2003; Galvao & Neto, 2012; de Vasconcelos *et al.*, 2018; Calderón *et al.*, 2019; García *et al.*, 2020). As an example, Marin *et al.* (2019) describe the application of an adventure serious game for teaching Effort Estimation in SE. The serious game, Back to Penelope, has been carefully designed to take into account the developer's viewpoint as well as the player's viewpoint. With this game, the authors provide a new way to practice how to measure the function points using class diagrams.

Morover, De Bortoli (2018) describes ludic activities like the black box, game processing, and the SE marathon and their application. The preliminary results show that these games are viable and generate more receptiveness by students in the teaching process.

By following, the results obtained from games implementation in SE courses are associated with variables like enjoyment level, realism level, and student perception are presented.

Riskware

Riskware is a game to introduce risk management in software projects. Its main purpose is that participants recognize the importance of planning the risks to be mitigated in a software development project before starting its execution. The learning goals of Riskware are:

1. Recognizing the importance of software project risk planning before the project start-up (proactive management) to take early actions for mitigating risks.
2. Identifying risks, as well as mitigating resources and controls, linked to software development projects.
3. Recognizing two factors—occurrence probabilities and impact measurement—for mitigating software development project risks.

All teams have a token for moving around the game board (See Figure 8). The winner is the first team to reach the end of the board representing the finish of the software product by the team. The game rules are as follows:

1. All players take hexagonal pieces and fit them in any order on the board stage according to the color.
2. Players should move their token by following lines from corner to corner of a hexagonal piece. Two arrows are the signals of the starting point.
3. Tokens should be moved step-by-step, from one corner to the next one. The board boundaries cannot be included in the path defined by a player.
4. Only forward moves are allowed (from the "begin" signal to the "end" signal).
5. One player turns have two actions: 1) moving the token to the next corner and 2) throwing the die for defining the risk to be selected. Related to the risk, the corner has three hexagonal pieces numbered with the pairs (1,2), (3,4), and (5,6). The number matching the die reveals the candidate risk to be materialized.
6. At the beginning of the game, each player receives COP$200.000. This game currency can be invested in buying controls/resources—valid during the entire game period—to mitigate risks and avoid risk materialization.
7. Once the game rules are explained, in the next 15 minutes all players should define the path to follow in the board and the controls/resources they want to buy.
8. In order to mitigate risks, players need both a control and a resource. If a player has only one of them, the risk is not mitigated.
9. If a risk is materialized and the player has both the resource and the control for mitigating the risk, the player can continue the game. In other cases, the player receives the defined impact of the materialized risk.
10. Three kinds of impact are defined: high, medium, and low. High impact implies losing two turns and medium impact means losing one turn. A game situation with low impact has two choices: 1) the player can pay half of the money needed to buy the control and the resource; or 2) if the player lacks the money or does not want to pay the money, his/her turn is lost.
11. The end of the game is reached when the first player comes to the "end" signal.
12. At the end of the game, each team receives a payment related to the advance level he/she reaches. The risk and payment sheet has information belonging to each board stage.

This videogame is highly flexible, as it can be taken to other application domains such as construction projects or investment projects, just by changing the initial configuration of risks, project stages, and controls and resources. This shows the potential of the videogame to be used in different engineering subjects related to project management (Gómez-Álvarez et al., 2016).

Figure 8. Riskware board example

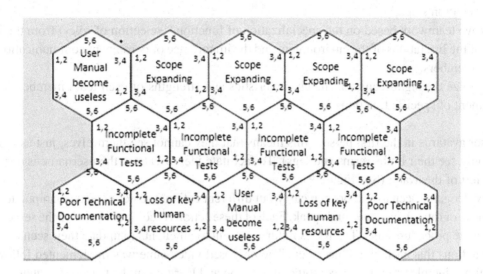

The Riskware videogame pilot generated the following results:

1. **Self – Assessment:** 95% and 85% of pilot participants consider having understood the game goals and rules, respectively.
2. **Enjoyment Level:** 90% of participants assess this level as Good, Very Good, and Excellent expressing that there was a permanent motivation of the participants for the subject.
3. **Realism Level:** 65% of participants affirm there is realism in the videogame. In this aspect, the possibility of making improvements in the video game functionalities is analyzed to consider other characteristics that help in the simulation of a work environment to manage software development project risks.
4. In the evaluation of the variable that measures the stimulation of creative thinking, a 90% valuation was obtained. Where it is evidenced that the participants consider that the video game manages to stimulate different thinking and awakens creativity to seek a winning strategy while performing associated activities.

TeamWork Videogame

TeamWork is a virtual reality-based videogame incorporating gamification principles for promoting and improving teamwork in engineering students (Gasca-Hurtado *et al.*, 2015). Taking advantage of the benefits of virtual reality as an alternative for student's motivation, this videogame with multiuser interaction leads to collaborative virtual environments that promote the development of social skills in teamwork, making decisions, and achieving intended goals. This videogame seeks to promote in participants the following learning goals:

1. Identify the importance of defining a plan for the development of a project.

2. Recognize the importance of collaboration, considering the need to establish agreements before the execution stage.
3. Improve teamwork based on the specialization of functions (selection of roles) from the recognition of the limitations of the environment and the importance of permanent communication among team members.
4. Recognize the significance of the characteristics and strengths of each team member for the assignment of specific functions.

The user avatar is in the first person, this means that they cannot see themselves, just as in real life, they can only see their limbs (arms and legs). To facilitate identification, the username is displayed in the upper left of the avatar (See Figure 9).

In the videogame scenario, users can carry out different actions: select objects, manipulate selected objects (move or rotate), navigate, and speak. Each of these actions is communicated to the server through a RPC (remote procedure call). The RPCs in turn are sent to all clients to update their scenario according to the actions that each client has taken. The proposed videogame was implemented following the gamification principles required to combine motivation and learning in the teaching strategy.

Figure 9. Avatar selection videogame interface. Source:(Gasca-Hurtado et al., 2015)

Particularly, this video game seeks to promote teamwork in engineering students, emphasizing the importance of identifying the strengths of each team member to contribute to the achievement of the proposed objectives (role specialization).

In general, the incorporation of educational videogames based on virtual-reality in the teaching-learning process facilitate the engagement and motivation of students to play an important role in improving learning outcomes. Therefore, the goal of many educational games is to enable learners to actively engage in games. In particular, the application of virtual reality technology can greatly improve the sense of presence and interaction that are deficient in educational games, stimulate learners' interest, and enhance their engagement. For all the above, educational games and virtual reality are a trend to innovate the SE teaching process and promote creativity in students (Gao *et al.*, 2018).

Support Approaches

Assessment Proposal of Didactic Strategies

The application of teaching and learning strategies requires an assessment approach for measuring the evolution of student learning and enhancing the educational activities conducted by teachers.

Manrique *et al.* (2015) present an assessment proposal of teaching and learning strategies in software process improvement. This approach is based on learning domains of the Bloom taxonomy (Anderson *et al.*, 2001), describing a three-domain structure or components (See Figure 10): 1) the cognitive and psychomotor domain, 2) the instrumental domain (directly oriented to the teaching proposal/method), and 3) the affective domain. Each component of the proposal is based on templates for guiding the questionnaire application. The questionnaires are data collection instruments for measuring students' perception regarding each strategy and the satisfaction in the learning experience. Such an assessment approach serves as a base model to ensure that training and assessment be planned to deliver all the necessary development for students, and a template by which the professor can assess the validity and coverage of any existing method.

Figure 10. Components of the Assessment proposal
Source:(Manrique-Losada et al., 2015)

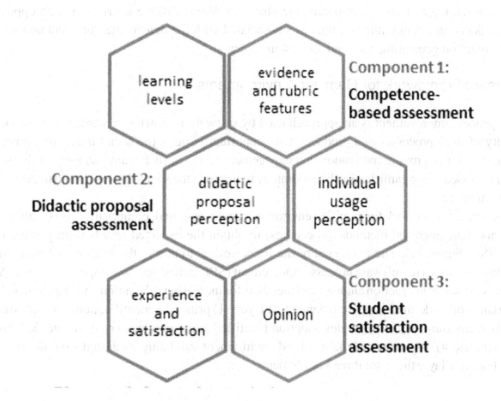

The component 1 (cognitive and psychomotor domain) comprises the following categories: knowledge, comprehension, application, analysis, synthesis, and evaluation, which are defined as learning levels of templates supporting the assessment. Besides, it is included in such a template the following features for complementing the assessment: 1) evidence features, specifying the abilities/skills related to each learning level, the application level of competence, and the learning level achieved; and 2) rubric features. Comprising the subject (specific topic being assessed) and the subject weight, defined by the instructor, representing a score/percentage, which quantitatively assesses the achievement of such competence.

The assessment method is a questionnaire and its goal is to measure student satisfaction regarding the didactic instrument. For applying the questionnaire, a previous pilot with the professors of this area was developed. The questionnaire method was applied using a no-probabilistic sample by means of snowball technique identifying the individuals (students) who can participate in the validation of the didactic instrument. A descriptive statistics to the data collected with the questionnaire is applied. The first analyzed variable is the *level of enjoyment* where 53% of participants gave a high score ("very good – 4"). The level of enjoyment is a feature related to the gamification goals, for this reason, identifying the level perceived by the students from the didactic instrument is relevant. Another analyzed variable is associated with the *level of the difficulty* of the instrument in comparison to game features. For this variable, the questionnaire results show a good level of difficulty related to instrument rules easily understood by the students.

Finally, the variable *closeness to the reality* of the instrument is analyzed. This variable is represented in the instrument for the distribution by phases as a simulation of the software development process. In accordance with the questionnaire results, 50% of the students argue that the level of closeness to reality is very good – (4), against 30% of students that assign a good level. This result is very important for our research because of the collection of quality metrics for defects management is an expensive and time–consuming activity. Additionally, the phase distribution of the instrument is an opportunity to show students, in a funny manner, the costs associated with the defects measurement and the early defects elimination generating a special interest in students.

Assessment Framework for Gamified Environments

Software process improvement is an approach used by software industries to increase the productivity and quality of their processes and products. One important issue is the social interaction among the team members for improving motivation and engagement levels in such team members. This situation could be addressed using gamification like a strategy to improve the social factors related to the software development process.

An assessment framework for gamified environments was proposed, comprising layers with the basic components (fundamentals, methods, procedures) to obtain the expected results from gamified environments (See Figure 11). The main goal of the framework is to ensure the proper implementation of gamification strategies in Software process improvement (SPI) initiatives. One important issue in SPI by industries is the social interaction among team members for increasing motivation and engagement levels.

The framework is defined as a pyramid with four layers: 1) principles identification that contextualizes the gamified environment; 2) principles adoption identified at the previous layer; 3) gamified environment design, and 4) assessment of the gamified environment validating its design from the principles adopted. For each layer there are three key elements:

Figure 11. Assessment framework for gamified environments
Source: (Gasca-Hurtado et al., 2018)

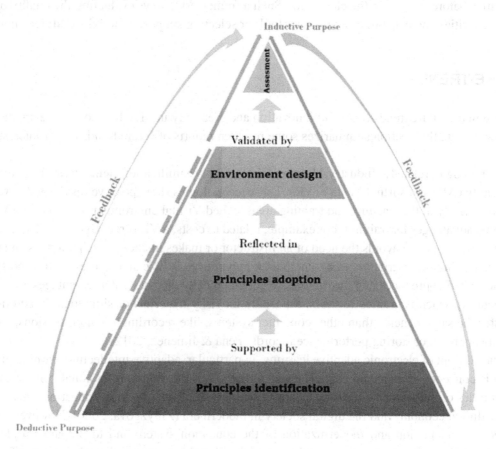

1. *Base component* includes the fundamental aspects for framework usage. Each layer has a basic starting point so that the framework user can establish the application basis of each layer.
2. *Procedural component* is equivalent to methods, procedures, and guidelines allowing obtain each layer goals and expected results.
3. *Results component* includes templates for indicating to framework user the structure of expected results in each layer. This component is a unique template that will be built layer by layer, as a result of following the instructions of the procedural component. Thus, in each results component, the template is improved regarding the previous layer.

This framework was applied to an environment called Video Scrum and allowed to verify the level of incorporation of gamification principles in such an environment (Gasca-Hurtado *et al.*, 2017).

Such a framework pretends to be the first guide to orientate from the contextualization of a gamification strategy for software process improvement initiatives to the assessment of the gamified environment. The assessment goal is verifying that the gamification principles are fulfilled in the gamification environment. For this reason, the proposed framework pretends to include several assessment strategies related to data analysis to measure the participants behavior.

By last, this assessment framework is an innovative instrument for evaluating gamified instruments or activities before using it in the classroom. Such a framework allows evaluating the quality of games or ludic activities and constitutes a professor tool for selecting support material for SE teaching.

FUTURE TRENDS

There are many future trends related to innovation and creativity in SE education, some are mentioned as follows. Then, this section summarizes some research reports of future trends of our interest.

- Technologies related to Industry 4.0 appropriate to apply gamification elements, such as Augmented Reality (AR) and Virtual Reality (VR). These technologies show positive results and novel initiatives mainly in the teaching and training areas, called Virtual environments (VEs). The VEs offer some advantages for training. For example, related to costs, a VE is reusable at a relative low cost. In some cases, VE avoids the need of an instructor or makes his/her participation less mandatory, thus leaving the instructors free to help their apprentices. VEs can also prevent transportation issues when apprentices and instructors are geographically distant. Other advantages are related to security, which is granted to users, especially for risky materials or situations. In addition, VEs offer the same benefits than other computer systems, like recording learning sessions, automatic data analysis, or storing performance records (Peña & Jiménez, 2012).
- The concept of electronic adaptive learning, in particular, adaptive intellectual learning platforms. This concept is considered as a center of formation of the value professional competencies and attitudes of the learner. Electronic adaptive learning is a novel trend in education since is part of the digital economy and the digital society in modern era (Zmyzgova, 2020). However, this trend requires adaptation and modernization of the education system and to prepare people for life and professional activity in the conditions of the digital society and digital economy (Prokofyev, 2017).
- Digital technologies that are important from the educational process implementation. They may include telecommunication technologies providing the creation of new generation communication networks; technologies of artificial intelligence and processing of large data (Big Data); AR and VR; cloud technologies; Internet of Things (IoT); blockchain technologies and others (Prokofyev et al., 2019).

Also, there are some future work lines related to the several results of the incorporation of new strategies or elements in SE education, in which we have been working.

- Launch a repository of open access instruments, called the digital bank of educational instruments. The goal is centralizing the educational instruments used by teachers, professors, or coaches to innovate in the classroom.
- Based on our assessment proposal, it is necessary to create assessment instruments based on competencies, improving their usability. An improvement proposal is the incorporation of technology, automating stages of the evaluation process.

Finally, we highlight others interesting future works lines such as:

- Technological platforms to support the teaching process. This line is related to digital transforming.
- Automatic generation of educational resources for different modalities and learning environments. This line is articulated of the eLearning research group.
- Competencies development for engineering teachers to achieve innovation in the classroom. This line is related to Industry 4.0.

CONCLUSION

Summarizing, promoting the innovation and creativity in the context of SE Education requires to develop, mainly: strategies, tools, and methodologies. Strategies, for organizing or planning the paths and actions to achieve the goals, with defined conditions and resources. Tools, for implementing the strategies based on automated, semi-automated and analog environments. In addition, methodologies for defining the whole framework to apply the tools and strategies designed in real educational contexts, based on aspects didactics and pedagogical. Further, it implies engagement of the professors and students, to develop and use the instruments to use in software engineering classes, and to evaluate the quality of these instruments, the learning achieved, and the level of motivation and creativity in the courses.

The application of teaching-learning strategies in SE requires methodologies, tools, and instruments to support the adequate usage in classroom, as well as transversal activities such as integration, application, training to professors and students, and assessment, among other. Further, the measurement and control of the evolution of student learning and enhancing the educational activities conducted by professors is an essential task.

REFERENCES

Ahmad, M., Rahim, L. A., & Arshad, N. I. (2015). An Analysis Of Educational Games Design Frameworks From Software Engineering Perspective. *Journal of Information and Communication Technology*, *14*, 123–151. doi:10.32890/jict2015.14.8

Alexandre, G. H. S., & Santos, S. C. (2018). Poster: PBL planner toolkit: A canvas-based tool for planning PBL in software engineering education. Proceedings - International Conference on Software Engineering, 153–154. 10.1145/3183440.3195060

Anderson, L., Krathwohl, D., & Bloom, B. (2001). *A taxonomy for learning, teaching, and assessing: A revision of Bloom's taxonomy of educational objectives* (1st ed.). Allyn & Bacon.

Baker, A., Navarro, E. O., & van der Hoek, A. (2003). An experimental card game for teaching software engineering. *Proceedings 16th Conference on Software Engineering Education and Training, 2003. (CSEE&T 2003)*, 216–223. 10.1109/CSEE.2003.1191379

Balaban, M., & Sturm, A. (2018). Software engineering lab- A n essential component of a software engineering curriculum. Proceedings - International Conference on Software Engineering, 21–30. 10.1145/3183377.3183395

Bobkowska, A. E. (2019). Exploration of creativity techniques in software engineering in training-application-feedback cycle. *Lecture Notes in Business Information Processing, 366,* 99–118. doi:10.1007/978-3-030-35646-0_8

Bosch, J. (2017). *Speed, Data, and Ecosystems: Excelling in a Software-Driven World.* CRC Press. doi:10.1201/9781315270685

Bourque, P., & Fairley, R. E. (2014). Guide to the Software Engineering Body of Knowledge (SWEBOK(R)): Version 3.0. IEEE Computer Society Press.

Buffardi, K. (2018). Tech startup learning activities: A formative evaluation. Proceedings - International Conference on Software Engineering, 24–31. doi:10.1145/3194779.3194781

Calderón, A., Trinidad, M., Ruiz, M., & O'Connor, R. V. (2019). An Experience of Use a Serious Game for Teaching Software Process Improvement. *Communications in Computer and Information Science, 1060,* 249–259. doi:10.1007/978-3-030-28005-5_19

Casallas, R., Davila, J. I., & Quiroga, J. P. (2002). Enseñanza de la ingeniería de software por procesos instrumentados. *Universidad de los. Andes.*

Conboy, K., Wang, X., & Fitzgerald, B. (2009). Creativity in agile systems development: A literature review. *IFIP Advances in Information and Communication Technology, 301,* 122–134. doi:10.1007/978-3-642-02388-0_9

Crawford, B., León de la Barra, C., Soto, R., & Monfroy, E. (2012). Agile software teams must be creatives. *Proceedings of 5th International Workshop on Co-operative and Human Aspects of Software Engineering, 1,* 20–26.

Dawson, R. (2000). Twenty dirty tricks to train software engineers. *Proceedings of the 22nd International Conference on Software Engineering,* 209–218. 10.1145/337180.337204

De Bortoli, L. Â. (2018). Non-conventional dynamics in a Software Engineering Course: practical and ludic activities. In *Proceedings of the XXXII Brazilian Symposium on Software Engineering* (pp. 328-337). 10.1145/3266237.3266257

de Vasconcelos, L. E. G., Oliveira, L. B., Guimarães, G., & Ayres, F. (2018). Gamification Applied in the Teaching of Agile Scrum Methodology. *Advances in Intelligent Systems and Computing, 738,* 207–212. doi:10.1007/978-3-319-77028-4_30

Devadiga, N. M. (2017). Software Engineering Education: Converging with the Startup Industry. Proceedings - 30th IEEE Conference on Software Engineering Education and Training, 192–196. 10.1109/CSEET.2017.38

Diniz, G. C., Silva, M. A. G., Gerosa, M. A., & Steinmacher, I. (2017). Using gamification to orient and motivate students to contribute to oss projects. *Proceedings - 2017 IEEE/ACM 10th International Workshop on Cooperative and Human Aspects of Software Engineering,* 36–42. 10.1109/CHASE.2017.7

Dorodchi, M., Al-Hossami, E., & Nagahisarchoghaei, M. (2019). Teaching an Undergraduate Software Engineering Course using Active Learning and Open Source Projects. Proceedings - Frontiers in Education Conference. 10.1109/FIE43999.2019.9028517

Durango, C., Zapata, C. M., & Zapata, C. M. (2018). Representación en el núcleo de la esencia de Semat de las Competencias de un Equipo de Desarrollo de Software. *Revista Entramado*.

Galvao, T., Neto, F., Bonates, M. F., & Campos, M. T. (2012). A serious game for supporting training in risk management through project-based learning. *Communications in Computer and Information Science, 248*, 52–61. doi:10.1007/978-3-642-31800-9_6

Gao, N., Xie, T., & Liu, G. (2018). A learning engagement model of educational games based on virtual reality. In *2018 International Joint Conference on Information, Media and Engineering (ICIME)* (pp. 1-5). IEEE. 10.1109/ICIME.2018.00010

García, I., Pacheco, C., León, A., & Calvo-Manzano, J. A. (2020). A serious game for teaching the fundamentals of ISO/IEC/IEEE 29148 systems and software engineering – Lifecycle processes – Requirements engineering at undergraduate level. *Computer Standards & Interfaces, 67*, 103377. doi:10.1016/j.csi.2019.103377

Garg, K., & Varma, V. (2008). People issues relating to software engineering education and training in India. *Proceedings of the 2008 1st India Software Engineering Conference*, 121–127. 10.1145/1342211.1342235

Gasca-Hurtado, G. P., Gómez-Álvarez, M. C., & Manrique-Losada, B. (2019). Using gamification in software engineering teaching: Study case for software design. *Advances in Intelligent Systems and Computing, 932*, 244–255. doi:10.1007/978-3-030-16187-3_24

Gasca-Hurtado, G. P., Gómez-Alvarez, M. C., Muñoz, M., & Mejía, J. (2016). Gamification proposal for defect tracking in software development process. In *European Conference on Software Process Improvement* (pp. 212-224). Springer. 10.1007/978-3-319-44817-6_17

Gasca-Hurtado, G. P., Gómez-Alvarez, M. C., Muñoz, M., & Mejía, J. (2017). Toward an assessment framework for gamified environments. *Communications in Computer and Information Science, 748*, 281–293. doi:10.1007/978-3-319-64218-5_23

Gasca-Hurtado, G. P., Gómez-Alvarez, M. C., Muñoz, M., & Mejía, J. (2018). Assessment Framework for Gamified Environments: A Gamification Assessment Model for Implementing the Framework. *Communications in Computer and Information Science, 896*, 240–253. doi:10.1007/978-3-319-97925-0_20

Gasca-Hurtado, G. P., Gómez-Álvarez, M. C., & Zepeda, V. V. (2018). Gamification experience of an educational environment in software engeening: Gamifying a course of agility for software process improvement. *Iberian Conference on Information Systems and Technologies*, 1–6. 10.23919/CISTI.2018.8399233

Gasca-Hurtado, G. P., Peña, A., Gómez-Álvarez, M. C., Plascencia-Osuna, Ó. A., & Calvo-Manzano, J. A. (2015). Realidad virtual como buena práctica para trabajo en equipo con estudiantes de ingeniería. RISTI - Revista Iberica de Sistemas e Tecnologias de Informacao, 16, 76–91. doi:10.17013/risti.16.76-91

Gómez-Álvarez, M. C., Gasca-Hurtado, G. P., & Garcia, C. (2016). Juegos serios como estrategia de enseñanza del proceso de gestión de riesgos de software: Prototipo de un videojuego. In 2016 IEEE 11th Colombian Computing Conference, CCC 2016 - Conference Proceedings. 10.1109/ColumbianCC.2016.7750804

Gómez-Álvarez, M. C., Gasca-Hurtado, G. P., Manrique-Losada, B., & Arias, D. M. (2016). Método de diseño de instrumentos pedagógicos para ingeniería de software. *Iberian Conference on Information Systems and Technologies*. 10.1109/CISTI.2016.7521377

Gómez-Álvarez, M. C., Sanchez-Dams, R., & Baron-Salazar, A. (2017). Trouble hunters: A game for introductory subjects to computer engineering. *Proceedings of the 2016 42nd Latin American Computing Conference*. 10.1109/CLEI.2016.7833398

Gómez-Álvarez, M.C., Zapata, C.M. & Astudillo, H. (2019). *SETMAT (Software Engineering Teaching Method and Theory): una teoría para la enseñanza de Ingeniería de Software*. Academic Press.

Groth, D. P., & Robertson, E. L. (2001). It's all about process: Project-oriented teaching of software engineering. *Software Engineering Education Conference, Proceedings*, 7–17. 10.1109/CSEE.2001.913814

Guerrero Armas, A. (2009). La importancia de la creatividad en el aula. Temas para la educación, 1(5), 1-7.

Gunkel, D. J. (2017). Rage against the machine: Rethinking education in the face of technological unemployment. In Surviving the Machine Age: Intelligent Technology and the Transformation of Human Work (pp. 147–162). Springer International Publishing. doi:10.1007/978-3-319-51165-8_10

Hernandez-de-Menendez, M., & Morales-Menendez, R. (2019). Technological innovations and practices in engineering education: A review. *International Journal on Interactive Design and Manufacturing*, *13*(2), 713–728. doi:10.100712008-019-00550-1

Hof, S., Kropp, M., & Landolt, M. (2017). Use of Gamification to Teach Agile Values and Collaboration: A multi-week Scrum simulation project in an undergraduate software engineering course. In *Proceedings of the 2017 ACM Conference on Innovation and Technology in Computer Science Education* (pp. 323-328). 10.1145/3059009.3059043

Hollis, B., & Maiden, N. (2013). Extending agile processes with creativity techniques. *IEEE Software*, *30*(5), 78–84. doi:10.1109/MS.2012.171

Juliantari, N. K., Sudarsana, I. K., Sutriyanti, N. K., Astawa, I. N. T., Putri, I. D. A. H., & Saddhono, K. (2018). Educational games based in information technology as innovation evaluation activity in learning. *Journal of Physics: Conference Series*, *1114*(1), 012041. doi:10.1088/1742-6596/1114/1/012041

Kurkovsky, S., Ludi, S., & Clark, L. (2019). Active learning with LEGO for software requirements. *Proceedings of the 50th ACM Technical Symposium on Computer Science Education*, 218–224. 10.1145/3287324.3287444

Laskowski, M. (2015). Implementing gamification techniques into university study path - A case study. *IEEE Global Engineering Education Conference*, 582–586. 10.1109/EDUCON.2015.7096028

Lemos, J., Alves, C., Duboc, L., & Rodrigues, G. N. (2012). A systematic mapping study on creativity in requirements engineering. *Proceedings of the ACM Symposium on Applied Computing*, 1083–1088. 10.1145/2245276.2231945

Lin, Y. T. (2019). Impacts of a flipped classroom with a smart learning diagnosis system on students' learning performance, perception, and problem solving ability in a software engineering course. *Computers in Human Behavior*, *95*, 187–196. doi:10.1016/j.chb.2018.11.036

López Carrillo, D., Calonge García, A., Rodríguez Laguna, T., Ros Magán, G., & Lebrón Moreno, J. A. (2019). Using Gamification in a Teaching Innovation Project at the University of Alcalá: A New Approach to Experimental Science Practices. *Electronic Journal of e-Learning*, *17*(2), 93-106.

López Díaz, R. A. (2017) ¿La creatividad: un lugar olvidado en la educación? In Estrategias de enseñanza creativa: investigaciones sobre la creatividad en el aula. Academic Press.

Mahmoudi, H., Pashavi, G., Koushafar, M., & Saribagloo, J. A. (2015). The Effect of Computer Games on Speed, Attention and Consistency of Learning Mathematics among Students. *Procedia: Social and Behavioral Sciences*, *176*, 419–424. doi:10.1016/j.sbspro.2015.01.491

Manrique-Losada, B., Gasca-Hurtado, G. P., & Gómez-Álvarez, M. C. (2015). Assessment proposal of teaching and learning strategies in software process improvement. *Revista de la Facultad de Ingeniería*, *77*, 105–114.

Manrique-Losada, B., González-Calderon, G., & Gasca-Hurtado, G. P. (2011). *A Proposal For Software Engineering Education Based On A Joint Project. Software Engineering: Methods. Modeling, And Teaching.*

Marín, B., Vera, M., & Giachetti, G. (2019). *An Adventure Serious Game for Teaching Effort Estimation in Software Engineering.* IWSM-Mensura.

Marina, J. (1994). *Teoría de la inteligencia creadora.* Anagrama.

Matturro, G., & Raschetti, F. (n.d.). *A Systematic Mapping Study on Soft Skills in Software Engineering.* Jucs.Org. Retrieved June 15, 2020, from http://www.jucs.org/jucs_25_1/a_systematic_mapping_study/jucs_25_01_0016_0041_matturo.pdf

Means, A. J. (2018). Learning to save the future: Rethinking education and work in an era of digital capitalism. In *Learning to save the Future: Rethinking Education and Work in an Era of Digital Capitalism.* Taylor and Francis. doi:10.4324/9781315450209

Mivehchi, L., & Rajabion, L. (2020). A framework for evaluating the impact of mobile games, technological innovation and collaborative learning on students' motivation. *Human Systems Management*, *39*(1), 27–36. doi:10.3233/HSM-190543

Moreno-Guerrero, A. J., Rodríguez-Jiménez, C., Gómez-García, G., & Ramos Navas-Parejo, M. (2020). Educational Innovation in Higher Education: Use of Role Playing and Educational Video in Future Teachers' Training. *Sustainability*, *12*(6), 2558. doi:10.3390u12062558

Nascimento, D. M. C., Chavez, C. F. G., & Bittencourt, R. A. (2019). The Adoption of Open Source Projects in Engineering Education: A Real Software Development Experience. Proceedings - Frontiers in Education Conference. 10.1109/FIE.2018.8658908

OMG. (2015). *Kernel and Language for Software Engineering Methods (Essence)-Version 1.1.* Object Management Group.

Palacin-Silva, M., Khakurel, J., Happonen, A., Hynninen, T., & Porras, J. (2017). Infusing Design Thinking into a Software Engineering Capstone Course. *Proceedings - 30th IEEE Conference on Software Engineering Education and Training*, 212–221. 10.1109/CSEET.2017.41

Paravizo, E., Chaim, O. C., Braatz, D., Muschard, B., & Rozenfeld, H. (2018). Exploring gamification to support manufacturing education on industry 4.0 as an enabler for innovation and sustainability. *Procedia Manufacturing, 21*, 438–445. doi:10.1016/j.promfg.2018.02.142

Patrício, R., Moreira, A. C., & Zurlo, F. (2018). Gamification approaches to the early stage of innovation. *Creativity and Innovation Management, 27*(4), 499–511. doi:10.1111/caim.12284

Portela, C., Vasconcelos, A., Oliveira, S., & Souza, M. (2017). The Use of Industry Training Strategies in a Software Engineering Course: An Experience Report. Proceedings - 30th IEEE Conference on Software Engineering Education and Training, 29–36. 10.1109/CSEET.2017.16

Prokofyev, K. G., Dmitrieva, O. V., Zmyzgova, T. R., & Polyakova, E. N. (2019). Modern Engineering Education as a Key Element of Russian Technological Modernization in the Context of Digital Economy. doi:10.2991/iscfec-18.2019.160

Prokofyev, K. G., Polyakova, E. N., Dmitrieva, O. V., & Zmyzgova, T. R. (2017). Digital economy of the Russian Federation as a directing factor for the development of professional personnel in the IT sphere. *Proceedings of the Regional scientific-practical conference The Concept of Development of the Productive Forces of the Kurgan Region*, 90-96.

Puerta, L. N. Z., & Alvarez, M. C. G. (2018). A methodological proposal to learn to program through the development of video games. *Iberian Conference on Information Systems and Technologies*, 1–6. 10.23919/CISTI.2018.8399326

Qian, M., & Clark, K. R. (2016). Game-based Learning and 21st century skills: A review of recent research. *Computers in Human Behavior, 63*, 50–58. doi:10.1016/j.chb.2016.05.023

Ribes, M.D. (2011). *El juego inf. y su metodología*. Eduforma, Ediciones.

Rivas & Revelo. (2017). *El proyecto integrador como proceso investigativo en el aula: Proyecto de Investigación. Fundación Academia de Dibujo Profesional*. Available: http://fido.palermo.edu/servicios_dyc/encuentro2007/02_auspicios_publicaciones/actas_diseno/articulos_pdf/A6029.pdf

Runeson, P. (2001). Experiences from teaching PSP for freshmen. *Software Engineering Education Conference Proceedings*, 98–107. 10.1109/csee.2001.913826

Shackelford, R., Lunt, B., McGettrick, A., Sloan, R., Topi, H., Davies, G., . . . Lunt, B. (2006). Computing Curricula 2005: The Overview Report. Proceedings of the 37th SIGCSE Technical Symposium on Computer Science Education - SIGCSE '06, 38(1), 456. 10.1145/1121341.1121482

Simpson, R., & Storer, T. (2017). Experimenting with Realism in Software Engineering Team Projects: An Experience Report. Proceedings - 30th IEEE Conference on Software Engineering Education and Training, 87–96. 10.1109/CSEET.2017.23

Singer, L., & Schneider, K. (2012). It was a bit of a race: Gamification of version control. In *2012 Second International Workshop on Games and Software Engineering: Realizing User Engagement with Game Engineering Techniques*, 5–8. 10.1109/GAS.2012.6225927

Slomanson, W. R. (2014). Blended Learning: A Flipped Classroom Experiment. *Journal of Legal Education, 64*, 93–102. doi:10.2307/24716075

Smart, K. L., & Csapo, N. (2007). Learning by doing: Engaging students through learner-centered activities. *Business Communication Quarterly*, *70*(4), 451–457. doi:10.1177/10805699070700040302

Sternberg, R. (1997). *Inteligencia exitosa*. Paidós.

Su, C. H. (2016). The effects of students' motivation, cognitive load and learning anxiety in gamification software engineering education: A structural equation modeling study. *Multimedia Tools and Applications*, *75*(16), 10013–10036. doi:10.100711042-015-2799-7

Taran, G. (2007). Using games in software engineering education to teach risk management. *Software Engineering Education Conference Proceedings*, 211–218. 10.1109/CSEET.2007.54

Towey, D., Chen, T. Y., Kuo, F. C., Liu, H., & Zhou, Z. Q. (2017). Metamorphic testing: A new student engagement approach for a new software testing paradigm. *Proceedings of 2016 IEEE International Conference on Teaching, Assessment and Learning for Engineering*, 218–225. 10.1109/TALE.2016.7851797

Towey, D., & Ng, Y.-k., R., & Wang, T. (2016). Open Educational Resources (OERs) and Technology Enhanced Learning (TEL) in Vocational and Professional Education and Training (VPET). *Proceedings of the IEEE International Conference on Teaching, Assessment, and Learning for Engineering*, 301–305. 10.1109/TALE.2016.7851808

Towey, D., & Walker, J. (2018). Traditional Higher Education Engineering versus Vocational and Professional Education and Training: What can we Learn from Each Other? *International Conference on Open and Innovative Education (ICOIE 2018)*.

Xie, S. X. (2018). *Smart classroom and university classroom teaching innovation. DEStech Transactions on Computer Science and Engineering*. IECE.

Zapata, C. M. (2007). *Requirements game: teaching software project management*. Academia.Edu. Retrieved February 18, 2020, from https://www.academia.edu/download/32419252/v10i1p3.pdf

Zapata, C. M., & Duarte, M. I. (2008). Consistency game: a didactic strategy for software engineering. *Revista Universidad de Zulia*, *31*(1). http://tjfeonline.com/admin/archive/117.09.20141410966981.pdf

Zhu, R., Hardy, D., & Myers, T. (2019). Co-designing with adolescents with autism spectrum disorder: From ideation to implementation. In *Proceedings of the 31st Australian Conference on Human-Computer-Interaction* (pp. 106-116). 10.1145/3369457.3370914

Zmyzgova, T. R., Polyakova, E. N., & Karpov, E. K. (2020). Digital Transformation of Education and Artificial Intelligence. In *2nd International Scientific and Practical Conference "Modern Management Trends and the Digital Economy: from Regional Development to Global Economic Growth" (MTDE 2020)* (pp. 824-829). Atlantis Press.

Chapter 8
Lessons Learned About Gamification in Software Engineering Education

Beatriz Marín

https://orcid.org/0000-0001-8025-0023

Universidad Diego Portales, Chile & Universidad Politécnica de Valencia, Spain

ABSTRACT

Software engineering courses traditionally mix theoretical aspects with practical ones that are later used in the development of projects. Teaching software engineering courses is not easy because in many cases the students lack motivation to exercise the topics prior to project development. This chapter presents the application of gamification on some topics of a software engineering course to engage students and increase their motivation. The authors argue that with the proper motivation, the students can better exercise the topics and obtain stronger knowledge. The authors have created five games to help in the learning process of the software engineering course. The games are related to risk management, BPMN modeling, Scrum process, design and inspection of class diagrams, and COSMIC functional size measurement. Gamification has been applied during four years in the software engineering course, resulting in an improved learning experience for the students. Finally, lessons learned are presented and discussed.

INTRODUCTION

Nowadays students have many distractions and it is difficult to capture their attention for long periods by using traditional teaching methods, such as a lecturer in front of the class using a blackboard to present the contents (Kirkwood & Price, 2005). Different elements to engage students with the contents and motivate their learning process are needed.

Software engineering courses at university level traditionally focus on theoretical and practical contents that the students put in practice in small projects and later apply in capstone projects (Schefer-Wenzl & Miladinovic, 2018). Teaching software engineering courses is not an easy task, since the students must learn complex concepts related to software development, concepts related to project management, as

DOI: 10.4018/978-1-7998-7552-9.ch008

Copyright © 2021, IGI Global. Copying or distributing in print or electronic forms without written permission of IGI Global is prohibited.

well as soft skills such as leadership, teamwork, and negotiation, among others (Marques et al., 2018). Despite the importance of the software engineering contents, in many cases the students lack motivation to exercise these contents prior to the development of the capstone project.

Gamification has been defined as the use of game elements such as badges or leaderboards to increase the motivation or engagement of students with regard to certain topics (Deterding et al., 2011) (Dicheva et al., 2015). Serious games are defined as games created for teaching/learning serious topics through a gamified learning experience (Fitz-Walter et al., 2011) (Landers, 2014). Considering the advantages demonstrated by the use of gamification and serious games in computer science education (Vargas-Enríquez et al., 2015) (Reis da Silva et al., 2015) (B. Marín et al., 2019), we argue that gamification and serious games are a good alternative to increase the motivation and engagement of software engineering students.

Much research has been conducted on the use of gamification on software engineering education, which mainly provides experiences about gamification or serious games for isolated topics of software engineering. The purpose of this chapter is to present the application of gamification to different topics of a software engineering course. The researchers of this chapter have designed, developed, and applied five serious games for five different topics of software engineering in order to foster the students' motivation at a software engineering course. These games are the following ones:

1. The *RISE* game, related to the identification and management of risks in software projects.
2. The *Scrumption* game, focused on the management of a project following the Scrum process for software development.
3. The *BPMN* game, related to the correction of BPMN diagrams, in which the student must decide what kind of conceptual construct better represents a specific business scenario.
4. The *Classutopia* game, focused on the design of class diagrams and defect detection on the diagrams.
5. Finally, the *BTP* game, related to functional size measurement and effort estimation by using the COSMIC measurement method.

Among these five games, the *RISE* game is the only one that must be played in teams; the remaining four games are played individually. The authors have applied these games in a software engineering course during four years, obtaining as a result that the use of gamification improves the learning process through a better engagement of students with the contents to be learned. Motivation for learning these and other topics of the software engineering course has also been increased. However, the authors also found some drawbacks in the use of gamification in software engineering courses, e.g. when it is used as the only means to teach, without lectures.

This chapter aims to demonstrate the feasibility of the use of gamification in software engineering as well as to provide lessons learned. Therefore, the contribution of this chapter is twofold: 1) it presents the design, development, and application of gamification and serious games for specific software engineering topics, and; 2) it presents lessons learned about the application of gamification and serious games in software engineering, including the limitations or drawbacks identified. These contributions can be useful for researchers, lecturers, and practitioners.

The rest of the chapter is organized as follows. The background section reviews prior work. Next, the gamification and serious games developed are presented, and the results of their application are presented. Lessons learned and future research directions are then discussed. Finally, our main conclusions are presented.

BACKGROUND

Many publications have studied the use of gamification in software engineering education, as evidenced in the literature reviews published on this topic.

(Pedreira et al., 2015) present a systematic mapping that comprises 29 studies about gamification in software engineering. These studies apply gamification mainly to software development, and a few studies gamified the requirements phase, the verification and validation phase, and project management (planning, assessment and control, etc.). The main gamification elements used were point-based reward system, badges, and social reputation.

(Alhammad & Moreno, 2018) state that most gamification efforts in software engineering are related to improving the engagement and in a lesser extent to improving the theoretical knowledge. This review comprises 21 primary studies. The results of the review indicate that most of the studies focus on software construction (programming) and that the most frequently used gamification elements are points and leaderboards.

(Muñoz et al., 2017) identify the use of gamified elements in software development teams. They review 31 primary studies, in which they identify eleven gamification elements. The leaderboard was identified as the most commonly applied element, and the second one was the points system. The authors observe that these elements improve student's participation.

(de A. Souza et al., 2018) conducted a systematic mapping to identify the gaps and future research of gamification in software engineering. In this work, 156 studies about gamification were selected from 1974 to 2016. The majority of these studies (59%) focus on the software process. The areas of software quality and of software modeling and analysis were the least considered (6.4% each). The gamification elements mainly used were leaderboards and points. The authors observe that gamification in software engineering education is a promising area for further research, especially for those knowledge areas less supported.

(Schefer-Wenzl & Miladinovic, 2018) apply the challenge concept (or rewarding mechanism) in a software engineering course in which students are part of teams that create the requirements specification and the high-level design of a same project description. Later, the different teams compete each other by sharing the specifications defined. If a group finds a problem in the specifications of another group, they win a point; if not, the group that shares the specification wins the point. Nevertheless, the authors did not find evidence of the evaluation of the approach or the perception of the students on the approach.

In the work presented by (Gasca-Hurtado et al., 2019), gamification was used to create a pedagogic instrument for teaching software design. To this end, the students worked in teams in the design of a car, in which they recognized the importance of the Personal Software Process framework. This strategy was piloted with 20 students, and the results indicate that the enjoyment level and creative thinking was considered good or very good by the majority of students. However, the closeness to reality was not rated as good or very good by the majority of the students.

A game focused on effort estimation is presented by (Calderón et al., 2017). The authors propose a simulation game called *Prodec* based on Albretch function points. This game deals with activities that cover the processes defined in ISO 25100.

There are some approaches that apply gamification to testing techniques, such as the *Bug Hunter* gamified platform (Jesus et al., 2019). Using this platform students can be rewarded by their achievements related to testing concepts and participation on tutorials, among others. It has a leaderboard and a forum that can be used by students to socialize. The authors conducted an experiment to evaluate the platform in comparison to traditional testing classes. Regarding the motivation, the students that used the gamified platform obtained higher values in interest, enjoyment, and perceived choice. The students that did not use the gamified platform perceived more pressure during the experiment and they felt more competent than the students using the gamified platform. Regarding the performance, the students that did not use the gamified platform obtained better marks.

Code Defenders (Rojas et al., 2017) is a game used to teach mutation testing and unit testing. The authors run an experiment and concluded that the participants that used the gamified platform wrote stronger test cases than the participants that did not. In addition, the participants enjoyed more writing test cases when they played Code Defenders.

There are some approaches that apply gamification to Scrum, such as the *PIG* game (Maxim et al., 2016), which simulates that the student is a Scrum master. This game provides an external tutorial to learn how to play, but the work does not present the results of the evaluation with students. *SCRUMI* is a virtual board game with questions about Scrum that students must answer (De Souza et al., 2017). *SimScrumF* is a Scrum simulator that promotes the students' engagement in the learning of agile concepts (Begosso et al., 2019). This game simulates different situations of the Scrum process. Depending on client satisfaction, the students earn more or less points.

The application of formal methods can provide benefits in software development. In (Prasetya et al., 2019), the FormalZ game is presented, which focuses on pre- and post-conditions of software. The main idea of FormalZ is to improve the engagement of students with formal specifications topics that often are experienced as dry topics. To evaluate FormalZ, an experiment with 30 subjects was run. The results indicate that most of the subjects perceived the approach as positive, but there is no evidence to confirm the improvement in engagement and learning.

Software engineering education was recognized as challenging by (Vos et al., 2019) because the subject is not considered exciting by students and teachers must deal with an increasing number of students. To tackle these limitations, the authors advocate the improvement of in-class engagement through the application of gamified quizzes, the improvement of out-class engagement through the use of the FormalZ game, and the improvement of the engagement specifically for software testing by using Code Defenders. They develop storytelling components for FormalZ and Code Defenders to improve the learning experience. The authors do not provide details of the application of the proposal.

In the majority of the cases reported, gamification in software engineering has been useful to improve motivation, content comprehension, and retention of students (Fernandes & Correa, 2017). Nevertheless there are also some studies that evidence that gamification has not been useful for software engineering courses (Berkling & Thomas, 2013). Students remarked that not all of them enjoyed the games and that they viewed the gamified platform as a barrier to access the contents that they needed to study for the exams.

In summary, there are several pieces of work that have applied gamification and serious games to software engineering courses. The authors specially review the pieces of work related to less investigated knowledge areas. The authors identify that prior work most often presents gamified experiences for only one topic of software engineering courses. In contrast, the authors use gamification for different topics of a software engineering course during four years. In this chapter the authors try to clarify if it is worth using gamification to improve the learning experience of different topics of software engineering courses, and to present some relevant lessons learned.

GAMIFICATION IN SOFTWARE ENGINEERING COURSES

In order to foster the students' motivation at software engineering courses, the authors have designed, developed, and applied gamification to different topics of software engineering. The authors focus on areas that have received little attention in related work, namely software quality and software modeling.

The authors provide below details of five serious games that were created for different topics. The RISE game, the Scrumption game, and the BTP game deal with different topics of software quality; risks management, scrum process, and functional size measurement, respectively. The BPMN and Classutopia games deal with different topics of software modeling; business process modeling and class diagram modeling, respectively.

The RISE Game

The *RISE* game was created to support the identification of five main risks that commonly occur in the development of a software project.

The *RISE* game has two main phases: first the creation of teams and the management of a project by using a mobile application, and second the construction of a product by using Legos.

In the first phase, the mobile application is used by the lecturer to indicate the amount of money assigned to each project, define the main requirements for the product, and assign a role to each student (project leader, analyst, designer, constructor, or quality assurance). The lecturer can see statistics of the teams (Figure 1).

Later, the mobile application is used by the teams, which can manage the project and accomplish the challenges proposed by the game in order to understand the main risks in software development. Initially, the project leaders must hire different roles to develop the project, whose goal is to construct a bridge with Legos taking into account the requirements and using efficiently the resources assigned. The hiring process occurs face to face in the classroom. For each student hired in the project, the total amount of money in the project is diminished according to a cost. When the project leaders complete their teams, they can start working on bridge construction. The first phase of the RISE game ends when all the teams are completed and ready to start the challenges to construct the bridge.

In the second phase of the RISE game, the bridge is constructed with Legos. Even though the traditional software development cycle comprises requirements specification, analysis, design, construction, testing, deployment, and maintainability, because of time restrictions the researchers group these phases: definition and analysis of software, with Risk1 - poor requirements specification; design and construction, with Risk2 - change of platform, Risk3 - expansion of the scope of the project, and Risk4 - losing a key member of the team; and testing, deployment, and maintainability of the software, with Risk5 - incomplete functional testing. In these phases the teams need to accomplish the challenges presented in the mobile application.

At the definition and analysis phase, the players see a brief introduction of the game and a set of requirements defined by the lecturer. Some requirements are valid and some are incomplete. For instance, Figure 2 – A shows the following requirements for the bridge: "the bridge must have 10cm of length", "the bridge must have 10 of height", "the bridge must cross two tables", "the bridge must support one car", and "the bridge must have 3 of width". Students must identify the incomplete requirements and ask the lecturer for a correction. When all the requirements are validated, they can pass to the next phase.

Figure 1. Screenshots of the mobile application used by the lecturer to define the money of a project and assign roles (A), to define the requirements and test cases for the product (B), and to see final statistics of the teams (C)

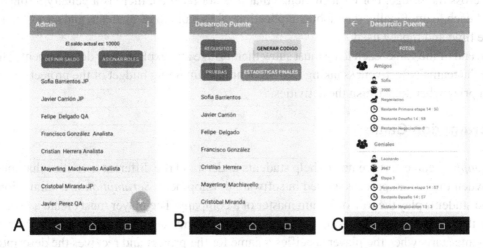

When the students are at the design and construction phase, the mobile application shows a message that requires the teams to change the bridge with another team randomly selected. The mobile application also presents a change in the requirements (see Figure 2 – B). Later, the constructor is fired from all the teams, so that the project leader needs to start negotiating and to hire another constructor (see Figure 2 – C).

Figure 2. Screenshots of the mobile application used by the teams to validate requirements (A), to change the platform and to change a requirement (B), and to hire a new constructor (C)

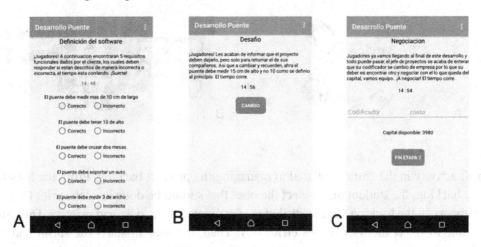

When the teams have changed the bridges and hired a new constructor, they go to the final part related to testing, deployment, and maintainability. Here the students must test the bridge in relation to the requirements. The mobile application presents the test cases defined by the lecturer. The teams must indicate whether the bridges pass the test cases or not; for instance, if a car can cross the bridge or if two cars can cross the bridge. For each challenge that it is not reached, there is a penalty in the amount of money of each team. Finally, the mobile application takes a photo of the team and saves their statistics about the time and money used.

At the end of the game, each team must show their bridge and explain their development. The authors compare the teams' effectiveness taking into account the remaining budget of the project. All the teams receive a prize when they finish the activities.

The Scrumption Game

The *Scrumption* game was created to help students understand the different activities that must be performed when the Scrum process is used in software development. *Scrumption* is a simulation game in which the students play the role of Scrum master of a company. The player must create a team and work fulfilling the Scrum process by using the corresponding events and artefacts defined by Scrum.

The game starts when the player specifies a name for the project and receives the description of the case. The performance of the player will be evaluated taking into account budget, time, and quality. The student, playing the role of Scrum master, must configure the time needed for the sprints and the deadline to deliver the final product (Figure 3 – A). After that, the student must select the members of the Scrum team (Figure 3 – B). The product owner is defined by the game. The student must select four to eight members in order to fulfill the recommended practice of having Scrum teams with six to ten members (remember that the Scrum master and the product owner are also members of the team).

Figure 3. Screenshots of the Scrumption game used by the students to configure the time of the project and the sprints (A) and to select the team (B)

The next activity in the game is related to managing the product backlog. From the list of tasks defined in the backlog, the student must select the ones that should be done in each sprint (Figure 4 – A). Each user history in the backlog has the attributes of estimated time, risk, and priority. Thus, the student should be able to select the user stories efficiently. Then, the student starts the sprint and the Scrum team works on the development of user stories (Figure 4 – B). During the sprint, there are some alerts that the student must solve, which appear randomly depending on the user stories selected for the sprint (Figure 4 – C). The student must make decisions, which increase or decrease the quality of the product and the motivation of the team.

Figure 4. Screenshots of the Scrumption game used by the students to select user stories (A), to see the progress of the sprint (B), and to receive an alert (C)

If the students can finish the sprint, the game shows the statistics of the sprint regarding the tasks done, the remaining budget, the morale of the team, the quality of the product, and the progress of the project (see Figure 5 – A). Then the player performs the next sprint's selection of user stories and makes the decisions about the alerts presented. In the final step the product is launched and the game provides statistics about the time, budget, team morale, and quality of the product. Finally, depending on the quality of the product, the game indicates if the student wins or fails the round (see Figure 5 – B).

Figure 5. Screenshots of the Scrumption game with the sprint statisctics (A) and the project statisctics (B)

The BTP Game

The BTP game was created to improve the estimation skills of students by using the COSMIC functional size measurement method (Beatriz Marín et al., 2019). This is a role-playing game in which the student takes the role of Ada, a young astronaut aground in an inhospitable planet that must return to her mother ship.

During the game, the student needs to estimate the functional size of the class diagrams that represent elements of the Ada space ship in order to repair it (see Figure 6 – A). To do the estimation applying the COSMIC functional size, the game provides a tutorial that helps the students. The student sends the droids owned by Ada to implement the elements needed to repair the spaceship. The droids use the effort estimated with COSMIC for each class diagram. The game has four scenes: crash landing, motion, hard cut, and scape velocity. At the beginning, just the first scene (crash landing) is unlocked, and the other scenes are unlocked when the student wins the previous scene. In each scene, there are three class diagrams that must be estimated, starting with the smallest diagram, and then going to the largest diagrams.

The student needs to correctly estimate the functional size, and next the droids must implement the class in the assigned time, during the time allocated to the scene. In each scene the time is interpreted

Figure 6. Screenshots of the BTP game in the scene to estimate the COSMIC Function Points of class diagrams (A), and with the successful estimation feedback (B)

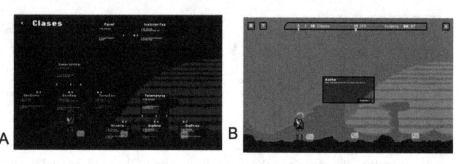

taking into account the context; for example in the crash landing scene the time represents the oxygen available (see Figure 6 – B), and in the scape velocity scene it is interpreted as the time needed to achieve the scape. If the student estimates wrong, for instance overestimating, the droids use more time to implement and the student can lose the scene. As a reward for good estimations, the student can unlock the following scenes.

The BPMN Game

The *BPMN* game was created to help students understand the conceptual constructs of BPMN diagrams. The player takes the role of a junior assistant of a company that must fulfill the task entrusted by his boss. To do so, the player must create a BPMN model to represent the process that must be followed to fulfill each task entrusted. The student must select concepts from a set of available BPMN constructs. This game has 3 levels: basic, medium, and advanced. The medium and advanced levels are initially locked, and when the student passes the basic level, they are progressively unlocked.

At the first level, the boss explains the different tasks that the junior assistant must perform in the correct order. The player must pay attention to the tasks to understand the complete process. Then, an incomplete BPMN model is presented to the player (Figure 7 – A). Starting from this incomplete model, the student must complete the model using the concepts provided for that level (Figure 7 – B). When the student selects a concept, it is included in the BPMN model (Figure 7 – C) until the diagram is completed. At the basic level, the available concepts are activities, exclusive gateways, objects, one lane, start event, and end event. At the medium level, the available concepts are the concepts of the basic level plus more lanes, parallel gateways, and intermediate events. At the advanced level, the available concepts are the

Figure 7. Screenshots of the BPMN game, first without elements (A), next with the selection of concepts (B), and finally with the BPMN diagram with the activity added (C)

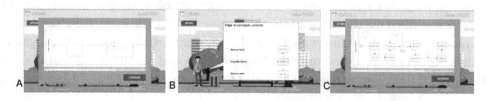

concepts of the medium level plus messages, time events, and inclusive gates. At the end of each level, feedback on the diagram is presented to the student.

During the modeling tasks of each level, the student must answer three questions that are related to the comprehension of the semantics of the conceptual constructs and to the correction of excerpts of BPMN models presented in the questions (Table 1). For each question, the feedback is shown immediately.

Table 1. Questions in the BPMN game

Level	Type	Question
1	Comprehension	Which of the following set of activities has the adequate level of detail to perform the process?
1	Comprehension	What is the correct gate that must be used to open the door of the car?
1	Correction	The following BPMN diagram represents the process, but after the car is found, it is not possible to continue the process. Why?
2	Comprehension	In this process there is a new participant. Is the participant out of the scope of the diagram or must he/she perform activities in the process?
2	Comprehension	When a lane is added to a pool, must a start event for the lane be included?
2	Correction	In the following BPMN diagram the design of tickets is not working. Why?
3	Comprehension	In this process there is a new participant. Must this role be included in the pool or must you add a new pool with the corresponding process of the new role?
3	Comprehension	How can you add the activities of the client in the process?
3	Correction	Which conceptual construct must be used to represent the three options to print the tickets?

At the end of each level, the number of BPMN concepts used, the correct answers, the elapsed time, the points obtained, and the percentage of success is shown to the student (Figure 8 – A). The level is reached when the success percentage is high enough to go to the next level and unlock the corresponding concepts.

At the end of the game, the students can register their name in the leaderboard (Figure 8 – B). This allows the students to compare their performance with others and encourages the students to improve their performance in the game. In addition, there are ten badges that the students can obtain when they accomplish the following milestones: when they reach the first level, when they reach the second level, when they reach the third level, when they answer correctly all the questions of the first level, when they answer correctly all the questions of the second level, when they answer correctly all the questions of the third level, when they complete the three levels, when they register three times their name in the leaderboard, and finally, it is possible to earn a badge when the students complete one level with 100% of successful percentage (which is calculated taking into account the amount of elements used correctly in each BPMN diagram). Figure 8 – C shows an example of badges obtained.

The Classutopia Game

The *Classutopia* game was created to help students practice with class diagrams (Marín et al., 2018). *Classutopia* is a role-playing game in which students play the role of a robot that must correct defective class diagrams. To do so, first the student must create a class diagram of the robot and next complete the

Figure 8. Screenshots of the BPMN game with the statistics of a successful level (A), registering the name in the leaderboard (B), and showing the badges obtained (C)

challenges by identifying defects in class diagrams related to different difficulty levels. This game allows the student to create class diagrams, understand class diagrams, and recognize class diagrams flaws.

During the game, the student can build or improve the class diagram of the robot (Figure 9 – A) or go to the missions (Figure 9 – B). The game provides 3 missions, each one related to a different level of difficulty. At the beginning, just the first mission is unlocked. In this mission, the student must identify defects in the attributes of the class diagram. When the student wins this mission, mission 2 is unlocked, which is related to the identification of defects in attributes and methods. When the student wins mission 2, mission 3 is unlocked, which is related to the identification of defects in attributes, methods, and associations.

Figure 9. Screenshots of the Classutopia game in the scene to build the class diagram of the robot (A), and with the defective class diagram that must repair during the mission (B)

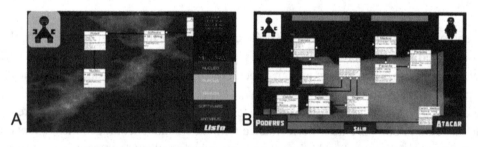

In each mission, the robot must identify the defects and repair the class diagram. There is a bar that represents the life of the robot, and time passes during the mission. The opponent of the robot is a magician that attacks the robot when the student does not identify the defects correctly. During the battle, the robot can use special powers, such as defense or a more powerful attack. To use the special powers, the student must answer questions related to the conceptual constructs, for instance what the meaning of a composition is, or when an inheritance relationship should be used, among others. Finally, when the student wins the mission, some advanced parts of the robot are unlocked, so that the student can rebuild the robot with the advanced parts. When the student adds the advanced parts (such as an antivirus), the characteristics (attack, defense, speed, and unique skills) of the robot are modified.

The defects in each mission are randomly injected, so that the students can play several times each mission in order to unlock all the advanced parts of the robot and improve it for the next battles. This allows the students to practice as many times as they want. The defects injected correspond to: Classes without name, Classes without id, Classes with repeated attributes, Classes with attributes without data type, Classes without creation service, Classes with service without return, Classes without visualization of attributes, Associations of wrong type, Associations without cardinality, Minimum cardinality of 1 at both ends, and Descending cardinality at one end of the association.

RESULTS OF THE GAMIFICATION IN SOFTWARE ENGINEERING COURSES

This section presents the results of the gamification applied in the software engineering course by using the games presented above. The software engineering course at Diego Portales University (Chile) is a fourth-year course of the Engineer degree in Computer Science and Telecommunications. This course is obligatory for all the students of the degree. It is an in-person course in which the students must learn about the development cycle, all its phases, and different standards, in addition to concepts related to the management of the project and soft skills such as teamwork, negotiation, and leadership.

The authors present the results obtained from the application of each game related to software quality (i.e., *RISE*, *Scrumption* and *BTP*) and to software modeling (i.e. *BPMN* and *Classutopia*). This section also presents the interpretation and discussion of the results.

Results of the Application of RISE

In order to evaluate the perception of the use of *RISE*, the researchers applied the game during the second semester of 2016. This course had 16 students. The lectures were performed by using a PowerPoint presentation to explain the risks in software projects. In the next class, the students had to answer a questionnaire at the beginning. In this questionnaire the name of the student, their previous experience (in order to obtain knowledge about whether they had experience working in a company), and five risks that they remembered from the previous lectures were asked.

The results of the initial questionnaire were as follows. Twelve students did not have experience working in companies, three students just worked during one to three months, and a student had been working during one year. The authors argue that the participation in real projects can help the students to recognize and remember the risks. Regarding the risks that they remembered, 12 students remembered that bad estimations is a risk, eight students recognized that poor requirements specification is a risk, and just one student remembered the risk related to losing a key member of the team and the risk related to change of platform. Students did not remember further risks. No student remembered five different risks.

At the following lecture, the subjects started playing the *RISE* game. In this session, the lecturer explained the goal of the game, assigned the roles to the students, the students conducted interviews (Figure 10 – A), and finally the teams were registered in the mobile application. This took 45 minutes. In the next session, the lecturer gave a Lego box to each team and the students used the mobile application and Legos to play (Figure 10 – B). At the end, the teams presented their bridges (Figure 10 – C) and received a prize. This took 45 minutes.

At the following session, the students answered another questionnaire in which five risks that they remembered were asked. One student did not attend to this session, thus 15 students answered. All the students remembered the 5 risks presented in the *RISE* game. Therefore, the effectiveness of using gamification to help in the learning process of risks of software projects was demonstrated. In addition, the researchers also asked the students about the perception of using a gamified approach with the widely

Figure 10. Photos of the students playing RISE, negotiating the roles to create the teams (A), building the bridge with Legos and answering the challenges presented through the mobile application (B), and presenting the four bridges created by the teams (C)

used TAM questionnaire (Moody, 2003). This questionnaire has 16 questions to evaluate the perceptions of the ease of use (PEOU), the perception of usability (PU), and the intention to use (ITU) with a 5-point Likert scale.

The results of the TAM questionnaire show that the average PEOU is 4.32, which indicates that the majority of the participants agreed or totally agreed that applying serious games facilitates the learning of risks. Regarding PU, the average was 4.2, which indicates that the majority of the participants agreed or totally agreed that *RISE* is efficient and effective to learn about risks related to software projects. Regarding ITU, the average was 3.96, which is a value close to agree. An explanation to this value is that the participants were students that did not have the intention to later teach about risks, but they expected to apply their learning in future projects.

In summary, after the application of *RISE* the authors conclude that the use of serious games is a teaching/learning technique that can be effective, efficient, and perceived as easy to learn by students in comparison to traditional lectures using PowerPoint.

Results of the Application of Scrumption

In order to evaluate the perception of use of *Scrumption*, this game was applied during the second semester of 2017. The course had 10 students. The use of the game was a voluntary extra activity of the course. The activity was performed before teaching Scrum. Nevertheless, at this moment of the course the students had attended lectures about waterfall, prototyping, the spiral model, and RUP. Moreover, the lecturer explained that there were other software processes such as Scrum and XP that used user stories to identify the requirements of the software product.

Eight students participated in the activity. First, the lecturer explained the goal of the game, which was related to understanding how to apply the Scrum process. Next, the lecturer provided the students with tablets with the *Scrumption* game. The students played during 30 minutes. When they finished playing, the researchers asked them to answer what they understood about the Scrum process and to complete a perception questionnaire about the usability of the game. The researchers also provided a blank space at the end of the questionnaire for suggestions.

The researchers analyzed the answers of the students that played *Scrumption*. All of them learned that Scrum is a software process that defines tasks that must be performed in sprints to develop a product. They also identified the product backlog with the user stories that must be managed during the sprints by the Scrum team. They also identified that the Scrum team corresponds to people, in addition to the

Scrum master and the product owner. Thus, the authors argue that the main idea of Scrum was learned by students.

For the perception of usability, the researchers used the usability metric for user experience (UMUX) questionnaire (Finstad, 2010), which has only four questions to evaluate the perception of usability. A 7-point Likert scale was used from 1 (totally disagree) to 7 (totally agree) to rate the answers of the students (see Table 2).

Table 2. Results of the UMUX questionnaire for Scrumption

Component	Question	Average
Effectiveness	*Scrumption* meets my requirements.	6.86
Satisfaction	Using *Scrumption* is a frustrating experience.	1.43
Overall usability	*Scruption* is easy to use.	5.85
Efficiency	I have to spend too much time correcting things with *Scrumption*.	2.14

The results indicate that the majority of the students totally agreed that *Scrumption* met their requirements, that is, that it could be used to understand how to follow the Scrum process. Regarding the satisfaction, the sentence states that using *Scrumption* is a frustrating experience, obtaining 1.43. This result is located between the totally disagree and disagree values, therefore the students recognized that using *Scrumption* was not a frustrating experience.

Regarding the overall usability perception, the result was near the agree value. The researchers reviewed the comments by the students and found that two students suggested that it would be better to interact with a keyboard for answering the alerts of *Scrumption* instead of the tablet. The authors observe that the result could be affected by these comments, nevertheless we think that it will be an interesting improvement for future versions of *Scrumption*. Regarding the efficiency, the result was near the disagree value, which means that the students did not feel that they needed to spend too much time correcting things with *Scrumption*.

In summary, the authors argue that using *Scrumption* can be effective for learning how to apply Scrum and that it can be perceived as an aid in learning by students.

Results of the Application of BTP

The researchers recorded the information of two applications of *BTP*. The first application was performed in the first semester of 2018, and the second application in the second semester of 2018. In both cases, the students were enrolled in the software engineering course and they had not received yet the lectures about the COSMIC measurement method. The participation was voluntary in both cases.

In the first application, the researchers aimed to evaluate the usability of using *BTP* to learn how to estimate with COSMIC. To do so, the researchers used the UMUX questionnaire, and students answered using a 5-point Likert scale (see Table 3). Ten students participated in this evaluation. The authors gave a brief introduction of the game and explained the aim of the study. The students played *BTP* during 30 minutes and at the end of the evaluation they answered the questionnaire.

The results indicate that the majority of the students agreed or totally agreed that *BTP* allowed them to learn how to estimate using COSMIC, resulting in an average of 3.9 points. In addition, the overall perception of usability was that *BTP* was easy to use. Nevertheless, regarding the second question and the fourth question, the researchers asked students why they considered somehow frustrating or that they needed to correct too many things using *BTP* since the values were between disagree and neutral. The students argued that they needed an example with each step of the application of COSMIC to do the estimation from class diagrams in addition to the tutorial related to how to measure using COSMIC. Consequently, the researchers modified the game and improved the tutorial for the second application.

Table 3. Results of the UMUX questionnaire for BTP

Component	Question	Average of the first application	Average of the second application
Effectiveness	Does BTP allow you to learn how to estimate by using the COSMIC method?	3.9	3.73
Satisfaction	Is playing BTP a frustrating experience?	2.6	3.1
Overall usability	Is BTP easy to use?	4.0	2.7
Efficiency	Do you spend too much time making corrections with BTP?	2.7	2.96

For the second application, the researchers improved the tutorial and recoded the estimation performed by the students in order to evaluate the effectiveness of using *BTP*. The authors briefly explained the aim of the evaluation to the students and then they played *BTP* during 30 minutes. At the end, the students answered the UMUX questionnaire, and the researchers also asked the students about how many attempts they thought that the game provided to reach a correct estimation and if they thought that they had used this number of attempts. The researchers included a blank space for suggestions.

Thirty students participated voluntarily in the second evaluation. Regarding the perception of effectiveness, there was a clear tendency to agree, as 19 students agreed or totally agreed that *BTP* allowed them to learn how to estimate by using COSMIC and ten students were neutral about this statement. For the remaining questions there was not a clear tendency.

Regarding the effectiveness, authors observe that student estimations were higher than real values, with an average of 9.5% over the correct value. Regarding the final questions, 70% of the students thought that they used the maximum number of attempts to estimate correctly, 20% perceived that they were more effective (using fewer than the maximum number of attempts), and 10% perceived that they were ineffective despite they use fewer attempts than the maximum allowed.

Regarding the suggestions that researchers received, ten students felt nervous about measuring using COSMIC since they had not had lectures on the topic. This can explain the results obtained in the UMUX questionnaire. Moreover, some students indicated that they preferred to use a touch screen instead of a mouse and a keyboard to play *BTP*.

Results of the Application of BPMN Game

The authors applied the *BPMN* game to the software engineering course during the first semester of 2018. All the students received lectures about BPMN and had done an exercise in class. Eleven students participated voluntarily in the study. The aim of the study was to know the perceptions about the game and also to collect suggestions for improvement.

The authors briefly explained the goal of the game and then the students played during 30 minutes. When they finished playing, they had to answer a perception questionnaire. The researchers used the UMUX questionnaire to evaluate the perception of usability. The students had to answer using a 7-point Likert scale. At the end of the questionnaire, the researchers asked students to leave their comments about the *BPMN* game.

Table 4 presents the results of the UMUX questionnaire in the evaluation of the *BPMN* game. As it can be observed, the subjects agreed that the game met their requirements, that is, that the *BPMN* game can be used to exercise their knowledge about BPMN diagrams. In addition, the subjects agreed that the *BPMN* game is easy to use and disagreed that using the *BPMN* game is a frustrating experience. Nevertheless, the result of the perception of efficiency reveals that some subjects needed more time to answer than others. The authors regard this as an improvement opportunity that could be addressed for instance by adding a tutorial to improve the perception of the time used to correct things with the *BPMN* game.

Table 4. Results of the UMUX questionnaire for BPMN game

Component	Question	Average
Effectiveness	BPMN meets my requirements.	5.73
Satisfaction	Using BPMN is a frustrating experience.	2.91
Overall usability	BPMN is easy to use.	6.18
Efficiency	I have to spend too much time correcting things with BPMN.	3.91

Regarding the comments, six students stated that the constructed BPMN model should be shown at the end of each level in order to be able to quickly identify their mistakes and better understand the feedback provided. The feedback is presented narratively currently. All the students stated that using the *BPMN* game was fun, that the context was fun, and that the feedback helped them to learn about how to model BPMN diagrams. In addition, all the students stated that the use of badges and a leaderboard encouraged them to continue learning.

Results of the Application of Classutopia

The researchers applied the *Classutopia* game during the first semester of 2017. All the students received lectures about conceptual modeling and class diagrams and had done exercises during the lectures. Researchers conducted the evaluation in order to know whether students find benefits in the use of *Classutopia* as a complementary strategy to the traditional classes to improve their learning about conceptual modeling of class diagrams.

Thirteen students participated voluntarily in the evaluation. The authors briefly explained the context of the game and the goal of this evaluation. Next, the students played during 30 minutes. All the students could learn how to build the robot and to detect defects in the basic level. Eleven subjects were able to learn how to build the robot and to detect defects at the basic and medium levels. Seven subjects could learn how to build the robot and to detect defects in the class diagrams at the basic, medium, and advanced levels.

Afterwards, the students had to answer a questionnaire with six questions in order to indicate their perception about the usability of the game to improve their learning of class diagrams. The students answered with a 5-point Likert scale (from 1– totally disagree to 5 – totally agree).

Table 5. Results of the questionnaire to assess Classutopia

Question	Average
1. Classutopia facilitates the understanding of a class diagram.	4.30
2. Classutopia helps in determining how to correct a class diagram.	4.07
3. Classutopia helps in understanding the concepts of the class diagram.	3.92
4. I find Classutopia easy to understand.	3.46
5. Classutopia allows you to learn about the design of a class diagram in an easier way than by using text.	4.00
6. In general, I found Classutopia to be useful	4.76

As it can be observed in Table 5, the majority of the students agreed or totally agreed that *Classutopia* helped in the comprehension of the class diagrams and in the understanding of how to construct a correct class diagram (questions 1 and 2). Regarding question 3, four students totally agreed with the sentence, four students agreed with the sentence, and five students answered neutral, thus the authors recognized a tendency to agree that *Classutopia* helps in understanding the concepts of the class diagram. Regarding question 4, just two students did not find *Classutopia* easy to understand. One of them argued that it was necessary to have a tutorial to understand how it worked, and the other student argued that more details about how the special powers of the robot worked were needed. Nevertheless, the students agreed that the use of *Classutopia* allowed them to learn easily the design of class diagrams (question 5), and in general they found *Classutopia* useful (question 6).

Interpretation and Discussion of the Results

In all the evaluations to the gamified platforms, the students completed a perception questionnaire. We believe that the responses were honest, since the participation was voluntary and the final marks of students did not depend on their perceptions of the gamified platforms.

The results evidence that the majority of the participants agreed or totally agreed that applying gamification and serious games facilitate the learning of the different topics. In particular, the results show that the gamification related to software quality through the *RISE, Scrumption,* and *BTP* games appears to be effective to help students learn these topics. In the gamification related to software design through the *BPMN* and *Classutopia* games, the students argued that the use of gamified elements such as badges, leaderboards, and powers encouraged them to continue playing, and correspondingly, to continue learning these topics.

In addition, the authors observe that the students that participated in the studies were more engaged and motivated to learn the remaining topics of the software engineering course, even though these topics were not taught using gamified elements. The authors believe that using gamification allows students to be more comfortable with the course, creating a relaxed space open to learn the topics of the course. Therefore, the authors argue that using gamification can improve the entire learning experience of students. Nevertheless, the authors plan to conduct additional studies to investigate the correlation between the final marks obtained by the students and the use of the gamified platforms.

LESSONS LEARNED AND FUTURE RESEARCH DIRECTIONS

The development and validation of serious games that use gamification to improve the learning experience of students of software engineering courses has allowed us to identify some relevant lessons learned, as well as limitations and future research directions.

Lesson 1: The use of a collaborative strategy in the game improves the effectiveness of using gamification in the learning process. The authors consider that using a collaborative game, there is more socialization of the concepts presented in the game and it is possible to take advantage of the learning among students, reinforcing the concepts learned. In this paper, the authors present five games that we developed and applied to a software engineering course. Four of them are designed to be used individually and just one was designed to be played collaboratively. When the authors analyze the results of the evaluation experiences, they observe that the use of a collaborative strategy for a game seems to improve the learning effectiveness. The results of the application of *RISE* support this claim.

Lesson 2: The use of concrete elements increases the motivation of students. Even though students of century XXI enjoy the use of videogames and they perceived that the use of serious games was funnier than traditional classes using blackboards or PowerPoint, when researchers added concrete elements to the learning experience they perceived it even funnier because in many cases they remembered when they played as kids. Therefore, the researchers can take advantage of these memories and increase the motivation for learning. The results provide evidence of this lesson. The authors argue that the combination of concrete elements such as Legos or cards with videogames improve the motivation of students for learning since they regard the learning activities as funnier.

Lesson 3: The use of gamification in the learning process can support the entire Bloom's taxonomy. Bloom's learning taxonomy presents six levels: remember, understand, apply, analyze, evaluate, and create. Taking into account the variety and number of topics that must be taught in a software engineering course, lecturers need to decide upon the level of the taxonomy that students will acquire for each topic in order to teach all the topics in the assigned hours for the course. Typically, it is not possible to obtain the maximum level for all the topics of the course. The researchers have demonstrated that it is possible to create serious games that help students to reach the entire Bloom taxonomy, such as *Classutopia*. This game helps students remember the concepts of class diagrams by the use of questions, enables the understanding of class diagrams presented in each mission, supports the application of the concepts known when the students interpret the concepts presented, enables the analysis of each class diagram when the students examine the diagrams, facilitates evaluation due to the identification of defects, and also supports diagram creation when the students design the class diagram for the robot. Therefore, the use of this game in one session allows students to enact the entire Bloom's taxonomy. For this reason, the authors argue that the use of serious games also allows lecturers to efficiently use the hours assigned to a course because by using these games students acquire the knowledge faster than exercising with pen and paper.

Lesson 4: It is not useful to learn complex concepts using gamification without previous lectures about these topics. Software estimation is not easy to teach, since students must learn the concepts that should be measured taking into account a measurement method. The measurement methods require that the students estimate the time needed to implement the software in an objective way, taking into account the functionality that must be implemented instead of the skills of developers. This is the case - for example - of the COSMIC measurement method, that supports the measurement of functional size via the identification of the functional processes and the data movements that occur in the functional processes. The researchers created a game to teach how to apply COSMIC, but they did not teach students previously. Instead, they provided a tutorial and a guided example about how to apply COSMIC to class diagrams. Even though the results indicate that the estimations were higher than the correct estimation in almost 10%, the students did not feel confident in their results. The students indicated that they felt nervous because they had not received classes on COSMIC previously, thus they felt pressure to play and finally felt somehow frustrated using the game. In this case, the researchers realized that it is not useful to use serious games to learn complex concepts when the students have not received lectures about these topics before. It adds anxiety to students.

Lesson 5: It is funnier to learn when the game has an interesting narrative. The authors observed that students smiled when they started the games and the context was presented. For each game developed for the course, the researchers tried to create narratives that could be interesting to the students, for instance in *Classutopia* the player is taking the role of a robot that must defeat a magician. In *BTP* the player is taking the role of a young astronaut that must repair her spaceship by constructing systems that allow her to survive during her voyage back to the mother ship. In synthesis, the authors argue that the narrative helps in engaging students.

Lesson 6: The use of rewards in the game increases the motivation and engagement of students. It is well-known that using rewards such as badges increases the motivation of students, generating on them the desire of playing to win badges. Authors observed this behavior in the *BPMN* game. Moreover, the authors observed that when the rewards won can be used in the game, then the motivation is even increased further. The authors observed that in the *Classutopia* game the students wanted to continue playing after the evaluation, just for fun and curiosity because they could use the rewards to construct a better robot to fight against the magician.

Lesson 7: The use of a leaderboard is important for self-esteem of students. Several publications postulate that the use of a leaderboard is important to socialize the results obtained in the game. In addition to that, authors observed that the use of a leaderboard was important for self-esteem of the students. In particular, the authors observed that in the *BPMN* game the students felt satisfaction when they wrote their initials on the leaderboard, and also when they shared the results. In contrast, in the *RISE* game there is not a leaderboard, all teams win, and at the end of the evaluation the students asked insistently which team was the best.

In summary, the use of gamification is worthwhile for software engineering courses because it can improve the engagement of students and facilitate the teaching of the different skills that the students must acquire in the course. In addition, gamification of engineering courses can help students to learn in an asynchronous way. This is tremendously important in situations where students cannot have the possibility to attend the lectures, for instance due to health restrictions by the pandemic, or because students have different learning styles. The students could then access different gamified elements depending on the characteristics of their learning style.

Besides the lessons learned about the application of gamification and serious game to the software engineering course, the authors also identify some limitations and future research opportunities. One of the limitations of the studies is that different questionnaires were used to evaluate the perception of usability. It would be better to use the same questionnaire and the same scale for the answers, but the researchers aimed to use well-known questionnaires in order to strengthen the validity of the results. Therefore, the authors identify the creation of a specific questionnaire to evaluate serious games as an opportunity for future research. This questionnaire applied to software engineering topics should have questions related to the perception of usability as well as questions related to the effectiveness of learning the specific topics. In addition, it would be interesting to know the expectations of the students about gamification, since it is an important factor for its acceptance. Recent studies have started to research on this topic (Chih-Hung Chung, 2019).

When the researchers started applying gamification to the software engineering course, they selected the theme of the first game (RISE), then they established the educational purpose, and finally they refined the game, following the guidelines by (Gomez, 2015). Using this general framework, it was difficult to understand the elements that the researchers wanted to gamify. As a consequence, in the following developments the researchers used another framework to define the mechanics, dynamics, and aesthetics of a game (Hunicke et al., 2004). Using this framework facilitated the development of the games, but the definition of metrics related to the mechanics and dynamics was not easy. Therefore, the authors identify the need for a framework that better supports the development of serious games and with which someone could define the mechanics, dynamics, and aesthetics, as well as to integrate the metrics that will be measured from the use of the game. An initial prototype of a design framework is presented by (Bucchiarone et al., 2019), which uses a model-driven approach to define a domain specific language for gamification. Nevertheless, this initial approach lacks the proper definition of storytelling, flashy user interfaces, and metrics of user experience. The authors advocate the use of model-driven engineering to accelerate the definition of a framework to design serious games and integrate the metrics in the development of games.

Considering that different students have different learning styles, such as visual, verbal, auditory, physical, social, and solitary learning, among others, the authors argue that with the help of gamification and serious games, lecturers can design different elements to improve the learning experience of all the students considering their learning styles. Nevertheless, nowadays the different learning styles are not fully considered at university-level courses, in which the lecturers need to teach to the majority of the students, and the remaining students need to apply greater effort to try to understand, which in some cases is not possible and causes a higher drop-out. An interesting new research topic related to gamification is the personalization of the gamified elements in order to incorporate the different learning styles, which could lead to similarities in the learning curve of students and therefore improve the efficiency of learning. This has been analyzed by (Buckley & Doyle, 2017) and (Hassan et al., 2019), providing some initial insights about adaptive gamification.

Taking into account that the software engineering course that the authors teach is in the four year of the degree, they want to analyze if learning is deeper when the students have participated in a gamified course. In addition, the authors want to analyze the final marks obtained by students that participate in gamified courses since they observed that they were also more motivated to learn all the topics of the course. Even though the researchers have analyzed the perception of usability for each serious game developed and the effectiveness of some of them, the authors believe that the final marks of students can bring the possibility of analyzing their learning performance. Finally, the authors want to investigate if the students' behavior in class change after they play some of the games.

As a final remark, in order to advance the research on the topics above, it is of paramount importance to conduct more empirical evaluations and also replications of the studies.

CONCLUSION

In this paper the use of gamification and serious games in a software engineering course was presented. Five serious games (*RISE*, *Scrumption*, *BPMN*, *Classutopia*, and *BTP*) that have been used to support the learning of different topics of the course were presented. With these serious games the authors provide evidence that it is feasible to use gamification in software engineering courses, in particular in knowledge areas less researched such as software quality and software modeling.

The evaluation of these serious games was performed with different cohorts of students. In all the evaluations the researchers aimed to know about their perception of usability. To this end, the researchers used well-known questionnaires such as TAM and UMUX. The results indicate that the students perceived as useful the use of serious games and gamification to support the learning process. Nevertheless, it is important to use these games as a complement to the regular lectures.

After four years applying gamification and serious games for the software engineering course, the authors draw some lessons learned. They include the benefits in using concrete elements, the engagement gained with an interesting narrative, or the support of the entire Bloom's taxonomy using a serious game. The authors argue that these lessons can help researchers and lecturers when they decide upon how to apply gamification to a software engineering course. They also discuss some limitations of the work and provide insights for future research.

Future work will focus on the lines of future research presented in the previous section. First of all, the authors aim to define a questionnaire that enables the evaluation of the perception of the usefulness of gamification in addition to the effectiveness of the use of the games in specific topics of the software engineering course. In addition, the authors aim to create a framework that provides students with the capability to access the different serious games and that allows researchers to visualize their progress in each game and also to obtain their answers as well as comments or suggestions. The authors argue that by having this framework they can observe the learning effectiveness of students in an integrated way, facilitating the decisions upon the topics in the lectures to pay more attention to. The authors also aim to create - or integrate - serious games for other important topics taught in the software engineering course, such as testing. Finally, we plan to continue conducting studies about the use of serious games in the software engineering course with the aim of strengthening the findings.

REFERENCES

Alhammad, M., & Moreno, A. (2018). Gamification in software engineering education: A systematic mapping. *Journal of Systems and Software*, *141*, 131–150. doi:10.1016/j.jss.2018.03.065

Begosso, L. R., Franco, L. H. B., Cunha, D. S. d., & Begosso, L. C. (2019). SimScrumF: a game for supporting the process of teaching Scrum. *Proceedings of the 9th International Conference on Information Communication and Management*. 10.1145/3357419.3357426

Berkling, K., & Thomas, C. (2013). Gamification of a Software Engineering course and a detailed analysis of the factors that lead to it's failure. *International Conference on Interactive Collaborative Learning (ICL)*. 10.1109/ICL.2013.6644642

Bucchiarone, A., Cicchetti, A., & Marconi, A. (2019). GDF: A Gamification Design Framework Powered by Model-Driven Engineering. *ACM/IEEE 22nd International Conference on Model Driven Engineering Languages and Systems Companion (MODELS-C)*.

Buckley, P., & Doyle, E. (2017). Individualising gamification: An investigation of the impact of learning styles and personality traits on the efficacy of gamification using a prediction market. *Computers & Education*, *106*, 43–55.

Calderón, A., Ruiz, M., & O'Connor, R. V. (2017). Coverage of the ISO 21500 standard in the context of software project management by a simulation-based serious game. *International Conference on Software Process Improvement and Capability Determination*.

Chung. (2019). Students' Acceptance of Gamification in Higher Education. International Journal of Game-Based Learning, 9(2). Advance online publication. doi:10.4018/IJGBL.2019040101

de A. Souza, M., Veado, L., Moreira, R., Figueiredo, E., & Costa, H. (2018). A systematic mapping study on game-related methods for software engineering education. *Information and Software Technology, 95*, 201-218.

De Souza, A., Duarte, R., Marinho, J., & Rodrigues, L. (2017). SCRUMI: A Board Serious Virtual Game for Teaching the SCRUM Framework. *IEEE/ACM 39th International Conference on Software Engineering Companion (ICSE-C)*.

Deterding, S., Dixon, D., Khaled, R., & Nacke, L. (2011). *From game design elements to gamefulness: defining gamification*. 15th International Academic MindTrek Conference: Envisioning Future Media Environments, Tampere, Finland.

Dicheva, D., Dichev, C., Agre, G., & Angelova, G. (2015). Gamification in Education: A Systematic Mapping Study. *Journal of Educational Technology & Society, 18*(3).

Fernandes, P., & Correa, C. (2017). *Game Elements in a Software Engineering Study Group: A Case Study*. IEEE/ACM 39th International Conference on Software Engineering: Software Engineering Education and Training Track (ICSE-SEET), Buenos Aires.

Finstad, K. (2010). The Usability Metric for User Experience. *Interacting with Computers, 22*(5), 323–327. doi:10.1016/j.intcom.2010.04.004

Fitz-Walter, Z., Tjondronegoro, D., & Wyeth, P. (2011). Orientation passport: using gamification to engage university students. *23rd Australian Computer-Human Interaction Conference*, Canberra, Australia. 10.1145/2071536.2071554

Gasca-Hurtado, G. P., Gómez-Álvarez, M. C., & Manrique-Losada, B. (2019). Using Gamification in Software Engineering Teaching: Study Case for Software Design. [*New Knowledge in Information Systems and Technologies*.]. *WorldCIST*, *19*, 2019.

Gomez, M. C. (2015). *Diseño de un instrumento pedagógico para la enseñanza de la mejora de procesos software*. Academic Press.

Hassan, M. A., Habiba, U., Majeed, F., & Shoaib, M. (2019). Adaptive gamification in e-learning based on students' learning styles. *Interactive Learning Environments*, 1–21. Advance online publication. doi:10.1080/10494820.2019.1588745

Hunicke, R., LeBlanc, M., & Zubek, R. (2004). MDA: A formal approach to game design and game research. *AAAI Workshop on Challenges in Game AI*. http://www.aaai.org/Papers/Workshops/2004/WS-04-04/WS04-04-001.pdf

Jesus, G. M. d., Paschoal, L. N., Ferrari, F. C., & Souza, S. R. S. (2019). Is It Worth Using Gamification on Software Testing Education? An Experience Report. *Proceedings of the XVIII Brazilian Symposium on Software Quality*. 10.1145/3364641.3364661

Kirkwood, A., & Price, L. (2005). Learners and learning in the twenty-first century: What do we know about students' attitudes towards and experiences of information and communication technologies that will help us design courses? *Studies in Higher Education*, *30*(3), 257–274. doi:10.1080/03075070500095689

Landers, R. (2014). Developing a Theory of Gamified Learning: Linking Serious Games and Gamification of Learning. *Simulation & Gaming*, *45*(6), 752–768. doi:10.1177/1046878114563660

Marín, B., Frez, J., Cruz-Lemus, J. A., & Genero, M. (2019, November). An Empirical Investigation on the Benefits of Gamification in Programming Courses. *ACM Transactions on Computing Education (TOCE)*, *19*(1), 22.

Marín, B., Larenas, F., & Giachetti, G. (2018). Learning Conceptual Modeling Design Through the Classutopia Serious Game. *International Journal of Software Engineering and Knowledge Engineering*, *28*(11&12), 1679–1699. doi:10.1142/S0218194018400235

Marín, B., Vera, M., & Giachetti, G. (2019). An Adventure Serious Game for Teaching Effort Estimation in Software Engineering. *IWSM-Mensura 2019: Joint Proceedings of the International Workshop on Software Measurement and the International Conference on Software Process and Product Measurement*.

Marques, M., Ochoa, S., Bastarrica, M., & Gutierrez, F. (2018). Enhancing the Student Learning Experience in Software Engineering Project Courses. *IEEE Transactions on Education*, *61*(1), 63–73. doi:10.1109/TE.2017.2742989

Maxim, B., Kaur, R., Apzynski, C., Edwards, D., & Evans, E. (2016). An Agile Software Engineering Process Improvement Game. *IEEE Frontiers in Education Conference (FIE)*.

Moody, D. L. (2003). The Method Evaluation Model: A Theoretical Model for Validating Information Systems Design Methods. *Proceedings of the 11th European Conference on Information Systems.*

Muñoz, M., Hernández, L., Mejia, J., Gasca-Hurtado, G. P., & Gómez-Alvarez, M. C. (2017). State of the Use of Gamification Elements in Software Development Teams Systems. *Software and Services Process Improvement. EuroSPI 2017.*

Pedreira, O., García, F., Brisaboa, N., & Piattini, M. (2015). Gamification in software engineering – A systematic mapping. *Information and Software Technology, 57,* 157–168.

Prasetya, I. S. W. B., Leek, C. Q. H. D., Melkonian, O., Tusscher, J. t., Bergen, J. v., Everink, J. M., . . . Zon, W. M. v. (2019). Having fun in learning formal specifications Proceedings of the 41st International Conference on Software Engineering: Software Engineering Education and Training. 10.1109/ ICSE-SEET.2019.00028

Reis da Silva, T., Medeiros, T., & da Silva Aranha, E. (2015). The use of games on the teaching of programming: a systematic review. ESELAW 2015, Lima, Peru.

Rojas, J. M., White, T. D., Clegg, B. S., & Fraser, G. (2017). Code defenders: crowdsourcing effective tests and subtle mutants with a mutation testing game. *Proceedings of the 39th International Conference on Software Engineering.* 10.1109/ICSE.2017.68

Schefer-Wenzl, S., & Miladinovic, I. (2018). Teaching Software Engineering with Gamification Elements. *International Journal of Advanced Corporate Learning, 11*(1).

Vargas-Enríquez, J., García-Mundo, L., Genero, M., & Piattini, M. (2015). Análisis de uso de la gamificación en la enseñanza de la informática. *Actas de las XXI Jornadas de la Enseñanza Universitaria de la Informática (JENUI 2015).*

Vos, T. E. J., Prasetya, I., Fraser, G., Martinez-Ortiz, I., Perez-Colado, I., Prada, R., ... Silva, A. R. (2019). IMPRESS: Improving Engagement in Software Engineering Courses Through Gamification. *Proceedings of the 20th International Conference on Product-Focused Software Process Improvement (PROFES).*

Chapter 9

Boosting the Competitiveness of Organizations With the Use of Software Engineering

Mirna Muñoz

https://orcid.org/0000-0001-8537-2695

CIMAT, A. C. Unidad Zacatecas, Mexico

ABSTRACT

Software has become the core of organizations in different domains because the capacity of their products, systems, and services have an increasing dependence on software. This fact highlights the research challenges to be covered by computer science, especially in the software engineering (SE) area. On the one way, SE is in charge of covering all the aspects related to the software development process from the early stages of software development until its maintenance and therefore is closely related to the software quality. On the other hand, SE is in charge of providing engineers able to provide technological-base solutions to solve industrial problems. This chapter provides a research work path focused on helping software development organizations to change to a continuous software improvement culture impacting both their software development process highlighting the human factor training needs. Results show that the implementation of best practices could be easily implemented if adequate support is provided.

INTRODUCTION

Nowadays in most organizations, the capacity of their products, systems, and services increasingly depends on software. The software allows them to compete, adapt and survive in a highly changing environment (Muñoz, Mejía & de León, 2020).

The importance acquired by the software industry becomes an opportunity for organizations of this domain, all of them (large, SMEs and SVEs), to have constant growth, and in most cases their survival. This opportunity brings a high demand for them to develop high-quality software. In this context, software development organizations have an increasing need to improve their software development process in an effort to meet the demand of the software industry (Muñoz et al., 2016).

DOI: 10.4018/978-1-7998-7552-9.ch009

Copyright © 2021, IGI Global. Copying or distributing in print or electronic forms without written permission of IGI Global is prohibited.

Software Engineering is an area of Computer Science, which covers all the aspects related to the software development process from the early stages of software development until its maintenance (Pressman, 2002). The foundation of Software Engineering is the process because it defines a framework for a set of key areas that must be established for the effective delivery of software engineering technology (Pressman, 2002).

Due to the importance of the Process, the Software Process Improvement is a research field within the Software Engineering area that has emerged from the need to respond to the problems involved in software development offering to software development organizations the opportunity of increasing its efficiency, taking as base that the efficiency in software development depends largely on the quality of the processes used to create it (Williams, 2008).

In this context, Software Process Improvement (SPI) becomes an obvious and logical way to address the increasing need to be competitive in the software industry (Cuevas et al, 2002). However, although there are many organizations motivated to improve their software processes, very few know how best to do so. Therefore, introducing process improvement has been a path full of obstacles for most organizations, and always away from the original path (Potter & Sakry, 2006; Morgan, 2009). Moreover, most improvement efforts fail, stakeholders feel frustrated, and they are more convinced that they must continue doing their work as before and the resistance to change increases (Calvo-Manzano et al., 2010).

The goal of this chapter is to present a path of a research that has been developed since 2005, which aims to implement Software Process Improvement in a smooth and continuous way, depending on the improvement pace accepted by the organization, and addressing four aspects to be taken into account for a success SPI such as people, models and standards, methods and methodologies; and software tools (Cuevas et al, 2002). By this way, the rejection attitudes regarding the implementation of SPI are prevented; therefore, the resistance to change are reduced.

After the introduction, this chapter is structured as follows: Section 2 shows four aspects covered in this research; Section 3 presents the research path developed; Section provides 4 discussion, conclusions and future trends.

BACKGROUND

As exposed in the introduction section, according to Cuevas (Cuevas et al, 2002) four aspects should be taken into account to achieve a successful SPI: *people, models and standards, methods and methodologies; and software tools*. This way allows software development organizations to establish "how" to define and improve their software development process that will help them to provide high-quality software to meet the requirements of software market.

This section provides an overview of the four aspects this research took as base toward the reinforcement of the development processes of SDOs.

- *People.* It refers to the qualified professionals able to work with international models and standards to enhance the quality and effectiveness of software developed. Moreover, they are required to be able to work on teams. Then, this chapter covers the research done, on the one way, analyzing the training provided by professionals at universities (Muñoz et al., 2019b), and the research focused on motivate and organize talented people to integrate high effective teams (Muñoz et al., 2019c).

- *Models and standards.* It refers to the process improvement models and standards targeted for the software industry, to contribute to the development of quality products within budget and schedule, by optimizing efforts and resources. Then, this chapter focus not on the development of new models and standards, but in the correct implementation of them (Mejía, Muñoz & Muñoz, 2016; Muñoz, Mejía & Gasca-Hurtado, 2014), including the work done to help software development organizations, large (Calvo-Manzano et al., 2010), SMEs (Muñoz, Mejía & Gasca-Hurtado, 2014) and VSEs (Laporte et al., 2017; Muñoz, Mejía & Laporte, 2019) in the implementation of best practices provided by international models and standards to increase its competitiveness.

- *Methods and methodologies.* It refers to the set of defined steps that indicates how to build software in a systematic way (Pressman, 2002). However, these methods and models are not used by engineers due to they prefer craftsman software development. Then, this chapter focuses on supporting the reinforcement of software development methods and methodologies, and how to get users to accept it, according to the specific features of the software development organization (Cuevas et al., 2007; Muñoz et al., 2019).

- *Software tools.* It refers to the development of automatic or semi-automatic approaches to facilitate and support the implementation of processes or methods (Pressman, 2002). Then, this chapter focuses on those software tools both semi-automatic and automatic that have been developed to support people in tasks related to training (Muñoz Peña & Hernández, 2019), process definition and improvement (Duron & Muñoz, 2013; Muñoz-Mata et al., 2015), and to help teams in the use of engineering best practices (Muñoz et al, 2017; Ibarra & Muñoz, 2018).

RESEARCH PATH DEVELOPED TO BOOST THE COMPETITIVENESS OF SOFTWARE DEVELOPMENT ORGANIZATIONS USING SOFTWARE ENGINEERING

The research path to boost the competitiveness of software development organizations by using software engineering started in 2006, focusing on the implementation of SPI in a pace supported by software development organizations, and has been growing up highlighting the human factor as key element for the success in the implementation of improvements in software development process.

Then, this section will describe how has been addressing the research by providing a review of the focused problems, and the research achievements covering the four aspects mentioned in the previous section: people, models and standards, methods and methodologies, and software tools. All together build what in this chapter is called "the research path". It is important to highlight that throughout the development of this research the four aspect has been addressed due to its importance in the Software Engineering area.

Context, Problems and Research Achievements Related to the "Models and Standards" Aspect

This is considering the first step of the path because this research was performed during the PhD studies of the author. The research context was set on that even when a set of success stories related to software process improvements in organizations have been published (Software Engineering Institute, 2007; Gibson, Goldensen & Kost, 2006), the introduction of process improvements represented serious problems to most organizations becoming a path with a lot of obstacles (Potter & Sakry, 2006; Morgan, 2009), having none (Goldenson, 2007) or very limit success (Conradi & Fuggeta, 2002). The problem addressed are focused on helping software development organization to implement software process improvements with better results.

As result of performing this research, it was proposed a methodology that allows software development organizations to improve their development processes in a smooth and continuous way, depending on their business goals but in a pace supported by them. The methodology was named as *methodology for process improvement through basic components and focusing on the resistance to change* (MIGME-RRC) (Calvo-Manzano et al., 2010).

As Figure 1 shows, MIGME-RRC is composed of four phases: (1) identifying internal best practices; (2) assess the organizational performance; (3) analyze external best practices, and (4) implement improvements. All of them supported by activities that addressed the reduction of resistance to change (change management and knowledge management). Due to this methodology represents the foundation of the research path. Next each phase is briefly described.

Figure 1. MIGME-RRC methodology (Calvo-Manzano et al., 2010)

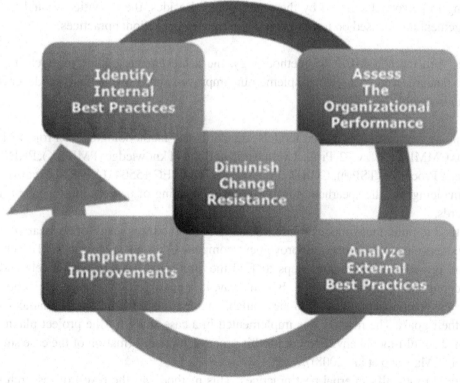

- **Identify Internal Best Practices:** This phase aims to start the implementation of the improvement but in a different way that assessments. It is focused on identifying the practices that are carry out within the organization. After the identification of the practices, it is possible to get an overview of the current organizational processes.

- **Assess the Organizational Performance:** This phase aims to evaluate the performance of the formalized practices regarding the coverage of the organizational business goals. This way allows identifying most and less covered business goals, and then, prioritizing the business goals needs.
- **Analyze External Best Practices:** This phase aims to build multi-model environments as reference to introduce the best practices within the organizational processes. Depending on the business goals the methodology allows provide a set of practices from different models and standards in such way that the organization has a candidate practices to be implemented focusing on their business goals needs and the way they work. A multi-model environment for this research work involves cultural aspects and the knowledge, which advises the use of the mix of best practices from more than one model or standard in a process, in order to achieve the organization's business goals (Muñoz, Mejía & Gasca, 2014).
- **Implement Improvements:** This phase aims to introduce best practices for improving the organizational processes. The way proposed by this methodology is integrating internal and external best practices, so that the organizational knowledge and experience is reinforced by external practices of a multi-model environment.
- **Activities to Reduce Change Resistance:** The methodology uses interviews and validations meeting to personnel selected by the organization. Besides, the activities related to knowledge management are focused on formalizing the current organizational practices.

Together with the MIGME-RRC methodology, the achievements of this research, regarding the models and standards were focused on implementing improvements by using multi-model environments, having as main results:

1. A mapping among the most used models, standards and methodologies for Project Management such as CMMI-DEV® v1.2, Project Management Book of knowledge (PMBOK), PRINCE2, Team Software Process® (TSP®), COBIT, ISO9001 and ISO/IEC 15504 (Calvo-Manzano et al., 2008). This mapping was the spearhead toward the understanding of process improvement models and standards.
2. A method to build multi-model environments. This method was result of a research who aims to incorporate elemental process improvement components in an organization. To achieve it, the method provides the minimum steps to find the similarities among the models and standards considered within a specific scope. By this way, it is possible to help an organization to choose those best practices compliant with the available models and standards in the market and that best meet their goals. The method was implemented in a case study for the project planning process obtained a multi-model environment for this process (more information of the case study is found in (Calvo-Manzano et al., 2008)).
3. A method to identify internal best practices. This method was the result of research focused on reducing the resistance to change starting the SPI analyzing the practices currently carried out in the organization so that if the practices are identified, it is possible to get an overview of the organizational current processes. Besides, the method allows involving relevant stakeholders since the beginning. The results of the case study executed to analyzed the viability of the method shown that using the method enable the extraction, collection, and formalization of the tacit knowledge

of the organization in an organizational process (more information of the case study is found in (Calvo-Manzano et al., 2010)).

4. A case study performed in a multinational software development organization that allows confirming that people only accept assimilated changes with identified benefits, by this way the improvements are perceived as an evolution of their work (Calvo-Manzano et al., 2010).

5. The application of knowledge management to support the use of multi-model environments in software process improvements. This research aims to reinforce the use of multi-model environments by applying knowledge management technologies such is the case of ontologies. As result of this research a model process ontology was obtained. Besides, the ontology was proved encompassing a set of international models and standards such as CMMI®-v1.2, TSP®, PMBOK, ISO/IEC 15504 and ISO/IEC 12207 (more information of the case study is found in (Muñoz, Mejía & Muñoz, 2013)).

6. A methodology for establishing multi-model environments. This methodology is an evolution of the method published in (Calvo-Manzano et al., 2008). This research adds a new phase to the previous method base on an adaptation of the goal question metric (GQM) method to identify and formalize the business goals of an organization. This methodology focused on a gap that was detected in a set of SMEs on Mexico regarding the establishment of business goals. This methodology was validated by performing a case study in a SME, the results shown that the methodology allows providing a proposal of practices implementation sequence covering the need to provide a guide of how to implement the improvement (more information of the case study is found in (Muñoz, Mejía & Gasca-Hurtado, 2014)).

7. The participation as a member of the team in charge to translate the CMMI-Dev model v1.2 and 1.3 to the Spanish Language.

Recently, the author was expanded the work focusing on very small entities and the use of international standards getting as result:

1. An analysis of the weaknesses that VSEs present in the implementation of the international standard ISO/IEC 29110. Due to the importance of involving VSEs in a continuous improvement, this analysis is part of a project to support VSEs in the implementation of ISO/IEC 29110 to reinforce their software development process. The analysis provides a comparative between the state of art and the state of practices of VSEs toward the implementation of an international standard. The results show as main weakness in activities related to the execution of verification and validation to the project artifacts as well as the lack of definition of test cases and test procedures (Muñoz, Peralta & Laporte, 2019).

Context, Problems and Research Achievements Related to the "Software Tools" Aspect

The results of implementing the MIGME-RRC methodology highlighted the need to support the use and implementation of processes. Therefore, as part of a postdoctoral stay, a research focused on the development of software applications to be used by software development organizations, which facilitate the implementation and use of software process improvements, was performed.

The research context was set on that even when organizations were motivated to implement software process improvements, not all have the knowledge to do that. To achieve it, Small and Medium Enterprises (SMEs) were focused due to their importance in worldwide industry economy (Pino, García & Piattini, 2008), (Garcia, Pacheco & Cruz, 2010). SMEs cover two type of companies the small enterprises which are companies with between 25 and 50 employees, and medium enterprises which are companies that have between 50 and 249 employees (Muñoz et al., 2012). The problem addressed in this research are focused on facilitating the implementation of improvements taking into account that they do not invest much on software process improvements (Muñoz et al., 2012).

To perform this research, in-depth software process improvement analysis in SMEs were performed covering three steps: (1) to understand the SMEs work culture; (2) to understand the needs of SMEs to implement SPI initiatives, and (3) to analyze the existing support to allow SMEs implementing SPI (Muñoz et al., 2012).

As results of the first step were established a set of features classified in four categories, as next listed (Muñoz et al., 2012):

1. **Organization:** It refers to the SME environment, and it has 6 features (high innovation and adoption, agile for change, daily changes, limited customer with high dependency, focus on practices, and project with short delivery time).
2. **Staff:** It refers to the human resources working in a SME, and it has 3 features (limited staff, many activities, and lack of process culture).
3. **Software Process:** It refers to the importance of the processes for SME, and it has 2 features (minimum training related to process, and poorly formalization of process and procedures).
4. **Software Process Improvement:** It refers to how is performed activities related to the implementation of improvements, and it has 3 features (all staff involved, lack of resources and lack of support).

As result of the second step were identified a set of success factors toward the implementation of software process improvements in SPI (Muñoz et al., 2012):

1. *Regarding the organization*, there were highlighted the availability of resources as well as an efficient communication mechanism.
2. *Regarding the staff*, there were identified the commitment of stakeholders and senior management commitments; the involvement of stakeholder, and the training on process and on SPI.
3. *Regarding the software process*, an adequate assessment frequency was highlighted.
4. *Regarding the implementation of improvements*, there were highlighted the use of guides in order to base the improvement programs on real organizational needs, the uses of incremental approaches, to provide the support and infrastructure required, and the selection of adequate reference model and/or standard.

Finally, as result of the third step were identified that most of tools were focused on the first step of the SPI but not on the rest of the SPI cycle. Therefore, there were established a set of nine requirements that a support tool should meet to help SMEs in the implementation of SPI (Muñoz et al., 2012):

1. **Process Assessment:** It refers to provide a fast assessment to the organizational processes.

2. **Snapshot of Process:** It refers to get an overview of the organizational process at specific time.
3. **Guide the Process Selection:** It refers to support in the selection of the processes to be improved.
4. **Process Modeling:** It refers to provide the resources that allows SMEs the formalization, and storage of their organizational processes.
5. **Facilitate the Improvement Implementation:** It refers to provide information of roles, and activities to be performed during the implementation of an improvement.
6. **Low Cost:** It refers to not implying a great investment for the SME.
7. **Self- Training:** It refers to the training included as part of the tool.
8. Efficient communication: it refers to enable the communication channels and knowledge sharing among people involved in the SPI.
9. **Useful Information:** It refers to provide visible information regarding the achievements of goals related to the amount of work to do as part of the SPI.

The achievements of this research, regarding the software tools were focused on providing software tools as support for the implementation of process improvements, having as main results:

1. A tool for the selection of strategies for implementing software process improvements in VSEs. This tool is a result of a research that addressed the gap of the existence of software tools that support SMEs in the implementation of process improvement initiatives taking into account the way an organization develop software projects (Duron & Muñoz, 2013).
2. A tool for providing a starting point to help SMEs for implementing software process improvements. This tool is a result of a research that addressed the lack of knowledge on how to start a process improvement effort. Therefore, this tool allows addressing the improvements effort in a software development organization based on the identification of their main problems, to achieve it this tool used a set of patterns to provide a starting point regarding the model, standard or agile methodology to be used as reference and focusing on the organization current needs, features and work culture. The tool was implemented in four SMEs of Mexico providing them the information regarding the model, process and practices that should be implemented to reduce the problems (more information of the case study is found in (Muñoz-Mata, Mejía-Miranda & Valtierra-Alvarado, 2015), (Muñoz et al., 2015).
3. A tool for using a method for lightening software processes through optimizing the selection of software engineering best practices. This tool resulted from a research that focused on lightening software processes, especially SMEs, so that the processes are optimized based on practices that add more value to the SME. More information about the method and the tool resulted from this research, as well as the case study of its application is found in (Muñoz, Mejía & Miramontes, 2016).
4. A tool for reinforcing the implementation of multi-model environments in software process improvements using knowledge management. This tool is focused on the reinforcement of multi-model environments using ontologies, it allows performing an analysis of process improvement opportunities helping SMEs to know the level of coverage of its current project management process related to activities, tools, metrics and measures proposed by different models and standards. The tool and case study performed to validate this tool is found in management (Mejía, Muñoz & Muñoz, 2016).

5. A study of tools for assessing the implementation and use of agile methodologies. This study aims to identify a correct way to assess the implementation of an agile methodology. To achieve it, a set of 41 diagnostic assessment tools found in literature were analyzed, to identify the agile elements covered by them (Muñoz et al, 2017b).

Context, Problems and Research Achievements Related to the "Human Factor" Aspect

During the execution of the research from the models and standards and support tools aspects, there were detected the importance of the human factor as main actor to become reality the implementation, and use of Software Engineering. An important fact is that you can have the best models, standards, software tools, but if you have people who do not want to use it, those resources will not work.

Due to the importance of this factor, this research was starting since 2012 and has been reaching so that, this factor becomes a pivot of the other three factors. It is important to mention that this research has been done since the author started working in the Software Engineering unit at the Mathematic Research Center.

The research context was set on that the approaches created in software process improvement area are focused on providing formal process descriptions, where models and standards of best practices have been developed. However, the human factor has been forgotten. Therefore, even when organizations are motivated to implement improvements the lack of having a SPI culture becomes a really challenge to achieve it.

The problem addressed in this research are focused on analyzing the SPI needs from the human perspective, because most of times the failure in the implementation of SPI, and even in the development of software projects are not related to technical issues but on human issues.

It is important to highlight that this research covers as human factor: (1) people working in a SPI initiative; (2) people working on software development teams, (3) engineers related to software development, and (4) undergraduates related to software engineering. Then, the achievements on researching in the human factor will be listed according to the work developed for each of them.

1. **Research Work Related to People Working in a SPI Initiative:** The research developed in this topic is focused on providing triggers to involve people and get its commitment regarding the implementation of success SPI initiatives. The achievements of this research have been:
   a. A characterization of SPI from the human perspective. Performing this research work it was possible to characterized the SPI needs and related problems from SMEs focusing on aspects such as organization, people, processes, financial resources, projects and models and standards. Besides, as result a set of patters to address the identified problems were defined (Muñoz et al., 2014), (Muñoz et al., 2014b), (Muñoz-Mata, Mejía-Miranda & Valtierra-Alvarado, 2015).
   b. The creation of strategies to implement best practices according to the work culture of an organization. These strategies aim to provide a set of steps to implement an improvement initiative according to the way of work of a SME regarding the development of a software project (Duron & Munoz, 2013).
2. **Research Work Related to People Working of Software Development Teams:** The research developed in this topic is focused on developing a method to integrate high effective development teams. This research has been growing up becoming multidisciplinary, and adding other topics

such as gamification, interactive styles, and virtual environments allowing to collaborate with other researchers. The achievements of this research have been:

a. An exploratory model to integrate high effective teams. This model aims to join topics such as software development methodology, interactive styles, virtual environments, and gamification to propose an innovative way to integrate effective teams. (Muñoz et al., 2016) (Muñoz et al., 2017). This method was developed in collaboration with the University of Guadalajara of Mexico.

b. A comparative analysis in which the implementation of an international standard is performed between team using adaptative and predictive software development methodologies. This analysis aims to identify the differences that VSEs using three development methodologies (traditional, agile and hybrid) to identify the differences regarding the implementation of an international standard (Muñoz et al., 2019d).

3. **Research Work Related to Engineers Working with Software Development:** The research developed in this topic is to provide the resources to help software engineers to develop soft kills that will reinforce them to be able to work as a team member. The achievements have been:

a. The use of gamification to identify team members profiles, this research includes gamification, teams, and virtual environments to identify those gamification elements that can be useful for identifying team members that can be have a better performance in the integration of a team. Besides, virtual environments are used to provide an attractive way (Hernández et al., 2016; Hernández et al, 2017; Muñoz et al., 2018c; Muñoz, Peña & Hernández, 2019). This research was developed in collaboration with the University of Guadalajara of Mexico.

4. **Research Work Related to Undergraduates Related to Software Engineering:** The research developed in this topic is related to analyze the gap among the software industry requirements, and the knowledge provided at universities. Then, the needs in the academic field, especially regarding the knowledge to be provided to students, are highlighted. The achievements of this research have been:

a. Analysis of the coverage among national and international standards, and a set of Mexican universities curricula, this research is focused on identify the gaps regarding the requested knowledge to work with quality standards and the knowledge provided at universities related with curricula related to Computer Science. Besides, this research covered an extension of the analysis in which it is analyzed the knowledge provided in Computer Science curricula at universities versus the knowledge requested in industry (Muñoz et al, 2015b; Muñoz et al, 2016b; Muñoz et al, 2016c; Muñoz et al, 2017c). This analysis was developed in collaboration with the University of Guadalajara of Mexico.

b. The implementation of the international standard ISO/IEC 29110 in Software Development Centers (SDCs). A SDC provides students the opportunity to get the experience of working under international standards to produce high-quality software products, as mentioned before one of the main problems SE has is the lack of knowledge transfer among software engineering researchers and the academy, then this research was focused on analyzing the implementation of a method to support a SDC in the implementation and use of an international standard. By this way, it is possible to reinforce the students' knowledge regarding the use of best practices to develop software for real customers. (Muñoz, Mejía & Laporte, 2018b; Muñoz et al., 2019b).

Context, Problems and Research Achievements Related to the "Methods and Methodologies" Aspect

Software engineering is relative a young area within Computer Science, therefore to provide the way "for doing something" has a high value. The context of this research was set on that most of software development organizations lack of experience and knowledge in the implementation of SPI, then it is necessary to provide a structured way to implement SPI, then it is necessary to provide "how" they can easily achieve it in an optimal way. The development of methods and methodologies has been mainly focused on SMEs and VSEs because they have limited resources (time, budget and human resources) to implement SPI, and therefore, to jump into a continuous software process improvement culture. The achievements of this research have been:

1. A method for establishing strategies to implement software process improvements. This method is the result of a research who is focused on providing strategies for the implementation of SPI based on the contextual aspects in which the software is developed, so that, the strategy is provided according to the organization needs and their work culture regarding project management (Muñoz et al., 2016).

2. A method that allows optimizing software process focusing on software engineering best practices. This method is the result of a research who aimed to addresses the optimization of an organizational software processes through optimizing the selection of software engineering practices while promoting a culture of continuous improvement (Muñoz, Mejía & Miramontes, 2016).

3. A method for developing catalogs to facilitate the implementation of software engineering practices. This method is the result of research who aimed to implement best practices tailored according to the size and type of the company and to get the tools and techniques that enable them to achieve it. Therefore, the method provides six steps to build catalogs of tools and techniques that can be easy adopted by the organization related to the targeted process (García et al, 2016). This method was developed in a collaboration with the Universidad de Medellín of Colombia.

4. A method to help VSEs to increment their competitiveness using the Basic profile of the international standard ISO/IEC 29110 This method is the result of a research who aimed to transfer the knowledge of SE researchers to industry, the method offers a set of steps that allows support the implementation of an international standard to VSEs. Besides, the method was proved in a set of VSEs of the Zacatecas Region, more information about the case study was published in (Muñoz, Mejía & Laporte, 2018; Muñoz, Mejía & Laporte, 2019). This method was built with in project to boost the VSEs that has been executed in collaboration with the secretary of economy of Zacatecas, Mexico, and another achievement of this research has been helping 19 VSEs to be certified in the basic profile of ISO/IEC 29110 (NYCE, 2020).

Another important result was to be invited to build the guide to help VSEs using agile environments to implement best practices of the basic profile of ISO/IEC 29110, as well as in the translation of the entry profile of the ISO/IEC 29110 to Spanish language.

5.   A Proposal to Avoid Issues in the DevOps Implementation: A Systematic Literature Review. This research aims to provides a guideline that allows establishing a generic DevOps process reinforced with the proven practices of the Basic profile of the ISO/IEC 29110 (Muñoz, Negrete & Mejía, 2019).

DISCUSSION, CONCLUSION AND FUTURE TRENDS

Discussion

Software Engineering (SE) pursue the establishment and use of software engineering practices, so that it boosting organizations (large, SMEs and VSEs), to obtain high-quality software products and services that are economical, reliable, and efficient to meet the needs of software market.

Even when Software Engineering is young area in Computer Sciences, it has becoming indispensable because the core of a great amount of organizations in different industrial domains is the software. The software allows software development organizations to generate software products, and services capable of providing high-performance solutions to problems of different domains (industrial, agricultural, aeronautics, Information and Communication Technologies, among others).

The above-mentioned highlights the opportunity for software development organizations to produce high-quality software products and services to satisfy market needs.

In this context, this chapter provides the results of a research performed since 2005, which is focused on software process improvement, covering the four aspects:

- **Models and Standards:** In this aspect, the main research results have been focused on the right implementation of models and standards for organizations (large, MSEs and VSEs).
- Support tools: in this aspect, the main results have been focused on providing support to facilitate the implementation of the SPI since the beginning and throughout all improvement implementation.
- **Human Factor:** In this aspect, the main results have been focused on the one hand to provide the resources to facilitate the implementation of SPI in organizations as well as the integration of effective teams using innovative way such as the use of gamification, interactive styles and virtual environments. On the other hand, to provide resources that serve as an input to reduce the gap between academic and industry knowledge requirements. Besides, to provide innovative ways to make the Software engineering topic training attractive for students and SE professionals.
- **Methods and Methodologies:** In this aspect, the main results have been focused on providing a guide to reduce the gap of "how" to implement and use best practices based on the organizational work culture and current needs.

All together has been integrating the research path toward boosting the competitiveness of software development organizations.

However, there is too much work to do, so this chapter aims to serve as base for the development future research in SE.

CONCLUSION

Software development organizations have increased their importance around the world because they create valuable products, and services to achieve the software market requirements. This fact provides an opportunity to them to a steady grow up, and its market survival. Besides, it brings the responsibility to researchers to provide the support to help them in the improvement of their development processes.

However, transferring the Software Engineering knowledge developed by researchers to the industry is a gap that should be reduced. In this context, this chapter provided a research path that has had an impact towards diminishing that gap, and providing the support that enables software development organizations to get advantage of the resources resulting of research works.

The author of this chapter hopes this could inspire young researchers to continue reducing the gap between industry and academic areas, because research can benefit industry but industry can benefit academic being the main source of challenges and problems to be solve. In this context, some finding that could be highlighted as challenges in SPI of the factors addressed in this chapter are next listed:

- **Models and Standards:** Regarding this factor, they should be broadened so that all type of software development organizations (large, SMEs, and VSEs) continue keeping the use of software engineering best practices no matter the domain they are providing software because no only the quality feature, but also security together are becoming very important and critical features that all software must achieve.

- **Software Tools:** One of the main findings regarding this factor is that they are an increasing demanding of tools that make it easy the implementation and use of software development processes, providing the required support that processes' users need to perform their daily tasks. One important aspect to highlight is that more than ever, these tools should allow knowledge sharing and resources among teams. Besides, software tools should take into account the type of new software services that software development organizations are demanding such as: infrastructure as a service, platform as a service, and software as a service.

- **People:** This factor is from the point of view of the author the one that could have most challenges because having the best models and standards, software tools and methods, and methodologies if people don't want to use it, nothing can be done. Therefore, it is important to change people's culture toward a continuous improvement culture in the early stages at universities, changing the view they perceived the usefulness of software engineering. Besides, for professionals working in teams and as part of software development organizations, keeping them in a continuous knowledge transfer from research results that can help them to get better results through the implementation of new resources to achieve both quality and security while perceiving them as an evolution of the way they work.

- **Methods and Methodologies:** Regarding this factor, they should be carefully analyzed and evolve according to the new needs of shape, design, develop, prove and deploy software, so that the use of them can help software development organizations to meet with time, budget and effort of software development projects while enabling the implementation of SPI in software development organizations.

FUTURE TRENDS

As mentioned in the Discussion section, in Software Engineering area there is too much to do. As Computer Science is progressing, new challenges in Software Engineering arise. Then, the research path provided in this chapter is growing up considering new topics with high impact in the four factors: (1) the reinforcement of DevOps development with engineering practices; (2) the use of Artificial Intelligence (AI) techniques applied to Software Engineering; (3) the reinforcement of AI with SE; (4) the reinforcement of software development organizations using agile methods for software development; (5) the reinforcement of resources to bring a practical Software Engineering to the academy using gamification and serious games; and (6) the development of soft skills to undergraduates, and engineers using Artificial Intelligence and gamification.

All above topics are the future trends that as researcher, the author of this chapter will work in next years.

ACKNOWLEDGMENT

The author would like to thanks all the coauthors of the papers included in this chapter and who has been shared this research path. The author would also like to thanks Gonzalo Cuevas, Jose A. Calvo Manzano, Tomas San Feliu, and Claude Y. Laporte for sharing their knowledge and experiences. Special thanks to Jezreel Mejía for his valuable time, effort, and support during this entire research period. Besides, I would like to thanks two strong women Adriana Peña and Gloria Gasca for keep with me throughout this path. Finally, I would like to thanks all my students Brenda Duron, Claudia Valtierra, Juan Jose Miramontes, Saul Hernández, Luis Ángel Hernández, Manuel Peralta, and Mario Rodriguez for their effort in the development of specific parts of this research path.

REFERENCES

Calvo-Manzano, J.A., Cuevas, G., Gómez, G., Mejía, J., Muñoz, M., & San Feliu, T. (2010). *Journal of Software Maintenance and Evolution: Research and Practice*. Doi:10.1002mr.505

Calvo-Manzano, J. A., Cuevas, G., Muñoz, M., & San Feliu, T. (2008). Process similarity study: Case study on project planning practices based on CMMI-DEV v1.2. EuroSPI 2008 Industrial Proceedings.

Conradi, H., & Fuggetta, A. (2002). Improving software process improvement. *Software IEEE, 19*(4), 92–99. doi:10.1109/MS.2002.1020295

Cuevas, G., Calvo Manzano, J., San Feliu, T., Mejia, J., Muñoz, M., & Bayona, S. (2007). Impact of TSPi on Software Projects. *Electronics, Robotics and Automotive Mechanics Conference (CERMA 2007)*, 706-711, 10.1109/CERMA.2007.4367770

Cuevas, G., De Amescua, A., San Feliu, T., Arcilla, M., Cerrada, J. A., Calvo-Manzano, J. A., & García, M. (2002). *Gestión del Proceso Software*. Universitaria Ramon Areces.

Durón, B., & Muñoz, M. (2013). Selección de estrategias para la implementación de mejoras. *Revista electrónica de Computación, Informática, Biomédica y Electrónica (ReCIBE), 3*, 1-15.

García, I., Pacheco, C., & Cruz, D. (2010). Adopting an RIA based tool for supporting assessment, implementation and learning in software in software process improvement under the NMX-I-059/02-NYCE-2005 standard in small software enterprises. *Eighth ACIS International Conference on Software Engineering Research. Management and Application.* 10.1109/SERA.2010.14

García, Y. M., Muñoz, M., Mejía, J., Martínez, J., Gasca-Hurtado, G. P., & Hincapié, J. A. (2016). Method for Developing Catalogs focused on Facilitating the implementation of Best Practices for Project Management of Software Development in SMEs, *Proceedings of the 5th International Conference in Software Process Improvement (CIMPS 2016), 1-8.* 10.1109/CIMPS.2016.7802805

Gibson, D., Goldenson, D., & Kost, K. (2006). *Performance results of CMMI-based process improvement*. Technical Report CMU/SEI-2006-TR-004 ESC-TR-2006-004, Software Engineering Institute (SEI), Carnegie Mellon University.

Goldenson D. (2007). Teach views, performance outcomes from process improvement. *Software Technology News, 10*(1).

Hernández, L., Muñoz, M., Mejia, J., & Peña, A. (2016). Gamification in software engineering team works: A systematic literature review, *Proceedings of the 5th International Conference in Software Process Improvement (CIMPS 2016), 1-8.*

Hernández, L., Muñoz, M., Mejia, J., Peña, A., Calvo-Manzano, J. A., & San Feliu, T. (2017). Proposal for identifying teamwork roles in software engineering through the construction of a virtual rube goldberg machine. *6th International Conference on Software Process Improvement (CIMPS), 1-8.* 10.1109/CIMPS.2017.8169953

Ibarra, S., & Muñoz, M. (2018). Support tool for software quality assurance in software development. *International Conference on Software Process Improvement CIMPS 2018, 13-19.* 10.1109/CIMPS.2018.8625617

Laporte, C. Y., Muñoz, M., Mejía, J., & O'Connor, R. (2017). Applying Software Engineering Standards in Very Small Entities. *IEEE Software*, 99-103.

Mejía J., Muñoz E., & Muñoz M. (2016). Reinforcing the applicability of Multi-model Environments for Software Process Improvement using Knowledge Management. Science of Computer Programming, Elsevier, Vol. SCICO, Pag.1-13. doi:10.1016/j.scico.2015.12.002

Morgan, P. (2009). Process improvement—Is it a lottery? *Software Development Magazine*. Available at: http://www.methodsandtools.com/archive/archive.php?id=52

Muñoz, M., Hernández, L., Mejía, M., Peña, A., Rangel, N., Torres, C., & Sauberer, G. (2017). A model to integrate highly effective teams for software development. In System, Software and services Process Improvement. Springer International Publishing AG. Doi:10.1007/978-3-319-64218-5_51

Muñoz, M., Mejía, J., Calvo-Manzano, J. A., Gonzalo, C., San Feliu, T., & De Amescua, A. (2012). Expected Requirements in Support Tools for Software Process Improvement in SMEs. *2012 IEEE Ninth Electronics, Robotics and Automotive Mechanics Conference*, 135-140. doi: 10.1109/CERMA.2012.29

Muñoz, M., Mejía, J., Calvo-Manzano, J. A., San Feliu, T., Corona, B., & Miramontes, J. (2017b). Diagnostic Assessment Tools for Assessing the Implementation and/or Use of Agile Methodologies in SMEs: An Analysis of Covered Aspects. *Software Quality Professional, 19*(2), 16-27.

Muñoz, M., Mejía, J., & de León, M. (2020). Investigación en el área de Mejora de Procesos de Software in Ingeniería de Software en México: Educación, Industria e Investigación. Academia Mexicana de Computación.

Muñoz, M., Mejía, J., Duron, B., & Valtierra, C. (2014). Software process improvement from a human perspective. In *New Perspectives in Information System and Technologies*. Springer International Publishing.

Muñoz, M., Mejia, J., & Gasca-Hurtado, G.P. (2014). A Methodology for Establishing Multi-Model Environments in Order to Improve Organizational Software Processes. *International Journal of Software Engineering and Knowledge Engineering, 24*, 909-933.

Muñoz, M., Mejía, J., Gasca-Hurtado, G. P., Gómez-Alvarez, M. C., & Duron, B. (2016). Method to Establish Strategies for Implementing Process Improvement According to the Organization's Context, System, Software and Services Process Improvement. Springer International Publishing.

Muñoz, M., Mejía, J., Gasca-Hurtado, G. P., Valtierra, C., & Duron, B. (2014b). Covering the human perspective in software process improvement. In *System, Software and Services Process Improvement*. Springer Berlin Heidelberg.

Muñoz, M., Mejía, J., Gasca-Hurtado, G. P., Vega-Zepeda, V., & Valtierra, C. (2015). Providing a Starting Point to Help SMEs in the Implementation of Software Process Improvements. In System, Software and Services Process Improvement. Springer.

Muñoz, M., Mejía, J., & Laporte, C. Y. (2018). *Reinforcing Very Small Entities Using Agile Methodologies with the ISO/IEC 29110. In Trends and Applications in Software Engineering. Springer.* https://doi-org.svproxy01.cimat.mx/10.1007/978-3-030-01171-0_8

Muñoz, M., Mejía, J., & Miramontes, J. (2016). Method for Lightening Software Processes through Optimizing the Selection of Software Engineering Best Practices. In Trends and Applications in Software Engineering. Springer International.

Muñoz, M., Mejía, J., & Muñoz, E. (2013). Knowledge management to support using muti-model environments in software process improvement. European System, Software & Service Process Improvement & Innovation EuroSPI 2013, 1-10.

Muñoz, M., Mejía, J., Peña, A., Lara, G., & Laporte, C. Y. (2019b, October). Transitioning international software engineering standards to academia: Analyzing the results of the adoption of ISO/IEC 29110 in four Mexican universities. *Computer Standards & Interfaces, 66*, 103340. doi:10.1016/j.csi.2019.03.008

Muñoz, M., Mejía, M., & Laporte, C. Y. (2018b). Implementación del Estándar ISO/IEC 29110 en Centros de Desarrollo de Software de Universidades Mexicanas: Experiencia del Estado de Zacatecas. *Revista Ibérica de Sistemas y Tecnologías de Informatión (RISTI), 29*(10).

Muñoz, M., Mejía, M., & Laporte, C. Y. (2019). Implementing ISO/IEC 29110 to Reinforce four Very Small Entities of Mexico under Agile Approach. *IET Software*, (March), 1–11. doi:10.1049/iet-sen.2019.0040

Muñoz, M., Mejía, M., Peña, A., & Rangel, N. (2016). Establishing Effective Software Development Teams: An Exploratory Model, System. In Software and Services Process Improvement. Springer International.

Muñoz, M., Negrete, M., & Mejía, J. (2019). Proposal to Avoid Issues in the DevOps Implementation: A Systematic Literature Review. In Á. Rocha, H. Adeli, L. Reis, & S. Costanzo (Eds.), *New Knowledge in Information Systems and Technologies. WorldCIST'19 2019. Advances in Intelligent Systems and Computing* (Vol. 930, pp. 666–677). Springer. https://doi-org.svproxy01.cimat.mx/10.1007/978-3-030-16181-1_63

Muñoz, M., Peña, A., & Hernández, L. (2019). Gamification in Virtual reality Environments for the integration of Highly Effective Teams. In Virtual Reality Designs. Science Publishers.

Muñoz, M., Peña, A., Mejía, J., Gasca-Hurtado, G. P., Gómez-Álvarez, M. C., & Hernández, L. (2018c). *Gamification to Identify Software Development Team Members' Profiles. In Systems, Software and Services Process Improvement. Springer*. https://doi-org.svproxy01.cimat.mx/10.1007/978-3-319-97925-0_18

Muñoz, M., Peña, A., Mejía, J., Gasca-Hurtado, G. P., Gómez-Alvarez, M. C., & Hernández, L. (2019c, April). Applying gamification elements to build teams for software development. *IET Software, 13*(2), 99–105. doi:10.1049/iet-sen.2018.5088

Muñoz, M., Peña, A., Mejía, J., Gasca-Hurtado, G. P., Gómez-Álvarez, M. C., & Laporte, C. Y. (2019d). A Comparative Analysis of the Implementation of the Software Basic Profile of ISO/IEC 29110 in Thirteen Teams That Used Predictive Versus Adaptive Life Cycles. In A. Walker, R. O'Connor, & R. Messnarz (Eds.), *Systems, Software and Services Process Improvement. EuroSPI 2019. Communications in Computer and Information Science* (Vol. 1060, pp. 179–191). Springer. doi:10.1007/978-3-030-28005-5_14

Muñoz, M., Peña, A., Mejía, J., & Lara, G. (2015b). *Analysis of Coverage of Moprosoft Practices in Curricula Programs Related to Computer Science and Informatics, Trends and Applications in Software Engineering Series: Advances in Intelligent Systems and Computing 405* (Vol. 405). Springer Berlin Heidelberg.

Muñoz, M., Peña, A., Mejía, J., & Lara, G. (2016b). Actual State of the Coverage of Mexican Software Industry Requested Knowledge Regarding the Project Management Best Practices. Computer Science and Information Systems (ComSIS), 13, 849-873.

Muñoz, M., Peña, A., Mejía, J., & Lara, G. (2016c). Coverage of the University Curricula for the Software Engineering Industry in Mexico. *IEEE Latin America Transactions, 14*, 2383-2389.

Muñoz, M., Peña, A., Mejía, J., & Lara, G. (2017c). ISO/IEC 29110 and Curricula Programs Related to Computer Science and Informatics in Mexico: Analysis of practices coverage. Springer International Publishing AG. doi:10.1007/978-3-319-69341-5_1

Muñoz, M., Peralta, M., & Laporte, C.Y. (2019). Análisis de las debilidades que presentan las Entidades Muy Pequeñas al implementar el estándar ISO/IEC 29110: Una comparativa entre estado del arte y el estado de la práctica. *RISTI, 34*(10).

Muñoz-Mata, M., Mejía-Miranda, J., & Valtierra-Alvarado, C. (2015). Helping Organizations to Address their Effort toward the Implementation of Improvements in their Software Process. *Revista Facultad de Ingeniería, 77*, 115-126.

NYCE. (2020). *Companies certified to ISO/IEC 29110-4-1:2011 standard*. Retrieved at https://www.nyce. org.mx/wp-content/uploads/2020/01/PADRON-DE-EMPRESAS-CERTIFICADAS-EN-LA-NORMA-ISO-IEC-29110-4-1-16-01-2020.pdf

Pino, J. F., García, F., & Piattini, M. (2008). Software process improvement in small and medium software enterprises: A systematic review. *SQJournal, 16*, 237–261.

Potter, N., & Sakry, M. (2006). *Making Process Improvement Work: A Concise Action Guide for Software Managers and Practitioners* (pp. 2–5). Addison-Wesley.

Pressman, R. S. (2002). *Ingeniería de Software: Un enfoque práctico. 5a edición*. McGraw-Hill.

Software Engineering Institute. (2007). *CMMI Performance Results. TATA Consultancy Services*. Software Engineering Institute (SEI), Carnegie Mellon University. Available at: http://www.sei.cmu.edu/cmmi/results/org29.html#BC2

Williams, T. (2008). How do organizations learn lessons from projects and do they? *IEEE Transactions on Engineering Management, 55*(2), 248–266. doi:10.1109/TEM.2007.912920

KEY TERMS AND DEFINITIONS

CMMI-DEV® v1.2: It is a capability and maturity model for software process improvement proposed by the Software Engineering Institute. This model aims to provide support to organizations for products and services development. It has a collection of best practices that address the development and maintenance of the activities that cover the product life cycle.

COBIT: Is an open standard, which structure provides best practices through a process domain and environment, and presents activities within a logical and manageable structure.

DevOps: It is a set of practices emerging to bridge the gaps between operation and developer teams to achieve a better collaboration.

ISO 9001-2000-Quality Management System: It is a standard focused on the efficiency of a quality management system to achieve customer requirements, covering the requirements for quality systems that support all product lifecycle, including initial agreements on deliverables, design, development and product support.

ISO/IEC 15504: Information Technology-Process Assessment: It is an international standard that provides a structured focus for the process assessment. It is five part "assessment model and indicators guide", it contains a set of software engineering best practices for each process: customers and suppliers, engineering, support, management, and organization.

Large Organizations: Is the term used to refer to an enterprise having from 51 to 250 people.

Multi-Model Environment: It involves all cultural aspects and the knowledge that makes advisable to use in each process a mix of best practices from more than one model or standard to achieve the organization's business goals.

PRINCE2: Methodology based on project management that present a ser of processes easy tailored and scalable for manage all type pf projects. It was designed to provide a common language through all stakeholders involved in the project. It describes how to divide a project in manage steps, enabling efficient control for resources, as well as a regular process through the project.

Project Management Book of Knowledge (PMBOK): Reference model that has project management process, tools, and techniques, and provides a set of high-level business process for all type of industry.

Small and Medium Enterprises: SMEs by its acronym is the term used to refer to an enterprise having from 25 to 50 people.

Software Engineering: It is the establishment and use of robust, targeted engineering principles to obtain economic, reliable, efficient software that satisfies the user needs.

Software Process Improvement: It is a field of research and practice, arising out of the need to solve software development issues. It covers the actions taken by organizations to change processes, according to the business needs and achieving their business goals more effectively.

Team Software Process® (TSP®): Methodology for developing software in teams, where they should plan and estimate their product, achieve their commitments, and improve their productivity and quality. TSP aims to provide a defined process, to recognize the process importance, and to know, base of available information, how to improve a process.

Very Small Entities: VSE by its acronym is the term used to refer to an enterprise, organization (e.g., public or non-profit organization), project or department having up to 25 people.

Chapter 10
Software Architecture:
Developing Knowledge, Skills, and Experiences

Perla Velasco-Elizondo

Universidad Autónoma de Zacatecas (UAZ), México

ABSTRACT

What is software architecture? A clear and simple definition is that software architecture is about making important design decisions that you want to get right early in the development of a software system because, in the future, they are costly to change. Being a good software architect is not easy. It requires not only a deep technical competency from practicing software architecture design in industry, but also an excellent understanding of the theoretical foundations of software architecture are gained from doing software architecture research. This chapter describes some significant research, development, and education activities that the author has performed during her professional trajectory path to develop knowledge, skills, and experiences around this topic.

INTRODUCTION

What is software architecture? To say it simple: software architecture is about making the design decisions that you want to get right early in the development of a software system, because future changes are costly. Today, software architecture development is necessary as never before; no organization begins a complex software system without a suitable software architecture.

Within the context of the software life cycle (Sommerville, 2011), software architecture is an artifact produced during the design phase. A software architect, or the software architecture design team, is responsible for defining software architecture. Being a good software architect is not an easy matter (Rehman et al., 2018), (Shahbazian, Lee & Medvidovic, 2018). The author considers that, it not only requires deep technical competency which comes from practicing software architecture design in industry; but also a very good understanding of the theoretical foundations of software architecture gained from doing software architecture research.

DOI: 10.4018/978-1-7998-7552-9.ch010

Copyright © 2021, IGI Global. Copying or distributing in print or electronic forms without written permission of IGI Global is prohibited.

Dr. Velasco-Elizondo finds the topic of software architecture fascinating. This chapter describes some of the significant research, education and, coaching activities she has undertaken during her professional trajectory path to develop knowledge, skills and experiences on this topic. She hopes that this material helps to encourage readers and, particularly, other women to get involved in science, technology and engineering.

This chapter will cover the following sections:

- **Getting it right: software architecture foundations**. This section describes how software architecture foundations are conceived and an example of why preserving them in practice is not always straightforward. It will discuss how to tackle this shortcoming with the proposal of exogenous connectors.

- **Practicing it right: software architecture methods**. In this section, the notion of software architecture lifecycle is introduced. Relevant methods for software architecture development are then briefly discussed within the context of this lifecycle, as well as some limitations related to the difficulty of adopting these methods in practice. Finally, an explanation of why and how technology has to be considered as a first-class design concept in order to tackle one of these limitations will be given.

- **Automating technology selection**. This section presents a software tool, recently developed, which uses information retrieval, natural language processing and sematic web techniques to address the problem of automating NoSQL database technologies search.

- **Software architecture education**. This section describes two educational projects Dr. Velasco-Elizondo has led to promote knowledge and practical experiences on software architecture design and development.

- **Hands on.** Dr. Velasco-Elizondo has had the opportunity to work, as a coach, with practicing software architects and developers helping them to deploy software architecture practices and methods. In this section some of these works will be described.

GETTING IT RIGHT: SOFTWARE ARCHITECTURE FOUNDATIONS

Software architecture has always existed as part of the discipline of Software Engineering. This section describes how software architecture foundations are conceived and gives an example of why preserving them in practice is not always straightforward. The proposed use of exogenous connectors to tackle this shortcoming is also included.

Foundations in Theory

Back when systems were relatively "less complex and small", abstract diagrams were drawn to give stakeholders a better understanding of software designs when describing them. Later, systems went beyond simple algorithms and data structures becoming more complex and larger in size. Therefore, similar in practice to other branches of engineering, more structured diagrams were essential to describe software system designs and communicate regarding aspects such as their main parts and responsibilities, their communication and data model, etc.

Software architecture foundations were built from a high-level model that consists of elements, form, and rationale (Perry, & Wolf, 1992). Elements are first-class constructs representing either computation, data, or connectors. Form is defined in terms of the properties of, and the relationships among, the elements. The rationale provides the underlying basis for the architecture in terms of architectural significant requirements, a.k.a. architectural drivers (Bass, Clements, & Kazman, 2012). In alignment with these foundations, in their seminal book Bass, Clements and Kazman defined software architecture as the set of structures needed for reasoning about the system, which comprises software elements (i.e. computation and data), relations among them (i.e. connectors), and the properties of both (Bass, Clements, & Kazman, 2012). In software architecture design, reasoning is vital as it supports designers in making justifiable decisions (Tang et al., 2008). Thus, all these authors agree that effective reasoning about architectural constructs and their relationships requires a high degree of understanding of these foundations.

Thus, components and connectors have become the basis of many software architecture development approaches. For example, Architecture Description Languages (ADLs) have always defined architectures of software systems in terms of components and connectors connecting them (Shaw & Garlan, 1996). Also, the current version of the Unified Modeling Language (UML) uses connectors to compose components into architectures of software systems.

Foundations in Practice

Despite software architecture foundations and well-specified software architecture design, this nonetheless, tends to erode over time (de Silva & Balasubramaniam, 2012). A number of reasons for design erosion have been identified. One reason relates to the manner in which software architecture is implemented in practice. Software architecture foundations define a component as the principal unit of computation (or data storage) in a system, while connector is the communication mechanism to allow components to interact. However, in existing system implementation approaches, communication originates in components, and connectors are only channels for passing on the control flow to other components. Connectors are mechanism for message passing, which allows components to invoke one another's functionality by method calls (or remote procedure calls), either directly or indirectly, via these channels. Thus components in these approaches mix computation with communication, since in performing their computation they also initiate method calls and manage their returns, via connectors. Consequently, in terms of communication, components implementations are not loosely coupled.

Having components containing very specific communication information hinders their reuse. Software reuse has been defined as "the systematic use of existing software assets to construct new or modified assets" (Mohagheghi & Conradi, 2007). Software reuse is an important topic in Software Engineering as it is widely accepted that it is a means of increasing productivity, saving time, and reducing the cost of software development. Separating computation from communication means that system specific composition details are not in components and therefore components can be reused many times for constructing different systems.

With these shortcomings in mind, this work proposes exogenous connectors to support component composition (Lau & Wang, 2007).

Exogenous Connectors

Exogenous connectors are first-class architectural constructs, which as their name suggests, encapsulate *loci* of communication outside components. By analyzing the control flow required in software systems, a set of useful communication schemes—here defined as specific connector types—has been identified and a catalogue of connectors proposed (Velasco-Elizondo, 2010). The communication schemes are analogous to either control-flow structures that can be found in most programming languages or to behavioral patterns. Behavioral patterns are design solutions that describe common communication schemes among objects. Table 1 contains the connectors in this catalogue and their corresponding descriptions.

Table 1. A catalogue of exogenous connectors

Name	Description
Sequencer	Provides a composition scheme where the computation in the composed components is executed sequentially one after another.
Pipe	Provides a composition scheme where the computation in the composed components is executed sequentially one after another and the output of an execution is the input of the next one and so forth.
Selector	Provides a composition scheme where the computation in only one of the composed components is executed based on the evaluation of a Boolean expression
Observer	Provides a composition mechanism where once the computation in the "publisher" component has been performed; the computation in a set of "subscribers" components is executed sequentially.
Chain of responsibility	Provides a composition mechanism where more than one component in a set can handle a request for computation.
Exclusive choice sequencer	Provides a composition mechanism where once the computation in a "predecessor" component has been performed, the computation of only one component in a set of "successor" components is executed.
Exclusive choice pipe	A version of the exclusive choice sequencer with internal data communication among the "predecessor" and in a set of "successor" components.
Simple merge sequencer	Provides a composition mechanism where once the computation in only one component in a set of "predecessor" components has been performed, the computation in a set of "successor" component is executed.
Simple merge pipe	A version of the simple merge sequencer with internal data communication between the "predecessor" and the "successor" component.

Figure 1 shows an example of a system architecture with exogenous connectors. It consists of a hierarchy of connectors K1-K5 representing the system's communication, sitting on top of components that provide the computation performed by the system. A connector works as a composition operator that promotes compositionality. That is, when applied to components it yields another component, which is called *composite component*. A composite component can in turn be a subject of further composition. This is illustrated in Figure 1 by the inner dotted boxes.

The control flow in the resulting system is fixed and encapsulated by the corresponding connector structure. A system with exogenous connectors has a set of possible execution paths, but when the system is executed, only one execution path is carried out. The dotted line in Figure 1 shows one possible control flow path for the system represented by the architecture. The execution of the system starts with the connector at the highest level. Thus, the connector K5 invokes the computation in the composite component (containing C1 and C2 components) by calling its top-level connector K4. After that, the connector K5 calls the composite component (containing two composite components: C3 and C4-C6 components). Internally, its top-level connector K3 calls both inner composite components. After this sequence of executions is completed, the control flow is returned back through the hierarchy until reaching the top-level connector K5 that delivers the result of the executions.

Figure 1. An example of a system architecture with exogenous connectors

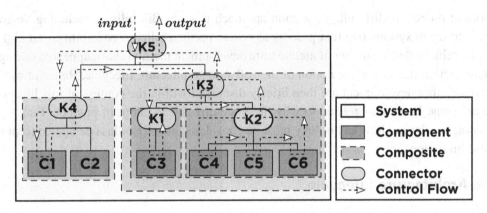

As it can be implied, exogenous connectors support an algebraic approach to component composition, namely, an approach inspired by algebra where the functionality in components is hierarchically composed into a new one of the same type. The resulting function can be further composed with other functions, yielding a more complex one. More formally, for an arbitrary number of levels (*L*), the connector type hierarchy can be defined in terms of dependent types and polymorphism as follows:

$L1 \circ$ Component $\circledR$ Result;
$L2 \circ L1 \times \ldots \times L1 \circledR$ Result;
For $2 < i \pounds n$, $Li \circ L(j_1) \times \ldots \times L(j_m) \circledR$ Result, for some *m*;
where $j_k \hat{I} \{1, \ldots, (i - 1)\}$ for $1 \pounds k \pounds m$,
$\{ L1, i = 1$
and $L(i) = \ldots$
$L1, i = n$.

Exogenous Connectors in Practice

Since they were proposed, exogenous connectors have been utilized in a variety of systems designs and implementations. Recent examples include IoT end-user smart homes (Arellanes & Lau, 2019) and vehicle control systems (Di Cola et al., 2015). These implementation exercises have all demonstrated the elimination of design erosion caused by not preserving components and connectors as first-class constructs at implementation time. Additionally, the use of exogenous connectors lead to a bottom-up, architecture centered development from reusable constructs. These reusable constructs include both, components and connectors.

Still under investigation is the fact that the use exogenous connectors to design and code system architectures inevitably leads to big hierarchies of connectors. Refactoring techniques for connectors can provide just such a facility.

PRACTICING IT RIGHT: SOFTWARE ARCHITECTURE DEVELOPMENT METHODS

If an important process is difficult, a common approach in many disciplines, including Software Engineering, is to try to systematize that process to ensure predictability, repeatability, and high-quality outcomes. To achieve that, a number of architecture development methods have appeared during the last decade. This section introduces the notion of the software architecture lifecycle. Relevant methods for software architecture development are then briefly discussed within the context of this lifecycle. Also discussed are some limitations related to why these are difficult to adopt in practice. Finally, there is an explanation of why and how technology must be considered as a first-class design concept to tackle one of these limitations.

Software Architecture Lifecycle

Ideally, software architecture development should be carried out within the context of a software architecture lifecycle, which provides a set of stages to follow, with its corresponding activities, to developing it (Cervantes, Velasco-Elizondo, & Kazman, 2013). In general, this lifecycle comprises the following stages, which are depicted in Figure 2:

1. **Requirements,** which focuses on identifying and prioritizing architectural requirements.
2. **Design,** which focuses on identifying and selecting the different constructs that compose the architecture and satisfy architectural requirements.
3. **Documentation**, which focuses on creating the documents that describe the different constructs that compose the architecture, in order to communicate it to different system stakeholders.
4. **Evaluation**, which focuses on assessing the software architecture design to determine whether it satisfies the architectural requirements.

METHODS TO SOFTWARE ARCHITECTURE DEVELOPMENT

For the purpose of this work, a *method* is assumed to be a series of detailed steps—with the corresponding instructions for implementation—to accomplish an end. Table 2 lists a set of well-known methods in software architecture development. It is generally considered that most of them exhibit limitations to effectively adopting them in practice, namely: (i) they do not cover all the stages of the architecture lifecycle, (ii) combining them is not always practical and efficient and (iii) they say very little about technology. Next, these limitations are further explained.

As Table 2 shows, most of the methods, apart from ACDM and RUP, do not cover all the stages of the architecture lifecycle. RUP covers them. However, RUP is a general approach to software develop-

Figure 2. Software architecture life cycle

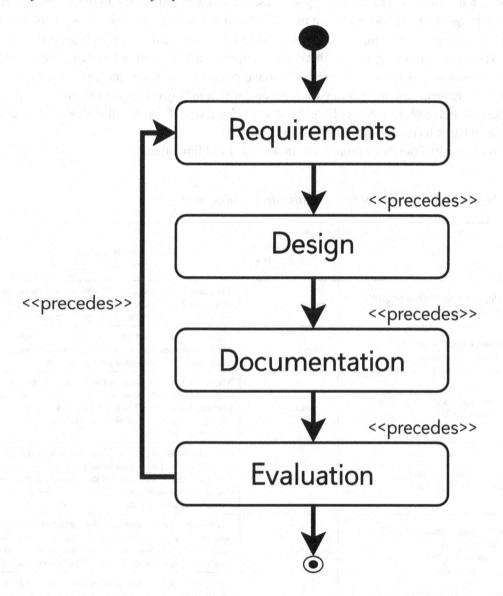

ment and the guidance that it provides with respect to each of the stages in the architecture lifecycle is very general.

The fact that architecture methods generally focus on a particular stage of the lifecycle requires, when doing software architecture development, selecting more than one method. However, the existence of more than one method to choose from for a particular stage of the lifecycle can complicate the selection. Besides, choosing an appropriate combination of the methods is not all that is required. One must also identify how the selected methods should be, practically and efficiently, used together. This is not trivial because different authors have defined these methods "in isolation". They are defined in terms of different activities, artifacts, and terminology. Thus, once an appropriate combination of methods is chosen, the architect must often modify them to avoid mismatches, omissions and/or repetitions.

Finally, architectural design is about applying a set of design decisions to satisfy architectural requirements and design decisions often involve the use of design concepts. *Design concepts* refer to a body of generally accepted architectural design solutions that can be used to create high quality architectural designs. There is a common agreement that design concepts include *reference architectures*, *deployment patterns*, *architectural patterns,* and *tactics*. Design concepts are abstract, and differ from the concepts that software architects use in their day-to-day work, which mostly come from technologies. Software architecture design methods say very little about technology, despite the fact that it is very critical to the success of and architecture design (Hofmeister et al., 2007).

Next section will describes a proposal to tackle this third limitation.

Table 2. Well-known methods for software architecture development

	Name	Software architecture lifecycle staged covered	Description
1	Quality Attribute Workshop (QAW) (Barbacci et al., 2003)	Requirements	It is a facilitated scenario-based method for defining the architectural *quality attributes* involving the stakeholders in a workshop. No other requirements types are considered.
2	Attribute Driven Design (ADD) (Cervantes & Kazman, 2016)	Design	It is an iterative method for designing software architectures in which, the designer decomposes the architecture into greater detail, considering *architectural requirements*.
3	The 4+1 view model (Kruchten, 1995)	Documentation	It is a model used for documenting software architectures, considering multiple, concurrent views from the viewpoint of different stakeholders. The four views of the model are *logical, development, process and physical*. The *use case* view serves as the 'plus one' view.
4	Views and Beyond (V&B) (Clements et al., 2010)	Documentation	It is a method and a collection of techniques for documenting software architectures, considering the following view types giving a different perspective of the structure of the system. The considered view types are: *module, component-and-connector* and the *allocation*.
7	The Software Architecture Analysis Method (SAAM) (Kazman et al., 1996)	Requirements, Evaluation.	It is a method for evaluating software architecture designs to point out the places where it fails to meet its *quality attribute requirements* and show obvious alternative designs that would work better. No other requirements types are considered.
8	Architecture Tradeoff Analysis Method (ATAM) (Clements, Kazman, & Klein, 2002)	Requirements, Evaluation	It is a method for evaluating software architecture designs relative to *quality attribute requirements* in order to expose architectural risks that potentially inhibit the achievement of an organization's business goals. No other requirements types are considered.
9	ARID (Clements et al., 2008)	Evaluation	It is a lightweight method for evaluating partial software architecture designs in its early stages. It combines aspects from ATAM and SAAM in a more tactical level.
9	Architecture Centric Design Method (ACDM) (Lattanze, 2009).	Requirements, Design, Documentation, Evaluation.	It is an iterative approach to software development; its feature is an emphasis on architecture. It say very little about technology.
10	RUP (Kroll, Kruchten, & Booch, 2003)	Requirements, Design, Documentation, Evaluation.	It is an iterative approach to software development. It say very little about technology.

Technology as a First-Class Design Concept and its use in Architectural Design Methods

In (Cervantes, Velasco-Elizondo, & Kazman, 2013) the idea of considering technologies as a first-class design concept was explicitly stated for the first time. A demonstration of how to use in ADD, a well-known method to architecture design, was also presented. Next, a recent case to demonstrate it is used.

Consider the development of an online system to apply for a place at a primary school. Via this system parents/tutors will be able to perform function such as creating an account, finding a school, filling out an application, and submitting an application. According to the software architecture lifecycle depicted in Figure 2, before starting architecture design the development team should have the architectural requirements identified. Architectural requirements include: (*i*) user requirements, which are the functions the users can perform via the software system; (*ii*) quality attributes, which are properties of software systems that are of interest in terms of it being developed or operated, e.g. maintainability, testability, performance, security; and (*iii*) constraints, which are already taken (design) decisions, i.e. mandated technologies, laws and standards that must be complied with.

These architectural requirements are outlined, in general terms, in Table 3.

Table 3. Architectural requirements for a system to apply for a place at a primary school

Architecture Requirements	Description
User requirements	UR1 - Find a school UR2 - Fill out application
Quality attributes	QA1 - Performance. A user performs a school search during peak load; the system processes the query in under 10 seconds. QA2 - Availability. A random event causes a failure to the system during normal operation; the system must be providing services again within 30 seconds of the failure. QA3 - Security. An unknown user from a remote location attempts to access the system during normal operation; the system blocks the access to this user the 99.99% of the times.
Constraints	C1- The system must run in Internet Explorer n+, Firefox 3+, Chrome 6+, and Safari 5+. C2- The system must use information stored in a MariaDB 10+ database.

Architectural patterns are proven good architecture design structures, which can be reused, e.g. layers, pipes and filters, MVC. Tactics are a proven good means to achieve a single quality attribute requirement, e.g. replication, concurrency, authentication. Considering the former, let's suppose that the architect used the ADD method, which defines the below steps, and also used architectural patterns, tactics and technologies.

1. Confirm that information about requirements is sufficient.
2. Choose a system element to decompose.
3. Identify candidate architectural drivers.
4. Choose a design concept that satisfies the drivers.
5. Instantiate architectural elements and allocate responsibilities.
6. Define interfaces for the instantiated elements.
7. Verify and refine requirements and make them constraints for instantiated elements.

8.   Repeat these steps for the next element.

Table 4 shows three design iterations of how the design process can be performed when technologies are first-class design concepts in ADD.

Table 4. Three design iterations using technologies as first-class design concepts in ADD

	Drivers (ADD step 3)	Element to decompose (ADD step 2)	Design decisions (ADD step 4)
1	User requirements Constraints	The system as a whole	Layers pattern
2	QA1 - Performance QA3 – Security	Presentation layer Business logic layer	Increase resource efficiency performance tactic – Cloudfare Detect intrusion security tactic – Cloudfare Detect service denial security tactic - Cloudfare
3	QA2 - Availability		Monitor availability tactic - Zabbix Ping/Eco availability tactic - Zabbix

The first iteration was intended to decompose the entire system (ADD step 2) and the primary concern was to define the overall system structure and allocate responsibilities to elements that the development team could develop independently. The architect decided to create a layered system using the Layers Architecture Pattern; which is a n-tiered pattern where the components are organized in horizontal layers (Clements et al., 2011). Although the layered architecture pattern does not specify the number and types of layers that must exist in the pattern, most layered architectures consist of four standard layers: presentation, business, persistence, and database.

In iteration 2, the architect decided to use several design concepts—say tactics and technologies—to address performance and security quality attributes. The *increase resource efficiency* tactic suggests looking at the ways algorithms use a resource to process an event and optimizing them to reduce their processing time. The *detect intrusion* tactic suggests monitoring traffic coming into a system against known patterns of attacks. The *detect service denial* is a tactic for detecting a special type of attack in which the system become overwhelmed with a flood of unauthorized access attempts and cannot do anything else (Sangwan, 2014). Cloudfare[1] is a technology that implements all these tactics.

With regard to performance, Cloudfare can automatically determine which resources are static, such as HTML pages, javascript files, stylesheets, images, and videos, and help cache this content at the network edge, which improves website performance. In terms of security, Cloudfare can stop attacks directed at a website by providing security from malicious activity, including denial-of-service attacks, malicious bots, and other nefarious intrusions.

In iteration 3, the architect decided to use the following tactics and technologies to address the availability quality attribute. Zabbix[2] is a monitoring software tool for diverse IT components, including networks, servers, virtual machines, and cloud services. Zabbix provides monitoring metrics, among others network utilization, CPU load and disk space consumption. Zabbix implements the ping/echo and monitor security tactics. The *monitor* tactic uses a process that continuously monitors the status of different elements of the system (Sangwan, 2014). This tactic often uses the ping/echo tactic to periodically ping an element for its status and can receive an echo indicating it was operating normally (Sangwan, 2014).

In this example, design continues along other iterations, making design decisions ranging from selecting architecture patterns and tactics to implementation options provided by technologies.

Important Considerations

As reported (Cervantes, Velasco-Elizondo, & Kazman, 2013) this approach has been applied successfully to several projects at a large company in Mexico City that develops software for government and private customers. More recently, it has been applied for refactoring existing systems and developing new ones at the Secretary of Education of Zacatecas state. For example, the online system to apply for a place at a primary school, described above, was unable to consistently handle 12,000 users at once –which is the expected load in peak time, and exhibited security breaches last time that it was in production. Using this approach the architecture of the system was redesigned and its implementation ran without incidents in 2020.

The proposed approach has been observed to be more realistic in the sense that design activities produce architectures that can be executed—and therefore tested—before they are implemented. However, it is important to consider that technology selection cannot be arbitrary, as it depends on factors such as: the development team's level of knowledge of each technology, the technology type (i.e. commercial or open source), the technology's maturity and level of support from its community, etc.

AUTOMATING TECNOLOGY SELECTION

When software architects design software architectures, they make the decision to promote a set of architectural requirements and aim for an optimal choice in the necessary trade-offs for a particular context. Assuming that software architecture can be specified in a formal manner, and its design can be done systematically via realistic design methods, a basic research question arises: could it be possible to automate software architecture development at least to some degree? The automation of software architecture design would be beneficial not only for increasing the productivity of a software architect, but also in improving the quality of the resulting architectures.

This section presents a recent tool developed, which uses natural language processing and semantic web techniques to the problem of automating technology searches (Esparza, 2019).

WHAT TECHNOLOGY SELECTION REALLY INVOLVES

The process of developing an architecture design starts by considering architectural requirements. Architectural requirements include (Cervantes et al., 2016): (*i*) user requirements, (*ii*) quality and (*iii*) constraints. Among these requirements, quality attributes and constraints are those that shape the architecture the most significantly (Cervantes et al., 2016). The process of creating an architecture design then continues by linking architecturally significant requirements to design decisions; this involves the use of design concepts that satisfy requirements. An example might be using the broker architectural pattern as a design concept to satisfy a scalability quality attribute. Next, these design decisions should be systematically linked to the implementation alternatives through the use of specific technologies, for example, selecting RabbitMQ[3] to implement the broker architectural pattern.

Table 5. Well-known tools to support technology search

	Signature		Query						Tools description				Third party info						Results					Technical details						Quality attributes				
	Support update	Automatic filing	Multiple counts	License type	Operation System Platform	Products' uses	Categories / Subcategories	Competitic technologies	Description	License type / Date	Developer / Official page	Vendors	Companies using the products	Use cases	Links to other resources	Recommendations of other products	User's research	Integration with other platform	OSS Images	Code examples	Intermediate's statistics	Reuse	Products' popularity charts	Size	Platform	Implementation language	Compatible technologies	APIs	Features and design	Performance	Usability	Availability	Scalability	Security
Softonic	S	S	S	S	S	S	S	-	S	S	S	S	-	-	-	S	-	-	S	S	-	S	-	S	S	-	-	-	-	-	S	-	-	-
Softpedia	S	-	S	S	S	S	S	-	S	S	S	S	-	-	-	S	-	-	S	S	S	S	-	S	S	-	-	-	-	-	-	-	-	-
Wolfram Alpha	S	P	S	S	S	S	-	-	S	S	S	-	-	-	-	-	-	-	-	-	S	-	-	S	-	S	-	-	-	-	-	-	-	-
AlternativeTo	S	-	S	-	S	S	S	-	S	S	S	-	S	-	-	S	S	-	S	-	S	S	-	-	S	-	-	-	-	-	-	-	-	-
SlackShare	S	P	S	-	-	S	S	-	S	-	S	-	S	S	-	S	S	S	-	-	S	S	-	-	-	-	-	-	-	-	-	-	-	-
G2 Crowd	S	-	S	-	-	S	S	-	S	S	S	-	-	-	-	S	S	-	S	-	-	S	-	-	-	-	-	-	-	-	-	S	S	S
StackOverflow	S	-	-	-	-	S	-	-	S	S	S	S	-	P	S	S	-	-	S	P	S	S	-	S	S	S	S	S	S	-	-	-	S	-
DBEngine	S	-	S	-	-	S	S	-	S	S	S	S	-	P	P	-	-	-	S	P	-	S	S	-	S	S	S	S	S	-	-	-	-	-

S = supported; P = partially supported; – = non supported;

Technology selection involves five main factors to consider: (*i*) deciding which technologies are available to realize the decisions made; (*ii*) determining whether the available tools to support this technology choice (e.g. IDEs, simulators, testing tools, and so on) are adequate for development to proceed; (*iii*) determining the extent of internal familiarity and external support available for the technology (e.g. courses, tutorials, examples and so on); (*iv*) determining the side effects of choosing a technology, such as a required coordination model or constrained resources; and (v) determining whether a new technology is compatible with the existing stack (Cervantes et al., 2013).

As a result, technology selection is a multicriteria decision-making problem. Furthermore, given the steadily growing number of technologies, deciding which options are available to implement the selected design decisions requires being aware of the range of existing. This can be particularly challenging for inexperienced software architects.

The problem of selecting a software technology can be defined in terms of two sub-problems as follows:

1. **Technology Search**: Finding technologies that allow the implementation of specific design decisions.
2. **Technology Selection**: Selecting a technology to use from among those available.

The following section elaborates on aspects of the first sub-problem: technology search.

EXISTING SUPPORT FOR TECHNOLOGY SEARCH

Table 5 compares a set of well-known tools to support technology search. This comparison is next briefly explained.

The "Repository" section describes the way in which the tools structure and maintain information about technology products in a repository. "Frequent Update" refers to the frequency of content updates. "Automatic filling" refers to whether the information for each technology is added manually or automatically. "Multiple sources" indicates whether the technology information is obtained from more than one source.

The "Query" section groups aspects related to the facility of formulating a query considering factors such as "Type of License", "Operating System Platform", "Name of the (Technology) Product", "Category", and "Compatible Technologies".

The "Results" section is about the aspects related to the query's results. The aspects are grouped into four categories. The first one, "Basic description" includes general information about the technology. The second category, "Third party links" refers to general information elements from third parties that complement the basic description. The third section, "Technical details", contains technical information elements. Finally, the "Quality attributes" section includes the quality attributes of the technology.

Three letters are used in Table 5 to describe the level of support for information in the sections previously described, namely S = supported; P = partially supported; - = non supported. It is therefore possible to state the following findings.

The support for formulating queries is limited. Most tools support queries based on the name of the technology and the category to which it belongs. The remainder of the factors are not well supported in the reviewed tools.

The resulting information is incomplete. Most of the tools cover all the requirements in the "Basic description" section. However, the necessary elements of the "Links to third parties" section are included

Figure 3. A screenshot of the result of a query in NoSQLFinder

in very few tools. With regards to the "Technical details" section, only two of the tools support most of the elements. Finally, information about quality attributes is limited.

NOSQLFINDER

NoSQLFinder is a functional prototype tool that helps architects to perform technology searches. NoSQLFinder uses information from various information sources, such as AlternativeTo, StackOverflow, DBpedia. Due to scope, in this prototype the focus was on supporting the search of NoSQL databases while taking into account many of the aspects described in Table 5. The design and implementation of

Figure 4. A screenshot of a database card in NoSQLFinder

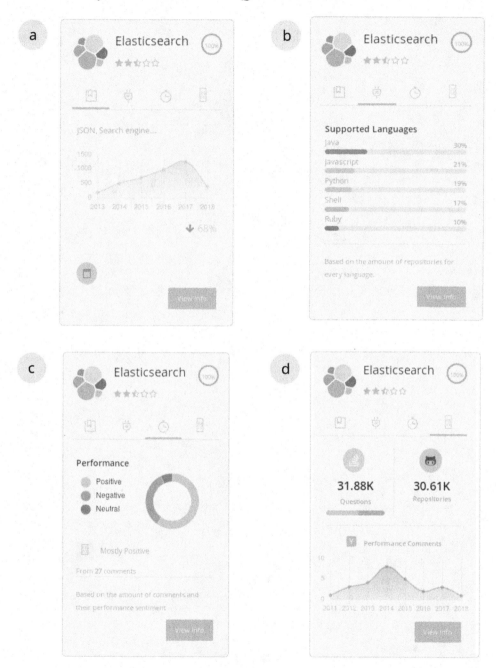

NoSQLFinder involves the use of data extraction, linked data, semantic Web and sentiment analysis techniques. NoSQLFinder is reachable via http://dataalchemy.xyz

Figure 3 shows a screenshot of the result of a query in NoSQLFinder. Each technology is shown as a card containing the following information sections: general popularity, supported programming languages, feedback from other users about its performance, and popularity among sites frequently visited by developers like StackOverflow and Github, see Figure 4 a, b, c, and d respectively.

Figure 5. A screenshot of part of the dashboard with information for a database in NoSQLFinder

When a user selects a specific card, all the information about the corresponding database is displayed on a dashboard. The dashboard is organized into four sections that represent the categories of information elements in Table 5, namely "Basic description", "Third party links", "Technical details", "Quality attributes". Figure 5 shows a screenshot of part of this dashboard.

FUTURE WORK

The design and implementation of NoSQLFinder has been a great learning experience. Firstly, it was an opportunity to learn various semantic Web techniques for collecting and integrating data. Secondly, various sentiment analysis techniques in order to determine and measure the degree of user satisfaction with respect to a quality attribute from text in natural language, were learned.

We plan to generate a more robust version of the tool for searching technologies. To this end, it was planned to explore the following lines of future work: support for more quality attributes, the use of machine-learning techniques to better evaluate what people say about technologies' quality attribute, and the inclusion of other types of technologies besides NoSQL databases.

SOFTWARE ARCHITECTURE EDUCATION

Software architecture development requires not only deep technical experience, but also understanding of the body of knowledge concerning software architecture, as expressed in terms of design concepts and software architecture development methods. Mastering software architecture development requires combining both experience and knowledge to ensure high quality outcomes when developing architecture.

This section describes two educational projects created to promote software architecture knowledge and experiences.

Summer School on Software Engineering

Dr. Velasco-Elizondo is an experienced teacher. Since 2012, the she has taught software architecture to students in under- and post-graduate programs in Software Engineering and has contributed to the definition of software architecture courses in these academic programs. Dr. Velasco-Elizondo put this experience to further use in 2012, when she founded one of the few Summer Schools on Software Engineering in Mexico, which she still run each summer. In each edition of the Summer School the topic of software architecture has been present in some form.

In the Summer Schools on Software Engineering, participating students represent private and public institutions located in various states of Mexico. Attendees have lauded the School as "an excellent forum to learn exciting topics that are related to way software systems are designed and implemented". They also welcomed the opportunity to "meet with colleagues and share experiences".

In the 2019 edition of the School three courses were offered: An introduction to NOSQL databases, Agile Techniques for Risks Management and Colored Backlogs with Scrum. Scrum is an agile project management framework that can be used for software development projects with the goal of incrementally delivering a software product by supplying working requirements every 2-4 weeks. In Scrum, a backlog is a list of tasks and/or requirements that need to be completed. In the third course it was learned and practiced a technique for ensuring that architectural requirements get addressed and prioritized applying the concept of color in a Scrum backlog as follows:

- Green – functional user requirements.
- Yellow – Architectural infrastructure to support the quality requirements.
- Red – Defects that are identified and need to be addressed.

- Black – Technical debt that builds up as the product is built and key decisions are deferred or poor work done. Technical debt is a term in software development that reflects the implied cost of additional rework caused by choosing a fast and dirty solution instead of using a better approach that would take longer.

Colored Backlogs is a technique proposed by Dr. Philippe Kruchten.

Software Architecture Book

Within the context of Software Engineering, the development of software architecture deals with structuring a software system to satisfy architectural requirements, namely, user functional requirements, quality attributes and constraints. This technological moment requires people to interact with many software systems that increasingly have more complex quality attribute requirements such as performance and availability. This increasing complexity is why software architecture development is an important topic.

Taking into account their experience as specialized teachers of Software Engineering, as well as the years of collaboration and consulting with the software development industry, Dr. Velasco-Elizondo and their colleagues identified the lack of an introductory book of software architecture in Spanish. They therefore decided to write this book, which is titled "Software Arquitectura: Conceptos y Ciclo de Desarrollo", published in 2015 (Cervantes, Velasco-Elizondo & Castro, 2016).

The book places an important emphasis on software architecture foundations but also provides practical examples that allow these foundations to be related to real practice. Practitioners, and master and undergraduate students interested in design and development of software systems are the main prospective readers of this book. The book has seven chapters, covering the following topics.

Chapter 1 presents the introduction to the topic of software architecture by introducing the basic concepts and the notion of a software architecture development lifecycle defining these stages: requirements, design, documentation, and evaluation.

Chapter 2 discusses the requirements stage. To provide an initial context, the term "requirement" as used in the field of Software Engineering is described. Then the focus is on the specific aspects of the requirements stage, including fundamental concepts, activities, and a review of well-known methods to systematically perform the activities necessary to this stage.

Chapter 3 is about the design stage. This chapter begins by describing the concept and levels of design in general and then lays out the architecture design process. Next is a discussion of the design principles and concepts that are used as part of the architecture design process. A review of some well-known methods to design architectures is then presented.

Chapter 4 explores the documentation stage, initially establishing the importance of documenting software architectures. There is a particular focus on how to create documentation to effectively communicate a software architecture design to different stakeholders. Initially, the meaning of sufficient documentation is discussed in a general way, followed by an exploration of what this concept means in software architecture and why documentation is important. Relevant concepts, notations, as well as methods that can be used to support activities at this stage are also included. The chapter concludes with a list of useful recommendations for generating good quality architectural documentation.

Chapter 5 is about the evaluation stage. Once a software architecture is designed and documented, it is possible to start constructing the system. However, before doing so, it is vital to ensure that the software architecture is correct and satisfies the architectural requirements. Evaluating software architectures enables the detection of breaches and risks, which can otherwise cause of delays or serious problems when implementing software architectures. This chapter begins by discussing the concept of evaluation in general terms, and then the moves to what this means for software architectures. The chapter also includes the description of some relevant methods used to evaluate software architectures.

Chapter 6 discusses the influence of software architecture in the implementation of a software system. The work of the architect is often considered to be finished when an architecture design has been defined, evaluated, and satisfactorily meets the architectural requirements. However, the lack of follow-up during the implementation of the system is often the cause when the architecture's design is not properly implemented.

Chapter 7 describes how to perform the stages of the software architecture development lifecycle in projects that use agile methods. Within the context of Software Engineering, agile methods are a set of widely used lightweight methods currently used to support systems development relying on self-organizing, interdisciplinary, and highly flexible teams. In this chapter the content is described around Scrum, a very popular agile method today.

Importantly, the topics in each chapter are explained via a case study, which is included in full as an appendix of the book. Furthermore, the book provides a set of questions and as well as references to other information sources so that readers can reinforce and build on their knowledge of the material presented in this book.

Hands on

Since 2008 Dr. Velasco-Elizondo has had the chance to work, as a coach, with practicing software architects and developers helping them to deploy software architecture practices and methods. Dr. Velasco-Elizondo strongly believes in lean and agile principles and she had also being able to apply them within the context of software architecture design.

In this section some of these experiences are described.

SmartFlow MVP

Internet of Things (IoT) is the technology enabling the communication of a variety of devices via the Internet in order to exchange data. IoT is composed of network of sensors, actuators, and devices that allow the development of new systems and services to monitor and control process or services. Dr. Velasco-Elizondo had the opportunity to contribute to the design and implementation of a minimum viable product (MVP) of a system of this kind for the mining industry domain. Specifically, she served as the Scrum Master of the Scrum Team developing the SmartFlow MVP. A minimum viable product (MVP) is a version of a product with just enough features to satisfy early customers and provide feedback for future product development.

SmartFlow MVP was a system that used RFID tags to support real-time exchange of data with a series of RFID readers through radio waves. RFID tags are a type of tracking devices that use smart barcodes in order to identify items. RFID is short for radio frequency identification. Any entity of interest circulating in a mine tunnel, i.e. miner, vehicle, had a RFID tag attached. An RFID transmitted its location and other relevant data to RFID readers. RFID readers sent the received data to a software system that processed and displayed it for different applications, i.e. access control, collision control, and evacuation control.

The use of Scrum for the development of the SmartFlow MVP was favored. Considering the agile nature of Scrum, it was considered that the Scrum Team were much more likely to get the MVP shipped on time and on budget. In this project Dr. Velasco-Elizondo and the team had the opportunity to deploy a set of practices to make agile architecting feasible. The following practices were integrated in a customized version of Scrum for this project: (1) visualizing requirements using the colored backlog technique (2) developing an architectural spike in a Sprint 0 (3) visualizing technical debt using the colored backlog techniques and (4) keeping the architecture documentation updated. An architecture spike is an experiment to reduce risk and to improve the technical understanding of the system to build and the technology choices to build it.

Visualizing architectural requirements using a colored backlog allowed the Scrum Team to better plan its releases and be aware of architectural requirements. Developing an architectural spike helped the Scrum Team to early determine whether the defined architecture was proper to support the architectural requirements; particularly quality attributes. Visualizing technical debt using a colored backlog helped the Scrum Team not only to be aware of it, but also to prioritize it in sprint planning just like normal requirements. Finally, as Simon Brown advises the focus was given to describing in the architecture documentation only the aspects that Scrum Team could not get from the code (Brown, 2014).

Refactoring an School Enrollment System

Working as a Principal Technical Assistant at the Secretary of Education of Zacatecas state, has giving Dr. Velasco-Elizondo the chance to contribute in the refactoring work a development team performed to pay technical debt of a school enrollment system. Parents and tutors to apply for a place at a primary school in Zacatecas state using this system.

In short, refactoring is a technical term in Software Engineering to refer of the activity of modifying the internal structure of code of a system without changing its behavior. Refactoring is important to maintain the long-term quality of a system code. If there is technical debt and developers do not perform some refactoring on a regular basis, technical debt will creep into the system. In this project it was made sure to have good reasons for doing it. In this case id was necessary to improve performance, scalability, security and test coverage. These quality requirements were understood as architectural and therefore, it leads to the process to select design concepts to realize them; and then select technologies to implement them.

Besides following a systematic and quality attribute driven approach to refactoring and learning new technologies, another good thing this project generated was the design and delivering of a course that helped the development team "to link theory to practice". That is, to better understand the undelaying design decisions and design concepts and the technology choices to implement them.

CONCLUSION

It is common to hear discussions of academic–practitioner relationships that focus on the gap between academics and practitioners, between rigor and applicability, between theory and practice or similar terms. The gap between academics and practitioners has been of concern for decades. For these reasons Dr. Velasco-Elizondo is very satisfied with the opportunities a have taken to develop what she wants to become: a software architecture academic-practitioner. Thus, in this chapter the author has described some significant research, education and coaching activities the author has performed during her professional career to develop knowledge, skills and experiences related to this desire.

Often researchers tend think that they already have enough to do with our research. In her experience, "working outside an office" helps not only to develop business awareness but also to strengthen soft skills, networking, self-awareness, and practical ways to apply research and demonstrate its potential impact. The connected world of today means that software is everywhere; thus, software architecture design is everywhere too. How can a software architect come up with the simplest possible design to make sure a software system fits into the long-term goals? Well, it demands a potent blend of thoughtful design with constant experimentation. This is exactly how people learn to tackle complexity and therefore, everything else in life.

Dr. Velasco-Elizondo hopes the material communicated in this chapter will inspire readers, specifically female readers. Do you know that women did very first jobs in Software Engineering history? Ada Lovelace was the first computer programmer in history. Grace Hopper developed the first computer compiler and made programming easier for all of us. Margaret Hamilton developed the on-board flight software for the lunar lander of the Apollo 11 mission. How, then, did was developed the myth that girls do not belong in Software Engineering? Although the effort to involve women in these fields has been rising in recent years, stereotypes still exist and are preventing women to have equal opportunities to access to education and work in STEM. These stereotypes are flat wrong. It does not make sense to think that talent, ideas, efforts should be wasted simply because they come from a woman, rather than a man. In most software development projects, different decisions are taken. (Bhat et al., 2020) provides a getting-started guide for prospective researchers who are entering the investigation phase of research on architectural decision-making.

Keep always an unfulfilled desire that is waiting to be fulfilled, when one is not hungry enough, one never will find the motivation to do anything. Never be satisfied, be curious to learn more and more. Be willing to keep trying the things people say cannot be done. In other words, and as many important people have said, Dr. Velasco-Elizondo encourages you to "stay hungry, stay foolish".

REFERENCES

Arellanes, D., & Lau, K. K. (2019). Workflow Variability for Autonomic IoT Systems. In *Proceedings of the International Conference on Autonomic Computing*, (pp. 24-30). Umea, Sweden: IEEE.

Barbacci, M., Ellison, R. J., Lattanze, A. J., Stafford, J. A., Weinstock, C. B., & Wood, W. G. (2003). *Quality Attribute Workshops (QAWs), Third Edition*. Technical Report CMU/SEI-2003-TR-016, Software Engineering Institute, Carnegie Mellon University.

Bass, L., Clements, P. C., & Kazman, R. (2012). *Software Architecture in Practice*. Addison-Wesley Professional.

Bhat, M., Shumaiev, K., Hohenstein, U., Biesdorf, A., & Matthes, F. (2020). The Evolution of Architectural Decision Making as a Key Focus Area of Software Architecture Research: A Semi-Systematic Literature Study. In *Proceedings of the IEEE International Conference on Software Architecture*, (pp. 69-80). IEEE.

Brown, S. (2014). *Software Architecture for Developers - Technical leadership by coding, coaching, collaboration, architecture sketching and just enough up front design.* Leanpub.

Buschmann, F., Meunier, R., Rohnert, H., Sommerlad, P., & Stal, M. (1996). *Pattern-Oriented Software Architecture Volume 1: A System of Patterns.* Wiley Publishing.

Cervantes, H., & Kazman, R. (2016). *Designing Software Architectures: A Practical Approach.* Addison-Wesley Professional.

Cervantes, H., Velasco-Elizondo, P., & Castro, L. (2016). *Arquitectura de software: conceptos y ciclo de desarrollo.* Cengage Learning.

Cervantes, H., Velasco-Elizondo, P., & Kazman, R. (2013). A Principled Way to Use Frameworks in Architecture Design. *IEEE Software, 30*(2), 46–53. doi:10.1109/MS.2012.175

Clements, P., Bachmann, F., Bass, L., Garlan, D., Ivers, J., Reed, L., & Nord, R. (2011). *Documenting Software Architectures: Views and Beyond.* Addison-Wesley Professional.

Clements, P., Kazman, R., & Klein, M. (2002). *Evaluating Software Architectures: Methods and Case Studies.* Addison-Wesley Professional.

Clements, P., Kazman, R., & Klein, M. (2008). *Evaluating Software Architectures Methods and Case Studies.* Addison-Wesley.

de Silva, L., & Balasubramaniam, D. (2012). Controlling software architecture erosion: A survey. *Journal of Systems and Software, 85*(1), 132–151. doi:10.1016/j.jss.2011.07.036

Di Cola, S., Lau, K.-K., Tran, C., & Qian, C. (2015). An MDE tool for defining software product families with explicit variation points. In *Proceedings of the International Conference on Software Product Line,* (pp. 355–360). New York, NY: Association for Computing Machinery. 10.1145/2791060.2791090

Esparza, M. (2019). *NoSQLFinder: un buscador de bases de datos NoSQL basado en técnicas de web semántica y análisis de sentimientos* (BSc Thesis).

Hofmeister, C., Kruchten, P. B., Nord, R., Obbink, H., Ran, A., & America, P. (2007). A general model of software architecture design derived from five industrial approaches. *Journal of Systems and Software, 80*(1), 106–126. doi:10.1016/j.jss.2006.05.024

Kazman, R., Abowd, G., Bass, L., & Clements, P. (1996). Scenario-Based Analysis of Software Architecture. *IEEE Software, 13*(6), 47–55. doi:10.1109/52.542294

Kroll, P., Kruchten, P. B., & Booch, G. (2003). The rational unified process made easy. Addison-Wesley Professional.

Kruchten, P. B. (1995). The 4+1 View Model of Architecture. *IEEE Software, 6*(12), 42–50. doi:10.1109/52.469759

Lattanze, A. J. (2009). *Architecting Software Intensive Systems: A practitioners guide.* CRC Press.

Lau, K., & Wang, Z. (2007). Software Component Models. *IEEE Transactions on Software Engineering, 33*(10), 709–724. doi:10.1109/TSE.2007.70726

Mohagheghi, P., & Conradi, R. (2007). Quality, productivity and economic benefits of software reuse: A review of industrial studies. *Empirical Software Engineering*, *12*(5), 471–516. doi:10.100710664-007-9040-x

Perry, D. E., & Wolf, A. L. (1992). Foundations for the study of software architecture. *SIGSOFT Software Engineering Notes*, *17*(4), 40–52. doi:10.1145/141874.141884

Rajkumar, R., Lee, I., Sha, L., & Stankovic, J. (2010). Cyber-physical systems: the next computing revolution. In *Proceedings of the design automation conference*, (pp 731–736). IEEE.

Rehman, I., Mirakhorli, M., Nagappan, M., Uulu, A. A., & Thornton, M. (2018). Roles and impacts of hands-on software architects in five industrial case studies. In *Proceedings of International Conference on Software Engineering*, (pp 117–127). Association for Computing Machinery. 10.1145/3180155.3180234

Sangwan, R. S. (2014). *Software and Systems Architecture in Action*. Auerbach Publications. doi:10.1201/b17575

Shahbazian, A., Lee, Y. K., Brun, Y., & Medvidovic, N. (2018). Making well-informed software design decisions. In *Proceedings of the 40th International Conference on Software Engineering*, (pp. 262–263). Association for Computing Machinery. 10.1145/3183440.3194961

Shaw, M., & Garlan, D. (1996). *Software Architecture: Perspectives on an Emerging Discipline*. Prentice Hall.

Sobrevilla, G., Hernández, J., Velasco-Elizondo, P., & Soriano, S. (2017). Aplicando Scrum y Prácticas de Ingeniería de Software para la Mejora Continua del Desarrollo de un Sistema Ciber-Físico. *ReCIBE*, *6*(1), 1–15.

Sommerville, I. (2011). *Software engineering*. Pearson.

Tang, A., Tran, M. H., Han, J., & Vliet, H. V. (2008). Design Reasoning Improves Software Design Quality. In S. Becker, F. Plasil, & R. Reussner (Eds.), Lecture Notes in Computer Science: Vol. 5281. *Quality of Software Architectures, Models and Architectures* (pp. 28–42). Springer. doi:10.1007/978-3-540-87879-7_2

Velasco-Elizondo, P., & Lau, K. (2010). A catalogue of component connectors to support development with reuse. *Journal of Systems and Software*, *83*(7), 1165–1178. doi:10.1016/j.jss.2010.01.008

ENDNOTES

1   See https://www.cloudflare.com/
2   See https://www.zabbix.com/
3   See https://www.rabbitmq.com/

Chapter 11
Developing a Model and a Tool for the Formation of Project Teams

Margarita André Ampuero
Universidad Tecnológica de La Habana, Cuba

Ana Lilian Infante Abreu
Universidad Tecnológica de La Habana, Cuba

ABSTRACT

Given the importance of team quality in the success of a project, this chapter presents a summary of the results obtained in 10 years of work, dedicated to the study and development of models and tools for the formation of project teams, from identifying the diversity of factors that can be taken into account in different contexts. The main characteristics of a model and versions of a configurable tool that support the model are described, which facilitates its application in different contexts and allows experimenting with different algorithms and solution methods to identify those that offer the best results.

INTRODUCTION

Today organizations recognize the quality of the team as a key factor in the success or failure of projects (Gutierrez et al., 2016; Afshar at al., 2018; Pavlov & Yahontova, 2019). However, team forming had evolved, from the assigning people to tasks or roles to forming teams as a whole. For example, the software projects in the beginning were developed by one or two people who assumed all the phases of the process. Currently, given the increase in the volume and complexity of highly demanded software products, projects must be faced in teams.

As defined in the Guide for Project Management - PMBOK (PMI, 2017) a project team "consists of individuals with assigned roles and responsibilities who work collectively to achieve a shared project goal".

Therefore, human resources must be properly managed in order to successfully complete the project.

DOI: 10.4018/978-1-7998-7552-9.ch011

Copyright © 2021, IGI Global. Copying or distributing in print or electronic forms without written permission of IGI Global is prohibited.

Human resource management includes processes to identify, acquire and manage the needed resources. Identifying the human resources, implies defining the roles to be covered, their responsibilities, the number of needed people and the required competences to perform each role, as well as the required level in each competence. After identifying the resources, it is necessary to acquire them to form the team (PMI, 2017).

Once the team is already developing the project, it is possible, even necessary, to improve its performance (for example: developing the competences of its members), but the team formation is key.

However, it is a complex process since it must not only take into account the competences. There are other factors to consider, some of an individual nature, such as workload, and other collective factors, such as interpersonal relationships.

Software project teams, for example, must be formed with competent personnel. The software industry is highly competitive since it demands to have quality products in the shortest possible time. Additionally, the development of Information and Communication Technologies is growing at a dizzying pace. Therefore, different roles were defined, most of which have a high functional dependency. As a consequence, incompatibilities between members need to be minimized.

This process becomes more complex when the amount of people to be considered and the amount of roles to be covered in the team increases, because the number of possible combinations to be evaluated increases significantly. This situation makes the process difficult to carry out, without the help of decision support systems that include algorithms for solving mathematical models, which represent the problem to be solved in the most objective way.

In order to face this problem, an investigation was carried out, whose main objective was to develop a model and a tool to support the process of forming project teams.

BACKGROUND

The last decade has seen an increase in work related to team formation as a whole, mainly since the research of Zakarian & Kusiak (1999), which identifies team formation as an optimization problem. Previously, many works considered only individual factors such as: staff competences or workload.

Research in this area addresses different aspects, including: the application context, the number of formed teams, the techniques, algorithms and approaches used in the solution, the development of tools to support the proposals and the factors to be considered.

The proposed solutions are associated to different contexts. Most of them focus on team formation of social network experts and student teams. Some allow to form one and others, multiple teams. Among the main techniques used are: the multi-criteria technique, exact techniques such as integer programming and approximate techniques such as heuristic and metaheuristic algorithms to solve optimization problems, in some cases with a monobjective approach and in others, with a multiobjective approach. There are investigations where support tools for the solution are documented.

Figure 1 shows the main factors taken into account in the analyzed works that address team formation.

Most of the analyzed investigations use a professional approach, because they take into account factors such as: the competences, experience and interest of people to perform tasks, roles or projects.

Competences and interest in performing tasks or roles were the most considered individual factors. In fact, some works only took into account competences. Budak et al. (2019) proposes to form sports club teams based on the skills of the athletes to cover the different positions. Other studies emphasize

Figure 1. Individual and collective factors considered in team forming

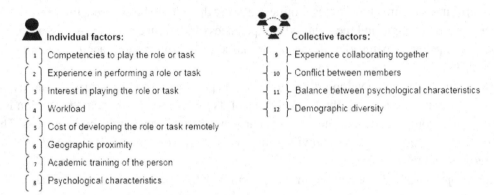

the need for effective leadership to ensure the success of the team. Ginnett (2019) focuses on analyzing the vital role that a competent captain plays in the success of a flight, although points out the importance of good relationships between crew members.

In some investigations the main purpose is to evaluate the algorithm performance. Kader and Zamli (2020) evaluated Jaya's algorithm (in comparison with other optimization algorithms) in the solution of the team formation problem, taking into account the experts' skills.

On the other hand, the interest in performing the task, role or project is one of the most used factors in researches addressing the formation of student teams (Del Val et al., 2014; Alberola et al., 2016a; Alberola et al., 2016b; Amarasinghe et al., 2017). Both Agrawal & Jariwala (2017) and Cavdur et al. (2018) take into account, the interest in the project and the students competences.

The most considered collective factors are: the experience of collaborating together, the conflict or affinity between members and the balance between psychological characteristics.

The first two factors represent the relationships between team members. In several investigations, especially those related to the team's formation in social networks, these relationships express the experience of collaborating together, called the cost of communication (Bredereck et al., 2018; Jeong et al., 2018). In general, the goal is to find competent individuals who, together, can execute tasks while minimizing the cost of communication (Ashenagar and others, 2016; Basiri and others, 2017).

Several works use graphs to represent relationships between members. Jeong et al. (2018) use them to represent the effectiveness of communication between social network experts, while Liemhetcharat and Veloso (2017) use graphs to capture interactions between learning agents. Bulmer and others (2020) to assign students to projects, consider the students' skills and project requirements, as well as the students' underlying relationships as a social network graph.

Han et al. (2017) also use the cost of communication, but additionally consider geographical proximity to form teams in social coding sites. Jin et al. (2019) propose the selection of the most competent and cooperative members, using the cooperative effect indicator to numerically describe the interpersonal relationship between members.

Not in all cases the relationship between members is expressed in terms of their collaboration. Afshar et al. (2018) propose the formation of soccer teams considering the abilities of the players and the harmony of the team. Brilhante et al. (2016) propose to form groups of tourists considering the interest for a proposed destination (instead of a task or role) and the friendship relations between the members.

Di Martinelly & Meskens (2017) propose to form teams of competent nurses to perform surgical interventions where there is good affinity between the members and time restrictions are met. Pavlov and Yahontova (2019) also propose assigning competent people to the roles but minimizing incompatibilities between members by taking into account the psychological socio-types. To determine the socio-type, it is necessary to use tests based on Jung typology, such as the Myers-Briggs Type Indicator (MBTI).

Relationships between the members is therefore an important factor in team formation. A current research trend is to propose measures to determine it, either by expressing the degree of affinity, incompatibility or cooperation.

Regarding the balance between psychological characteristics, the investigations use this factor looking for diversity in the team and that the members complement each other. Some studies propose to form teams with a diversity of psychological types (Bergey and King, 2014; DuPont and Hoyle, 2015), while others propose to form teams, in which all the team roles are present (André et al., 2010; Alberola et al., 2016a). Balmaceda et al. (2014) consider three factors: psychological types, team roles, and social relationships.

Team roles, as proposed by Belbin (Belbin, 1981) are a group of behavioral patterns expected and attributed to someone who occupies a certain position in a social unit.

On the other hand, demographic diversity was the least considered collective factor. Gender has been used along with other characteristics such as age and nationality, to ensure diversity or to achieve homogeneity of teams.

Bergey & King (2014) developed a tool to create equally diverse students teams. They propose to form teams with competent members that are balanced according to the gender and psychological types. Bahargam et al. (2018) address the automatic formation of teams in social networks. The authors define an efficient measure to control the faultlines of teams, in order to manage diversity and prevent them from being divided into subgroups. Sex, nationality and age are identified among the characteristics that can cause the team to be subdivided.

As a result of the analysis, it was possible to identify that most of the investigations take into account both individual and collective factors in the team formation. However, although there is agreement about the factors identified, only some works consider more than two factors (Bergey & King, 2014; Balmaceda, 2014; Alberola et al., 2016a; Ashenagar et al., 2016; Farasat & Nikolaev, 2016; Gutierrez et al., 2016; Basiri et al., 2017; Ebadi et al., 2017; Han et al., 2017).

There are few investigations where, even considering two or more factors, the problem is addressed using a multiobjective approach (Infante et al., 2014; Ashenagar et al., 2016; Farasat & Nikolaev, 2016). Generally, a monobjective approach is employed using a function that combines various factors.

In general, as part of the analyzed works, no tool is developed or documented to support the solution. The few works in which the tool is documented (Bergey & King, 2014; Alberola et al., 2016b; Brilhante et al. 2016; Amarasinghe et al. 2017; Ding et al., 2017; Ebadi et al., 2017), it is not configurable, which limits its application in a context for which it was not developed. As a consequence, it is necessary to define models that take into account the diversity of factors, to develop tools that allow selecting them according to the needs of the decision-maker, and to apply solution methods and algorithms to solve the problem from a multiobjective approach.

At the conclusion of the analysis, it is worth highlighting the active participation of women in this area of research. In over 60% of the research analyzed, at least one of the authors is a woman, and in even more than 30%, women are the main authors.

A CONCEPTUAL FRAMEWORK

In everyday life there are many problems in which it is a matter of optimizing (maximizing or minimizing) a certain value. A combinatorial optimization problem consists in finding the best (optimal) solution from a finite set of alternative solutions, exploring the (usually large) search space. The quality or optimality of the solutions will be defined by the capacity of these solutions to minimize or maximize a certain function, called objective function. However, the decision-making process for real-world problems often involves consideration of multiple objectives. Thus, optimization is the task of finding one or more solutions that correspond to the minimization or maximization of one or more objectives and that satisfy all restrictions, if any (Chong & Zak, 2013).

Optimization problems involving a single objective function often have a single optimal solution (monobjective). On the other hand, multiobjective optimization problems simultaneously consider several objective functions which are often in conflict, such as minimizing costs and maximizing the quality of a product. The result is a set of alternatives called Pareto's optimal solutions or non-dominated solutions (Miettinen, 2008). In this type of problem, multiple criteria must be satisfied, which often conflict, and there is no single solution that simultaneously satisfies all of them. Therefore, the obtained solutions must be in accordance with the preferences of the decision-maker.

Team formation is a multiobjective combinatorial optimization problem because it tries to find solutions (teams), evaluating a set of possible combinations (assignment of people to roles), ensuring compliance with established restrictions and trying, for example, to maximize staff competences and minimize incompatibilities between members.

There are different ways to represent the preferences of decision makers in multiobjective optimization problems (Coello et al., 2007).

The weighted factors method is based on the idea of converting the multiobjective problem into a scalar problem by constructing a single objective function which is the sum of the initial objective functions, weighted by a weight. The lexicographic method only requires establishing the priority of the objectives, it is not necessary to define the weight for each objective. Although it is easier for the decision-maker to prioritize objectives than to assign them weights, both methods require that these be defined early in the process, in many cases without any basis for doing so. In many situations, the decision-maker is clear about the objectives to be considered, but not about the priority or weight to be assigned to each objectives. With the pure multiobjective method, it is not necessary to define neither the priority nor the weights. This method reflects the multiobjective reality of the problem because it treats the objectives separately (Coello et al., 2007).

Exact and approximate techniques are used to solve optimization problems. Exact techniques allow the optimal solution to be obtained, but have a high computational cost, because the execution time grows exponentially as the size of the problem increases. Even in some cases, it is impossible to find the solution because of the required time. The approximate techniques, on the other hand, allow to obtain "good solutions" in a reasonable time, exploring the search space efficiently.

Among the approximate techniques, heuristics and metaheuristics stand out.

Heuristics is defined as a procedure that attempts to describe a good feasible, but not necessarily an optimal, solution to the specific problem at hand. However, sometimes it is not necessary to develop specific-purpose heuristics to address problems.

Metaheuristic algorithms are named after Fred Glover (Glover, 1986), who describes a metaheuristic as "the master strategy that guides and modifies other heuristics to produce solutions beyond those normally generated in the search for a local optimum. Heuristics guided by a "meta" strategy may be a high-level procedure or may contain a description of the movements that allow one solution to be transformed into another, along with an associated evaluation rule".

These algorithms only specify the general strategy to guide specific aspects of the search, allowing them to be adapted by a local heuristic to a specific application. The tendency of metaheuristics is to start by obtaining a solution or a set of solutions, and to initiate a search for improvements guided by certain principles.

One of the most used ways to classify metaheuristics divides them into: trajectory-based and population-based. Trajectory-based metaheuristics start from a point, search for its neighborhood and update the current solution, forming a path, from one point to another. In contrast, population-based metaheuristics work with a set of solutions in each iteration, which are improved iteratively through an intelligent process of exploration of the search space (Miettinen, 2008). In the last decades a large number of metaheuristic algorithms (variants of them and hybrids) have been developed and applied in the solution of monobjetive and multiobjective problems.

MAIN RESULTS OF THE RESEARCH

The research was organized in four stages. Figure 2 shows the objectives of each stage.

Figure 2. Objectives by stage of the research

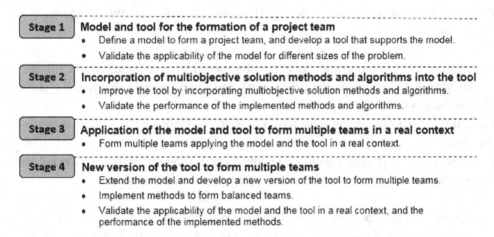

Stage 1: Model and Tool for the Formation of a Project Team

André et al (2011) defined a formal model for forming a software project team, based on the study of related work and the results of a survey applied to industry experts. The model took into account individual factors identified in related works such as: required technical and generic competences to perform each role, workload and psychological characteristics. As a novel element, it also incorporated collective factors such as: the balance of the team based on psychological characteristics and incompatibility relationships between members and between roles.

The model were designed to form a unique team and includes four objective functions:

- Maximize the competences of people in the assigned role or roles.
- Minimize incompatibilities between members of a project team.
- Balance the load of team personnel.
- Minimize the cost of working remotely

The last objective is only applicable in organizations facing this variant of development.
The model proposes to calculate:

- The index of a person's competence to perform a role considering: the level of the person in each required competence to perform the role, and the weight of the competence in each role, weighted according to its importance.
- A person's workload, adding up the load already assigned (in projects under development) with the workload of the roles assigned in the team undergoing forming.
- The cost of a person working remotely considering: the location of the person with respect to the place where the project is developed, and the impact of developing the role remotely.

Additionally, André et al. (2010) developed a study that identified Myers-Briggs, Belbin and 16PF, as three of the most used tests in the related investigations to team formation. As a main result of the study, patterns useful for team forming were identified and incorporated into the model as restrictions. The identified patterns were:

- The person assigned to the role of project leader should have as preferred: the Shaper role or the Co-ordinator role (according to the Belbin test), and should have as subtype, E_ _J (according to the Myers-Briggs test).
- In the team, at least one person must have the Belbin´s Plant role as a favorite (according to the Belbin test).
- The preference for performing action roles must exceed the preference for mental roles and the preference for mental roles must exceed the preference for social roles.

Given the quantity of incorporated factors in the model and with the purpose of validating its applicability, a tool called Teamsoft+ was developed. André & Baldoquín (2010) documented the tool, which is configurable because allow the selection of the objectives and restrictions to consider in the team formation, depending on the application context. Given the feasibility of using metaheuristic algorithms in the solution of multiobjective combinatorial problems (Coello et al., 2007), in this first version of the tool Teamsoft+, trajectory-based monobjective algorithms were implemented such as: Tabu Search (Glover, 1986), Simulated Annealing (Kirkpatrick, 1983), Hill Climbing (Rich & Knight, 1994) of Better Climb with Restart, and hybrids of GRASP (Feo & Resende, 1995) with these three algorithms. In addition, the weighted factors method (Coello et al., 2007) was implemented to solve the problem.

For the treatment of restrictions, the rejection technique was used, which only accepts feasible solutions. A solution is considered feasible if it meets all the restrictions of the problem.

André et al. (2011) developed experiments for different sizes of the problem (medium and large organizations), using Teamsoft+ tool. As a result, good (feasible) solutions were obtained in acceptable run times (no more than 3 minutes).

At the conclusion of this stage of the investigation, a set of valuable results were obtained:

- A formal model was designed to form a project team, which allows considering a set of factors, both individual and collective.
- A flexible tool was developed (Teamsoft+). The tool supports the model and allows the decision-maker to select the objective functions and restrictions to be considered in the forming process.
- A set of recognized metaheuristic algorithms were implemented in the tool to solve the problem.
- The applicability of the model was validated, demonstrating that the implemented algorithms offer good solutions in reasonable execution times.

However, a set of limitations were identified for improvement in the following stages:

- Although the proposed model responds to a multiobjective combinatorial optimization problem, the only solution method implemented was weighted factors, which does not fully reflect the multiobjective reality of the problem. The method treats the problem as monobjective based on weighting the objectives, turning it into a problem of single objective. The application of the method has two other disadvantages: the decision maker must assign weights to the objective functions (which can be difficult), and the same solutions can be obtained for different combinations of weights.
- As a consequence, in addition to methods, it is necessary to incorporate multiobjective algorithms in the tool to solve the problem.
- The architecture of the Teamsoft+ tool was not designed with the use of class libraries in mind. This practice is widespread today because it facilitates the reuse of algorithms already implemented in such libraries.
- The rejection technique, used for the treatment of restrictions, results in a significant part of the generated solutions were rejected because they breached at least one restriction.

Stage 2: Incorporation of Multiobjective Solution Methods and Algorithms into the Tool

In order to solve the detected first three limitations in the previous stage, Infante et al., (2014) developed a new version of Teamsoft+.

Taking into account the "No Free Lunch" theorem (Wolpert & Macread, 1997), according to which there is no algorithm that is absolutely better than another when compared in all possible functions and even, establishing a function for a type of problem, an algorithm can be more efficient than another depending on the size of the problem to be solved and the resource to be optimized (quality of the solution or execution time), it was decided to incorporate in the tool different multiobjective algorithms to evaluate its performance.

However, the algorithms were not directly implemented in the tool. Teamsoft+ incorporated the BICIAM class library, which provides a large number of metaheuristic algorithms to solve optimization problems. It allowed to reuse the implemented algorithms and take advantage of the good practices of

BICIAM, which, using design patterns, facilitates the incorporation of problems, algorithms and solution methods, by separating the logic of metaheuristics from the logic of the problem.

It was necessary to modify BICIAM to guarantee its use in solving multiobjective optimization problems.

Two solution methods were incorporated into BICIAM: lexicographical and pure multiobjectives. These methods allow the decision maker to select several factors (objective functions) to form the team, without the need to assign a weight to each factor. The lexicographic method only needs to prioritize the objectives.

With the pure multiobjective method, a set of solutions is obtained (various team proposals). It is an advantage over the previous methods, which only provide a solution (only one team is proposed).

The inclusion of the three methods in the tool facilitates the work of decision-makers because they can select the most appropriate method in each case.

Additionally, seven multiobjective trajectory-based algorithms were incorporated into BICIAM, because they have been used successfully in the solution of a wide variety of optimization problems and are easier to implement than the population-based (because they have fewer parameters). The algorithms incorporated were variants of the Hill Climbing (Multiobjective Stochastic, Multiobjective with Reset and Multiobjective for a greater distance), variants of the Simulated Annealing (Multiobjective of Ulungu and Teghem, and Multiobjective Multicase), Multiobjective Tabu and Multiobjective GRASP.

Because no real data or international test databases were available for this type of problem, an algorithm was developed to generate the data required by the model and evaluate the performance of the algorithms in the different scenarios. The data was generated, following patterns identified from surveys and tests applied to a group of specialists.

In the developed experiments by Infante et al. (2014), good results were obtained with the three multiobjective variants of Hill Climbing and the multiobjective variant of Simulated Annealing. These algorithms provided good solutions in acceptable execution times for all the problem sizes analyzed (medium, large and especially large organizations).

The worst performing algorithms were: Multiobjective Simulated Annealing of Ulungu, GRASP + Multiobjective Simulated Annealing of Ulungu, GRASP + Multiobjective Tabu Search and Multiobjective Tabu Search, especially in scenarios corresponding to large and very large organizations. The application of GRASP (in the hybrid algorithms), to build an initial solution as part of the execution of the different algorithms, did not report better results than when the initial solution was randomly generated.

Among the main results achieved at the end of this stage are:

- The incorporation of BICIAM in the tool facilitated the reuse of the algorithms already implemented in the library.
- The modifications made to BICIAM allow it to be used to solve multiobjective optimization problems.
- The library extension, incorporating seven trajectory-based multiobjective, facilitated to carry out experiments.
- The incorporation in the tool of the solution methods, lexicographic and pure multiobjective, helped to meet the different preferences of the decision-maker.
- Experiments demonstrated that multiobjective trajectory-based algorithms obtain good results in the solution of this problem (even in different sizes of the problem), especially the multiobjective variants of Hill Climbing and the multiobjective variant of Simulated Annealing.

Considering the good results achieved by multiobjective trajectory algorithms in solving this problem, the authors set a new objective, to apply the model and use the tool in solving this problem in a real scenario, in this case, the formation of student teams.

Stage 3: Application of the Model and the Tool to Form Multiple Teams in a Real Context

The researchers had to face a new challenge. Both the model and the tool were designed to form a unique team, and in the academic context to develop projects, several teams must be formed.

In (Infante et al., 2020a) the authors analyzed more than 40 papers dealing with the formation of one or more teams and decided to apply the proposed model by André al. (2011) and the Teamsoft+ tool to form student teams. The authors made this decision because the model takes into account the vast majority of factors and the tool allows the decision maker to select the required factors (as it is configurable). Moreover, to solve the problem, it is possible to use both approaches (monobjective and multiobjective).

The strategy was to carry out several executions until the required teams were formed, because the tool only forms one team at a time.

Infante et al. (2020a) developed an experiment, whose objective was to form the required eleven project teams for the Software Engineering 3 (IS3) course, using Teamsoft+. This course is carried out in the 4th year of the career Informatics Engineering at the Universidad Tecnológica de La Habana. The objective of the IS3 course is to develop a real project playing roles and exercising teamwork, because this competence is very important for future graduates (López et al., 2018).

Eight roles must be covered in each team: project leader, planner, quality specialist, configuration manager, analyst, architect, programmer and tester.

The next step was to determine the factors to consider in the formation of the student teams.

In the work related to the formation of teams in the academic context, the factors considered are justified, based on the study of the state of the art. However, in these investigations it is not documented whether the students' criteria were taken into account. For this reason the authors, before the experiment, applied surveys to the students of the five years of the career to identify according to their criteria, which factors should be taken into account in the formation of teams.

Two rounds were executed, 350 students of the career (84%) participated in one of the two rounds:

- 71% of the students participated in the first round, with at least 50% of the students from each academic year.
- 78% of the students participated in the second round, with at least 70% of the students from each academic year.

In the first round, a survey was applied to identify the factors to be considered. At the end of this round, all factors were listed. Factors expressing the same idea were unified and criteria expressed by less than five students were eliminated. As a result of the first round, 15 factors were obtained.

It is important to explain how one of the identified factors in the first round was the presence of at least one woman on the team. This factor was not selected for the second round because it was only proposed by four first-year students. However, when the authors applied the survey in the second round, they reported the rejected factors and asked the students their opinion about them. The students unanimously rejected the inclusion of gender as a form factor because they did not consider it relevant to the team's success.

In the second round the students ordered the factors. The order of preference of the factors by academic year was identified, applying consensus rankings. In general, the order given to the factors by the students of the different academic years was similar, the differences were small. The ten best ranked factors, regardless of the student's academic year, were:

- Have generic competences such as: responsibility, commitment, teamwork, communication skills and logical reasoning.
- Have technical competences to play the roles of the project.
- Affinity or incompatibility relationships between members.
- Interest in the project.
- Experience working together.
- Interest in playing the role or task.

The factors considered less important were: geographical proximity of the members, ability to learn, student's academic index, creativity and presence of a leader in the team.

Once the coincidence between the proposed factors by the students and the identified factors in the related works was verified, the next step was to select the factors to be considered in the formation of the student teams.

Infante et al. (2020a) selected two objective functions from proposed model by André et al. (2011): maximize competences and minimize incompatibilities between members. The third objective function "Balance the workload" was not selected because students should have no additional workload. The fourth objective function was also not selected, as none member needed to work at distance.

In addition, the following restrictions were considered:

- Each role must be covered by a student.
- A student may not perform at the same time roles considered incompatible, such as: programmer and tester.
- The student assigned to a role must have the defined competence level for this role.
- The three role categories proposed by Belbin (action roles, mental roles and social roles) must be represented in the team.
- In the team, the preference for playing action roles should be greater than the preference for playing mental roles.
- In the team, the preference for playing mental roles should be greater than the preference for playing social roles.
- The student who plays the role of Project leader must have among their preferred Belbin roles: Shaper or Co-ordinator.

Although the students did not identify the balance between the psychological characteristics, Infante et al. (2020a) decided to select it, taking into account the number of papers that point out the importance of this factor in the formation of teams.

Three instruments were applied to the 85 students enrolled in the course IS3 to determine generic competences: communication skills, teamwork and analytical capacity.

The obtained grades by the students in certain subjects and the achieved score in Belbin roles were used to determine the level of the students in the required technical competences to perform the different roles of the project. For example, to calculate the level of competence of a student who will play the role of Programmer, the obtained grades in the following subjects were considered: Introduction to programming, Object-oriented design and programming, Data structure 1, Structure of Data 2 and Web Programming.

Belbin and Myers-Briggs tests were applied to all the students to evaluate their psychological characteristics. To determine interpersonal relationships, a survey was applied to students where they had to specify with which students they did not want to work in the project because they had unfavorable personal or work relationships in previous projects.

The results of the instruments and tests applied to the students, linked to the different factors, were analyzed from a gender perspective. Although more than 75% of the students in the career are men, no relevant differences were identified.

Two methods were implemented in the Teamsoft+ tool to form the eleven project teams required in the IS3 course. In both methods, the team formation was carried out in two stages, according to PM-BOK (PMI, 2017). First, the project leader was assigned and after, team forming was completed with the participation of the project leaders.

The first method (Prioritize Project Leaders) first assigns project leaders to all teams and then completes the formation of all teams.

The second method (Without prioritizing the Project Leaders) forms complete teams, one by one. In each team, first the project leader is assigned and then the rest of the roles are assigned. The main disadvantage of this method is not having people with the necessary characteristics and competences to play the role of project leader when the last teams are formed because they were assigned to other roles in the first teams.

The experiment allowed evaluating the performance of different multiobjective algorithms in solving this problem. Five algorithms were executed, four trajectory-based algorithms (Ulungu Multiobjective Simulated Annealing, Multiobjective Multicase Simulated Annealing, Multiobjectivo Stochastic Hill Climbing for a greater distance, Multiobjective Hill Climbing with Restart) and a population-based algorithm (NSGAII).

Infante et al. (2020a) used non-parametric statistical techniques to compare the obtained results in the metrics (error rate, generational distance and dispersion) by the different algorithms. The Keel tool (Alcala-Fdez et al., 2011) was used for the execution of the non-parametric tests.

In order to solve the identified fourth limitation in the first stage of the investigation, two other restrictions treatment techniques were implemented in the tool: penalization and preservation. The penalty technique allows accepting no feasible solutions by penalizing the objective function. The preservation technique proposes to obtain a representation of the problem or an operator that always guarantees to obtain feasible solutions.

The penalty technique was applied, combined with rejection (90% of iterations with penalty and 10% with rejection), with the aim of obtaining a feasible solution at the end of the search.

The developed experiment by Infante et al. (2020a), showed that only complete teams were formed using the penalty technique with the algorithms of Multiobjective Stochastic Hill Climbing, Multiobjective Hill Climbing with Restart and Multiobjective Multicase Simulated Annealing. The rest of the algorithms obtained a significant percentage of solutions, where the last one or the last two teams were not formed.

Greater number of complete teams were formed applying the first method, because the project leaders were selected at the beginning of the process. On the contrary, applying the second method, the last two or three teams were not completed, because it was more difficult to find a project leader who complied with all the imposed restrictions.

In addition, it was found that the teams were unbalanced as the most competent students were assigned to the first teams, even to roles for which a high level of competence is not required. Therefore, roles requiring a higher level of competence were not covered in the last teams, because no students were available.

Among the achieved main results at the end of this stage are:

- Multiple project teams were formed in a real context using the Teamsoft+ tool, even though both the model and the tool were designed to form a single team.
- The flexibility of the tool allowed for the selection of functions and restrictions appropriate to that context.
- It was possible to obtain complete teams applying the penalty technique.
- Again, multiobjective variants of Hill Climbing and the multiobjective variant of Simulated Annealing obtained good results in solving the problem.

Although complete teams of students can be formed using the tool Teamsoft+, the results suggest to extend the model and the tool to allow multiple teams to be formed in each execution. Additionally, new methods must be implemented to ensure balanced teams are formed.

Stage 4: New Version of the Tool to Form Multiple Teams

Infante et al. (2020b) extended the proposed model by André et al. (2011), taking into account the results of the experiments, the identified factors in the related works and the applied surveys to the students, which were described in the previous stages.

Table 1 shows the considered factors in each model and the objective functions, associated with each factor.

Table 1. Objective functions included in each model version

Factors considered	Objective functions included in each version of the model	
	Team formation (André et al., 2011)	**Formation of multiple teams (Infante et al., 2020b)**
Competences	Maximize	Maximize Balance between the teams
Workload	Balance within the team	Balance within the team Balance between the teams
Cost to develop at a distance	Minimize	Minimize Balance between the teams
Interest in playing the role	-	Maximize Balance between the teams
Incompatibilities between members	Minimize	Minimize Balance between the teams
Presence of Belbin's roles	-	Maximize Balance between the teams

The extended model allow the formation of one or multiple project teams at the same time. The main improvements and extensions included by Infante et al. (2020b) in the proposed model are:

- An objective function to maximize the interest of the people for playing the roles.
- An objective function to maximize the presence of Belbin's roles in the team. In the previous model there is a restriction that requires the presence of all Belbin roles in the team, but in the new model also this factor is incorporated as an objective function, which allows greater flexibility.
- Several objective functions for the formation of multiple project teams which guarantee the balance between the formed teams according to the different factors considered.
- Three new restrictions in the formation of multiple project teams:
  ○ All people have to be part of a team in at least one role.
  ○ The number of people a team can have is restricted to a fixed amount.
  ○ Each person must be assigned to only one project.

A new version of the Teamsoft+ tool, based on the extended model by Infante et al. (2020b), was developed. The new version allows to form multiple teams because in each execution, different team proposals are generated. This allows the decision maker to evaluate the proposals and select the most suitable.

The tool allows, as in previous versions, to select the objectives and restrictions of the model, to consider in the teams formation.

The BICIAM class library was incorporated into the new version of Teamsoft+. This allows reusing the large number of monobjective and multiobjective algorithms implemented in the library.

Similar to the previous version, three methods were implemented to solve the problem (weighted factors, lexicographic and pure multiobjective).

In addition, four methods were implemented in the tool for the formation of multiple teams:

- Two methods begin by first assigning the project leader and after, form rest of each team, either one at a time or simultaneously.
- The other two methods form the entire teams (without first assigning the project leader), either one at a time or simultaneously.

Simultaneous formation involves assigning the required people to cover the highest priority role in each project, and continuing until assigning the required people to cover the lowest priority role in each project. On the contrary, one-by-one formation, assigns the necessary people to all the roles of a project, before assigning people to the roles of the next project. The simultaneous formation methods aim to form balanced teams.

The capacity for select objective functions, restrictions and, methods and algorithms to solve the problem, facilitate decision-making and experimentation. Furthermore, it allows the tool to be used in different contexts, whenever a set of parameters are configured. For example: to form the cabin crews, a problem addressed by Ginnett (2019), the different parameters must be configured (e.g. the roles: captain and first officer).

An organization should perform the following steps to form teams using the Teamsoft+ tool:

Steps to form Teams Using the Teamsoft+ Tool

In the tool, four elements are key in team's formation, these are: people, competences, roles and projects.

Step 1: Configure parameters related to key elements, such as:

- Levels: competences, importance of competences, workload, incompatibility among members and cost of working remotely,
- Required generic and technical competences,
- Roles to be played by the team members (e.g. programmer and architect),
- The required generic competences to perform each role and for each competency, the required minimum level,
- Incompatible roles (e.g. Programmer and tester),
- Level of the cost of playing each role remotely (e.g. High for the architect and Low for the programmer),
- Groups where the people in the organization are located (example: departments in the business context and faculties, years and class groups, in the academic context).

Step 2: Record the data involved in the formation process.
About people:

- General data such as: Name, surname and identity number, group, preferred and avoided functional roles, level in each technical and generic competence, level of incompatibility with people in the organization and psychological characteristics (psychological type and the preferred and avoided team roles).

About the project:

- General data such as: Name and locality or province where it will be developed, structure of the project which includes the required roles (ordered by level of importance for the project), amount of people to be assigned to each role, level of workload of each role, the required technical competences by the project and for each one, its importance and the required minimum level to perform each role.

Step 3: Configure parameters for team's formation, such as:

- Select the projects and groups of people to be considered. It is possible to select the whole organization or part of it. For example, a company department or a class group of the faculty.
- Select the general restrictions to consider in the formation:
  - Define the maximum amount of roles a person can play.
  - Define if a person can only be assigned to a project.
  - Define if all the people in the selected group should be assigned.
  - If required, define the amount of people to be assigned per project.
- Select the team formation method to use.
- Select the method of solving the problem to be used (weighted factors, lexicographic and pure multiobjective).
- Select the solution algorithm to use.

The possibility of selecting the algorithm to use, facilitates the development of experiments to evaluate the behavior of the algorithms in solving the problem. However, it is a disadvantage when the decision maker is not an expert. A variant is to establish a default algorithm. However, the algorithm can vary its performance depending on the size of the problem. This aspect should be improved in future versions of the tool.

Step 4: Form the teams. The steps to execute depend on the selected method to form the teams. There are two possible scenarios:

- If the decision-maker selected a team-building method that prioritizes the project leader's assignment, the next step is to select the factors to be considered in the assignment and to establish the restrictions associated with each of them. Possible factors are: competences, workload, interest in the role, psychological characteristics and cost of distance work.

- If the decision maker selected a team formation method that does not prioritize the assignment of the project leader, or if the project leader has already been assigned, the next step is to select the solution method to be used. Then, the factors to be considered are selected and restrictions are set for each of them. The following objective functions can be selected for team formation: maximizing competencies, minimizing incompatibilities between members, balancing workload, minimizing the cost of distance work, maximizing interest in performing the roles and maximizing the presence of Belbin's roles. Depending on the factors considered, other objective functions can be selected to balance the teams based on these factors (as shown in Table 1).

Infante et al. (2020b) developed a new experiment, now using the new version of the tool. The objective was the same as in the previous experiment, to form the student teams for the IS3 course. The eleven student teams must be complete (all roles must be covered) and must be balanced.

The structure of the teams is homogeneous, in terms of the roles to be covered and the needed competences to perform these roles. All students must be assigned to a project.

The experimentation carried out allowed validating that the tool is highly configurable.

In the formation of the teams, the following factors were taken into account: technical and generic competences, incompatibilities between members, interests to play each role and psychological characteristics (using the Belbin's test). The workload and cost to develop software at distance are not being considered because these factors are not applicable in this context.

In addition to the data collected for the previous experiment, a survey was applied to the students where they had to define the functional roles preferred and avoided.

Weighted factors are used as the solution method. The following weights were assigned to the selected objective functions: Maximize the competences (0.1), Balance the level of competences between the teams (0.2), Minimize incompatibilities between members (0.1), Balance the incompatibilities between the teams (0.2), Maximize interest to play each role (0.1), Balance the interest between the teams (0.1), Maximize the presence of Belbin's roles in the teams (0.1) and Balance the presence of Belbin's roles between the teams (0.1).

The Hill Climbing algorithm was selected, taking into account the good results obtained by the algorithm in the previous experiments (Infante et al., 2014; Infante et al., 2020a).

In the experiment two of the implemented four methods for the formation of multiple teams were applied:

- **Method 1:** Form complete teams one by one (without first assigning to the project leaders).
- **Method 2:** Form teams simultaneously (without first assigning to project leaders).

Project leaders were not assigned first, because it was decided to respect the priority of the roles established when defining the structure.

Finally, entire teams were formed using the new version of the Teamsoft+ tool (even applying both methods). Table 2 shows the evaluation of each project team for the different factors and the balance index. The evaluations of the first team formed are shown in the column titled T1 and so on, for the rest of the eleven teams.

Table 2. Evaluation of each factor by team and balance index (Infante et al., 2020b)

Solution method	Factor	Evaluation of each factor by team											Balance index
		T1	T2	T3	T4	T5	T6	T7	T8	T9	T10	T11	
1	Competences	0,95	0,47	0,71	0,52	0,62	0,90	0,71	0,90	0,81	0,62	0,71	1,38
	Incompatibilities	0,5	0,52	0,52	0,52	0,5	0,5	0,5	0,5	0,5	0,5	0,5	0,09
	Interest to play each role	0,69	0,62	0,62	0,62	0,81	0,75	0,81	0,69	0,69	0,93	0,92	1,02
	Presence of Belbin´ roles	1	0,89	1	1	1	0,89	1	1	0,78	0,89	0,78	0,84
2	Competences	0,85	0,71	0,71	0,71	0,71	0,52	0,62	0,66	0,81	0,71	0,54	0,81
	Incompatibilities	0,5	0,5	0,5	0,5	0,5	0,5	0,5	0,5	0,5	0,52	0,50	0,04
	Interest to play each role	0,81	0,87	0,75	0,69	0,75	0,63	0,63	0,69	0,75	0,57	0,75	0,75
	Presence of Belbin´ roles	0,89	1	1	1	1	0,89	0,89	0,78	0,89	1	1	0,72

Although both methods allow to form complete teams, applying the second method, a better balance is obtained between the teams (as observed in Table 2). The balance index represents the deviation of each index in relation to the average, so the ideal value is 0.

FUTURE WORK

Among the objectives to be fulfilled in the following research stages are:

- Development of experiments to evaluate the performance of different trajectory-based and population-based multiobjective algorithms for different problem sizes, using the different methods for the formation of multiple teams and strategies for the treatment of restrictions.
- Incorporation into the model of factors such as: presence of the different psychological types and demographic diversity.
- Configuration by default the appropriate solution algorithm (according to the characteristics of the organization), to avoid the decision maker (non-expert) having to select it.

RESEARCH TRENDS

Different trends are identified in this area of research:

- Definition of more complete models to represent the problem more objectively.
- Development of simpler and more efficient algorithms.
- Performance evaluation of different algorithms in the solution of the problem in various contexts.
- Development of flexible tools to facilitate the work of decision makers.
- Efficient and more objective measures to determine the relationships between people, taking into account aspects such as: previous cooperation, evolution of the relationship and psychological characteristics.

Other trends are more linked to the formation of teams not focused on one organization, given the rise of global projects:

- Analysis of different factors, such as cultural intelligence, in the performance and satisfaction of global teams (Henderson et al., 2018).
- Factors to consider in entrepreneurial team formation (Lazar et al., 2020).
- Measures that can be efficiently used to evaluate impact on team cohesion and performance.

CONCLUSION

Given the importance of the team in the success of any kind of projects, the amount of researches related to team formation has increased in recent years. The participation of women in this area of research is significant. In a large part of the works analyzed, women have participated as co-authors and have even led several investigations.

As a main result of this research, a formal model was defined for the formation of one or multiple project teams. The model considers a large amount of factors, both individual and collective. As a novel element, the model included not only a group of objective functions to maximize or minimize these factors (as appropriate) within the team, but other functions to balance the teams according to the different factors.

The new version of the Teamsoft+ tool supports the model to form multiple teams. The flexibility of the tool allows the decision maker to select the objective functions, the restrictions, the solution method and algorithm, as well as the team formation method to use. The tool can be used in different contexts to form one or multiple teams, it is only necessary to configure parameters associated with four key elements of the model: people, competences, roles and projects.

The incorporation of BICIAM in the tool allowed reusing a large number of metaheuristic algorithms. At the same time, the modifications made to the library enable it to be used in order to solve multiobjective optimization problems.

The multiobjective methods and algorithms incorporated into BICIAM facilitated the development of experiments. The experiments carried out during the research showed that the multiobjective trajectory-based algorithms obtain good results in the solution of this problem (even in different sizes of the problem), especially the multiobjective variants of Hill Climbing and the multiobjective variant of Simulated Annealing.

The implementation in the tool of methods for the simultaneous formation of teams and the incorporation of objective functions to balance the teams, associated with different factors, allowed to form complete and balanced teams.

REFERENCES

Afshar, J., Roudsari, A. H., Lee, C., Eom, C., Lee, W., & Arora, N. (2018). Harmonic Mean Based Soccer Team Formation Problem. In *Proceedings of the 7th International Conference on Emerging Databases: Technologies, Applications, and Theory* (pp. 240-246). Springer Singapore. 10.1007/978-981-10-6520-0_25

Agrawal, V., & Jariwala, A. (2017). *Web-based tools for supporting student-driven Capstone Design Team formation* [Paper presentation]. *124th ASEE Annual Conference and Exposition*. Columbus, OH, USA.

Alberola, J. M., Del val, E., Sanchez-Anguix, V., & Julián, V. (2016b). A general framework for testing different student team formation strategies, In Methodologies and Intelligent Systems for Technology Enhanced Learning (pp. 23-31). Springer Verlag.

Alberola, J. M., Del Val, E., Sánchez-Anguix, V., Palomares, A., & Teruel, M. D. (2016a). An artificial intelligence tool for heterogeneous team formation in the classroom. *Knowledge-Based Systems*, *101*, 1–14. doi:10.1016/j.knosys.2016.02.010

Alcala-Fdez, J., Fernández, A., Luengo, J., Derrac, J., García, S., Sánchez, L., & Herrera, F. (2011). KEEL Data-Mining Software Tool: Data Set Repository, Integration of Algorithms and Experimental Analysis Framework. *Journal of Multiple-Valued Logic and Soft Computing*, *17*(2), 255–287.

Amarasinghe, I., Hernández-Leo, D., & Jonsson, A. (2017). Towards data-informed group formation support across learning spaces. In *Joint 6th Multimodal Learning Analytics Workshop and the Second Cross-LAK Workshop* (pp. 31-38). MMLA-CrossLAK.

André, M., & Baldoquín, G. (2010). A decision support system for assigning human resources to software project teams. *Revista de Investigación Operacional*, *31*(1), 61–69.

André, M., Baldoquín, G., & Acuña, S. T. (2010). Identification of patterns for the formation of software development projects teams. *International Journal of Human Capital and Information Technology Professionals*, *1*(3), 11–24.

André, M., Baldoquín, G., & Acuña, S. T. (2011). Formal model for assigning human resources to teams in software projects. *Information and Software Technology*, *53*(3), 259–275. doi:10.1016/j.infsof.2010.11.011

Ashenagar, B., Eghlidi, N. F., Afshar, A., & Hamzeh, A. (2016). Team formation in social networks based on local distance metric. In *Proceedings of the 12th International Conference on Fuzzy Systems and Knowledge Discovery* (pp. 946-952). IEEE.

Bahargam, S., Golshan, B., Lappas, T., & Terzi, E. (2019). A team-formation algorithm for faultline minimization. *Expert Systems with Applications*, *119*, 441–455. doi:10.1016/j.eswa.2018.10.046

Balmaceda, J. M., Schiaffino, S., & Andrés Díaz-Pace, J. (2014). Using constraint satisfaction to aid group formation in CSCL. *Inteligencia Artificial*, *17*(52), 35–45.

Basiri, J., Taghiyareh, F., & Ghorbani, A. (2017). Collaborative team formation using brain drain optimization: A practical and effective solution. *World Wide Web (Bussum)*, *20*(6), 1385–1407. doi:10.100711280-017-0440-6

Belbin, M. (1981). *Management Teams: Why They Succeed or Fail*. Butterworth Heinemann.

Bergey, P., & King, M. (2014). Team machine: A decision support system for team formation. *Decision Sciences Journal of Innovative Education*, *12*(2), 109–130. doi:10.1111/dsji.12027

Bredereck, R., Chen, J., Hüffner, F., & Kratsch, S. (2018). Parameterized complexity of team formation in social networks. *Theoretical Computer Science*, *717*, 26–36. doi:10.1016/j.tcs.2017.05.024

Brilhante, I., Macedo, J. A., Nardini, F. M., Perego, R., & Renso, C. (2016). Group finder: An item-driven group formation framework. In *Proceedings of the 17th IEEE International Conference on Mobile Data Management* (pp. 8-17). IEEE. 10.1109/MDM.2016.16

Budak, G., Kara, İ., İç, Y. T., & Kasımbeyli, R. (2019). New mathematical models for team formation of sports clubs before the match. *Central European Journal of Operations Research*, *27*(1), 93–109. doi:10.100710100-017-0491-x

Bulmer, J., Fritter, M., Gao, Y., & Hui, B. (2020). FASTT: Team Formation Using Fair Division. Canadian Conference on Artificial Intelligence. In *Advances in Artificial Intelligence* (pp. 92-104). Elsevier.

Cavdur, F., Sebatli, A., Kose-Kucuk, M., & Rodoplu, C. (2019). A two-phase binary-goal programming-based approach for optimal project-team formation. *The Journal of the Operational Research Society*, *70*(4), 689–706. doi:10.1080/01605682.2018.1457480

Chong, E. K. P., & Zak, S. H. (2013). *An introduction to optimization*. John Wiley & Sons.

Coello, C., Lamont, G. B., & Veldhuizen, D. A. (2007). *Evolutionary Algorithms for Solving Multi-Objective Problems*. Springer.

Del Val, E., Alberola, J. M., Sanchez-Anguix, V., Palomares, A., & Teruel, M. D. (2014). A team formation tool for educational environments. In *Trends in Practical Applications of Heterogeneous Multi-Agent Systems* (pp. 173–181). Springer Verlag. doi:10.1007/978-3-319-07476-4_21

Di Martinelly, C., & Meskens, N. (2017). A bi-objective integrated approach to building surgical teams and nurse schedule rosters to maximise surgical team affinities and minimise nurses' idle time. *International Journal of Production Economics*, *191*, 323–334. doi:10.1016/j.ijpe.2017.05.014

Ding, C., Xia, F., Gopalakrishnan, G., Qian, W., & Zhou, A. (2017). TeamGen: An Interactive Team Formation System Based on Professional Social Network. In *Proceedings of the 26th International Conference on World Wide Web Companion* (pp. 195-199). 10.1145/3041021.3054725

DuPont, B., & Hoyle, C. (2015). *Automation and optimization of engineering design team selection considering personality types and course-specific constraints* [Paper presentation]. *122nd ASEE Annual Conference and Exposition*, Seattle, WA, USA.

Ebadi, A., Tighe, P. J., Zhang, L., & Rashidi, P. (2017). DisTeam: A decision support tool for surgical team selection. *Artificial Intelligence in Medicine*, *76*, 16–26. doi:10.1016/j.artmed.2017.02.002 PMID:28363285

Farasat, A., & Nikolaev, A. G. (2016). Social structure optimization in team formation. *Computers & Operations Research*, *74*, 127–142. doi:10.1016/j.cor.2016.04.028

Feo, T. A., & Resende, M. G. C. (1995). Greedy randomized adaptive search procedures. *Journal of Global Optimization*, *6*(2), 109–133. doi:10.1007/BF01096763

Ginnett, R. C. (2019). Crews as groups: Their formation and their leadership. In *Crew resource management* (pp. 73–102). Academic Press. doi:10.1016/B978-0-12-812995-1.00003-8

Glover, F. (1986). Future Paths for Integer Programming and Links to Artificial Intelligence. *Computers & Operations Research*, *13*(5), 533–549. doi:10.1016/0305-0548(86)90048-1

Gutiérrez, J. H., Astudillo, C. A., Ballesteros-Pérez, P., Mora-Melià, D., & Candia-Véjar, A. (2016). The multiple team formation problem using sociometry. *Computers & Operations Research*, *75*, 150–162. doi:10.1016/j.cor.2016.05.012

Han, Y., Wan, Y., Chen, L., Xu, G., & Wu, J. (2017). Exploiting geographical location for team formation in social coding sites. In *Proceedings of the 21st Pacific-Asia Conference on Knowledge Discovery and Data Mining* (pp. 499-510). Springer International Publishing. 10.1007/978-3-319-57454-7_39

Henderson, L. S., Stackman, R. W., & Lindekilde, R. (2018). Why cultural intelligence matters on global project teams. *International Journal of Project Management*, *36*(7), 954–967. doi:10.1016/j.ijproman.2018.06.001

Infante, A. L., André, M., Rosete, A., & López, Y. (2020a). Methods for the formation of multiple teams of students applying a multiobjective approach. *Revista de Ingeniería Industrial*, *41*(1), 20–39.

Infante, A. L., André, M., Rosete, A., Naredo, J. A., & Durán, A. (2020b, March). *A decision support tool for multiple team formation problems* [Paper presentation]. *14th International Conference on Operations Research (ICOR)*, La Habana, Cuba.

Infante, A. L., André, M., Rosete, A., & Rampersaud, L. (2014). Formation of software project teams applying multi-objective metaheuristic algorithms. *Revista Iberoamericana de Inteligencia Artificial*, *17*(54), 1–16. doi:10.4114/intartif.vol17iss54pp1-16

Jeong, Y., Pan, Y., Rathore, S., Kim, B., & Park, J. H. (2018). A parallel team formation approach using crowd intelligence from social network. *Computers in Human Behavior*, *101*, 429–434. doi:10.1016/j.chb.2018.07.018

Jin, C. X., Li, F. C., Zhang, K., Xu, L. D., & Chen, Y. (2019). A cooperative effect-based decision support model for team formation. *Enterprise Information Systems*, *14*(1), 110–132. doi:10.1080/17517575.2019.1678071

Kader, Md. A., & Zamli, K. Z. (2020). Adopting Jaya Algorithm for Team Formation Problem. In *Proceedings of the 9th International Conference on Software and Computer Applications* (pp. 62–66). ACM.

Kirkpatrick, S., Gelatt, C. D., & Vecchi, M. P. (1983). Optimization by Simulated Annealing. *Science*, *220*(4598), 671–680. doi:10.1126cience.220.4598.671 PMID:17813860

Lazar, M., Miron-Spektor, E., Agarwal, R., Erez, M., Goldfard, B., & Chen, G. (2020). Entrepreneurial team formation. *The Academy of Management Annals*, *14*(1), 29–59. doi:10.5465/annals.2017.0131

Liemhetcharat, S., & Veloso, M. (2017). Allocating training instances to learning agents for team formation. *Autonomous Agents and Multi-Agent Systems*, *31*(4), 905–940. doi:10.100710458-016-9355-3

López, Y., André, M., Infante, A. L., Escalera, K., & Verona, S. (2018). Evaluation of the performance of roles in software development teams. Use of rating scales. *Ingeniare. Revista Chilena de Ingeniería*, *26*(3), 486–498.

Miettinen, K. (2008). Introduction to Multiobjective Optimization: Noninteractive Approaches. In *Multiobjective optimization: interactive and evolutionary approaches* (pp. 1–26). Springer Berlin Heidelberg.

Pavlov, D., & Yahontova, I. (2020). Formation of Effective Leading Project Teams: A Multi-Objective Approach. In *Proceedings of the 6th International Conference on Social, economic, and academic leadership* (pp. 84-90). Atlantis Press. 10.2991/assehr.k.200526.013

PMI. (2017). *A Guide to the Project Management Body of Knowledge (PMBOK Guide)* (6th ed.). Project Management Institute.

Rich, E., & Knight, K. (1991). *Artificial Intelligence* (2nd ed.). McGraw-Hill Education.

Wolpert, D. H., & Macready, W. G. (1997). No free lunch theorems for optimization. *IEEE Transactions on Evolutionary Computation*, *1*(1), 67–82. doi:10.1109/4235.585893

Zakarian, A., & Kusiak, A. (1999). Forming teams: An analytical approach. *IEEE Transactions*, *31*(1), 85–97. doi:10.1080/07408179908969808

KEY TERMS AND DEFINITIONS

Belbin Test: It allows to identifying the preferred and avoided team roles of each person, among the nine defined roles, which are grouped into three categories: mental roles (Plant, Monitor Evaluator and Specialist), action roles (Shaper, Implementer, and Completer Finisher) and social roles (Coordinator, Resource Investigator, and Teamworker).

Feasible Solution: It satisfies the entire restrictions foreseen in the optimization problem. When at least one restriction of the problem is not met, the solution is considered not feasible.

Generic Competences: These are also called transversal and define characteristics referring to the general behavior of the person, independently of the specific technical knowledge. For example: communication skills and analytical skills.

Myers-Briggs Type Indicator: This test measures four different dimensions of human preferences: Extroversion (E), Introversion (I), Intuition (N), Sense (S), Emotion (F), Thinking (T), Judgment (J), and Perception (P). From the values of each dimension, identify the psychological type of the person among the 16 possible types.

Technical Competences: These are associated with specific technical knowledge and skills of each position or role.

Chapter 12
Connecting the Dots Between Human Factors and Software Engineering

Mary Sánchez-Gordón
https://orcid.org/0000-0002-5102-1122
Østfold University College, Norway

ABSTRACT

Software engineering (SE) is a human-intensive activity where human factors play a fundamental role. As such, SE is an inherently sociotechnical endeavor on which different social and technical aspects are involved. In fact, it is recognized that successful SE not only depends on technical or process issues, but also it is influenced by human factors. They have been proved to have impact on software process and their study is a growing research field. The summary presented in this chapter highlights the results obtained in a five-year effort research aiming at understanding the role that human factors play in SE. As a result, a holistic view of human factors on software process is given.

INTRODUCTION

Software Engineering (SE) is concerned with all aspects of software production, beyond the technical processes of software development and tools, SE also includes people (Sommerville, 2010). This chapter summarizes the main results obtained by the author after five years of research. The main research goal was to build a bridge between human factors (called human aspects in SE) and software development in order to improve the software process and help developers in their very complex and high demanding daily job (M.-L. Sánchez-Gordón & O'Connor, 2016; M.-L. Sánchez-Gordón, O'Connor, Colomo-Palacios, & Herranz, 2016; M.-L. Sánchez-Gordón, Colomo-Palacios, et al., 2016; M.-L. Sánchez-Gordón, 2017; M.-L. Sánchez-Gordón et al., 2017; M. Sánchez-Gordón & Colomo-Palacios, 2018, 2019b, 2019a, 2020b, 2020a; M. Sánchez-Gordón et al., 2020). The journey started long time ago, 1997, when the author was working in Ecuador as a programmer in a small software company while finishing a degree in Computer Science. At that point, the author realized that technical knowledge is not enough to ensure

DOI: 10.4018/978-1-7998-7552-9.ch012

Copyright © 2021, IGI Global. Copying or distributing in print or electronic forms without written permission of IGI Global is prohibited.

the success of a software project. The human activity of all stakeholders –project manager, software developers, testers, and so on– has an influence in the daily work and the results of the project. *How to improve the software process?* was an open question that the author tried to answer for each software project –regardless the size and sector– in which the author was involved over 15 years.

Over the time, that question was so challenging that led the author to enroll in a PhD program in 2013. The first research effort reports on a grounded theory study in order to *understand the gap between software process practices and actual practice in small software companies* (M.-L. Sánchez-Gordón & O'Connor, 2016). The focus was on small companies due to the vast majority of them in software industry. As a result, three areas of concern were identified: customer, software product, and development tasks coordination and tracking. The three software companies involved in the study stated that they used their homegrown software process to work. Although software quality standards were not a major concern for those companies, all participants displayed a sincere interest on improving their way of working. In particular, the project managers displayed standard benefits awareness and barriers toward its adoption. They also agreed that best practices such as those including in the lifecycle processes described in ISO/IEC 29110 standard could be helpful, even though they will not immediately adopt it. By reviewing the literature available related to how to improve the software process in small software companies, one can conclude that despite the importance of this research area for software industry it has been relatively scarce study. Although there is a large number of concerns and factors influencing the software development process (Marks et al., 2017), people are essential in the software process and in its assessment and improvement (Sampaio et al., 2013). In fact, the software development process is acknowledged as a *"socio-technical system"* (Fuggetta & Di Nitto, 2014). Therefore, the author understood that human factors influencing the software development process in small software companies deserve to be further investigated to achieve a software process improvement.

The starting point was the study of *software process* along with the related standards in small enterprises. From there, hard and *soft skills* were identified by reviewing literature and then the definition of *culture* was explored in a relatively new agile approach called DevOps. At the end of this review, empathy seemed to be behind DevOps culture because it is claimed that DevOps dissolves the barriers between developers and operators. From there, the study of *emotions* emerged like an important driver and it was also explored. Finally, given that *diversity of people and ideas are good for our field* (Capretz, 2014) the last study is about *diversity*.

BACKGROUND

The study of human factors in SE is a growing research field (Lenberg et al., 2015) in which it is recognized that successful SE not only depends on technical or process issues, but also is influenced by human factors (Capretz, 2014). Indeed, it was realized early in the development of SE field (Weinberg, 1971; Gannon, 1979). Although SE work would be seen as human and technical aspects separately, in practice, it is difficult to disentangle the way people do things from the methods, techniques, and technologies they use (França et al., 2020). Thus, SE is a human–intensive activity where human factors play a critical role. As such, SE is an inherently socio-technical endeavor (Capretz, 2014) on which different social and technical aspects are involved. For instance, the collaboration and communication that take place among stakeholders are fundamental activities to lead complex software projects to success (Pressman, 2009). Likewise, the human factors –people– are fundamental in any software process improvement

(SPI) initiative since it requires commitment and responsibility to achieve effective, efficient, and quality processes (Korsaa et al., 2013).

In early days, research concerned with organizational, social or psychological factors was scarce whereas much of the research and practice were focused largely on technological or process-related factors (Perry et al., 1994). In last two decades, although, agile methods have emphasized the value of people –teams and their communication and collaboration–, it can still not be considered to be in the SE mainstream (Lenberg et al., 2015). There are conferences that have names that allude to this research area but they are focused mainly on the human–computer interaction or on usability, e.g. human-centered SE (HCSE) and conference on human factors in computing systems (CHI). However, workshops have addressed concerns close to this topic over the years. Three good examples are the workshop on cooperative and human aspects of software engineering (CHASE), the workshop on emotion awareness in SE (SEmotion), and the workshop on human factors in software development processes (HuFo). Since 2008, the CHASE has been held in conjunction with the largest conference within SE (ICSE). It has highlighted cooperative and human aspects of SE and emphasized that SE activities typically happen in the context of a group or team (Dittrich et al., 2020). The SEmotion is also part of the ICSE conference since 2016 but it aims to create an international, sustainable forum for researchers and practitioners interested in the role of affect in software. Finally, since the same year, the HuFo has been held in conjunction with the PROFES conference. HuFo has highlighted human factors in software product engineering and processes (Abrahao et al., 2020).

The relation of human factors and the software engineering has also been a subject of study in some previous studies. The human factors have different levels of impact in the SE process varying from organizational and interpersonal to individual (Fazli & Bittner, 2017). Thus, human factors in SE processes have been studied from different perspectives and there are some secondary studies about this topic.

Contributions to this field include a systematic literature review (SLR) directly focused on human factors in software development conducted by (Pirzadeh, 2010). The author proposed the following categories to human factors: (i) organizational, (ii) interpersonal and (iii) individual. More recently, a definition of the research area behavioral software engineering (BSE) was proposed by (Lenberg et al., 2015). The authors present 55 BSE concepts and a brief description of them from a SLR. The most common concepts were communication (39 publications), group composition (24), job satisfaction (24) and leadership (23). In addition, personality was identified in 31 publications although no explicit search was conducted for it. A recent systematic mapping study to identify existing research on soft skills in SE was conducted by (Matturro et al., 2019). After reviewing, 44 studies were selected, and 30 main categories of soft skills were identified. Among them, communication skills, team work, analytical skills, organizational skills, and interpersonal skills are mentioned as such in at least half of the reviewed studies. The focus is on all the soft skills related to the practice of SE reported in literature, and not just on the specific factors such as motivation (Beecham et al., 2008) or personality (Cruz et al., 2015). Finally, a SLR was carried out by (Machuca-Villegas et al., 2020) in order to classify social and human factors related to productivity in software development teams. This ongoing research selected 13 factors and their definitions in the light of three concepts: work team, software development, and gamification.

Culture also plays an important role for the success of SE projects. A SLR was conducted to analyze cultural influences on collaborative work in SE (Fazli & Bittner, 2017). The findings point out that there are differences e.g. in communication styles, interaction in teams, decision-making, and more during collaboration. Authors concluded that the ignorance of cultural differences in distributed agile teams can lead to significant problems such as severe misunderstanding and conflicts in distributed projects.

Therefore, in-depth-studies on culture and collaboration in global software engineering (GSE) teams should be conducted in order to better understand and manage their dynamics. In the same vein, a SLR was conducted by (Marinho et al., 2018) in order to identify specific practices for managing cultural differences in Global Software Development (GSD). As a result, 12 implementable cultural practices were found in 19 studies to "provide a cultural knowledge base", "understand and make team members aware of cultural differences", and "plan responses to mitigate occurrences of cultural misunderstandings".

Diversity in SE is another aspect related to human beings. Research on equity, diversity and inclusion has been a mainstay of IEEE Computer Society and ACM. Two relevant examples are the International Conference on Software Engineering (ICSE) and the International Conference on Global Software Engineering (ICGSE). In 2018, a SRL conducted by (Menezes & Prikladnicki, 2018) found only 28 papers related to SE. The majority of them were focused on gender diversity aspects (18), followed by disabilities (7), ethnicity (3), age (1), personality (1), and other papers (3) discussing diversity generically without any type specifically. On the other hand, a systematic mapping study published in 2019 determined how diversity is being considered in SE. This mapping study conducted by (Silveira & Prikladnicki, 2019) found 221 papers from 2001 to 2018. In the identity diversity perspective, the papers address gender diversity (129), followed by cultural diversity (67), age/generation diversity (10), ethnicity (7), LGBTQI (2), and only one paper dealing with disabilities. From the cognitive diversity perspective, the authors classiδed 61 papers because most of the 221 papers address identity diversity as the main topic. The 61 papers address diversity of background (24), followed by personality (17), psychological (7), thinking (7), functional (4), and ethics (2). However, regarding agile methodologies, very few studies (12) out of the total were found to be related.

Despite the efforts made, SE is a relatively new field in which there are many open questions (Erdogmus et al., 2018). In particular, the article "Bringing the Human Factor to Software Engineering" by (Capretz, 2014) was a source of inspiration and ideas for the author of this chapter because Capretz highlighted that *"the study of human factors in SE will not be a silver bullet that solves all problems but it could offer different insights and fresh approaches to answering some open questions"*. In this chapter, the aim is to bring together the results and experiences from the author and her colleagues after a 5-years research effort on human factors in SE in a single source. The chapter should be useful for SE practitioners and researchers interested in this field.

CONNECTING THE DOTS

This section summarizes the main results obtained by the author and her colleagues at the end of the period of five years, with the main goal of bridging the gap between human factors and SE. Research has focused on how the human aspects of a technical discipline as SE can improve the software process and understanding emotions, culture, and diversity in SE and software development (see Figure 1).

On Software Process

In general, if the people within an organization are not managed effectively, they could potentially cause disruptions to the implementation process. However, the human factor management requires moving beyond traditional mechanisms in order to increase motivation through engagement. One way to achieve this goal is gamification, therefore, the relationship between gamification and human factors in quality

Figure 1. Connecting the dots between human factors and software engineering

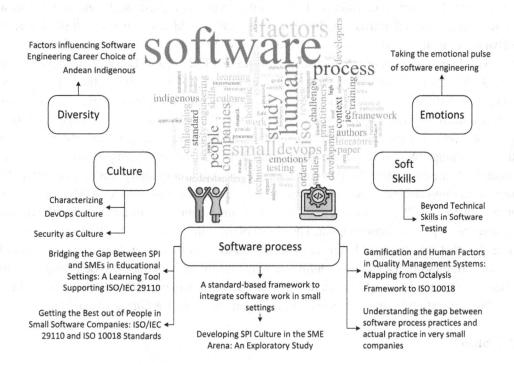

management systems (QMS) were identified by carrying out a *mapping from octalysis framework to ISO 10018 standard* (M.-L. Sánchez-Gordón, Colomo-Palacios, et al., 2016). The findings revealed that gamification can be designed for addressing all human factors in order to improve QMS, in particular initiatives focus on software process. The identified factors are: communication, leadership, empowerment, engagement, attitude and motivation, networking, recognition and rewards, teamwork and collaboration, education and learning, creativity and innovation, awareness, responsibility and authority, and recruitment. To explore the feasibility of such approach, a learning tool for the ISO/IEC 29110 standard was designed with twofold objectives to *understand the project management process of the basic profile* (M.-L. Sánchez-Gordón, O'Connor, Colomo-Palacios, & Sánchez-Gordón, 2016), and to *bridge the gap between software process improvement and SMEs in educational settings* (M.-L. Sánchez-Gordón, O'Connor, Colomo-Palacios, & Herranz, 2016). The findings indicated that the proposed learning tool created a positive learning experience, and therefore could be used as a strategy to support education and promote the ISO/IEC 29110 standard.

Despite the appealing previous results, *getting the best out of people in small software companies* (M.-L. Sánchez-Gordón, 2017) is hard due to the concerns and perceived shortcomings present in this type of companies. Therefore, a holistic view of human factors on software process in small software companies were proposed based on best practices of the ISO/IEC 29110 and ISO 10018 standards. To sum up, it is important having an effective involvement of people with the necessary competences that goes beyond common sense: encouraging teamwork, networking, positive attitudes, empowerment, and engagement as a result of leadership behavior. It is also worth noting that a high degree of people involvement could foster creativity and innovation. Finally, recruitment processes become less critical when an organization has a low staff turnover.

The previous studies allowed to build a *standard-based framework to integrate software work in small settings* (M.-L. Sánchez-Gordón et al., 2017) that supports the establishment of mechanisms to incorporate human factors that traditionally have been partially addressed or not addressed at all by the small software companies. This framework, called Samay –Quechua word meaning spirit or soul–, was developed based upon reviews of relevant standards –ISO/IEC 29110, ISO 10018, OMG Essence, and ISO/IEC 33014– and previously published studies in this field. The results of the expert review and validation supported the view that Samay could support practitioners when small software companies want to start improving their ways of work. At this point, the author and her colleagues realized that training is one way to enhance individual capabilities and organizational productivity in order to gain competitive advantage (Noe et al., 2014; Zhao et al., 2014). However, training is also one of the challenges small software companies face. In consequence, an exploratory study was carried out to *develop software process improvement culture in the small-medium sized enterprises arena* (M. Sánchez-Gordón & Colomo-Palacios, 2019b). This study was based on game attributes in order to design the training for an agnostic software process improvement. The object of the training was Samay Framework. As a result, the trainees felt that they improved their knowledge and most of them were more encouraged to know more about the framework. Despite that online training (synchronous mode) was delivered, after almost all training sessions, the levels of arousal and pleasure were incremented. The holistic view of training process in this context gives the confidence in the alignment of the training goals and business goals.

On Soft Skills

Beside aforementioned human factors, personality traits and soft skills are influencing the software process. In recent years, it is increasingly discussed in the SE community that technical, also known as hard skills, and non-technical, also known as soft skills, are equally important (Garousi et al., 2019). In fact, there are several studies related to soft skills in SE, e.g. (Florea & Stray, 2019a, 2019b; Matturro et al., 2019). However, the term "soft" is not the only one used in the literature, there are other frequently used terms as synonyms that slightly differ in meaning. These terms range from non-cognitive abilities, 21st century skills, intangible skills, human factors, interpersonal skills, generic competencies, to social & emotional intelligence and people skills (Matturro et al., 2019).

In particular, soft skills in testing has been recognized as a toolbox to approach work (van Veenendaal, 2020) but there is a lack of empirical research in this topic. As a consequence, an exploratory study which goes *beyond technical skills in software testing automated and manual testing* was done (M. Sánchez-Gordón et al., 2020). This study aimed to identify what are the most valued skills with regards to these different types of testing. To do so, a survey was designed to collect data from software practitioners. The questionnaire covers 35 skills grouped into four categories for non-technical (soft) skills: cognitive skills, communication skills, social skills, and open and adaptable to change skills. Additionally, three categories for technical (hard) skills were evaluated: domain knowledge, testing skills, and tools knowledge. The perceived importance of the 34 skills in each type of testing was identified on a five-point scale –from 1-Not at all important to 5-Very Important.

The results of this exploratory study came from 72 practitioners. Despite the small sample size, they provide empirical evidence about the high importance that software practitioners give to hard and soft skills alike. By analyzing the remaining skill related to "tools knowledge" (open-closed question), one can see that practitioners master a large spectrum of testing tools. Furthermore, a null hypotheses H_0: μ_{sx}(Manual) = μ_{sx}(Automated) was tested using Wilcoxon signed-rank test with Bonferroni-Holm correction. This non-parametric statistical test method was used because the normality test revealed that the data does not follow a normal distribution. The results show that there is no significant difference in the respondents' perceived value of these skills between the testing approaches. However, the top few skills are a mix of both hard and soft skills and it seems that one cannot isolate one from the other.

On Culture

Culture is a very complex concept and difficult to grasp. Most of the available definitions of culture share a common ground and describe similar views on culture with mostly identical attributes and elements. The iceberg model of culture proposed by (Hall, 1976) has two layers and it is often used as a reference. The first layer is the unconscious part, which basically means the invisible one, while the second, on contrast, is visible and conscious. Moreover, the first one is formed by values, norms, attitudes and beliefs while the second aggregates all phenomena that are caused by the first layer and have empirical evidence, often described as behavior and cultural artifacts. In general, many members of a social group are not aware of the fact that there are different ways of thinking, acting, behaving and feeling in different social groups (Gray, 2016). According to (Marinho et al., 2018), the complex interaction of different values, attitudes, behavioral patterns, beliefs and communication approaches of stakeholders of a project can give rise to misunderstanding and misinterpretation of intent. In turn, such a misunderstanding can result in conflict, mistrust and under-utilization of expertise.

Given DevOps is receiving increasing attention from practitioners and researchers, a SLR was carried out to characterize DevOps Culture (M. Sánchez-Gordón & Colomo-Palacios, 2018). DevOps is acknowledged as an evolution of agile software development which is informed by a lean principles background (Lwakatare et al., 2016). The findings are based on the 23 primary studies founded during 2013-2018. They revealed that seven out of thirteen attributes identified in this SLR were the most frequently ones: (i) Communication, (ii) Collaboration, (iii) Feedback (Continuous and immediate), (iv) Responsibility (personal/mutual), (v) Improvement cycle, (vi) Sharing Knowledge, (vii) Transparency, (viii) Commitment and agreement, (ix) New personnel and ideas, (x) Leadership, (xi) Blameless, (xii) Experimentation, and (xiii)Trust. By analyzing the findings, the emotional phenomenon experienced by people emerged as another aspect in the soft side of DevOps. In this case, empathy seems to be behind DevOps culture since "dissolves the barriers between self and other" (Pavlovich & Krahnke, 2012) as DevOps dissolves the barriers between developers and operators (Ebert et al., 2016).

When security is implemented into a DevOps toolchain, behavioral changes are also needed in order to create a security culture. In this context, DevSecOps has emerged as one of the approaches to lessen or –at best– solve some of the issues (Myrbakken & Colomo-Palacios, 2017). Therefore, to better understanding security as culture a SLR on the cultural side of DevSecOps was conducted (M. Sánchez-Gordón & Colomo-Palacios, 2020b). Although the time period for the SLR was not limited, only 11 papers were founded from 2016 to 2019. The identified attributes were classified based on the categorization scheme for DevOps culture proposed in our previous study. However, 2 out of 13 attributes were renamed to best suit our findings: (i) "New personnel and ideas" to "Hiring new personnel"; and (ii) "Improvement cycle" to "Continuous improvement mindset". DevSecOps culture not only move some security practices to an earlier phase of the software lifecycle but also help to adopt a different way of working, one that draws attention to cross-team collaboration in the light of security. For instance, a security champion could help to make sure that security is not overlooked in the process. The findings reveal that culture is a key element that should be adequately addressed in DevSecOps to face some security issues.

On Emotions

Emotions are a crucial part in our daily lives, however the definition of the term emotion is still discussed among the research community (Osuna et al., 2020). Software is a product of human activities that entails our social interaction and cognitive aspects (Capretz, 2014) in which emotions are also elicited. An extensive interaction between emotion and cognition in human beings –e.g., perception, attention, learning, and decision making– have revealed by research areas such as psychology and neuroscience (Osuna et al., 2020). Thus, characteristics such as human behavior (Lenberg et al., 2015) and affects –emotions and moods– are always present in software work. For instance, people's facial expression, voice intonation, and body posture are shaped by the emotion states experienced so that the understanding of emotional signals in work environments becomes an important aspect that influences factors such as communication and verbal and non-verbal behavior (Osuna et al., 2020). In other words, SE involves people in a broad range of activities where personality traits, moods, and emotions play a key role. For successful SE projects, stakeholders often need to experience positive affect (such as trust, appreciation, positive feelings associated to rewarding, and so on), to agree on display rules for emotions and moods, and to hold mutual commitment to the project goals. According to (Graziotin et al., 2015), affective reactions of the individuals influence all of the human factors, but it is worth noting that human factors such as satisfaction, motivation, affective commitment, and well-being are not affects per se –even happiness is considered a peripheral affect.

In this sense, a SLR of empirical studies was conducted to *take the emotional pulse of software engineering* (M. Sánchez-Gordón & Colomo-Palacios, 2019a). This SLR aims to identify, evaluate, and synthesize research on software developers' emotions as well as the measures used to assess its existence. This review includes 66 studies published in the period 2005-2018. Although one can conclude that this field is not mature enough yet, the results provide a state of the art in this research area that could benefit researchers by providing the latest trends and identifying the corresponding research gaps.

The findings of the SLR helped to identify 40 discrete emotions in the primary studies. The most frequent emotions were: anger, fear, disgust, sadness, joy, love and happiness. Although 22.74% of all primary studies used only a discrete approach to measure emotions, two different dimensional approaches were founded in 46.96% of studies: VAD –valence, arousal, and dominance– and polarity –positive, negative, and neutral. However, it is worth to note that the approach-avoidance dimension so far was not explored. The remaining 30.30% used both (discrete and dimensional) approaches. Most of the studies used software practitioners and datasets from industrial context as subjects. Although they may not be representative of the whole software industry, the evidence is enough to support that software developers not only feel emotions, but also display them in artifacts and communications during their daily work.

On Diversity

As software organizations become global, diversity becomes a central feature of software development teams (Hazzan & Dubinsky, 2006). Diversity can be expressed in different ways such as nationalities, gender, minorities, cultures, life styles and world views (Hazzan & Dubinsky, 2006). Therefore, diversity is a big challenge in SE. Some studies point out that diversity builds better teams and delivers better results, among other benefits (Silveira & Prikladnicki, 2019). To ensure that the organizations get the best possible return on their investment, people management should focus on respect for differences, equal treatment, inclusion, and motivation (Sommerville, 2010). There is also evidence supporting that the participation of minorities during the development process from the initial phase contributes to better creativity in finding solutions for different projects (Menezes & Prikladnicki, 2018).

According to a large survey carried out in United States (Trauth et al., 2012), there is not only a comparatively low representation of women in STEM but also, there are other underrepresented minorities such as Blacks and Latinos. Indeed, diversity and especially gender is being studied in SE and has gained relevance in the last few years (Menezes & Prikladnicki, 2018; Silveira & Prikladnicki, 2019). However, ethnicity is still an understudied topic in SE. Even more, according to (Gren, 2018), more diverse studies that investigate diversity aspects in combination are important and needed in empirical research, better known as *intersectionality*. To bring diversity and inclusion into the mainstream of the software development process, the SE community needs a better understanding of the career choice of underrepresented minorities. Career choice is recognized as a major life decision that is a complex and multifaceted phenomenon. Although there are theoretical approaches to explain and predict STEM career choices (Kvasny et al., 2015), qualitative approaches are still needed in order to identify the factors that shape career choice of underrepresented minorities (Joshi et al., 2016). In Latin America, it would be interesting to know how Andean indigenous people's career interest develops and is modified over time.

Being close to nature and community is an essential constituent to the indigenous worldview, and basic to their belief systems and attitudes (Kharkongor & Albert, 2014). Thus, the culture and thinking of indigenous people are focused on sustainable development which has become mainstream and indeed an urgent and prominent objective for governments worldwide (OECD, 2017) as the adoption of the UN Sustainable Development Goals (SDGs) shown. However, indigenous people are a widely diverse group itself, in which individuals and communities are living at different geographic locations in the continuum between the traditional ways of life and the modern (Kharkongor & Albert, 2014). Therefore, indigenous people are diverse, within and across nations (OECD, 2017), and their continuing evolution has been influenced by dominant societies and globalization (Kharkongor & Albert, 2014). The estimated number of indigenous people ranges between 300 and 370 million worldwide. Based on the latest censuses available in Latin America (Freire et al., 2015), in 2010 there were about 42 million indigenous people in the region –representing nearly 8% of the total population–, and they speak over 500 languages. Although it is difficult to estimate increases in the indigenous population across the region, the only country that reported a decrease in its indigenous population in the past decade is Bolivia.

Taking all above, an exploratory study about the *factors influencing software engineering career choice of Andean indigenous* was conducted (M. Sánchez-Gordón & Colomo-Palacios, 2020a). In this study, 10 interviews were conducted during September–October 2019, 8 participants came from four different Quechua communities in Ecuador and 2 participants came from Aymara community in Bolivia. The qualitative data analysis was based on open coding, axial coding, and selective coding that are coding techniques part of grounded theory. The findings reveal seven factors that make up the career choice of indigenous people. The factors are Social Support, Exposure to digital technology, Autonomy of Use, Digital Skill, Purpose of Use, Identity, and Work ethic. Raising the voices of indigenous men and women, this study contributes to better understand of this phenomenon while promoting equity of opportunities within the scope of SE.

FUTURE TRENDS

There are a lot of opportunities for future empirical research on human factors in SE. One of the most obvious is a replication of previous exploratory studies in order to provide further evidence that helps the area mature. In this case, the possibility of getting negative results is one of the most important benefits of replication studies.

It would be interesting to know to what extent the productivity of hard skills stems from their combination with soft skills. The balance of hard and soft skills should be differentiated according to software practitioner' needs, i.e. where a project manager/software developer/tester is in her/his career. In particular, further studies should also look at which skills are essential for a head start in the labor market and to what extend such skills could be developed by software practitioner in their daily work. In addition, SE could benefit from advances in other research areas such as cognitive science. For instance, further research should devise more "intuitive" notations for documentation. Intuitive means the nonverbal and partially verbal knowledge about how the software really works.

Sentiment analysis tools have been evaluated only on English datasets, therefore, it would be interesting to experiment with data from different languages such as Spanish. Moreover, future research on emotions should focus on the impact caused by emotions of different stakeholders on practices and artifacts in different context of software projects. In particular, basic emotions could be studied to get more insights about their effect and how to apply the measurements. However, it seems that the question posed by Ekman (Ekman, 2016) holds true in SE domain: will compelling evidence for more than just five emotions (anger, fear, disgust, sadness, and happiness) be forthcoming in the coming years, or is that all that can be empirically established?

Culture is an influence and restriction factor for actions so that an individual has consequently two roles: it carries culture, and on the other hand, it has a formative influence on it. Therefore, it should be interesting to know to what extent the adaption to a cultural standard as DevOps culture is easier than changing it. Moreover, it could be interesting to explore the influence of cultural awareness and cultural intelligence (CQ) in GSD.

As mentioned before, it is widely discussed that there are some underrepresented profiles in Software Engineering. Therefore, new strategies should be explored in order to create a more diverse and inclusive SE community that ensures equity and sustainability. Further research in role models and mentoring could help to this end.

CONCLUSION

Research has focused on understanding the role that people play in SE and how the human factors of a technical discipline can affect final results and improve the software process. The human factors in SE can be studied from different perspectives such as sociological, management and technical aspects. Although there is a growing interest from academic and practitioners, unfortunately, the human factors in SE do not receive the attention they deserve as previously mentioned (Capretz, 2014).

This chapter presented a summary which highlights the main results obtained by the author during a 5-years effort research. Above all, the takeaway message of all the studies presented is that human factors, skills, emotions, culture and diversity could be positive impact in any software project. However, several threats to validity could have affected the results of the findings of the different studies summarized in this chapter. In this sense, methodologically sound research approaches and protocols were designed for each study. A lot of attention was paid to minimize the threats to validity in each study. In particular, the primary threat to validity was the small sample size in the empirical studies. Therefore, further research in the field is certainly needed, and venues for discussion, like CHASE and SEmotion, are an added value for researchers and software practitioners.

By connecting the dots between human factors and SE, the author hopes that this effort will foster interest in research on the strengthening of the software industry, particularly in Latin America, by promoting human factors. Drawing attention to professionals in the local software industry could produce solutions tailored to local needs and capabilities as mentioned in (UNCTAD, 2012). Even more, given the rapid growing of software industry, the subsequent huge demand for technical jobs is not being filled and the diversity crisis in software development is becoming a major concern. That calls us to pay attention not only in women as software professionals but also in other underrepresented minorities like Black people and Indigenous people. In this context, an intersectional perspective could provide new insights about how social identities such as race, sexuality, and gender interact to reproduce structural inequalities (Lambert & Akinlade, 2019). As an analytical tool, intersectionality can be seen as "*a way of understanding and analyzing the complexity in the world, in people, and in human experiences*" (Collins & Bilge, 2016). In other words, intersectionality is a way to examine how power relations are intertwined and mutually dependent. It means that SE research should consider not only the gender dynamic but also other social and cultural constructs of one's identity, including but not limited to race, class, ethnicity, sexuality, nationality, age, dis/ability, and immigrant status.

As a Latin American woman and researcher in the SE field, the author of this chapter would like to add some final thoughts for novel researchers. In general, research is a very competitive and demanding job that not only requires time and effort but also creativity among other soft skills. A variety of quantitative and qualitative methodologies can be fruitfully deployed to conduct the research. Likewise, different disciplines and interdisciplinary approaches can and should be integrated to pursue SE research. In fact, research is influenced, to some extent, by all the human factors mentioned in this chapter. For instance, research communities are made up of different types of people with distinct technical and cultural backgrounds. In this context, an intersectional perspective which focuses on the interplay and complexity between different social identities of underrepresented minorities groups can provide a useful starting point to address some of the challenges that arise in SE research community as a result of these differences. Along this 5-years journey, the author of this chapter scrutinized four facets –identity, values, motivations, and skills– of herself to identify the strengths that could allow her to overcome drawbacks. In this way, she developed a growth mindset to learn from her experiences and act on what she has learned. From her perspective, continuous learning and continuous improvement mindset are fundamentals; however she is also guided by her cultural heritage so that she follows an approach that represents her identity and her ancestors. Two examples are the Samay framework references to a Quechua word and her ways of work that her colleagues from more individualist societies acknowledge and appreciate as one of the features of a more collectivist society.

Finally, research as software are rarely produced by only one individual therefore to connect the dots, a set of studies was conducted by the author and some colleagues. In this sense, one cannot connect the dots looking forward one can only connect them looking backwards. So, novel researchers have to trust that the dots will somehow connect in their future. This approach has never let her down, and it has made all the difference in her personal and professional life.

ACKNOWLEDGMENT

The author would like to thank all the participants and coauthors of the selected papers in this chapter who shared this journey. The author would also like to thanks to Harald Holone and Monica Kristiansen, Dean and Head of studies from Østfold University College for their support. Special thanks to Ricardo Colomo-Palacios for his tirelessness time and effort to share his knowledge and professional experiences during this entire research period.

REFERENCES

Abrahao, S., Baldassarre, M. T., da Silva, F. Q. B., & Romano, S. (2020). Call for papers—HuFo 2019. *PROFES Workshops*.

Beecham, S., Baddoo, N., Hall, T., Robinson, H., & Sharp, H. (2008). Motivation in Software Engineering: A systematic literature review. *Information and Software Technology, 50*(9–10), 860–878. doi:10.1016/j.infsof.2007.09.004

Capretz, L. F. (2014). Bringing the Human Factor to Software Engineering. *IEEE Software, 31*(2), 104–104. doi:10.1109/MS.2014.30

Collins, P. H., & Bilge, S. (2016). *Intersectionality*. John Wiley & Sons.

Cruz, S., da Silva, F. Q. B., & Capretz, L. F. (2015). Forty years of research on personality in software engineering: A mapping study. *Computers in Human Behavior, 46*, 94–113. doi:10.1016/j.chb.2014.12.008

Dittrich, Y., Fagerholm, F., Baldassare, M. T., & Wiese, I. (2020). Call for papers—CHASE 2020. *IEEE ICSE Workshops*.

Ebert, C., Gallardo, G., Hernantes, J., & Serrano, N. (2016). DevOps. *IEEE Software, 33*(3), 94–100. doi:10.1109/MS.2016.68

Ekman, P. (2016). What Scientists Who Study Emotion Agree About. *Perspectives on Psychological Science, 11*(1), 31–34. doi:10.1177/1745691615596992 PMID:26817724

Erdogmus, H., Medvidović, N., & Paulisch, F. (2018). 50 Years of Software Engineering. *IEEE Software, 35*(5), 20–24. doi:10.1109/MS.2018.3571240

Fazli, F., & Bittner, E. (2017). Cultural Influences on Collaborative Work in Software Engineering Teams. *50th Hawaii International Conference on System Sciences, HICSS 2017*, 454–463. http://hdl.handle.net/10125/41205

Florea, R., & Stray, V. (2019a). The skills that employers look for in software testers. *Software Quality Journal*, 1–31. doi:10.100711219-019-09462-5

Florea, R., & Stray, V. (2019b). A Global View on the Hard Skills and Testing Tools in Software Testing. *Proceedings of ICGSE, 2019*, 143–151. doi:10.1109/ICGSE.2019.00035

França, C., da Silva, F. Q. B., & Sharp, H. (2020). Motivation and Satisfaction of Software Engineers. *IEEE Transactions on Software Engineering*, *46*(2), 118–140. doi:10.1109/TSE.2018.2842201

Freire, G., Schwartz Orellana, S. D., Zumaeta Aurazo, M., Costa, D. C., Lundvall, J. M., Viveros Mendoza, M. C., Lucchetti, L. R., Moreno Herrera, L. L., & Sousa, L. D. C. (2015). *Indigenous Latin America in the twenty-first century: The first decade* (No. 98544). The World Bank. http://documents.worldbank.org/curated/en/145891467991974540/Indigenous-Latin-America-in-the-twenty-first-century-the-first-decade

Fuggetta, A., & Di Nitto, E. (2014). Software Process. *Proceedings of the on Future of Software Engineering*, 1–12. 10.1145/2593882.2593883

Gannon, J. D. (1979). Human Factors in Software Engineering. *Computer*, *12*(12), 6–7. doi:10.1109/MC.1979.1658569

Garousi, V., Giray, G., Tuzun, E., Catal, C., & Felderer, M. (2019). Closing the Gap Between Software Engineering Education and Industrial Needs. *IEEE Software*, 1–1. doi:10.1109/MS.2019.2914663

Gray, D. (2016). *Liminal Thinking: Create the Change You Want by Changing the Way You Think*. Two Waves Books.

Graziotin, D., Wang, X., & Abrahamsson, P. (2015). The Affect of Software Developers: Common Misconceptions and Measurements. *2015 IEEE/ACM 8th International Workshop on Cooperative and Human Aspects of Software Engineering*, 123–124. 10.1109/CHASE.2015.23

Gren, L. (2018). On gender, ethnicity, and culture in empirical software engineering research. *Proceedings of the 11th International Workshop on Cooperative and Human Aspects of Software Engineering - CHASE '18*, 77–78. 10.1145/3195836.3195837

Hall, E. T. (1976). *Beyond culture*. Anchor Press.

Hazzan, O., & Dubinsky, Y. (2006). Can Diversity in Global Software Development Be Enhanced by Agile Software Development? *International Workshop on Global Software Development for the Practitioner*, 58–61. 10.1145/1138506.1138520

Joshi, K. D., Kvasny, L., Unnikrishnan, P., & Trauth, E. (2016). How Do Black Men Succeed in IT Careers? The Effects of Capital. *49th Hawaii International Conference on System Sciences*, 4729–4738. 10.1109/HICSS.2016.586

Kharkongor, G. C., & Albert, S. (2014). Career Counseling among Indigenous Peoples. In G. Arulmani, A. J. Bakshi, F. T. L. Leong, & A. G. Watts (Eds.), *Handbook of Career Development: International Perspectives* (pp. 539–554). Springer New York. doi:10.1007/978-1-4614-9460-7_30

Korsaa, M., Johansen, J., Schweigert, T., Vohwinkel, D., Messnarz, R., Nevalainen, R., & Biro, M. (2013). The people aspects in modern process improvement management approaches. *Journal of Software: Evolution and Process*, *25*(4), 381–391. doi:10.1002mr.570

Kvasny, L., Joshi, K. D., & Trauth, E. (2015, March 15). *Understanding Black Males' IT Career Choices*. iConference 2015, Newport Beach, CA. https://www.ideals.illinois.edu/handle/2142/73428

Lambert, J. R., & Akinlade, E. Y. (2019). Immigrant stereotypes and differential screening. *Personnel Review*, *49*(4), 921–938. doi:10.1108/PR-06-2018-0229

Lenberg, P., Feldt, R., & Wallgren, L. G. (2015). Behavioral software engineering: A definition and systematic literature review. *Journal of Systems and Software*, *107*, 15–37. doi:10.1016/j.jss.2015.04.084

Lwakatare, L. E., Kuvaja, P., & Oivo, M. (2016). Relationship of DevOps to Agile, Lean and Continuous Deployment. *International Conference on Product-Focused Software Process Improvement*, 399–415. 10.1007/978-3-319-49094-6_27

Machuca-Villegas, L., Gasca-Hurtado, G. P., Restrepo Tamayo, L. M., & Morillo Puente, S. (2020). Social and Human Factor Classification of Influence in Productivity in Software Development Teams. In M. Yilmaz, J. Niemann, P. Clarke, & R. Messnarz (Eds.), *Systems, Software and Services Process Improvement* (pp. 717–729). Springer International Publishing., doi:10.1007/978-3-030-56441-4_54

Marinho, M., Luna, A., & Beecham, S. (2018). Global Software Development: Practices for Cultural Differences. In M. Kuhrmann, K. Schneider, D. Pfahl, S. Amasaki, M. Ciolkowski, R. Hebig, P. Tell, J. Klünder, & S. Küpper (Eds.), *Product-Focused Software Process Improvement* (pp. 299–317). Springer International Publishing. doi:10.1007/978-3-030-03673-7_22

Marks, G., O'Connor, R. V., & Clarke, P. M. (2017). The Impact of Situational Context on the Software Development Process – A Case Study of a Highly Innovative Start-up Organization. In A. Mas, A. Mesquida, R. V. O'Connor, T. Rout, & A. Dorling (Eds.), *Software Process Improvement and Capability Determination* (pp. 455–466). Springer International Publishing. doi:10.1007/978-3-319-67383-7_33

Matturro, G., Raschetti, F., & Fontán, C. (2019). A Systematic Mapping Study on Soft Skills in Software Engineering. *Journal of Universal Computer Science*, *25*(1), 16–41.

Menezes, Á., & Prikladnicki, R. (2018). Diversity in Software Engineering. *Proceedings of the 11th International Workshop on Cooperative and Human Aspects of Software Engineering*, 45–48. 10.1145/3195836.3195857

Myrbakken, H., & Colomo-Palacios, R. (2017). DevSecOps: A Multivocal Literature Review. *International Conference on Software Process Improvement and Capability Determination*, 17–29. 10.1007/978-3-319-67383-7_2

Noe, R. A., Clarke, A. D. M., & Klein, H. J. (2014). Learning in the Twenty-First-Century Workplace. *Annual Review of Organizational Psychology and Organizational Behavior*, *1*(1), 245–275. doi:10.1146/annurev-orgpsych-031413-091321

OECD. (2017). *Promising Practices in Supporting Success for Indigenous Students*. OECD Publishing. https://read.oecd-ilibrary.org/education/promising-practices-in-supporting-success-for-indigenous-students_9789264279421-en

Osuna, E., Rodríguez, L.-F., Gutierrez-Garcia, J. O., & Castro, L. A. (2020). Development of computational models of emotions: A software engineering perspective. *Cognitive Systems Research*, *60*, 1–19. doi:10.1016/j.cogsys.2019.11.001

Pavlovich, K., & Krahnke, K. (2012). Empathy, Connectedness and Organisation. *Journal of Business Ethics, 105*(1), 131–137. doi:10.100710551-011-0961-3

Perry, D. E., Staudenmayer, N. A., & Votta, L. G. (1994). People, organizations, and process improvement. *IEEE Software, 11*(4), 36–45. doi:10.1109/52.300082

Pirzadeh, L. (2010). *Human Factors in Software Development: A Systematic Literature Review*. Chalmers University of Technology. https://odr.chalmers.se/handle/20.500.12380/126748

Pressman, R. (2009). *Software Engineering: A Practitioner's Approach* (7th ed.). McGraw-Hill Science.

Sampaio, A., Sampaio, I. B., & Gray, E. (2013). The need of a person oriented approach to software process assessment. *2013 6th International Workshop on Cooperative and Human Aspects of Software Engineering (CHASE)*, 145–148. 10.1109/CHASE.2013.6614752

Sánchez-Gordón, M., & Colomo-Palacios, R. (2018). Characterizing DevOps Culture: A Systematic Literature Review. In I. Stamelos, R. V. O'Connor, T. Rout, & A. Dorling (Eds.), *Software Process Improvement and Capability Determination* (pp. 3–15). Springer International Publishing. doi:10.1007/978-3-030-00623-5_1

Sánchez-Gordón, M., & Colomo-Palacios, R. (2019a). Taking the emotional pulse of software engineering—A systematic literature review of empirical studies. *Information and Software Technology, 115*, 23–43. doi:10.1016/j.infsof.2019.08.002

Sánchez-Gordón, M., & Colomo-Palacios, R. (2019b). Developing SPI Culture in the SME Arena: An Exploratory Study. In A. Walker, R. V. O'Connor, & R. Messnarz (Eds.), *Systems, Software and Services Process Improvement* (pp. 222–234). Springer International Publishing. doi:10.1007/978-3-030-28005-5_17

Sánchez-Gordón, M., & Colomo-Palacios, R. (2020a). Factors influencing Software Engineering Career Choice of Andean Indigenous. *Proceedings of the ACM/IEEE 42nd International Conference on Software Engineering: Companion Proceedings*, 264–265. 10.1145/3377812.3390899

Sánchez-Gordón, M., & Colomo-Palacios, R. (2020b). Security as Culture: A Systematic Literature Review of DevSecOps. *Proceedings of the IEEE/ACM 42nd International Conference on Software Engineering Workshops*, 266–269. 10.1145/3387940.3392233

Sánchez-Gordón, M., Rijal, L., & Colomo-Palacios, R. (2020). Beyond Technical Skills in Software Testing: Automated versus Manual Testing. *Proceedings of the IEEE/ACM 42nd International Conference on Software Engineering Workshops*, 161–164. 10.1145/3387940.3392238

Sánchez-Gordón, M.-L. (2017). Getting the Best out of People in Small Software Companies: ISO/IEC 29110 and ISO 10018 Standards. *International Journal of Information Technologies and Systems Approach, 10*(1), 45–60. doi:10.4018/IJITSA.2017010103

Sánchez-Gordón, M.-L., Colomo-Palacios, R., & Herranz, E. (2016). Gamification and Human Factors in Quality Management Systems: Mapping from Octalysis Framework to ISO 10018. *EuroSPI, 2016*, 234–241. doi:10.1007/978-3-319-44817-6_19

Sánchez-Gordón, M.-L., de Amescua, A., O'Connor, R. V., & Larrucea, X. (2017). A standard-based framework to integrate software work in small settings. *Computer Standards & Interfaces, 54*(3), 162–175. doi:10.1016/j.csi.2016.11.009

Sánchez-Gordón, M.-L., & O'Connor, R. V. (2016). Understanding the Gap Between Software Process Practices and Actual Practice in Very Small Companies. *Software Quality Journal, 24*(3), 549–570. doi:10.100711219-015-9282-6

Sánchez-Gordón, M.-L., O'Connor, R. V., Colomo-Palacios, R., & Herranz, E. (2016). Bridging the Gap Between SPI and SMEs in Educational Settings: A Learning Tool Supporting ISO/IEC 29110. *Proceedings of the IEEE/ACM 42nd International Conference on Software Engineering Workshops*, 3–14. 10.1007/978-3-319-44817-6_1

Sánchez-Gordón, M.-L., O'Connor, R. V., Colomo-Palacios, R., & Sánchez-Gordón, S. (2016). A Learning Tool for the ISO/IEC 29110 Standard: Understanding the Project Management of Basic Profile. *Proceedings 16th International Conference on Software Process Improvement and Capability DEtermination (SPICE 2016), 609*, 270–283. 10.1007/978-3-319-38980-6_20

Silveira, K. K., & Prikladnicki, R. (2019). A Systematic Mapping Study of Diversity in Software Engineering: A Perspective from the Agile Methodologies. *Proceedings of the 12th International Workshop on Cooperative and Human Aspects of Software Engineering*, 7–10. 10.1109/CHASE.2019.00010

Sommerville, I. (2010). *Software Engineering* (9th ed.). Addison-Wesley.

Trauth, E. M., Cain, C. C., Joshi, K. D., Kvasny, L., & Booth, K. (2012). Embracing Intersectionality in Gender and IT Career Choice Research. *Proceedings of the 50th Annual Conference on Computers and People Research*, 199–212. 10.1145/2214091.2214141

UNCTAD. (2012). *Information economy report 2012: The software industry and developing countries.* United Nations Publications.

van Veenendaal, E. (2020). Next-Generation Software Testers: Broaden or Specialize! In S. Goericke (Ed.), *The Future of Software Quality Assurance* (pp. 229–243). Springer International Publishing., doi:10.1007/978-3-030-29509-7_18

Weinberg, G. M. (1971). *The psychology of computer programming* (Vol. 932633420). Van Nostrand Reinhold.

Zhao, J., Qi, Z., & de Pablos, P. O. (2014). Enhancing enterprise training performance: Perspectives from knowledge transfer and integration. *Computers in Human Behavior, 30*, 567–573. doi:10.1016/j.chb.2013.06.041

KEY TERMS AND DEFINITIONS

Behavioral Software Engineering: Is the study of cognitive, behavioral and social aspect software engineering performed by individuals, groups or organizations.

ISO 10018: Is a standard entitled "Quality management – Guidance for people engagement". It provides guidance on engaging people in an organization's quality management system, and on enhancing their involvement and competence within it. ISO 10018 is applicable to any organization, regardless of size, type, or activity.

ISO/IEC 29110: Is a series of international standards and guides entitled "Systems and Software Engineering – Lifecycle Profiles for Very Small Entities (VSEs)". A Very Small Entity (VSE) is an enterprise, an organization, a department, or a project having up to 25 people.

ISO/IEC 33014: Is a standard entitled "Information technology — Process assessment — Guide for process improvement". It provides informative guidance on using process assessment as part of a complete framework and method for performing process improvement as part of a continual improvement activity.

LGBTQI: Pertaining collectively to people who identify as lesbian, gay, bisexual, transgender, queer (or those questioning their gender identity or sexual orientation), and intersex.

OMG Essence: Is a standard entitled "Kernel and Language for Software Engineering Methods". The kernel provides the common ground for defining software development practices. It includes the essential elements that are always prevalent in every software engineering endeavor, such as Requirements, Software System, Team, and Work. These elements have states representing progress and health, so as the endeavor moves forward the states associated with these elements progress.

Chapter 13
How Do We Interact in Collaborative Virtual Reality?
A Nonverbal Interaction Perspective

Adriana Peña Pérez Negrón
 https://orcid.org/0000-0001-6823-2367
CUCEI, Universidad de Guadalajara, Mexico

ABSTRACT

Nonverbal interaction includes most of what we do; the interaction resulted from other means than words or their meaning. In computer-mediated interaction, the richness of face-to-face interaction has not been completely achieved. However, multiuser virtual reality, a computer-generated environment that allows users to share virtual spaces and virtual objects through their graphic representation, is a highly visual technology in which nonverbal interaction is better supported when compared with other media. Still, like in any technology media, interaction is accomplished distinctively due to technical and design issues. In collaborative virtual reality, the analysis of nonverbal interaction represents a helpful mechanism to support feedback in teaching or training scenarios, to understand collaborative behavior, or to improve this technology. This chapter discussed the characteristics of nonverbal interaction in virtual reality, presenting advances in the automatic interpretation of the users' nonverbal interaction while a spatial task is collaboratively executed.

INTRODUCTION

Virtual reality (VR) is a three-dimensional (3D) computer-generated scenario with which the user can interact, navigating through it, or modifying objects. Furthermore, in a multiuser situation, the user will interact not only with the virtual environment but also with others through different channels, verbal and no verbal actions. While verbal communication is easily achieved, nonverbal interaction in VR is constrained due to design and technological issues. It is then important to understand how users accomplish interaction through a graphical representation to improve the users' experience in general, and for the design of particular situations. In this context, the automatic analysis of nonverbal interaction in VR

DOI: 10.4018/978-1-7998-7552-9.ch013

Copyright © 2021, IGI Global. Copying or distributing in print or electronic forms without written permission of IGI Global is prohibited.

represents a not trivial task to enhance such interactions' comprehension, providing stakeholders with immediate feedback.

VR primary purpose is to produce a feeling of presence by generating the users' perceptual transfer into the virtual environment (VE). Although immersion, as a state of mind, depends on the users' willingness, the interaction design plays a significant role in the immersion sensation. In turn, the interaction design is hardly based on the computer input/output devices.

From a technical point of view, desktop-based VR is considered the less immersive because the user can interact simultaneously with the real world. At the other edge is Immersive Virtual Reality (IVR), which surrounds the user with the VE, so that the user can interact only with the virtual scenario. The two leading technologies to achieve IVR are the CAVE™, see Figure 1, a 10'X10'X10' theater made up of three rear-projection screens for walls, and a down projection screen for the floor (Cruz-Neira, Sandin, & Defanti, 1993). And the head-mounted display (HMD), a device that displays the scenario for each eye with a different perspective, see Figure 2. Between desktop VR and IVR is semi-immersive VR, a variety of technologies that can consist of big screens, semicircular displays, or tactile gadgets such as virtual gloves as input devices.

The user interaction with the VE is part of the Human-Computer Interaction (HCI) field of study. And it is composed of four basic actions (Mine, 1995):

1. *Navigation*, the displacement in the virtual space.
2. *Selection*, the action of pointing or grabbing an object.
3. *Manipulation*, the modification of the state of an object (e.g., moving or rotating it).
4. *System control*, the set of application features usually through menus.

HCI in VR can follow similar to real-life approaches, such as grabbing an object by a hand-arm movement. However, it mostly follows a metaphor, a representative action to perform the interaction with the VE. In turn, a metaphor can follow a similar to real-life approach; however, this is not always possible or advisable. For example, following the grabbing an object instance, in VR, objects are usually grabbed or selected through the mouse or a game controller, different from extending the arm to touch them. However, people only can grab real objects at their reach, which is not an impediment in virtual situations where the user can select objects that appear at a long distance. Some metaphors to grab remote objects are a ray or a gun target pointer to indicate the object to be grabbed, and a click most likely will trigger the selection action. Afterward, the object has to present some indicative change for the user to be aware of the object selection. A metaphor for the user interaction is then the users' actions and the design mechanism that supports the users' awareness.

A key feature for VR users is that they require a proxy to interact with the virtual world and the actors on it, which is also its representation in the environment; their avatar.

Avatar

An avatar can be as simple as a pointer to indicate the user's position in the virtual scenario, or it can have, for example, a humanoid representation. Nowadays, it is possible to create avatars highly similar to the user, for example, through 3D scan reconstruction. Economou et al. (2017) achieved very realistic avatars by what they call "replicants", a dynamic full-body 3D reconstruction of the user in real-time of both geometry and texture.

Figure 1. Cave Automatic Virtual Environment (CAVE) (Cruz-Neira, Sandin, & Defanti, 1993)

A user can manipulate the avatar in three different forms (Capin et al., 1998):

1. *Directly controlled* through body trackers. A process also known as poppet avatars, where the user's natural motion and live performance are mapped to realistically reproducing them in the VE (Apostolakis & Daras, 2015).
2. *User-guided*, defining tasks and movements through a computer input device.
3. *Semi-autonomous*, here the avatar has an internal state that depends on its goals, and the user modifies this state, typically via animations.

There is also similar to real-life interaction for the avatar directly controlled, or through metaphors in the user-guided and semi-autonomous approaches.

Figure 2. Head-mounted display (HMD)

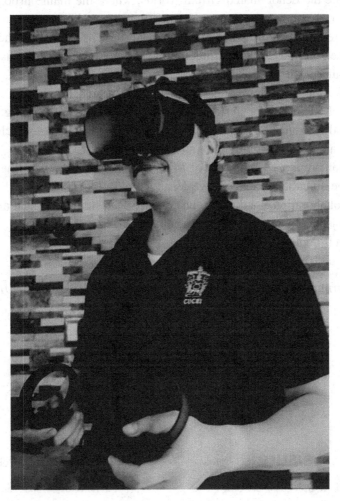

The avatar features play a fundamental role to interact with others (Kolesnichenko, McVeigh-Schultz, & Isbister, 2019). The impact of the selected metaphors and the input/output devices will derive in the users' immersion and presence sensations. In a multiuser situation, this has implications for the actors in the environment.

Collaborative Virtual Environments (CVE)

According to Schroeder (2011), multiuser virtual environments (MUVE) fall into two main categories: leisure uses for gaming and socializing, and instrumental uses for research and prototype systems.

The most significant number of MUVE is in the leisure category, mainly in massive multiplayer online role-playing games (MMORPG) or massive multiplayer online (MMO), in which, as its name indicates, a large number (thousands) of people can play simultaneously. In MMO, the players have great control over their appearance and the word they inhabit. One of the most popular MMORPG is World of Warcraft™ released in 2004 by Blizzard Entertainment that has kept its popularity by eight major extended packs.

For socialization are the denominated virtual worlds, where the main purpose is to spend time in open activities, contrary to games that have a defined purpose and a manufactured conflict. Same as MMO, the user has great control over the appearance and the virtual world. The most popular one is Second Life™, launched on June 2003, by Linden Lab. Although its popularity has suffered a decrease, it is still the most popular virtual world.

In the instrumental category, systems are usually aimed for a small number of users and short periods. An essential number of VR prototype systems have been developed for training in the industry (Peña & Jiménez, 2012), and in education (Peña, 2010). Other instrumental uses include travel, real state, electronic commerce, and health, although not always in a multiuser modality.

VE for collaboration are a particular case of MUVE treated differently in the research community (Schroeder, 2011); the so-called Collaborative Virtual Environments (CVE) developed for research purposes. In which, collaboration at a distance has mainly been studied for spatial tasks, (Peña, Lara & Estrada, 2020), and object-centered tasks to study human behavior (Peña, Rangel, & Maciel, 2015). The MUVE categorization is depicted in Figure 3.

Figure 3. Multiuser virtual environments (MUVE) categorization (Schroeder, 2011)

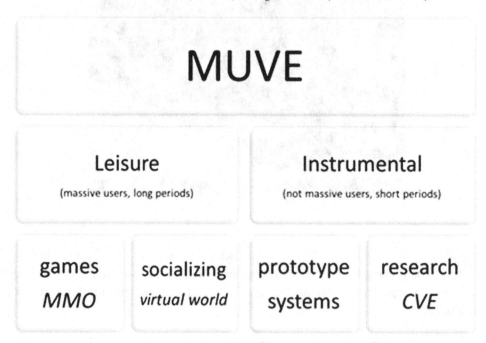

Different technology tools to collaborate at a distance are available, such as collaborative documents and videoconferences; however, CVE is the only technology that allows sharing a common space and objects at a distance; this has a significant implication on the task to be performed.

Spatial Tasks in CVE

Despite its advantages, for a task that requires interpersonal skills such as negotiation, argumentation, or to reach an agreement, CVE might not be the best option. This disadvantage is mainly because of the avatars' lack of facial expressions. Even though there are advances in providing avatars with this feature, those approaches are mostly based on animations that require the users' intervention provoking nonspontaneous responses, or through face tracking not easily available. Besides, eye-contact, a powerful resource to get feedback in face-to-face negotiation, has not been adequately achieved in CVE, although not required without facial expressions. Recently, Mixed Reality (MX) has been proposed as an alternative for this drawback; by placing video cameras, the face of the user, some gestures, and postures can be superimposed in the user's avatar in the CVE (Teo et al. 2019).

However, it should be noted that in the context of collaboration, while for interpersonal interaction, eye-gaze and facial expressions are critical, instrumental interaction further relies on body movements and gestures (Schroeder, 2011). The human body continually provides information regarding presence, identity, attention, activity status, availability, and mood; it establishes a social distance to regulate interaction; and it supports speech with nonverbal communication (Economou, et al. 2017).

In this context, the comprehension of the nonverbal interaction in CVE should support better-designed applications. Likewise, in the case of applications, for example, on education or training, the understanding of collaborative interaction in spatial tasks among users should be helpful to give feedback of the session. Therefore, the automatic analysis of nonverbal interaction in CVE represents a helpful tool to give insights of the users' nonverbal interaction. This chapter presents a research line for the automation of retrieval and interpretation of the nonverbal interaction in CVE, in which the users are performing a task that requires the use of the space and the manipulation of objects.

BACKGROUND

The actors displaying nonverbal interaction that can inhabit the CVE are the users and intelligent virtual agents (IVA). IVA are embodied interactive characters that exhibit human-like qualities to interact with humans or other IVA. They communicate using human modalities to simulate real-time perception, cognition, and actions (Ayllet et al., 2013). The study of IVA nonverbal interaction has been mainly conducted to generate believable, natural behavior. In this area, research has focused in different topics such as the human interactant perception, dynamics of attitudes adjusting the attitude according to the interactant or the situation, or the IVA behavior to match its nonverbal display to certain circumstances (Dermouche & Pelachaud, 2020; Economou et al., 2017; Guerrero-Vásquez et al. 2018).

Nonverbal behavior automatically tracked from people in real-world conditions has been analyzed to determine, for example, participation and learning attitude in Collaborative Learning (Hayashi et al. 2014), or to understand cultural background and the topic of conversation (Shahrour & Russell, 2015).

As the avatar has a great impact on the users' perception and their display of nonverbal behavior in CVE, this is a topic of interest in the research community. Economou, et al. (2017), conducted a study to evaluate their platform for human representation in CVE based on the users' experience. They found that an aesthetical pleasing and realistic representation aids realism in the activity, effectively identifying user roles and personalities, and properly supporting turn-taking in communication. They concluded that their platform in the future should include improving 3D reconstruction techniques, AI for the analysis of the users' behavior and engagement, recording of the user actions, and supporting private communication.

Herrera, Oh, & Bailenson (2020) compared how the nonverbal behavioral realism of the users' avatar in a CVE impact the self-presence (the psychological state of associating the virtual presence with the actual self), the social presence (the sense of being in the virtual with someone else), and interpersonal attraction (rapport) in dyadic interaction. For the study, they used three conditions in IVR: static hands in a full-body avatar; head and hands tracked from the user with arms movement automatically inferred, and; floating head and hands directly controlled by the user. Results showed greater self and social presence, and interpersonal attraction, when using the third condition, which represents the most natural movements although from a not full-body avatar.

The purpose of the interaction should have a great impact on the design of the avatar, for virtual worlds, Kolesnichenko, McVeigh-Schultz, & Isbister (2019) conducted a study by interviewing designers about the practices for the users' avatar available interaction mechanisms. Main results reported that teleportation is the most used form of navigation in social VR or virtual worlds, and that using small distances is the practice that better suits social interactions. Regarding appearance, avatars tend to have a simplistic format to scaled-down the polygons for better performance over the Internet. A protective bubble around the avatar seems to be a common practice to avoid others from invading the "personal space". Furthermore, they use social mechanics like the handshake, and the avatars usually have a system to express emotions through emoji images. These practices have somehow proved to be effective for nonverbal interaction in VR for socializing.

The recent interest in Affective Computing (AC) has encouraged the study of nonverbal interaction to understand the users' affective state. Oh et al. (2016), based on the premise that smiling affects positively interpersonal outcomes, conducted a study to understand if by tracking the users' smile and enhancing it in their avatars, they perceived a more positive communication experience. By a linguistic analysis, they found that the participants used more positive words to describe their interaction experience in the VE under the enhanced smile condition.

As VR does not have to follow the real-life rules; another enhancing practice for nonverbal behavior was presented by Mayer et al. (2020). They observed that deictic gestures that guide others' attention to a certain area present a systematic misinterpretation in both real-life and VR. Deictic gestures are mainly performed by extending the arm and the index finger; the authors assumed that errors were caused by both the pointer and the observer's interpretation. They adjusted the pointer gesture, making a correction through a model that rotate the arm; this modification was made visible in the VE only for the observer. Results showed a 22.99% improvement in the observer's accuracy to specify where the pointer was previously indicating.

Regarding performing a task, Sun, Shaikh, & Won (2019) presented a study with tracked movements from users during a collaborative and a competitive task in IVR. The collaborative task consisted on instructing the participants to generate ideas with their conversational partner, and in the competitive task they were instructed to generate more ideas for themselves. They compared humanoid avatars with cuboid avatars. Results showed natural synchrony between pairs with both types of avatars; interaction synchrony represents people's rapport, collaboration, and positive social interaction.

Specifically, in spatial tasks to understand the impact of the avatar during interaction, Smith & Neff (2018) highlighted the role of being embodied in VR with faithful users' movements rendered into their avatars in a study conducted to investigate communication behavior in dyads. They compared face-to-face with full-body avatars and not embodied conditions. Users' experiences along with annotations of verbal and nonverbal behavior were collected. Thirty dyads completed two tasks, negotiating an apartment layout and placing furniture. They found that the full-body avatar provided a high level of social presence similar to face-to-face interaction, while the users perceived the not embodied condition as "feeling lonely" presenting a degraded communication.

Gamelin, et al. (2020) conducted a study for the effects in dyads carrying on a spatial task, comparing avatars based on 2.5D streamed point-cloud and 3D pre-constructed avatars that replicated the users' movements. Two spatial tasks were applied, one consisted of verbally guiding a participant to select two cubes from a set of ten, and the second one to select a 3-row pattern among eight rows of a virtual grid. The performance was evaluated by the time to complete the tasks and the number of errors. They concluded that for spatial collaboration while the kinematic fidelity is advisable, a moderate visual fidelity is sufficing.

Collaborative tasks require to be aware of the presence and participation of the others. Specially for spatial tasks, nonverbal interaction provides a great number of informational cues. Despite several studies related to nonverbal interaction in CVE, there are not enough insights about the nonverbal interaction that users display through their avatars, a human-human nonverbal interaction mediated by the CVE. Also, most of the studies are intended to understand the users' experience or performance. This chapter deals with the automatic analysis of this type of nonverbal interaction.

NONVERBAL INTERACTION IN CVE

When we interact with others, the communication channels convey more than the meaning of the words. The tone of voice, eye contact, and body movements or actions enrich communication giving support to mutual comprehension, fundamental for collaborative work; nonverbal interaction transmits communicative intentions, feelings, and even attitudes (Bolinger, 1985).

Nonverbal interaction is roughly understood as the interaction that takes place by other means than words, assuming words as the verbal element. A useful definition, but as indicated by Knapp & Hall (2007), this does not account the complex phenomenon, where "other than words" refers to the type of signal produced (its encoding) and the perceived code to interpret the symbol (its decoding), which paradoxically can include words. Another important aspect of nonverbal behavior is the different degrees of awareness and control we put on it (coding), or the awareness degree when decoding it by the perceived stimulus, denoting several variations.

Patterson (1982) proposed a functional classification for the analysis of nonverbal exchange, see Figure 4. According to him, each nonverbal behavior can be either to inform something or to regulate interaction. But they also can function to express intimacy, exercise social control, or facilitate service or task goals, in which case, patterns of behavior over time can be observed. Intimacy reflex the degree of union or openness among two persons. In general, such intimacy is manifested through high levels of spontaneous nonverbal involvement. The social-control involves influence to change others' behavior, trying to persuade them. Compared with expressing intimacy, the social-control will continue or intensify to achieve persuasion, and nonverbal involvement will be less spontaneous and more self-conscious and managed. And service-task category will reflect only a task relationship with an impersonal nonverbal involvement.

Figure 4. Nonverbal interaction functional classification by Patterson (1982)

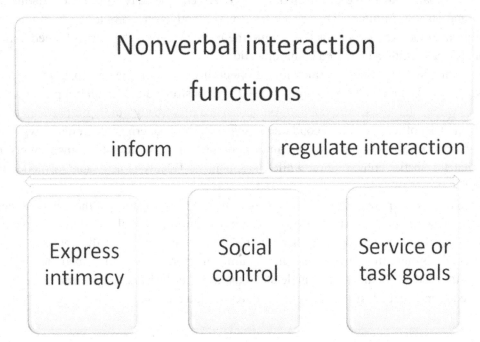

The involvement in service or task goal interaction is barely variable, with impersonal nonverbal behavior, not engaged with personality or emotions (Patterson, 1982); this is the type of nonverbal interaction patters expected in a spatial task accomplishment. As mentioned, a spatial task is the most likely type to be carried on in CVE, and this is a task in which people will center their attention on the space and the objects, where co-presence is desirable (Spante et al., 2003; Schroeder, 2011). Under these considerations, the coding and decoding of the nonverbal exchange will be narrowed, facilitating somehow its automatic analysis; however, this is not a straightforward and complex task that remains under development.

In CVE can be assumed, to a certain point, that the more similar HCI to real-life it will be an increase in the spontaneity of the users' display of nonverbal behavior (Peña, Rangel & Lara, 2015; Herrera, Oh, & Bailenson, 2020), which will change over time as the users get more familiar with the application. And this can be applied also for the interaction metaphors and the avatar features. In virtual scenarios, our means to interact is our avatar that in a multiuser situation will support collaboration and the co-presence feeling.

Knapp & Hall (2007) classified the areas of study of nonverbal behavior as the environmental structures and conditions within which nonverbal interaction takes place, the physical characteristics of the interacting people, and their behaviors, all of which represent specifications in CVE (Peña, Rangel & Lara, 2015).

The Interaction Environment

Our immediate surrounding area affects our mood and actions; its elements affect people's interactions even when they might not be part of them. In this category are the studies related to the physical environment such as furniture, lighting, temperature, or noises, and it includes *Proxemics*, the study of the use and perception of our personal space (Hall, 1968).

The physical environment in CVE is represented by the virtual scenario and the objects on it. But unlike in real-life, most of the objects on it will have a purpose, and that purpose should be hardly related to the task at hand. These conditions will cause the users to focus on a few things with constant engagement because there is an ongoing reason to be in the virtual scenario (Spante et al., 2003). In such conditions, the objects are a significant aspect of the analysis of nonverbal interaction. And regarding Proxemics, it has been found that people tend to keep personal distance through their avatars, similar to what they do in the real world (Han, 2019).

Physical Characteristics

A person's physical characteristics also impact how others perceive a person; this, in turn, will impact how they treat and interact with that person. These studies' scope also includes artifacts, such as clothes, hairstyles, and skin decoration, like cosmetics or tattoos. In CVE the avatar should be designed mainly to maintain a consistent identity (Schroeder, 2011), to support the others' identification, awareness of co-presence, and location, all significant aspects for spatial tasks.

The most common practice in CVE is the use of humanoid avatars to facilitate collaboration. An avatar that looks human is expected to exhibit somehow human-like behavior. However, there is scarce evidence of the effects of different levels of behavioral realism on the nonverbal behavior in CVE interactions (Herrera, Youn & Bailenson, 2020).

Along with appearance, the avatar's physical characteristics that will impact the interaction with others are its doable movements, the animations linked to it, and how the user controls it. All of which will derive in a lesser or greater spontaneity for nonverbal behavior (Peña, Rangel & Lara, 2015).

Body Movements and Positions

Body movements include gestures, gazes, facial expressions, and postures. Postures are typically studied in conjunction with other nonverbal signals to establish the degree of attention or involvement, and rapport when, for example, an interactor mimics the others postures.

Facial expressions are body movements mostly related to emotional states and regulatory gestures, which provide feedback and manage interaction flow. The gaze is the eye movement to see someone; mutual gaze or eye contact is when the interactants look to each other, but eye behavior also indicates what, when, and how we look. And gestures, which main categorization is speech dependent when they have a well-known verbal translation, and speech-related when they accompany speech. Most body movements studied are limb movement, hands, and head movements (Knapp & Hall, 2007). In CVE this is closely related to the doable movements of the avatar and its animations for postures.

Based on this classification, a model for nonverbal interaction cues was presented in Peña, Muñoz, & Lara (2019). For the model is presented a taxonomy braked into Environmental factors discussed in the section 'The Interaction Environment'; *Kinesics*, the study of what is called the body language, all body movements except physical contact (Argyle, 1990); *Paralanguage*, the physical mechanisms to produce nonverbal vocal qualities and sound (Juslin et al., 2005); and Proxemics.

The selected cues for each category were made following their expression likelihood in CVE based on technical issues, the avatars' most common designs, but mainly on their possibility of been automatically retrieved. However, it is important to mention that this is not intended to be an exhaustive list. Next, the taxonomy shows the selected cues, with a brief rationalization for their selection in cursive.

TAXONOMY OF NONVERBAL CUES FOR AUTOMATIC ANALYSIS

- **Environmental factors**
  - Object cues. *Manipulatives as part of the interaction in spatial tasks*
- **Kinesics**
  - Body movements. *The most common ones*
    - § Facial expressions. *When they are available*
    - § Gestures. *The most commons ones*
- Hand movements. *To select and manipulate objects*
- Head movements. *To change the point of view*
  - Body positions. *Available mainly through animation*
    - § Crunch
    - § Sit
    - § Squat
    - § Standup
- **Paralanguage**. *The easiest to retrieve*
  - Vocalization pause. *To determine pause or vocalization*
    - § Speech rate. *A comparative measure among participants*
- **Proxemics**. *Easy to retrieve cues*
  - Position
  - Navigation
    - § Walk
    - § Run
    - § Fly

For the model (Peña, Muñoz & Lara, 2019), based on the users' logs are presented the states to identify when a nonverbal cue is taking place or when the conditions change in the environment. Different UML state diagrams are described to create the proper algorithm for the automatic retrieval of the nonverbal cues from the environment, which allows analysis while the task is being accomplished (see Peña, Muñoz, & Lara, 2019 for details). In this same model, the identification of the individual cues is then proposed as a means to understand group performance.

AUTOMATIC ANALYSIS OF NONVERBAL INTERACTION

The automatic analysis of nonverbal interaction has been proposed to understand the complex phenomenon of collaboration in CVE. Collaboration represents a joint effort of two or more persons to complete a task or achieve a common goal. By collaborating with others, people expect to get better outcomes or require less effort than individual labor. However, collaboration requires coordination, negotiation, and consensus to establish the synchronous activities required to achieve the joint goal.

This section presents three approaches for analysis that have been proposed to understand the accomplishment of a collaborative task, based on nonverbal cues automatically collected in CVE. The first approach is to distinguish task stages, the second one to distinguish collaboration from other structures of working together such as division of labor, and the third proposal to get insights regarding collaboration based on layers of complexity for nonverbal cues.

Distinguishing Task Stages

When taking care of a task in CVE, people will follow certain stages. *Salutation*, in this stage people will recognize others' appearances, while small-talk is expected. An *environment recognition* is then required when the users are there for the first time because, unlike in real-life, they will need to explore the environment and understand how to interact with it. Afterward, is expected a *plan-implement-review cycle* to take care of the task.

In Peña & de Antonio (2010a), a first exploratory study was conducted in a real-life situation to understand the extent to which nonverbal cues were useful for the analysis of nonverbal interaction in CVE. Seven groups of triads were formed, 11 males and ten females, each group had at least one male and one female. Voluntary participants were Computer Science students, graduated students, or teachers. In the groups were not mixed students and teachers to enhance the symmetry of action, knowledge, and status, proper for collaboration.

The study consisted of furniture arrangement in a department sketch. Two analyses were conducted: a summary analysis based on frequencies to get individual participation; and a structural analysis for group behavior (Gabner et al., 2003).

Results on the frequencies of individual participation showed, according to experts' opinions, that each person's degree of influence in the task achievement is correlated with the time they speak and the time they manipulate objects. That is, the participants with higher speaking time and manipulation were perceived as with higher participation in the accomplishment of the task. Other collected measures were: time or duration of floor maintenance (the timel they keep speaking regardless others interventions in the conversation), gazes to a peer, being the target of a peer's gaze, and the number or frequency of utterance, floor maintenance, interventions in the shared workspace, gazes directed to a peer, gazes received from a peer, mutual gazes, and the hand pointing gesture.

Results based on the group behavior showed that it was possible to distinguish the stages in the task accomplishment of Planning, Implementation, Implementation due to division of labor, Implementation due to evaluation, and Evaluation, based on the number of utterances, pointing gestures, gazes, and the number of object manipulations.

Following this study (Peña & de Antonio, 2010a), a proposal was made in Peña & de Antonio (2010b). In this paper, several selected nonverbal cues are described for its automatic retrieval: the amount of talk, object manipulation, gazes, deictic gestures, Proxemics, head movements, body postures, and facial expressions. Also, it was highlighted the importance of determining *discussion periods* formed on turns of talk. When people collaborate, during discussion periods, they share knowledge regarding the task to create a common ground, and they can get consensus about possible actions to achieve goals (Clark & Brennan, 1991).

Discussion periods can be inferred automatically under some considerations. A discussion period is a talking turns interchange of two or more people, but they have to be differentiated from a question-answer interchange or the statements people do alongside their actions, directed to no one in particular (Heath et al., 1994).

A talking turn begins when a person starts to speak, and it is kept as long as that person is not interrupted. In a computer system, the talking turn can be established by the user's vocalization, but we make pauses when we talk. For the automatic recognition of a pause, the end of the utterance is usually accounted if a pause in the range of 500 to 2000 ms occurs (Brdiczka, Maisonnasse, & Reignier, 2005), and the answer to a question goes in a smaller range of around 500 ms (Johnson & Leigh, 2001). Therefore, two seconds of silence can be functional to determine the talking-turn end. Summarizing, the discussion period can be established if an exchange of talking-turns takes place, with pauses no longer of two seconds (Peña, 2014).

A scheme to identify the stages and the primary cues to be observed is presented in Figure 5.

Figure 5. Distinguishing task stages during a collaborative task accomplishment (adapted from Peña & de Antonio, 2010b)

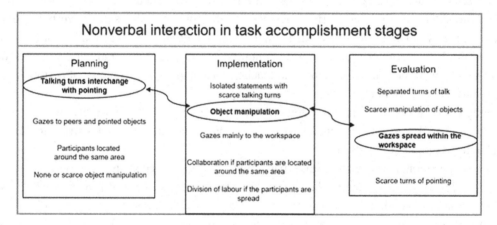

Establishing Collaboration

People working together does not necessarily mean that they are collaborating. Although collaboration might be the proper strategy to follow, for example, in Collaborative Learning or in certain training situations, this might not always be the case. Based on the nonverbal cues displayed by the users' avatars, another exploratory study was conducted to analyze different nonverbal interactive patterns to establish different working together situations.

In Peña & de Antonio, (2009), four different working situations were settled through indications for furniture arrangement: collaboration, division of labor, hierarchical situation, and brute force approaches. In collaboration is expected equal participation from the group members. Division of labor distinguishes collaboration from cooperation because group members split the work, solve sub-tasks individually, and then assemble those parts to an outcome (Dillenbourg, 1999). When people work together, some members might prefer to lead or be led, emerging a hierarchical situation where one or some members take control, giving orders to the others to achieve the goal. Likewise, if the group decides not to discuss or follow a plan, they will try to solve the task by just taking care of the implementation, not following any order, a brute force approach.

In two CAVE systems remotely connected, two participants at a distance with head, one hand, and eye-tracking transmitted their physical movements to their avatars. They controlled the system through a game controller. They were asked to arrange furniture following the next instructions to propitiate collaborative, division of labor, hierarchical, and brute force working together situations:

Collaborative trial. Participants were asked to arrange the furniture in a shared room by mutual consensus.
Hierarchical trial. A participant was asked to lead the other to place a billiard table into a room, as shown in Figure 6.
Division of labor trial. Furniture had only two colors, one for each participant to place them.
Brute force trial. Participants were instructed to arrange the furniture as quickly as they could.

Figure 6. Following instructions to place a billboard table in a room

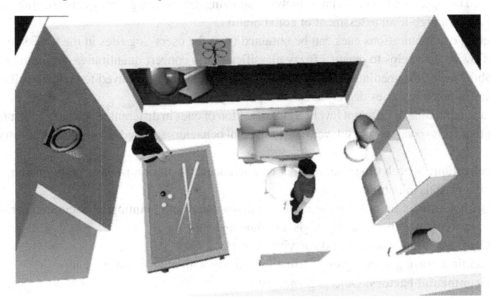

Because of the use of the space in this task, Proxemics could be observed. Besides, due to the gaze tracker, an analysis regarding what each participant was looking at any time was also available. Results showed that during the implementation stage:

- Discussion periods diminished in the division of labor and brute force strategies.

- Participants were around the same area for collaboration and the hierarchical situation, in contrast with being in separate areas for division of labor and brute force strategies.
- Both participants' manipulation of objects at the same time happens mostly in the division of labor and brute force strategies.
- During collaboration gazes were mainly on the objects and to each other; in the hierarchical situation mainly from the one that gave directions to the one that was following them; in division of labor mainly to the working area; and, around their area and to each other in the brute force situation.

It is important to highlight that Exploring the scenario, Planning, and Reviewing stages were present only in the collaborative situation, the most crucial feature to determine collaboration in contrast with the other working together situations.

High-Level Indicators for Collaboration

Once established that distinctive rates of nonverbal interaction cues could represent a useful approach to determine the participants' involvement in the task (Peña & de Antonio, 2010a), it was decided to go further by comparing participants' rates among them. In Casillas, Peña & Gutierrez (2019) was proposed an inference mechanism to evaluate collaboration in CVE based on expert human rules for nonverbal interaction. This approach is a multi-layer analysis, applying data filtering, fuzzy classification, and rules inference to get a high-level assessment of collaboration.

Nonverbal communications cues can be obtained from the users' log files in the CVE session. The constant flow of data helps to create a fuzzy classification to convert quantitative data into qualitative data, establishing a low, medium, and high level of nonverbal cues displayed to analyze collaboration by the rates of nonverbal cues displayed by each participant.

From a combination of different levels, a classification of cues in different task stages generates a first inference that corresponds to a first layer. The nonverbal behaviors selected as primitive indicators were:

- **Vocalization:** Speech time rate, number of utterances, discussion periods participation, and discussion periods initiation
- **Pointing Gesture:** Pointing in the implementation stage, and pointing in discussion periods
- Head movement in discussion periods: nodding and shaking
- **Navigation:** Without objects and carrying objects.
- **Proxemics:** Staying within-group formation, staying with other(s) participant(s).
- **Environmental Factors:** Objects manipulation.

In Table 1 are presented examples of inferences from different degrees in low-level indicators. On the first column is the categorization of the nonverbal cues, the next four columns are the different cues for each selected categorization, and an example of degree (i.e., high, medium, low), the fifth last column shows the inferences resulted of the combination of the different degrees of cues for each categorization.

Categories in Table 1 correspond to an area of study. As can be observed in the Taxonomy of nonverbal cues for automatic analysis previously discussed, as follows: Vocalization corresponds to the Paralanguage area, Pointing and Head movements are from Kinesics, and Navigation and Position are part of Proxemics, and Object manipulation is an Environmental factor.

Table 1. Examples of inferences by category resulting from a combination of cues degrees.

Vocalization	Speech time	Number of utterances	Discussion periods participation	Discussion periods initiator	Inferences
	High	High	High	High	leadership in strategy
	Medium	Medium	Medium	High	influence in strategy
Pointing gesture	**Implementation stage**	**Discussion periods**			
	High	High			influence in strategy and task
	Medium	Medium			influence in strategy and task
Head movements in discussion periods	**Nodding**	**Headshake**			
	High	High			high involvement in strategy
	Medium	Low			involvement in strategy
Navigation	**Without objects**	**Carrying objects**			
	Long-distance	Long-distance			high involvement in strategy and task
	Regular distance	Small distance			involvement in strategy
Position	**Group formation**	**From specific member(s)**			
	Close	Far away			not involved in the main group
	Close	Close			involved in a group and a subgroup
Object manipulation					
	High				taking care of task accomplishment
	Medium				involved in task accomplishment

From all the degrees of combinations of nonverbal cues were then obtained the 29 low-level indicators (Inferences in Table 1), next listed and that represent a second layer over the primitive indicators to get low-level indicators:

LOW LEVEL INDICATOR OF NONVERBAL BEHAVIOR

1 Paralanguage_LeadershipInStrategy
2 Paralanguage_HighInfluenceInStrategy
3 Paralanguage_InfluenceInGroupCohesion
4 Paralanguage_InfluenceInStrategy
5 Paralanguage_LowParticipationInStrategy
6 Paralanguage_NotParticipativeInSrategy
7 Paralanguage_ParticipationInStrategy
8 Paralanguage_Talkative

1 KnsesicsHead_InvolvementInStrategy_High

2 KnsesicsHead_InvolvementInStrategy

3 KnsesicsHead_InvolvementInStrategy_Low

4 KnsesicsHead_InvolvementInStrategy_Not

1 KnsesicsPointing_InfluenceInStrategyAndTask

2 KnsesicsPointing_InfluenceInStrategy

3 KnsesicsPointing_InfluenceInTask

4 KnsesicsPointing_LowInfluenceInTaskAndStrategy

1 ProxemicsNavigation_InvolvementInStrategy

2 ProxemicsNavigation_HighInvolvementInStrategy

3 ProxemicsNavigation_HighInvolvementInStrategyAndTask

4 ProxemicsNavigation_HighInvolvementInTask

5 ProxemicsNavigation_InvolvementInTaskAndStrategy

6 ProxemicsNavigation_LowInvolvementInStrategyAndTask

1 ProxemicsPosition_NotInvolvedInAGroup

2 ProxemicsPosition_InvolvedInAGroup

3 ProxemicsPosition_InvolvedInMainGroup

4 ProxemicsPosition_InvolvedInAGroupAndSubgroup

1 EnviromentalObject_TakingCareOfTaskAccomplishment

2 EnviromentalObject_InvolvedInTaskAccomplishment

3 EnviromentalObject_NotInvolvedInTaskAccomplishment

Then a third layer over the low-level indicators from the combination of the 29 low-level indicators gives way to high-level indicators. In this case is taken one low-level indicator of each category: Paralanguague (8), KinesicsHead (4), KinesicsPointing (4), ProxemicsNavigation (6) ProxemicsPosition (4), and EnviromentalObject (3), where the numbers in parenthesis represent the total of low-level indicators in that category. Next are presented two examples of high-level indicators:

Example 1. 1 Paralanguage_LeadershipInStrategy + 2 KnesicsPointing_InfluenceInStrategy + 4 KnsesicsHead_InvolvementInStrategy_Not +3 ProxemicsNavigation_InvolvementInStrategy + 1 ProxemicsPosition_NotInvolvedInAGroup +1 EnviromentalObject _TakingCareOfTaskAccomplishment = *Highly involvement with high participation in strategy, not involved in group dynamics, and taking care of the task.*

Example 2. 5 Paralanguage_LowParticipationInStrategy + 3 KnsesicsPointing_InfluenceInTask + 2 KnsesicsHead_InvolvementInStrategy +2 ProxemicsNavigation_HighInvolvementInStrategy + 1 ProxemicsPosition_NotInvolvedInAGroup + 1 EnviromentalObject_TakingCareOfTaskAccomplishment = *Not participating in strategy but highly involved on it, not involved in group dynamics, and taking care of the task.*

The approach was applied in a desktop-based CVE developed in the OpenSim™ platform. Five females and nine males in the range of 18 to 25 years old undergraduate students of Computer Science voluntarily participated, constituting seven dyads. The task consisted of forming a figure with 14 cuboid pieces placed in a circle, where participants had humanoid avatars. Dyads had three sessions, in which they assemble cuboid figures. In the application, text files saved the time stamp, the users' name, the avatars, and objects positions at each program cycle. Data collected was the participants' average time for navigation with or without holding an object, manipulation of objects, nodding, and headshakes in discussion periods. Also, the audio was transcribed to get a rate of the number of words, utterance, and when starting a conversation.

According to the authors, the approach produced the expected results by describing the type of collaboration each participant had during the session. However, results only validate the categorization, and not if it matches the users' performance or an expert perception.

As pointed out by the authors, the selection of the primitive cues or the inferences might change at any layer according to the task at hand or different experts' opinions. Even though, the layered approach is still a valuable tool to understand the collaborative process. Also, collaboration process can be consulted at any time of the session, helpful for online feedback (Casilla, Peña & Gutierrez, 2019).

Along with advances on the automatic analysis of collaboration, some proposal has been to apply the analysis of nonverbal cues automatic retrieval.

AUTOMATIC ANALYSIS OF NONVERBAL INTERACTION APPLICATIONS

The automatic analysis of nonverbal interaction, as stated, can give feedback at any time of the collaborative session. Such feedback can be useful in different situations. In this section are discussed two applications of such analysis conducted by the author and colleagues. The first one is a facilitator for Collaborative Learning, and the second one was applied in Affective Computing.

Collaboration Facilitator for Collaborative Learning

Although most pedagogical virtual tutors or facilitators are task-oriented, in Peña (2014), the proposed facilitator monitors only aspects of collaboration, offering advice in this regard. Common ground is required to take care of a collaborative task (Clark & Brennan, 1991); it is a mechanism that takes place during a conversation, the discussion periods, which are particularly important in a Collaborative Learning situation.

In this case, the facilitator for collaboration "observes" the sequence of stages in the task by determining the manipulation of objects and discussion periods through the log files, as shown in Figure 7 in a UML states chart. After the initial stage, the students might formulate a plan on how to accomplish the task, or they might jump into the implementation. If a discussion period takes place, the Planning stage is assumed, but if they go directly to manipulate objects, then the Implementation stage is assumed. During the Implementation stage, if a discussion period appears, the state changes to the Reviewing stage. If the discussion period ends and the session continues, the state changes back to the Implementation stage, or the session is ended.

The automatic stage recognition is used by the facilitator to send text messages encouraging discussion periods. Table 2, shows in the first column the stage where the message is sent, in the second column an ID for each message, then the content of the message in the third column, and in the fourth column is described the condition that triggers that message.

Another task of the facilitator is to try to balance participation, in this case, the formula taken from the real-life situation from Peña & de Antonio (2010a) was applied to establish under or over participation (see Peña, Aguilar, & Casillas, 2012 for details on the formula). In this case, the facilitator sends a personalized message for the participant, with his/her name and the text: "you should try to increase participation" for under participation, or "you should try to involve your peers" for over participation.

Figure 7. Stage determination by the collaborative facilitator (Peña, 2014)

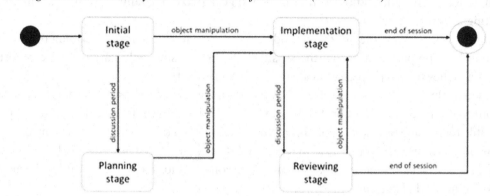

Table 2. Text messages sent by the collaborative facilitator based on stages recognition

Stage	Message	Text of the Message	Triggered condition
Initial	Messsage_0	Your first step could be to talk about how to solve the task	3000 ms from session starts with no discussion period or Implementation
Initial	Message_1	Maybe you want to consider having a plan before starting the task	Implementation starts without one discussion period
Implement	Message_2	A review of what you have done until now could be advisable	3000 ms in Implementation stage without a discussion period
Implement	Message_3	You should try to work as a team	The three participants implementing at the same time
Implement	Message_4	Before leaving the session, you might want to review your outcome	Finishing the session without one discussion period in the Implementation stage

The facilitator performance was evaluated in a desktop CVE shown in Figure 8, in which three people decide how to arrange furniture in a scale model of an apartment. The user cannot see his/her avatar. For the message to disappear from the screen, the participant had to agree or disagree on it.

Ninety students forming 30 triads evaluated the facilitator messages during the session. Results showed that for group messages, participants agreed on 84% of them, and in the case of personal messages, the rate was 81% of agreement. Following the message advice, that is, changing somehow the condition that triggered the message occurred 65.3% of the time.

A post-questionnaire was applied to participants; the answers had a 1 to 5 scale as follows: 1) not at all; 2) little; 3) regular; 4) good enough, and; 5) completely. The questions were aimed to understand the feeling of presence getting a 3.42 mean, the feeling of co-presence getting a 3.82 mean, agreement on the task outcome getting a 3.41 mean, and messages appropriateness that got a 3.34 mean.

The fact that the messages were on the screen until the user decided to agree or disagree with it was necessary to understand the user perception; however, participants might be just trying to take them out of sight to continue with the task. Also, although participants agreed with the message, they not always followed the advice. Finally, the facilitator should be proved in other contexts.

Figure 8. CVE for three users to arrange furniture in a department sketch.

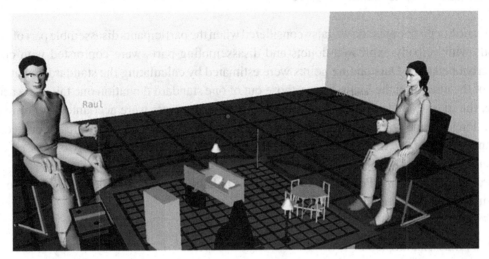

Affective Behavior

The interest in the affective component in computers has grown under the research area of Affective Computer, aimed to study the relation between emotions and computers (Picard, 1997). The evaluation of computer users' affective state through questionnaires presents the inconvenience of the changes in the people's emotional state moment-by-moment. Body measures using trackers overcome this questionnaire inconvenience. However, they are not easy to implement and can be perceived by the user as invasive. A third approach is based on task measures, an indirect evaluation based on the fact that our affective state influences our behavior on subsequent tasks (Picard & Daily, 2005). Under such consideration in Peña et al. (2016), the use of nonverbal interaction analysis was proposed to understand users' affective behavior.

There are a number of elements to be considered in the analysis of affective behavior, the stimulus, the reaction speed, the physiological conditions, the context, the interaction circumstance, or the presence of certain persons (Kantor, 1929). The former representing an important element within a collaborative situation, where people express themselves through their interaction with others.

The study in Peña et al. (2016) hypnotized that in an engaging situation, the implementation of a task can be momentarily interrupted when the participants feel frustrated, puzzled, or confused (Csikszentmihályi, 1991; Kort & Reilly, 2002). This expected change in the interaction flow was observed in implementation by object manipulation, navigation, and the number of participants' utterances. In navigation, considering that an overview of the scenario in a spatial task might be due to a review situation. And more prolonged than usual utterances could represent explanations or negotiation on confusing periods.

An exploratory study was conducted in a desktop CVE. Eight participants forming four dyads worked on an assembling task forming a figure with cuboid parts, see Figure 9. The verbally expressed difficulties by the participants during the sessions were manually classified and identified as follows:

- Doubts about the final figure shape
- Doubts about the pieces, like concern about not having enough pieces or the proper ones
- Doubts on the course of action, concerns about what his/her partner was doing

- Doubts about how to handle the pieces

A confusion or puzzle episode was also considered when the participants disassemble part of the figure. Periods with verbally expressed doubts and disassembling parts were contrasted with changes in the nonverbal behavior. Outstanding points were estimated by calculating the standard deviation on the duration of the utterance; the longest ones, those out of one standard deviation one tail, were accounted. Likewise, the most extended times in navigation outstanding points were accounted. As of implementation the longest time with no activity and one standard deviation one tail, were accounted. Results showed that 81.6% of the times, the atypical behavior corresponded to a verbally expressed difficulty or a dissemble situation.

According to the authors (Peña et al. 2016), this is a holistic situation to understand affective behavior that requires further investigation, but results were encouraging.

Figure 9. CVE assembling task.

FUTURE RESEARCH DIRECTIONS

The presented Taxonomy of nonverbal cues for automatic analysis (Peña, Muñoz, & Lara, 2019), should be enhanced as an ontological model, representing the domain items of knowledge defining not only the classification of concepts but their relationships (Jepsen, 2009). An ontology structure will support sharing common understanding with structured information, reusing the domain knowledge, making explicit assumptions, separating domain knowledge from operational knowledge, and analyzing the domain knowledge (Noy, & McGuinness, 2001).

The application of the analysis of nonverbal behavior can represent an impact in education and training CVE where the feedback for the users, teachers, or trainers is required. Therefore, it is important to continue this research path, where nonverbal analysis can complement the verbal analysis and task performance.

In the area of human behavior, the analysis of nonverbal interaction can be both ways. To understand how to improve CVE and to understand nonverbal interaction in an environment where the user will not feel observed, giving way to spontaneous behavior and the possibility of recording all the users' interventions for computer analysis (Peña, Lara & Estrada, 2020).

New technologies are putting on the table new was to display nonverbal interaction in CVE; this is the case of MR. Also, enhanced nonverbal cues is an interesting new trend, for which nonverbal interaction restrictions or misinterpretation can be solved through different techniques. In this case, the use of virtual bodies to support spatial tasks should lead to new codding and decoding strategies that can be supported by, for example, AI. IVA supporting the users' nonverbal interaction could also be another line of research, where the IVA can interpret or emphasize the users' interactions to enhance interaction.

Another trend is the emotional state of mind of the user. Its interpretation through his/her nonverbal interaction can also support a task's performance since emotions guide our behavior in ways we can now explore.

Finally, the focused interaction achieved through a virtual scenario with narrowed distractors such as objects not useful for the task, or social distractions could be an interesting research area.

The study of human behavior has expanded to new technologies; this represents a considerable challenge that will continuously be changing.

CONCLUSION

There are scares studies on the nonverbal behavior that users express through their visual representation, their avatar, in CVE; most of them aimed to create believable characters (Gobron, et al 2012). In this chapter are presented advances for the automatic analysis of nonverbal interaction in this technology media.

It is important to emphasize that the proposals in this chapter correspond to a situation where a spatial collaborative task is carried on, for which CVE represent the best media for geographically distant participants.

Different analyses conducted to a Taxonomy for nonverbal interaction of the users' avatars, by considering technical characteristics and limitations (Peña, Muñoz, & Lara 2019). Also, by comparing the real-life conditions, because the richness of our nonverbal behavior is still barely accomplished in computer-generated scenarios, the areas of study in nonverbal interaction were adjusted for CVE (Peña, Rangel, & Lara, 2015). However, we have to consider that humans have a long history of adapting the communication methods, since the telegraph or the telephone to nowadays social networks, we use the available communication cues to understand others.

Two applications for nonverbal behavior in CVE were presented. The creation of a facilitator for collaboration in Collaborative Learning was developed (Peña, 2014), and it was also presented a holistic approach to understanding the affective state of the computer users, based on their nonverbal behavior analysis (Peña et al., 2016).

In CVE the teamwork performance and each actor participation can be automatically analyzed. This analysis can give proper feedback on time for students, teachers, apprentices, and trainers when using this media for education and training purposes. Furthermore, this analysis will also support the design of CVE that better support the users' nonverbal interaction.

This research received no specific grant from any funding agency in the public, commercial, or not-for-profit sectors.

REFERENCES

Ammi, M., & Katz, B. F. (2015). Intermodal audio–haptic intermodal display: Improvement of communication and interpersonal awareness for collaborative search tasks. *Virtual Reality (Waltham Cross)*, *19*(3-4), 235–252. doi:10.100710055-015-0273-5

Apostolakis, K. C., & Daras, P. (2015, August). Natural user interfaces for virtual character full body and facial animation in immersive virtual worlds. In *International Conference on Augmented and Virtual Reality* (pp. 371-383). Springer. 10.1007/978-3-319-22888-4_27

Argyle, M. (1990). *Bodily communication* (2nd ed.). International Universities Press.

Aylett, R., & Ballin, D. (2013). *Intelligent virtual agents*. Springer Berlin/Heidelberg.

Bailenson, J. N., Yee, N., Merget, D., & Schroeder, R. (2006). The effect of behavioral realism and form realism of real-time avatar faces on verbal disclosure, nonverbal disclosure, emotion recognition, and copresence in dyadic interaction. *Presence (Cambridge, Mass.)*, *15*(4), 359–372. doi:10.1162/pres.15.4.359

Bolinger, D. (1985). *Intonation and its parts: Melody in spoken English*. Edward Arnold.

Brdiczka, O., Maisonnasse, J., & Reignier, P. (2005, October). Automatic detection of interaction groups. In *Proceedings of the 7th international conference on Multimodal interfaces* (pp. 32-36). Academic Press.

Capin, T. K., Pandzic, I. S., Magnenat Thalmann, N., & Thalmann, D. (1998). Realistic avatars and autonomous virtual humans in: VLNET networked virtual environments. In R. A. Earnshaw & J. Vince (Eds.), *Virtual worlds in the Internet* (pp. 157–174). IEEE Computer Society Press.

Casillas, L., Peña, A., & Gutierrez, A. (2019). Automatic Approach to Evaluate Collaborative Interaction in Virtual Environments. In *Handbook of Research on Technology Integration in the Global World* (pp. 1–23). IGI Global. doi:10.4018/978-1-5225-6367-9.ch001

Clark, H. H., & Brennan, S. E. (1991). Grounding in communication. In *Perspectives on socially shared cognition* (pp. 127–149). American Psychological Association. doi:10.1037/10096-006

Cruz-Neira, C., Sandin, D. J., & Defanti, T. A. (1993). Surround-screen projection based virtual reality: The design and implementation of the CAVE. *Computer Graphics*, *27*, 135–142.

Csikszentmihályi, M. (1991). *Flow: The psychology of optimal experience*. HarperCollins.

Dermouche, S., & Pelachaud, C. (2020). *Leveraging the Dynamics of Non-Verbal Behaviors For Social Attitude Modeling. IEEE Transactions on Affective Computing*.

Dillenbourg, P. (1999). What do you mean by collaborative learning? In *Collaborative learning: Cognitive and computational approaches* (pp. 1–19). Elsevier.

Economou, D., Doumanis, I., Argyriou, L., & Georgalas, N. (2017). User experience evaluation of human representation in collaborative virtual environments. *Personal and Ubiquitous Computing, 21*(6), 989–1001. doi:10.100700779-017-1075-4

Gabner, K., Jansen, M., Harrer, A., Herrmann, K., & Hoppe, H. U. (2003). Analysis methods for collaborative models and activities. *International Conference on Computer Supported Collaborative Learning*, 369-377.

Gamelin, G., Chellali, A., Cheikh, S., Ricca, A., Dumas, C., & Otmane, S. (2020). Point-cloud avatars to improve spatial communication in immersive collaborative virtual environments. *Personal and Ubiquitous Computing*, 1–18.

Gobron, S., Ahn, J., Garcia, D., Silvestre, Q., Thalmann, D., & Boulic, R. (2012). An event-based architecture to manage virtual human non-verbal communication in 3d chatting environment. In *International Conference on Articulated Motion and Deformable Objects* (pp. 58-68). Springer. 10.1007/978-3-642-31567-1_6

Guerrero-Vásquez, L. F., Landy-Rivera, D. X., Bravo-Torres, J. F., López-Nores, M., Castro-Serrano, R., & Vintimilla-Tapia, P. E. (2018, June). AVATAR: Contribution to Human-Computer interaction processes through the adaptation of semi-personalized virtual agents. In *2018 IEEE Biennial Congress of Argentina (ARGENCON)* (pp. 1-4). IEEE. 10.1109/ARGENCON.2018.8646055

Hall, E. T. (1968). Proxemics Text. *Current Anthropology, 9*, 2–3.

Han, X. (2019). *Investigating Proxemics between avatars in virtual reality* (Unpublished master dissertation). KTH Royal Institute of Technology, Sweden.

Hayashi, Y., Morita, H., & Nakano, Y. I. (2014). Estimating collaborative attitudes based on non-verbal features in collaborative learning interaction. *Procedia Computer Science, 35*, 986–993. doi:10.1016/j.procs.2014.08.184

Heath, C., Jirotka, M., Luff, P., & Hindmarsh, J. (1994). Unpacking collaboration: The interactional organisation of trading in a city dealing room. *Computer Supported Cooperative Work, 3*(2), 147–165. doi:10.1007/BF00773445

Herrera, F., Oh, S. Y., & Bailenson, J. N. (2020). Effect of Behavioral Realism on Social Interactions Inside Collaborative Virtual Environments. *PRESENCE: Virtual and Augmented Reality, 27*(2), 163–182. doi:10.1162/pres_a_00324

Jepsen, T. C. (2009). Just what is an ontology, anyway? *IT Professional, 11*(5), 22–27. doi:10.1109/MITP.2009.105

Johnson, A., & Leigh, J. (2001). Tele-immersive collaboration in the CAVE research network. In *Collaborative Virtual Environments* (pp. 225–243). Springer. doi:10.1007/978-1-4471-0685-2_12

Juslin, P. N., Scherer, K. R., Harrigan, J., & Rosenthal, R. (2005). Vocal expression of affect. In J. Harrigan, R. Rosenthal, & K. R. Scherer (Eds.), *The new handbook of methods in nonverbal behavior research* (pp. 65–135). Oxford University Press.

Kantor, J. R. (1924). *Principles of psychology*. The Principia Press. doi:10.1037/10752-000

Knapp, M., & Hall, J. (2007). *Nonverbal communication in human interaction* (7th ed.). Thomson Wadsworth.

Kort, B., & Reilly, R. (2002, June). An affective module for an intelligent tutoring system. In *International Conference on Intelligent Tutoring Systems* (pp. 955-962). Springer. 10.1007/3-540-47987-2_95

Kolesnichenko, A., McVeigh-Schultz, J., & Isbister, K. (2019, June). Understanding Emerging Design Practices for Avatar Systems in the Commercial Social VR Ecology. In *Proceedings of the 2019 on Designing Interactive Systems Conference* (pp. 241-252). 10.1145/3322276.3322352

Mayer, S., Reinhardt, J., Schweigert, R., Jelke, B., Schwind, V., Wolf, K., & Henze, N. (2020, April). Improving Humans' Ability to Interpret Deictic Gestures in Virtual Reality. In *Proceedings of the 2020 CHI Conference on Human Factors in Computing Systems* (pp. 1-14). 10.1145/3313831.3376340

Mine, M. (1995). *ISAAC: A virtual environment tool for the interactive construction of virtual worlds.* UNC Chapel Hill Computer Science Technical Report TR95-020.

Noy, N. F., & McGuinness, D. L. (2001). *Ontology development 101: A guide to creating your first ontology.* Academic Press.

Oh, S. Y., Bailenson, J., Krämer, N., & Li, B. (2016). Let the avatar brighten your smile: Effects of enhancing facial expressions in virtual environments. *PLoS One, 11*(9), e0161794. doi:10.1371/journal.pone.0161794 PMID:27603784

Patterson, M. L. (1982). A sequential functional model of nonverbal exchange. *Psychological Review, 89*(3), 231–249. doi:10.1037/0033-295X.89.3.231

Peña, A. (2010). Collaborative virtual environment for distance learning When to use 3D? *Innovación Educativa (México, D.F.), 10*(52), 25–33.

Peña, A. (2014). A Collaboration Facilitator Model for Learning Virtual Environments. *Computer Science and Information Technology. HRPUB, 2*(2), 100–107. doi:10.13189/csit.2014.020207

Peña, A., Aguilar, R.A., & Casillas, L. A. (2012). The Users' Avatars Nonverbal Interaction in Collaborative Virtual Environments for Learning. *Virtual Reality and Environments*, 69-94.

Peña, A., & de Antonio, A. (2009). Using Avatar's Nonverbal Communication to monitor Collaboration in a Task-oriented Learning Situation in a CVE. In *Workshop on Intelligent and Innovative Support for Collaborative Learning Activities* (p. 19). Academic Press.

Peña, A., & de Antonio, A. (2010a). Nonverbal communication as a means to support collaborative interaction assessment in 3D virtual environments for learning. In *Monitoring and assessment in online collaborative environments: Emergent computational technologies for E-learning support* (pp. 172–197). IGI Global. doi:10.4018/978-1-60566-786-7.ch010

Peña, A., & de Antonio, A. (2010b). Inferring interaction to support collaborative learning in 3D virtual environments through the user's avatar Non-Verbal Communication. *International Journal of Technology Enhanced Learning, 2*(1-2), 75–90. doi:10.1504/IJTEL.2010.031261

Peña, A., & Jiménez, E. (2012). Virtual Environment for Effective Training. *Revista Colombiana de Computación*, *13*(1), 45–58.

Peña, A., Lara, G., & Estrada, E. (2020). Navigation in Virtual Environments. In *Virtual Reality Designs* (pp. 10–26). CRC Press.

Peña, A., Muñoz, E., & Lara, G. (2019). A model for nonverbal interaction cues in collaborative virtual environments. *Virtual Reality (Waltham Cross)*, 1–14.

Peña, A., Rangel, N., & Lara, G. (2015). Nonverbal interaction contextualized in collaborative virtual environments. *Journal on Multimodal User Interfaces*, *9*(3), 253–260. doi:10.100712193-015-0193-4

Peña, A., Rangel, N. E., & Maciel, O. E. (2015). Comparison of the effects of oral and written communication on the performance of cooperative tasks, *International Review of Social Science. Academy of IRMBR*, *3*(11), 487–499.

Peña, A., Rangel, N. E., Muñoz, M., Mejia, J., & Lara, G. (2016). Affective Behavior and Nonverbal Interaction in Collaborative Virtual Environments. *Journal of Educational Technology & Society*, *19*(2), 29–41.

Picard, R. W. (Ed.). (1997). *Affective computing*. MIT Press.

Picard, R. W., & Daily, S. B. (2005). Evaluating affective interactions: Alternatives to asking what users feel. In *CHI Workshop on Evaluating Affective Interfaces: Innovative Approaches* (pp. 2219-2122). New York, NY: ACM.

Smith, H. J., & Neff, M. (2018, April). Communication behavior in embodied virtual reality. In *Proceedings of the 2018 CHI Conference on Human Factors in Computing Systems* (pp. 1-12). Academic Press.

Schroeder, R. (2010). *Being There Together: Social interaction in shared virtual environments*. Oxford University Press. doi:10.1093/acprof:oso/9780195371284.001.0001

Shahrour, G. J., & Russell, M. J. (2015). Recognizing an individual, their topic of conversation, and cultural background from 3D body movement. *World Acad Sci Eng Technol Int J Comput Electr Autom Control Inf Eng*, *9*(1), 311–316.

Spante, M., Heldal, I., Steed, A., Axelsson, A., & Schroeder, R. (2003). Strangers and friends in networked immersive environments: Virtual spaces for future living. In *Proceeding of Home Oriented Informatics and Telematics*. HOIT.

Sun, Y., Shaikh, O., & Won, A. S. (2019). Nonverbal synchrony in virtual reality. *PLoS One*, *14*(9), e0221803. doi:10.1371/journal.pone.0221803 PMID:31525220

Teo, T. F., Hayati, A. A., Lee, G., Billinghurst, M., & Adcock, M. (2019, November). A technique for mixed reality remote collaboration using 360 panoramas in 3d reconstructed scenes. In *25th ACM Symposium on Virtual Reality Software and Technology* (pp. 1-11). 10.1145/3359996.3364238

ADDITIONAL READING

Blascovich, J., & Bailenson, J. (2011). *Infinite reality: Avatars, eternal life, new worlds, and the dawn of the virtual revolution.* William Morrow & Co.

Fairchild, A. J., Campion, S. P., Garcia, A. S., Wolff, R., Fernando, T., & Roberts, D. J. (2016). A mixed reality telepresence system for collaborative space operation. *IEEE Transactions on Circuits and Systems for Video Technology, 27*(4), 814–827. doi:10.1109/TCSVT.2016.2580425

Hrimech, H., Alem, L., & Merienne, F. (2011). How 3D interaction metaphors affect user experience in collaborative virtual environment. *Advances in Human-Computer Interaction, 2011*, Article ID 172318, 11 pages doi:10.1155/2011/172318

Knapp, M., & Hall, J. (2007). *Nonverbal communication in human interaction* (7th ed.). Thomson Wadsworth.

Peña, A., Lara, G., & Orozco, H. R. (Eds.). (2020). *Virtual Reality Designs.* CRC Press.

Ryan, W. S., Cornick, J., Blascovich, J., & Bailenson, J. N. (2019). Virtual reality: Whence, how and what for. In *Virtual Reality for Psychological and Neurocognitive Interventions* (pp. 15–46). Springer. doi:10.1007/978-1-4939-9482-3_2

Scarborough, J. K., & Bailenson, J. N. (2014). Avatar psychology. The Oxford handbook of virtuality, 129-144.

Schroeder, R. (2010). *Being There Together: Social interaction in shared virtual environments.* Oxford University Press. doi:10.1093/acprof:oso/9780195371284.001.0001

KEY TERMS AND DEFINITIONS

Avatar: The graphic representation of an actor in a virtual reality environment.
CVE: Collaborative virtual environments, multiusers virtual reality designed for research purposes.
MUVE: Computer-generated scenarios for multiusers to interact.
Nonverbal Interaction: The interaction accomplished by other means than words or their meaning.

Chapter 14
Virtual Reality in Object Location

Graciela Lara López
CUCEI, Universidad de Guadalajara, Mexico

ABSTRACT

Currently, virtual reality (VR) is a computer technology that is growing in terms of developments and discoveries. Virtual reality has been introduced in different areas due to the growing interest it has caused in people. The development of applications with virtual reality is increasingly varied, covering activities, tasks, or processes of everyday life in the fields of industry, education, medicine, tourism, art, entertainment, design, and modeling of objects, among others. This chapter will focus on describing the latest advances and developments in virtual reality within the scope of representing reality in the process of locating objects. With the support of virtual environments and intelligent virtual agents, the author has managed to develop a computational model that generates indications in natural language, for the location of objects considering spatial and cognitive aspects of the users.

INTRODUCTION

Currently, Virtual Reality (VR) is one of the technologies with a very broad growth projection within companies and research centers. However, it is contradictory to see that this technology is very alien to certain groups of the population due to various situations, such as: not having a clear idea of what (VR) is, not having accessibility to it, not being within the people's particular interests due to age, among others. Before these situations, it is necessary and useful to specify that the term of Virtual Reality (VR) was popularized in 1989 by Jaron Lanier, emerging in the field of video games and entertainment. Several experts have tried to define the term Virtual Reality. Below are 2 of the definitions of experts that have had more relevance in this area:

- "Virtual Reality is a computer system used to create an artificial world in which the user has the impression of being in that world with the ability to navigate through the world and manipulate objects in the world" (Manetta & Blade, 1995).

DOI: 10.4018/978-1-7998-7552-9.ch014

Copyright © 2021, IGI Global. Copying or distributing in print or electronic forms without written permission of IGI Global is prohibited.

- "Virtual Reality is a paradigm that uses computers and human-computer interfaces (HCI) to create the effect of a three-dimensional (3D) world in which the user interacts directly with virtual objects" (Bryson, 1996).

Basing on these definitions, is defined Virtual Reality as the interactive simulation that involves all the senses, generated by the computer, explorable, visually and manipulable in real time, giving the sensation of presence in the environment.

Virtual Reality like a research tool has addressed different uses and generated amazing advantages, to observe aspects never before explored in the development of specialized solutions that respond to the needs of both researchers and industrialists in their various areas. Virtual Reality allows the simulation of spaces that have not been built, is the technology that manages to represent reality where the human being cannot be located for being difficult or risky.

On the other hand, the Virtual Reality is increasingly present in different areas, the main uses and applications of Virtual Reality have been extended to varied fields and sectors such as: a) Simulation: medicine, industrial, military, transportation, education, training and engineering; b) Modeling: particles, physical environments and human characteristics; c) Design: space, products, tools and prototypes; d) Representation of reality: objects, situations and people.

Increasingly, society demands innovative applications with technical support from Virtual Reality, so that users can develop and facilitate the retention of knowledge, better conceive physical spaces, practice risk sports, visit museums or galleries, train personnel in tasks or high risk processes, applying medical treatments to overcome phobias, trauma or disabilities, that is, applications that offer experiences that help and motivate users, beyond just offering entertainment.

In this context and considering that virtual environments are a valuable resource for training within industries, digital education or to carry out virtual visits in museums, was observed the need to support these activities with the location of objects. Therefore, the author of this chapter has developed some mechanisms to simulate this process and thus improve the learning and construction of user knowledge of these activities within Virtual Environments.

In accordance with Manetta & Blade (1995) a Virtual Environment is defined as realistic simulations of interactive scenes. For Vizcaíno (2011) a virtual environment is also recognized as a synthetic environment. Vizcaíno (2011) cited that Virtual Reality allows us to describe visual simulations of the physical reality that surrounds the human being, thus managing to simulate imaginary environments and scenes, or impossible for breaking physical laws. With the use of highly realistic virtual environments, an infinite range of possibilities has been opened to design and develop intelligent virtual systems that answer questions to users about different topics such as: health and diet plans, physical training, search routes or location.

Focusing specifically on the task of locating objects in the real world, it has been working on the development of a computational model for the generation of directions for object location in virtual environments, taking into account the characteristics of the objects, users and the plane of the virtual environment.

As part of the properties of objects, physical characteristics such as: color, size, shape, texture, changes in position, perceptual salience from an individual approach and from a contextual approach have been studied and modeled. Also, the cognitive and perceptual characteristics of users are essential during a search process. Likewise, the lighting of each space or plane are characteristics with practical and decorative effects that also influence the localization process, without forgetting the occlusions that prevent or hinder the vision of the objects.

Furthermore, it has been examined that a particularly useful technique in the process of locating objects in the real world is the handling of reference objects. These elements are used as a support to give directions in the location of objects. These objects are considered really effective and essential resources. For this reason, the interest in the study of salience and the design of algorithms that could obtain this characteristic arose, for each object contained in each virtual environment.

To select the best reference object, several variables that can influence have been analyzed, such as:

- The physical characteristics of the object (color, size, shape, texture, orientation), from a 3D approach.
- The spatial location of the object with respect to the point of view of the observer.
- Previous knowledge of the objects or the environment where the object to be located is located.
- The perceptual and cognitive characteristics of the users.

Along with the computational model developed for the generation of indications in the location of objects, an Intelligent Virtual Systems has been implicitly developed, which combines knowledge of various multidisciplinary areas such as Virtual Reality, Informatics, Applied Psychology, Optics, as well as the handling of Space Language, to understandably answer questions about the location of a particular object within a 3D environment.

The development of this research has aimed to provide a support tool, which can be coupled in a virtual environment to carry out activities such as: the study of academic content, the training in the operation of industrial equipment, navigate inside a virtual museum, among other activities, where the location of objects is a task of necessary to achieve the goals of the user.

BACKGROUND

As a task prior to the development of all research, it was necessary to identify and describe the precedents on the research topic, to understand the nature of the problem, of course based on references from the existing literature. This allowed in-depth research to identify some computational model that incorporated all or some of the glimpsed elements, for the proposed new model.

The author of this chapter in (Lara, De Antonio & Peña,2016), a review of the computer systems found was presented, as well as a discussion of progress in recent years regarding this line of research. Through a systematic search using different search string criteria, a set of 20 related papers were selected.

As part of the criteria for project selection, the following were considered: a) that the systems used the spatial language for the location of objects, allowing to discover that the process of locating objects has been investigated and analyzed in both real and virtual environments in 2D and 3D; b) the presence of linguistics and psychology, semantics and syntax, two fields that are related to the study of frames of reference, the implementation of a perceptual salience model and cognitive maps, which support understanding and the generation of spatial language; c) interaction with humans or robots; and d) the application of some algorithm that will apply the AI.

Table 1 presents the list of 20 projects selected for its analysis, as well as the name of their developer: The main results obtained of the analysis were next:

Table 1. Computer systems analyzed

Name and year	Developed by:
SHRDLU (1971)	Terry Winograd (at the MIT Artificial Intelligence Laboratory)
VITRA (VIsual TRAnslator) Fraunhofer Institute (IITB, Karlsruhe) project	Unknown
2D Images	
CITYTOUR System (1986 -1988)	Elizabeth André, Guido Bosch, Gerd Herzog and Thomas Rist
SOCCER System (1986 - 1988)	
3D Images Workbench (1992 - 1995)	Herzog, Blocher, Gapp, Stopp, Wahlster, André, Rist, Nagel, Enkelmann, Zimmermann Wazinski.
Constrained Connectionist System (1996)	Terry Regier
Scene Describer (1999)	Alicia Abella and John R. Kender
Virtual Director System (2000)	Amitabha Mukerjee Kshitij Gupta, Siddharth Nautiyal, Mukesh P Singh and Neelkanth Mishra
Attentional Vector Sum Model (2001)	Terry Regier and Laura A. Carlson
Describer System (2002)	Deb K. Roy
Situated Language Interpreter System (2003)	John D. Kelleher
System for Spatial Knowledge Representation for Human-Robot Interaction (2003 - 2006)	Reinhard Moratz, Thora Tenbrink, John Bateman and Kerstin Fischer
Bishop System (2004)	Peter Gorniak and Deb Roy
Space Case (2005 - 2006)	Kate Lockwood, Ken Forbus, Daniel T. Halstead and Jeffrey Usher
GLIDES System (2006)	Paul Williams, Risto Miikkulainen, Williams and Miikkulainen,
Situated Artificial Communicators (2006)	Gert Rickheit and Ipke Wachsmuth
Reference Object Choice in Spatial Language: Machine and Human Models (2010)	Michel Barclay
Moscaret (2013)	Thanh-Hai Trinh

1. Most systems considered the use of semantics as an important aspect for its implementation.
2. Fifteen of the systems considered the development of a semantic model, in order to have a correct interpretation of symbols and words.
3. Eleven of the systems had as their main objective in its development the location of objects.

4. All the works reviewed refer to spatial relationships, from visual perception and natural language, generating linguistic expressions.

5. Nine of the systems considered the aspect of perceptual salience from the physical characteristics of the objects.

6. All systems are systems that were implemented in a virtual environment, with variable dimensions such as: textual, 2D or 3D.

7. The Human-Computer interaction mode was the most common interaction, with 16 systems. Only 4 systems considered an interaction with robots.

8. It was observed that several systems considered the use of reference objects, linguistic expressions and / or spatial reference frames.

9. Artificial Intelligence as a scientific field of informatics was applied in the development of six of the selected systems. With the support of neural networks, knowledge bases and Bayesian networks, it has been possible to develop models that simulate human intelligence associated with the process of locating objects. The complete analysis was published in (Lara *et al.* 2016).

At the end of this analysis, three projects were identified, which were closer to the new proposal that the author has been developed in recent years. Table 2 presents a summary of the areas that distinguish each of the analyzed models, compared to the proposal. Column 1 lists the name of the system and your developer; column 2 specifies whether an object salience model was used; column 3 indicates whether the system includes a perceptual user model; column 4 refers to whether a cognitive user model is used; column 5 refers to whether a reference object selection algorithm was implemented; Column 6 describes whether the system implemented an algorithm to determine the most convenient spatial relationship between the user and the object to be located, and finally, Column 7 shows whether an algorithm was applied to generate indications for the location of objects.

A general description of the key aspects of these three project, is presented below:

Table 2. Analysis of computer systems applying spatial language and perceptual salience and other aspects VS new model

Author / System	Salience Model (Object)	Perceptual Modeling (User)	Cognitive Modeling (User)	Reference object selection algorithm	Algorithm to determine Spatial Relation	Algorithms for the generation Indications for Location (Objects)
Attentional Vector Sum Model *Terry Regier and Laura A. Carlson (2001)*	✓	û	û	✓	✓	✓
Describer System *Deb K. Roy (2002)*	✓	û	û	✓	✓	✓
Situated Language Interpreter System *Gert Rickheit and Ipke Wachsmuth (2006)*	✓	û	û	û	✓	✓
New model	✓	✓	✓	✓	✓	✓

1. **Attentional Vector Sum Model:** Computational model that predicts linguistic expressions considering spatial language. This model is supported by selected reference objects based on their irregular geometric shapes. The authors use sinusoidal equation functions to determine if the path to a reference point is horizontal or vertical. Attention to the reference object is weighted by an algorithm that considers the sum of vectors between the reference and the object to be located. The authors do not describe at any time the development of a perceptual salience model. They use as (Gapp, 1995) the center of mass, the orientations and the distance of the object, to select the reference object. They test the model with various experiments using 2D images (Regier & Carlson, 2001).

2. **Describer System:** In this computer system, a learning algorithm is implemented and evaluated that describes objects in visual scenes in a spoken way. Scenes that are represented by a set of 2D images. Through descriptions in natural language, the algorithm obtains probabilistic structures that encode the visual semantics of the structure of phrases, word classes and individual words. This has as its main objective the evaluation and semantic understanding by human judges of the performance of oral descriptions generated automatically with respect to the descriptions generated by humans. The system does not include the implementation of an object salience model. However, color, size and position were the three basic characteristics for the description of the object (Roy, 2002).

3. **Situated Language Interpreter System:** This computer system implements location-oriented interpretation of spatial language. The system was supported by three aspects: a) an algorithm of visual salience of the objects based on the user's visualization volume; b) a semantic model for expressions containing projective prepositions; and c) the abstraction to trace the candidate paths of a location expression, where it is ensured to choose the most prominent reference object. The system allows users to move around in a virtual environment and manipulate objects. At the same time, the system allows the user to select different types of frames of reference (Kelleher, 2003).

It is worth mentioning that the search to find new advances related to the development of this type of projects has continued. However, few have been the findings. Next, a set of more recent works related to this line of research is described.

(Hou & Skubic, 2016), they implemented a spatial language generation system to reveal the location of an object within a 3D environment. The interface allows a robot to interact with a human. Through a short and precise description an object is searched, with respect to the reference objects and a spatial relationship. The authors consider three fundamental aspects: 1) acquire precise information so that users perceive the objects to be located; 2) find the match of human spatial language syntax and human language habit; and 3) use the fewest number of words. Within the system an environment is modeled where the robot builds an environmental model, to detect all the objects to be located, the information of all the objects in the environment is stored in a relationship entity model. The information includes geometric characteristics such as: size, shape, and orientation of objects.

In (Tian, Wang & Wang, 2017), was proposed a project, which consists of a multitasking learning system with the support of a multitasking neural network, for the location of objects. In this model, a neural network consisting of three modules was developed: the first module extracts the shared characteristics of an image of traffic scenes, to generate low-level characteristics and gather information from different levels; the second module comprises a training algorithm; and the third module executes a performance algorithm.

The authors considered the task of locating objects from a bounding box of an object, with the architecture of the multitasking neural network, to extract high-level semantic information, then obtained the limit information considered low-level that is combined end-to-end for object location. The innovation of this model is exemplified in the design of an object location algorithm that integrates a set of parameters of low level of computational complexity, to locate the position of the object. It is worth mentioning that the model does not include the development of a salience model. However, they consider the shape of objects from their limit.

For their part, (Chen, Kovvuri, Gao & Navatia, 2017) proposed a multimodal spatial regression system with a semantic context (MSRC), which predicts the location of objects. Starting from a query and the information of the context related to a question, the system operates a spatial regression network through bounding boxes. Given a 2D image and a natural language query phrase, a grounding system locates the objects mentioned in the image. The phrases of a query can be related semantically to provide useful clues, in the location of basic objects. The authors do not cite a salience model, nor a spatial reference frame during the location of objects.

On the other hand, (Yousaf & Wolter, 2017) presented the proposal of an algorithm to extract spatial information, through descriptions of places in natural language. Spatial information is context dependent. The algorithm considers a lexicon of spatial prepositions, processing sentence by sentence. The authors label each part of their speech, considering a superior sentence structure, where they consider the noun phrase of the subject and the prepositional phrase, then locate additional nouns by means of short sentences. The authors do not give very extensive details of their research, as it is still in a developmental stage. However, the advances are quite interesting in relation to the research area of this chapter.

Finally, (D'Agostini *et al.* 2018) implemented an intelligent virtual system that assists users with mild cognitive problems when carrying out daily activities such as the preparation of elementary foods. The system is made up of several modules that manage animations of actions that users develop, taking into account the user's condition and the environmental context. As part of the actions of the users are: reach, move, mix, tilt and grab.

In this proposal, the location of objects occurs within the plane of a kitchen. Through the development of a sensor fusion module capable of specifying the precision of objects in real time, the system considers two main tasks: 1) to capture the position of the environment, that is, the location of the user and the objects; and 2) implement an assistant with contextualized augmented reality animations.

Support actions are managed by different states that change from one to another, according to what the user performs. The data is exchanged through a message queue server. The system does not consider a salience model, nor does it consider specific characteristics of the objects. However, they extract three types of characteristics: 1) relative distance between nodes; 2) velocity of each node (in the human body reference frame); and 3) azimuth and altitude of the vector connecting the torso to arm nodes (elbow and wrist). Likewise, the authors consider relevant, to accurately calculate the user's point of view in real time so that the virtual images are aligned with the objects in the real world.

The analysis carried out, as well as the deep search to find new discoveries of this topic within the consulted literature from 1971 a 2018, have made it possible to verify that none of these systems gathered all the identified elements, for the process of locating objects in virtual environments, from the perspective of the new model. Reason why the interest and motivation arose, to start developing a model that was innovative, useful and relevant in various real-life activities, where (VR) was an auxiliary to simulate a relatively complex activity.

In the next section, it is explained how the model for the localization of objects using Virtual Reality has been developing, presenting first the advances of a salience model, after the progress of the user modeling and the semantics of virtual worlds and, finally the advances with the algorithms for generating indications. It is worth mentioning that all the designs and computational algorithms described below are the contribution of the work that has been developed over several years.

MODEL FOR THE LOCATION OF OBJECTS USING VIRTUAL REALITY

The task of locating objects in the real world can become complex and variable, this depends on the circumstances of the environment and the characteristics of each user. Often users who train or explore a place through a virtual system spend a lot of time searching for objects that are hidden with other objects or simply do not remember where they saw them before (See Figure 1).

Figure 1. User locating an object

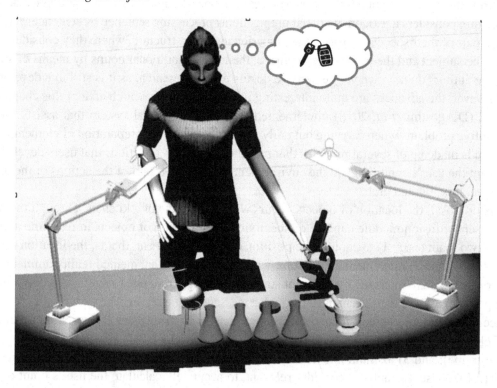

In order to simplify and make the process of locating objects more agile within virtual learning or training environments, has been worked on the design of computational models that allow the selection of reference objects based on their perceptual salience, that is, objects that stand out from among all the objects contained within a virtual environment through their physical characteristics such as: color, size, shape and texture. For each of these characteristics, computational algorithms have been designed, developed and tested, that allow the extraction of each of these features, from two approaches: the individual and from the context. Next, the computational salience model proposed by the author is explained.

Computational Model of Perceptual Saliency for 3D objects Based on their Color, Size and Shape

Objects are inert material things of small, medium or large size that are perceived by sight or felt by the touch of human beings. Considering this definition, it can be said that objects have various physical characteristics, which make them more prominent than others, that is, more relevant. The visual salience or also known as the perceptual salience of an object is associated with the interaction of its basic characteristics with respect to the surrounding objects (Gapp, 1995; Hoffman & Singh, 1997; Stoia, 2007). According to (Kapur, 2003), visual saliency is a process of association of objects and their representation in order to attract attention and capture thinking and behavior.

The main purpose for which a salient computational model for 3D objects within virtual environments was developed was to select the best reference object. In the process of locating objects, a reference object is a resource that allows determining the position of another object within space. Thus, a reference object allows a user to be directed towards another object, person or a certain purpose.

In relation to this contribution, the author has worked on the development and validation of a computational salience model, which can determine the intrinsic and contextual salience of each object present in a virtual environment, thus identifying the most prominent object from the environment.

The salience model consists mainly of three parts: a) the individual salience measure of a 3D object, b) the salience measure of an object with respect to its context, and c) the general salience measure (also called "global salience"). Each of these parts is described in general terms below:

Individual Salience Measure

For the calculation of the individual salience of a 3D object it was necessary to carry out a process of extraction of characteristics of each object. This process has been called "characterization". In the first instance, the author only worked with the color, size and shape of the objects, but it has been necessary to add other characteristics such as: the texture and orientation.

The characterization process consists of the abstraction and quantification of each of the characteristics of the 3D object, in a virtual environment. To carry out this process, the author considered a set of previously selected criteria, to treat each characteristic. The information obtained is normalized to obtain an individual measure of salience.

The criteria taken into account to measure the salience by color of an object, from its individual form were: consider the color space of the CIE-Lab model and discard the RGB model, since the first model is oriented more towards the human eye and it allows quantifying the color differences that can be expressed in terms of human perception, while the second is less intuitive because it is more hardware-oriented.

Determining which color is the most salient, in view of users is a complex task. For this reason, a list of colors analyzed by Choungourian (1968) was taken into account, which includes the colors: red, orange, yellow, yellow-green, Green, blue-green, blue and purple. From this list and considering a computational algorithm, distances of the color of the object are measured with the list of colors proposed by Choungourian (1968), a salience value is assigned to each color coordinate, and finally is data are averaged and weighted to assign a salience value ranging from [0 - 1].

For the case of size salience, the volume measurement based on a voxelization process was considered. The 3D object goes through a voxelization process, the number of voxels is obtained. Then the number of voxels is multiplied by the size of the voxel. Finally, a similar weight to the color is made, to obtain a measure of salience with a value ranging from [0 - 1].

Without a doubt, the most complex challenge for the implementation of this salience model was to obtain a salience measure of the shape of the objects in the environment, from the individual and contextual perspective. Firstly, the way in which the shape of an object was characterized from its individual focus will be analyzed. Here, the author considered using the voxelization process. Later, it was assumed that the flat surfaces of an object are less prominent than those of pointy surfaces. Taking into account this assumption, the full space and empty space of the Bounding Box that surrounds the 3D objects were measured, and a measure of salience was also assigned [0 - 1]. For more information on the implementation of this proposal see (Lara *et al.* 2018a).

The latest advance in the development of this salience model is the proposal of a texture salience measure, from a two-dimensional approach using the central idea of a salience map. Texture is a visual appearance characteristic which depends on the effects of contrast (light and shadow). The proposal is to obtain the color of each pixel in the RGB coordinate system, then those coordinates are transformed into the CIE-Lab model format, the value of saliency by texture image is calculated, by the average of the sum of saliency by pixel and the total of pixel of texture image.. For more information on the implementation of this proposal see (Lara *et al.* 2018b).

Measure of Salience from the Context

The general strategy for measuring salience with respect to the context of an object, from its color, size and shape characteristics, consists of a process where the weighted average of the color, size and shape is calculated. Then the distance of the color, size and shape from the context is calculated. To establish a mathematical salience value, the following operations are performed: a) a standard normal distribution considering that the color, size and shape distances have a normal distribution, and b) a proportional distribution that determines a normalized salience value of [0 - 1].

An important aspect to consider in this contextual salience model was that although the human beings live in a three-dimensional world, we only see in two dimensions. In other words, the human visual system only receives centred projections on plane images of two dimensions. This is why the representation of the color and size of an object with respect to its context was extracted from a 2D projection in this model of contextual salience, except in the shape, since the human mind transforms and organizes the perceived elements into something to be integrated into a whole.

For the representation of the shape of an object from the context, the Zernike descriptors were used. Also known as descriptors of geometric moments with orthogonal bases, which make a vector representation of the object.

General Salience Measure

With the sum of the individual salience measure and the salience measure with respect to the context, the general salience (global salience) is obtained with a normalized value of [0 - 1].

Using User Modeling and Semantics of Virtual Worlds

Around the development of this research, the author has implemented processes that allow modeling intelligent virtual systems, which are related to the profile of the different users that interact with the virtual environments and their characteristics. The purpose of this is that the generation of indications is adapted to the needs and characteristics of the users. Currently, computer advances allow the design and implementation of explicit user models, with their knowledge and experiences of the different objects present in the virtual environment.

Through data ontologies, the author have modeled users where their cognitive and perceptual attributes are simulated. Similarly, the use of data ontologies has allowed representing the semantics of virtual environments, which is necessary for the generation of indications, in which the properties of the objects and the spatial relationships between the objects are stored.

With the implementation of these data ontologies it has been possible to make a concrete representation of the knowledge of users and virtual environments. These data ontologies have also made it possible to have a standardized information storage format. For the representation of these ontologies, a visual OWL (Web Ontology Language) has been used, with a representation of graphs.

In this context, it is necessary to mention that for the design of any data ontology it is necessary to identify the characteristics of the object classes to be represented, in this case there were two object classes: the user class and the world class. Next, is described how the two ontologies for these two classes were designed, within the indication generation model for location of objects.

User Modeling

Each person is very different from another, so it was necessary to select personal characteristics, which allow obtaining useful aspects, for the generation of indications. An individual can have physical and cognitive characteristics, which form them fully in the particular.

The characteristics analyzed and selected for user modeling were classified into four types:

1. **Basic Characteristics:** Considered as the qualities, properties, abilities or attributes that constitute an individual, that is, they are the elements that all human beings have such as: name, age, gender, among others. These attributes were called personal data and it contains static information. It is worth mentioning that these attributes have been useful during the development of the experimentation processes.
2. **Cognitive Characteristics:** These characteristics are those that allow to carry out any task and are used continuously, to learn and remember information at the moment when it is required to maintain and distribute the attention of an individual. With these skills you can recognize sounds, process stimuli, perform calculations, or mentally represent objects.

After analyzing these characteristics, the general ability to remember the spatial location of an object was selected, that is, the location memory (Mol) that a user possesses. Obviously, visual memory intervenes here, to remember the characteristics and position of objects within the virtual environment, where the location of objects takes place. The way in which it was decided to measure the (Mol) was using the Rey–Osterrieth complex figure test (ROCF) which is a widely used neuropsychological test for visual perception and long term visual memory. After obtaining the results of the ROCF test, a scale to evaluate the (Mol) was proposed. This complete proposal was published in (López, 2016).

3. **Perceptual Characteristics:** These characteristics represent the visual stimulus, which is considered subjective, selective and temporary. Subjective because the reactions to the same stimulus can be very different from one individual to another. Selective because individuals cannot have complete vision at the same time, from their central or peripheral vision. And temporary because it is a short-term manifestation. Considering these aspects, the perceptual characteristics with which it was decided to work, were those that managed to deduce the way in which users visually perceived a scene, such as visual acuity and / or color blindness.

The main objective of modeling visual acuity was, to know at what distance a user sees a blurred object, that is, we sought to know at what distance a user can see clearly. This feature provides a user's performance limit to distinguish spatial details from a visual object in ideal lighting conditions, a fundamental aspect for the generation of indications. The Snellen test was used to retrieve the information on this characteristic. Here users correctly identify the letters in a graph or table. On the other hand, the color blindness of the users was modeled, since this characteristic is a visual deficiency that causes a series of changes in the colors seen, which would affect during the selection of the best reference object. For more information on the implementation of these two characteristics see (López, G. L., 2016).

4. **Knowledge and Experience Characteristics:** Other characteristics of individuals that differentiate them from the rest and make them unique are the knowledge they have about certain specific objects, and the objects present within an environment, as well as the area of knowledge to which each object belongs and the areas of knowledge of the user.

The main objective of modeling these characteristics was to obtain the degree of familiarity that users possess about the objects contained within a virtual environment, as well as the level of mastery of some areas of knowledge, to infer the probability of recognizing objects related to that area.

During the development of this research, it was considered to represent a set of personal characteristics related to a user or types of users. Modeling a user within a virtual environment requires analyzing their behavior during the development of a real-world activity or task, considering key elements such as objects or conditions of the users within the environment. For this reason, modeling a user is a great challenge since it represents effort, to model it from a conceptual representation, to personalize and adapt the environments, according to the physical and internal needs of them.

Virtual Environment Modeling

Another important aspect in the development of this computational model for generating indications in the location of objects has undoubtedly been to have a semantic description of the virtual environment, based on the concept of object. Two types of objects can be defined, geometric objects and semantic objects. A semantic object is the specific meaning shared by the author and the end user of the environment, and can be associated with one or more geometric objects. Under this theoretical approach and using a data ontology, the semantic description of each virtual environment was developed. This ontology is called world ontology.

The characteristics analyzed and selected for modeling the virtual environment were divided into two types:

- **Common Characteristics:** They are the attributes or properties that make objects unique and special, they contain static information. These properties are visible or not visible, several of them are based on the structure of the object and are defined by observation. These characteristics consider the name, color, size, volume, shape, color coordinates, and position coordinates, among others.
- **Measures of Salience:** These are the properties that represent a measure of salience from different variables, which include individual salience of an object, salience from the context of an object, among others. These measures of salience have been obtained using the algorithms mentioned in the previous section (Computational model of perceptual saliency for 3D objects based on their color, size and shape).

It is important to mention that two types of objects are displayed within a virtual environment: content objects and structure objects. A content object is like a decoration object or other objects such as chairs, sofas, lamps, among others. A structural type object is one that delimits virtual space such as a wall, ceiling, or window. Both types of objects were organized within the data ontology, both are labeled, but only the content objects are selected as reference objects.

Generating Automatic Indications to Locate Object in Evs

The main goal of the development of this research has been to design a software component that in an intelligent way generates directions in natural language for a user to be able to locate objects in a virtual environment.

For the design of this software component three cases were analyzed:

1. The object to be located (OL) is in the same room that the user, but not in the user's field of view.
2. The OL is in another room, and therefore not at the sight of the viewer.
3. The OL is in the user's field of view.

Based on these cases, some algorithms have been designed and developed, to reflect aspects of spatial knowledge of users and thus generate those indications intelligently, so that users can locate objects within a room from their field of vision, or outside their field of view. These algorithms can be adapted to different training areas such as to operate the dashboard of an airplane cabin, or the control of a manufacturing machine, among other options.

The solution designed for the development of these algorithms is described below.

1. The first algorithm designed is responsible for selecting the best reference object within the virtual environment, taking into account the user's prior knowledge with respect of the types of objects present in the scene and the probability that the user remembers the location of the objects by their perceptual salience. With the use of reference objects it has been possible to generate indications in natural language, to help users locate specific objects within a virtual environment.

For the development of this algorithm, it was decided to measure the user's prior knowledge with a numerical measure established by himself. There were three established measures: High at (1), Medium (.5), and Low (0). On the other hand, the probability that the user remembers the location of objects due to their salience, is calculated by a mathematical expression, which includes several variables such as time of oblivion, viewing time, among others. All these mathematical equations have been contributions to the development of this investigation.

2.   The second algorithm performs the process of selecting a relevant spatial relationship between the object to be located and the reference object. For the design of this algorithm it was necessary to go into the knowledge of spatial language and its syntax. Spatial language is actually natural language with spatial references, useful for giving instructions on the location of an object.

For the generation of spatial language, various spatial terms or propositions were analyzed, which were combined with a wide collection of linguistic expressions for the generation of indications. The prepositions or spatial relationships selected for their programming were: On / Under, Close to, Left, Right, Above, Below, In front of, Behind, Inside, Between, and First, second, third, etc. These prepositions were identified as the most used, according to a study carried out with 28 users, where they were asked to generate sentences to indicate the location of an object.

Several criteria were established to program the computational procedure for each of these spatial relationships, since all objects have their own relative location, which is combined with a spatial reference frame. Also, various mathematical representations were considered for the implementation of some of these spatial relationships. The development of this algorithm was especially relevant for the location of the reference object, since it is actually this object that guides the user's view towards the object to be located.

3.   The third algorithm is the one that generates the indications for the location of objects, in each of the aforementioned cases. Each sentence contains information necessary to facilitate the process of locating objects. The sentence structure includes: a locate object, the spatial relationship, a reference object, and the object's most salient property. This expression in the form of a sentence is based on the linguistic structure proposed by (Kelleher, 2003).

There are three novel contributions in this framework: a visual saliency algorithm, a semantic model for locative expressions in natural language containing projective prepositions, and a discourse model that generates indications for the location of objects within a virtual environment. For more information on the implementation of these algorithms see (López, G. L., 2016).

FUTURE TRENDE

There are several directions that are planned to follow to extend this work. The task chosen for this initial research is of a very generic nature, but the underlying algorithms can be applied to numerous practical applications in various areas.

In the future, it is intended to expand the visual characteristics of objects, with characteristics derived from the context such as orientation and change of position of an object.

Further refine the measures of salience of the shape of an object since being one of the most diverse, complex and less relevant characteristics, it was given less weight than the other characteristics. Also, it was thought to be the least salient feature after color and size. A couple of experiments proved otherwise. In the view of the users, it turned out to be more salient than size, thus recognizing color as the most salient feature, followed by shape and finally size.

For this reason, the author is working on the development of a salience new metric based on the points (vertices) of the object. The metric has been designed, implemented and validated with a group of 40 users, testing an experiment that includes 100 objects with abstract shapes and 100 objects with non-abstract shapes, to verify that the salience of the shape of an object can be measured based on your points. Currently, the results are being analyzed to be possibly published, in a short time.

Regarding the salience model with respect to the context, a Multilayer Neural Network is under development. The main objective of the development of this network is to help predict the most salient objects of any virtual environment. At the same time, the author seeks to contrast the results of his experiments with users and the results that the network returns, and verify that its salience model is efficient.

The aim is to improve the selection algorithm of the best reference object, in order to refine some aspects detected in the calculation of the probability of memory, with respect to the central and peripheral vision times.

Also, it is planned to experiment with tasks that involve more complex linguistic constructions. For this reason, the author works with the development of a software tool whose main function is that of a word classifier. It also performs a classification of spatial relationships. With this it is intended that our algorithm generates linguistic expressions with greater affinity, that is, they allow the understanding of speech based on the most widely used language of users. These future lines of research are still in an initial stage, the author only mentions some details towards the final results.

CONCLUSION

The work carried out under the line of investigation of "Virtual Reality in the location of objects" in recent years has been a significant challenge in the area of computing that has had to be faced. It has been a task aimed at generating technological knowledge, to respond to a problem, that is, to a need of the environment with an approach that directly connects (VR) with the fabric of other areas such as: Applied Psychology, Optics, and Mathematics among others.

The (VR) together with the simulation have helped human beings to solve real world challenges, at the same time changing their way of living, working and communicating.

The work presented here represents the first advances in this direction, under the aspects discussed. Far from there being a definitive solution, to the need addressed it is evident that it has already become one of the great challenges for communication between users and virtual environments during the task of locating objects.

The proposal of the model for the generation of indications in the location of objects in virtual environments, has consisted in defining an architecture for a Deterministic Intelligent System that serves as a base, to develop other architectures that can specify systems that solve other needs such as: learning, training on site or complex places, among others.

In addition, the problem has been addressed from different parts, in which functions of the requirements that are posed to the task of locating objects can be added. Those parts have been: the salience model for 3D objects, the user modeling and semantics of virtual environments, the component for the automatic generation of indications for the location of objects in virtual environments. New algorithms such as the texture salience measurement has been incorporated, without any complexity, being activated or deactivated when necessary.

On the other hand, the review of the existing works revealed, on the one hand, that the aspects selected for the design and development of this model would be useful, to address all the ideas gathered. It has also been useful to know the work of other researchers, to see the way in which they usually approach the extraction of the physical characteristics of an object, and reveal the deficiencies that usually exist in their developments. Faced with this situation, the decision was made to design new algorithms for the extraction or characterization of physical characteristics of an object. The need to develop a salience model for 3D objects within virtual environments with the flexibility of incorporating new functions, and demonstrate the flexibility of the design of the new model.

In addition, it has been considered necessary to include practical and comfortable elements such as data ontologies, to manage a unified information storage style, and thus have information related to users and in the virtual environment.

The representation of cognitive and perceptual characteristics has allowed to endow the intelligent system with physical features of the users, to generate indications more related to each type of user. Representing these characteristics can improve the user experience within the virtual environment, since the personalized instructions offered to each user, regarding their position within the environment, will make the task of localization easier.

The incorporation of natural language through written or voice prompts within the model makes the virtual environment a friendlier environment.

It has been proven that virtual reality facilitates the manipulation of objects within an inbuilt environment. It is also possible to simulate user characteristics from complex models and from different perspectives. Finally, through computational algorithms we have implemented natural language as a support tool in the object location process, for the training process. The development of this research has made it possible to offer users predefined indications, combining various aspects of both virtual environment and as of themselves.

In view of the foregoing, the fact of new contributions regarding the systems analyzed in the state of the matter can be concluded.

ACKNOWLEDGMENT

Graciela Lara Lopez would like to thank Dr. Angelica De Antonio Jiménez, for sowing in her the taste for virtual environments, as well as her guidance and accompaniment, for a long time of the development of this research.

REFERENCES

Bryson, S. (1996). Virtual Reality in Scientific Visualization. *Communications of the ACM, 39*(5), 62–71. doi:10.1145/229459.229467

Chen, K., Kovvuri, R., Gao, J., & Nevatia, R. (2017, June). MSRC: Multimodal spatial regression with semantic context for phrase grounding. In *Proceedings of the 2017 ACM on International Conference on Multimedia Retrieval* (pp. 23-31). 10.1145/3078971.3078976

Choungourian, A. (1968). *Color Preferences and Cultural Variation: AmSci*. Southern Universities Press. doi:10.2466/pms.1968.26.3c.1203

D'Agostini, J., Bonetti, L., Salem, A., Passerini, L., Fiacco, G., Lavanda, P., Motti, E., Stocco, M., Gashay, K. T., Abebe, E. G., Alemu, S. M., Haghani, R., Valtolini, A., Strobbe, C., Covre, N., Santolini, G., Armellini, M., Sacchi, T., Ronchese, D., . . . De Cesso, M. (2018, April). An augmented reality virtual assistant to help mild cognitive impaired users in cooking a system able to recognize the user status and personalize the support. In *2018 Workshop on Metrology for Industry 4.0 and IoT* (pp. 12-17). IEEE. 10.1109/METROI4.2018.8428314

Gapp, K.-P. (1995). *Object Localization: Selection of Optimal Reference Objects, Fed*. Rep. of Germany, Universität des Saarlandes.

Hoffman, D. D., & Singh, M. (1997). Salience of visual parts: Elsevier. *Cognition*, *68*(1), 29–78. doi:10.1016/S0010-0277(96)00791-3 PMID:9187064

Huo, Z., & Skubic, M. (2016, May). Natural spatial description generation for human-robot interaction in indoor environments. In *2016 IEEE international conference on smart computing (SMARTCOMP)* (pp. 1-3). IEEE.

Kapur, S. (2003). Psychosis as a state of aberrant salience: A framework linking biology, phenomenology, and pharmacology in schizophrenia. *The American Journal of Psychiatry*, *160*(1), 13–23. doi:10.1176/appi.ajp.160.1.13 PMID:12505794

Kelleher, J. D. (2003). *A Perceptually Based Computational Framework for the Interpretation of Spatial Language Dublin City University* (PhD Thesis). Academic Press.

López, G. L. (2016). *Modelo computacional para la generación de indicaciones en la localización de objetos en entornos virtuales: aspectos espaciales y perceptivos* (Doctoral dissertation). Universidad Politécnica de Madrid.

Lara, G., De Antonio, A., & Peña, A. (2018a). A computational model of perceptual saliency for 3D objects in virtual environments. *Virtual Reality (Waltham Cross)*, *22*(3), 221–234. doi:10.100710055-017-0326-z

Lara, G., Peña, A., Rolon, C., Muñoz, M., & Estrada, E. (2018b). A Computational Measure of Saliency of the Texture Based a Saliency Map by Color. In *International Conference on Software Process Improvement* (pp. 206-215). Springer.

Manetta, C., & Blade, R. A. (1995). Glossary of virtual reality terminology. *International Journal of Virtual Reality*, *1*(2), 35–39. doi:10.20870/IJVR.1995.1.2.2604

Regier, T., & Carlson, L. A. (2001). Grounding Spatial Language in Perception: An Empirical and Computational Investigation. *Journal of Experimental Psychology. General*, *130*(2), 273–298. doi:10.1037/0096-3445.130.2.273 PMID:11409104

Roy, D. K. (2002). Learning Visually-Grounded Words and Syntax for a Scene Description Task. *Computer Speech & Language, 16*(3-4), 1–39. doi:10.1016/S0885-2308(02)00024-4

Stoia, L. (2007). *Noun phrase generation for situated dialogs* (PhD thesis). Ohio State University.

Tian, Y., Wang, H., & Wang, X. (2017). Object localization via evaluation multi-task learning. *Neurocomputing, 253*, 34–41. doi:10.1016/j.neucom.2017.01.098

Vizcaíno Recio, P. (2011). *Sistemas inteligentes para mundos virtuales*. Academic Press.

Yousaf, M., & Wolter, D. (2017, November). Spatial Information Extraction from Natural language Place Description for Incorporating Contextual Variables. In *Proceedings of the 11th Workshop on Geographic Information Retrieval* (pp. 1-2). 10.1145/3155902.3155910

KEY TERMS AND DEFINITIONS

Data Ontology: Is a concrete representation of knowledge. Likewise, it is a specification of a conceptualization. A data ontology is represented as an organized knowledge structure.

Descriptor: Is a mapping from the 3D object space to some highdimensional vector space.

Saliency: Is the process of the association of objects and their representation that attracts attention and captures people's thinking and behavior.

Spatial Reference Frames: Is a structure to specify the object's spatial composition and position; a coordinate system to give directions from different points in space or a mental representation of positions, such as up, down or side.

Voxelization: Is the segmentation of an object into small cubic portions, a unit called voxel, which conform and represent the three-dimensional object.

Chapter 15
An Overview of Applications of Artificial Intelligence Using Different Techniques, Algorithms, and Tools

Yadira Quiñonez

iD https://orcid.org/0000-0002-7604-8532

Universidad Autonoma de Sinaloa, Mexico

ABSTRACT

Technology is currently a crucial benchmark in any application area. In general, society is immersed in the era of digitalization; therefore, incorporating digital technology in different application areas has been more accessible. Nowadays, claiming that adopting artificial intelligence systems in any area is already an emerging need. In this chapter, several artificial intelligence techniques are presented, as well as algorithms and tools that have been used to provide a variety of solutions such as artificial neural networks, convolutional neural networks architecture, AI models, machine learning, deep learning, and bio-inspired algorithms focused mainly on ant colony optimization, response threshold models, and stochastic learning automata. Likewise, the main applications that use AI techniques are described, and the main trends in this discipline are mentioned. This chapter ends with a critical discussion of artificial intelligence advances.

INTRODUCTION

Artificial Intelligence (AI) has had incredible growth since its beginnings until today. Significant progress has been made in different applications, such as computer vision, speech recognition, robotics, semantic parsing, transfer learning, natural language processing, machine learning, and deep learning. In general, there are different fields of application of artificial intelligence; the classification of these fields is directly related to four main areas. First, Natural Language Processing, where the main objective is to capture, process, and respond in natural language to make the machines understand human speech, both

DOI: 10.4018/978-1-7998-7552-9.ch015

Copyright © 2021, IGI Global. Copying or distributing in print or electronic forms without written permission of IGI Global is prohibited.

speaking and writing (Grisot, 2018). Second, through Image Processing or Computer Vision is possible to capture, store, and edit images using different algorithms to perform the analysis (Bhowmik, 2018). Third, using Robotics, it can create computer-controlled mechanical systems that allow performing a variety of different tasks (Waidyasekara, 2020). Fourth, to collect, store, and process various information to derive recommendations or instructions to act on Expert Systems is necessary (Singholi, 2018).

Robotics is one of the most characteristic areas of AI; numerous advances have been developed that have allowed contributing to different areas of application. Traditionally, robotics applications focused on mainly in the industrial sector. In the last two decades, the field of application of robotics has been extended to other sectors, for example, robots for construction, domestic robots, assistance robots, robots in medicine, robots defense, rescue and security (Waidyasekara, 2020). In the last years, automation and control have become a topic of interest for researchers from different areas. mainly, the industrial robotics (Grau, 2017; Yenorkar, 2018) and in the robotic systems applied in the medical area, such as tele-operated surgery (Burgner-Kahrs, 2015) and surgical pattern cutting (Murali, 2015). currently, there are continuous technological developments and various applications such as prostheses (Allen, 2016), orthoses (Niyetkaliyev, 2017), exoskeletons (Tehmat, 2018), and devices for teleoperation to improve human capabilities (Quiñonez, 2020a).

Also, Unmanned Aerial Vehicles (UAV) has been an object mainly study in autonomous exploration in urban environments, exploration, and generation of three-dimensional maps. In this sense, calculating the appropriate movements for a machine to reach a specific point in space is a great challenge. Some works have been developed that focus on the execution of complex algorithms to obtain solutions related to autonomous navigation using reactive algorithms (Quiñonez, 2018), and images classification in real time using convolutional neural networks (Quiñonez, 2020b). On the other hand, Computer Vision (CV) has a multitude of applications in different areas (Rashed, 2019; Kumar, 2019). Certainly, robotics is one of the primary beneficiaries (Ansari, 2020a), because computer vision is one of the most used techniques based on image analysis (Rohan, 2019). Several techniques form the computer vision field, and besides that, they are consistently combined with machine learning algorithms (Ansari, 2020b). In the last decades, pattern recognition has become an exciting research line in the area of robotics and computer vision (Quiñonez, 2015). The classical techniques of pattern recognition more used are template matching, statistical classification, syntactic or structural matching, and neural networks.

The remainder of this paper is organized as follows: section background introduces an overview of previous related works on the application of different techniques of AI, such as IoT applications, machine learning, deep learning, and the most common application domains. In the section of techniques, algorithms, and tools; the main AI techniques, the characteristics, the applications, the different algorithms, and the architectures used for each of the techniques are described in detail. Also, different artificial intelligence platforms are mentioned that allow developers to create their projects in a faster and easier way. In section future trends, a summary of artificial intelligence trends is presented according to the Accenture Technology Vision 2019 Report. Finally, the conclusion section, it summarizes the conclusions of the paper.

BACKGROUND

Artificial intelligence is a topic that has become increasingly relevant in recent years. Currently, AI is already shaping our everyday lives; several scientific progress and automation of many processes have served to solve complex industrial and social problems and to create new and innovative products and solutions. In the last decade, improving daily activities, creating new products, and services have caught the attention of society in general, industry, academia, and research. IoT is a current trend of technological development. It is possible to create new applications that generate new opportunities such as in the economy and society. When it is talking about IoT technology, a scenario is described where any physical object can be turned into a terminal connected to the internet in a domestic environment, to control and monitor different things at home remotely from anywhere and at any time through an internet connection (Vashi, 2017). In the fourth industrial revolution, a set of technologies brings the possibility to transform traditional scheduling approach to the smarter scheduling system. In this sense, there are many IoT applications in different fields, such as e-commerce (Yu, 2017; Liu, 2019), smart home (Malche, 2017; Li, 2019), smart city (Brincat, 2019; Kazmi, 2018), intelligent transportation (Luo, 2019; Sodhro, 2019), agriculture (Ruan, 2019; Togneri, 2019), wearable device (Cirani, 2015; Sharma, 2019), healthcare (Zhu, 2019; Alabdulatif, 2019), and many other domains (Balliu, 2019; Gupta, 2019).

Currently, Machine Learning (ML) is common in all sectors and industries. However, in a particular way, it is transforming healthcare because robust algorithms and prediction models' high levels of precision are used. These algorithms are useful in identifying complicated patterns within a large amount of data. Some of the most common application domains are the recognition of personal characteristics (Choi, 2014; Huang, 2016), face recognition (Atallah, 2018; Jafri, 2020), the handwritten digits recognition (Larasati, 2017; Zhao, 2020), digital forensic analysis (Yang, 2018), traffic sign recognition (Natarajan, 2018; hu, 2018), sentiment analysis (Gutiérrez, 2019), among others.

Some areas of application in healthcare are disease identification, personalized medicine, clinical trial research, medical image segmentation, digital health records, epidemic outbreak prediction, and surgical robotics (Maes, 2019). In the work of Shailaja et al. present a review of the different applications of ML in healthcare as well as describe the techniques used for the prediction of various diseases (Shailaja, 2018). In this research work of Mir and Dhage (2018), has been proposed the use of big data analytics and machine learning in the healthcare domain, to help in early diagnosis of disease on the diabetes patients and be able to help professionals in decision-making for diagnosis. They used four classifiers based on machine learning algorithms, which are naive bayes, support vector machine, random forest, and simple cart classifiers on the diabetes patient dataset using Weka.

Deep Learning (DL) methods have the advantage of being able to learn the features from the input data automatically; it is characterized by to store and access tremendous amount of data. Deep learning techniques increase learning capacity and provide a decision support system at scales that are transforming the future of health care. In the medical applications, the commonly used deep learning algorithms include Convolution Neural Network (CNN) (Liu, 2018; Yamashita, 2018), Recurrent Neural Network (RNN) (Choi, 2017; Khodabakhshi, 2017), Deep Belief Network (DBN) (Chen, 2018; San, 2016), Deep Neural Network (DNN) (Chen, 2017; Gharehbaghi, 2018), and Generative Adversarial Network (GAN) (Emami, 2018; Seeliger, 2018).

TECHNIQUES, ALGORITHMS, AND TOOLS

AI methods or techniques are presented as an alternative to solve complex systems that cannot be resolved using traditional methods. Over the past two decades, a variety of intelligent algorithms have been modeled, including artificial neural networks, evolutionary computing, swarm intelligence, artificial immune systems, fuzzy systems, deductive reasoning, expert systems, machine learning, deep learning, and all these intelligent algorithms are part of the field of AI. Figure 1 shows a summary of the main areas of AI, as well as the most used algorithms and techniques.

Figure 1. Main areas, algorithms, and techniques of artificial intelligence

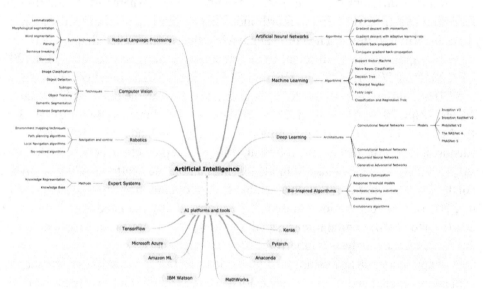

Artificial Neural Networks

Artificial Neural Networks (ANN) have been studied since the '60s until today by various researchers in the scientific community to solve problems in many different application areas. This is mainly based on the functioning of the human brain; they are dynamic auto-adaptive systems, which adjust to the elements that composed the system and adapted to the system's new conditions. As its name indicates, the ANN is composed of several interconnected neurons, where its input parameters are the set of signals received from the environment. After calculations are performed using an activation function (Guresen, 2011), and finally to obtain the output signal. That means, with these systems, it is possible to process information in real-time to create artificial models that solve severe problems, such as time series prediction, data extraction, classification problems, pattern recognition, adaptive control, among others.

In the last decades, pattern recognition has become an interesting research line in the area of robotics and computer vision. The classical techniques of pattern recognition more used are template matching, statistical classification, syntactic or structural matching, and neural networks. As is known, the "knowledge" acquired by neural networks is obtained through a learning algorithm, in which the weights are adjusted by iterations until to achieve desired outputs within the accuracy level established. The back-propagation algorithm is the most used method in the literature; however, over time they have developed new techniques that are more stable and allow convergence faster, such as gradient descent with momentum, gradient descent with adaptive learning rate, gradient descent with momentum, and adaptive learning rate, resilient back-propagation, conjugate gradient back-propagation with fletcher-reeves update, conjugate gradient back-propagation with Powell-Beale restarts, BFGS quasi-newton back-propagation, scaled conjugate gradient back-propagation, among other. A brief description of these algorithms is presented in (Jain, 2000).

Robots' autonomous navigation is one of the main problems among the robots due to its complexity and dynamism as it depends on environmental conditions as the interaction between themselves, persons, or any unannounced change in the environment. Pattern recognition has become an exciting research line in robotics and computer vision; however, the problem of perception extends beyond that of classification; the main idea is training a specified structure to perform the classifying a given pattern. In this work (Quiñonez, 2015), the application of neural network and pattern recognition techniques with back-propagation learning procedures for autonomous robot navigation has been proposed. The work's objective was to achieve that a robot is capable of performing a path in an unknown environment through pattern recognition identifying four classes that indicate what action to perform. The ROS platform and the TurtleBot 2 robot were used to test these results. According to the simulation results, it can conclude that a more significant amount of data entering the network can generate overfitting affecting the generalization of the network because it tends to identify the images only when exactly replicating the conditions in which they were taken. In another work (Quiñonez, 2009), a control architecture for multi-robot systems in dynamic environments was proposed. The low-level behaviors were obtained through artificial neural networks and evolutionary algorithms to achieve collaborative behaviors in a multi-robot system. For example, cooperative tasks were established in a surveillance scenario to emphasize cooperation and competition between robots.

Machine Learning

Machine Learning is a dynamic field of research; it is considered one of the essential AI areas. The main objective is to develop techniques that allow computers to learn from a set of data and make predictions of such data; that is, it allows systems to learn directly from examples, data, and experience (Louridas, 2016). ML approaches are divided into three learning categories: supervised, semi-supervised, and unsupervised. Supervised learning involves labeling the data, such as "acceptable" and "not acceptable," and then the ML network is training with the labeled data. This means that it is necessary to know the data to be able to label them. In unsupervised learning, there is no need to label the data, and the algorithm is used to train the data, which tries to identify the defects on its own. Semi-supervised learning uses the two learnings mentioned before; this means that the ML algorithm uses both labeled and unlabeled data. There are different techniques used in ML, such as Support Vector Machine, Naive Bayes Classification, Decision Tree, K-Nearest Neighbor, Fuzzy Logic, and Classification and Regression Tree (Shailaja, 2018).

The last two decades have awakened different researchers' interest and dedication because it is possible to develop prediction models based on only the information available about a problem. This information can be numerical, qualitative, or mixed. Therefore, it can be said that ML is the result of merging statistical techniques: the calculation power and computational processing. Its main applications have been pattern recognition, natural language processing, and computational learning (Liu, 2017).

Deep Learning

Deep learning is a subfield of machine learning and one of the most famous scientific research trends. In recent years, it has made significant progress and is considered one of the most potent tools because it can handle many data through computational models formed by multiple layers of processing (LeCun, 2015). The field of application is increasingly high; large technology companies such as Google, Facebook, and Microsoft have developed and improved algorithms to process large amounts of information. Thanks to technological advances concerning the most potent data processing units and large capacity storage units, this has been achieved. As a result of this, it has been possible to develop algorithms and models to perform complex operations (Awad, 2015), such as computer vision (Wu, 2017; Goswami, 2018), speech recognition (Sustika, 2017), robotics (Miyajima, 2017), semantic parsing (Heck, 2014), transfer learning (Moriya, 2018), natural language processing (Alshahrani, 2016; He, 2018), among others. In general, there are several deep neural network architectures (Mehta, 2018; Hesamian, 2019; Prabhat, 2020); the most commonly used are: Convolutional Neural Network (CNN), Convolutional Residual Networks (CRNs), Recurrent Neural Network (RNN), Generative Adversarial Networks (GAN), among other. In this work, the CNN architecture is addressed.

Convolutional Neural Networks Architecture

In recent years, the CNN architecture has received substantial attention by different researchers, mainly from the information processing and machine learning community (Gu, 2018). It has become trendy due to thanks to the high-performance GPUs or CPU clouds. CNN is the current architecture for image classification, image segmentation, object recognition, and face recognition. These networks assume explicitly that the input data are images; thereby, a CNN consists of a stack of convolutional modules that carry out feature extraction. They are usually composed of a set of layers that can be grouped by their functionalities. Therefore, the computational complexity of CNN is determined by the convolutional layers, and the number of parameters is related to the fully connected layers (Cheng, 2018). One of the main fields of application by convolutional neural networks is the automotive industry.

In general, CNN consists of a stack of convolutional modules that carry out feature extractions; they are usually composed of a set of layers that can be grouped by their functionalities. Three types of layers are used: Convolutional Layers, Pooling Layers, and Classification Layers. Basically, in the convolution step, the input image features are extracted, and each image is considered a matrix of pixel values. Then, a matrix called filter, kernel, or feature detector is obtained to slide the filter over the image and to compute the dot product; this procedure is called Convolved Feature or Feature Map. Three parameters control the size of the convolved map: Depth (number of filters used for the convolution operation); Stride (number of pixels to slide the filter matrix over the input matrix), and Zero-padding (it is recommended to pad the input matrix with zeros around the border to apply the filter at the edges of the input image matrix). Additionally, every time the convolution operation is performed, at the same time, the procedure called ReLU is carried out, which consists of replacing all negative pixel values in the feature map by zero (Yamashita, 2018; Habibi, 2017).

Pooling Layers are inserted periodically between successive convolutional layers. Its principal function is to progressively reduce the spatial size of the data of the images that are extracted by the convolutional layers to reduce the number of parameters and calculations in the network. It is also used to control overfitting. This layer operates independently in each depth segment of the input data and reduces its spatially; it can be used different types of pooling: Max, Average, Sum. Max Pooling extracts the most substantial element from the map, stores its maximum value, and discards the other values. It can also take the average or the sum of all the elements from the map. However, max pooling is the algorithm that is commonly used in CNN's. The features extracted by the convolutional layers and reduced by the pooling layers are classified in the classification layer. In the fully connected layer, all the nodes are connected to the layer's nodes that precede it. In the fully connected layer, each node of the layer is connected to nodes in the layer that precedes it. That is, in this layer, the Multi-Layer Perceptron and a SoftMax activation function in the output layer are used to use these features to classify the input image into several classes according to the training dataset (Yamashita, 2018; Habibi, 2017).

Transfer learning is a technique that dramatically shortens the process by taking a piece from a model that has been previously trained in a specific task and reuses it in a new model. According to Pan and Yang (2010), "transfer learning techniques try to transfer the knowledge from some previous tasks to a target task when the latter has fewer high-quality training data". This means that it is possible to use the knowledge that a model has learned in a specific task from a large amount of training data in another new task with little objective training data (Weiss, 2016). Recently, in the work of Liang et al. (2019) present a summary of the different types of transfer learning, such as Transitive Transfer Learning, Life-long Transfer Learning, Transfer Reinforcement Learning, and Adversarial Transfer Learning. Also, it mentions the most relevant applications for transfer learning.

Architectures

The Inception V3 model is a deep convolutional neural network and has been designed to perform computational calculations efficiently using 12 times fewer parameters than other models; this allows it to be implemented in less powerful systems (Szegedy, 2016). Inception RastNet V2 was born from the implementation of a more simplified and optimized architecture of Inception V3 and the use of residual connections. Residual connections were introduced by He et al. (2016). These connections allow short-cuts in the model for training very deep architectures.

The MobileNet V2 model is characterized by replacing traditional convolutional layers by "depthwise separable convolutions" to reduce the computational load required by traditional layers and maintain the same accuracy (Sandler, 2018). This architecture is specifically designed for mobile and resource-constrained environments; design models for mobile devices is an excellent challenge because these models must be small and fast, and at the same time, accurate (Tan, 2019). The NASNet-A convolutional network is mainly characterized by using the Neural Architecture Search (NAS) framework (Zoph, 2018). This algorithm considers the most appropriate neural network architecture for each model and uses reinforce-ment learning as a search method to optimize architecture configurations. The first tests carried out used the CIFRA-10 dataset, then transferred the learned architecture to ImageNet. According to the results, the algorithm can recognize objects in real-time with high accuracy. Finally, the PNASNet-5 model is the precursor network of NASNet. This architecture was produced automatically using an improved version of the NAS algorithm. This algorithm is called Progressive Neural Architecture Search, and it is more efficient than reinforcement learning-based methods and evolutionary algorithms (Liu, 2018).

In other previous works, the mentioned models were analyzed and tested using the TensorFlow plat-form. According to the results in this work (Quiñonez, 2019), the Inception V3 model presents better results and high performance in the training, validation, and testing phases than the Inception ResNet V2 model. It can be said that Inception V3 is the one that best adapts and offers an optimal and stable precision in the general behavior of the system. In another work (Quiñonez, 2020), three models have been analyzed: Inception V3, MobileNet V2, and NASNet-A (large) trained in the TensorFlow platform. According to the results, the NASNet-A (large) model presents better results and high performance in the training, validation, and testing phases than the Inception V3 and MobileNet V2 models. It can be deduced that the NASNet-A (large) model did not suffer over-fitting; even though it did not obtain the highest training precision, this can be confirmed in the test stage's accuracy.

In other previous works, the mentioned models were analyzed and tested using the TensorFlow platform. According to the results in this work (Quiñonez, 2019), the Inception V3 model presents better results and high performance in the training, validation, and testing phases than the Inception ResNet V2 model. It can be said that Inception V3 is the one that best adapts and offers an optimal and stable precision in the general behavior of the system. In another work (Quiñonez, 2020), three models have been analyzed: Inception V3, MobileNet V2, and NASNet-A (large) trained in the TensorFlow platform. According to the results, the NASNet-A (large) model presents better results and high performance in the training, validation, and testing phases than the Inception V3 and MobileNet V2 models. It can be deduced that the NASNet-A (large) model did not suffer over-fitting; even though it did not obtain the highest training precision, this can be confirmed in the test stage's accuracy.

Bio-Inspired Algorithms

In the last two decades, several investigations have focused on biological inspiration applications as they provide fascinating examples of functional collective behavior (Robinson, 1992), characterized by rapid changes, high uncertainty, indefinite richness, and limited availability of information. These examples have been useful to study and apply these findings to the design of multi-robot systems. The first works inspired in the behavior of social insects (e.g., ants, bees, birds, and fishes) concerning the study of group behavior have been presented in (Langer, 1994; Mataric, 1995). Most bio-inspired algorithm research focuses on robotics and is designed for specific tasks and different environments to cope with uncertain situations and react quickly to unforeseen changes in the environment. Pfeifer et al. (2007) have presented a study about self-organization, embodiment, and biologically inspired robotics. Recently, in this work of Zeng et al. (2020) proposed a bio-inspired approach that could enable the robot to learn compliant behavior from the interactions and collaborations with the human partner.

Bio-inspired algorithms have been studied by different researchers in computer science, mathematics, and biology; these algorithms are based on the principles and inspiration of biological evolution. Various algorithms are developed in other fields for information processing, decision-making, and optimization objectives, such as genetic algorithms, evolutionary algorithms, response threshold models, learning automata-based probabilistic algorithms, and ant colony optimization algorithms. In this work, it has experimented with different techniques; first, the application of response threshold models inspired by division of labor in social insects, secondly, the application of reinforcement learning algorithm based on learning automata theory, and finally, ant colony optimization-based deterministic algorithms (Quiñonez, 2012; De Lope, 2015).

Ant Colony Optimization

Communities or colonies of social insects have been intensely studied by some researchers (Robinson, 1992), as they provide fascinating examples of functional collective behavior. From a biological standpoint, it has attracted much interest specifically for the way they carry out the division of labor, the fact that members of a colony specialize in specific roles. An insect colony works as an integrated unit capable of processing large amounts of information in a distributed manner. Insect societies are characterized by the division of labor, communication between individuals, and the ability to solve complex problems. These characteristics have long been a source of inspiration and subject of numerous studies, acquiring great relevance for many researchers both in robotics and biology. In this sense, Ant Colony Optimization (ACO) is a meta-heuristic approach introduced in the early 1990s by Dorigo et al. (1992). The general idea of the ACO approach is to solve combinatorial optimization problems based on the behavior of real ants; more specifically, the inspiring source is how ants can find the shortest paths between food sources their nest (Blum, 2005). ACO algorithms are stochastic search procedures based on a probabilistic model (Dorigo, 2005), called by the authors "the pheromone model."

ACO algorithms are based on the following ideas: first, each path followed by an ant is associated with a candidate solution for a given problem. Second, when an ant follows a path, the amount of pheromone deposited on that path is proportional to the quality of the target problem's solution. Moreover, when an ant has to choose between two or more paths, the path(s) with a larger pheromone has a higher probability of being chosen by the ant. As a result, the ants eventually converge to a short path, hopefully, the optimum or a near-optimum solution for the target problem. In essence, the design of an ACO algorithm involves the specification of an appropriate representation of the problem, a method to enforce the construction of valid solutions, a problem-dependent heuristic function, and a rule for pheromone updating.

In this work of de Lope et al. (2012), has been proposed a solution to the self-coordination problem of multi-robot systems in the distribution of heterogeneous multi-tasks by applying Ant Colony Optimization-based deterministic algorithms as well as Learning Automata-based probabilistic algorithms. The efficiency of the methods has been evaluated in terms of the optimal distribution of the existing tasks in such a way that they are all executed using the minimum number of robots. Based on the results, it can be spoken of multi-tasks selection instead of multi-tasks allocation, which means as the agents or robots select the tasks instead of being assigned a task by a central controller.

Response Threshold Models

In insect societies, many factors contribute to an individual's decision to perform a task, including genotypic, environmental, temporal, morphological, physiological, and social factors. However, specific signals can be dominant in stimulating the performance of a particular task. Within a group of insects, an individual performs a task if it observes sufficient signals indicating demand for the task to be completed. These signals might be environmental or in the form of messages from fellow members of society. Such signals can be categorized according to the task to perform, hence the name task-associated stimulus or hereafter stimulus.

Threshold models are based on an understanding of the decentralized mechanisms that underlie the organization of natural swarms such as ants, bees, birds, and fish. Social insects provide one of the best-known examples of self-organized biological behavior. Using local and limited communication, they can accomplish impressive behavioral feats: maintaining the colony's health and caring for their young. A social insect colony operates without any central control, no one is in charge, and no colony member directs another's behavior. With this decentralized way to work (Kube, 2000), social insect colonies are formed by highly cooperative groups that are experts at manipulating and exploiting their environment, defending resources and brood, and allow for task specialization among group members.

The response threshold model assumes that individuals have an inherent threshold to respond to specific task stimuli. In a group, the individuals with the lowest threshold for a task will perform this task more often. The division of labor emerges from the differences between individuals in their thresholds. Different versions of the response threshold model have looked at the effect of threshold reinforcement (Merkle, 2004), colony size (Gautrais, 2002; Jeanson, 2007), number of tasks (Gove, 2009), and genetic diversity (Eckholm, 2011). These studies assume that task stimuli are well-mixed in the environment; Therefore, individuals' cues to choose tasks are global.

Eric Bonabeau et al. (1998) have proposed a simple mathematical model of response thresholds to regulate labor division in insect societies. In this model, it is assumed that each task is associated with a stimulus or set of stimuli so that individuals detect the information of the different stimulus intensity. Therefore, they can assess the demand for a particular task when they contact the stimulus associated. The underlying idea is straightforward when a stimulus exceeds the threshold of an individual's response. An individual is likely to respond to stimuli and engage in the task because the stimulus level associated with that task exceeds its threshold. The intensity of a stimulus decreases as the individual performs the task; therefore, individuals with high thresholds are unlikely to perform the task when other individuals, with lower thresholds, maintain the stimulus intensity below their thresholds. However, when individuals with low thresholds do not complete the task, individuals with high thresholds may engage in task performance because the stimulus intensity exceeds their thresholds.

In a previous work (Quiñonez, 2011b; de Lope, 2013), it was proposed and presented a bio-inspired solution based on response threshold models to solve the problem corresponding to the multi-tasks distribution. More specifically, it addresses the self-election of heterogeneous and specialized tasks by autonomous robots instead of the usual multi-tasks allocation problem in multi-robot systems. An external controller distributes the existing tasks among the individual robots. According to the results obtained, it has been shown that the bio-inspired threshold model can be efficiently applied to solve this self-coordination problem in multi-robot systems.

Stochastic Learning Automata

Learning Automata have made a significant impact and have attracted considerable interest in the last two decades. The first research on learning automata models was developed in Mathematical Psychology (Narendra, 1989), which describes the use of stochastic automata with updating of action probabilities, resulting in a reduction in the number of states comparison with deterministic automata. They can be applied to a broad range of modeling and control problems, control of manufacturing plants, pattern recognition, path planning for the manipulator, among others. An important point to note is that the decisions must be made with very little knowledge concerning the environment to guarantee robust behavior without the system's complete knowledge. In a purely mathematical context, the goal of a learning system is the optimization of a function not known explicitly.

In many problems involving modeling the behavior of a system, sometimes there is insufficient detailed information to determine how the system behaves, or the system's behavior is so complicated that an accurate description of it becomes irrelevant or impossible. In that case, probabilistic and deterministic models are often useful. Probabilistic algorithms model a problem or search for a problem space using a probabilistic model of candidate solutions. Many metaheuristics and computational intelligence algorithms may be considered probabilistic, although the difference with algorithms is the explicit (rather than implicit) use of the tools of probability in problem-solving. In deterministic models, right decisions bring about good outcomes. Given a particular input, it will always produce the same correct output, and the underlying machine will ever pass through the same sequence of states. Therefore, the outcome is deterministic. A straightforward model for deterministic algorithms is the mathematical function, just as a function always produces the same output given a specific input. The difference is that algorithms describe precisely how the output is obtained from the input, whereas abstract functions may be defined implicitly.

Stochastic learning automata operating in stationary and non-stationary random environments have been studied extensively (Thathachar, 2002). Several algorithms have been proposed in the literature (e.g., LR-I algorithm, LR-P algorithm, pursuit algorithm) for the automaton to update its action probability vector. Stochastic learning automata's objective is to determine how past actions and responses should guide the choice of the action at any stage, so when a specific action is performed, the environment provides a random response that is either favorable or unfavorable (Maravall, 2011).

In this sense, a learning automaton is a model for making adaptation decisions using only stochastic information from the environment and not based on detailed models or estimates. It learns to choose the optimal actions of a specific and finite set of actions called its action set, based only on noisy feedback from its environment. At each time instant, the automaton randomly chooses its action set based on its current action probability distribution. That is, the automaton uses the feedback from the environment to updates the action probability distribution and to select the next action.

In another work (Quiñonez, 2011a; de Lope, 2013), it has been presented a solution through automata learning probabilistic based algorithm, applied to the self-coordination problem of multi-robot systems, taking into account the distribution of heterogeneous multi-tasks in a team of mobile robots. The performance indexes or learning curves obtained for each task corresponding to load $L_{i(t)}$ versus time, confirm that the robots can select the existing tasks autonomously and individually without the intervention of any global and central tasks scheduler. It has been shown that the algorithm can be efficiently applied to solve this self-coordination problem in multi-robot systems obtaining truly decentralized solutions.

Artificial Intelligence Platforms

Currently, different artificial intelligence platforms allow developers to create their projects in a faster and easier way. First, TensorFlow (TensorFlow, 2020) is a powerful artificial intelligence library developed and supported by the Google Brain team in 2015 to facilitate the processing of large amounts of data in machine learning and deep neural network research. The TensorFlow architecture works in three parts: first, the data is preprocessed. Second, the model is built, and finally, the model is trained and estimated. TensorFlow is designed to perform complex numerical computations due to its flexible architecture. It allows its implementation in various platforms such as CPUs, GPUs, and TPUs, allowing developers to experiment with new optimizations and training algorithms. Second, Microsoft Azure (Microsoft Azure, 2020) is a collaborative tool that provides an interactive visual workspace that enables you to build easily, test, and deploy predictive analytic models using state-of-the-art machine learning algorithms. Besides, it is possible to quickly scale out model training in the cloud and use any python open source frameworks and tools. Third, Amazon Machine Learning (Amazon ML, 2020) is a powerful and cloud-based service that allows developers to integrate machine learning models into applications in a simple way. Amazon ML allows us to easily obtain predictions for applications using simple APIs without writing a custom prediction code.

FUTURE TRENDS

Nowadays, technology is a fundamental benchmark in any application area, science in coexistence with technology has allowed the creation of tools and devices that simplify daily activities. In the last decade, improving daily activities and creating new products and services has caught society's attention in general, industry, academia, and research. There have been numerous advances and technological developments for different personal applications, at home, in education, in organizations, and the manufacturing industry is no exception since it has become a great interest topic. In this sense, with the emergence of new computer technologies, different algorithms and techniques of Artificial Intelligence, Robotics, Internet of Things (IoT), Cyber-Physical Systems, Big Data Analytics, Cloud Computing, Machine Learning, and Deep Learning have been used to model, control, optimize and process the data generated from the behavior of intelligent manufacturing systems.

Currently, society, in general, is immersed in the era of digitalization. Therefore, companies invest in digital technologies and adopt artificial intelligence systems, mainly due to economic factors. It is possible to reduce operating costs and higher revenues due to the sales market expansion. Moreover, with these systems, organizations acquire technological advantages that allow them to increase the efficiency of resources and reduce the cost of error; this means, with the incorporation of digital technology, expectations and capacities in organizations increase. So, where is Artificial Intelligence headed, and what should we do about it?

According to the Accenture Technology Vision 2019 report, mentions that 83% of business and IT executives agree that digital demographics give their organizations a new way to identify market opportunities for unmet customer needs, and IT leaders report that AI will have the most significant impact on their organizations over the next three years. Organizations are adopting solutions based on artificial intelligence to improve business operations and increase profitability. It is related to the digitally "saturated" technological industries, such as telecommunications, automotive, financial services, consumer goods, transportation, and logistics companies. Digital-born companies are completely changing their transformations and are facilitating consumers with digital products and services. In the other hand, according to the Living in an AI world 2020 report, technology insiders in the KPMG survey says: "more than 751 business insiders from five industries (retail, financial services, healthcare, transportation, and technology) agree to AI adoption in the technology industry". This means that companies that incorporate AI technology comprehensively could double their revenue stream.

It is time to stop, take a look, and ask ourselves: where do some of the world's largest and most influential companies that have invested, researched, and adopted AI in organizations? For example, what do these companies do to be so successful for Google, Facebook, and Amazon? The answer is quite simple; they are companies that are leading in AI deployment at for years, they have invested in and committed to incorporating AI into their organizations. In this context, to be at the forefront, transform the business and deploy the right technology, it is necessary to take into account these considerations in organizations: the rapid shift from experimental to applied technology, automation, AI, analytics, and low-code platforms are converging, enterprise demand is growing, new organizational capabilities are critical, internal governance emerging as a key area, the need to manage AI, and rise of AI-as-a-service, then it can be said that, according to these considerations, artificial intelligence could change the competitive landscape in organizations.

CONCLUSION

These investigations have been directed towards finding efficient and robust methods that serve to solve complex problems in different areas. Nowadays, it can be considered a fully established scientific discipline because emerging new areas of knowledge attempt to improve the effectiveness, efficiency, performance, and robustness of the algorithms, techniques, and tools used. In recent years, a substantial amount of development has emerged in the field of artificial intelligence. Several studies in the literature by some researchers from the scientific community focus on creating intelligent machines and devices capable of imitating the functions and movements of human beings. Therefore, this chapter describes different artificial intelligence techniques, algorithms, and tools that have been used to provide a variety of solutions such as artificial neural networks, convolutional neural networks architecture, AI models, machine learning, deep learning, and bio-inspired algorithms focused mainly on ant colony optimization, response threshold models, and stochastic learning automata.

As a result of modeling a wide variety of AI algorithms, numerous technological advancements have been obtained that focus mainly on mass automation of services to increase productivity, flexibility, quality, and, above all, improve security and reduce people's risk tasks. In this sense, new technologies offer organizations new capabilities to drive a radical change in the workplace. Hence, companies need to adopt new technological strategies that allow them to generate new opportunities to offer better products, services, and meet consumers. However, reaching these intelligent environments is necessary to extend the infrastructure to dynamic environments.

The use of artificial intelligence in various social, economic, and educational areas has been increasing considerably. However, the use of AI for medical diagnosis in different specialties has been widely studied because this is a great variety and high data volume. Therefore, with current AI algorithms, it is possible to train the data, classify it and segment the images to find patterns that maximize precision through historical patterns and detect rapid changes to provide a faster and more effective diagnosis; in this case, it is very common to use deep learning algorithms because its main characteristic is that it can process a high volume of data. At this time, you may be wondering if AI can replace doctors, the answer is no because it is always necessary for the specialist to be present at the time of diagnosis; rather, it is about uniting the experience and knowledge of the specialist doctor with the AI data processing speed, to maximize diagnostic accuracy, minimize errors and make results faster and more effective.

Finally, it is essential to mention that it is already common to be surrounded by an endless number of devices that can be controlled remotely from anywhere, at any time, by anything and anyone. Therefore, incorporating artificial intelligence technology in any area is already an emerging need. In the last year, months perhaps, who has not heard that AI is the future? It is even a topic that generates controversy among people. So, it can be said that the companies that use these technologies have certain advantages over those that do not use them, mainly because they maximize their benefits and face new challenges

REFERENCES

Accenture Technology Vision. (2019). *Full Report*. Retrieved June 1, 2020, from https://www.accenture.com/_acnmedia/PDF-94/Accenture-TechVision-2019-Tech-Trends-Report.pdf

Alabdulatif, A., Khalil, I., Yi, X., & Guizani, M. (2019). Secure Edge of Things for Smart Healthcare Surveillance Framework. *IEEE Access: Practical Innovations, Open Solutions*, 7, 31010–31021. doi:10.1109/ACCESS.2019.2899323

Allen, S. (2016). New prostheses and orthoses step up their game: Motorized knees, robotic hands, and exosuits mark advances in rehabilitation technology. *IEEE Pulse*, 7(3), 6–11. doi:10.1109/MPUL.2016.2539759 PMID:27187533

Alshahrani, S., & Kapetanios, E. (2016). Are Deep Learning Approaches Suitable for Natural Language Processing? In E. Métais, F. Meziane, M. Saraee, V. Sugumaran, & S. Vadera (Eds.), *Natural Language Processing and Information Systems* (pp. 343–349). Springer. doi:10.1007/978-3-319-41754-7_33

Amazon Machine Learning. (2020). *Machine Learning on AWS Documentation*. Retrieved June 1, 2020, from https://aws.amazon.com/machine-learning/

Ansari, S. (2020a). Industrial Application: Real-Time Defect Detection in Industrial Manufacturing. In Building Computer Vision Applications Using Artificial Neural Networks. Apress.

Ansari, S. (2020b). Building a Machine Learning–Based Computer Vision System. In *Building Computer Vision Applications Using Artificial Neural Networks*. Apress. doi:10.1007/978-1-4842-5887-3_4

Atallah, R. R., Kamsin, A., Ismail, M. A., Abdelrahman, S. A., & Zerdoumi, S. (2018). Face Recognition and Age Estimation Implications of Changes in Facial Features: A Critical Review Study. *IEEE Access: Practical Innovations, Open Solutions*, 6, 29290–28304. doi:10.1109/ACCESS.2018.2836924

Awad, M., & Khanna, R. (2015). *Efficient Learning Machines*. Apress. doi:10.1007/978-1-4302-5990-9

Azure, M. (2020). *Azure Documentation*. Retrieved June 1, 2020, from https://docs.microsoft.com/en-us/azure/

Balliu, M., Bastys, I., & Sabelfeld, A. (2019). Securing IoT Apps. *IEEE Security and Privacy*, 17(5), 22–29. doi:10.1109/MSEC.2019.2914190

Bhowmik, D., & Appiah, K. (2018). Embedded Vision Systems: A Review of the Literature. In N. Voros, M. Huebner, G. Keramidas, D. Goehringer, C. Antonopoulos, & P. Diniz (Eds.), *Applied Reconfigurable Computing. Architectures, Tools, and Applications* (pp. 204–216). Springer. doi:10.1007/978-3-319-78890-6_17

Blum, C. (2005). Ant colony optimization: Introduction and recent trends. *Physics of Life Reviews*, 2(4), 353–373. doi:10.1016/j.plrev.2005.10.001

Bonabeau, E., Theraulaz, G., & Deneubourg, J. (1998). Fixed response thresholds and the regulation of division of labor in insect societies. *Bulletin of Mathematical Biology*, 60(4), 753–807. doi:10.1006/bulm.1998.0041

Brincat, A. A., Pacifici, F., & Mazzola, F. (2019). IoT as a Service for Smart Cities and Nations. *IEEE Internet of Things Magazine*, 2(1), 28–31. doi:10.1109/IOTM.2019.1900014

Burgner-Kahrs, J., Rucker, D. C., & Choset, H. (2015). Continuum robots for medical applications: A survey. *IEEE Transactions on Robotics and Automation*, 31(6), 1261–1280. doi:10.1109/TRO.2015.2489500

Chen, G., Tsoi, A., Xu, H., & Zheng, W. J. (2018). Predict effective drug combination by deep belief network and ontology fingerprints. *Journal of Biomedical Informatics*, *85*, 149–154. doi:10.1016/j.jbi.2018.07.024 PMID:30081101

Chen, S., Cowan, C. F. N., & Grant, P. M. (1991). Orthogonal least squares learning for radial basis function networks. *IEEE Transactions on Neural Networks*, *2*(2), 302–309. doi:10.1109/72.80341 PMID:18276384

Chen, T. E., Yang, S., Ho, L. T., Tsai, K. H., Chang, Y. F., Lai, Y. H., Wang, S. S., Tsao, Y., & Wu, C. C. (2017). S1 and S2 heart sound recognition using deep neural networks. *IEEE Transactions on Biomedical Engineering*, *64*(2), 372–380. doi:10.1109/TBME.2016.2559800 PMID:28113191

Choi, E., Schuetz, A., Stewart, W. F., & Sun, J. (2017). Using recurrent neural network models for early detection of heart failure onset. *Journal of the American Medical Informatics Association*, *24*(2), 361–370. PMID:27521897

Choi, W., Chao, Y. W., Pantofaru, C., & Savarese, S. (2014). Discovering Groups of People in Images. In D. Fleet, T. Pajdla, B. Schiele, & T. Tuytelaars (Eds.), *Computer Vision* (pp. 417–433). Springer.

Cirani, S., & Picone, M. (2015). Wearable Computing for the Internet of Things. *IT Professional*, *17*(5), 35–41. doi:10.1109/MITP.2015.89

de Lope, J., Maravall, D., & Quiñonez, Y. (2012). Decentralized Multi-tasks Distribution in Heterogeneous Robot Teams by Means of Ant Colony Optimization and Learning Automata. In E. Corchado, V. Snášel, A. Abraham, M. Woźniak, M. Graña, & S. B. Cho (Eds.), *Hybrid Artificial Intelligent Systems* (pp. 103–114). Springer. doi:10.1007/978-3-642-28942-2_10

de Lope, J., Maravall, D., & Quiñonez, Y. (2013). Response threshold models and stochastic learning automata for self-coordination of heterogeneous multi-task distribution in multi-robot systems. *Robotics and Autonomous Systems*, *61*(7), 714–720. doi:10.1016/j.robot.2012.07.008

de Lope, J., Maravall, D., & Quiñonez, Y. (2015). Self-organizing techniques to improve the decentralized multi-task distribution in multi-robot systems. *Neurocomputing*, *163*, 47–55. doi:10.1016/j.neucom.2014.08.094

Dorigo, M. (1992). *Optimization, learning and natural algorithms* (Doctoral dissertation). Dipartimento di Elettronica, Politecnico di Milano, Milan.

Dorigo, M., & Blum, C. (2005). Ant colony optimization theory: A survey. *Theoretical Computer Science*, *344*(2-3), 243–278. doi:10.1016/j.tcs.2005.05.020

Eckholm, B., Anderson, K., Weiss, M., & DeGrandi-Hoffman, G. (2011). Intracolonial genetic diversity in honeybee (Apis mellifera) colonies increases pollen foraging efficiency. *Behavioral Ecology and Sociobiology*, *65*(5), 1037–1044. doi:10.100700265-010-1108-8

Emami, H., Dong, M., Nejad-Davarani, S. P., & Glide-Hurst, C. K. (2018). Generating synthetic CTs from magnetic resonance images using generative adversarial networks. *Medical Physics*, *45*(8), 3627–3636. doi:10.1002/mp.13047 PMID:29901223

Gautrais, J., Theraulaz, G., Deneubourg, J. L., & Anderson, C. (2002). Emergent polyethism as a consequence of increased colony size in insect societies. *Journal of Theoretical Biology, 215*(3), 363–373. doi:10.1006/jtbi.2001.2506 PMID:12054843

Gharehbaghi, A., & Babic, A. (2018). Structural risk evaluation of a deep neural network and a Markov model in extracting medical information from phonocardiography. *Studies in Health Technology and Informatics, 251*, 157–160. PMID:29968626

Goswami, T. (2018). Impact of Deep Learning in Image Processing and Computer Vision. In J. Anguera, S. Satapathy, V. Bhateja, & K. Sunitha (Eds.), Microelectronics, Electromagnetics and Telecommunications (pp. 475-485). Springer. doi:10.1007/978-981-10-7329-8_48

Gove, R., Hayworth, M., Chhetri, M., & Rueppell, O. (2009). Division of labour and social insect colony performance in relation to task and mating number under two alternative response threshold models. *Insectes Sociaux, 56*(3), 319–331. doi:10.100700040-009-0028-y

Grau, A., Indri, M., Bello, L. L., & Sauter, T. (2017). Industrial robotics in factory automation: from the early stage to the Internet of Things. In *Proceedings of Conference of the IEEE Industrial Electronics Society* (pp. 6159-6164). IEEE Press. 10.1109/IECON.2017.8217070

Grisot, C. (2018). Application to Natural Language Processing and Machine Translation. In *Cohesion, Coherence and Temporal Reference from an Experimental Corpus Pragmatics Perspective. Yearbook of Corpus Linguistics and Pragmatics* (pp. 263–288). Springer. doi:10.1007/978-3-319-96752-3_7

Gu, J., Wang, Z., Kuen, J., Ma, L., Shahroudy, A., Shuai, B., Liu, T., Wang, X., Wang, G., Cai, J., & Chen, T. (2018). Recent Advances in Convolutional Neural Networks. *Journal Pattern Recognition, 77*, 354–377. doi:10.1016/j.patcog.2017.10.013

Gupta, K., & Johari, R. (2019). IOT based Electrical Device Surveillance and Control System. In *Proceedings of International Conference on Internet of Things: Smart Innovation and Usages* (pp. 1-5). IEEE Press. 10.1109/IoT-SIU.2019.8777342

Guresen, E., & Kayakutlu, G. (2011). Definition of artificial neural networks with comparison to other networks. *Procedia Computer Science, 3*, 426–433. doi:10.1016/j.procs.2010.12.071

Gutiérrez, L., Bekios-Calfa, J., & Keith, B. (2019). A Review on Bayesian Networks for Sentiment Analysis. In J. Mejia, M. Muñoz, Á. Rocha, A. Peña, & M. Pérez-Cisneros (Eds.), *Trends and Applications in Software Engineering* (pp. 111–120). Springer. doi:10.1007/978-3-030-01171-0_10

Habibi, A. H., & Jahani, H. E. (2017). Guide to Convolutional Neural Networks. Springer Nature. doi:10.1007/978-3-319-57550-6

He, K., Zhang, X., Ren, S., & Sun, J. (2016). Deep residual learning for image recognition. In *Proceedings of Conference on Computer Vision and Pattern Recognition* (pp. 770-778). Las Vegas, NV: IEEE Press.

He, X., & Deng, L. (2018). Deep Learning in Natural Language Generation from Images. In L. Deng & Y. Liu (Eds.), *Deep Learning in Natural Language Processing* (pp. 289–307). Springer. doi:10.1007/978-981-10-5209-5_10

Heck, L., & Huang, H. (2014). Deep learning of knowledge graph embeddings for semantic parsing of Twitter dialogs. In *Proceedings of Global Conference on Signal and Information Processing* (pp. 597-601). Atlanta, GA: IEEE Press. 10.1109/GlobalSIP.2014.7032187

Hesamian, M. H., Jia, W., He, X., & Kennedy, P. (2019). Deep Learning Techniques for Medical Image Segmentation: Achievements and Challenges. *Journal of Digital Imaging, 32*(4), 582–596. doi:10.100710278-019-00227-x PMID:31144149

Hu, W., Zhuo, Q., Zhang, C., & Li, J. (2018). Fast Branch Convolutional Neural Network for Traffic Sign Recognition. *Intelligent Transportation Systems, 9*(3), 114–126.

Huang, F., Sun, T., & Bu, F. (2016). Generation of person-specific 3D model based on single photograph. In *Proceedings of International Conference on Computer and Communications* (pp. 704-707). IEEE Press.

Jafri, S., Chawan, S., & Khan, A. (2020). Face Recognition using Deep Neural Network with "Liveness-Net. In *Proceedings of International Conference on Inventive Computation Technologies* (pp. 145-148). IEEE Press.

Jain, A. K., Duin, R. P. W., & Mao, J. (2000). Statistical pattern recognition: A review. *IEEE Transactions on Pattern Analysis and Machine Intelligence, 22*(1), 4–37. doi:10.1109/34.824819

Jeanson, R., Fewell, J. H., Gorelick, R., & Bertram, S. (2007). Emergence of increased division of labor as a function of group size. *Behavioral Ecology and Sociobiology, 62*(2), 289–298. doi:10.100700265-007-0464-5

Kazmi, A., Serrano, M., & Soldatos, J. (2018). VITAL-OS: An Open Source IoT Operating System for Smart Cities. *IEEE Communications Standards Magazine, 2*(2), 71–77. doi:10.1109/MCOMSTD.2018.1700016

Khodabakhshi, M. B., & Moradi, M. H. (2017). The attractor recurrent neural network based on fuzzy functions: An effective model for the classification of lung abnormalities. *Computers in Biology and Medicine, 1*(84), 124–136. doi:10.1016/j.compbiomed.2017.03.019 PMID:28363113

Kube, R. C., & Bonabeau, E. (2000). Cooperative transport by ants and robots. *Robotics and Autonomous Systems, 30*(1-2), 85–101. doi:10.1016/S0921-8890(99)00066-4

Kumar, A., & Das, S. D. (2019). Bird Species Classification Using Transfer Learning with Multi-stage Training. In C. Arora & K. Mitra (Eds.), *Computer Vision Applications* (pp. 28–38). Springer. doi:10.1007/978-981-15-1387-9_3

Langer, D., Rosenblatt, J. K., & Hebert, M. (1994). A Behavior-based system for off-road navigation. *Transactions on Robotics and Automation, 10*(6), 776–782. doi:10.1109/70.338532

Larasati, R., & KeungLam, H. (2017). Handwritten digits recognition using ensemble neural networks and ensemble decision tree. In *International Conference on Smart Cities, Automation Intelligent Computing Systems* (pp. 99-104). IEEE Press. 10.1109/ICON-SONICS.2017.8267829

LeCun, Y., Bengio, Y., & Hinton, G. (2015). Deep Learning. *Nature, 521*(7553), 436–444. doi:10.1038/nature14539 PMID:26017442

Li, W., Logenthiran, T., Phan, V., & Woo, W. L. (2019). A Novel Smart Energy Theft System (SETS) for IoT-Based Smart Home. *IEEE Internet of Things Journal, 6*(3), 5531-5539.

Liang, H., Fu, W., & Yi, F. (2019). A Survey of Recent Advances in Transfer Learning. In *Proceedings of International Conference on Communication Technology* (pp. 1516-1523). IEEE Press. 10.1109/ICCT46805.2019.8947072

Liu, C., Xiao, Y., Javangula, V., Hu, Q., Wang, S., & Cheng, X. (2019). NormaChain: A Blockchain-Based Normalized Autonomous Transaction Settlement System for IoT-Based E-Commerce. *IEEE Internet of Things Journal, 6*(3), 4680–4693. doi:10.1109/JIOT.2018.2877634

Liu, C., Zoph, B., Neumann, M., Shlens, J., Hua, W., Li, L. J., Fei-Fei, L., Yuille, A., Huang, K., & Murphy, K. (2018). Progressive Neural Architecture Search. In V. Ferrari, M. Hebert, C. Sminchisescu, & Y. Weiss (Eds.), *Computer Vision* (pp. 19–35). Springer.

Liu, W., Wang, Z., Liu, X., Zeng, N., Liu, Y., & Alsaadi, F. E. (2017). A survey of deep neural network architectures and their applications. *Neurocomputing, 234*, 11–26. doi:10.1016/j.neucom.2016.12.038

Liu, W., Zhang, M., Zhang, Y., Liao, Y., Huang, Q., Chang, S., Wang, H., & He, J. (2018). Real-Time Multilead Convolutional Neural Network for Myocardial Infarction Detection. *IEEE Journal of Biomedical and Health Informatics, 22*(5), 1434–1444. doi:10.1109/JBHI.2017.2771768 PMID:29990164

Louridas, P., & Ebert, C. (2016). Machine Learning. *IEEE Software, 33*(5), 110–115. doi:10.1109/MS.2016.114

Luo, X., Zhang, H., Zhang, Z., Yu, Y., & Li, K. (2019). A New Framework of Intelligent Public Transportation System Based on the Internet of Things. *IEEE Access: Practical Innovations, Open Solutions, 7*, 55290–55304. doi:10.1109/ACCESS.2019.2913288

Maes, F., Robben, D., Vandermeulen, D., & Suetens, P. (2019). The Role of Medical Image Computing and Machine Learning in Healthcare. In E. Ranschaert, S. Morozov, & P. Algra (Eds.), *Artificial Intelligence in Medical Imaging* (pp. 9–23). Springer. doi:10.1007/978-3-319-94878-2_2

Malche, T., & Maheshwary, P. (2017). Internet of Things (IoT) for building smart home system. In *Proceedings of International Conference on IoT in Social, Mobile, Analytics and Cloud* (pp. 65-70). IEEE Press.

Maravall, D., & de Lope, J. (2011). Fusion of learning automata theory and granular inference systems: ANLAGIS. Applications to Pattern Recognition and Machine Learning. *Neurocomputing, 74*(8), 1237–1242. doi:10.1016/j.neucom.2010.07.024

Matarić, M. J. (1995). From Local Interactions to Collective Intelligence. In L. Steels (Ed.), *The Biology and Technology of Intelligent Autonomous Agents* (pp. 275–295). Springer. doi:10.1007/978-3-642-79629-6_11

Mehta, A., Parekh, Y., & Karamchandani, S. (2018). Performance Evaluation of Machine Learning and Deep Learning Techniques for Sentiment Analysis. In Information Systems Design and Intelligent Applications (pp. pp 463-471). Springer. doi:10.1007/978-981-10-7512-4_46

Merkle, D., & Middendorf, M. (2004). Dynamic polyethism and competition for tasks in threshold reinforcement models of social insects. *Adaptive Behavior - Animals, Animats, Software Agents, Robots. Adaptive Systems*, *12*(3-4), 251–262.

Mir, A., & Dhage, S. N. (2018). Diabetes Disease Prediction Using Machine Learning on Big Data of Healthcare. In *Proceedings of International Conference on Computing Communication Control and Automation* (pp. 1-6). IEEE Press. 10.1109/ICCUBEA.2018.8697439

Miyajima, R. (2017). Deep Learning Triggers a New Era in Industrial Robotics. *IEEE MultiMedia*, *24*(4), 91–96. doi:10.1109/MMUL.2017.4031311

Moriya, S., & Shibata, C. (2018). Transfer Learning Method for Very Deep CNN for Text Classification and Methods for its Evaluation. In *Proceedings of Annual Computer Software and Applications Conference* (pp. 153-158). IEEE Press. 10.1109/COMPSAC.2018.10220

Murali, A., Sen, S., Kehoe, B., Garg, A., Mcfarland, S., Patil, S., Boyd, W. D., Lim, S., Abbeel, P., & Goldberg, K. (2015). Learning by observation for surgical subtasks: multilateral cutting of 3D viscoelastic and 2D Orthotropic Tissue Phantoms. In *Proceeding of International Conference on Robotics and Automation* (pp. 1202–1209). IEEE Press. 10.1109/ICRA.2015.7139344

Narendra, K. S., & Thathachar, M. A. L. (1989). *Learning automata: an introduction*. Prentice-Hall, Inc.

Natarajan, S., Annamraju, A. K., & Baradkar, C. S. (2018). Traffic sign recognition using weighted multi-convolutional neural network. *IET Intelligent Transport Systems*, *12*(10), 1396–1405. doi:10.1049/iet-its.2018.5171

Niyetkaliyev, A. S., Hussain, S., Ghayesh, M. H., & Alici, G. (2017). Review on design and control aspects of robotic shoulder rehabilitation orthoses. *IEEE Transactions on Human-Machine Systems*, *47*(6), 1134–1145. doi:10.1109/THMS.2017.2700634

Pan, S. J., & Yang, Q. (2010). A survey on transfer learning. *Transactions on Knowledge and Data Engineering*, *22*(10), 1345–1359. doi:10.1109/TKDE.2009.191

Pfeifer, R., Lungarella, M., & Iida, F. (2007). Self-organization, embodiment, and biologically inspired robotics. *American Association for the Advancement of Science*, *318*(5853), 1088–1093. doi:10.1126cience.1145803 PMID:18006736

Prabhat, N., & Kumar-Vishwakarma, D. (2020). Comparative Analysis of Deep Convolutional Generative Adversarial Network and Conditional Generative Adversarial Network using Hand Written Digits. In *Proceedings of International Conference on Intelligent Computing and Control Systems* (pp. 1072-1075). IEEE Press.

Quiñonez, Y., Barrera, F., Bugueño, I., & Bekios-Calfa, J. (2018). Simulation and path planning for quadcopter obstacle avoidance in indoor environments using the ROS framework. In J. Mejia, M. Muñoz, Á. Rocha, Y. Quiñonez, & J. Calvo-Manzano (Eds.), *Trends and Applications in Software Engineering* (pp. 295–304). Springer. doi:10.1007/978-3-319-69341-5_27

Quiñonez, Y., de Lope, J., & Maravall, D. (2009). Cooperative and Competitive Behaviors in a Multi-robot System for Surveillance Tasks. In R. Moreno-Díaz, F. Pichler, & A. Quesada-Arencibia (Eds.), *EUROCAST* (pp. 437–444). Springer. doi:10.1007/978-3-642-04772-5_57

Quiñonez, Y., de Lope, J., & Maravall, D. (2011b). Bio-inspired Decentralized Self-coordination Algorithms for Multi-heterogeneous Specialized Tasks Distribution in Multi-Robot Systems. In J. M. Ferrández, J. R. Álvarez Sánchez, F. de la Paz, & F. J. Toledo (Eds.), *Foundations on Natural and Artificial Computation* (pp. 30–39). Springer. doi:10.1007/978-3-642-21344-1_4

Quiñonez, Y., Lizarraga, C., Peraza, J., & Zatarain, O. (2020b). Image recognition in UAV videos using convolutional neural networks. *IET Software*, *14*(2), 176–181. doi:10.1049/iet-sen.2019.0045

Quiñonez, Y., Maravall, D., & de Lope, J. (2011a). Stochastic Learning Automata for Self-coordination in Heterogeneous Multi-Tasks Selection in Multi-Robot Systems. In I. Batyrshin & G. Sidorov (Eds.), *Advances in Artificial Intelligence* (pp. 443–453). Springer. doi:10.1007/978-3-642-25324-9_38

Quiñonez, Y., Maravall, D., & de Lope, J. (2012). Application of Self-Organizing Techniques for the Distribution of Heterogeneous Multi-Tasks in Multi-Robot Systems. In *Proceedings of Electronics, Robotics and Automotive Mechanics Conference* (pp. 66-71). IEEE Press 10.1109/CERMA.2012.19

Quiñonez, Y., Ramirez, M., Lizarraga, C., Tostado, I., & Bekios, J. (2015). Autonomous Robot Navigation Based on Pattern Recognition Techniques and Artificial Neural Networks. In J. Ferrández, J. Álvarez-Sánchez, F. de la Paz, F. Toledo-Moreo, & H. Adeli (Eds.), *Bioinspired Computation in Artificial Systems* (pp. 320–329). Springer. doi:10.1007/978-3-319-18833-1_34

Quiñonez, Y., Zatarain, O., Lizarraga, C., & Peraza, J. (2019). Using Convolutional Neural Networks to Recognition of Dolphin Images. In J. Mejia, M. Muñoz, Á. Rocha, A. Peña, & M. Pérez-Cisneros (Eds.), *Trends and Applications in Software Engineering* (pp. 236–245). Springer. doi:10.1007/978-3-030-01171-0_22

Quiñonez, Y., Zatarain, O., Lizarraga, C., Peraza, J., & Mejía, J. (2020a). Algorithm Proposal to Control a Robotic Arm for Physically Disable People Using the LCD Touch Screen. In J. Mejia, M. Muñoz, Á. Rocha, & J. Calvo-Manzano (Eds.), *Trends and Applications in Software Engineering* (pp. 187–207). Springer. doi:10.1007/978-3-030-33547-2_15

Rashed, H., Yogamani, S., El-Sallab, A., Das, A., & El-Helw, M. (2019). Depth Augmented Semantic Segmentation Networks for Automated Driving. In C. Arora & K. Mitra (Eds.), *Computer Vision Applications* (pp. 1–13). Springer. doi:10.1007/978-981-15-1387-9_1

Rehmat, N., Zuo, J., Meng, W., Liu, Q., Xie, S. Q., & Liang, H. (2018). Upper limb rehabilitation using robotic exoskeleton systems: A systematic review. *International Journal of Intelligent Robotics and Applications*, *2*(3), 283–295. doi:10.100741315-018-0064-8

Robinson, G. (1992). Regulation of division of labor in insect societies. *Annual Review of Entomology*, *37*(1), 637–665. doi:10.1146/annurev.en.37.010192.003225 PMID:1539941

Rohan, R. D., Patel, Z., Yadavannavar, S.C., Sujata, C., & Mudengudi, U. (2019). Image Segmentation and Geometric Feature Based Approach for Fast Video Summarization of Surveillance Videos. In Computer Vision Applications (pp. 79-88). Springer.

Ruan, J., Jiang, H., Zhu, C., Hu, X., Shi, Y., Liu, T., Rao, W., & Chan, F. T. S. (2019). Agriculture IoT: Emerging Trends, Cooperation Networks, and Outlook. *IEEE Wireless Communications, 26*(6), 56–63. doi:10.1109/MWC.001.1900096

San, P. P., Ling, S. H., & Nguyen, H. T. (2016). Deep learning framework for detection of hypoglycemic episodes in children with type 1 diabetes. In *Proceedings of Conference on Engineering in Medicine Biology Society* (pp. 3503-3506). IEEE Press. 10.1109/EMBC.2016.7591483

Sandler, M., Howard, A., Zhu, M., Zhmoginov, A., & Chen, L. (2018). MobileNet V2: inverted residuals and linear bottlenecks. In *Proceedings of Conference on Computer Vision and Pattern Recognition* (pp. 4510-4520). IEEE Press.

Seeliger, K., Güçlü, U., Ambrogioni, L., Güçlütürk, Y., & van Gerven, M. A. J. (2018). Generative adversarial networks for reconstructing natural images from brain activity. *NeuroImage, 181*, 775–785. doi:10.1016/j.neuroimage.2018.07.043 PMID:30031932

Shailaja, K., Seetharamulu, B., & Jabbar, M. A. (2018). Machine Learning in Healthcare: A Review. In *Proceedings of International Conference on Electronics, Communication and Aerospace Technology* (pp. 910-914). IEEE Press.

Sharma, V., Vineeta, Som, S., & Khatri, S. K. (2019). Future of Wearable Devices Using IoT Synergy in AI. In *Proceedings of International conference on Electronics, Communication and Aerospace Technology* (pp. 138-142). IEEE Press. 10.1109/ICECA.2019.8821915

Singholi, A. K. S., & Agarwal, D. (2018). Review of Expert System and Its Application in Robotics. In Intelligent Communication, Control and Devices (pp. 1253-1265). Springer. doi:10.1007/978-981-10-5903-2_131

Sodhro, A. H., Obaidat, M. S., Abbasi, Q. H., Pace, P., Pirbhulal, S., Yasar, A. U. H., Fortino, G., Imran, M. A., & Qaraqe, M. (2019). Quality of Service Optimization in an IoT-Driven Intelligent Transportation System. *IEEE Wireless Communications, 26*(6), 10–17. doi:10.1109/MWC.001.1900085

Sustika, R., Yuliani, A. R., Zaenudin, E., & Pardede, H. F. (2017). On comparison of deep learning architectures for distant speech recognition. In *Proceedings of International conferences on Information Technology, Information Systems and Electrical Engineering* (pp. 17-21). IEEE Press. 10.1109/ICITISEE.2017.8285488

Szegedy, C., Vanhoucke, V., Ioffe, S., Shlens, J., & Wojna, Z. (2016). Rethinking the inception architecture for computer vision. In *Proceedings of Conference on Computer Vision and Pattern Recognition* (pp. 2818-2826). IEEE Press. 10.1109/CVPR.2016.308

Tan, M., Chen, B., Pang, R., Vasudevan, V., Sandler, M., Howard, A., & Le, Q. V. (2019). MnasNet: Platform-Aware Neural Architecture Search for Mobile. In *Proceedings of Conference on Computer Vision and Pattern Recognition* (pp. 2815-2823). IEEE Press. 10.1109/CVPR.2019.00293

TensorFlow. (2020). *TensorFlow Documentation*. Retrieved June 1, 2020, from https://www.tensorflow.org/api_docs

Thathachar, M. A. L., & Sastry, P. S. (2002). Varieties of learning automata: An overview. *Transactions on Systems, Man, and Cybernetics, 32*(6), 711–722. doi:10.1109/TSMCB.2002.1049606 PMID:18244878

Togneri, R., Kamienski, C., Dantas, R., Prati, R., Toscano, A., Soininen, J. P., & Cinotti, T. S. (2019). Advancing IoT-Based Smart Irrigation. *IEEE Internet of Things Magazine, 2*(4), 20–25. doi:10.1109/IOTM.0001.1900046

Vashi, S., Ram, J., Modi, J., Verma, S., & Prakash, C. (2017). Internet of Things (IoT): A vision, architectural elements, and security issues. In *Proceedings of International Conference on IoT in Social, Mobile, Analytics and Cloud* (pp. 492-496). IEEE Press. 10.1109/I-SMAC.2017.8058399

Waidyasekara, K. G. A. S., Gamlath, M., & Pandithawatta, S. (2020). Application of Robotic Technology for the Advancement of Construction Industry in Sri Lanka: A Review. In *Proceeding of International Conference on Engineering, Project, and Production Management* (pp. 43-54). Springer. 10.1007/978-981-15-1910-9_4

Weiss, K., Khoshgoftaar, T. M., & Wang, D. J. (2016). A survey on transfer learning. *Journal of Big Data, 3*(9), 1–40.

Wu, Q., Liu, Y., Li, Q., Jin, S., & Li, F. (2017). The application of deep learning in computer vision. In *Proceedings of Chinese Automation Congress* (pp. 6522-6527). IEEE Press. 10.1109/CAC.2017.8243952

Yamashita, R., Nishio, M., Do, R. K. G., & Togashi, K. (2018). Convolutional neural networks: An overview and application in radiology. *Insights Into Imaging, 9*(4), 611–629. doi:10.100713244-018-0639-9 PMID:29934920

Yang, B., Sun, X., Cao, E., Hu, W., & Chen, X. (2018). Convolutional neural network for smooth filtering detection. *IET Image Processing, 12*(8), 1432–1438. doi:10.1049/iet-ipr.2017.0683

Yenorkar, R., & Chaskar, U. M. (2018). GUI based pick and place robotic arm for multipurpose industrial applications. In *Proceeding of International Conference on Intelligent Computing and Control Systems* (pp. 200-203). IEEE Press. 10.1109/ICCONS.2018.8663079

Yu, H., & Zhang, X. (2017). Research on the Application of IoT in E-Commerce. In *Proceedings of International Conference on Computational Science and Engineering and International Conference on Embedded and Ubiquitous Computing* (pp. 434-436). IEEE Press. 10.1109/CSE-EUC.2017.269

Zeng, C., Yang, C., & Chen, Z. (2020). Bio-inspired robotic impedance adaptation for human-robot collaborative tasks. *Science China. Information Sciences, 63*(7), 170–201. doi:10.100711432-019-2748-x

Zhao, H., & Liu, H. (2020). Multiple classifiers fusion and CNN feature extraction for handwritten digits recognition. *Granular Computing, 5*, 411-418.

Zhu, H., Wu, C. K., Koo, C. H., Tsang, Y. T., Liu, Y., Chi, H. R., & Tsang, K. F. (2019). Smart Healthcare in the Era of Internet-of-Things. *IEEE Consumer Electronics Magazine, 8*(5), 26-30.

Zoph, B., Vasudevan, V., Shlens, J., & Le, Q. V. (2018). Learning transferable architectures for scalable image recognition. In *Proceedings of Conference on Computer Vision and Pattern Recognition* (pp. 8697-8710). IEEE Press. 10.1109/CVPR.2018.00907

KEY TERMS AND DEFINITIONS

Automata: Is a machine designed to automatically follow a predetermined sequence of operations or respond to encoded instructions.

Bioinspired Algorithms: Are metaheuristics that imitate methods for solving optimization problems in natural processes.

Dataset: A data collection containing instances. Each column represents a feature in a typical dataset, and each row represents a member of the dataset.

Learning Automata: Are methods used to solve many problems that are too complex, highly non-linear, uncertain, incomplete, or non-stationary.

Self-Organization Theory: This theory explains the behavioral aspects of social insects; in particular, it shows how the complexity of the collective behavior of these insects may arise from the interaction among individuals who exhibit a simple behavior.

Supervised Learning: Supervised learning is used when it has full knowledge of each instance's actual values or labels. Basically, it uses a training dataset to develop a prediction model by consuming input data and output values.

Unsupervised Learning: Unsupervised learning is used when the attributes to be predicted are unknown in all instances. This learning generally involves learning structured patterns in the data by rejecting pure unstructured noise.

Chapter 16
Data Science Process for Smart Cities

Elsa Estrada
CUCEI, Universidad de Guadalajara, Mexico

Martha Patricia Martínez Vargas
CUCEA, Universidad de Guadalajara, Mexico

ABSTRACT

Smart cities have been proposed as information technology strategies to generate solutions for the benefit of large cities to improve their quality of life, through phenomena identification tools that use artificial intelligence. Some work has been aimed at developing the infrastructure for monitoring events and the Internet of things, others merely on data analytics without an application system context. This work cites various investigations on data science processes of the smart cities and reports some of its works whose main topics are planning for the start of a smart city, the framework for the analysis of smart cities, and smart cities big data algorithms for sensors location. In these cases, the experiences in these cases are described as well as the trend towards a new process with the form of monitoring-analysis-evaluation-found pattern-driving object-decision-making and the future of smart cities is finally discussed.

INTRODUCTION

The Smart Cities have been proposed as Information Technology (IT) strategies to generate solutions in favor of big cities for the benefit of their quality of life. The terms embedded in this paradigm are the Internet of Things (IoT), Big Data, and data analytics. They are implemented in a monitoring-analytics-dispatch process. Here apparently human supervision has no interference; so, the word Smart is often related to the automation process (Mentsiev, Engel, & Gudaeva, 2020) or with the mere use of technologies. But for Smart Cities, the principal actors are the government, industry, citizens, and the academy, (Thompson, 2016) therefore automation-technologies and communities are intertwined in these solutions. Some governments for example, London, Singapure, Seoul and New York have launched Smart City projects at the country level, promoting Open Data and citizen participation through their web portals,

DOI: 10.4018/978-1-7998-7552-9.ch016

Copyright © 2021, IGI Global. Copying or distributing in print or electronic forms without written permission of IGI Global is prohibited.

while the private sector and industry have emphatically enlisted in the issue of building infrastructure for monitoring events and the development of applications using sensors and data analytics. Citizens have also been involved in decision-making through popular applications for community projects, which aims to induce activities for the improvement process of the entire environment.

This chapter aims to propose and describe the processes, based on the study of the functions, artifacts, and software elements required in Smart City tools for the development of quality of life. This through the definition of Data Science methods and the report of works carried out whose topics are the Planning for the start of a Smart City, the Framework for the analysis of Smart Cities and Smart Cities Big Data algorithms for sensors location, aimed at the development of tools that stimulate leaders and citizens the ability to interpret the results of the analysis, exploiting Open Data and Big Data according to the paradigm of data science, finally discussing the delving into a new software process paradigm as monitoring-analysis-evaluation-pattern found-driving object - decision making, where the user participates in the evaluation of the pattern through the visualization and exchange of results, causing continuous algorithm changes as the shape of the data changes with the real world and the future of Smart Cities.

BACKGROUND

In the first part of this section, Smart City is studied as a concept and as a paradigm as well as its dimensions and areas of extension in the city. In the second part, the trajectories followed by its investigation and implementations are presented, envisioning the main challenge that is not to exclude the humans from this process. In the third part, Data Mining is analyzed and compared with Data Science, and Data Science with Big Data Analytics alluding to technologies and Machine Learning, optimization or bio inspired methods immersed in them. It also describes the importance of communication of analysis results, ethical and social aspects that contract errors in scientific models. The fourth part mentions the Smart Cities processes immersed in apps classified by the problems that these solutions attack with their respective Data Science process.

Smart Cities a Paradigm for the Development of Infrastructure and Society

The concept Smart City is a fuzzy term that also mixes different dimensions. According to the Intelligent Community Forum the word Smart is about applying technologies to make cities work better, operating as an automated factory (intelligentcommunity.org, 2018). For (Telecommunication standardization sector of ITU (2016) it is a Smart Sustainable City that uses Information and Communication Technology (ICT), as one of the basic means to improve the quality of life and all kinds of aspects of a city, for others, it is the replacement of human intervention in daily processes in the life of the city, by systems that use physical infrastructures made up of sensors, cameras, computers, and connection networks, suggesting that it is possible to replace man with Information Technology to help man which is debatable (Pavlou, 2018).

Monitoring appears as a sub-process of this paradigm, in the sense that environmental events are expected to be scanned and to be analyzed to observe patterns and reply to them automatically. "Such "smartness" in smart cities derives from the employment of many advanced Artificial Intelligence (AI) algorithms or the combination of several of them" (Tang, et al., 2017). Another perspective is the definition given from sub Factors or dimensions, that is, a set of characteristics that must be covered to determine if a community is a Smart City (Badr, Benahmed, Abdes-samed, & Ouardouz, 2016), an example of this is the BOYD COHEN model which proposes 6 dimensions: Smart Living, Smart People, Smart Economy, Smart Environment, Smart Government, Smart Economy, Smart Mobility, and Smart Environment. In the figure 1 a simplified model, wherein the center appears two people representing the urban community as the beneficiaries, the 6 symbols that surround them are the key areas related to the 6 factors or dimensions, which in turn measure another set of indicators, such as Health and Safety for the Smart Living, Education and Creativity for the Smart People, air and land cargo transportation for the Smart Economy, the use of natural resources, like fuel, for the Smart Environment, the open Government for the Smart Government, and sustainable transport systems for Smart Mobility.

Figure 1. Dimensions in a Smart City according to BOYD COHEN model (Cohen, 2014)

A peculiar characteristic of this paradigm is the presence of ICT as the central axis. So, it is constant that the index to be measured is the Internet connection, placing some cities as Smart for having a robust physical structure, interconnecting citizens in extended territories, and where speed, stability, and data transport capacity is accessible or available. An example in this case is the 5 generation (5G) that will act as the backbone of IoT and will pave the way for the development of Smart Cities (Sriganesh & Ramjee, 2018).

The ICT is also considered the elements that promote prosperity because they stimulate social inclusion that brings with it the reduction of poverty; other benefits result in solving the most urgent perceived problems of a population. Some problems are, for example, the lack of information on areas that have a lack of services such as water, electricity, schools, and unemployment opportunities.

In the Smart Government process or technique or aspect, technologies are involved in citizen participation; the concept of governance is carried out on websites whose social participation forums contain community projects that are open to the public for their knowledge and decision-making.

The IT has linked the Smart Environment and the Smart Living, generating the Smart Building concept, which establishes automated housing and building structures, with monitoring of the consumption of natural resources, as well as emergencies caused by fires, health, and insecurity, and providing better control in lighting and air conditioning. The indices to be measured here are the environmental factors: pollution, use of water, electricity, and gas, as well as the effort to protect nature.

Smart Cities Challenges

The troubling issues for society are the way of life that has led to the destruction of the environment and humanity. The problem of deterioration due to pollution and abuse of resource use has been the boom of the century leaving a little bit aside the exclusion that men experiences in the daily processes, where information systems intervene, which is seen for example when illegal use is made of their data for commercial purposes or the excessive career of technologies such as mobiles and purchase and sale systems, which require high business intelligence to analyze consumer buying habits. The monitoring of people who flow around buildings to know their patterns without requesting authorization, the aerial scanning of conurbation areas for the construction of geolocation maps without permission from the corresponding authorities or the monitoring of Internet accesses to promote products carried out by fraudulent actors, in summary this is the Tracking process (Yu, Macbeth, Modi, & Pujol, 2016) where is the action. Meanwhile, Smart Cities are presented as the panacea of urban complexes. For companies it represented an opportunity to ensure their productivity and life in the market, especially because of the need that appeared to design and build electronic components to build intelligent systems. For researchers, it became an overwhelming task, mainly because it was facing the problem of how to understand the limits and scope that IT should be developed under this framework.

But the research takes different aspects: first, some authors began this work by proposing surveys to identify those factors that are related to the quality of life, and based on these they built metrics to evaluate and compare cities in terms of efficiency and City Resilience (Li, Chen, & Luna-Reyes, 2017). In the second, the authors work focused on establishing systems and infrastructures that involve the intelligent dispatch of services and provision of resources such as the Smart Building, which are systems with mostly hardware elements, but also software, such as communication protocols. Leaning further this investigation towards the IoT and the 5 generation (5G) of mobile phone technology, that be adapted to city environments, allowing automation, remote device management, data collection through visitor kiosks, surveillance systems with video cameras, and monitoring of transportation systems. The reason for this investigation was based on the requirements of the optimal connectivity of automated systems in network infrastructure (Skouby & Lynggaard, 2014) to deploy the solutions.

In the third aspect are the works-oriented to the identification of patterns, such as the optimization of alternative routes for traffic, the creation of technologies for Business Intelligence or Smart Services that rely heavily on Data Mining, similarly, studies appear in the health field that relies on Data Analytics to build new possibilities of care, cure, and disease prevention (Asri, Mousannif, & Al Moatassime, 2019). In a fourth aspect, the investigations of systems that involve the analysis of Big Data are identified within what is known as the era of data exploitation. The excessive increase of information is generated in sensors, the Internet, and in the world of transactions of client information systems - server and intranet, whose main goal is prediction (AI Nuaimi, Al Neyadi, Mohamed, & Al-Jaroodi, 2015). The Open Data philosophy (Beckwith, Sherry, & Prendergast, 2019) is to establish a free access interface that citizens can exploit without privacy restrictions, approaching the science of Open Data, increasing the generation of tools that use information from multiple sources such as government, companies, and results of research experiments, supporting decision-making, encouraging innovation and interoperability, but at the same time, its permanence depends on how available the information is made by governments, and also on how relevant it is.

The challenges that are looming are: knowing the characteristics to be implemented in Smart City applications for decision-making using Data Science without excluding the individual in the pattern extraction process, finding the techniques that adaptively analyze new situations.

Data Science

In the first section, various approaches that surround Data Science are presented, such as Data Mining, the knowledge discovery in the Databases knowledge discovery (KDD) process, its relationship with statistics, and computer science that apply AI methods, including features of Process Science. The second section relates the relationship between Data Science and Big Data Analytics and lists the applications that have exploited analysis techniques and particular processes according to the topics: Public Services, Smart Grid, E-health-IoT, Transport and mobility, Political Services, and government monitoring.

Data Science, a Multidisciplinary Field

Data Science was born because data became valuable capital for scientists and companies. In the beginning, storage mattered and data management through computer systems and database managers whose scope was transactional and safeguard for historical files. Later, more sophisticated database management systems began to appear, to efficiently control large amounts of data. It was then becoming more urgent to exploit the data to support decision-making, which is why Data Mining appears as a development scheme for tools to convert raw data into meaningful information. According to (Han, Pei, & Kamber, 2011) Data Mining is a KDD process consisting of a sequence of steps, data cleaning, data integration, data transforming, Data Mining, pattern evaluation and knowledge presentation. In a survey carried out to determine the algorithms and Data Mining techniques that can be used in an intelligent computing system to gather the pattern involved and the information present in it, the following prominent algorithms were obtained: clustering algorithm, neural network algorithm, regression algorithm, and bayesian algorithm (Swamidason, 2019). From this perspective, Data Mining techniques are a field of statistics and computer science that apply AI methods such as Machine Learning.

But the valuable information is not only captured from the tables and facts of the databases, but it is also extracted from the user activities in the systems, this is a process called "Process Mining" and one of the areas where it is implemented in the industry, with this paradigm it is possible to discover patterns in the activities of the processes, "since Event logs may store additional information such as the resource" (WIREs Data Mining Knowl Discov, 2012).

Data Science is a very broad concept, it is a multidisciplinary field that uses scientific methods, systems, processes, algorithms, and unifies statistics, Data Analysis, and Machine Learning in order to understand a phenomenon, incorporating, of course, Data Mining and "Process Mining", and includes features of Process Science which approaches are process-centric, but often focus on modeling rather than learning from event data (Aalst, 2016), this covers stochastic processes (Graf Plessen & Bemporad, 2018), optimization, such as bioinspired algorithms (Yazdani & Jolai, 2016) business process, process automation, formal methods (Matsuo, 2017).

Data Science and Big Data Analytics

In addition, Data Science faces the era of Big Data, this was "include rapid advances in computing technologies and the resulting explosion of data" (Song & Zhu, 2016); these advances are closely related to CPU speed, network bandwidths, distributed systems for parallel processing as well as frameworks that support the use of sensors. An example is deep learning, which has progressed in two main areas: Big Data and computing power, both in the form of clusters of CPUs / GPUs (central / graphics processing units) and in the cloud (Baldi, 2018).

Some examples of applications that have exploited Big Data are mainly the Smart Grid case, E-health, the Internet of Things, Public utilities, Transportation and logistics, Political services and government monitoring (Oussous, Benjelloun, & Ait Lahcen, 2017). Table 1 shows an example of 5 types of applications and how they implement Big Data Analytics.

Data Science and Human Inclusion

Thus, data scientists discover behavior intelligence by looking into the activities, processes, dynamics, and impact of individual and group actors, or by the behavior and business quantifiers, owners, and users in the physical world (Cao, 2017).

Data Science (Blei & Smyth, 2017) focuses on exploiting large bursts of data for prediction, exploration, understanding, and intervention. This position emphasizes approximation and simplification of the results obtained while Data Mining focuses on the application of analysis techniques. For data science the relevance is in the techniques used to visualize and transmit the analysis that is done to better understand the outside world.

Ethical and Social Aspects of Data Science

The expansive and exploitative nature of the information carried out by Data Science has caused concern about the repercussion of the publication of results or knowledge, because the findings may be compromised by the veracity of the data sets and by the use of private data. This is a topic that faces significant consequences in the management and supervision of responsibilities, and the responsibilities in Data Science locating ethics (Leonelli, 2016). This refers directly to the participants of the process, both the one who provides the data and the one who applies the algorithms and interprets the models obtained and even the developer of the Data Mining tools.

Table 1. Tools that have exploited big data analytics

Big Data Applications	Big Data Analytics Implementation
Public Services	An important implementation is the Smart Meters, which are multiple meters that are used in electricity, gas, water, the heat used in houses, offices, and buildings to measure the utilization of estimated payment. They also provide data that gives feedback to the clients. The objective of this smart metering is to save on consumption. Clients can make smart decisions by analyzing their usage (Manoharan & Rathinasabapathy, 2018). Another implementation is the systems "Smart Street Lighting systems" which are like systems acting in street lighting lamps with a device that can perform the monitoring of all variables affecting the lamp and can control it. The information is used to send the central warning of maintenance (Carloto, et al., 2019).
Smart Grid	A Smart Grid allows electricity to flow from producer to consumer and to self-monitor and self-correct deficiencies to prevent community supply failures (Guizani & Anan, 2014). With the IoT and connected devices such as Smart Meters and sensors, it is possible to handle large volumes of data on energy consumption and production. Other solutions of Smart Grid is to extract knowledge from their components, some apply it to State Analytics on stream data to obtain information like: real-time electrical state, real-time grid topology, others in Customer Analytics apply to data on customer consumption, in orders to build demand profiles, and others perform active analytics so-called because they correlate data emitted from the systems involved within the Smart Grid (El Khaouat & Benhlima, 2016).
E-health- IoT	These solutions refer to implementations of technologies such as radio frequency identification –RFID, wireless sensor network -WSN, smart mobile technologies and wearable devices for monitoring Real-time patients, risk alarms, rehabilitation therapies, medications; to improve health applying Predictive modeling and Machine Learning on large sample sizes, with more patient data. It can uncover nuances and patterns that couldn't be previously uncovered (Scarpato, Pieron, Di Nunzio, & Fallucchi, 2017).
Transport and mobility	In (Torre-Bastida, Del Ser, Laña, Ilardia, Bilbao, & Campos-Cordobés, 2018) they present a recent classification and applications of Big Data paradigm: 1) Driver assistance, these solutions monitor the surroundings of the vehicle and warn of dangerous situations, 2) Traveler information refers to applications that, for example, use social media by crowdsourcing to provide information to the traveler, 3) Roadway operations and management in which vehicle data is used to identify congestion and limited access on roadways. Four traffic management referred to traffic model information by demand estimation and 4) analysis of congestion. This same work summarizes the analysis techniques used in the applications studied, some of which are: statistical and econometric models, neural networks, classification, heuristic algorithm, deep learning, optimization, and route planning.
Political Services and government monitoring	The emotional analysis based on social Big Data can help people's consumption aspect and opinions for government policy or company product evaluation, the Emotional Classification Process for natural language can be in two aspects: an analysis method based on the dictionary of emotions and the one based on in Machine Learning Newly-Coined Words and Emoticon Polarity for Social-Emotional Opinion Decision Jin Sol Yang (Yang & Chung, 2019).

It is also necessary "a methodology for ethics in AI and Data Science research" (D'Aquin, Troullinou, O'Connor, Cullen, Faller, & Holden, 2018) and one of its requirements is to include a varied set of skills, expertise, and experts to face ethical challenges that must be addressed as a conversation between computers, technologists, and social scientists, as well as legal ethics experts.

The panel "The Responsibility Challenge" detects that the Governments are starting to recognize the need to regulate data-driven algorithmic technology (Jagadish, Bonchi, Eliassi-Rad, Getoor, Gummadi, & Stoyanovich, 2019). Some examples mentioned were the European Union's General Data Protection Regulation, the New York City Automated Decisions Systems Law, and the Net Neutrality principle, which aims to protect individuals who are impacted by collection and analysis.

In the Speech for the Assembly on algorithmic, it is emphasized that inequalities increase since "a few know everything about us, while we know nothing about them", and with this "critical thinking and conscious exercise are lulled to sleep of freedom". This brings a risk to democratic societies because knowledge and wealth accumulate in the hands of a few (Hall, 2020).

Smart Cities processes Immersed in Apps

In (Thompson, 2016) they use a survey by which they identified seventy types of city-related mobile apps, where almost half of all are relative to "traveling in cities". Then in order of percentages from highest to lowest are "cultural issues" apps, the third highest-ranking app type "look into helping citizens to report faults, to local authorities", then the group of apps dedicated to "environment, food, safety and health", the group of apps related to" social and tourism", the group of apps" safety and security" and finally the group related to "business". In (Angelidou, Psaltoglou, Komninos, Kakderi, Tsarchopoulos, & Panori, 2017), they analyze 32 applications addressing environmental sustainability issues found in the Intelligent / Smart Cities Open Source, which is a community repository. This analysis was developed to answer questions about the type of digital applications of cities They can be used to address environmental issues, as well as to identify the main trends and detect gaps on technical and policy levels. In their findings, it is reported that a significant part of these applications is from sustainable mobility themes, as for other environmental challenges there are applications related to air pollution, biodiversity and natural habitat, waste management, energy consumption, and applications of water resources. The following describes the processes of these apps summarized in the subsequent list of Smart Cities Apps.

Apps Smart City

Routes, Times & Fuel Consumption: The processes executed by the apps used in traveling in cities that are usually implemented are the optimization of travel times, route, and fuel consumption. In (Goudarzi, 2018) a comparison is made of Machine Learning algorithms related to the prediction of travel times, these were Nearest Neighbor, Windowed Nearest Neighbor, Linear Regression. The study indicates that a shallow Artificial Neural Network (ANN) can provide more accurate prediction than the other algorithms.

- **Recommendations & Customer Preferences:** Regarding the processes implemented in apps of this type, there are those related to "cultural issues". Their emergence is affected by an evolution of processes of searching for citizen information caused by the culture itself, and that it went from searching in the internet to the discovery of patterns, with the appearance of popular recommendation systems, which often act as agents that discover the needs and preferences of users, such as tastes and options, supporting decision-making to benefit the client. These systems probe user trends that are usually exposed, for example, on social networks or video-sharing platforms with a large volume of content in the comments. For the development of these apps, both Big Data analytics and AI play an important role, for Big Data analytics the management, extraction, and filtering of Big streaming is carried out and with the AI is obtaining the model of suggestions. Nowadays there today in by day there are various systems to suggest commercial products, restaurants, museums, or preferences such as the dish of the day or the clothes to wear. An example is (Su, Giancarlo, Moscato, Picariello, & Esposito, 2019), which proposes a strategy for cultural items suggestion, which makes semantic searches and inferences that are based on Machine Learning and are capable of suggesting items of interest, the case was applied to museums when visiting a city.
- **Digital Services to Make Decisions by Authorities:** With the increasing population, citizen complaints towards the government also increase, with it also appear platforms that support sub-judice-type issues, family or interpersonal disputes, some with or without a government response.

An example is (ICSCET, IEEE Staff, 2018), which applies the analysis with map-reduce to recognize patterns based on location and based on types, offering an interface to both the local citizen and the authorities concerned. In this group, there are also e-government applications, in which they underline not only citizen participation in community projects, but they also focus on Smart Services applications such as document storage while applicators fill out these forms (Eniyal, V., Priya, S., Meeralakshmi, M., & Sivanantham, S., 2020).

- **Environment, Health Using Crowdsourcing, Social Media o IoT:** In Smart Cities, activities for the protection of the environment and care for the well-being of the person are implemented through applications that perform monitoring for data collection, which can be generating sensing data using IoT, social media, or crowdsourcing. On the subject of health, the systems allow continuous monitoring of the patient through mobile devices such as smartphones, smartwatches, or glucometers, among others. Smart health apps tend to use self-learning and self-improvement techniques, few use self-learning algorithms (ANN, genetic algorithms, ant colony optimization, and simulated annealing) others use Topology based and ontology-based heuristic algorithms and several, they focus on widely used distributed computing platforms for Big Data Analytics solutions such as Hadoop MapReduce and Apache Spark (Zeadally, Siddiqui, Baig, & Ibrahim, 2019). In Smart Home and Smart Environment systems where the increase in sensors is colossal along with the heterogeneity and massive structures of acquired data, the analysis methods can be used in middleware, and be developed with the assistance of deep learning methods (Kabalci, Kabalci, Padmanaban, Holm-Nielsen, & Blaabjerg, 2019).

DEVELOPED SOLUTIONS REPORT: SMART CITY TOOLS FOR SOCIAL INCLUSION AND DECISION MAKING

Although e-government applications such as Smart services applications are becoming popular because their processes make citizen inclusion and recognition of their dignity within the community by being active participants, the applications are exhibited as separate processes, it is, therefore, necessary that defined schemes are proposed within a data-driven e-government model: (Agbozo & Spassov, 2018), with the aim of aggregate at each level of government, all e-services that total the demands and requests to respond to them through a joint vision, and Open Data, for governments to unlock the value of data, available to them and data to drive the decision making process, taking advantage of the potential of Machine Learning. With them, it is noted that the collection, extraction and personalized organization of the Key Performance Indicators (KPI) measurement indicators-variables would be simplified.

Regarding the apps of both recommendations and preferences and travel planning for optimization of time and resources, it is perceived that they are not connected to an integrating monitor whose analysis has repercussions in obtaining actions to make tangible regional changes or is linked to an immediate decision-making. And although it is observed that a science and technology career is assumed to solve urban problems in all its senses, it is visualized that the Data Science processes applied in these tools are not capable of changing according to events, since in each solution the technique used, be it any Machine Learning, heuristic algorithm, deep learning, optimization and others remain fixed within the body of the systems that contain the computer programs.

Therefore, the research and development of Frameworks for Smart Cities app are proposed, which are summarized in three themes: the infrastructure of KPI Open Data, the Framework for the analysis of Smart Cities models and to support the Data Science for decision-making oriented to the intelligent dispatch of service petitions, and Smart Cities Big Data algorithms for sensors location.

Planning for the Start of a Smart City: A Metric Structure

When Smart City projects began to spread in Guadalajara Jalisco it happened at different levels, in the Academic, Government, and Industry. Ciudad Creative Digital was a project carried out between the Federal Government, the Government of Jalisco, the National Chamber of the Electronics, Telecommunications and Information Technology Industry and the Guadalajara City Council to promote the development of people, through creativity and quality of life. In this perspective, in 2014 a plan was developed to prepare Guadalajara to be a Smart City, this work culminated in the white paper entitled "Towards the preparation of the Guadalajara's Smart City Metrics Structure" (Vázquez-Castañeda & Estrada-Guzman, 2015), in this project is proposed a development and implementation of a metric structure to verify the status of the indicators, analyze and correlate them with KPI to improve the performance of the city, understanding the function of sharing the metrics with other cities to develop a standardization. The topics dealt within in this work were condensed and are shown in figure 2, in which the elements that support this structure appear. The stakeholders that are the actors for the implementation of a Smart City play a special role, so that with these the importance of determining their responsibilities and tasks as participants is highlighted. In this group the government dependencies, contracting authorities were located, such as project managers; that is, operators and citizens. It is recognized that success depends on the availability and immediacy of the analytics produced by the information of the stakeholders.

The measurement process is fundamental to understand and make decisions in a city. Some key areas that were considered for inclusion are the talent, innovation, connections and distinctiveness, and since these metrics require specifications, methods, and standards to make the comparison between cities and

Figure 2. Stakeholder interaction process with Open Data through the Smart City metric structure

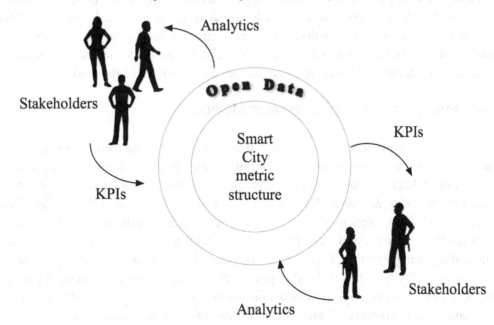

the correlation between indicators and KPIs. It is proposed to be addressed under the same framework, Open Data is required to promote the sharing of data and values between business and citizens, as well as promoting collaboration between universities, the government, and the industry. The data comes from public sources, private sources, and sources in networks like social media.

Results

Among the tools and standards analyzed for this purpose, the use of tree layers stands out: 1) File structures due to the multiple formats that proliferate, among them JSON, XML, and CSV formats are taken into account. 2) Protocols as IoT. 3) Kind of storage, since the periodicity of these, may vary, or there may be large volumes of data that require the selection of the type of storage for Big Data.

Experiences and Stakeholders Involved

The experience in (Vázquez-Castañeda & Estrada-Guzman, 2015) was that it allowed meeting with various stakeholders in the industry, academia, and government through dialogues and working groups, collaborating for a common objective, each contributing their talents and technological resources to achieve the goals established as a team. Likewise, guests were included in the workshops to share their experiences in the generation of patents and the need to promote the ability to innovate among citizens to create awareness of participation and belonging to their community. Another experience arose from the need to manipulate data without structures for manipulation with NoSQL for that information that is relevant for Smart Cities, so (Estrada-Guzman, Maciel, & Gómez, 2015) delves into key-value documents to store structures nested.

Framework for the Analysis of Smart Cities

The evolution of Smart Cities entails continuous changes that involve many variables, which could hinder the development of evaluation tools and methodologies. Among the tools and standards analyzed for this purpose, is the use of trees. The evolution of Smart Cities entails continuous changes that involve many variables, which could hinder the development of evaluation tools and methodologies. Most metric models are based on selecting KPIs according to the specific objectives of the model.

Cities assessment through KPIs Evaluation Method

As different organizations propose their indicators that generate different models, it is difficult to obtain a direct comparison between the models. To address this disadvantage in (Estrada, Maciel, Peña Pérez Negrón, López, Larios-Rosillo, & Ochoa-Zezzati, 2019) and in (Estrada E., Maciel, Peña Pérez Negrón, Lara López, Larios, & Ochoa, 2018), a Framework based on the application of Data Science to KPIs is proposed. This Framework represents an infrastructure that goes through the treatment of Open Data, facilitating the evaluation of the comparison of different models for decision-making, and up to the final stage of reporting attention. This Framework is based on four columns as components a) a tree structure to manage KPIs, b) a JSON (JavaScript Object Notation) designed document for intelligent service dispatch, c) Web applications for evaluations based on Smart People and, 4) the infrastructure for receiving and attending reports. Figure 3 shows the assembly of these components.

Figure 3. Smart City Architecture of the Framework to analysis and smart dispatch of services (Estrada E., Maciel, Peña Pérez Negrón, López, Larios-Rosillo, & Ochoa-Zezzati, 2019)

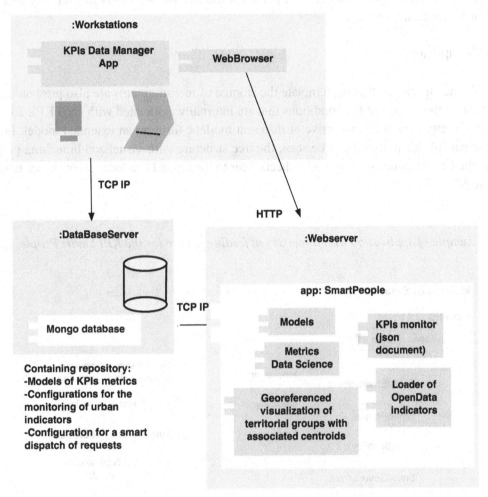

Knowing that different situations arise in each city, to which the city has to adapt this leads to continuous change in their evolution processes, which take into account various variables and the selection of the KPIs of a city to make decisions. In (Estrada, Peña Pérez Negrón, Lara López, & Casillas, 2018) the design and a prototype with the algorithms are presented, starting the implementation of the Framework to analyze and to make smart the dispatch process of services. This work is part of a global project to measure the quality of life of the city of Guadalajara, which is integrated into the territorial sector pattern identification tool that is based on Open Data analysis and geo-referenced visualization described below. The design provides a systematic approach for the constant evaluation and measurement of these factors, as well as for comparing different reports from different models.

Results

The applied approach is developed in three stages: analysis of the city metrics model, analysis of Open Data format and design and implementation of algorithms to process JSON objects in MongoDB. This work describes the functions of data loading (Data Adder), analysis and visualization of patterns (Analyzes of Metrics), and a model (Model) that performs the tree mode display of each key performance indicator or KPI with its source.

Models Component

On the Web, the algorithms that contemplate the storage of measurements are also presented to obtain a global view of the quality of life conditions that are internally associated with each KPI, allowing the evaluation of a city from the perspective of different models, forming an extended model. In figure 4 the graphic part of this proposal can be seen, the tree structure with visualized branching of KPIs according to the Cohen model is shown. The sheets refer to the Open Data location of the variables in the Internet world.

Figure 4. Example of application with a registry of feeding source for the KPI Smart People, Education branch

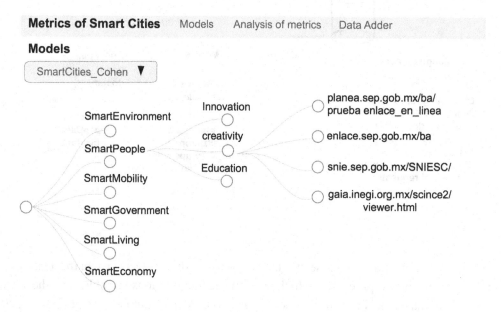

Analysis of Metrics

Sustainability and equity are some of the challenges that large cities face due to the constant incorporation of the surrounding population, which implies new ways of supplying services and resource management such as energy, drinking water, transportation, education, and care from the natural environment. Hence, event monitoring is an effective way to measure the efficiency and level of territorial equity. In the work (Estrada E., Maciel, Ochoa, Bernabe-Loranca, Oliva, & Larios, 2018) a tool for the visualization of patterns by the measurement of efficiency indicators is proposed, using Machine Learning techniques. The objective is to support decision-making through georeferenced analysis exploiting Open Data.

Figure 5. Implementation of the visualization process in Smart City tools for decision-making

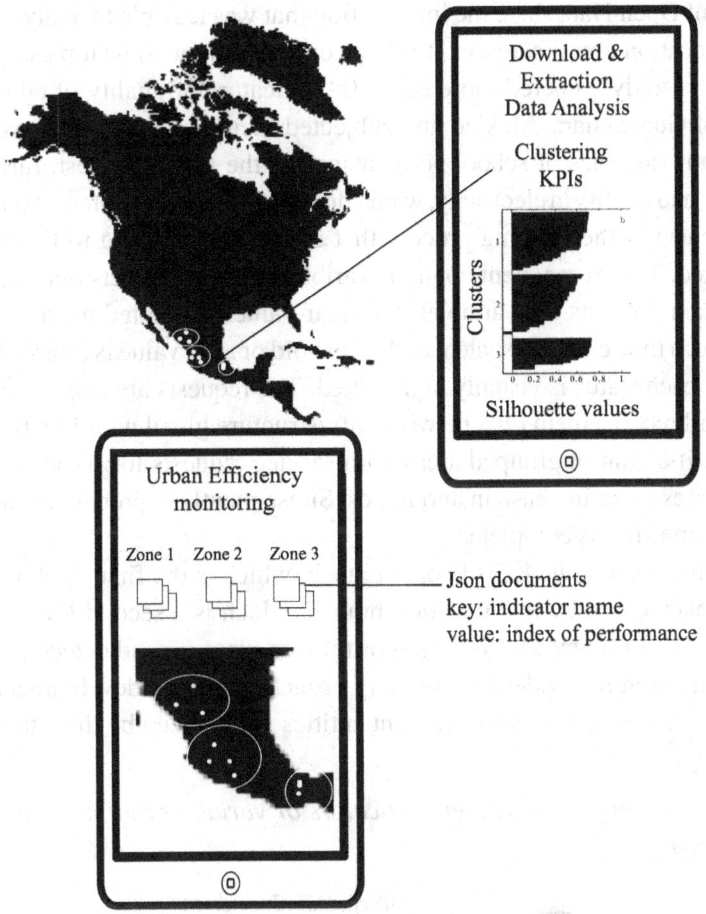

Figure 5 shows the result of this work, presenting a sketch in which three essential aspects prevail: Open Data, loading, and extraction for analysis, and georeferenced visualization. The map refers to Open Data, due to the existence of latent information specified in positioning points (latitude, longitude), they are displayed in white points and different regions, and they also keep underlying patterns (groupings) displayed by the white circles. The Download & Extraction Data Analysis screen belongs to the developed tool, in it the Open Data has information to be downloaded and extracted. It is analyzed by unsupervised learning algorithms, specifically clustering, and distance-based methods such as kmeans and fuzzy c-means.

The Urban Efficiency monitoring screen presents the function that carries out the display of the georeferenced visualization, being a fundamental part of the extension of the interpretation with the values of the centroids of clusters that appear as zone 1, zone 2 and zone 3. The georeferenced visualization happens because all the data that intervened in the training and tests are drawn using a color depending on the group assigned by calculating Euclidean distances, so that on the map it is possible to see reflected the agglomerations of data belonging to certain groups on specific territories, noting cases of trends of propagation of patterns towards certain directions.

An outstanding experience in (Estrada E., Maciel, Ochoa, Bernabe-Loranca, Oliva, & Larios, 2018) was the exploration of Open Data since the information that was feasible to analyze for this process was associated with geolocation coordinates and that was only found for some topics, including Air Quality and Education, so this study gathered more than 300 indicators of quality of education from primary schools in the city of Guadalajara, Mexico and subjected them to tests of kmeans and fuzzy c-means. The indicators contain variables of school performance in the ENLACE test, furniture infrastructure, computer equipment, and quality in electricity, water, drainage, pavement, Internet services, among others.

An annex component is the tracking process that consists of reacting to the review of the indicators that are monitored. This component contains various software objects that are involved in various scenarios. One of them presents the variables and their values consulted by area, name, password, or service request to which they can be dispatched. A threshold or alert value is established in each indicator and those who are in each status is visually highlighted. The requests are dispatched to various government entities who will receive them on a network infrastructure glued with Restful. The georeferenced view allows the identification of grouped areas with service requests for some common cause such as lack of certain resources or an increase in anomalies. Subsequently, a process of **monitoring-analysis-evaluation-decision-making** is completed.

Figure 6 shows this process, the KPIs People branch, which is the first level of abstraction of a city metrics model. It broken down by its Education branch, which is a second level and 6 of its indicator variables, which are monitored by a monitor (algorithm) to measure and detect atypical values or alert values that require attention for evidencing scarcity or lack of human development, and with this data structure, generate service requests to government entities symbolized by the letters sent.

Figure 6. Layers are breaking down by their indicators or variables that are scanned by a monitor to do the Smart Services dispatch

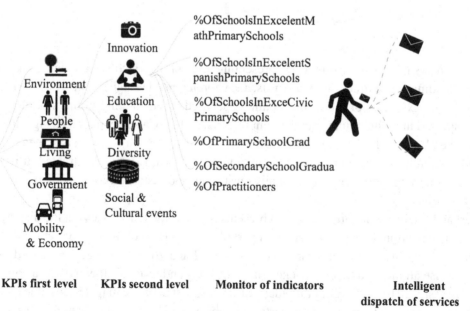

The monitor is a JSON document that also has the task of applying the Data Science algorithm, that is, it selects the corresponding one, which means that it is not a fixed algorithm. Thus, one of the results of the experience was the realization that most of the works base their findings on the application of a Data Science algorithm because it is a set of observations that are not expected to change, but in reality, does change therefore the need for the vision of non-static dynamic selection solutions for these algorithms. Proof of this is the variant presentation that Open data makes of its data.

Smart Cities Big Data Algorithms for Sensors Location

In (Estrada, Martínez Vargas, Gómez, Peña Pérez Negrón, Lara López, & Maciel, 2019) a method was proposed to obtain an algorithm development model that allows locating sensors using their information. It was developed with d the method with the data collected from environmental sensors, installed in the Guadalajara Metropolitan Area (ZMG), Mexico. This article suggests a classification scheme based on Machine Learning, using generated Big Data to build real-time patterns for the new sensor placement. Patterns will be recognized between the surroundings of sensor groups in which it has been sensed by monitoring processes such as low quality of life, to better fix the monitoring sensor, for new sensors, or the relocation of old sensors with the generated information by them through established hot-zones. The authors define the concept of "hot-zone" as a perimeter, an essential source of data for analysis. In a hot zone, constant activity can be found with substantial data to assess the quality of observation. These hot spots are used to locate or relocate new sensors.

A Recursive Search of Midpoints Within Hot-Zones

A process was designed to guide the implementation, which was detailed in four phases. The first three phases are based on the Data Mining process, and the fourth phase is the establishment of algorithms using selected techniques. The goal of the process is to resolve the hot spots. As an example, this process was implemented in the ZMG, for air pollution. In this case, the first algorithm for data training was designed to generate the classification model with a dynamic update. A second algorithm was designed for data labeling, which is activated after each data entry. The two algorithms are independent. Classification is carried out in parallel with the training process, while some data is classified, others are used for training to observe possible changes in patterns, or to decrease the processing time due to a possible reduction in the number of variables of the model. In this phase, a frequency matrix is generated that works in conjunction with a neighboring sensor matrix to identify hot spots and present their displays on a geo-referenced map.

Figure 7 shows an example of sensors scattered in a geo-referenced region. Two of the four sensors were identified as hot spots: Sensor 2 and Sensor 3 in contrast to sensors 1 and more distant ones represented by Sensor n; the range of the hot zone is reduced, getting closer to sensor 3, but could disappear backward, getting closer to sensor 2. The range of the hot zone will be reduced depending on sensor data and using the analogy of a binary search, it is that it takes one of two routes recursively. This process will generate another geo-referenced dynamic map with the distinguished sensors in the hot-zone and the new sensor location.

Figure 7. A recursive search of midpoints within hot-zones Source: IGI, 2014

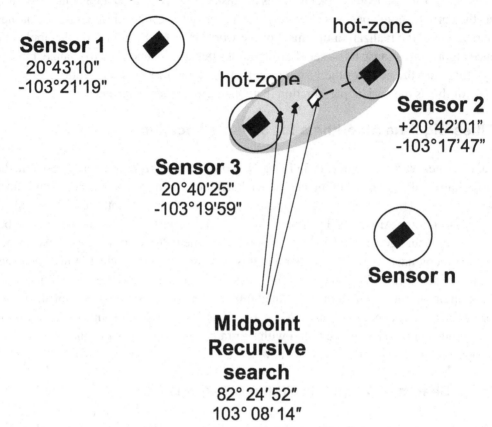

Results

The result in Estrada, Martínez Vargas, Gómez, Peña Pérez Negrón, Lara López, & Maciel, 2019's work,describes that to consider that a single Data Mining technique cannot always be a point of reference for a variant of measurement areas of a city, because, in the case of the environment, monitoring variables tend to change, the 20-year history of environmental sensing shows that air quality standards and norms have been adjusted over time.

FUTURE TRENDS

Although there is a race at the speed of competition in the liberation of technology for both AI and its family of techniques: Soft Computing, intelligent computing, evolutionary computing, and others, whose solutions have used Data Science algorithms such as those already mentioned, the results as Data structure are not available to the public and decision-making authorities. So, the trend will be in promoting the opening of their repositories, otherwise, this advantage of valuable elements of Open Data will disappear from processes of citizen-government linkage. Here an area of opportunity is glimpsed to propose the schematization of the analysis results used in the technologies.

On the development of Smart Cities by Data Science processes, the danger that this paradigm runs can be discussed if it does not consider that technological advance must occur at all levels of reasoning, that is, for example, ¿Does a Smart City identify itself for having 5G?, although the users are only consumers of technology that do not contribute anything of themselves to society, or ¿Does a city is a Smart City compared to another in the world because the KPIs that evaluates are rated well as opposed to others that are not because they qualify at a lower level?, and the citizens of these Smart City do not know where the resources for these technologies are sponsored or the hidden intentions of industries and governments, not to mention the monitoring they do of the user without their consent. A trend towards the development of tools where the government communicates the deficiencies or research opportunities to the various organizations, such as the academy, for the resolution of massive situations, instead of the release of tools only to provoke demand for articles and services. And since today's problems result in issues of mental health, river pollution, recycling, poverty due to discrimination, diseases and epidemics, Data Science processes are inclined to provide mechanisms for locating causes of the observed phenomena, by territorial location, emerging a new way of conceiving computer programs which are outlined as monitoring-analysis-evaluation-pattern found -**driving object**- decision-making, where the driving object is rescued as a set of factors causing a phenomenon, which response to unknowns.

The opportunity to study Data Science topics is opened now as a conversation not only between computers, technologists, social scientists, and legal experts in ethics; It also opens for the own evaluation of citizens' interests. Finally, it is discussed whether the authors want a Smart City or to the City of God (Hipponensis, 426), from which Saint Augustine of Hippo describes as one that frees us from lies and errors, persecuting the true God, where man is not excluded, nor is the technology it is imposed as its god.

CONCLUSION

Data science processes are essential in the analysis of everyday phenomena, their design must materialize community-wide solutions, the veracity of which is tested by the recipients, and the dynamic ability to change the algorithm according to the agreement with the requirements must also be included in its design user and changing environment validations. Therefore, the word Smart, although it tends to mean automation by AI and thus attracts giants from industry and businesses that promote the sensors so that they execute mechanical actions at the same time using the IoT, incorporates the promotion of human inclusion as a paradigm of community processes, monitoring, and evaluation of specific indicators such as education, poverty, use of natural resources that invite awareness of the transcendental or that has consequences with sustainability, being rather a term related to the word "Track" and given some projects of collaborative participation by digital means and the philosophy of Open Data to promote the habit of sharing, it resembles the word "Share".

As future work, research will be channeled into the outline of tools with user interfaces that become increasingly closer to the user's abstraction in a dynamic way, adding functionalities to capture the user's perception of himself and his surroundings, offering Visualizations of causes and solutions of realities through the exploitation of scientific algorithms and processes that contain the option to share information with other citizens and the government with the right to also access the exchange of analysis.

ACKNOWLEDGMENT

To Dr. Ruth Padilla Muñoz Rector of CUCEI and Dr. Marco Pérez Cisneros Director of the Electronics and Computing Division, who have supported both the research of Smart Cities and the training and updating of teachers and researchers, who offered noble and transcendent actions that led to the presentation of this work.

REFERENCES

Aalst, W. (2016). *Process Mining Data Science in Action*. Springer. doi:10.1007/978-3-662-49851-4

Agbozo, E., & Spassov, K. (2018). Establishing Efficient Governance through Data-Driven e-Government. In *Conference 11th International Conference on Theory and Practice of Electronic Governance*, New York: Association for Computing Machinery.

Angelidou, M., Psaltoglou, A., Komninos, N., Kakderi, C., Tsarchopoulos, P., & Panori, A. (2017). Enhancing sustainable urban development through smart city applications. *Journal of Science and Technology Policy Management*, 9(2), 146–169. doi:10.1108/JSTPM-05-2017-0016

Asri, H., Mousannif, H., & Al Moatassime, H. (2019). Reality mining and predictive analytics for building smart applications. *Journal of Big Data*, 6(66), 2–25. doi:10.118640537-019-0227-y

Badr, B., Benahmed, M., Abdes-samed, B., & Ouardouz, M. (2016). Ranking models of smart cities. In *2016 4th IEEE International Colloquium on Information Science and Technology (CiSt)* (pp. 872-879). Tangier, Morocco: IEEE.

Baldi, P. (2018). Deep Learning in Biomedical Data Science. *Annual Review of Biomedical Data Science*, 1(1), 181–205. doi:10.1146/annurev-biodatasci-080917-013343

Beckwith, R., Sherry, J., & Prendergast, D. (2019). Data Flow in the Smart City: Open Data Versus the Commons. In M. Lange & M. Waal (Eds.), *The Hackable City* (pp. 205–221). Springer Singapore. doi:10.1007/978-981-13-2694-3_11

Blei, D. M., & Smyth, P. (2017). Science and data science. *Proceedings of the National Academy of Sciences of the United States of America*, 114(33), 8689–8692. doi:10.1073/pnas.1702076114 PMID:28784795

Cao, L. (2017). Data science: Challenges and directions. *Communications of the ACM*, 60(8), 59–68. doi:10.1145/3015456

Carloto, F. G., Dalla Costa, M. A., Barriquello, C. H., da Silva Spode, N., Maziero, L., & Dotto Vizzotto, W. (2019). The Role of a Smart Street Lighting into a Smart Grid Environment. In 2019 IEEE PES Innovative Smart Grid Technologies Conference - Latin America (ISGT Latin America). Gramado, Brazil: IEEE.

Cohen, B. (2014, November 20). The Smartest Cities in The World 2015: Methodology. *Fast Company: The future of business. General format.* https://www.fastcompany.com/3038818/the-smartest-cities-in-the-world-2015-methodology

D'Aquin, M., Troullinou, P., O'Connor, N., Cullen, A., Faller, G., & Holden, L. (2018). Towards an "Ethics by Design" Methodology for AI Research Projects. In *Proceedings AIES '18: Proceedings of the 2018 AAAI/ACM Conference on AI, Ethics, and Society.* ACM. 10.1145/3278721.3278765

El Khaouat, A., & Benhlima, L. (2016). Big data based management for smart grids. In *Renewable and Sustainable Energy Conference (IRSEC)* (pp. 1044-1047). Marrakech, Morocco: IEEE.

Eniyal, V., Priya, S., Meeralakshmi, M., & Sivanantham, S. (2020). Securing Technology and Government Services Enrollment-Stage. In *2020 6th International Conference on Advanced Computing and Communication Systems (ICACCS).* Coimbatore, India: IEEE.

Estrada, E., Maciel, R., Ochoa, A., Bernabe-Loranca, B., Oliva, D., & Larios, V. (2018). Smart City Visualization Tool for the Open Data Georeferenced Analysis Utilizing Machine Learning. *International Journal of Combinatorial Optimization Problems and Informatics, 9*(2), 25–40.

Estrada, E., Maciel, R., Peña Pérez Negrón, A., Lara López, G., Larios, V., & Ochoa, A. (2018). Framework for the Analysis of Smart Cities Models. In J. Mejia, M. Muñoz, Á. Rocha, A. Peña, & M. Pérez-Cisneros (Eds.), *Trends and Applications in Software Engineering, 865* (pp. 261–269). Springer, Cham.

Estrada, E., Maciel, R., Peña Pérez Negrón, A., López, G., Larios-Rosillo, V., & Ochoa-Zezzati, C. (2019). A framework to support the data science of Smart City models for decision-making oriented to the intelligent dispatch of service petitions. *IET Software, 14*(2), 159–164. doi:10.1049/iet-sen.2019.0044

Estrada, E., Martínez Vargas, M. P., Gómez, J., Peña Pérez Negrón, A., Lara López, G., & Maciel, R. (2019). Smart Cities Big Data Algorithms for Sensors Location. *MDPI in Applied Sciences, 9*(19), 1–14. doi:10.3390/app9194196

Estrada, E., Peña Pérez Negrón, A., Lara López, G., & Casillas, L. (2018). Algoritmos para el control de indicadores clave de desempeño para Smart Cites. Proceedings Research in Computing Science.

Estrada-Guzmán, E., Maciel, R., & Gómez, L. (2015, July 7). NoSQL method for the metric analysis of Smart Cities. *IEEE-CCD Smart Cities White Paper.* https://smartcities.ieee.org/images/files/pdf/mtxgdl_nosql.pdf

Goudarzi, F. (2018). Travel Time Prediction: Comparison of Machine Learning Algorithms in a Case Study. In *2018 IEEE 20th International Conference on High Performance Computing and Communications; IEEE 16th International Conference on Smart City; IEEE 4th Intl. Conference on Data Science and Systems,* (pp. 1404-1407). Exeter, UK: IEEE.

Graf Plessen, M., & Bemporad, A. (2018). Stock Trading via Feedback Control: Stochastic Model Predictive or Genetic? *Journal of Modern Accounting and Auditing, 14*(1), 35–47. doi:10.17265/1548-6583/2018.01.004

Guizani, M., & Anan, M. (2014). Smart Grid Opportunities and Challenges of Integrating Renewable Sources: A Survey. In *Wireless Communications and Mobile Computing Conference, IWCMC, International,* (pp. 1098-1105). Nicosia, Cyprus: IEEE.

Hall, C. (2020, February 28). *Address prepared by pope Francis, read by h.e. archbishop Paglia, president of the pontifical academy for life*. http://www.vatican.va/content/francesco/en/speeches/2020/february/documents/papa-francesco_20200228_accademia-perlavita.html

Han, J., Pei, J., & Kamber, M. (2011). *Data Mining: Concepts and Techniques* (3rd ed.). Elsevier. http://myweb.sabanciuniv.edu/rdehkharghani/files/2016/02/The-Morgan-Kaufmann-Series-in-Data-Management-Systems-Jiawei-Han-Micheline-Kamber-Jian-Pei-Data-Mining.-Concepts-and-Techniques-3rd-Edition-Morgan-Kaufmann-2011.pdf

Hipponensis, A. (426). *The City of God*. Roma: Opening text.

ICSCET. IEEE Staff. (2018). Smart E-Grievance System for Effective Communication in Smart Cities. In *Conference: 2018 International Conference on Smart City and Emerging Technology (ICSCET)*, (pp. 1-4). Mumbai, India: IEEE.

intelligentcommunity.org. (2018). *ICF. Intelligent Community Forum*. https://www.intelligentcommunity.org/

Jagadish, H., Bonchi, F., Eliassi-Rad, T., Getoor, L., Gummadi, K., & Stoyanovich, J. (2019). The Responsibility Challenge for Data. *SIGMOD '19:* In *Proceedings of the 2019 International Conference on Management of Data*. Association for Computing Machinery.

Kabalci, Y., Kabalci, E., Padmanaban, S., Holm-Nielsen, J., & Blaabjerg, F. (2019). Internet of Things Applications as Energy Internet in Smart Grids and Smart Environments. *Electronics (Basel)*, *8*(9), 972. doi:10.3390/electronics8090972

Leonelli, S. (2016). Locating ethics in data science: Responsibility and accountability in global and distributed knowledge production systems. *Philosophical Transactions of the Royal Society A*, *374*(2083), 1–12. doi:10.1098/rsta.2016.0122 PMID:28336799

Li, K., Chen, Y., & Luna-Reyes, L. F. (2017). City Resilience as a Framework to Understand Smart Cities: Dimensions and Measurement. In *Proceedings of the 18th Annual International Conference on Digital Government Research*. Association for Computing Machinery. 10.1145/3085228.3085249

Manoharan, A., & Rathinasabapathy, V. (2018). Smart Water Quality Monitoring and Metering Using Lora for Smart Villages. In *2nd International Conference on Smart Grid and Smart Cities*. Kuala Lumpur: IEEE.

Matsuo, S. (2017). How formal analysis and verification add security to blockchain-based systems. In *Proceedings of the 17th Conference on Formal Methods in Computer-Aided Design*. FMCAD Inc. 10.23919/FMCAD.2017.8102228

Mentsiev, A., Engel, M., & Gudaeva, D.-M. (2020). Impact of IoT on the automation of processes in Smart Cities: Security issues and world experience. *Journal of Physics: Conference Series*, *1515*, 1–7. doi:10.1088/1742-6596/1515/2/022026

Nuaimi, A. I. (2015). Applications of big data to smart cities. *Journal of Internet Services and Applications*, *6*(25), 2–15. doi:10.118613174-015-0041-5

Oussous, A., Benjelloun, F.-Z., & Ait Lahcen, A. (2017). Big Data technologies: A survey. *Journal of King Saud University – Computer and Information Sciences, 30*(4), 431-448.

Pavlou, P. (2018). Internet of Things – Will Humans be Replaced or Augmented? *GfK Marketing Intelligence, 10*(2), 43–48. doi:10.2478/gfkmir-2018-0017

Scarpato, N., Pieron, A., Di Nunzio, L., & Fallucchi, F. (2017). E-health-IoT Universe: A Review. *International Journal on Advanced Science. Engineering and Information Technology, 7*(6), 2328–2336.

Skouby, K., & Lynggaard, P. (2014). Smart home and smart city solutions enabled by 5G, IoT, AAI and CoT services. In *2014 International Conference on Contemporary Computing and Informatics (IC3I)*. Mysore, India: IEEE. 10.1109/IC3I.2014.7019822

Song, I.-Y., & Zhu, Y. (2016). Big data and data science: What should we teach? *Expert Systems: International Journal of Knowledge Engineering and Neural Networks, 33*(4), 364–373. doi:10.1111/exsy.12130

Sriganesh, R., & Ramjee, P. (2018). Impact of 5G Technologies on Smart City Implementation. *Wireless Personal Communications, 100*(1), 161–176. doi:10.100711277-018-5618-4

Su, X., Giancarlo, S., Moscato, V., Picariello, A., & Esposito, C. (2019). An Edge Intelligence Empowered Recommender System Enabling Cultural Heritage Applications. *IEEE Transactions on Industrial Informatics, 15*(7), 4266–4275. doi:10.1109/TII.2019.2908056

Swamidason, I. T. J. (2019). Survey of data mining algorithm's for intelligent computing system. *Journal of Trends in Computer Science and Smart Technology, 1*(1), 14-23.

Tang, B., Chen, Z., Hefferman, G., Pei, S., Wei, T., He, H., & Yang, Q. (2017). Incorporating Intelligence in Fog Computing for Big Data Analysis in Smart Cities. *IEEE Transactions on Industrial Informatics, 13*(5), 2140–2150. doi:10.1109/TII.2017.2679740

Telecommunication standardization sector of ITU. (2016). *Recommendation ITU-T Y.4900/L.1600*. http://handle.itu.int/11.1002/1000/12627-en?locatt=format:pdf&auth

Thompson, E. M. (2016). What makes a city 'smart'? *International Journal of Architectural Computing, 14*(4), 358–371. doi:10.1177/1478077116670744

Torre-Bastida, A. I., Del Ser, J., Laña, I., Ilardia, M., Bilbao, M. N., & Campos-Cordobés, S. (2018). Big Data for transportation and mobility: Recent advances, trends and challenges. *IET Intelligent Transport Systems, 12*(8), 742–755. doi:10.1049/iet-its.2018.5188

van der Aalst, W., Adriansyah, A., & van Dongen, B.WIREs Data Mining Knowledge Discovery. (2012). Replaying history on process models for conformance checking and performance analysis. *WIREs Data Mining and Knowledge Discovery, 2*(2), 182–192. doi:10.1002/widm.1045

Vázquez-Castañeda, C., & Estrada-Guzman, E. (2015, August 20). *Towards the preparation of the Guadalajara's SmartCity Metrics Structure*. IEEE-GDL CCD Smart Cities White Paper. https://smartcities.ieee.org/images/files/pdf/whitepapermtx_v8.pdf

Yang, J., & Chung, K. (2019). Newly-Coined Words and Emoticon Polarity for Social Emotional Opinion Decision. In 2019 IEEE 2nd International Conference on Information and Computer Technologies. Kahului, HI: IEEE. 10.1109/INFOCT.2019.8711413

Yazdani, M., & Jolai, F. (2016). Lion Optimization Algorithm (LOA): A nature-inspired metaheuristic algorithm. *Journal of Computational Design and Engineering*, *3*(1), 24–36. doi:10.1016/j.jcde.2015.06.003

Yu, Z., Macbeth, S., Modi, K., & Pujol, J. (2016). Tracking the Trackers. In *Proceedings of the 25th International Conference on World Wide*. Web Conferences Steering Committee. 10.1145/2872427.2883028

Zeadally, S., Siddiqui, F., Baig, Z., & Ibrahim, A. (2019). Smart healthcare: Challenges and potential solutions using the internet of things (IoT) and big data analytics. *PSU Research Review*, ahead-of-print.

KEY TERMS AND DEFINITIONS

Apps Smart City: Applications that resolve problems of services and lack of resources in smart cities through data analytics.

Big Data: Set of analytical techniques and methods for large volumes of data with the final obtaining of computing solutions.

Data Analytics: A process that is conformed by method and statistics techniques, computation, data mining, and big data as well as the sequence of steps to follow that culminate with the visualization of patterns to the solution to a problem.

Data-Driven Visualization: Visualization techniques for the display of the results after the analysis emphasizing the ease of decision-making through the graphical interface.

Intelligent Dispatch: Protocol and processes for the automatic sending of requests and attention to massive services in smart cities.

Internet of Things: Hardware and software infrastructure with a network approach that uses sensors to capture data by monitoring events.

Machine Learning: Supervised and unsupervised learning methods and techniques.

Open Data: Philosophy and web services for computer analytics that provide free access to data sets with content from different fields such as economy, environment, education, among others.

Smart People: Factors and technologies that contribute to the development of education, culture, human values, inclusion for citizens.

Chapter 17
Railway Engineering:
Timetable Planning and Control, Artificial Intelligence and Externalities

Aranzazu Berbey Alvarez
https://orcid.org/0000-0003-4278-5478
Universidad Tecnológica de Panamá, Panama

Jessica Guevara-Cedeño
https://orcid.org/0000-0002-7273-6848
Universidad Tecnológica de Panamá, Panama

ABSTRACT

This chapter is a case study of the dissemination of railway engineering research in Latin America developed by a railway engineering research group. The leader of the group is a female researcher. The authors aim to inspire to other women researchers in Latin American and Caribbean (LAC) countries who are trying to develop research in IT areas, many times facing serious difficulties, incomprehension, and great challenges. This chapter is divided in set sections like introduction, background, development of railway engineering research. This third section is divided into subsections like timetable planning and trains control, characterization of Panama metro line 1, dwelling times, fuzzy logic, artificial intelligence, social-economics railway externalities, and environmental railway externalities. The fourth section presents the results of the relationship between research activity and teaching of railway engineering obtained in this case study. Finally, the authors present a brief vision about future and emerging regional trends about railway engineering projects.

INTRODUCTION

This chapter presents a case study on the efforts of a Latin American railway engineering research group, including research activities, railway engineering courses, and other complementary activities. Railway engineering is a multidisciplinary engineering discipline focused on the design, construction, operation, inspection, and evaluation of rail transportation systems like metro, railroad, commuter train,

DOI: 10.4018/978-1-7998-7552-9.ch017

Copyright © 2021, IGI Global. Copying or distributing in print or electronic forms without written permission of IGI Global is prohibited.

tramway, light rail, and monorail. This high-tech discipline includes a range of engineering disciplines like civil engineering, computer engineering, electrical engineering, mechanical engineering, industrial engineering, telecommunications engineering, and railway externalities.

In the Latin America and Caribbean (LAC) context of urban transport systems, avenues of research are emerging that exploit nontraditional sources of data like big data and satellite information (Yañez-Pagans et al., 2019). Several studies explore ways to improve the operational efficiency of systems (Yañez-Pagans et al., 2019). Those seeking to promote behavioral changes in transport use can generate learning that is useful to both public and private actors involved. The science of artificial intelligence (AI) can develop rule-based expert systems, evolutionary optimization techniques, neural networks, and fuzzy logic related to solutions in railway transportation systems.

In general, transportation problems in the LAC are common. Fay et al. (2017) indicated that the LAC region has limited integration among transport modes, especially rail and road. For the rail infrastructure, Fay et al. (2017) indicated that density is less than 5 kilometers per thousand square kilometers for countries with a rail network as compared to 16 kilometers per thousand square kilometers for countries in the Organisation for Economic Co-operation and Development (OECD). In freight cargo, Mowatt (Mowatt & Cerra, 2017) found that the most mentioned constraint to export growth was infrastructure weaknesses and transportation costs. In the LAC, constraints were due to geography, including lack of adequate roads and railways, inefficiencies at ports and airports, and high costs when getting goods to market. To improve transport systems in Latin America, design systems must give priority to intermodality when transporting passengers and freight, which will make guided transport systems (metro and rail networks) the backbone of sustainable transport (Clemente, 2013).

The OECD, World Trade Organization (WTO), and the Inter-American Development Bank (IDB) (OECD et al., 2010) presented a snapshot of aid for trade on the ground about the LAC case stories. The publication indicated that projects to develop regional maritime transport and railroad networks were underway (OECD et al., 2010). For this reason, the IDB provided grant financing for feasibility studies and technical assistance in the region.

BACKGROUND

Railway engineering is considered a high technology development field with various research lines in prestigious universities, railroad research centers, and professional railway engineering associations. AI, a branch of computer sciences engineering performs tasks like visual perception, speech recognition, decision making, and translation between languages. This allows a computer program to think and learn like intelligent agents. Rail mobility, in coordination with the application of AI, can solve urban massive transit problems. There is extensive scientific literature regarding multiple applications of AI techniques in railway transportation systems. Table 1 presents these examples.

Table 1 shows a set of fuzzy logic applications in the railway transportation systems. Calic, Selmic, Macura, and Nikolic (Calic et al., 2019), Khosravi et al. (2017), Kaleybar and Farshad (2016), and Karakose et al. (2015) presented a scientific publication on topics like energy consumption prediction, railway traction, and pantograph-catenary systems. Calic et al. (2019) provided the Wang-Mendel method, combining numerical and linguistic information into a common framework (a fuzzy rule as a tool for energy consumption prediction). Khosravi et al. (2017) presented a fuzzy logic-based vector control of permanent magnet synchronous motor using stacked matrix converter for railway traction applications.

Table 1. Fuzzy logic application in railway engineering

Authors	Year	1	2	3	4	5	6	7	Institution, University, or Center
Calic et al.	2019	x							University of Belgrade (Serbia)
Milosavljević et al.	2018		x						School of Railway Applied Studies (Serbia)
De Aguiar, Amaral, Vellasco, & Ribeiro	2018		x					x	Federal University of Juiz de For a (Brazil), Pontifical Catholic University of Rio de Janeiro (Brazil)
Rozova, Sustr, Soušek, & Sohajek	2018		x	x					University of Pardubice (Czechia)
Dindar, Kaewunruen, & An	2018		x	x					University of Birmingham (UK)
Metin, Ulu, Paksoy, & Yücel	2018				x				Yildiz Technical University (Turkey)
Sasidharan, Burrow, Ghatoaora, & Torbaghan	2017			x	x				University of Birmingham (UK)
Zhang	2017		x				x		National Research Center of Railway Safety Assessment Beijing Jiaotong University (China)
De Aguiar, De Nogueira, Vellasco, & Ribeiro	2017		x					x	Federal University of Juiz de For a (Brazil), Pontifical Catholic University of Rio de Janeiro (Brazil)
Jamshidi, Núñez, Dollevoet, & Li	2017			x	x				Delft Univ. of Technology (The Netherlands)
Khosravi, Fazel, & Abdollahi	2017	x							Iran University of Science and Technology (Iran)
An, Qin, Jia, & Chen	2016			x					University of Birmingham (UK), Beijing Jiaotong University (China)
Menéndez, Martínez, Sanz, & Benitez	2016			x					Vías y Construcciones (Spain), Fundacion Cartif (Spain), Universidad de Granada (Spain)
Leonardi	2016			x					University of Reggio Calabria (Italy)
Kaleybar & Farshad	2016	x							Iran University of Science and Technology (Iran)
Karakose et al.	2015	x							Firat University (Turkey)
Pattanaik & Yadav	2015		x						Birla Institute of Technology (India)
Pamučar, Atanasković, & Milicic	2015		x						University of Defence (Serbia), University of Novi Sad (Serbia)

(1): Energy consumption prediction, railway traction, pantograph-catenary systems, (2): Safety and security railway engineering, train control system, level crossing system, (3): Risk, management, planning, mitigation decisions, infrastructure, maintenance decisions, (4): Vibrations estimation, (5): Simulation, Montecarlo technique, prediction, (6): Big data, (7): Adaptive filter theory

Kaleybar and Farshad (Kaleybar & Farshad, 2016) presented a control strategy of railway power quality compensator for alternating current (AC) traction power supply systems using a recessive self-tuning proportional-integral (PI) controller based on fuzzy logic adopted in the current control system. Karakose et al. (Karakose et al., 2015) presented an arc detection method based on fuzzy logic using S-transform for pantograph-catenary systems.

An et al. (2016), Menéndez et al. (2016), and Leonardi (2016) developed their work in relative topics like risk, management, planning, mitigation decisions, rail infrastructure, and maintenance decisions. For example, An et al. (An et al., 2016) presented a modified fuzzy analytical hierarchy process (FAHP) approach that employs the fuzzy multiplicative consistency method for the establishment of pairwise comparison matrices in risk decision making analysis in the railway risk decision making process. Menéndez et al. (2016) presented a development of a smart framework based on fuzzy and computational intelligence techniques to support infrastructure maintenance decisions in railway corridors. Leonardi (Leonardi, 2016) outlined an evaluation framework that integrates fuzzy logic with multicriteria decision making in the context of infrastructure railway planning.

Milosavljević, Jeremić, and Vujović (2018), Pattanaik and Yadav (Pattanaik & Yadav, 2015), and Pamučar et al. (Pamučar et al., 2015) presented a scientific publication on aspects like safety and security railway engineering, train control system, and level crossing system. Milosavljević, Jeremić, and Vujović (Milosavljevic et al., 2019) developed a fuzzy logic application for train braking distance determination. Pattanaik and Yadav (Pattanaik & Yadav, 2015) presented a decision support model for an automated railway level crossing system using fuzzy logic control (FLC). The FLC model recognizes railway events as the arrival and departure of trains. The generated output action signals include the warning siren and control actions for the opening and closing of gates. Pamučar et al. (2015) worked with the modeling of a fuzzy logic-based approach that offers adequate support to management when prioritizing railway-level crossings without barriers with automatic signaling and/or interlocking systems.

Rozova et al. (2018) presented fuzzy prediction diagnostic as a crisis management solution in the railway transport regarding the security system of the Czech Republic. Dindar et al. (Dindar et al., 2018) reviewed adequate risk analysis techniques for railway turnout systems, mentioning the fuzzy logic technique and other analysis tools in uncertain conditions.

Metin et al. (Metin et al., 2018) noted that, to mitigate bridge vibrations, a semiactive magnetorheological (MR) damper with FLC is positioned at the ends of the bridge. Sasidharan et al. (Sasidharan et al., 2017) reviewed risk management applications for the railway industry. Regarding the integration of Monte Carlo with fuzzy reasoning, Sasidharan et al. (2017) found it could be especially pertinent to the railway industry as it would enable uncertainties associated with data and the credibility of expert judgement to gain a better understanding of risks and impacts of risk mitigation decisions. Zhang (Zhang, 2017) presented an analysis method based on the fuzzy RDF model and uncertain reasoning for high-speed train control system big data. De Aguiar et al. (De Aguiar et al., 2018) introduced the set-concept, which is derived from the adaptive filter theory. This concept is used with the training procedure of type-1 and singleton/nonsingleton fuzzy logic systems to reduce computational complexity and increase convergence speed. It also presents different criteria for its use with set-membership. Jamshidi et al. (Jamshidi et al., 2017) proposed a methodology based on a set of fuzzy key performance indicators in combination with a fuzzy Takagi-Sugeno interval model to predict squat evolution for different scenarios over a time horizon in railway infrastructures.

DEVELOPMENT OF RAILWAY ENGINEERING RESEARCH IN PANAMA

A Brief History of Railway Transportation Systems in Panama

The Panama Metro Line 1 is the first metro system in Central America. However, rail technologies are not new in the Isthmus of Panama. For example, the Panama Interoceanic Railroad, inaugurated in 1855, was the first transcontinental or trans-isthmian railroad (CPRR.org, 1988; Lienhard, 1988; Mahler, 2006; The Panama Railroad, 2008)The Chiriquí Railroad, whose construction began on April 23, 1914, was inaugurated April 22, 1916. Its development took place during the administration of President Dr. Belisario Porras. The Chiriquí Railroad's extension reached 81 kilometers (Berrío-Lemm, 2010; BPP, 2008; Castro-Stanziola, 2006; Panamá Vieja Escuela, 2014; Redacción de TVN noticias, 2017; Serracin,

2014). The project was the idea of President Pablo Arosemena in 1911 to connect Panama City with David City. It originally included a branch to the province of Los Santos. However, it was not carried out due to its excessive budget. President Porras, through Law No. 20 of February 19, 1913 (Gobierno de Panamá, 1913), authorized the feasibility studies of a provincial railway under the contract of the American company, R. W. Hubbard. In 1928, under the presidency of Rodolfo Chiari, the La Concepción railway track was extended to the town of Puerto Armuelles. A railway station was later built. The Chiriquí Land Company, a subsidiary of the United Fruit Company, obtained permission to build more branches to transport its banana crops (Wikipedia, 2020). Subsequently, a branch was built to the town of Boquete in the Chiriquí mountains. The Chiriquí Railroad ceased operation in the mid-1980s, mainly due to its high operating and maintenance costs and the existence of land routes that connected populations in a more efficient manner.

Prior to the construction and commissioning of the Panama metro network (Atencio, 2016; CEPAL, 2013; Metro de Panama(2017), 2017; Metro de Panama(2018), 2018; Metro de Panamá(2018), 2018; Metro de Panama & Consorcio línea 2, 2015; Republica de Panama & Consorcio linea 1, 2010), Panama City had an urban rail system, the urban tram, to transport passengers (Alonso, 2003; Bermúdez, 1996; Celerier, 2013; Morrison, 2003, 2008; Upegui, 2009; Vergara, 2015).This tram system operated until Saturday, April 31, 1941 at 6:00 p.m. More than 70 years later, the Panama metro began operations. The first metro line was inaugurated on April 5, 2014 (Panama Metro, 2019); the second metro line of Panama City was inaugurated on April 25, 2019 (González-Jiménez, 2019)(Rivera, 2019).

The Panama Metro Line 1 is 16 km. This metropolitan subway connects the north (at the San Isidro station) to the south (to the Albrook station). This final station connects with the National Bus Terminal of Transport's Albrook Bus Terminal, which serves the entire country and the city. In addition, this station is close to the local airport, Marcos A. Gelabert International Airport, and the Panama Canal Railroad (Berbey-Álvarez et al., 2019) (see Figure 1).

The first line of the Panama Metro has both elevated and subterranean tracks operated with a catenary-guided transport system (Berbey et al., 2014). The Albrook zone contains a storage facility and maintenance facility for rolling stock (a surface of 10 hectares). The operations control center (OCC) is also located in the Albrook facility zone. Rolling stock float trains have several three and five electric unit coaches, with a maximum capacity of 800 and 1,000 passengers per train, respectively (Metro de Panamá(2018), 2018). The dwelling time ranges from 25 to 30 seconds.

Timetable Planning and Train Controls

The control train systems' engineering applications monitor and control the trains' movements and protection systems. A regular interval timetable is characterized by train services in a fixed time pattern (Demitz et al., 2010). According to Hansen (Hansen, 2010), the timetable quality is governed by precise running time, realistic recovery times, optimal headway, and buffer times. Headway is the time distance between two consecutives vehicles in a transit system (Campion, G., Van Breusegem, V., Pinson, P. y Bastin, 1985) Rice, 1974; Sasama & Ohkawa, 1983; (VanBreusegem et al., 1991).In the case of Panama Metro Line 1, the headway is 3 minutes with 20 seconds between 6:00 a.m. and 8:00 a.m. (i.e., 18 trains/hour). It is 4 minutes with 30 seconds(i.e., 14 trains/hour) in off-peak hours (Metro de Panamá, 2020b).

In this line of ideas, Berbey-Alvarez, San Segundo, and de Dios Sanz Bobi (Berbey et al., 2008), Berbey, Caballero, Galán, and Sanz-Bobi (2009), and Berbey et al. (2014) proposed a Lyapunov-based index for designing a real-time rescheduling algorithm for metro lines. A modified real-time discrete

Figure 1. Scheme of Panama Metro Line 1 (Phase 1 and Phase 2) (Berbey-Alvarez, 2013)

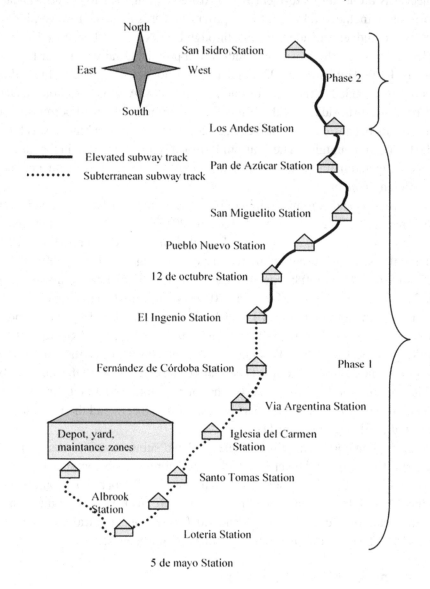

space state model was proposed regarding the saturation effects in the metro line. The direct method of Lyapunov was applied to analyze the stability of the metro line system. As a result of this analysis, a stability index and establishment of three stability zones were proposed to indicate the current state of the system. The proposed algorithm allowed for a real-time rescheduling of the timetable for the trains under medium delay.

According to Google Scholar and ResearchGate Web platforms, research by Berbey-Alvarez et al. (2008, 2009, 2014) was cited by other authors (Kampczyk, Dybel, & Dybel, 2020; Khosrosereshki & Moaveni, 2019; Lai & Ip, 2017; Lai, Chen, Yan, & Li, 2018; (Moaveni & Karimi, 2017). This summary is discussed in Table 2.

Table 2. Summary of cited works

Authors	Year	1	2	3	4	Institution, University, or Center
Lai et al.	2018	x				National Taiwan University (Taiwan)
Moaveni & Karimi	2017		x			K. N. Toosi University of Technology (Iran)
Lai et al.	2017	x				National Taiwan University (Taiwan)
Khosrosereshki & Moaveni	2019			x		Iran University of Science and Technology (Iran) K. N. Toosi University of Technology (Iran)
Kampczyk et al.	2020				x	AGH University of Science and Technology (Poland)
(1): Simulation, (2): Predictive control, (3): Rail traffic regulation, (4): Welded rail						

Lai et al. (Y.-C. (Rex) Lai et al., 2018) presented a simulation-based method of capacity utilization evaluation to account for uncertainty in recovery time. Moaveni and Karimi (2017) developed a study about subway traffic regulation using model-based predictive control by considering the passengers' dynamic effect. Lai et al. (Y.-C. Lai & Ip, 2017) presented an integrated framework for assessing service efficiency and stability of rail transit systems. Khosrosereshki and Moaveni (2019) published a paper on metro traffic regulation by considering the effect of transfer stations. Kampczyk et al. (2020) presented a study on the second difference in rail temperature of a continuous welded rail.

The tables 2 and 3 and their respective discussions try to show neutral objective evidence about the impact of the research activities carried out by PRERG through their citations by other authors. In the world academia, the impact by scientists is usually measured by an academic metric as their citations. The citations represent the dissemination of knowledge among scientists. It is a way to understand how much our scientific work may have had an impact if at all.

Characterization of Panama Metro Line 1

According to Pyrgidis (Pyrgidis, 2016), rail transport systems can move at grade, underground, and above the ground (elevated). The characterization of Panama Metro Line 1 was possible thanks to a research project of the same manner (Berbey-Álvarez et al., 2011). The general objective of this project was conducted using a framework of academic and research activities about the Panama Metro Line 1 project. In this work, a methodology was proposed on the time estimation of train movement partial services of the Panama Metro Line 1. First, nominal train services were estimated as the basis for estimating partial train services. For this reason, members of the Panama Railway Engineering Research Group (PRERG) considered technical information of the conceptual engineering about the Panama Metro Line 1. This conceptual engineering, functional, technical, and contractual specification corresponded to:

- Conceptual operation engineering (Secretaría del Metro de Panamá, 2010b) (Republica de Panama & Consorcio linea 1, 2010)
- Railway track systems and geometric conceptual design(Secretaría del Metro de Panamá, 2010a)
- Signaling and train control (Metro de Panamá, 2010)
- Rolling stock (Metro de Panama, 2010)(SMP. Secretaria del Metro de Panamá., 2010)(Secretaria del Metro de Panama, 2010)
- Railway stations' architecture (Secretaria del Metro de Panamá(2010), 2010)

- Railway stations' conceptual design (J. Velasco, Fernandez, et al., 2010c, 2010a, 2010b; J. Velasco, J. Fernandez, et al., 2010)

To validate this proposal, results were simulated using a set of scenarios that characterized the proposed model. The cause of the partial train's services could be an incidence, failure, breakdown of rolling stock, rail break, damage to the catenary, etc. This work would be limited to partial train's services because of the temporary immobilization of a train on the railway track.

Finally, PRERG published a paper as result of this project. It was used as a supporting tool for the active teaching and learning methodology in railway engineering courses (A. Berbey-Alvarez et al., 2015).

Dwelling Times, Fuzzy Logic, and AI

Matters around station dwelling times can be tackled with fuzzy logic and AI because the fuzzy set theory provides the mathematical technique for the systematic handling of imprecise data (Leonardi, 2016). In other words, Menéndez et al. (Menéndez et al., 2016) considered that fuzzy logic has become a successful approach to address complex problems. Fuzzy logic succeeds in formulating human knowledge and expert experience for the decision-making process. This allows for the managing and representation of imprecise information and vagueness found in the context of the railway industry. For example, the estimation of station dwelling time is critical for an acceptable railway timetable plan (Kikuchi & Miljkovic, 1999) because the line capacity in metro and high-frequency suburban railways is determined by both station dwelling times and factors like line speed or train acceleration (Berbey-Alvarez, Sanchez, Caballero, & Calvo, 2014). Fuzzy logic is based on observations using decisions based on imprecise and nonnumerical information. Fuzzy models are mathematical equations that represent imprecise information in which the correct values of these variables are real numbers between 0 and 1.

PRERG presented a new approach that combines the origin destination matrices method with the application of fuzzy logic using the Panama Metro Line 1 as a case study. PRERG presented an extension and practical application of previous research, using three fundamental levels of passenger flow in the membership function for a train's coach. Finally, PRERG proposed the application of the proposed algorithm to predict more realistic effects.

The works of Berbey-Alvarez et al. (2014) were cited by many authors, including Oh et al. (Oh et al., 2020), Cristóbal et al. (Cristóbal et al., 2018), Yang, Shiwakoti, and Tay (Yang et al., 2019), Feng et al. (Feng et al., 2017), Van-Ma et al. (Van-Ma et al., 2017), Becker and Schreckenberg (2018), Fabian, Sánchez-Martínez, and Attanucci (Fabian et al., 2018), D'Acierno et al. (D'Acierno et al., 2017), Carvajal, Cucala, and Fernández (Carvajal et al., 2016), He, Zhang, Keyu, and Lu (He et al., 2019), Li, Huang, and Schonfeld (Li et al., 2018), Di Maio, Botte, Montella, and D'Acierno (Di Maio et al., 2020). The summary of the citations are presented in Table 3.

For example, Oh et al. (Oh et al., 2020) presented a case study about dwelling time estimation using real-time train operations and smart card-based passenger data in Seoul, South Korea. Cristobal et al. (2018) presented an article about applying time-dependent attributes to represent demand in road mass transit systems. Yang et al. (2019)'s study explored train dwell time models as developed in the last 40 years. Feng et al. (2017) presented an algorithm by optimizing the energy-efficient metro train timetable and control strategy in off-peak hours. Van-Ma et al. (2017) developed a study about a fuzzy-based adaptive streaming algorithm for reducing entropy rate of an ASH bitrate fluctuation to improve mobile quality of service. Becker and Schreckenberg (2018) presented a case study on the influence

Table 3. Summary of citations by other authors

Authors	Year	1	2	3	4	5	6	7	Institution, University, or Center
Oh et al.	2020	X					x		Korea University, Khalifa University of Science and Technology, Abu Dhabi, Korea Railroad Research Institute
Cristobal et al.	2018	X							University of Las Palmas de Gran Canaria (Spain)
Yang et al.	2019	X		x					RMIT University, Melbourne (Australia)
Feng et al.	2017	X	x						Central South University (China), Beijing Jiaotong University (China)
Van-Ma et al.	2017					x			Chonnam National University (Korea), Electronics and Telecommunications Research Institute (Korea)
Becker & Schreckenberg	2018	X					x		Universität Duisburg-Essen Physik von Transport und Verkehr (Germany)
Fabian et al.	2018	X	x				x		Massachusetts Institute of Technology, Cambridge (USA), Massachusetts Bay Transportation Authority, Boston (USA)
D'Acierno et al.	2017	X					x		University of Naples (Italy), D'Appolonia
Carvajal et al.	2016				X	x			Institute for Research in Technology, Pontifical Comillas University (Spain)
He et al.	2019							x	Southwest Jiaotong University (China), National United Engineering Laboratory of Integrated and Intelligent Transportation (China), China Railway Economic and Planning Research Institute (China)
Li et al.	2018	X							Beijing Jiaotong University (China), University of Maryland (USA)
Di Maio et al.	2020	X							Federico II University of Naples (Italy)
1: Timetable, passenger flow, dwell time; 2: Train's control; 3: Review; 4: Energy consumption; 5: Fuzzy logic; 6: Case study; 7: Machine learning									

of stochastic dwell times on railway traffic simulations. Fabian et al. (2018) presented a study featured in Improving High-Frequency Transit Performance Through Headway-Based Dispatching: Development and Implementation of a Real-Time Decision-Support System on a Multi-Branch Light Rail Line. D'Acierno et al. (2017) developed a methodology for determining dwell times consistent with passenger flows in the case of metro services. Carvajal et al. (2016) used AI techniques like fuzzy logic and the fuzzy train tracking algorithm for the energy efficient operation of CBTC equipped metro lines. He et al. (He et al., 2019) developed a machine-learning-based integrated pedestrian facilities planning and staff assignment problem in transfer stations. Li et al. (Li et al., 2018) presented a study about metro timetabling for time-varying passenger demand and congestion at stations. Di Maio et al. (Di Maio et al., 2020) presented an analytical formulation to determine each bus stop's corresponding dwell time to increase the reliability of the planned service.

Social-Economics Railway Externalities

The externalities concept corresponds to the cost that affects a third party who did not pay for this benefit. For example, in the case of railway transportation, externalities occur when the consumption of a transportation service private price equilibrium cannot reflect real costs for the general society. Types of railway externalities can include social, economic, environmental, and energy. Externalities can be either positive or negative.

Vehicle congestion in cities, which produces an annual loss of millions of dollars, affects productivity sensitively. The social benefits of mass transit systems have a positive impact on the dynamics of metropolitan areas. Berbey-Alvarez et al. (2017) presented a railway externalities study related to the saving of travel time and economic utility. This study operated under various projected scenarios and compared with real data of passenger mobilization of the Panama Metro Line 1 (2014-2016). It discussed an estimation on the saving of travel times and economic utility through 2035 in Panama City. According to ResearchGate, the study has 850 reads. Figure 1 reveals a general scheme of this methodology by estimated social, economic, and environmental externalities (Guevara-Cedeño, 2013).

Figure 2. Methodology of externalities (Guevara-Cedeño, 2013)

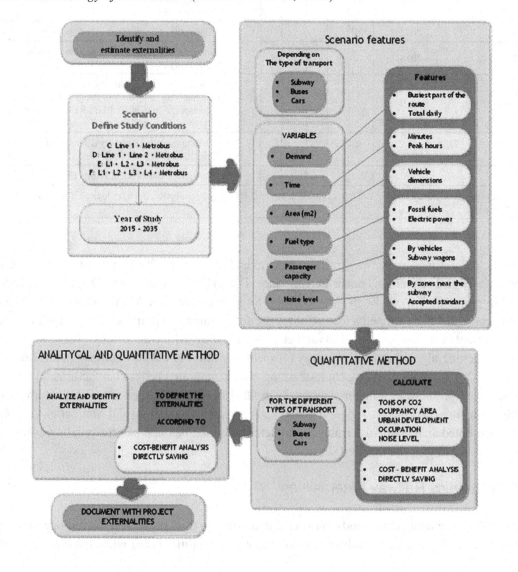

Environmental Railway Externalities

The methodology to determine carbon dioxide (CO_2) emissions for Panama Metro Line 1 was based on the original (American Public Transportation Association, 2009) approach of the APTA climate change standards working group. The APTA methodology calculates the average cost of taking public transit by determining the cost of an average monthly transit pass of local public transit agencies across the country (American Public Transportation Association, 2020).

Berbey-Alvarez et al. (2017, 2019) and Guevara-Cedeño, Aguilar, Torabi, and Berbey-Alvarez (Guevara-Cedeño et al., 2018) published an analysis of CO_2 emissions in the Panama Metro Line 1 using the APTA methodology (2015-2017). Their work has been used as reading and assessment materials in individual short exams (Berbey-álvarez, 2017; Aranzazu Berbey-Alvarez, 2014) in railway engineering courses in the Technological University of Panamá.

RELATIONSHIP BETWEEN RESEARCH ACTIVITY AND TEACHING OF RAILWAY ENGINEERING IN PANAMA

A Global Brief of Railway Engineering in Higher Education

In the LAC context, Kohon (Kohon, 2011) published a study on Latin America's railway transportation sector.Kohon's (2011) study, a technical note financed by the IDB, considered railway training a priority. According to Kohon (2011), the training of new generations of human resource experts was still insufficient. In the field of public management, the training involved professionals in the development of strategies, policies, planning, and regulations associated with rail transportation. In the field of railway companies, the training involved professionals and technicians of medium and higher levels. Kohon (Kohon, 2011) mentioned that initiatives in Argentina and Brazil are limited to the field of railway companies. In addition to strengthening these initiatives, they must consider the possibility of training resources from countries that, for reasons of scale, cannot generate their own training.

However, this situation is not exclusive to the LAC regionLautala et al. (2010) and Lautala, Tyler-Dick, Mckinney, and Clarke (2013) considered that the national emphasis on highway transportation and lack of demand for graduates in rail-related fields led to decades of neglect surrounding rail transportation and engineering education by universities in the United States. However, the Tuning Transatlantic Cooperation in Rail Higher Education (TUNRail) project evaluates teaching and learning practices of railway systems in European and U.S. institutions of higher education by defining the level of collaboration between the academic programs and railway industry (Marinov et al., 2011).

Kalidova and Neduzha (Kalivoda & Neduzha, 2017) presented a study about enhancing the scientific level of engineering training of railway transport professionals. This study confirmed that international cooperation promotes the strengthening of contacts between universities, improves the quality of students' training, is a factor the professional development of future specialists, and raises the scientific level of engineering training of railway transport specialists.

Rizzetto et al. (2015) presented other interesting European experiences regarding a postgraduate course titled "Railway Infrastructure and Systems Engineering." This postgraduate course is a case of cooperation between academia and railway industry transport. Lautala (Lautala, 2007) presented a benchmarking study to investigate the upcoming demand for university graduates by Class I railroads and engineering consultants. The study looked at whether current methods are adequate to attract, educate, recruit, train, and retain engineering students in the railroad profession.

Lautala and Tyler-Dick (2017) presented the results of the Railway Engineering Education Symposium (REES). Marinov et al. (Marinov et al., 2013) analyzed the current state of supply and demand for higher education in rail logistics. Their work revealed a spectrum of courses and programs related to rail, freight transport, and logistics.

There is still a strong need for specific training and education on operations management skills. These skills will improve company performance, efficiency, and quality of service.

Jing, You-Ming, and Li-Yan (2017) proposed a revised method based on education professional certification standards. Its curriculum, which was based on the supplementary standard of engineering certification, aimed to improve the capacity of staff in the rail transit operation. Another curricular review experience is presented in Kaewunruen (Kaewunruen, 2017). The railway engineering curriculum in the civil engineering program was critically reviewed and evaluated, enhancing core technical skills alongside those required for systems-thinking solutions. Comparative evaluations were based on the review and evaluation of both the academic and railway industry sectors.

Railway Engineering in Panamaniam Higher Education

In 2009, Berbey-Alvarez et al. (2009) founded the PRERG) at the Technological University of Panamá. This group included members of Spain. It later incorporated members of the University of Granada, Spain. The PRERG was founded in its long-term vision and growth of the railway engineering professional workforce in Panama.

According to Streitzig, Schön, Griese, and Oetting (Streitzig et al., 2013), education is a central aspect for winning and qualifying employees for railway operation and research. According to Tyler-Dick, Schlake, and Lautala (2018) and Tyler-Dick, Lautala, and Schlake (2019), students must be introduced to railway concepts before they decide on the direction of their studies. In doing so, student interest in rail courses will increase and, in turn, satisfy industry demands for interns. The tables 4 and 5 summarize efforts of railway engineering teaching at the Technological University of Panamá.

The PRERG work generated by the research and development (R&D) activity has been used as a supporting tool for the active teaching and learning methodology in a railway engineering course. Table 5 shows a resume of the engineering course oriented to railway and engineering transportation.

Table 4. Summary of railway engineering seminaries

Speaker´s Affiliation	Title	Year	Sponsors
Technological University of Panamá Universidad Politécnica de Madrid	*Sistemas y Tecnologías de Transporte Urbano Ferroviario*	2010	Aecid, Metro de Panamá, UTP
Universidad Tecnológica de Panamá Universidad de Granada	*Sistema de Ingeniería Ferroviaria I*	2014	AUIP, Metro de Panama, UTP
Universidad Tecnológica de Panamá Universidad de Granada	*Diseño geométrico y mecánica de la vía férrea*	2015	UTP

Source: (Calvo-Poyo & Berbey-Álvarez, 2014), (Lorente-Gutierrez & Berbey-Álvarez, 2015), Sanz-Bobi, Berbey-Álvarez, Caballero, and Alvarez (2009), (Sanz-Bobi et al., 2009, 2010)

Table 5. Resume of engineering course oriented to railway and engineering transportation

Group	Subject	Students	Year
1IE141	Tópicos de actualización tecnológica	39	2014
1IE143	Tópicos de actualización tecnológica	37	2014
1IE143	Tópicos de actualización tecnológica	39	2015
1IE141	Tópicos de actualización tecnológica	39	2016
1IE143	Tópicos de actualización tecnológica	39	2017

Source: (Vicerrectoría académica, 2020)

Engineering students were able to better comprehend the Panama Metro Network through the use of Panama Metro professional technical documents related to Lines 1 and 2. However, these resources must be adapted through a stronger understanding by engineering students. Therefore, it is important that the railway engineering professors have a solid background. Railway engineering backgrounds should include three components: (1) higher engineering education; (2) R&D; and (3) professional activities in the railway industry.

In the same direction, a group of papers regarding railway engineering education in undergraduate engineering courses was published (Berbey-álvarez et al., 2017; A Berbey-Alvarez, 2015; A Berbey-Alvarez et al., 2018; Berbey Álvarez, 2016). With the objective of developing the R&D activity with engineering students, Berbey-Alvarez developed a final subject project guide (Berbey-Álvarez, 2017; A Berbey-Alvarez, 2019) so engineering students could present scientific posters and articles in congress (Alvarado et al., 2012; Cogley-Brown, Berbey Álvarez, et al., 2014; Cogley-Brown, Berbey-Alvarez, et al., 2014; Monrroy, 2018). Consequently, regarding the PRERG's activities, the scientific papers generated by the R&D activity were used as supporting tools for the active teaching and learning methodology in railway engineering courses at the Technological University of Panamá, particularly in the faculty of electrical engineering. For example, Monrroy's (2018) scientific paper on the main characteristics of the electrical system of the Panama Metro Line 2 was published with electromechanical engineering students. Important points were developed, including substations, catenary systems, cables, protection systems, power supply systems, and other electrical aspects of the rail transportation system. Therefore, it is possible to construct a didactic resource with and by students of engineering and related careers in the courses of engineering and rail transportation.

Table 6 shows the citations of Berbey et al. (Berbey et al., 2013), (Berbey-álvarez et al., 2017), and (A Berbey-Alvarez & Caballero-George, 2012). The table's citations often correspond to bachelor's theses and scientific papers presented in congress. These citations represent the dissemination of knowledge among both undergraduate and graduate students. Our citation in master thesis, bachelor thesis and scientific papers in congress is a sample of how much our scientific work in PRERG has had an impact.

Additionally, the faculty of civil engineering's subject, Terminales de Trasbordo (Cod. 8771)" is designed for bachelor's students in maritime port engineering (UTP, 2016e). In the field of Panamanian private universities, the "Universidad Interamericana de Panamá" (UIP) includes a subject titled "Transporte Terrestre y Ferroviario" (code 202-00009) in cycle 7 of the bachelor's degree in transportation and logistics engineering (UIP, 2019).

Table 6. Summary of citations of PRERG

Works	Authors	Year	1	2	3	Institution, University, Center
(Berbey et al., 2013)	Sarmiento	2020	x			Universidad de Buenos Aires (Argentina)
	Conde	2017	x			Universidad de San Andres (Argentina)
	Amaya-Usaquen	2015		x		Universidad Piloto de Colombia (Colombia)
	Muñoz-Portero	2016		x		Universidad Carlos III de Madrid (Spain)
	Madrid-Naz	2018		x		Universidad de Sevilla (Spain)
	Doicela-Gómez	2018		x		Universidad Central de Ecuador (Ecuador)
	Berrezueta-Merchan	2016		x		Universidad Politecnica Salesiana (Ecuador)
(Berbey-álvarez et al., 2017)	Carretón et al.,	2018			x	Universidad de Las Palmas de Gran Canaria (Spain)
Berbey et al. (2012)	Amaya-Usaquen	2015			x	Universidad Piloto de Colombia (Colombia)
(Berbey et al., 2010)	Benavides et al.,	2017			x	Universidad técnica de norte (Ecuador)
Berbey-Alvarez & Caballero-George (2012).	Alzate-Torres et al.,	2018			x	Universidad Nacional de Colombia (Colombia)
(1); Master's thesis, (2): Bachelor's thesis, (3): Scientific paper						

Railway Professional and Technical Training in Panama

The Instituto Técnico Superior de Panamá Oeste (ITSPO) provides railway training for professional and technical skills (Richards, 2016). The ITSPO installed a railway track section and a tramway to develop these professional skills (Presidencia de la República de Panamá, 2017)(Ministerio de Educación, 2016) (Zeballos, 2016). The ITSPO was created by a cooperation and technical assistance agreement in the field of education between the Ministries of Education of Panama (MEDUCA) and France. According to MEDUCA, three companies support this railway professional and technical training (Ministerio de Educación, 2016). First, Alstom donated the rolling stock. Second, the TSO CIM company built a railway track section so students can complete their hours of laboratory practice. Third, Schneider Electric donated the educational equipment for electricity and industrial automation.

REGIONAL FUTURE TRENDS

This section presents a brief vision about future and emerging regional trends. It explores railway engineering projects like the Panama Monorail Line 3, Maya Train, Bogota Metro, and Mesoamerican Train.

The Panama Metro Network operates Lines 1 and 2 in Panama City. The next railway, Line 3, is a monorail that departs from Albrook Station before traveling to Arraiján, Nuevo Chorrillo, and Ciudad del Futuro. The first phase corresponds to 26.7 kilometers and 14 stations (Martínez-Palacios, 2019). Phase one's estimated demand is 20,000 passengers in one direction at peak hours. Each train will have six wagons. Line 3 will have two circuits: East Circuit (Albrook – Nuevo Chorrillo [17.5km]) and Complete Circuit (Albrook – Ciudad del Futuro [25.85km]) (Metro de Panamá, 2020a).

The Maya Train will be a 1,525 kilometer railway line in Mexico's Yucatan Peninsula. It will cross the states of Tabasco, Campeche, Chiapas, Yucatan, and Quintana Roo. This railway line will have 17 stations with rolling stock to provide cargo and passenger transportation services. The maximum speed of the passenger rolling stock will be 160 kilometers per hour (Comisión de asuntos frontera sur, 2019; Flores et al., 2019; Mexico., 2020) (Martínez-Palacios, 2019).

The Mesoamerican Train, connecting Mexico with Panama (Rieles multimedio, 2020), is part of the Mesoamérica project, integrated by Mexico, Guatemala, Belize, Honduras, El Salvador, Nicaragua, Costa Rica, Panama, Colombia, and the Dominican Republic. The project includes a portfolio of projects in eight strategic areas: (1) energy; (2) transport; (3) telecommunications; (4) commercial facilitation and competitiveness; (5) health; (6) environment; (7) risk management; and (8) housing (EFE, 2013).

The Bogota Metro Line 1 will be a 23.96 kilometer elevated mass rapid transit line. Bogota Metro Line 1 will accommodate 72,000 passengers per hour in each direction. The trains will achieve an average speed of 43 kilometers per hour, reaching the south from the north in approximately 27 minutes (Metro de Bogotá, 2015; Verdict media, 2022).

Dussel-Peters, Armony, and Cui (Dussel-Peters et al., 2018) examined the connections between China and the LAC. Their research showed the expansion of an emerging field of study, including significant implications for the future relationship between China and Latin America. In the future, the railway transportation systems and other LAC infrastructure developments will play a critical role (Koleski & Blivas, 2018).

CONCLUSION

Rail mobility, including the application of AI, can solve problems related to urban massive transit and freight cargo. There is extensive scientific literature on the multiple applications of AI techniques in the railway transportation system. Fuzzy logic, a key tool, models expert knowledge to improve the decision-making process as a consequence of more adequately representing imprecise information and vagueness in the railway industry. The methods addressed demonstrate the application of technologies for solving pollution and economic problems in rail transport, which are means of human development.

Railway engineering should have a relevant place within university curricula and engineering disciplines. For example, railway engineering courses should be part of curricula design within civil engineering, computer engineering, electrical engineering, mechanical engineering, industrial engineering, telecommunications engineering, and others.

The authors have been able to contribute knowledge in the development of railway studies for Panama and in the research community. At present, the PRERG continues with research railway engineering activities. In addition, the female leader of this research group has submitted her first book for publication, titled *Fundamentos de la Ingeniería ferroviaria: la vía* (Editorial Tecnologica of the Technological University of Panamá).

ACKNOWLEDGMENT

The authors wants to express her gratitude to various institutions, including: Universidad Tecnológica de Panamá, IFARHU (Panamá); SENACYT (Panamá); Universidad Politécnica de Madrid (Spain);

Universidad de Granada (Spain); Fundación Carolina (Spain); Panama Metro Authority (Panama); Universidad de Chile (Chile); Instituto Justo Arosemena (Panama); Dr. Belisario Porras School (Panama); and Miguel de Unamuno School (Spain).

REFERENCES

Alonso, R. (2003). *AlonsoRoy.com - Escritos Históricos de Panamá: R.I.P. para el tranvía eléctrico.* https://web.archive.org/web/20110719121230/http://www.alonsoroy.com/era/era10.html

Alvarado, F., Jiménez, G., López, K., Pacheco, E., Roa, N., Solís, A., Tejada, M., & Berbey-Álvarez, A. (2012). Sistemas de ventilación mayor y aires acondicionados de la línea 1 del metro de Panamá. (Mención Honorífica) Del 19 al 22 de octubre del 2016, Hotel Wyndham Pana. In Apanac (Ed.), *XVI Congreso Nacional de Ciencia y Tecnología. Asociación panameña para el avance de la ciencia.* Apanac.

American Public Transportation Association. (2009). *APTA climate change standards working group. Recommended practice for quantifying greenhouse gas emissions from transit.* APTA.

American Public Transportation Association. (2020). *Transit Savings Report Methodology.* News and Publications.APTA. https://www.apta.com/news-publications/transit-savings-report-methodology/#:~:text=APTA calculates the average cost,transit agencies across the country.

An, M., Qin, Y., Jia, L. M., & Chen, Y. (2016). Aggregation of group fuzzy risk information in the railway risk decision making process. *Safety Science, 82,* 18–28. doi:10.1016/j.ssci.2015.08.011

Atencio, C. (2016). *El Metro de Panamá, entre los mejores del mundo.* Periódico La Estrella de Panamá. http://laestrella.com.pa/panama/nacional/metro-entre-mejores-mundo/23927947

Berbey. (2010). A fuzzy logic inference approach for the estimation of the passengers flow demand. Proceedings of the International Conference on Fuzzy Computation and 2nd International Conference on Neural Computation, ICFC 2010 - International Conference on Fuzzy Computation, 125–129. doi:10.5220/0003057701250129

Berbey. (2013). Trenes: Material rodante del transporte ferroviario. *Prisma, 4*(1), 33–37.

Berbey. (2008). Lyapunov based stability analysis for metro lines. *Urban Transport XIV. Urban Transport and the Environment in the 21st Century.*

Berbey, A., Sánchez, V., Caballero, R., & Calvo, F. (2014). Passenger's flow for a train's coach and dwelling time using fuzzy logic. In *Proceedings of 2014 International Work Conference on Bio-inspired Intelligence (IWOBI),* (pp. 30–36). IEEE. 10.1109/IWOBI.2014.6913934

Berbey-Alvarez, A. (2014). *Portafolio de la asignatura de Tópicos de actualización tecnológica (TAT) orientada a ingeniería y transporte ferroviario.* Academic Press.

Berbey-Álvarez, Guevara-Cedeño, J., Alvarez, H., & Mihailovs, F. (2019). Panama metro line 1: Analysis of CO2 emissions from 2015 to 2017. Principles for an eco-transportation city. *Procedia Computer Science, 149,* 467–474. doi:10.1016/j.procs.2019.01.164

Berbey-Alvarez, A. (2015). Estudio de Caso: Tópicos de actualización tecnológica. Academic Press.

Berbey Álvarez, A. (2016). ¿Cómo evaluar la inserción de la investigación en la docencia universitaria? Caso de estudio: Tópicos de Actualización Tecnológica. In E. Universidad de las Palmas de la Gran Canaria (Ed.), InnoeducaTIC2016. III Jornadas Iberoamericanas de Innovación educativa en el Ámbito de las TIC, Las Palmas de Gran Canaria, 17-18 de noviembre 2016. Academic Press.

Berbey-álvarez, A. (2017). *Portafolio de la asignatura TAT desarrollado durante los años 2014, 2015 y 2016*. Vigente.

Berbey-Álvarez, A. (2017). Guía para desarrollo de proyecto de investigación. Proyecto final de la asignatura Tópicos de actualización Tecnológica. Facultad de Ingeniería Eléctrica. Universidad Tecnológica de Panamá.2014, Actualizada 2016.

Berbey-Alvarez, A. (2019). Guía para el desarrollo del proyecto final de la asignatura. Academic Press.

Berbey-álvarez, A., Alvarez, H., Castillo, G., Torre, I. D. La, Panamá, U. T. De, Eléctrica, F. D. I., Edificio, N., Panamá, R. De, & Valladolid, U. De. (2017). *El poster científico : recurso de la docencia e investigación*. Academic Press.

Berbey-Alvarez, A., Álvarez, H., Castillo-Sánchez, G., & De LaTorre-Diez, I. (2018). Acción tutorial para la mentoría en la iniciación científica. In *V Jornadas Iberoamericanas de Innovación Educativa en el Ámbito de las TIC y las TAC Las Palmas de Gran Canaria, 15 y 16 de noviembre de 2018*. https://www.researchgate.net/profile/Aranzazu_Berbey-Alvarez

Berbey-Alvarez, A., & Caballero-George, R. (2012). Un enfoque de lógica borrosa para el modelado de los flujos de pasajeros y el tiempo de parada. In Laccei 2012 (Ed.), *Tenth LACCEI Latin American and Caribbean Conference for Engineering and Technology (LACCEI'2012) "Megaprojects: Building Infrastructure by Fostering Engineering Collaboration, Efficient and Effective Integration and Innovative Planning" July 23 - 27, 201* (p. 9). Laccei 2012.

Berbey-Álvarez, A., Caballero-George, R., Alvarez, H., & Guevara-Cedeño, J. (2011). *Caracterización de la línea 1 del Metro de Panamá*. Sistema de Información Científica de La UTP - SicUTP. http://www.investigadores.utp.ac.pa/proyectos/882

Berbey-Alvarez, A., Merchan, F., Guevara-Cedeño, J., Cogley, A., & Caballero, R. (2015). Caracterización de la línea 1 del Metro de Panamá. In LACCEI (Ed.), *Latin American and Caribbean Consortium of Engineering Institutions, the thirteenth latinamerican and caribbean conference for engineering and technology Santo Domingo, Dominican Republic. 2015*. LACCEI. 10.18687/LACCEI2015.1.1.239

Berbey-Alvarez, A., Sanchez, V., Caballero, R., & Calvo, F. (2014). Passenger's flow for a train's coach and dwelling time using fuzzy logic. In *2014 International Work Conference on Bio-Inspired Intelligence: Intelligent Systems for Biodiversity Conservation, IWOBI 2014 - Proceedings* (pp. 30–36). IEEE. 10.1109/IWOBI.2014.6913934

Bermúdez, R. J. (1996). Ricardo J. Bermúdez en la cultura arquitectónica y literaria de Panamá. Compilación, clasificación y prólogo de Samuel A. Gutiérrez Tomo I. La Prensa. Panamá.

Berrío-Lemm, V. (2010). *Belisario Porras Barahona*. Panamá y Su Historia. https://panahistoria.wordpress.com/2010/10/27/belisario-porras-barahona/

BPP. (2008). *El ferrocarril que Chiriquí perdió*. Breve Historia Del Ferrocarril Nacional de Chiriqui. Charco Azul. https://charcoazul.wordpress.com/2008/07/18/el-ferrocarril-que-chiriqui-dejo-perder/

Calic, J., Selmic, M., Macura, D., & Nikolic, M. (2019). Fuzzy Logic Application in Green Transport - Prediction of Freight Train Energy Consumption. *International Journal for Traffic and Transport Engineering*, *9*(3), 35–44. doi:10.7708/ijtte.2019.9(3).04

Calvo-Poyo, F., & Berbey-Álvarez, A. (2014). Sistema de Ingeniería Ferroviaria I. Universidad Tecnológica de Panamá. Patrocinado por: Asociacion Universitaria Iberoamericana de Postgrado(AUIP)y la Secretaria del Metro de Panamá(Panamá).

Campion, G., Van Breusegem, V., Pinson, P. y Bastin, G. (1985). Traffic regulation of an underground railway transportation system by state feedback. *Optimal Control Applications & Methods, 6*, 385–402.

Carvajal, W., Cucala, A., & Fernández, A. (2016). Fuzzy train tracking algorithm for the energy efficient operation of CBTC equipped metro lines. *Engineering Applications of Artificial Intelligence, 53*, 19–31. doi:10.1016/j.engappai.2016.03.011

Castro-Stanziola, H. (2006). *El ferrocarril de Chiriquí*. Periódico La Prensa. https://web.archive.org/web/20100415110132/http://mensual.prensa.com/mensual/contenido/2006/11/26/hoy/vivir/807497.html

Celerier, L. (2013). *The Streetcars (Tranvias) of Panama*. EcoCircuitos Panama Travel Blog Adventure, Conservation and Education. https://ecocircuitospanama.wordpress.com/2013/01/08/the-streetcars-tranvias-of-panama/

CEPAL. (2013). Situación actual de los metros y ferrocarriles de América Latina. *Boletin FAL, 326*, 1–16.

Cogley-Brown, A., Berbey-Alvarez, A., & Caballero-George, R. (2014). Estimación de los servicios parciales de la línea 1 del metro de Panamá.. XII Encuentro Iberoamericano de Mujeres Ingenieras, Arquitectas y Agrimensoras. Perspectiva de La Mujer Profesional Iberoamericana, Ante Las Tendencias de La Ingeniería y Arquitectura Sostenible".

Cogley-Brown, A., Berbey Álvarez, A., & Caballero-George, R. (2014). Estimación de los servicios parciales de la línea 1 del metro de Panamá. In Editorial Tecnológica (Ed.), XII Encuentro Iberoamericano de Mujeres Ingenieras, Arquitectas y Agrimensoras. Perspectiva de la mujer profesional Iberoamericana, ante las tendencias de la ingeniería y arquitectura sostenible". Editorial Tecnológica.

Comisión de asuntos frontera sur. (2019). *Ficha técnica del tren maya: Aspectos legislativos, ambientales, económicos y socio-culturales*. Author.

CPRR.org. (1988). *The Panama Railroad*. Central Pacific Railroad Photographic History Museum. http://cprr.org/Museum/

Cristóbal, T., Padrón, G., Lorenzo-Navarro, J., Quesada-Arencibia, A., & García, C. (2018). Applying Time-Dependent Attributes to Represent Demand in Road Mass Transit Systems. *Entropy (Basel, Switzerland)*, *20*(133), 1–18. doi:10.3390/e20020133

D'Acierno, L., Botte, M., & Placido, A. (2017). Methodology for Determining Dwell Times Consistent with Passenger Flows in the Case of Metro Services. *Urban Rail Transit, 3*, 73–89.

De Aguiar, E. P., Amaral, R. P. F., Vellasco, M. M. B. R., & Ribeiro, M. V. (2018). An enhanced singleton type-2 fuzzy logic system for fault classification in a railroad switch machine. *Electric Power Systems Research, 158*(May), 195–206. doi:10.1016/j.epsr.2017.12.018

de Panamá, G. (1913). *Sobre tierras balvias e indultadas.* Asamblea Nacional. República de Panamá. https://docs.panama.justia.com/federales/leyes/20-de-1913-feb-21-1913.pdf

Demitz, J., Hübschen, C., & Albrecht, C. (2010). Timetable stability -using simulation to ensure quality in a regualr interval timetable. In I. Hansen (Ed.), *Timetable planning and information quality* (pp. 11–24). WIT press.

Di Maio, A., Botte, M., Montella, B., & D'Acierno, L. (2020). The Definition of Bus Fleet Operational Parameters: The Dwell Time Estimation. *2020 IEEE International Conference on Environment and Electrical Engineering and 2020 IEEE Industrial and Commercial Power Systems Europe (EEEIC / I&CPS Europe).* 10.1109/EEEIC/ICPSEurope49358.2020.9160592

Dindar, S., Kaewunruen, S., & An, M. (2018). Identification of appropriate risk analysis techniques for railway turnout systems. *Journal of Risk Research, 21*(8), 974–995. doi:10.1080/13669877.2016.1264452

Dussel-Peters, E., Armony, A., & Cui, S. (2018). *Building development for a new era. China's infraestructure projects in Latin America and the Caribbean.* Academic Press.

EFE. (2013). *Evalúan la creación de ferrocarril que conecte a Mesoamérica.* Portafolio.

Fabian, J., Sánchez-Martínez, G. E., & Attanucci, J. P. (2018). Improving High-Frequency Transit Performance through Headway-Based Dispatching: Development and Implementation of a Real-Time Decision-Support System on a Multi-Branch Light Rail Line. *Transportation Research Record: Journal of the Transportation Research Board, 2672*(8), 363–374. doi:10.1177/0361198118794534

Feng, J., Li, X., Liu, H., Gao, X., & Mao, B. (2017). Optimizing the Energy-Efficient Metro Train Timetable and Control Strategy in Off-Peak Hours. *Energies, 10*(436), 20. doi:10.3390/en10040436

Flores, A., Deniau, Y., & Prieto-Diaz, S. (2019). *El Tren Maya . Un nuevo proyecto de articulación territorial en la Península de Yucatán.* Academic Press.

González-Jiménez, R. (2019). *Varela inaugura la segunda línea del Metro de Panamá.* Inversión. Periódico La Prensa. https://www.prensa.com/economia/Varela-inaugura-segunda-Metro-Panama_0_5289970977.html

Guevara-Cedeño, J., Aguilar, J., Torabi, R., & Berbey-Alvarez, A. (2018). Electric mobility in Panama: A review. In U. da Madeira (Ed.), *ES2DE 2018. International Conference on Energy and Sustainability in Small Developing Economies.* IEEE.

Hansen, I. A. (2010). State of the art of railway operations research. In I. Hansen (Ed.), *Timetable planning and information quality* (pp. 35–47). WIT Press. doi:10.2495/978-1-84564-500-7/04

He, B., Zhang, H., Keyu, W., & Lu, G. (2019). Machine Learning based integrated pedestrian facilities planning and staff assignment problem in transfer stations. *8th International Conference on Railway Operations Modelling and Analysis - RailNorrk¨oping 2019*, 387–408.

Jamshidi, A., Núñez, A., Dollevoet, R., & Li, Z. (2017). Robust and predictive fuzzy key performance indicators for condition-based treatment of squats in railway infrastructures. *Journal of Infrastructure Systems*, 23(3), 1–13. doi:10.1061/(ASCE)IS.1943-555X.0000357

Kaewunruen, S. (2017). Underpinning systems thinking in railway engineering education. *Australasian Journal of Engineering Education*, 22(2), 107–116. doi:10.1080/22054952.2018.1440481

Kaleybar, H. J., & Farshad, S. (2016). A comprehensive control strategy of railway power quality compensator for AC traction power supply systems. *Turkish Journal of Electrical Engineering and Computer Sciences*, 24(6), 4582–4603. doi:10.3906/elk-1404-250

Kalivoda, J., & Neduzha, L. O. (2017). Enhancing the Scientific Level of Engineering Training of Railway Transport Professionals. *Science and Transport Progress. Bulletin of Dnipropetrovsk National University of Railway Transport*, 0(6(72)), 128–137. doi:10.15802tp2017/119050

Karakose, E., Gencoglu, M. T., Karakose, M., Yaman, O., Aydin, I., & Akin, E. (2015). A new arc detection method based on fuzzy logic using S-transform for pantograph–catenary systems. *Journal of Intelligent Manufacturing*, 19. Advance online publication. doi:10.100710845-015-1136-3

Khosravi, M., Fazel, S. S., & Abdollahi, V. (2017). Fuzzy logic-based vector control of permanent magnet synchronous motor using stacked matrix converter for railway traction aplications. *Railway Research*, 4(2), 41–56.

Kikuchi, S., & Miljkovic, D. (1999). *Method To Preprocess Observed Traffic Data for Consistency Application of Fuzzy Optimization Concept.* Transportation Research Record 1679 Paper No. 99-0129 73.

Kohon, J. (2011). *Más y mejores trenes.* BID.

Koleski, K., & Blivas, A. (2018). China's Engagement with Latin America and the Caribbean. Congressional Research Service.

Lai, Y.-C., Chen, K.-T., Yan, T.-H., & Li, M.-H. (2018). Simulation-Based Method of Capacity Utilization Evaluation to Account for Uncertainty in Recovery Time. *Transportation Research Record: Journal of the Transportation Research Board, 2672*(10), 202–214.

Lai, Y.-C., & Ip, C.-S. (2017). An integrated framework for assessing service efficiency and stability of rail transit systems. *Transportation Research Part C, Emerging Technologies*, 79, 18–41. doi:10.1016/j.trc.2017.03.006

Lautala, P. (2007). *From classroom to rail industry- A rail engineer in the making.* Academic Press.

Leonardi, G. (2016). A fuzzy model for a railway-planning problem. *Applied Mathematical Sciences*, 10(January), 1333–1342. doi:10.12988/ams.2016.63106

Li, K., Huang, H., & Schonfeld, P. (2018). Metro Timetabling for Time-Varying Passenger Demand and Congestion at Stations. *Journal of Advanced Transportation, 2018*, 27. doi:10.1155/2018/3690603

Lienhard, J. (1988). *No. 1208: The Panama Railroad*. The Engines of Our Ingenuity. https://uh.edu/engines/epi1208.htm

Lorente-Gutierrez, J., & Berbey-Álvarez, A. (2015). *Diseño Geométrico y Mecánica de la Vía Férrea*. Universidad Tecnológica de Panamá.

Mahler, S. (2006). *The New Panama Railroad: World's Ninth Wonder*. Britannica Blog. http://blogs.britannica.com/2007/04/the-new-panama-railroad-ninth-wonder-of-the-world/

Marinov, M., Fraszczyk, A., Zunder, T., Rizzetto, L., Ricci, S., Todorova, M., Dzhaleva, A., Karagyozov, K., Trendafilov, Z., & Schlingensiepen, J. (2013). A supply-demand study of practice in rail logistics higher education. *Journal of Transport Literature*, 7(2), 338–351. doi:10.1590/S2238-10312013000200018

Marinov, M., Pachl, J., Lautala, P., Macario, R., Reis, V., & Riley-Edwards, J. (2011). Policy-Oriented Measures for Tuning and Intensifying Rail Higher Education on both Sides of the Atlantic. *4th International Seminar on Railway Operations Modelling and Analysis (IAROR)*, 17.

Martínez-Palacios, A. (2019). Nota técnica Proyecto del Tren maya. Instituto Mexicano para la competividad (IMCO).

Menéndez, M., Martínez, C., Sanz, G., & Benitez, J. M. (2016). Development of a Smart Framework Based on Knowledge to Support Infrastructure Maintenance Decisions in Railway Corridors. *Transportation Research Procedia*, *14*, 1987–1995. doi:10.1016/j.trpro.2016.05.166

Metin, M., Ulu, A., Paksoy, M., & Yücel, M. (2018). Vibration mitigation of railway bridge using magnetorheological damper. In Intech (pp. 18–29). doi:10.5772/intechopen.71980

Metro de Bogotá. (2015). *Proyecto Primera Línea del Metro de Bogotá*. Sistema Metro.

Metro de Panama. (2010a). *Ingeniería conceptual. Especificaciones funcionales, técnicas y contractuales TOMO II.- Equipamientos. II.7 Material rodante*. Secretaria del Metro de Panama.

Metro de Panamá. (2010b). *Ingenieria conceptual. Especificaciones funcionales, técnicas y contractuales Tomo II Equipamiento. II.4.2 Señalizacion y control de trenes. Puesto de mando CCO, Torre de control y estaciones. Línea 1*. Secretaria del Metro de Panamá.

Metro de Panama & Consorcio línea 2. (2015). *Contrato-MPSA-014-2015*. Metro de Panama.

Metro de Panama. (2017). *Metro de Panama*. Wikipedia. https://es.wikipedia.org/wiki/Metro_de_Panamá

Metro de Panama. (2018a). *Parametros de Operación línea 1*. https://www.elmetrodepanama.com/parametros/

Metro de Panamá. (2018b). *Official Web Page of Panama Metro*. https://www.elmetrodepanama.com/

Metro de Panamá. (2020a). *Línea 3 del metro de Panamá*. Pagina Web Institucional Del Metro de Panamá.

Metro de Panamá. (2020b). *Parametros*. Operaciones. https://www.elmetrodepanama.com/parametros/

Mexico., G. de. (2020). *Información del proyecto. Tren maya. Anexo técnico*. Academic Press.

Milosavljevic, M., Jeremic, D., & Vujovic, D. (2019). Train Braking Distance Calculation Using Fuzzy Logic. doi:10.20544/tts2018.p57

Ministerio de Educación. (2016). *Visita al Tranvía Modelo CITADIS 302*. Nota de Prensa.

Moaveni, B., & Karimi, M. (2017). Subway Traffic Regulation Using Model-Based Predictive Control by Considering the Passengers Dynamic Effect. *Arabian Journal for Science and Engineering*, *12*(7), 3021–3031. Advance online publication. doi:10.100713369-017-2508-0

Monrroy, A. (2018). Suministro de la Energía Eléctrica de la Línea 2 del Metro de Panamá : Ingeniería Conceptual comentada Supply of the Electric Power of Line 2 of the Panama Metro : Conceptual Engineering commented. In Universidad Tecnologica de Panama (Ed.), *2018: 3er Congreso Internacional de Ciencias y Tecnologías para el Desarrollo Sostenible 2018* (p. 17). Universidad Tecnologica de Panamá. https://revistas.utp.ac.pa/index.php/memoutp/article/view/1796/2587

Morrison, A. (2003). *Electric Transport Inaugurations in Latin America*. Electric Transport Inaugurations in Latin America. http://www.tramz.com/

Morrison, A. (2008). *The Tramways of Panama City Colombia-Panama*. http://www.tramz.com/co/pa/pa.html

Mowatt, R., & Cerra, V. (2017). Trade policy issues in Latin America and the Caribbean: Views from country authorities. Academic Press.

OECD, WTO, & IDB. (2010). *Latin american and caribbean Case Stories : A snap of Aid for Trade on the ground*. Author.

Oh, Y., Byon, Y., Song, J., Kwak, H., & Kang, S. (2020). Dwell Time Estimation Using Real-Time Train Operation and Smart Card-Based Passenger Data : A Case Study in Seoul, South Korea. *Applied Sciences (Basel, Switzerland)*, *10*(476), 12. doi:10.3390/app10020476

Pamučar, D., Atanasković, P., & Milicic, M. (2015). Modeling of fuzzy logic systems for investment management in the railway infraestructure. *Technical Gazette*, *22*(5), 1185–1192. doi:10.17559/TV-201406261104653

Panamá Vieja Escuela. (2014). *La historia del ferrocarril de Chiriqui*. Panamá Vieja Escuela. https://www.panamaviejaescuela.com/historia-ferrocarril-chiriqui/

Pattanaik, L. N., & Yadav, G. (2015). Decision support model for automated railway level crossing system using fuzzy logic control. *Procedia Computer Science*, *48*(C), 73–76. doi:10.1016/j.procs.2015.04.152

Presidencia de la República de Panamá. (2017). *Memoria de la presidencia*. Memoria.

Pyrgidis, C. N. (2016). Railway transportation systems. Design, construction and operation. Taylor and Francis Group. doi:10.1201/b19472

Redacción de TVN noticias. (2017). *El Ferrocarril de Chiriquí en el Panamá de ayer*. Variedad. https://www.tvn-2.com/variedad/Ferrocarril-Chiriqui-Panama-ayer_0_4911258844.html

Republica de Panama & Consorcio linea 1. (2010). *Contrato-N°SMP-28-2010*. Secretaria del Metro de Panama.

Richards, R. (2016). *Nuevo Instituto Técnico Superior de Panamá Oeste capacitará sobre mantenimiento del Metro*. Nacionales.

Rieles multimedio. (2020). *Mexico: Parlacen respalda tren mesoamericano de Panamá a Chiapas*. REvista Rieles Multimedio.

Rivera, L. (2019). *Presidente Varela entrega la Línea 2 del Metro de Panamá, obra construida con "transparencia y eficiencia."* Metro de Panamá. https://www.elmetrodepanama.com/presidente-varela-entrega-la-linea-2-del-metro-de-panama-obra-construida-con-transparencia-y-eficiencia/

Sanz-Bobi, J., Berbey-Álvarez, A., Caballero, R., & Alvarez, H. (2009). *C/025994/09 - Cooperación interuniversitaria para la ejecución de acciones dirigidas a la ejecución y desarrollo otorgada según la publicación de BOE de enero del 2009 dentro del Programa de Convocatoria de ayudas para programas de cooperación interuniver*. Aecid.

Sanz-Bobi, J., Vazquez-Brunel, J., & Berbey-Álvarez, A. (2010). Sistemas y Tecnologías de Transporte Urbano Ferroviario. Universidad Tecnologica de Panamá. Patrocinado por la Aecid(España) y la Secretaria del Metro de Panamá(Panamá).

Sasidharan, M., Burrow, M. P. N., Ghataora, G. S., & Torbaghan, M. E. (2017). *A Review of Risk Management Applications for Railways*. Railway Engineering., doi:10.25084/raileng.2017.0065

Secretaría del Metro de Panamá. (2010a). Ingeniería conceptual. Especificaciones funcionales, técnicas y contractuales. Tomo II. Equipamientos. II. Sistemas de vías. II.1.2. Ingeniería conceptual diseño geométrico. *Línea, 1*, 1–60.

Secretaría del Metro de Panamá. (2010b). *Ingeniería conceptual. Especificaciones funcionales, técnicas y contractuales Tomo II Equipamientos. II. O. Normas generales. II.0.1. Ingeniería conceptual de la operación. Línea 1*. Secretaría del Metro de Panamá.

Secretaria del Metro de Panamá. (2010c). *Ingenieria Conceptual, Especificaciones funcionales, tecnicas y contractuales. Tomo I Obras civiles I.6. Secretaria del Metro de Panamá Arquitectura de estaciones. 1.6.1. memoria descriptiva, N°1, 17/03/2010*.

Secretaria del Metro de Panama. (2010d). *Nota Tecnica*.

Serracin, E. (2014). *La historia olvidada del ferrocarril de Bugaba*. http://www.soydebugaba.com/blog/la-historica-y-olvidada-estacion-del-ferrocarril-de-bugaba

SMP. Secretaria del Metro de Panamá. (2010). *II.7 Material rodante. Pliego de cargos. Diseño y construcción de la línea 1 del metro de Panamá. 2010*. Secretaria del Metro de Panama.

Streitzig, C., Schön, S., Griese, S., & Oetting, A. (2013). Practical education of young academics for railway operation and research. *EURO – ZEL 2013 21st International Symposium*, 240–245.

The Panama Railroad. (2008). *The Panama Rail road*. The Panama Railroad. http://www.panamarailroad.org/

Upegui, O. (2009). *The Golden Era of Streetcars in Panama*. Lingua Franca. https://epiac1216.wordpress.com/2009/03/05/the-golden-era-of-streetcars-in-panama/

Van-Ma, L., Park, J., Nam, J., Ryu, H., & Kim, J. (2017). A Fuzzy-Based Adaptive Streaming Algorithm for Reducing Entropy Rate of DASH Bitrate Fluctuation to Improve Mobile Quality of Service. *Entropy (Basel, Switzerland)*, *19*(477), 1–18. doi:10.3390/e19090477

VanBreusegem, V., Campion, G., & Bastin, G. (1991). Traffic Modeling and State Feedback control for Metro lines. *IEEE Transactions on Automatic Control, 36*(7).

Velasco, J., & Fernandez, J. (2010a). Diseño Conceptual Geometrico-Via Argentina. Secretaria del Metro de Panama.

Velasco, J., & Fernandez, J. (2010b). Diseño Conceptual Geometrico Linea 1-Iglesia del Carmen. Secretaria del Metro de Panama.

Velasco, J., & Fernandez, J. (2010c). Diseño conceptual geometrico Linea 1-San Miguelito. Secretaria del Metro de Panama.

Velasco, J., & Fernandez, J. (2010d). Diseño conceptual geometrico-5 de mayo. Secretaria del Metro de Panama.

Verdict media. (2022). *Bogota Metro*. Railway Tecnology.

Vergara, Y. (2015). *Estación del Metro en San Isidro abre sus puertas a los usuarios*. Transporte. TVN 2. https://www.tvn-2.com/nacionales/transporte/Estacion-Metro-San-Isidro-usuarios_0_4278322129.html

Vicerrectoría académica. (2020). *Evaluacion del desempeño docente. Resultado Individual por Profesor*. Universidad Tecnologica de Panamá.

Yañez-Pagans, P., Martinez, D., Mitnik, O. A., Scholl, L., & Vazquez, A. (2019). Urban transport systems in Latin America and the Caribbean: Lessons and challenges. *Latin American Economic Review*, *28*(1), 15. Advance online publication. doi:10.118640503-019-0079-z

Yang, J., Shiwakoti, N., & Tay, R. (2019). Train dwell time models – development in the past forty years. *Australasian Transport Research Forum 2019 Proceedings*, 1–12.

Zeballos, E. (2016). *Capacitarán en mantenimiento del Metro*. Periodico El Siglo.

Zhang, D. (2017). High-speed train control system big data analysis based on the fuzzy RDF model and uncertain reasoning. *International Journal of Computers, Communications & Control*, *12*(4), 577–591. doi:10.15837/ijccc.2017.4.2914

KEY TERMS AND DEFINITIONS

Algorithm: Is a set of well-defined rules in a procedure with the objective to find a corrected solution of a problem.

Artificial Intelligence: A branch of computer sciences engineering performs tasks like visual perception, speech recognition, decision making, and translation between languages. This allows a computer program to think and learn like intelligent agents.

Blocking Time: Is the period in which a section track authorized the use of one train and the section track is blocked to all other trains.

Control Trains: Is an engineering system for monitoring and controlling train movement's support to train protection system.

Delay: Is a time deviation of a train with respect your original timetable.

Dwelling Time: Is a period when a train stops in a railway station until the train moves again to the next station.

Externalities: The externalities concept corresponds to the cost that affects a third party who did not pay for this benefit. For example, in the case of railway transportation, externalities occur when the consumption of a transportation service private price equilibrium cannot reflect real costs for the general society. Types of railway externalities can include social, economic, environmental, and energy. Externalities can be either positive or negative.

Fuzzy Logic: Is based on observations using decisions based on imprecise and nonnumerical information. Fuzzy models are mathematical equations that represent imprecise information in which the correct values of these variables are real numbers between 0 and 1.

Headway: The time distance between two successive trains on the railway track.

Railway Engineering: Is a multidisciplinary engineering discipline focused on the design, construction, operation, inspection, and evaluation of rail transportation systems like metro, railroad, commuter train, tramway, light rail, and monorail. This high-tech discipline includes a range of engineering disciplines like civil engineering, computer engineering, electrical engineering, mechanical engineering, industrial engineering, telecommunications engineering, and railway externalities.

Recovery Time: Is a period to correct small delays in the trains.

Stability: The capacity of any system to recover its original state.

Station: According UIC 406, is a point of a railway network where the train can overtake, crossing or running in reverse direction. The station is a defined place where the trains stop to passengers leave it.

Train Diagram: Is a distance-time graphic where is showed the train paths, running times, dwelling time on a railway line.

Compilation of References

Aalst, W. (2016). *Process Mining Data Science in Action*. Springer. doi:10.1007/978-3-662-49851-4

Abascal, J., Arrue, M., Garay, N., & Tomás, J. (2002). USERfit Tool. A Tool to Facilitate Design for All. In *Universal Access Theoretical Perspectives* (pp. 141–152). Practice, and Experience.

Abrahao, S., Baldassarre, M. T., da Silva, F. Q. B., & Romano, S. (2020). Call for papers—HuFo 2019. *PROFES Workshops*.

Accenture Technology Vision. (2019). *Full Report*. Retrieved June 1, 2020, from https://www.accenture.com/_acnmedia/PDF-94/Accenture-TechVision-2019-Tech-Trends-Report.pdf

Adya, M., Samant, D., Scherer, M. J., Killeen, M., & Morris, M. W. (2012). Assistive / rehabilitation technology, disability, and service delivery models. *Cognitive Processing*, *13*(S1), 75–78. doi:10.100710339-012-0466-8 PMID:22820864

Aebersold, M., Rasmussen, J., & Mulrenin, T. (2020). Virtual Everest: Immersive Virtual Reality Can Improve the Simulation Experience. *Clinical Simulation in Nursing*, *38*, 1–4. doi:10.1016/j.ecns.2019.09.004

Afshar, J., Roudsari, A. H., Lee, C., Eom, C., Lee, W., & Arora, N. (2018). Harmonic Mean Based Soccer Team Formation Problem. In *Proceedings of the 7th International Conference on Emerging Databases: Technologies, Applications, and Theory* (pp. 240-246). Springer Singapore. 10.1007/978-981-10-6520-0_25

Agbozo, E., & Spassov, K. (2018). Establishing Efficient Governance through Data-Driven e-Government. In *Conference 11th International Conference on Theory and Practice of Electronic Governance*, New York: Association for Computing Machinery.

Agrawal, V., & Jariwala, A. (2017). *Web-based tools for supporting student-driven Capstone Design Team formation* [Paper presentation]. *124th ASEE Annual Conference and Exposition*. Columbus, OH, USA.

Ahmad, M., Rahim, L. A., & Arshad, N. I. (2015). An Analysis Of Educational Games Design Frameworks From Software Engineering Perspective. *Journal of Information and Communication Technology*, *14*, 123–151. doi:10.32890/jict2015.14.8

Aizpurua, A., Harper, S., & Vigo, M. (2016). Exploring the relationship between web accessibility and user experience. *International Journal of Human-Computer Studies*, *91*, 13–23. doi:10.1016/j.ijhcs.2016.03.008

Alabdulatif, A., Khalil, I., Yi, X., & Guizani, M. (2019). Secure Edge of Things for Smart Healthcare Surveillance Framework. *IEEE Access: Practical Innovations, Open Solutions*, *7*, 31010–31021. doi:10.1109/ACCESS.2019.2899323

Alberola, J. M., Del val, E., Sanchez-Anguix, V., & Julián, V. (2016b). A general framework for testing different student team formation strategies, In Methodologies and Intelligent Systems for Technology Enhanced Learning (pp. 23-31). Springer Verlag.

Alberola, J. M., Del Val, E., Sánchez-Anguix, V., Palomares, A., & Teruel, M. D. (2016a). An artificial intelligence tool for heterogeneous team formation in the classroom. *Knowledge-Based Systems*, *101*, 1–14. doi:10.1016/j.knosys.2016.02.010

Alcala-Fdez, J., Fernández, A., Luengo, J., Derrac, J., García, S., Sánchez, L., & Herrera, F. (2011). KEEL Data-Mining Software Tool: Data Set Repository, Integration of Algorithms and Experimental Analysis Framework. *Journal of Multiple-Valued Logic and Soft Computing, 17*(2), 255–287.

Aleksandrova, O. (2019). Accessibility of Assistive Technologies as a Factor in the Successful Realization of the Labor Potential of Persons with Disabilities : Russia ' s Experience. *Societies (Basel, Switzerland), 9*(70).

Alessa, D., & Gonzales, K. S. (2020, April 14). Perceptions of service learning in pharmacy education: A systematic review. *Currents in Pharmacy Teaching and Learning, 8.* Advance online publication. doi:10.1016/j.cptl.2020.04.005 PMID:32624146

Alexandre, G. H. S., & Santos, S. C. (2018). Poster: PBL planner toolkit: A canvas-based tool for planning PBL in software engineering education. Proceedings - International Conference on Software Engineering, 153–154. 10.1145/3183440.3195060

Alhammad, M., & Moreno, A. (2018). Gamification in software engineering education: A systematic mapping. *Journal of Systems and Software, 141,* 131–150. doi:10.1016/j.jss.2018.03.065

Allemang, D., Hendler, J., & Gandon, F. (2020). *Semantic Web for the Working Ontologist* (3rd ed.). ACM Books. doi:10.1145/3382097

Allen, S. (2016). New prostheses and orthoses step up their game: Motorized knees, robotic hands, and exosuits mark advances in rehabilitation technology. *IEEE Pulse, 7*(3), 6–11. doi:10.1109/MPUL.2016.2539759 PMID:27187533

Alonso, R. (2003). *AlonsoRoy.com - Escritos Históricos de Panamá: R.I.P. para el tranvía eléctrico.* https://web.archive. org/web/20110719121230/http://www.alonsoroy.com/era/era10.html

Alshahrani, S., & Kapetanios, E. (2016). Are Deep Learning Approaches Suitable for Natural Language Processing? In E. Métais, F. Meziane, M. Saraee, V. Sugumaran, & S. Vadera (Eds.), *Natural Language Processing and Information Systems* (pp. 343–349). Springer. doi:10.1007/978-3-319-41754-7_33

Alvarado, F., Jiménez, G., López, K., Pacheco, E., Roa, N., Solís, A., Tejada, M., & Berbey-Álvarez, A. (2012). Sistemas de ventilación mayor y aires acondicionados de la línea 1 del metro de Panamá. (Mención Honorífica) Del 19 al 22 de octubre del 2016, Hotel Wyndham Pana. In Apanac (Ed.), *XVI Congreso Nacional de Ciencia y Tecnología. Asociación panameña para el avance de la ciencia.* Apanac.

Alves, F. J., Carvalho, E. A. D. E., Aguilar, J., Brito, L. L. D. E., & Bastos, G. S. (2020). Applied Behavior Analysis for the Treatment of Autism : A Systematic Review of Assistive Technologies. *IEEE Access, 8*(1968).

Amado-Salvatierra, H. R., Hilera, J. R., Tortosa, S. O., Rizzardini, R. H., & Piedra, N. (2016). Towards a Semantic Definition of a Framework to Implement Accessible e-Learning Projects. [). IICM.]. *Journal of Universal Computer Science, 22,* 921–942.

Amarasinghe, I., Hernández-Leo, D., & Jonsson, A. (2017). Towards data-informed group formation support across learning spaces. In *Joint 6th Multimodal Learning Analytics Workshop and the Second Cross-LAK Workshop* (pp. 31-38). MMLA-CrossLAK.

Amazon Machine Learning. (2020). *Machine Learning on AWS Documentation.* Retrieved June 1, 2020, from https:// aws.amazon.com/machine-learning/

American Public Transportation Association. (2009). *APTA climate change standards working group. Recommended practice for quantifying greenhouse gas emissions from transit.* APTA.

American Public Transportation Association. (2020). *Transit Savings Report Methodology*. News and Publications. APTA. https://www.apta.com/news-publications/transit-savings-report-methodology/#:~:text=APTA calculates the average cost,transit agencies across the country.

Ammi, M., & Katz, B. F. (2015). Intermodal audio–haptic intermodal display: Improvement of communication and inter-personal awareness for collaborative search tasks. *Virtual Reality (Waltham Cross)*, *19*(3-4), 235–252. doi:10.100710055-015-0273-5

Anderson, L., Krathwohl, D., & Bloom, B. (2001). *A taxonomy for learning, teaching, and assessing: A revision of Bloom's taxonomy of educational objectives* (1st ed.). Allyn & Bacon.

André, M., & Baldoquín, G. (2010). A decision support system for assigning human resources to software project teams. *Revista de Investigación Operacional*, *31*(1), 61–69.

André, M., Baldoquín, G., & Acuña, S. T. (2010). Identification of patterns for the formation of software development projects teams. *International Journal of Human Capital and Information Technology Professionals*, *1*(3), 11–24.

André, M., Baldoquín, G., & Acuña, S. T. (2011). Formal model for assigning human resources to teams in software projects. *Information and Software Technology*, *53*(3), 259–275. doi:10.1016/j.infsof.2010.11.011

Angeli, C., & Valanides, N. (2019). Developing Young children's computational thinking with educational robotics: An interaction effect between gender and scaffolding strategy. *Computers in Human Behavior*, *105*. Advance online publication. doi:10.1016/j.chb.2019.03.018

Angelidou, M., Psaltoglou, A., Komninos, N., Kakderi, C., Tsarchopoulos, P., & Panori, A. (2017). Enhancing sustainable urban development through smart city applications. *Journal of Science and Technology Policy Management*, *9*(2), 146–169. doi:10.1108/JSTPM-05-2017-0016

An, M., Qin, Y., Jia, L. M., & Chen, Y. (2016). Aggregation of group fuzzy risk information in the railway risk decision making process. *Safety Science*, *82*, 18–28. doi:10.1016/j.ssci.2015.08.011

Ansari, S. (2020a). Industrial Application: Real-Time Defect Detection in Industrial Manufacturing. In Building Computer Vision Applications Using Artificial Neural Networks. Apress.

Ansari, S. (2020b). Building a Machine Learning–Based Computer Vision System. In *Building Computer Vision Applications Using Artificial Neural Networks*. Apress. doi:10.1007/978-1-4842-5887-3_4

Apostolakis, K. C., & Daras, P. (2015, August). Natural user interfaces for virtual character full body and facial animation in immersive virtual worlds. In *International Conference on Augmented and Virtual Reality* (pp. 371-383). Springer. 10.1007/978-3-319-22888-4_27

Arellanes, D., & Lau, K. K. (2019). Workflow Variability for Autonomic IoT Systems. In *Proceedings of the International Conference on Autonomic Computing*, (pp. 24-30). Umea, Sweden: IEEE.

Argyle, M. (1990). *Bodily communication* (2nd ed.). International Universities Press.

Aris, N., & Orcos, L. (2019). Educational robotics in the stage of secondary education: Empirical study on motivation and STEM skills. *Education in Science*, *9*(2), 73. doi:10.3390/educsci9020073

Asanka, P. D., & Perera, A. S. (2018). Defining Fuzzy Membership Function for Fuzzy Data Warehouses. *4th International Conference for Convergence in Technology*, 1-5.

Asanka, P. D., & Perera, A. S. (2019). Linguistics Analytics in Data Warehouses Using Fuzzy Techniques. *IEEE International Research Conference on Smart Computing and Systems Engineering (SCSE)*, 165-171. 10.23919/SCSE.2019.8842764

Ashenagar, B., Eghlidi, N. F., Afshar, A., & Hamzeh, A. (2016). Team formation in social networks based on local distance metric. In *Proceedings of the 12th International Conference on Fuzzy Systems and Knowledge Discovery* (pp. 946-952). IEEE.

Asri, H., Mousannif, H., & Al Moatassime, H. (2019). Reality mining and predictive analytics for building smart applications. *Journal of Big Data*, 6(66), 2–25. doi:10.118640537-019-0227-y

Atallah, R. R., Kamsin, A., Ismail, M. A., Abdelrahman, S. A., & Zerdoumi, S. (2018). Face Recognition and Age Estimation Implications of Changes in Facial Features: A Critical Review Study. *IEEE Access: Practical Innovations, Open Solutions*, 6, 29290–28304. doi:10.1109/ACCESS.2018.2836924

Atencio, C. (2016). *El Metro de Panamá, entre los mejores del mundo*. Periódico La Estrella de Panamá. http://laestrella.com.pa/panama/nacional/metro-entre-mejores-mundo/23927947

Awad, M., & Khanna, R. (2015). *Efficient Learning Machines*. Apress. doi:10.1007/978-1-4302-5990-9

Aylett, R., & Ballin, D. (2013). *Intelligent virtual agents*. Springer Berlin/Heidelberg.

Azure, M. (2020). *Azure Documentation*. Retrieved June 1, 2020, from https://docs.microsoft.com/en-us/azure/

Badr, B., Benahmed, M., Abdes-samed, B., & Ouardouz, M. (2016). Ranking models of smart cities. In *2016 4th IEEE International Colloquium on Information Science and Technology (CiSt)* (pp. 872-879). Tangier, Morocco: IEEE.

Bahargam, S., Golshan, B., Lappas, T., & Terzi, E. (2019). A team-formation algorithm for faultline minimization. *Expert Systems with Applications*, 119, 441–455. doi:10.1016/j.eswa.2018.10.046

Bailenson, J. N., Yee, N., Merget, D., & Schroeder, R. (2006). The effect of behavioral realism and form realism of real-time avatar faces on verbal disclosure, nonverbal disclosure, emotion recognition, and copresence in dyadic interaction. *Presence (Cambridge, Mass.)*, 15(4), 359–372. doi:10.1162/pres.15.4.359

Baker, A., Navarro, E. O., & van der Hoek, A. (2003). An experimental card game for teaching software engineering. *Proceedings 16th Conference on Software Engineering Education and Training, 2003. (CSEE&T 2003)*, 216–223. 10.1109/CSEE.2003.1191379

Balaban, M., & Sturm, A. (2018). Software engineering lab- A n essential component of a software engineering curriculum. Proceedings - International Conference on Software Engineering, 21–30. 10.1145/3183377.3183395

Baldi, P. (2018). Deep Learning in Biomedical Data Science. *Annual Review of Biomedical Data Science*, 1(1), 181–205. doi:10.1146/annurev-biodatasci-080917-013343

Balliu, M., Bastys, I., & Sabelfeld, A. (2019). Securing IoT Apps. *IEEE Security and Privacy*, 17(5), 22–29. doi:10.1109/MSEC.2019.2914190

Balmaceda, J. M., Schiaffino, S., & Andrés Díaz-Pace, J. (2014). Using constraint satisfaction to aid group formation in CSCL. *Inteligencia Artificial*, 17(52), 35–45.

Banco Mundial, & Organización Mundial de la Salud. (2011). *Informe mundial la discapacidad*. Author.

Barbacci, M., Ellison, R. J., Lattanze, A. J., Stafford, J. A., Weinstock, C. B., & Wood, W. G. (2003). *Quality Attribute Workshops (QAWs), Third Edition*. Technical Report CMU/SEI-2003-TR-016, Software Engineering Institute, Carnegie Mellon University.

Basiri, J., Taghiyareh, F., & Ghorbani, A. (2017). Collaborative team formation using brain drain optimization: A practical and effective solution. *World Wide Web (Bussum)*, 20(6), 1385–1407. doi:10.100711280-017-0440-6

Bass, L., Clements, P. C., & Kazman, R. (2012). *Software Architecture in Practice*. Addison-Wesley Professional.

Bauer, S. M., Elsaesser, L.-J., & Arthanat, S. (2011). Assistive products for persons with disabilities – classification and terminology. In *Disability and Rehabilitation* (pp. 243–259). Assistive Technology.

Bayeck, R. (2016). Exploratory study of MOOC learners' demographics and motivation: The case of students involved in groups. *Open Praxis*, *8*(3), 223–233. doi:10.5944/openpraxis.8.3.282

Beckwith, R., Sherry, J., & Prendergast, D. (2019). Data Flow in the Smart City: Open Data Versus the Commons. In M. Lange & M. Waal (Eds.), *The Hackable City* (pp. 205–221). Springer Singapore. doi:10.1007/978-981-13-2694-3_11

Beecham, S., Baddoo, N., Hall, T., Robinson, H., & Sharp, H. (2008). Motivation in Software Engineering: A systematic literature review. *Information and Software Technology*, *50*(9–10), 860–878. doi:10.1016/j.infsof.2007.09.004

Begosso, L. R., Franco, L. H. B., Cunha, D. S. d., & Begosso, L. C. (2019). SimScrumF: a game for supporting the process of teaching Scrum. *Proceedings of the 9th International Conference on Information Communication and Management*. 10.1145/3357419.3357426

Belbin, M. (1981). *Management Teams: Why They Succeed or Fail*. Butterworth Heinemann.

Benavides, F., Otegui, X., Aguirre, A., & Andrade, F. (2013). Robótica educativa en Uruguay: de la mano del robot butiá. *XV Congreso Internacional de Informática en la Educación*.

Berbey Álvarez, A. (2016). ¿Cómo evaluar la inserción de la investigación en la docencia universitaria? Caso de estudio: Tópicos de Actualización Tecnológica. In E. Universidad de las Palmas de la Gran Canaria (Ed.), InnoeducaTIC2016. III Jornadas Iberoamericanas de Innovación educativa en el Ámbito de las TIC, Las Palmas de Gran Canaria, 17-18 de noviembre 2016. Academic Press.

Berbey. (2008). Lyapunov based stability analysis for metro lines. *Urban Transport XIV. Urban Transport and the Environment in the 21st Century*.

Berbey. (2010). A fuzzy logic inference approach for the estimation of the passengers flow demand. Proceedings of the International Conference on Fuzzy Computation and 2nd International Conference on Neural Computation, ICFC 2010 - International Conference on Fuzzy Computation, 125–129. doi:10.5220/0003057701250129

Berbey. (2013). Trenes: Material rodante del transporte ferroviario. *Prisma*, *4*(1), 33–37.

Berbey, A., Sánchez, V., Caballero, R., & Calvo, F. (2014). Passenger's flow for a train's coach and dwelling time using fuzzy logic. In *Proceedings of 2014 International Work Conference on Bio-inspired Intelligence (IWOBI)*, (pp. 30–36). IEEE. 10.1109/IWOBI.2014.6913934

Berbey-Alvarez, A. (2014). *Portafolio de la asignatura de Tópicos de actualización tecnológica (TAT) orientada a ingeniería y transporte ferroviario*. Academic Press.

Berbey-Alvarez, A. (2015). Estudio de Caso: Tópicos de actualización tecnológica. Academic Press.

Berbey-Álvarez, A. (2017). Guía para desarrollo de proyecto de investigación. Proyecto final de la asignatura Tópicos de actualización Tecnológica. Facultad de Ingeniería Eléctrica. Universidad Tecnológica de Panamá.2014, Actualizada 2016.

Berbey-Alvarez, A. (2019). Guía para el desarrollo del proyecto final de la asignatura. Academic Press.

Berbey-Alvarez, A., & Caballero-George, R. (2012). Un enfoque de lógica borrosa para el modelado de los flujos de pasajeros y el tiempo de parada. In Laccei 2012 (Ed.), *Tenth LACCEI Latin American and Caribbean Conference for Engineering and Technology (LACCEI'2012) "Megaprojects: Building Infrastructure by Fostering Engineering Collaboration, Efficient and Effective Integration and Innovative Planning" July 23 - 27, 201* (p. 9). Laccei 2012.

Berbey-álvarez, A., Alvarez, H., Castillo, G., Torre, I. D. La, Panamá, U. T. De, Eléctrica, F. D. I., Edificio, N., Panamá, R. De, & Valladolid, U. De. (2017). *El poster científico : recurso de la docencia e investigación.* Academic Press.

Berbey-Alvarez, A., Álvarez, H., Castillo-Sánchez, G., & De LaTorre-Diez, I. (2018). Acción tutorial para la mentoría en la iniciación científica. In *V Jornadas Iberoamericanas de Innovación Educativa en el Ámbito de las TIC y las TAC Las Palmas de Gran Canaria, 15 y 16 de noviembre de 2018.* https://www.researchgate.net/profile/Aranzazu_Berbey-Alvarez

Berbey-Álvarez, A., Caballero-George, R., Alvarez, H., & Guevara-Cedeño, J. (2011). *Caracterización de la línea 1 del Metro de Panamá.* Sistema de Información Científica de La UTP - SicUTP. http://www.investigadores.utp.ac.pa/proyectos/882

Berbey-Alvarez, A., Merchan, F., Guevara-Cedeño, J., Cogley, A., & Caballero, R. (2015). Caracterización de la línea 1 del Metro de Panamá. In LACCEI (Ed.), *Latin American and Caribbean Consortium of Engineering Institutions, the thirteenth latinamerican and caribbean conference for engineering and technology Santo Domingo, Dominican Republic. 2015.* LACCEI. 10.18687/LACCEI2015.1.1.239

Berbey-álvarez, A. (2017). *Portafolio de la asignatura TAT desarrollado durante los años 2014, 2015 y 2016.* Vigente.

Berbey-Álvarez, Guevara-Cedeño, J., Alvarez, H., & Mihailovs, F. (2019). Panama metro line 1: Analysis of CO2 emissions from 2015 to 2017. Principles for an eco-transportation city. *Procedia Computer Science, 149*, 467–474. doi:10.1016/j.procs.2019.01.164

Berger, R. (2016). *España 4.0 El reto de la transformación digital de la economía.* Observatorio de la Industria 4.0. Recuperado de https://observatorioindustria.org/informes/

Bergey, P., & King, M. (2014). Team machine: A decision support system for team formation. *Decision Sciences Journal of Innovative Education, 12*(2), 109–130. doi:10.1111/dsji.12027

Berkling, K., & Thomas, C. (2013). Gamification of a Software Engineering course and a detailed analysis of the factors that lead to it's failure. *International Conference on Interactive Collaborative Learning (ICL).* 10.1109/ICL.2013.6644642

Bermúdez, R. J. (1996). Ricardo J. Bermúdez en la cultura arquitectónica y literaria de Panamá. Compilación, clasificación y prólogo de Samuel A. Gutiérrez Tomo I. La Prensa. Panamá.

Berrío-Lemm, V. (2010). *Belisario Porras Barahona.* Panamá y Su Historia. https://panahistoria.wordpress.com/2010/10/27/belisario-porras-barahona/

Beyene, W. M. (2016). Realizing inclusive digital library environments: opportunities and challenges. In *20th International Conference on Theory and Practice of Digital Libraries* (pp. 3–14). 10.1007/978-3-319-43997-6_1

Bhat, M., Shumaiev, K., Hohenstein, U., Biesdorf, A., & Matthes, F. (2020). The Evolution of Architectural Decision Making as a Key Focus Area of Software Architecture Research: A Semi-Systematic Literature Study. In *Proceedings of the IEEE International Conference on Software Architecture*, (pp. 69-80). IEEE.

Bhowmik, D., & Appiah, K. (2018). Embedded Vision Systems: A Review of the Literature. In N. Voros, M. Huebner, G. Keramidas, D. Goehringer, C. Antonopoulos, & P. Diniz (Eds.), *Applied Reconfigurable Computing. Architectures, Tools, and Applications* (pp. 204–216). Springer. doi:10.1007/978-3-319-78890-6_17

Bizer, C., Heath, T., & Berners-Lee, T. (2009). Linked Data - The Story So Far. *International Journal on Semantic Web and Information Systems, 5*, 1–22.

Blei, D. M., & Smyth, P. (2017). Science and data science. *Proceedings of the National Academy of Sciences of the United States of America, 114*(33), 8689–8692. doi:10.1073/pnas.1702076114 PMID:28784795

Blum, C. (2005). Ant colony optimization: Introduction and recent trends. *Physics of Life Reviews*, *2*(4), 353–373. doi:10.1016/j.plrev.2005.10.001

Bobkowska, A. E. (2019). Exploration of creativity techniques in software engineering in training-application-feedback cycle. *Lecture Notes in Business Information Processing*, *366*, 99–118. doi:10.1007/978-3-030-35646-0_8

Bødker, S. (2015). Third-Wave HCI, 10 Years Later, Participation and Sharing. Magazines Interaction, 22(5).

Bolinger, D. (1985). *Intonation and its parts: Melody in spoken English*. Edward Arnold.

Bonabeau, E., Theraulaz, G., & Deneubourg, J. (1998). Fixed response thresholds and the regulation of division of labor in insect societies. *Bulletin of Mathematical Biology*, *60*(4), 753–807. doi:10.1006/bulm.1998.0041

Bonacin, R., Rodrigues, M. C. C. B., & Antônio, M. (2009). An Agile Process Model for Inclusive Software Development. In *Enterprise Information Systems* (pp. 807–818). Springer. doi:10.1007/978-3-642-01347-8_67

Bosch, J. (2017). *Speed, Data, and Ecosystems: Excelling in a Software-Driven World*. CRC Press. doi:10.1201/9781315270685

Bourque, P., & Fairley, R. E. (2014). Guide to the Software Engineering Body of Knowledge (SWEBOK(R)): Version 3.0. IEEE Computer Society Press.

BPP. (2008). *El ferrocarril que Chiriquí perdió*. Breve Historia Del Ferrocarril Nacional de Chiriqui. Charco Azul. https://charcoazul.wordpress.com/2008/07/18/el-ferrocarril-que-chiriqui-dejo-perder/

Brdiczka, O., Maisonnasse, J., & Reignier, P. (2005, October). Automatic detection of interaction groups. In *Proceedings of the 7th international conference on Multimodal interfaces* (pp. 32-36). Academic Press.

Bredereck, R., Chen, J., Hüffner, F., & Kratsch, S. (2018). Parameterized complexity of team formation in social networks. *Theoretical Computer Science*, *717*, 26–36. doi:10.1016/j.tcs.2017.05.024

Brilhante, I., Macedo, J. A., Nardini, F. M., Perego, R., & Renso, C. (2016). Group finder: An item-driven group formation framework. In *Proceedings of the 17th IEEE International Conference on Mobile Data Management* (pp. 8-17). IEEE. 10.1109/MDM.2016.16

Brincat, A. A., Pacifici, F., & Mazzola, F. (2019). IoT as a Service for Smart Cities and Nations. *IEEE Internet of Things Magazine*, *2*(1), 28–31. doi:10.1109/IOTM.2019.1900014

Brown, S. (2014). *Software Architecture for Developers - Technical leadership by coding, coaching, collaboration, architecture sketching and just enough up front design*. Leanpub.

Bryson, S. (1996). Virtual Reality in Scientific Visualization. *Communications of the ACM*, *39*(5), 62–71. doi:10.1145/229459.229467

Bucchiarone, A., Cicchetti, A., & Marconi, A. (2019). GDF: A Gamification Design Framework Powered by Model-Driven Engineering. *ACM/IEEE 22nd International Conference on Model Driven Engineering Languages and Systems Companion (MODELS-C)*.

Buckley, P., & Doyle, E. (2017). Individualising gamification: An investigation of the impact of learning styles and personality traits on the efficacy of gamification using a prediction market. *Computers & Education*, *106*, 43–55.

Budak, G., Kara, İ., İç, Y. T., & Kasımbeyli, R. (2019). New mathematical models for team formation of sports clubs before the match. *Central European Journal of Operations Research*, *27*(1), 93–109. doi:10.100710100-017-0491-x

Buffardi, K. (2018). Tech startup learning activities: A formative evaluation. Proceedings - International Conference on Software Engineering, 24–31. doi:10.1145/3194779.3194781

Bulmer, J., Fritter, M., Gao, Y., & Hui, B. (2020). FASTT: Team Formation Using Fair Division. Canadian Conference on Artificial Intelligence. In *Advances in Artificial Intelligence* (pp. 92-104). Elsevier.

Burgner-Kahrs, J., Rucker, D. C., & Choset, H. (2015). Continuum robots for medical applications: A survey. *IEEE Transactions on Robotics and Automation, 31*(6), 1261–1280. doi:10.1109/TRO.2015.2489500

Buschmann, F., Meunier, R., Rohnert, H., Sommerlad, P., & Stal, M. (1996). *Pattern-Oriented Software Architecture Volume 1: A System of Patterns.* Wiley Publishing.

Caballero Chi, L. O. (2017). *Incorporación de técnicas de HCI en un proceso ágil mediante patrones (Tesis Doctoral).* Escuela Técnica Superior de Ingenieros Informáticos, Universidad Politécnica de Madrid.

Caballero, Y. A., & Muñoz-Repiso, A. G.-V. (2017). Development of computational thinking and collaborative learning in kindergarten using programmable educational robots. *Proceedings of the 5th International Conference on Technological Ecosystems for Enhancing Multiculturality,* 1-6. Obtenido de https://dl.acm.org/doi/abs/10.1145/3144826.3145353

Cabero, J., & Valencia, R. (2021). And COVID-19 transformed the educational system: Reflections and experiences to learn. *International Journal of Educational Research and Innovation, 15,* 217–227. doi:10.46661/ijeri.5246

Calderón, A., Ruiz, M., & O'Connor, R. V. (2017). Coverage of the ISO 21500 standard in the context of software project management by a simulation-based serious game. *International Conference on Software Process Improvement and Capability Determination.*

Calderón, A., Trinidad, M., Ruiz, M., & O'Connor, R. V. (2019). An Experience of Use a Serious Game for Teaching Software Process Improvement. *Communications in Computer and Information Science, 1060,* 249–259. doi:10.1007/978-3-030-28005-5_19

Calic, J., Selmic, M., Macura, D., & Nikolic, M. (2019). Fuzzy Logic Application in Green Transport - Prediction of Freight Train Energy Consumption. *International Journal for Traffic and Transport Engineering, 9*(3), 35–44. doi:10.7708/ijtte.2019.9(3).04

Calle-Jimenez, T., Sanchez-Gordon, S., Rybarczyk, Y., Jadán, J., Villarreal, S., Esparza, W., Acosta-Vargas, P., Guevara, C., & Nunes, I. L. (2019). Analysis and improvement of the web accessibility of a tele-rehabilitation platform for hip arthroplasty patients. In Advances in Human Factors and Systems Interaction. Advances in Intelligent Systems and Computing (pp. 233-245). Cham, Switzerland: Springer. doi:10.1007/978-3-319-94334-3_24

Calle-Jimenez, T., Sanchez-Gordon, S., & Luján-Mora, S. (2014). Web accessibility evaluation of massive open online courses on geographical information systems, In *Proceedings of the Global Engineering Education Conference (EDUCON)* (pp. 680-686). 10.1109/EDUCON.2014.6826167

Calvo-Manzano, J. A., Cuevas, G., Muñoz, M., & San Feliu, T. (2008). Process similarity study: Case study on project planning practices based on CMMI-DEV v1.2. EuroSPI 2008 Industrial Proceedings.

Calvo-Manzano, J.A., Cuevas, G., Gómez, G., Mejia, J., Muñoz, M., & San Feliu, T. (2010). *Journal of Software Maintenance and Evolution: Research and Practice.* Doi:10.1002mr.505

Calvo-Poyo, F., & Berbey-Álvarez, A. (2014). Sistema de Ingeniería Ferroviaria I. Universidad Tecnológica de Panamá. Patrocinado por: Asociacion Universitaria Iberoamericana de Postgrado (AUIP) y la Secretaria del Metro de Panamá (Panamá).

Campion, G., Van Breusegem, V., Pinson, P. y Bastin, G. (1985). Traffic regulation of an underground railway transportation system by state feedback. *Optimal Control Applications & Methods, 6,* 385–402.

Cao, L. (2017). Data science: Challenges and directions. *Communications of the ACM, 60*(8), 59–68. doi:10.1145/3015456

Capin, T. K., Pandzic, I. S., Magnenat Thalmann, N., & Thalmann, D. (1998). Realistic avatars and autonomous virtual humans in: VLNET networked virtual environments. In R. A. Earnshaw & J. Vince (Eds.), *Virtual worlds in the Internet* (pp. 157–174). IEEE Computer Society Press.

Capretz, L. F. (2014). Bringing the Human Factor to Software Engineering. *IEEE Software, 31*(2), 104–104. doi:10.1109/MS.2014.30

Carloto, F. G., Dalla Costa, M. A., Barriquello, C. H., da Silva Spode, N., Maziero, L., & Dotto Vizzotto, W. (2019). The Role of a Smart Street Lighting into a Smart Grid Environment. In 2019 IEEE PES Innovative Smart Grid Technologies Conference - Latin America (ISGT Latin America). Gramado, Brazil: IEEE.

Carrera, S., Varas, M., & Urrutia, A. (2010). Transformación de esquemas multidimensionales difusos desde el nivel conceptual al nivel lógico. *Ingeniare. Revista Chilena de Ingeniería, 18*(2), 165–175.

Carvajal, W., Cucala, A., & Fernández, A. (2016). Fuzzy train tracking algorithm for the energy efficient operation of CBTC equipped metro lines. *Engineering Applications of Artificial Intelligence, 53*, 19–31. doi:10.1016/j.engappai.2016.03.011

Casallas, R., Davila, J. I., & Quiroga, J. P. (2002). Enseñanza de la ingeniería de software por procesos instrumentados. *Universidad de los. Andes.*

Casillas, L., Peña, A., & Gutierrez, A. (2019). Automatic Approach to Evaluate Collaborative Interaction in Virtual Environments. In *Handbook of Research on Technology Integration in the Global World* (pp. 1–23). IGI Global. doi:10.4018/978-1-5225-6367-9.ch001

Castro-Stanziola, H. (2006). *El ferrocarril de Chiriquí.* Periódico La Prensa. https://web.archive.org/web/20100415110132/http://mensual.prensa.com/mensual/contenido/2006/11/26/hoy/vivir/807497.html

Caswell, T., Henson, S., Jensen, M., & Wiley, D. (2008). Open Content and Open Educational Resources: Enabling Universal Education. *International Review of Research in Open and Distance Learning, 9*(1), 1–11. doi:10.19173/irrodl.v9i1.469

Cavdur, F., Sebatli, A., Kose-Kucuk, M., & Rodoplu, C. (2019). A two-phase binary-goal programming-based approach for optimal project-team formation. *The Journal of the Operational Research Society, 70*(4), 689–706. doi:10.1080/01605682.2018.1457480

Celerier, L. (2013). *The Streetcars (Tranvias) of Panama.* EcoCircuitos Panama Travel Blog Adventure, Conservation and Education. https://ecocircuitospanama.wordpress.com/2013/01/08/the-streetcars-tranvias-of-panama/

CEPAL. (2013). Situación actual de los metros y ferrocarriles de América Latina. *Boletin FAL, 326*, 1–16.

Cervantes, H., & Kazman, R. (2016). *Designing Software Architectures: A Practical Approach.* Addison-Wesley Professional.

Cervantes, H., Velasco-Elizondo, P., & Castro, L. (2016). *Arquitectura de software: conceptos y ciclo de desarrollo.* Cengage Learning.

Cervantes, H., Velasco-Elizondo, P., & Kazman, R. (2013). A Principled Way to Use Frameworks in Architecture Design. *IEEE Software, 30*(2), 46–53. doi:10.1109/MS.2012.175

Chen, G., Shen, J., Barth-Cohen, L., Jiang, S., Huang, X., & Eltoukhy, M. (2017). Assessing elementary students' computational thinking in everyday reasoning and robotics programming. *Computers & Education, 109*, 162–175. doi:10.1016/j.compedu.2017.03.001

Chen, G., Tsoi, A., Xu, H., & Zheng, W. J. (2018). Predict effective drug combination by deep belief network and ontology fingerprints. *Journal of Biomedical Informatics*, *85*, 149–154. doi:10.1016/j.jbi.2018.07.024 PMID:30081101

Chen, K., Kovvuri, R., Gao, J., & Nevatia, R. (2017, June). MSRC: Multimodal spatial regression with semantic context for phrase grounding. In *Proceedings of the 2017 ACM on International Conference on Multimedia Retrieval* (pp. 23-31). 10.1145/3078971.3078976

Chen, S., Cowan, C. F. N., & Grant, P. M. (1991). Orthogonal least squares learning for radial basis function networks. *IEEE Transactions on Neural Networks*, *2*(2), 302–309. doi:10.1109/72.80341 PMID:18276384

Chen, T. E., Yang, S., Ho, L. T., Tsai, K. H., Chang, Y. F., Lai, Y. H., Wang, S. S., Tsao, Y., & Wu, C. C. (2017). S1 and S2 heart sound recognition using deep neural networks. *IEEE Transactions on Biomedical Engineering*, *64*(2), 372–380. doi:10.1109/TBME.2016.2559800 PMID:28113191

Chen, X., Zou, D., Cheng, G., & Xie, H. (2020). Detecting latent topics and trends in educational technologies over four decades using structural topic modeling: A retrospective of all volumes of Computers & Education. *Computers & Education*, *151*(February), 103855. doi:10.1016/j.compedu.2020.103855

Chicaiza, J. (2016). Un enfoque basado en Linked Data para soportar la Búsqueda Personalizada de Recursos Educativos Abiertos (Thesis Doctoral). Technical University of Madrid (UPM) doi:10.20868/UPM.thesis.44387

Chicaiza, J., Piedra, N., & Valencia, M.-P. (2014). Consideraciones de accesibilidad en la producción y distribución de recursos educativos en formato PDF. Un caso de implementación para la formación Virtual Accesible en América Latina. *Proceedings of the V Congreso Internacional Sobre Calidad y Accesibilidad de La Formación Virtual (CAFVIR 2014).*

Chicaiza, J., Piedra, N., Lopez, J., & Tovar-Caro, E. (2017). Recommendation of Open Educational Resources. An Approach based on Linked Open Data. In *Proceedings of 2017 IEEE EDUCON Conference.* 10.1109/EDUCON.2017.7943018

Chicaiza, J., Cabrera-Loayza, M. C., Elizalde, R., & Piedra, N. (2020). Application of Data Anonymization in Learning Analytics. In *ACM International Conference Proceeding Series*, (vol.1, pp. 1–6). 10.1145/3378184.3378229

Chicaiza, J., Piedra, N., Lopez, J., & Tovar-Caro, E. (2014). Domain Categorization of Open Educational Resources based on Linked Data. *Communications in Computer and Information Science*, *468*, 15–28. doi:10.1007/978-3-319-11716-4_2

Chicaiza, J., Piedra, N., Lopez, J., & Tovar-Caro, E. (2015). A User Profile Definition in context of recommendation of Open Educational Resources. In *Proceedings of 2015 Frontiers in Education Conference, (FIE) 2015* (pp. 1–7). 10.1109/FIE.2015.7344314

Chicaiza, J., Piedra, N., Lopez, J., & Tovar-Caro, E. (2015). Promotion of self-learning by means of Open Educational Resources and semantic technologies. In *Proceedings of 2015 International Conference on Information Technology Based Higher Education and Training (ITHET)*, (pp. 1–6). 10.1109/ITHET.2015.7218024

Chih-Hsiung, T., Cherng-Jyh, Y., Sujo-Montes, L., & Sealander, K. (2018). Digital Lifelong-Learning Literacy. In R. Papa & S. Armfield (Eds.), *The Wiley Handbook of Educational Policy* (pp. 531–550). John Wiley & Sons.

Choi, E., Schuetz, A., Stewart, W. F., & Sun, J. (2017). Using recurrent neural network models for early detection of heart failure onset. *Journal of the American Medical Informatics Association*, *24*(2), 361–370. PMID:27521897

Choi, W., Chao, Y. W., Pantofaru, C., & Savarese, S. (2014). Discovering Groups of People in Images. In D. Fleet, T. Pajdla, B. Schiele, & T. Tuytelaars (Eds.), *Computer Vision* (pp. 417–433). Springer.

Chong, E. K. P., & Zak, S. H. (2013). *An introduction to optimization.* John Wiley & Sons.

Choungourian, A. (1968). *Color Preferences and Cultural Variation: AmSci*. Southern Universities Press. doi:10.2466/pms.1968.26.3c.1203

Chung. (2019). Students' Acceptance of Gamification in Higher Education. International Journal of Game-Based Learning, 9(2). Advance online publication. doi:10.4018/IJGBL.2019040101

Cirani, S., & Picone, M. (2015). Wearable Computing for the Internet of Things. *IT Professional, 17*(5), 35–41. doi:10.1109/MITP.2015.89

Clark, H. H., & Brennan, S. E. (1991). Grounding in communication. In *Perspectives on socially shared cognition* (pp. 127–149). American Psychological Association. doi:10.1037/10096-006

Clements, P., Bachmann, F., Bass, L., Garlan, D., Ivers, J., Reed, L., & Nord, R. (2011). *Documenting Software Architectures: Views and Beyond*. Addison-Wesley Professional.

Clements, P., Kazman, R., & Klein, M. (2002). *Evaluating Software Architectures: Methods and Case Studies*. Addison-Wesley Professional.

Clements, P., Kazman, R., & Klein, M. (2008). *Evaluating Software Architectures Methods and Case Studies*. Addison-Wesley.

Coello, C., Lamont, G. B., & Veldhuizen, D. A. (2007). *Evolutionary Algorithms for Solving Multi-Objective Problems*. Springer.

Cogley-Brown, A., Berbey Álvarez, A., & Caballero-George, R. (2014). Estimación de los servicios parciales de la línea 1 del metro de Panamá. In Editorial Tecnológica (Ed.), XII Encuentro Iberoamericano de Mujeres Ingenieras, Arquitectas y Agrimensoras. Perspectiva de la mujer profesional Iberoamericana, ante las tendencias de la ingeniería y arquitectura sostenible". Editorial Tecnológica.

Cogley-Brown, A., Berbey-Alvarez, A., & Caballero-George, R. (2014). Estimación de los servicios parciales de la línea 1 del metro de Panamá.. XII Encuentro Iberoamericano de Mujeres Ingenieras, Arquitectas y Agrimensoras. Perspectiva de La Mujer Profesional Iberoamericana, Ante Las Tendencias de La Ingeniería y Arquitectura Sostenible".

Cohen, B. (2014, November 20). The Smartest Cities in The World 2015: Methodology. *Fast Company: The future of business. General format*. https://www.fastcompany.com/3038818/the-smartest-cities-in-the-world-2015-methodology

Collins, P. H., & Bilge, S. (2016). *Intersectionality*. John Wiley & Sons.

Comisión de asuntos frontera sur. (2019). *Ficha técnica del tren maya: Aspectos legislativos, ambientales, económicos y socio-culturales*. Author.

Conboy, K., Wang, X., & Fitzgerald, B. (2009). Creativity in agile systems development: A literature review. *IFIP Advances in Information and Communication Technology, 301*, 122–134. doi:10.1007/978-3-642-02388-0_9

Connell, B. R., Jones, M., Mace, R., Mueller, J., Mullick, A., Ostroff, E., … Vanderheiden, G. (1997). *The principles of universal design*. Retrieved from https://projects.ncsu.edu/design/cud/about_ud/udprinciplestext.htm

Conradi, H., & Fuggetta, A. (2002). Improving software process improvement. *Software IEEE, 19*(4), 92–99. doi:10.1109/MS.2002.1020295

Cook, A. M., & Polga, J. M. (2015). *Assistive Technologies Principles and Practice* (4th ed.). Elsevier.

Coppes, A., Mesa, G., Viera, A., Fern, E., & Vallespir, D. (2009). *Una Metodolog´ıa para Desarrollo de Videojuegos*. In *38*°. JAIIO - Simposio Argentino de Ingeniería de Software.

Coughlan, T., Lister, K., Seale, J., Scanlon, E., & Weller, M. (2019). Accessible inclusive learning: Foundations. In REducational visions: Lessons from 40 years of innovation (pp. 51–73). Ubiquity Press.

CPRR.org. (1988). *The Panama Railroad*. Central Pacific Railroad Photographic History Museum. http://cprr.org/Museum/

Cravero, A., & Sepúlveda, S. (2012). A chronological study of paradigms for data warehouse design. *Ingenieria e Investigacion, 32*(2), 58–62.

Crawford, B., León de la Barra, C., Soto, R., & Monfroy, E. (2012). Agile software teams must be creatives. *Proceedings of 5th International Workshop on Co-operative and Human Aspects of Software Engineering, 1,* 20–26.

Cristóbal, T., Padrón, G., Lorenzo-Navarro, J., Quesada-Arencibia, A., & García, C. (2018). Applying Time-Dependent Attributes to Represent Demand in Road Mass Transit Systems. *Entropy (Basel, Switzerland), 20*(133), 1–18. doi:10.3390/e20020133

Cruz-Neira, C., Sandin, D. J., & Defanti, T. A. (1993). Surround-screen projection based virtual reality: The design and implementation of the CAVE. *Computer Graphics, 27,* 135–142.

Cruz, S., da Silva, F. Q. B., & Capretz, L. F. (2015). Forty years of research on personality in software engineering: A mapping study. *Computers in Human Behavior, 46,* 94–113. doi:10.1016/j.chb.2014.12.008

Csikszentmihályi, M. (1991). *Flow: The psychology of optimal experience.* HarperCollins.

Cuevas, G., Calvo Manzano, J., San Feliu, T., Mejia, J., Muñoz, M., & Bayona, S. (2007). Impact of TSPi on Software Projects. *Electronics, Robotics and Automotive Mechanics Conference (CERMA 2007),* 706-711, 10.1109/CERMA.2007.4367770

Cuevas, G., De Amescua, A., San Feliu, T., Arcilla, M., Cerrada, J. A., Calvo-Manzano, J. A., & García, M. (2002). *Gestión del Proceso Software.* Universitaria Ramon Areces.

D'Acierno, L., Botte, M., & Placido, A. (2017). Methodology for Determining Dwell Times Consistent with Passenger Flows in the Case of Metro Services. *Urban Rail Transit, 3,* 73–89.

D'Agostini, J., Bonetti, L., Salem, A., Passerini, L., Fiacco, G., Lavanda, P., Motti, E., Stocco, M., Gashay, K. T., Abebe, E. G., Alemu, S. M., Haghani, R., Valtolini, A., Strobbe, C., Covre, N., Santolini, G., Armellini, M., Sacchi, T., Ronchese, D., . . . De Cesso, M. (2018, April). An augmented reality virtual assistant to help mild cognitive impaired users in cooking a system able to recognize the user status and personalize the support. In *2018 Workshop on Metrology for Industry 4.0 and IoT* (pp. 12-17). IEEE. 10.1109/METROI4.2018.8428314

d'Aquin, M. (2012). *Linked Data for Open and Distance Learning Prepared for the Commonwealth of Learning.* http://oasis.col.org/handle/11599/219

d'Aquin, M. (2016). On the Use of Linked Open Data in Education: Current and Future Practices. In D. Mouromtsev & M. d'Aquin (Eds.), Lecture Notes in Computer Science: Vol. 9500. *Open Data for Education* (pp. 3–15). Springer. doi:10.1007/978-3-319-30493-9_1

D'Aquin, M., Troullinou, P., O'Connor, N., Cullen, A., Faller, G., & Holden, L. (2018). Towards an "Ethics by Design" Methodology for AI Research Projects. In *Proceedings AIES '18: Proceedings of the 2018 AAAI/ACM Conference on AI, Ethics, and Society.* ACM. 10.1145/3278721.3278765

Dagiene, V., Gudoniene, D., & Burbaite, R. (2015). *Semantic Web Technologies for e-learning: Models and implementation* (Vol. 26). Informatica. doi:10.15388/Informatica.2015.46

Dawson, R. (2000). Twenty dirty tricks to train software engineers. *Proceedings of the 22nd International Conference on Software Engineering,* 209–218. 10.1145/337180.337204 de A. Souza, M., Veado, L., Moreira, R., Figueiredo, E., & Costa, H. (2018). A systematic mapping study on game-related methods for software engineering education. *Information and Software Technology, 95*, 201-218.

De Aguiar, E. P., Amaral, R. P. F., Vellasco, M. M. B. R., & Ribeiro, M. V. (2018). An enhanced singleton type-2 fuzzy logic system for fault classification in a railroad switch machine. *Electric Power Systems Research, 158*(May), 195–206. doi:10.1016/j.epsr.2017.12.018

De Bortoli, L. Â. (2018). Non-conventional dynamics in a Software Engineering Course: practical and ludic activities. In *Proceedings of the XXXII Brazilian Symposium on Software Engineering* (pp. 328-337). 10.1145/3266237.3266257

de Lope, J., Maravall, D., & Quiñonez, Y. (2012). Decentralized Multi-tasks Distribution in Heterogeneous Robot Teams by Means of Ant Colony Optimization and Learning Automata. In E. Corchado, V. Snášel, A. Abraham, M. Woźniak, M. Graña, & S. B. Cho (Eds.), *Hybrid Artificial Intelligent Systems* (pp. 103–114). Springer. doi:10.1007/978-3-642-28942-2_10

de Lope, J., Maravall, D., & Quiñonez, Y. (2013). Response threshold models and stochastic learning automata for self-coordination of heterogeneous multi-task distribution in multi-robot systems. *Robotics and Autonomous Systems, 61*(7), 714–720. doi:10.1016/j.robot.2012.07.008

de Lope, J., Maravall, D., & Quiñonez, Y. (2015). Self-organizing techniques to improve the decentralized multi-task distribution in multi-robot systems. *Neurocomputing, 163*, 47–55. doi:10.1016/j.neucom.2014.08.094

de Panamá, G. (1913). *Sobre tierras balvias e indultadas.* Asamblea Nacional. República de Panamá. https://docs.panama.justia.com/federales/leyes/20-de-1913-feb-21-1913.pdf

De Santana, V. F., De Oliveira, R., Almeida, L. D. A., & Baranauskas, M. C. C. (2012). Web accessibility and people with dyslexia: a survey on techniques and guidelines. In *Proceedings of the International Cross-Disciplinary Conference on Web Accessibility* (pp. 1-9). 10.1145/2207016.2207047

de Silva, L., & Balasubramaniam, D. (2012). Controlling software architecture erosion: A survey. *Journal of Systems and Software, 85*(1), 132–151. doi:10.1016/j.jss.2011.07.036

De Souza, A., Duarte, R., Marinho, J., & Rodrigues, L. (2017). SCRUMI: A Board Serious Virtual Game for Teaching the SCRUM Framework. *IEEE/ACM 39th International Conference on Software Engineering Companion (ICSE-C).*

de Vasconcelos, L. E. G., Oliveira, L. B., Guimarães, G., & Ayres, F. (2018). Gamification Applied in the Teaching of Agile Scrum Methodology. *Advances in Intelligent Systems and Computing, 738*, 207–212. doi:10.1007/978-3-319-77028-4_30

Deepak, M. (2015). Open Educational Resources. In G. Thakur (Ed.), *Recent trends in ICT in education.* Laxmi Book Publication.

Dekhane, S. & Napier, N. (2017) Impact of participation vs non: participation in a programming boot camp (PBC) on women in computing. *Journal of Computing Sciences in Colleges, 33*(2).

Del Giorgio, H. R., & Mon, A. (2019B). Niveles de productos software en la industria 4.0. *International Journal of Information Systems and Software Engineering for Big Companies, 5*(2), 53–62.

Del Giorgio, H., & Mon, A. (2019A). *Las TICs en las Industrias.* Editorial Universidad Nacional de La Matanza.

Del Val, E., Alberola, J. M., Sanchez-Anguix, V., Palomares, A., & Teruel, M. D. (2014). A team formation tool for educational environments. In *Trends in Practical Applications of Heterogeneous Multi-Agent Systems* (pp. 173–181). Springer Verlag. doi:10.1007/978-3-319-07476-4_21

Delgado, M., Molina, C., Sánchez, D., Ariza, L. R., & Vila, M. A. (2003). A flexible approach to the multidimensional model: The fuzzy datacube. In *Conference on Technology Transfer*, (pp. 26-36). Springer.

Delgado, M., Molina, C., Sánchez, D., Vila, A., & Rodriguez-Ariza, L. (2004). A fuzzy multidimensional model for supporting imprecision in OLAP. *IEEE International Conference on Fuzzy Systems, 3*, 1331-1336. 10.1109/FUZZY.2004.1375362

Demitz, J., Hübschen, C., & Albrecht, C. (2010). Timetable stability -using simulation to ensure quality in a regualr interval timetable. In I. Hansen (Ed.), *Timetable planning and information quality* (pp. 11–24). WIT press.

Department of Trade and Industry, Consumer Affairs Directorate. (2000). *A Study of the Difficulties Disabled People Have when Using Everyday Consumer Products*. Author.

Dermouche, S., & Pelachaud, C. (2020). *Leveraging the Dynamics of Non-Verbal Behaviors For Social Attitude Modeling. IEEE Transactions on Affective Computing*.

Deterding, S., Dixon, D., Khaled, R., & Nacke, L. (2011). *From game design elements to gamefulness: defining gamification*. 15th International Academic MindTrek Conference: Envisioning Future Media Environments, Tampere, Finland.

Devadiga, N. M. (2017). Software Engineering Education: Converging with the Startup Industry. Proceedings - 30th IEEE Conference on Software Engineering Education and Training, 192–196. 10.1109/CSEET.2017.38

Di Cola, S., Lau, K.-K., Tran, C., & Qian, C. (2015). An MDE tool for defining software product families with explicit variation points. In *Proceedings of the International Conference on Software Product Line*, (pp. 355–360). New York, NY: Association for Computing Machinery. 10.1145/2791060.2791090

Di Maio, A., Botte, M., Montella, B., & D'Acierno, L. (2020). The Definition of Bus Fleet Operational Parameters: The Dwell Time Estimation. *2020 IEEE International Conference on Environment and Electrical Engineering and 2020 IEEE Industrial and Commercial Power Systems Europe (EEEIC / I&CPS Europe)*. 10.1109/EEEIC/ICPSEurope49358.2020.9160592

Di Martinelly, C., & Meskens, N. (2017). A bi-objective integrated approach to building surgical teams and nurse schedule rosters to maximise surgical team affinities and minimise nurses' idle time. *International Journal of Production Economics, 191*, 323–334. doi:10.1016/j.ijpe.2017.05.014

Di Martino, F., & Sessa, S. (2020). Fuzzy Transform for Data Classification. In *Fuzzy Transforms for Image Processing and Data Analysis*. Springer. doi:10.1007/978-3-030-44613-0_11

Dicheva, D., Dichev, C., Agre, G., & Angelova, G. (2015). Gamification in Education: A Systematic Mapping Study. *Journal of Educational Technology & Society, 18*(3).

Dietze, S., Drachsler, H., & Giordano, D. (2013). A Survey on Linked Data and the Social Web as facilitators for TEL recommender systems. In N. Manouselis, H. Drachsler, K. Verbert, & O. C. Santos (Eds.), Recommender Systems for Technology Enhanced Learning: Research Trends and Applications. Academic Press.

Dillenbourg, P. (1999). What do you mean by collaborative learning? In *Collaborative learning: Cognitive and computational approaches* (pp. 1–19). Elsevier.

Dindar, S., Kaewunruen, S., & An, M. (2018). Identification of appropriate risk analysis techniques for railway turnout systems. *Journal of Risk Research, 21*(8), 974–995. doi:10.1080/13669877.2016.1264452

Ding, C., Xia, F., Gopalakrishnan, G., Qian, W., & Zhou, A. (2017). TeamGen: An Interactive Team Formation System Based on Professional Social Network. In *Proceedings of the 26th International Conference on World Wide Web Companion* (pp. 195-199). 10.1145/3041021.3054725

Diniz, G. C., Silva, M. A. G., Gerosa, M. A., & Steinmacher, I. (2017). Using gamification to orient and motivate students to contribute to oss projects. *Proceedings - 2017 IEEE/ACM 10th International Workshop on Cooperative and Human Aspects of Software Engineering*, 36–42. 10.1109/CHASE.2017.7

Dittrich, Y., Fagerholm, F., Baldassare, M. T., & Wiese, I. (2020). Call for papers—CHASE 2020. *IEEE ICSE Workshops*.

Dorigo, M. (1992). *Optimization, learning and natural algorithms* (Doctoral dissertation). Dipartimento di Elettronica, Politecnico di Milano, Milan.

Dorigo, M., & Blum, C. (2005). Ant colony optimization theory: A survey. *Theoretical Computer Science*, *344*(2-3), 243–278. doi:10.1016/j.tcs.2005.05.020

Dorodchi, M., Al-Hossami, E., & Nagahisarchoghaei, M. (2019). Teaching an Undergraduate Software Engineering Course using Active Learning and Open Source Projects. Proceedings - Frontiers in Education Conference. 10.1109/FIE43999.2019.9028517

DuPont, B., & Hoyle, C. (2015). *Automation and optimization of engineering design team selection considering personality types and course-specific constraints* [Paper presentation]. *122nd ASEE Annual Conference and Exposition*, Seattle, WA, USA.

Durango, C., Zapata, C. M., & Zapata, C. M. (2018). Representación en el núcleo de la esencia de Semat de las Competencias de un Equipo de Desarrollo de Software. *Revista Entramado*.

Durón, B., & Muñoz, M. (2013). Selección de estrategias para la implementación de mejoras. Revista electrónica de Computación, Informática, Biomédica y Electrónica (ReCIBE), 3, 1-15.

Dussel-Peters, E., Armony, A., & Cui, S. (2018). *Building development for a new era. China´s infraestructure projects in Latin America and the Caribbean*. Academic Press.

Ebadi, A., Tighe, P. J., Zhang, L., & Rashidi, P. (2017). DisTeam: A decision support tool for surgical team selection. *Artificial Intelligence in Medicine*, *76*, 16–26. doi:10.1016/j.artmed.2017.02.002 PMID:28363285

Ebert, C., Gallardo, G., Hernantes, J., & Serrano, N. (2016). DevOps. *IEEE Software*, *33*(3), 94–100. doi:10.1109/MS.2016.68

Echeverría, & Vega. (2016). *Creación de prototipo funcional de aplicación móvil para configurar "smartags nfc" para personas ciegas y disminuidas visuales*. Universidad Católica del Norte.

Eckholm, B., Anderson, K., Weiss, M., & DeGrandi-Hoffman, G. (2011). Intracolonial genetic diversity in honeybee (Apis mellifera) colonies increases pollen foraging efficiency. *Behavioral Ecology and Sociobiology*, *65*(5), 1037–1044. doi:10.100700265-010-1108-8

Economou, D., Doumanis, I., Argyriou, L., & Georgalas, N. (2017). User experience evaluation of human representation in collaborative virtual environments. *Personal and Ubiquitous Computing*, *21*(6), 989–1001. doi:10.100700779-017-1075-4

EdX. (2018). *Age Demographics*. Retrieved from https://edx.readthedocs.io/projects/edx-insights/en/latest/enrollment/Demographics_Age.html

EFE. (2013). *Evalúan la creación de ferrocarril que conecte a Mesoamérica*. Portafolio.

Ekman, P. (2016). What Scientists Who Study Emotion Agree About. *Perspectives on Psychological Science*, *11*(1), 31–34. doi:10.1177/1745691615596992 PMID:26817724

El Khaouat, A., & Benhlima, L. (2016). Big data based management for smart grids. In *Renewable and Sustainable Energy Conference (IRSEC)* (pp. 1044-1047). Marrakech, Morocco: IEEE.

Emami, H., Dong, M., Nejad-Davarani, S. P., & Glide-Hurst, C. K. (2018). Generating synthetic CTs from magnetic resonance images using generative adversarial networks. *Medical Physics*, *45*(8), 3627–3636. doi:10.1002/mp.13047 PMID:29901223

Eniyal, V., Priya, S., Meeralakshmi, M., & Sivanantham, S. (2020). Securing Technology and Government Services Enrollment-Stage. In *2020 6th International Conference on Advanced Computing and Communication Systems (ICACCS)*. Coimbatore, India: IEEE.

Erdogmus, H., Medvidović, N., & Paulisch, F. (2018). 50 Years of Software Engineering. *IEEE Software*, *35*(5), 20–24. doi:10.1109/MS.2018.3571240

Esparza, M. (2019). *NoSQLFinder: un buscador de bases de datos NoSQL basado en técnicas de web semántica y análisis de sentimientos* (BSc Thesis).

Espinosa, A., Flores, E., Fuenzalida, C., Muñoz, Y., & Vega, V. (2016). *Creación de un Prototipo de una plataforma tecnológica para acceso inclusivo a audiolibros para personas ciegas y disminuidas visuales*. Universidad Católica del Norte.

Estivill-Castro, V. (2019). Inviting teachers to use educational robotics to foster mathematical problem-solving. *Advances in Intelligent Systems and Computing, 1023*.

Estrada, E., Peña Pérez Negrón, A., Lara López, G., & Casillas, L. (2018). Algoritmos para el control de indicadores clave de desempeño para Smart Cites. Proceedings Research in Computing Science.

Estrada, E., Maciel, R., Ochoa, A., Bernabe-Loranca, B., Oliva, D., & Larios, V. (2018). Smart City Visualization Tool for the Open Data Georeferenced Analysis Utilizing Machine Learning. *International Journal of Combinatorial Optimization Problems and Informatics*, *9*(2), 25–40.

Estrada, E., Maciel, R., Peña Pérez Negrón, A., Lara López, G., Larios, V., & Ochoa, A. (2018). Framework for the Analysis of Smart Cities Models. In J. Mejia, M. Muñoz, Á. Rocha, A. Peña, & M. Pérez-Cisneros (Eds.), *Trends and Applications in Software Engineering, 865* (pp. 261–269). Springer, Cham.

Estrada, E., Maciel, R., Peña Pérez Negrón, A., López, G., Larios-Rosillo, V., & Ochoa-Zezzati, C. (2019). A framework to support the data science of Smart City models for decision-making oriented to the intelligent dispatch of service petitions. *IET Software*, *14*(2), 159–164. doi:10.1049/iet-sen.2019.0044

Estrada, E., Martínez Vargas, M. P., Gómez, J., Peña Pérez Negrón, A., Lara López, G., & Maciel, R. (2019). Smart Cities Big Data Algorithms for Sensors Location. *MDPI in Applied Sciences*, *9*(19), 1–14. doi:10.3390/app9194196

Estrada-Guzmán, E., Maciel, R., & Gómez, L. (2015, July 7). NoSQL method for the metric analysis of Smart Cities. *IEEE-CCD Smart Cities White Paper*. https://smartcities.ieee.org/images/files/pdf/mtxgdl_nosql.pdf

Eysenbach, G. (2001). What is e-Health. *Journal of Medical Internet Research*, *3*(2), e20. doi:10.2196/jmir.3.2.e20 PMID:11720962

Fabian, J., Sánchez-Martínez, G. E., & Attanucci, J. P. (2018). Improving High-Frequency Transit Performance through Headway-Based Dispatching: Development and Implementation of a Real-Time Decision-Support System on a Multi-Branch Light Rail Line. *Transportation Research Record: Journal of the Transportation Research Board*, *2672*(8), 363–374. doi:10.1177/0361198118794534

Farasat, A., & Nikolaev, A. G. (2016). Social structure optimization in team formation. *Computers & Operations Research*, *74*, 127–142. doi:10.1016/j.cor.2016.04.028

Fasel, D., & Zumstein, D. (2009). A fuzzy data warehouse approach for web analytics. In World Summit on Knowledge Society, (pp. 276-285). Springer.

Fasel, D. (2009). A fuzzy data warehouse approach for the customer performance measurement for a hearing instrument manufacturing company. *IEEE Sixth International Conference on Fuzzy Systems and Knowledge Discovery, 7*, 285-289. 10.1109/FSKD.2009.266

Fasel, D., & Shahzad, K. (2010). A data warehouse model for integrating fuzzy concepts in meta table structures. *IEEE International Conference and Workshops on Engineering of Computer Based Systems*, 100-109. 10.1109/ECBS.2010.18

Fasel, D., & Shahzad, K. (2012). Fuzzy data warehouse for performance analysis. In *Fuzzy Methods for Customer Relationship Management and Marketing: Applications and Classifications* (pp. 217–251). IGI Global. doi:10.4018/978-1-4666-0095-9.ch010

Fazli, F., & Bittner, E. (2017). Cultural Influences on Collaborative Work in Software Engineering Teams. *50th Hawaii International Conference on System Sciences, HICSS 2017*, 454–463. http://hdl.handle.net/10125/41205

Feng, J., Li, X., Liu, H., Gao, X., & Mao, B. (2017). Optimizing the Energy-Efficient Metro Train Timetable and Control Strategy in Off-Peak Hours. *Energies, 10*(436), 20. doi:10.3390/en10040436

Feo, T. A., & Resende, M. G. C. (1995). Greedy randomized adaptive search procedures. *Journal of Global Optimization, 6*(2), 109–133. doi:10.1007/BF01096763

Fernandes, P., & Correa, C. (2017). *Game Elements in a Software Engineering Study Group: A Case Study*. IEEE/ACM 39th International Conference on Software Engineering: Software Engineering Education and Training Track (ICSE-SEET), Buenos Aires.

Finstad, K. (2010). The Usability Metric for User Experience. *Interacting with Computers, 22*(5), 323–327. doi:10.1016/j.intcom.2010.04.004

Fitz-Walter, Z., Tjondronegoro, D., & Wyeth, P. (2011). Orientation passport: using gamification to engage university students. *23rd Australian Computer-Human Interaction Conference*, Canberra, Australia. 10.1145/2071536.2071554

Florea, R., & Stray, V. (2019a). The skills that employers look for in software testers. *Software Quality Journal*, 1–31. doi:10.100711219-019-09462-5

Florea, R., & Stray, V. (2019b). A Global View on the Hard Skills and Testing Tools in Software Testing. *Proceedings of ICGSE, 2019*, 143–151. doi:10.1109/ICGSE.2019.00035

Flores, A., Deniau, Y., & Prieto-Diaz, S. (2019). *El Tren Maya . Un nuevo proyecto de articulación territorial en la Península de Yucatán*. Academic Press.

França, C., da Silva, F. Q. B., & Sharp, H. (2020). Motivation and Satisfaction of Software Engineers. *IEEE Transactions on Software Engineering, 46*(2), 118–140. doi:10.1109/TSE.2018.2842201

Freire, G., Schwartz Orellana, S. D., Zumaeta Aurazo, M., Costa, D. C., Lundvall, J. M., Viveros Mendoza, M. C., Lucchetti, L. R., Moreno Herrera, L. L., & Sousa, L. D. C. (2015). *Indigenous Latin America in the twenty-first century: The first decade* (No. 98544). The World Bank. http://documents.worldbank.org/curated/en/145891467991974540/Indigenous-Latin-America-in-the-twenty-first-century-the-first-decade

Fuggetta, A., & Di Nitto, E. (2014). Software Process. *Proceedings of the on Future of Software Engineering*, 1–12. 10.1145/2593882.2593883

Gabner, K., Jansen, M., Harrer, A., Herrmann, K., & Hoppe, H. U. (2003). Analysis methods for collaborative models and activities. *International Conference on Computer Supported Collaborative Learning*, 369-377.

Galindo, J., Urrutia, A., & Piattini, M. (Eds.). (2009). *Fuzzy databases: Modeling, design, and implementation*. IGI Global.

Galvao, T., Neto, F., Bonates, M. F., & Campos, M. T. (2012). A serious game for supporting training in risk management through project-based learning. *Communications in Computer and Information Science*, *248*, 52–61. doi:10.1007/978-3-642-31800-9_6

Gamelin, G., Chellali, A., Cheikh, S., Ricca, A., Dumas, C., & Otmane, S. (2020). Point-cloud avatars to improve spatial communication in immersive collaborative virtual environments. *Personal and Ubiquitous Computing*, 1–18.

Gannon, J. D. (1979). Human Factors in Software Engineering. *Computer*, *12*(12), 6–7. doi:10.1109/MC.1979.1658569

Gao, Y., Li, Y.-F., Lin, Y., Gao, H., & Khan, L. (2020). *Deep Learning on Knowledge Graph for Recommender System: A Survey*. http://arxiv.org/abs/2004.00387

Gao, N., Xie, T., & Liu, G. (2018). A learning engagement model of educational games based on virtual reality. In *2018 International Joint Conference on Information, Media and Engineering (ICIME)* (pp. 1-5). IEEE. 10.1109/ICIME.2018.00010

Gapp, K.-P. (1995). *Object Localization: Selection of Optimal Reference Objects, Fed.* Rep. of Germany, Universität des Saarlandes.

García, I., Pacheco, C., & Cruz, D. (2010). Adopting an RIA based tool for supporting assessment, implementation and learning in software in software process improvement under the NMX-I-059/02-NYCE-2005 standard in small software enterprises. *Eighth ACIS International Conference on Software Engineering Research. Management and Application.* 10.1109/SERA.2010.14

García, Y. M., Muñoz, M., Mejía, J., Martínez, J., Gasca-Hurtado, G. P., & Hincapié, J. A. (2016). Method for Developing Catalogs focused on Facilitating the implementation of Best Practices for Project Management of Software Development in SMEs, *Proceedings of the 5th International Conference in Software Process Improvement (CIMPS 2016)*, 1-8. 10.1109/CIMPS.2016.7802805

García, I., Pacheco, C., León, A., & Calvo-Manzano, J. A. (2020). A serious game for teaching the fundamentals of ISO/IEC/IEEE 29148 systems and software engineering – Lifecycle processes – Requirements engineering at undergraduate level. *Computer Standards & Interfaces*, *67*, 103377. doi:10.1016/j.csi.2019.103377

Garg, K., & Varma, V. (2008). People issues relating to software engineering education and training in India. *Proceedings of the 2008 1st India Software Engineering Conference*, 121–127. 10.1145/1342211.1342235

Garousi, V., Giray, G., Tuzun, E., Catal, C., & Felderer, M. (2019). Closing the Gap Between Software Engineering Education and Industrial Needs. *IEEE Software*, 1–1. doi:10.1109/MS.2019.2914663

Gasca-Hurtado, G. P., Peña, A., Gómez-Álvarez, M. C., Plascencia-Osuna, Ó. A., & Calvo-Manzano, J. A. (2015). Realidad virtual como buena práctica para trabajo en equipo con estudiantes de ingeniería. RISTI - Revista Iberica de Sistemas e Tecnologias de Informacao, 16, 76–91. doi:10.17013/risti.16.76-91

Gasca-Hurtado, G. P., Gómez-Álvarez, M. C., & Manrique-Losada, B. (2019). Using Gamification in Software Engineering Teaching: Study Case for Software Design. [*New Knowledge in Information Systems and Technologies.*]. *WorldCIST*, *19*, 2019.

Gasca-Hurtado, G. P., Gómez-Álvarez, M. C., & Manrique-Losada, B. (2019). Using gamification in software engineering teaching: Study case for software design. *Advances in Intelligent Systems and Computing*, *932*, 244–255. doi:10.1007/978-3-030-16187-3_24

Gasca-Hurtado, G. P., Gómez-Alvarez, M. C., Muñoz, M., & Mejía, J. (2016). Gamification proposal for defect tracking in software development process. In *European Conference on Software Process Improvement* (pp. 212-224). Springer. 10.1007/978-3-319-44817-6_17

Gasca-Hurtado, G. P., Gómez-Alvarez, M. C., Muñoz, M., & Mejía, J. (2017). Toward an assessment framework for gamified environments. *Communications in Computer and Information Science, 748*, 281–293. doi:10.1007/978-3-319-64218-5_23

Gasca-Hurtado, G. P., Gómez-Alvarez, M. C., Muñoz, M., & Mejía, J. (2018). Assessment Framework for Gamified Environments: A Gamification Assessment Model for Implementing the Framework. *Communications in Computer and Information Science, 896*, 240–253. doi:10.1007/978-3-319-97925-0_20

Gasca-Hurtado, G. P., Gómez-Álvarez, M. C., & Zepeda, V. V. (2018). Gamification experience of an educational environment in software engineering: Gamifying a course of agility for software process improvement. *Iberian Conference on Information Systems and Technologies*, 1–6. 10.23919/CISTI.2018.8399233

Gautrais, J., Theraulaz, G., Deneubourg, J. L., & Anderson, C. (2002). Emergent polyethism as a consequence of increased colony size in insect societies. *Journal of Theoretical Biology, 215*(3), 363–373. doi:10.1006/jtbi.2001.2506 PMID:12054843

Gharehbaghi, A., & Babic, A. (2018). Structural risk evaluation of a deep neural network and a Markov model in extracting medical information from phonocardiography. *Studies in Health Technology and Informatics, 251*, 157–160. PMID:29968626

Gibson, D., Goldenson, D., & Kost, K. (2006). *Performance results of CMMI-based process improvement.* Technical Report CMU/SEI-2006-TR-004 ESC-TR-2006-004, Software Engineering Institute (SEI), Carnegie Mellon University.

Ginnett, R. C. (2019). Crews as groups: Their formation and their leadership. In *Crew resource management* (pp. 73–102). Academic Press. doi:10.1016/B978-0-12-812995-1.00003-8

Giordano Lerena, R., & Páez Pino, A. (Eds.). (2018). Matilda y las mujeres en ingeniería en américa latina. Consejo Federal de Decanos de Ingeniería de Argentina CONFEDI. Latin American and Caribbean Consortium of Engineering Institutions.

Giordano Lerena, R., & Páez Pino, A. (Eds.). (2020). Matilda y las mujeres en ingeniería en américa latina II. Consejo Federal de Decanos de Ingeniería de Argentina CONFEDI. Latin American and Caribbean Consortium of Engineering Institutions.

Global Learning Consortium. (2020). *Accessibility.* Retrieved from https://www.imsglobal.org/activity/accessibility

Glover, F. (1986). Future Paths for Integer Programming and Links to Artificial Intelligence. *Computers & Operations Research, 13*(5), 533–549. doi:10.1016/0305-0548(86)90048-1

Gobron, S., Ahn, J., Garcia, D., Silvestre, Q., Thalmann, D., & Boulic, R. (2012). An event-based architecture to manage virtual human non-verbal communication in 3d chatting environment. In *International Conference on Articulated Motion and Deformable Objects* (pp. 58-68). Springer. 10.1007/978-3-642-31567-1_6

Goldenson D. (2007). Teach views, performance outcomes from process improvement. *Software Technology News, 10*(1).

Gómez-Álvarez, M. C., Gasca-Hurtado, G. P., & Garcia, C. (2016). Juegos serios como estrategia de enseñaza del proceso de gestión de riesgos de software: Prototipo de un videojuego. In 2016 IEEE 11th Colombian Computing Conference, CCC 2016 - Conference Proceedings. 10.1109/ColumbianCC.2016.7750804

Gómez-Álvarez, M.C., Zapata, C.M. & Astudillo, H. (2019). *SETMAT (Software Engineering Teaching Method and Theory): una teoría para la enseñanza de Ingeniería de Software*. Academic Press.

Gómez-Álvarez, M. C., Gasca-Hurtado, G. P., Manrique-Losada, B., & Arias, D. M. (2016). Método de diseño de instrumentos pedagógicos para ingeniería de software. *Iberian Conference on Information Systems and Technologies*. 10.1109/CISTI.2016.7521377

Gómez-Álvarez, M. C., Sanchez-Dams, R., & Baron-Salazar, A. (2017). Trouble hunters: A game for introductory subjects to computer engineering. *Proceedings of the 2016 42nd Latin American Computing Conference*. 10.1109/CLEI.2016.7833398

Gomez, M. C. (2015). *Diseño de un instrumento pedagógico para la enseñanza de la mejora de procesos software*. Academic Press.

González-Jiménez, R. (2019). *Varela inaugura la segunda línea del Metro de Panamá*. Inversión. Periódico La Prensa. https://www.prensa.com/economia/Varela-inaugura-segunda-Metro-Panama_0_5289970977.html

Goodman, J., Langdon, P. M., & Clarkson, P. J. (2006). Providing Strategic User Information for Designers: Methods and Initial Findings. In J. Clarkson, P. Langdon, & P. Robinson (Eds.), Designing Accessible Technology (pp. 41–51). Springer Link.

Gordon, M. (2018). In search of a universal human rights metaphor: Moral conversations across differences. *Educational Philosophy and Theory*, *50*(1), 83–94. doi:10.1080/00131857.2017.1336920

Gorissen, P. (2013). Open textbooks: trends and opportunities. In R. Jacobi, H. Jelgerhuis, & N. van der Woert (Eds.), Trend report: Open Educational Resources 2013 (pp. 1–114). Academic Press.

Goswami, T. (2018). Impact of Deep Learning in Image Processing and Computer Vision. In J. Anguera, S. Satapathy, V. Bhateja, & K. Sunitha (Eds.), Microelectronics, Electromagnetics and Telecommunications (pp. 475-485). Springer. doi:10.1007/978-981-10-7329-8_48

Goudarzi, F. (2018). Travel Time Prediction: Comparison of Machine Learning Algorithms in a Case Study. In *2018 IEEE 20th International Conference on High Performance Computing and Communications; IEEE 16th International Conference on Smart City; IEEE 4th Intl. Conference on Data Science and Systems*, (pp. 1404-1407). Exeter, UK: IEEE.

Gove, R., Hayworth, M., Chhetri, M., & Rueppell, O. (2009). Division of labour and social insect colony performance in relation to task and mating number under two alternative response threshold models. *Insectes Sociaux*, *56*(3), 319–331. doi:10.100700040-009-0028-y

Graf Plessen, M., & Bemporad, A. (2018). Stock Trading via Feedback Control: Stochastic Model Predictive or Genetic? *Journal of Modern Accounting and Auditing*, *14*(1), 35–47. doi:10.17265/1548-6583/2018.01.004

Granollers, T., Lorés, J., & Cañas, J. J. (2005). Diseño de Sistemas Interactivos Centrados en el Usuario. Academic Press.

Granollers, T. (2004). *Una metodología que integra la ingeniería del software, la interacción persona ordenador y la accesibilidad en el contexto de equipos de desarrollo multidisciplinares (Tesis Doctoral)*. Departament de Llenguatges i Sistemes Informàtics Universitat de Lleida.

Grau, A., Indri, M., Bello, L. L., & Sauter, T. (2017). Industrial robotics in factory automation: from the early stage to the Internet of Things. In *Proceedings of Conference of the IEEE Industrial Electronics Society* (pp. 6159-6164). IEEE Press. 10.1109/IECON.2017.8217070

Gray, D. (2016). *Liminal Thinking: Create the Change You Want by Changing the Way You Think*. Two Waves Books.

Graziotin, D., Wang, X., & Abrahamsson, P. (2015). The Affect of Software Developers: Common Misconceptions and Measurements. *2015 IEEE/ACM 8th International Workshop on Cooperative and Human Aspects of Software Engineering*, 123–124. 10.1109/CHASE.2015.23

Greenberg, R. I., Thiruvathukal, G. K., & Greenberg, S. T. (2020). Integrating Mathematics and Educational Robotics: Simple Motion Planning. *Advances in Intelligent Systems and Computing,* 262-269.

Gren, L. (2018). On gender, ethnicity, and culture in empirical software engineering research. *Proceedings of the 11th International Workshop on Cooperative and Human Aspects of Software Engineering - CHASE '18*, 77–78. 10.1145/3195836.3195837

Grisot, C. (2018). Application to Natural Language Processing and Machine Translation. In *Cohesion, Coherence and Temporal Reference from an Experimental Corpus Pragmatics Perspective. Yearbook of Corpus Linguistics and Pragmatics* (pp. 263–288). Springer. doi:10.1007/978-3-319-96752-3_7

Groth, D. P., & Robertson, E. L. (2001). It's all about process: Project-oriented teaching of software engineering. *Software Engineering Education Conference, Proceedings*, 7–17. 10.1109/CSEE.2001.913814

Guerrero Armas, A. (2009). La importancia de la creatividad en el aula. Temas para la educación, 1(5), 1-7.

Guerrero, H., & Vega, V. (2018). Usability analysis : Is our software inclusive? Guide for addressing accessibility in standards.

Guerrero-Vásquez, L. F., Landy-Rivera, D. X., Bravo-Torres, J. F., López-Nores, M., Castro-Serrano, R., & Vintimilla-Tapia, P. E. (2018, June). AVATAR: Contribution to Human-Computer interaction processes through the adaptation of semi-personalized virtual agents. In *2018 IEEE Biennial Congress of Argentina (ARGENCON)* (pp. 1-4). IEEE. 10.1109/ARGENCON.2018.8646055

Guevara-Cedeño, J., Aguilar, J., Torabi, R., & Berbey-Alvarez, A. (2018). Electric mobility in Panama: A review. In U. da Madeira (Ed.), *ES2DE 2018. International Conference on Energy and Sustainability in Small Developing Economies*. IEEE.

Guizani, M., & Anan, M. (2014). Smart Grid Opportunities and Challenges of Integrating Renewable Sources: A Survey. In *Wireless Communications and Mobile Computing Conference, IWCMC, International*, (pp. 1098-1105). Nicosia, Cyprus: IEEE.

Gu, J., Wang, Z., Kuen, J., Ma, L., Shahroudy, A., Shuai, B., Liu, T., Wang, X., Wang, G., Cai, J., & Chen, T. (2018). Recent Advances in Convolutional Neural Networks. *Journal Pattern Recognition*, *77*, 354–377. doi:10.1016/j.patcog.2017.10.013

Gunkel, D. J. (2017). Rage against the machine: Rethinking education in the face of technological unemployment. In Surviving the Machine Age: Intelligent Technology and the Transformation of Human Work (pp. 147–162). Springer International Publishing. doi:10.1007/978-3-319-51165-8_10

Gupta, K., & Johari, R. (2019). IOT based Electrical Device Surveillance and Control System. In *Proceedings of International Conference on Internet of Things: Smart Innovation and Usages* (pp. 1-5). IEEE Press. 10.1109/IoT-SIU.2019.8777342

Guresen, E., & Kayakutlu, G. (2011). Definition of artificial neural networks with comparison to other networks. *Procedia Computer Science*, *3*, 426–433. doi:10.1016/j.procs.2010.12.071

Gutiérrez, J. H., Astudillo, C. A., Ballesteros-Pérez, P., Mora-Melià, D., & Candia-Véjar, A. (2016). The multiple team formation problem using sociometry. *Computers & Operations Research*, *75*, 150–162. doi:10.1016/j.cor.2016.05.012

Gutiérrez, L., Bekios-Calfa, J., & Keith, B. (2019). A Review on Bayesian Networks for Sentiment Analysis. In J. Mejia, M. Muñoz, Á. Rocha, A. Peña, & M. Pérez-Cisneros (Eds.), *Trends and Applications in Software Engineering* (pp. 111–120). Springer. doi:10.1007/978-3-030-01171-0_10

Habibi, A. H., & Jahani, H. E. (2017). Guide to Convolutional Neural Networks. Springer Nature. doi:10.1007/978-3-319-57550-6

Hall, C. (2020, February 28). *Address prepared by pope Francis, read by h.e. archbishop Paglia, president of the pontifical academy for life.* http://www.vatican.va/content/francesco/en/speeches/2020/february/documents/papa-francesco_20200228_accademia-perlavita.html

Hall, E. T. (1968). Proxemics Text. *Current Anthropology, 9,* 2–3.

Hall, E. T. (1976). *Beyond culture.* Anchor Press.

Han, X. (2019). *Investigating Proxemics between avatars in virtual reality* (Unpublished master dissertation). KTH Royal Institute of Technology, Sweden.

Han, J., Pei, J., & Kamber, M. (2011). *Data Mining: Concepts and Techniques* (3rd ed.). Elsevier. http://myweb.sabanciuniv.edu/rdehkharghani/files/2016/02/The-Morgan-Kaufmann-Series-in-Data-Management-Systems-Jiawei-Han-Micheline-Kamber-Jian-Pei-Data-Mining.-Concepts-and-Techniques-3rd-Edition-Morgan-Kaufmann-2011.pdf

Hansen, I. A. (2010). State of the art of railway operations research. In I. Hansen (Ed.), *Timetable planning and information quality* (pp. 35–47). WIT Press. doi:10.2495/978-1-84564-500-7/04

Han, Y., Wan, Y., Chen, L., Xu, G., & Wu, J. (2017). Exploiting geographical location for team formation in social coding sites. In *Proceedings of the 21st Pacific-Asia Conference on Knowledge Discovery and Data Mining* (pp. 499-510). Springer International Publishing. 10.1007/978-3-319-57454-7_39

Hassan, M. A., Habiba, U., Majeed, F., & Shoaib, M. (2019). Adaptive gamification in e-learning based on students' learning styles. *Interactive Learning Environments,* 1–21. Advance online publication. doi:10.1080/10494820.2019.1588745

Hayashi, Y., Morita, H., & Nakano, Y. I. (2014). Estimating collaborative attitudes based on non-verbal features in collaborative learning interaction. *Procedia Computer Science, 35,* 986–993. doi:10.1016/j.procs.2014.08.184

Hazzan, O., & Dubinsky, Y. (2006). Can Diversity in Global Software Development Be Enhanced by Agile Software Development? *International Workshop on Global Software Development for the Practitioner,* 58–61. 10.1145/1138506.1138520

Heath, C., Jirotka, M., Luff, P., & Hindmarsh, J. (1994). Unpacking collaboration: The interactional organisation of trading in a city dealing room. *Computer Supported Cooperative Work, 3*(2), 147–165. doi:10.1007/BF00773445

He, B., Zhang, H., Keyu, W., & Lu, G. (2019). Machine Learning based integrated pedestrian facilities planning and staff assignment problem in transfer stations. *8th International Conference on Railway Operations Modelling and Analysis - RailNorrk̈oping 2019,* 387–408.

Heck, H. (2009). Assistive technologies. In *Technology Guide* (pp. 226–229). Springer., doi:10.1007/978-3-540-88546-7_44

Heck, L., & Huang, H. (2014). Deep learning of knowledge graph embeddings for semantic parsing of Twitter dialogs. In *Proceedings of Global Conference on Signal and Information Processing* (pp. 597-601). Atlanta, GA: IEEE Press. 10.1109/GlobalSIP.2014.7032187

He, K., Zhang, X., Ren, S., & Sun, J. (2016). Deep residual learning for image recognition. In *Proceedings of Conference on Computer Vision and Pattern Recognition* (pp. 770-778). Las Vegas, NV: IEEE Press.

Henderson, L. S., Stackman, R. W., & Lindekilde, R. (2018). Why cultural intelligence matters on global project teams. *International Journal of Project Management*, *36*(7), 954–967. doi:10.1016/j.ijproman.2018.06.001

Hernández, L., Muñoz, M., Mejia, J., & Peña, A. (2016). Gamification in software engineering team works: A systematic literature review, *Proceedings of the 5th International Conference in Software Process Improvement (CIMPS 2016)*, 1-8.

Hernandez-de-Menendez, M., & Morales-Menendez, R. (2019). Technological innovations and practices in engineering education: A review. *International Journal on Interactive Design and Manufacturing*, *13*(2), 713–728. doi:10.100712008-019-00550-1

Hernández, L., Muñoz, M., Mejia, J., Peña, A., Calvo-Manzano, J. A., & San Feliu, T. (2017). Proposal for identifying teamwork roles in software engineering through the construction of a virtual rube goldberg machine. *6th International Conference on Software Process Improvement (CIMPS)*, 1-8. 10.1109/CIMPS.2017.8169953

Herrera, F., Oh, S. Y., & Bailenson, J. N. (2020). Effect of Behavioral Realism on Social Interactions Inside Collaborative Virtual Environments. *PRESENCE: Virtual and Augmented Reality*, *27*(2), 163–182. doi:10.1162/pres_a_00324

Hersh, M. (2008). Disability and Assistive Technology Systems. In M. Hersh & M. A. Johnson (Eds.), *Assistive Technology for Visually Impaired and Blind People* (pp. 1–50). Springer-Verlag. doi:10.1007/978-1-84628-867-8_1

Hesamian, M. H., Jia, W., He, X., & Kennedy, P. (2019). Deep Learning Techniques for Medical Image Segmentation: Achievements and Challenges. *Journal of Digital Imaging*, *32*(4), 582–596. doi:10.100710278-019-00227-x PMID:31144149

He, X., & Deng, L. (2018). Deep Learning in Natural Language Generation from Images. In L. Deng & Y. Liu (Eds.), *Deep Learning in Natural Language Processing* (pp. 289–307). Springer. doi:10.1007/978-981-10-5209-5_10

Hipponensis, A. (426). *The City of God.* Roma: Opening text.

Hoffman, D. D., & Singh, M. (1997). Salience of visual parts: Elsevier. *Cognition*, *68*(1), 29–78. doi:10.1016/S0010-0277(96)00791-3 PMID:9187064

Hofmeister, C., Kruchten, P. B., Nord, R., Obbink, H., Ran, A., & America, P. (2007). A general model of software architecture design derived from five industrial approaches. *Journal of Systems and Software*, *80*(1), 106–126. doi:10.1016/j.jss.2006.05.024

Hof, S., Kropp, M., & Landolt, M. (2017). Use of Gamification to Teach Agile Values and Collaboration: A multi-week Scrum simulation project in an undergraduate software engineering course. In *Proceedings of the 2017 ACM Conference on Innovation and Technology in Computer Science Education* (pp. 323-328). 10.1145/3059009.3059043

Hollis, B., & Maiden, N. (2013). Extending agile processes with creativity techniques. *IEEE Software*, *30*(5), 78–84. doi:10.1109/MS.2012.171

Hooshyar, D., Pedaste, M., Saks, K., Leijen, Ä., Bardone, E., & Wang, M. (2020). Open learner models in supporting self-regulated learning in higher education: A systematic literature review. *Computers & Education*, *103878*. Advance online publication. doi:10.1016/j.compedu.2020.103878

Huang, F., Sun, T., & Bu, F. (2016). Generation of person-specific 3D model based on single photograph. In *Proceedings of International Conference on Computer and Communications* (pp. 704-707). IEEE Press.

Hunicke, R., LeBlanc, M., & Zubek, R. (2004). MDA: A formal approach to game design and game research. *AAAI Workshop on Challenges in Game AI.* http://www.aaai.org/Papers/Workshops/2004/WS-04-04/WS04-04-001.pdf

Huo, Z., & Skubic, M. (2016, May). Natural spatial description generation for human-robot interaction in indoor environments. In *2016 IEEE international conference on smart computing (SMARTCOMP)* (pp. 1-3). IEEE.

Hurtado, C., & Gutierrez, C. (2007). *Data warehouses and OLAP: concepts, architectures and solutions. In Chapter Handling Structural Heterogeneity in OLAP*. Idea Group, Inc.

Hu, W., Zhuo, Q., Zhang, C., & Li, J. (2018). Fast Branch Convolutional Neural Network for Traffic Sign Recognition. *Intelligent Transportation Systems*, *9*(3), 114–126.

Ibarra, S., & Muñoz, M. (2018). Support tool for software quality assurance in software development. *International Conference on Software Process Improvement CIMPS 2018*, 13-19. 10.1109/CIMPS.2018.8625617

ICSCET. IEEE Staff. (2018). Smart E-Grievance System for Effective Communication in Smart Cities. In *Conference: 2018 International Conference on Smart City and Emerging Technology (ICSCET)*, (pp. 1-4). Mumbai, India: IEEE.

Infante, A. L., André, M., Rosete, A., & López, Y. (2020a). Methods for the formation of multiple teams of students applying a multiobjective approach. *Revista de Ingeniería Industrial*, *41*(1), 20–39.

Infante, A. L., André, M., Rosete, A., Naredo, J. A., & Durán, A. (2020b, March). *A decision support tool for multiple team formation problems* [Paper presentation]. *14th International Conference on Operations Research (ICOR)*, La Habana, Cuba.

Infante, A. L., André, M., Rosete, A., & Rampersaud, L. (2014). Formation of software project teams applying multi-objective metaheuristic algorithms. *Revista Iberoamericana de Inteligencia Artificial*, *17*(54), 1–16. doi:10.4114/intartif.vol17iss54pp1-16

Iniesto, F. (2020). *An investigation into the accessibility of Massive Open Online Courses (MOOCs)* (PhD thesis). The Open University, London, UK.

Inmon, W. H. (2005). *Building the data warehouse*. John Wiley & Sons.

intelligentcommunity.org. (2018). *ICF. Intelligent Community Forum*. https://www.intelligentcommunity.org/

International Organization for Standardization. (2008a). Standard ISO 9241-171:2008 Ergonomics of human-system interaction – Part 171 Guidance on software accessibility.

International Organization for Standardization. (2008b). Standard ISO/IEC 24751-1:2008 Information technology – Individualized adaptability and accessibility in e-learning, education and training.

International Organization for Standardization. (2018). Standard ISO 9241-11:2018 Ergonomics of human-system interaction — Part 11: Usability: Definitions and concepts.

Jadán-Guerrero, J., Guevara, C., Lara-Alvarez, P., Sanchez-Gordon, S., Calle-Jimenez, T., Salvador-Ullauri, L., Acosta-Vargas, P., & Bonilla-Jurado, D. (2020a). Building hybrid interfaces to increase interaction with young children and children with special needs. In Advances in Human Factors and Systems Interaction. Advances in Intelligent Systems and Computing (pp. 306-314). Cham, Switzerland: Springer. doi:10.1007/978-3-030-20040-4_28

Jadán-Guerrero, J., Sanchez-Gordon, S., Acosta-Vargas, P., Alvites-Huamaní, C. G., & Nunes, I. L. (2020b). Interactive storytelling books for fostering inclusion of children with special needs. In Advances in Human Factors and Systems Interaction. Advances in Intelligent Systems and Computing (pp. 222-228). Cham, Switzerland: Springer. doi:10.1007/978-3-030-51369-6_30

Jafri, S., Chawan, S., & Khan, A. (2020). Face Recognition using Deep Neural Network with "LivenessNet. In *Proceedings of International Conference on Inventive Computation Technologies* (pp. 145-148). IEEE Press.

Jagadish, H., Bonchi, F., Eliassi-Rad, T., Getoor, L., Gummadi, K., & Stoyanovich, J. (2019). The Responsibility Challenge for Data. *SIGMOD '19:* In *Proceedings of the 2019 International Conference on Management of Data.* Association for Computing Machinery.

Jain, A. K., Duin, R. P. W., & Mao, J. (2000). Statistical pattern recognition: A review. *IEEE Transactions on Pattern Analysis and Machine Intelligence, 22*(1), 4–37. doi:10.1109/34.824819

Jamshidi, A., Núñez, A., Dollevoet, R., & Li, Z. (2017). Robust and predictive fuzzy key performance indicators for condition-based treatment of squats in railway infrastructures. *Journal of Infrastructure Systems, 23*(3), 1–13. doi:10.1061/(ASCE)IS.1943-555X.0000357

Jaschik, S. (2016). *University may remove online content to avoid disability law.* Retrieved from https://www.insidehighered.com/news/2016/09/20/berkeley-may-remove-free-onlinecontent-rather-complying-disability-law

Jeanson, R., Fewell, J. H., Gorelick, R., & Bertram, S. (2007). Emergence of increased division of labor as a function of group size. *Behavioral Ecology and Sociobiology, 62*(2), 289–298. doi:10.100700265-007-0464-5

Jeong, Y., Pan, Y., Rathore, S., Kim, B., & Park, J. H. (2018). A parallel team formation approach using crowd intelligence from social network. *Computers in Human Behavior, 101*, 429–434. doi:10.1016/j.chb.2018.07.018

Jepsen, T. C. (2009). Just what is an ontology, anyway? *IT Professional, 11*(5), 22–27. doi:10.1109/MITP.2009.105

Jesus, G. M. d., Paschoal, L. N., Ferrari, F. C., & Souza, S. R. S. (2019). Is It Worth Using Gamification on Software Testing Education? An Experience Report. *Proceedings of the XVIII Brazilian Symposium on Software Quality.* 10.1145/3364641.3364661

Jin, C. X., Li, F. C., Zhang, K., Xu, L. D., & Chen, Y. (2019). A cooperative effect-based decision support model for team formation. *Enterprise Information Systems, 14*(1), 110–132. doi:10.1080/17517575.2019.1678071

Johnson, A., & Leigh, J. (2001). Tele-immersive collaboration in the CAVE research network. In *Collaborative Virtual Environments* (pp. 225–243). Springer. doi:10.1007/978-1-4471-0685-2_12

Jordan, K. (2015). *MOOC Completion Rates: The Data.* Retrieved from http://www.katyjordan.com/MOOCproject.html

Joshi, K. D., Kvasny, L., Unnikrishnan, P., & Trauth, E. (2016). How Do Black Men Succeed in IT Careers? The Effects of Capital. *49th Hawaii International Conference on System Sciences*, 4729–4738. 10.1109/HICSS.2016.586

Juliantari, N. K., Sudarsana, I. K., Sutriyanti, N. K., Astawa, I. N. T., Putri, I. D. A. H., & Saddhono, K. (2018). Educational games based in information technology as innovation evaluation activity in learning. *Journal of Physics: Conference Series, 1114*(1), 012041. doi:10.1088/1742-6596/1114/1/012041

Juslin, P. N., Scherer, K. R., Harrigan, J., & Rosenthal, R. (2005). Vocal expression of affect. In J. Harrigan, R. Rosenthal, & K. R. Scherer (Eds.), *The new handbook of methods in nonverbal behavior research* (pp. 65–135). Oxford University Press.

Kabalci, Y., Kabalci, E., Padmanaban, S., Holm-Nielsen, J., & Blaabjerg, F. (2019). Internet of Things Applications as Energy Internet in Smart Grids and Smart Environments. *Electronics (Basel), 8*(9), 972. doi:10.3390/electronics8090972

Kader, Md. A., & Zamli, K. Z. (2020). Adopting Jaya Algorithm for Team Formation Problem. In *Proceedings of the 9th International Conference on Software and Computer Applications* (pp. 62–66). ACM.

Kaewunruen, S. (2017). Underpinning systems thinking in railway engineering education. *Australasian Journal of Engineering Education, 22*(2), 107–116. doi:10.1080/22054952.2018.1440481

Kaleybar, H. J., & Farshad, S. (2016). A comprehensive control strategy of railway power quality compensator for AC traction power supply systems. *Turkish Journal of Electrical Engineering and Computer Sciences*, *24*(6), 4582–4603. doi:10.3906/elk-1404-250

Kalivoda, J., & Neduzha, L. O. (2017). Enhancing the Scientific Level of Engineering Training of Railway Transport Professionals. *Science and Transport Progress. Bulletin of Dnipropetrovsk National University of Railway Transport*, *0*(6(72)), 128–137. doi:10.15802tp2017/119050

Kalyvioti, K., & Mikropoulos, T. (2013). A Virtual Reality Test for the Identification of Memory Strengths of Dyslexic Students in Higher Education. *J. UCS*, *19*(18), 2698–2721.

Kanter, A. S. (2015). *The development of disability rights under international law: From charity to human rights*. Routledge.

Kantor, J. R. (1924). *Principles of psychology*. The Principia Press. doi:10.1037/10752-000

Kapur, S. (2003). Psychosis as a state of aberrant salience: A framework linking biology, phenomenology, and pharmacology in schizophrenia. *The American Journal of Psychiatry*, *160*(1), 13–23. doi:10.1176/appi.ajp.160.1.13 PMID:12505794

Karakose, E., Gencoglu, M. T., Karakose, M., Yaman, O., Aydin, I., & Akin, E. (2015). A new arc detection method based on fuzzy logic using S-transform for pantograph–catenary systems. *Journal of Intelligent Manufacturing*, *19*. Advance online publication. doi:10.100710845-015-1136-3

Kazman, R., Abowd, G., Bass, L., & Clements, P. (1996). Scenario-Based Analysis of Software Architecture. *IEEE Software*, *13*(6), 47–55. doi:10.1109/52.542294

Kazmi, A., Serrano, M., & Soldatos, J. (2018). VITAL-OS: An Open Source IoT Operating System for Smart Cities. *IEEE Communications Standards Magazine*, *2*(2), 71–77. doi:10.1109/MCOMSTD.2018.1700016

Keates, S. (2007). Designing for Accessibility: A Business Guide to Countering Design Exclusion. Lawrence Erlbaum Associates.

Keates, S. (2004). Developing BS7000 Part 6 – Guide to Managing Inclusive Design. In *User-Centered Interaction Paradigms for Universal Access in the Information Society* (pp. 332–339). Springer. doi:10.1007/978-3-540-30111-0_29

Keates, S., Clarkson, P. J., & Street, T. (2003). Countering design exclusion : Bridging the gap between usability and accessibility. *Universal Access in the Information Society*, *2*(2), 215–225. doi:10.100710209-003-0059-5

Kelleher, J. D. (2003). *A Perceptually Based Computational Framework for the Interpretation of Spatial Language Dublin City University* (PhD Thesis). Academic Press.

Kharkongor, G. C., & Albert, S. (2014). Career Counseling among Indigenous Peoples. In G. Arulmani, A. J. Bakshi, F. T. L. Leong, & A. G. Watts (Eds.), *Handbook of Career Development: International Perspectives* (pp. 539–554). Springer New York. doi:10.1007/978-1-4614-9460-7_30

Khodabakhshi, M. B., & Moradi, M. H. (2017). The attractor recurrent neural network based on fuzzy functions: An effective model for the classification of lung abnormalities. *Computers in Biology and Medicine*, *1*(84), 124–136. doi:10.1016/j.compbiomed.2017.03.019 PMID:28363113

Khosravi, M., Fazel, S. S., & Abdollahi, V. (2017). Fuzzy logic-based vector control of permanent magnet synchronous motor using stacked matrix converter for railway traction aplications. *Railway Research*, *4*(2), 41–56.

Kikuchi, S., & Miljkovic, D. (1999). *Method To Preprocess Observed Traffic Data for Consistency Application of Fuzzy Optimization Concept*. Transportation Research Record 1679 Paper No. 99-0129 73.

Kimball, R., & Ross, M. (2011). *The data warehouse toolkit: the complete guide to dimensional modeling.* John Wiley & Sons.

Kirkpatrick, S., Gelatt, C. D., & Vecchi, M. P. (1983). Optimization by Simulated Annealing. *Science, 220*(4598), 671–680. doi:10.1126cience.220.4598.671 PMID:17813860

Kirkwood, A., & Price, L. (2005). Learners and learning in the twenty-first century: What do we know about students' attitudes towards and experiences of information and communication technologies that will help us design courses? *Studies in Higher Education, 30*(3), 257–274. doi:10.1080/03075070500095689

Kitchenham, B. (2007). *Guidelines for performing systematic literature reviews in software engineering.* EBSE Technical Report.

Knapp, M., & Hall, J. (2007). *Nonverbal communication in human interaction* (7th ed.). Thomson Wadsworth.

Kohon, J. (2011). *Más y mejores trenes.* BID.

Koleski, K., & Blivas, A. (2018). China's Engagement with Latin America and the Caribbean. Congressional Research Service.

Kolesnichenko, A., McVeigh-Schultz, J., & Isbister, K. (2019, June). Understanding Emerging Design Practices for Avatar Systems in the Commercial Social VR Ecology. In *Proceedings of the 2019 on Designing Interactive Systems Conference* (pp. 241-252). 10.1145/3322276.3322352

Konstantinou, N., & Spanos, D. E. (2015a). Technical Background. In *Materializing the Web of Linked Data* (pp. 17–49). Springer. doi:10.1007/978-3-319-16074-0_2

Konstantinou, N., & Spanos, D. E. (2015b). Deploying Linked Open Data: Methodologies and Software Tools. In *Materializing the Web of Linked Data.* Springer; doi:10.1007/978-3-319-16074-0_3

Korsaa, M., Johansen, J., Schweigert, T., Vohwinkel, D., Messnarz, R., Nevalainen, R., & Biro, M. (2013). The people aspects in modern process improvement management approaches. *Journal of Software: Evolution and Process, 25*(4), 381–391. doi:10.1002mr.570

Kort, B., & Reilly, R. (2002, June). An affective module for an intelligent tutoring system. In *International Conference on Intelligent Tutoring Systems* (pp. 955-962). Springer. 10.1007/3-540-47987-2_95

Kroll, P., Kruchten, P. B., & Booch, G. (2003). The rational unified process made easy. Addison-Wesley Professional.

Kruchten, P. B. (1995). The 4+1 View Model of Architecture. *IEEE Software, 6*(12), 42–50. doi:10.1109/52.469759

Kube, R. C., & Bonabeau, E. (2000). Cooperative transport by ants and robots. *Robotics and Autonomous Systems, 30*(1-2), 85–101. doi:10.1016/S0921-8890(99)00066-4

Kumar, A., & Das, S. D. (2019). Bird Species Classification Using Transfer Learning with Multistage Training. In C. Arora & K. Mitra (Eds.), *Computer Vision Applications* (pp. 28–38). Springer. doi:10.1007/978-981-15-1387-9_3

Kurkovsky, S., Ludi, S., & Clark, L. (2019). Active learning with LEGO for software requirements. *Proceedings of the 50th ACM Technical Symposium on Computer Science Education,* 218–224. 10.1145/3287324.3287444

Kvasny, L., Joshi, K. D., & Trauth, E. (2015, March 15). *Understanding Black Males' IT Career Choices.* iConference 2015, Newport Beach, CA. https://www.ideals.illinois.edu/handle/2142/73428

Lai, Y.-C., Chen, K.-T., Yan, T.-H., & Li, M.-H. (2018). Simulation-Based Method of Capacity Utilization Evaluation to Account for Uncertainty in Recovery Time. *Transportation Research Record: Journal of the Transportation Research Board, 2672*(10), 202–214.

Lai, Y.-C., & Ip, C.-S. (2017). An integrated framework for assessing service efficiency and stability of rail transit systems. *Transportation Research Part C, Emerging Technologies, 79*, 18–41. doi:10.1016/j.trc.2017.03.006

Lambert, J. R., & Akinlade, E. Y. (2019). Immigrant stereotypes and differential screening. *Personnel Review, 49*(4), 921–938. doi:10.1108/PR-06-2018-0229

Landers, R. (2014). Developing a Theory of Gamified Learning: Linking Serious Games and Gamification of Learning. *Simulation & Gaming, 45*(6), 752–768. doi:10.1177/1046878114563660

Langer, D., Rosenblatt, J. K., & Hebert, M. (1994). A Behavior-based system for off-road navigation. *Transactions on Robotics and Automation, 10*(6), 776–782. doi:10.1109/70.338532

Laporte, C. Y., Muñoz, M., Mejía, J., & O'Connor, R. (2017). Applying Software Engineering Standards in Very Small Entities. *IEEE Software*, 99-103.

Lara, G. A., Delgado, M., & Marín, N. (2013). Fuzzy multidimensional modelling for flexible querying of learning object repositories. In *International Conference on Flexible Query Answering Systems* (pp. 112-123). Springer. 10.1007/978-3-642-40769-7_10

Lara, G., De Antonio, A., & Peña, A. (2018a). A computational model of perceptual saliency for 3D objects in virtual environments. *Virtual Reality (Waltham Cross), 22*(3), 221–234. doi:10.100710055-017-0326-z

Lara, G., Peña, A., Rolon, C., Muñoz, M., & Estrada, E. (2018b). A Computational Measure of Saliency of the Texture Based a Saliency Map by Color. In *International Conference on Software Process Improvement* (pp. 206-215). Springer.

Larasati, R., & KeungLam, H. (2017). Handwritten digits recognition using ensemble neural networks and ensemble decision tree. In *International Conference on Smart Cities, Automation Intelligent Computing Systems* (pp. 99-104). IEEE Press. 10.1109/ICON-SONICS.2017.8267829

Laskowski, M. (2015). Implementing gamification techniques into university study path - A case study. *IEEE Global Engineering Education Conference*, 582–586. 10.1109/EDUCON.2015.7096028

Lattanze, A. J. (2009). *Architecting Software Intensive Systems: A practitioners guide.* CRC Press.

Lau, K., & Wang, Z. (2007). Software Component Models. *IEEE Transactions on Software Engineering, 33*(10), 709–724. doi:10.1109/TSE.2007.70726

Lautala, P. (2007). *From classroom to rail industry- A rail engineer in the making.* Academic Press.

Lazar, M., Miron-Spektor, E., Agarwal, R., Erez, M., Goldfard, B., & Chen, G. (2020). Entrepreneurial team formation. *The Academy of Management Annals, 14*(1), 29–59. doi:10.5465/annals.2017.0131

LeCun, Y., Bengio, Y., & Hinton, G. (2015). Deep Learning. *Nature, 521*(7553), 436–444. doi:10.1038/nature14539 PMID:26017442

Lemos, J., Alves, C., Duboc, L., & Rodrigues, G. N. (2012). A systematic mapping study on creativity in requirements engineering. *Proceedings of the ACM Symposium on Applied Computing*, 1083–1088. 10.1145/2245276.2231945

Lenberg, P., Feldt, R., & Wallgren, L. G. (2015). Behavioral software engineering: A definition and systematic literature review. *Journal of Systems and Software, 107*, 15–37. doi:10.1016/j.jss.2015.04.084

Leonardi, G. (2016). A fuzzy model for a railway-planning problem. *Applied Mathematical Sciences*, *10*(January), 1333–1342. doi:10.12988/ams.2016.63106

Leonelli, S. (2016). Locating ethics in data science: Responsibility and accountability in global and distributed knowledge production systems. *Philosophical Transactions of the Royal Society A*, *374*(2083), 1–12. doi:10.1098/rsta.2016.0122 PMID:28336799

Li, W., Logenthiran, T., Phan, V., & Woo, W. L. (2019). A Novel Smart Energy Theft System (SETS) for IoT-Based Smart Home. *IEEE Internet of Things Journal*, *6*(3), 5531-5539.

Liang, H., Fu, W., & Yi, F. (2019). A Survey of Recent Advances in Transfer Learning. In *Proceedings of International Conference on Communication Technology* (pp. 1516-1523). IEEE Press. 10.1109/ICCT46805.2019.8947072

Liemhetcharat, S., & Veloso, M. (2017). Allocating training instances to learning agents for team formation. *Autonomous Agents and Multi-Agent Systems*, *31*(4), 905–940. doi:10.100710458-016-9355-3

Lienhard, J. (1988). *No. 1208: The Panama Railroad*. The Engines of Our Ingenuity. https://uh.edu/engines/epi1208.htm

Li, K., Chen, Y., & Luna-Reyes, L. F. (2017). City Resilience as a Framework to Understand Smart Cities: Dimensions and Measurement. In *Proceedings of the 18th Annual International Conference on Digital Government Research*. Association for Computing Machinery. 10.1145/3085228.3085249

Li, K., Huang, H., & Schonfeld, P. (2018). Metro Timetabling for Time-Varying Passenger Demand and Congestion at Stations. *Journal of Advanced Transportation*, *2018*, 27. doi:10.1155/2018/3690603

Lin, Y. T. (2019). Impacts of a flipped classroom with a smart learning diagnosis system on students' learning performance, perception, and problem solving ability in a software engineering course. *Computers in Human Behavior*, *95*, 187–196. doi:10.1016/j.chb.2018.11.036

Liu, C., Xiao, Y., Javangula, V., Hu, Q., Wang, S., & Cheng, X. (2019). NormaChain: A Blockchain-Based Normalized Autonomous Transaction Settlement System for IoT-Based E-Commerce. *IEEE Internet of Things Journal*, *6*(3), 4680–4693. doi:10.1109/JIOT.2018.2877634

Liu, C., Zoph, B., Neumann, M., Shlens, J., Hua, W., Li, L. J., Fei-Fei, L., Yuille, A., Huang, K., & Murphy, K. (2018). Progressive Neural Architecture Search. In V. Ferrari, M. Hebert, C. Sminchisescu, & Y. Weiss (Eds.), *Computer Vision* (pp. 19–35). Springer.

Liu, W., Wang, Z., Liu, X., Zeng, N., Liu, Y., & Alsaadi, F. E. (2017). A survey of deep neural network architectures and their applications. *Neurocomputing*, *234*, 11–26. doi:10.1016/j.neucom.2016.12.038

Liu, W., Zhang, M., Zhang, Y., Liao, Y., Huang, Q., Chang, S., Wang, H., & He, J. (2018). Real-Time Multilead Convolutional Neural Network for Myocardial Infarction Detection. *IEEE Journal of Biomedical and Health Informatics*, *22*(5), 1434–1444. doi:10.1109/JBHI.2017.2771768 PMID:29990164

Lohre, R., Warner, J. J. P., Athwal, G. S., & Goel, D. P. (2020). The evolution of virtual reality in shoulder and elbow surgery. JSES International, 1–9. doi:10.1016/j.jseint.2020.02.005

López Carrillo, D., Calonge García, A., Rodríguez Laguna, T., Ros Magán, G., & Lebrón Moreno, J. A. (2019). Using Gamification in a Teaching Innovation Project at the University of Alcalá: A New Approach to Experimental Science Practices. *Electronic Journal of e-Learning*, *17*(2), 93-106.

López Díaz, R. A. (2017) ¿La creatividad: un lugar olvidado en la educación? In Estrategias de enseñanza creativa: investigaciones sobre la creatividad en el aula. Academic Press.

López, G. L. (2016). *Modelo computacional para la generación de indicaciones en la localización de objetos en entornos virtuales: aspectos espaciales y perceptivos* (Doctoral dissertation). Universidad Politécnica de Madrid.

Lopez, J., Piedra, N., & Chicaiza, J. (2015). Recommendation of OERs shared in social media based-on social networks analysis approach. Proceedings of Frontiers in Education Conference, FIE. 10.1109/FIE.2014.7044454

López, Y., André, M., Infante, A. L., Escalera, K., & Verona, S. (2018). Evaluation of the performance of roles in software development teams. Use of rating scales. *Ingeniare. Revista Chilena de Ingeniería, 26*(3), 486–498.

Lorente-Gutierrez, J., & Berbey-Álvarez, A. (2015). *Diseño Geométrico y Mecánica de la Vía Férrea*. Universidad Tecnológica de Panamá.

Louridas, P., & Ebert, C. (2016). Machine Learning. *IEEE Software, 33*(5), 110–115. doi:10.1109/MS.2016.114

Luo, X., Zhang, H., Zhang, Z., Yu, Y., & Li, K. (2019). A New Framework of Intelligent Public Transportation System Based on the Internet of Things. *IEEE Access: Practical Innovations, Open Solutions, 7*, 55290–55304. doi:10.1109/ACCESS.2019.2913288

Lwakatare, L. E., Kuvaja, P., & Oivo, M. (2016). Relationship of DevOps to Agile, Lean and Continuous Deployment. *International Conference on Product-Focused Software Process Improvement*, 399–415. 10.1007/978-3-319-49094-6_27

Machuca-Villegas, L., Gasca-Hurtado, G. P., Restrepo Tamayo, L. M., & Morillo Puente, S. (2020). Social and Human Factor Classification of Influence in Productivity in Software Development Teams. In M. Yilmaz, J. Niemann, P. Clarke, & R. Messnarz (Eds.), *Systems, Software and Services Process Improvement* (pp. 717–729). Springer International Publishing., doi:10.1007/978-3-030-56441-4_54

Maes, F., Robben, D., Vandermeulen, D., & Suetens, P. (2019). The Role of Medical Image Computing and Machine Learning in Healthcare. In E. Ranschaert, S. Morozov, & P. Algra (Eds.), *Artificial Intelligence in Medical Imaging* (pp. 9–23). Springer. doi:10.1007/978-3-319-94878-2_2

Mahler, S. (2006). *The New Panama Railroad: World's Ninth Wonder*. Britannica Blog. http://blogs.britannica.com/2007/04/the-new-panama-railroad-ninth-wonder-of-the-world/

Mahmoudi, H., Pashavi, G., Koushafar, M., & Saribagloo, J. A. (2015). The Effect of Computer Games on Speed, Attention and Consistency of Learning Mathematics among Students. *Procedia: Social and Behavioral Sciences, 176*, 419–424. doi:10.1016/j.sbspro.2015.01.491

Malche, T., & Maheshwary, P. (2017). Internet of Things (IoT) for building smart home system. In *Proceedings of International Conference on IoT in Social, Mobile, Analytics and Cloud* (pp. 65-70). IEEE Press.

Malinowski, E., & Zimanyi, E. (2008). *Advanced Data Warehouse Design: From Conventional to Spatial and Temporal Applications*. Springer.

Manetta, C., & Blade, R. A. (1995). Glossary of virtual reality terminology. *International Journal of Virtual Reality, 1*(2), 35–39. doi:10.20870/IJVR.1995.1.2.2604

Manoharan, A., & Rathinasabapathy, V. (2018). Smart Water Quality Monitoring and Metering Using Lora for Smart Villages. In *2nd International Conference on Smart Grid and Smart Cities*. Kuala Lumpur: IEEE.

Manrique-Losada, B., Gasca-Hurtado, G. P., & Gómez-Álvarez, M. C. (2015). Assessment proposal of teaching and learning strategies in software process improvement. *Revista de la Facultad de Ingeniería, 77*, 105–114.

Manrique-Losada, B., González-Calderon, G., & Gasca-Hurtado, G. P. (2011). *A Proposal For Software Engineering Education Based On A Joint Project. Software Engineering: Methods. Modeling, And Teaching.*

Maravall, D., & de Lope, J. (2011). Fusion of learning automata theory and granular inference systems: ANLAGIS. Applications to Pattern Recognition and Machine Learning. *Neurocomputing*, *74*(8), 1237–1242. doi:10.1016/j.neucom.2010.07.024

Marín, B., Frez, J., Cruz-Lemus, J. A., & Genero, M. (2019, November). An Empirical Investigation on the Benefits of Gamification in Programming Courses. *ACM Transactions on Computing Education (TOCE)*, *19*(1), 22.

Marín, B., Vera, M., & Giachetti, G. (2019). An Adventure Serious Game for Teaching Effort Estimation in Software Engineering. *IWSM-Mensura 2019: Joint Proceedings of the International Workshop on Software Measurement and the International Conference on Software Process and Product Measurement.*

Marina, J. (1994). *Teoría de la inteligencia creadora.* Anagrama.

Marín, B., Larenas, F., & Giachetti, G. (2018). Learning Conceptual Modeling Design Through the Classutopia Serious Game. *International Journal of Software Engineering and Knowledge Engineering*, *28*(11&12), 1679–1699. doi:10.1142/S0218194018400235

Marín, B., Vera, M., & Giachetti, G. (2019). *An Adventure Serious Game for Teaching Effort Estimation in Software Engineering.* IWSM-Mensura.

Marinho, M., Luna, A., & Beecham, S. (2018). Global Software Development: Practices for Cultural Differences. In M. Kuhrmann, K. Schneider, D. Pfahl, S. Amasaki, M. Ciolkowski, R. Hebig, P. Tell, J. Klünder, & S. Küpper (Eds.), *Product-Focused Software Process Improvement* (pp. 299–317). Springer International Publishing. doi:10.1007/978-3-030-03673-7_22

Marin, N., Pons, O., & Vila, M. A. (2000). Fuzzy types: A new concept of type for managing vague structures. *International Journal of Intelligent Systems*, *15*(11), 1061–1085. doi:10.1002/1098-111X(200011)15:11<1061::AID-INT5>3.0.CO;2-A

Marinov, M., Pachl, J., Lautala, P., Macario, R., Reis, V., & Riley-Edwards, J. (2011). Policy-Oriented Measures for Tuning and Intensifying Rail Higher Education on both Sides of the Atlantic. *4th International Seminar on Railway Operations Modelling and Analysis (IAROR)*, 17.

Marinov, M., Fraszczyk, A., Zunder, T., Rizzetto, L., Ricci, S., Todorova, M., Dzhaleva, A., Karagyozov, K., Trendafilov, Z., & Schlingensiepen, J. (2013). A supply-demand study of practice in rail logistics higher education. *Journal of Transport Literature*, *7*(2), 338–351. doi:10.1590/S2238-10312013000200018

Marks, G., O'Connor, R. V., & Clarke, P. M. (2017). The Impact of Situational Context on the Software Development Process – A Case Study of a Highly Innovative Start-up Organization. In A. Mas, A. Mesquida, R. V. O'Connor, T. Rout, & A. Dorling (Eds.), *Software Process Improvement and Capability Determination* (pp. 455–466). Springer International Publishing. doi:10.1007/978-3-319-67383-7_33

Marques, M., Ochoa, S., Bastarrica, M., & Gutierrez, F. (2018). Enhancing the Student Learning Experience in Software Engineering Project Courses. *IEEE Transactions on Education*, *61*(1), 63–73. doi:10.1109/TE.2017.2742989

Martínez-Palacios, A. (2019). Nota técnica Proyecto del Tren maya. Instituto Mexicano para la competividad (IMCO).

Matarić, M. J. (1995). From Local Interactions to Collective Intelligence. In L. Steels (Ed.), *The Biology and Technology of Intelligent Autonomous Agents* (pp. 275–295). Springer. doi:10.1007/978-3-642-79629-6_11

Matsuo, S. (2017). How formal analysis and verification add security to blockchain-based systems. In *Proceedings of the 17th Conference on Formal Methods in Computer-Aided Design.* FMCAD Inc. 10.23919/FMCAD.2017.8102228

Matturro, G., & Raschetti, F. (n.d.). *A Systematic Mapping Study on Soft Skills in Software Engineering.* Jucs.Org. Retrieved June 15, 2020, from http://www.jucs.org/jucs_25_1/a_systematic_mapping_study/jucs_25_01_0016_0041_matturo.pdf

Matturro, G., Raschetti, F., & Fontán, C. (2019). A Systematic Mapping Study on Soft Skills in Software Engineering. *Journal of Universal Computer Science*, 25(1), 16–41.

Maxim, B., Kaur, R., Apzynski, C., Edwards, D., & Evans, E. (2016). An Agile Software Engineering Process Improvement Game. *IEEE Frontiers in Education Conference (FIE)*.

Mayer, S., Reinhardt, J., Schweigert, R., Jelke, B., Schwind, V., Wolf, K., & Henze, N. (2020, April). Improving Humans' Ability to Interpret Deictic Gestures in Virtual Reality. In *Proceedings of the 2020 CHI Conference on Human Factors in Computing Systems* (pp. 1-14). 10.1145/3313831.3376340

Mazón, J. N., & Trujillo, J. (2008). An MDA approach for the development of data warehouses. *Decision Support Systems*, 45(1), 41–58. doi:10.1016/j.dss.2006.12.003

Means, A. J. (2018). Learning to save the future: Rethinking education and work in an era of digital capitalism. In *Learning to save the Future: Rethinking Education and Work in an Era of Digital Capitalism*. Taylor and Francis. doi:10.4324/9781315450209

Mehta, A., Parekh, Y., & Karamchandani, S. (2018). Performance Evaluation of Machine Learning and Deep Learning Techniques for Sentiment Analysis. In Information Systems Design and Intelligent Applications (pp. pp 463-471). Springer. doi:10.1007/978-981-10-7512-4_46

Mejía J., Muñoz E., & Muñoz M. (2016). Reinforcing the applicability of Multi-model Environments for Software Process Improvement using Knowledge Management. Science of Computer Programming, Elsevier, Vol. SCICO, Pag.1-13. doi:10.1016/j.scico.2015.12.002

Menéndez, M., Martínez, C., Sanz, G., & Benitez, J. M. (2016). Development of a Smart Framework Based on Knowledge to Support Infrastructure Maintenance Decisions in Railway Corridors. *Transportation Research Procedia*, 14, 1987–1995. doi:10.1016/j.trpro.2016.05.166

Menezes, Á., & Prikladnicki, R. (2018). Diversity in Software Engineering. *Proceedings of the 11th International Workshop on Cooperative and Human Aspects of Software Engineering*, 45–48. 10.1145/3195836.3195857

Mentsiev, A., Engel, M., & Gudaeva, D.-M. (2020). Impact of IoT on the automation of processes in Smart Cities: Security issues and world experience. *Journal of Physics: Conference Series*, 1515, 1–7. doi:10.1088/1742-6596/1515/2/022026

Merkle, D., & Middendorf, M. (2004). Dynamic polyethism and competition for tasks in threshold reinforcement models of social insects. *Adaptive Behavior - Animals, Animats, Software Agents, Robots. Adaptive Systems*, 12(3-4), 251–262.

Mesiti, M., Ribaudo, M., Valtolina, S., Barricelli, B. R., Boccacci, P., & Dini, S. (2011). Collaborative Environments: Accessibility and Usability for Users with Special Needs. In Community-Built Databases (pp. 319–340). Springer.

Metin, M., Ulu, A., Paksoy, M., & Yücel, M. (2018). Vibration mitigation of railway bridge using magnetorheological damper. In Intech (pp. 18–29). doi:10.5772/intechopen.71980

Metro de Bogotá. (2015). *Proyecto Primera Línea del Metro de Bogotá*. Sistema Metro.

Metro de Panama & Consorcio línea 2. (2015). *Contrato-MPSA-014-2015*. Metro de Panama.

Metro de Panama. (2010a). *Ingeniería conceptual. Especificaciones funcionales, técnicas y contractuales TOMO II.- Equipamientos. II.7 Material rodante*. Secretaria del Metro de Panama.

Metro de Panamá. (2010b). *Ingenieria conceptual. Especificaciones funcionales, técnicas y contractuales Tomo II Equipamiento. II.4.2 Señalizacion y control de trenes. Puesto de mando CCO, Torre de control y estaciones. Línea 1.* Secretaria del Metro de Panamá.

Metro de Panama. (2017). *Metro de Panama*. Wikipedia. https://es.wikipedia.org/wiki/Metro_de_Panamá

Metro de Panama. (2018a). *Parametros de Operación línea 1*. https://www.elmetrodepanama.com/parametros/

Metro de Panamá. (2018b). *Official Web Page of Panama Metro*. https://www.elmetrodepanama.com/

Metro de Panamá. (2020a). *Línea 3 del metro de Panamá*. Pagina Web Institucional Del Metro de Panamá.

Metro de Panamá. (2020b). *Parametros*. Operaciones. https://www.elmetrodepanama.com/parametros/

Mexico., G. de. (2020). *Información del proyecto. Tren maya. Anexo técnico*. Academic Press.

Miettinen, K. (2008). Introduction to Multiobjective Optimization: Noninteractive Approaches. In *Multiobjective optimization: interactive and evolutionary approaches* (pp. 1–26). Springer Berlin Heidelberg.

Mikroyannidi, E., Liu, D., & Lee, R. (2016). Use of Semantic Web Technologies in the Architecture of the BBC Education Online Pages. In D. Mouromtsev & M. d'Aquin (Eds.), Lecture Notes in Computer Science: Vol. 9500. *Open Data for Education* (pp. 67–85)., doi:10.1007/978-3-319-30493-9_4

Milosavljevic, M., Jeremic, D., & Vujovic, D. (2019). Train Braking Distance Calculation Using Fuzzy Logic. doi:10.20544/tts2018.p57

MINCyT. (2015). Industria 4.0: Escenarios e impactos para la formulación de políticas tecnológicas en los umbrales de la Cuarta Revolución Industrial (M. de Ciencia & P. Tecnología e Innovación, Eds.). Academic Press.

Mine, M. (1995). *ISAAC: A virtual environment tool for the interactive construction of virtual worlds*. UNC Chapel Hill Computer Science Technical Report TR95-020.

Ministerio de Educación. (2016). *Visita al Tranvía Modelo CITADIS 302*. Nota de Prensa.

Mir, A., & Dhage, S. N. (2018). Diabetes Disease Prediction Using Machine Learning on Big Data of Healthcare. In *Proceedings of International Conference on Computing Communication Control and Automation* (pp. 1-6). IEEE Press. 10.1109/ICCUBEA.2018.8697439

Misirli, A., & Komis, V. (2014). Robotics and Programming Concepts in Early Childhood Education: A Conceptual Framework for Designing Educational Scenarios. *Educational Software Use in Kindergarten*, 99-118.

Mivehchi, L., & Rajabion, L. (2020). A framework for evaluating the impact of mobile games, technological innovation and collaborative learning on students' motivation. *Human Systems Management*, *39*(1), 27–36. doi:10.3233/HSM-190543

Miyajima, R. (2017). Deep Learning Triggers a New Era in Industrial Robotics. *IEEE MultiMedia*, *24*(4), 91–96. doi:10.1109/MMUL.2017.4031311

Moaveni, B., & Karimi, M. (2017). Subway Traffic Regulation Using Model-Based Predictive Control by Considering the Passengers Dynamic Effect. *Arabian Journal for Science and Engineering*, *12*(7), 3021–3031. Advance online publication. doi:10.100713369-017-2508-0

Mohagheghi, P., & Conradi, R. (2007). Quality, productivity and economic benefits of software reuse: A review of industrial studies. *Empirical Software Engineering*, *12*(5), 471–516. doi:10.100710664-007-9040-x

Molina, C., Gómez, M. E., Torre, J. M., & Vila, M. A. (2005). Using Fuzzy Data Cube for Exploratory Analysis in Financial Economy. In *EUSFLAT Conf.* (pp. 424-429). Academic Press.

Molina, C., Rodriguez-Ariza, L., Sánchez, D., & Vila, M. A. (2006). A new fuzzy multidimensional model. *IEEE Transactions on Fuzzy Systems*, *14*(6), 897–912. doi:10.1109/TFUZZ.2006.879984

Mon, A., & Del Giorgio, H. (2018). Análisis de las tecnologías de la información y la comunicación y su innovación en la industria. In *Proceedings of XXIV Congreso Argentino de Ciencias de la Computación*, (pp. 1020-1029). Universidad Nacional del centro de la Provincia de Buenos Aires: Sedici Press.

Mon, A., & Del Giorgio, H. R. (2019). Usability in ICTs for Industry 4.0. In *Human-Computer Interaction 5th Iberoamerican Workshop, HCI-Collab*. Puebla, México: Springer.

Mon, De María, Querel, & Figuerola. (2018). Evaluation of technological development for the definition of Industries 4.0. In *Proceedings of 2018 Congreso Argentino de Ciencias de la Informática y Desarrollos de Investigación* (pp. 523-530). Universidad Nacional de San Martín, IEEE Explore.

Monrroy, A. (2018). Suministro de la Energía Eléctrica de la Línea 2 del Metro de Panamá : Ingeniería Conceptual comentada Supply of the Electric Power of Line 2 of the Panama Metro : Conceptual Engineering commented. In Universidad Tecnologica de Panama (Ed.), *2018: 3er Congreso Internacional de Ciencias y Tecnologías para el Desarrollo Sostenible 2018* (p. 17). Universidad Tecnologica de Panamá. https://revistas.utp.ac.pa/index.php/memoutp/article/view/1796/2587

Moody, D. L. (2003). The Method Evaluation Model: A Theoretical Model for Validating Information Systems Design Methods. *Proceedings of the 11th European Conference on Information Systems.*

Moreno-Guerrero, A. J., Rodríguez-Jiménez, C., Gómez-García, G., & Ramos Navas-Parejo, M. (2020). Educational Innovation in Higher Education: Use of Role Playing and Educational Video in Future Teachers' Training. *Sustainability*, *12*(6), 2558. doi:10.3390u12062558

Moreno, I., Muñoz, L., & Serracin, J. (2012). La robótica educativa, una herramienta para la enseñanza-aprendizaje de las ciencias y las tecnologías. *Teoría la Educación: Educación y Cultura en la Sociedad la Infinformación*, *13*(2), 74–90.

Morgan, P. (2009). Process improvement—Is it a lottery? *Software Development Magazine*. Available at: http://www.methodsandtools.com/archive/archive.php?id=52

Moriya, S., & Shibata, C. (2018). Transfer Learning Method for Very Deep CNN for Text Classification and Methods for its Evaluation. In *Proceedings of Annual Computer Software and Applications Conference* (pp. 153-158). IEEE Press. 10.1109/COMPSAC.2018.10220

Morrison, A. (2003). *Electric Transport Inaugurations in Latin America*. Electric Transport Inaugurations in Latin America. http://www.tramz.com/

Morrison, A. (2008). *The Tramways of Panama City Colombia-Panama*. http://www.tramz.com/co/pa/pa.html

Mowatt, R., & Cerra, V. (2017). Trade policy issues in Latin America and the Caribbean: Views from country authorities. Academic Press.

Muñoz, M., Hernández, L., Mejia, J., Gasca-Hurtado, G. P., & Gómez-Alvarez, M. C. (2017). State of the Use of Gamification Elements in Software Development Teams Systems. *Software and Services Process Improvement. EuroSPI 2017.*

Muñoz, M., Hernández, L., Mejía, M., Peña, A., Rangel, N., Torres, C., & Sauberer, G. (2017). A model to integrate highly effective teams for software development. In System, Software and services Process Improvement. Springer International Publishing AG. Doi:10.1007/978-3-319-64218-5_51

Muñoz, M., Mejía, J., & de León, M. (2020). Investigación en el área de Mejora de Procesos de Software in Ingeniería de Software en México: Educación, Industria e Investigación. Academia Mexicana de Computación.

Muñoz, M., Mejia, J., & Gasca-Hurtado, G.P. (2014). A Methodology for Establishing Multi-Model Environments in Order to Improve Organizational Software Processes. *International Journal of Software Engineering and Knowledge Engineering, 24*, 909-933.

Muñoz, M., Mejía, J., & Miramontes, J. (2016). Method for Lightening Software Processes through Optimizing the Selection of Software Engineering Best Practices. In Trends and Applications in Software Engineering. Springer International.

Muñoz, M., Mejía, J., & Muñoz, E. (2013). Knowledge management to support using muti-model environments in software process improvement. European System, Software & Service Process Improvement & Innovation EuroSPI 2013, 1-10.

Muñoz, M., Mejía, J., Calvo-Manzano, J. A., San Feliu, T., Corona, B., & Miramontes, J. (2017b). Diagnostic Assessment Tools for Assessing the Implementation and/or Use of Agile Methodologies in SMEs: An Analysis of Covered Aspects. *Software Quality Professional, 19*(2), 16-27.

Muñoz, M., Mejía, J., Duron, B., & Valtierra, C. (2014). Software process improvement from a human perspective. In *New Perspectives in Information System and Technologies*. Springer International Publishing.

Muñoz, M., Mejía, J., Gasca-Hurtado, G. P., Gómez-Alvarez, M. C., & Duron, B. (2016). Method to Establish Strategies for Implementing Process Improvement According to the Organization's Context, System, Software and Services Process Improvement. Springer International Publishing.

Muñoz, M., Mejía, J., Gasca-Hurtado, G. P., Valtierra, C., & Duron, B. (2014b). Covering the human perspective in software process improvement. In *System, Software and Services Process Improvement.* Springer Berlin Heidelberg.

Muñoz, M., Mejía, J., Gasca-Hurtado, G. P., Vega-Zepeda, V., & Valtierra, C. (2015). Providing a Starting Point to Help SMEs in the Implementation of Software Process Improvements. In System, Software and Services Process Improvement. Springer.

Muñoz, M., Mejía, M., & Laporte, C. Y. (2018b). Implementación del Estándar ISO/IEC 29110 en Centros de Desarrollo de Software de Universidades Mexicanas: Experiencia del Estado de Zacatecas. *Revista Ibérica de Sistemas y Tecnologías de Informactión (RISTI), 29*(10).

Muñoz, M., Mejía, M., Peña, A., & Rangel, N. (2016). Establishing Effective Software Development Teams: An Exploratory Model, System. In Software and Services Process Improvement. Springer International.

Muñoz, M., Peña, A., & Hernández, L. (2019). Gamification in Virtual reality Environments for the integration of Highly Effective Teams. In Virtual Reality Designs. Science Publishers.

Muñoz, M., Peña, A., Mejía, J., & Lara, G. (2016b). Actual State of the Coverage of Mexican Software Industry Requested Knowledge Regarding the Project Management Best Practices. Computer Science and Information Systems (ComSIS), 13, 849-873.

Muñoz, M., Peña, A., Mejía, J., & Lara, G. (2016c). Coverage of the University Curricula for the Software Engineering Industry in Mexico. *IEEE Latin America Transactions, 14*, 2383-2389.

Muñoz, M., Peña, A., Mejía, J., & Lara, G. (2017c). ISO/IEC 29110 and Curricula Programs Related to Computer Science and Informatics in Mexico: Analysis of practices coverage. Springer International Publishing AG. doi:10.1007/978-3-319-69341-5_1

Muñoz, M., Peralta, M., & Laporte, C.Y. (2019). Análisis de las debilidades que presentan las Entidades Muy Pequeñas al implementar el estándar ISO/IEC 29110: Una comparativa entre estado del arte y el estado de la práctica. *RISTI, 34*(10).

Muñoz, M., Mejía, J., Calvo-Manzano, J. A., Gonzalo, C., San Feliu, T., & De Amescua, A. (2012). Expected Requirements in Support Tools for Software Process Improvement in SMEs. *2012 IEEE Ninth Electronics*, *Robotics and Automotive Mechanics Conference*, 135-140. doi: 10.1109/CERMA.2012.29

Muñoz, M., Mejía, J., & Laporte, C. Y. (2018). *Reinforcing Very Small Entities Using Agile Methodologies with the ISO/IEC 29110. In Trends and Applications in Software Engineering. Springer.* https://doi-org.svproxy01.cimat.mx/10.1007/978-3-030-01171-0_8

Muñoz, M., Mejía, J., Peña, A., Lara, G., & Laporte, C. Y. (2019b, October). Transitioning international software engineering standards to academia: Analyzing the results of the adoption of ISO/IEC 29110 in four Mexican universities. *Computer Standards & Interfaces, 66*, 103340. doi:10.1016/j.csi.2019.03.008

Muñoz, M., Mejía, M., & Laporte, C. Y. (2019). Implementing ISO/IEC 29110 to Reinforce four Very Small Entities of Mexico under Agile Approach. *IET Software*, (March), 1–11. doi:10.1049/iet-sen.2019.0040

Muñoz, M., Negrete, M., & Mejía, J. (2019). Proposal to Avoid Issues in the DevOps Implementation: A Systematic Literature Review. In Á. Rocha, H. Adeli, L. Reis, & S. Costanzo (Eds.), *New Knowledge in Information Systems and Technologies. WorldCIST'19 2019. Advances in Intelligent Systems and Computing* (Vol. 930, pp. 666–677). Springer. https://doi-org.svproxy01.cimat.mx/10.1007/978-3-030-16181-1_63

Muñoz, M., Peña, A., Mejía, J., Gasca-Hurtado, G. P., Gómez-Álvarez, M. C., & Hernández, L. (2018c). *Gamification to Identify Software Development Team Members' Profiles. In Systems, Software and Services Process Improvement. Springer.* https://doi-org.svproxy01.cimat.mx/10.1007/978-3-319-97925-0_18

Muñoz, M., Peña, A., Mejía, J., Gasca-Hurtado, G. P., Gómez-Alvarez, M. C., & Hernández, L. (2019c, April). Applying gamification elements to build teams for software development. *IET Software, 13*(2), 99–105. doi:10.1049/iet-sen.2018.5088

Muñoz, M., Peña, A., Mejía, J., Gasca-Hurtado, G. P., Gómez-Álvarez, M. C., & Laporte, C. Y. (2019d). A Comparative Analysis of the Implementation of the Software Basic Profile of ISO/IEC 29110 in Thirteen Teams That Used Predictive Versus Adaptive Life Cycles. In A. Walker, R. O'Connor, & R. Messnarz (Eds.), *Systems, Software and Services Process Improvement. EuroSPI 2019. Communications in Computer and Information Science* (Vol. 1060, pp. 179–191). Springer. doi:10.1007/978-3-030-28005-5_14

Muñoz, M., Peña, A., Mejía, J., & Lara, G. (2015b). *Analysis of Coverage of Moprosoft Practices in Curricula Programs Related to Computer Science and Informatics, Trends and Applications in Software Engineering Series: Advances in Intelligent Systems and Computing 405* (Vol. 405). Springer Berlin Heidelberg.

Muñoz-Mata, M., Mejía-Miranda, J., & Valtierra-Alvarado, C. (2015). Helping Organizations to Address their Effort toward the Implementation of Improvements in their Software Process. *Revista Facultad de Ingeniería, 77*, 115-126.

Murali, A., Sen, S., Kehoe, B., Garg, A., Mcfarland, S., Patil, S., Boyd, W. D., Lim, S., Abbeel, P., & Goldberg, K. (2015). Learning by observation for surgical subtasks: multilateral cutting of 3D viscoelastic and 2D Orthotropic Tissue Phantoms. In *Proceeding of International Conference on Robotics and Automation* (pp. 1202–1209). IEEE Press. 10.1109/ICRA.2015.7139344

Myrbakken, H., & Colomo-Palacios, R. (2017). DevSecOps: A Multivocal Literature Review. *International Conference on Software Process Improvement and Capability Determination*, 17–29. 10.1007/978-3-319-67383-7_2

Nahhas, S., Bamasag, O., Khemakhem, M., & Bajnaid, N. (2018). *Added Values of Linked Data in Education: A Survey and Roadmap* (Vol. 7). Computers. doi:10.3390/computers7030045

Narendra, K. S., & Thathachar, M. A. L. (1989). *Learning automata: an introduction.* Prentice-Hall, Inc.

Nascimento, D. M. C., Chavez, C. F. G., & Bittencourt, R. A. (2019). The Adoption of Open Source Projects in Engineering Education: A Real Software Development Experience. Proceedings - Frontiers in Education Conference. 10.1109/FIE.2018.8658908

Natarajan, S., Annamraju, A. K., & Baradkar, C. S. (2018). Traffic sign recognition using weighted multi-convolutional neural network. *IET Intelligent Transport Systems*, *12*(10), 1396–1405. doi:10.1049/iet-its.2018.5171

Ningenia, L. (2016). *Qué es la Industria 4.0*. Recuperado de http://www.ningenia.com/2016/05/31/que-es-la-industria-4-0

Nishizawa, H., Shimada, K., Ohno, W., & Yoshioka, T. (2013). Increasing reality and educational merits of a virtual game. *Procedia Computer Science*, *25*, 32–40. doi:10.1016/j.procs.2013.11.005

Niyetkaliyev, A. S., Hussain, S., Ghayesh, M. H., & Alici, G. (2017). Review on design and control aspects of robotic shoulder rehabilitation orthoses. *IEEE Transactions on Human-Machine Systems*, *47*(6), 1134–1145. doi:10.1109/THMS.2017.2700634

Noe, R. A., Clarke, A. D. M., & Klein, H. J. (2014). Learning in the Twenty-First-Century Workplace. *Annual Review of Organizational Psychology and Organizational Behavior*, *1*(1), 245–275. doi:10.1146/annurev-orgpsych-031413-091321

Noy, N. F., & McGuinness, D. L. (2001). *Ontology development 101: A guide to creating your first ontology*. Academic Press.

Nuaimi, A. I. (2015). Applications of big data to smart cities. *Journal of Internet Services and Applications*, *6*(25), 2–15. doi:10.118613174-015-0041-5

NYCE. (2020). *Companies certified to ISO/IEC 29110-4-1:2011 standard*. Retrieved at https://www.nyce.org.mx/wp-content/uploads/2020/01/PADRON-DE-EMPRESAS-CERTIFICADAS-EN-LA-NORMA-ISO-IEC-29110-4-1-16-01-2020.pdf

OECD, WTO, & IDB. (2010). *Latin american and caribbean Case Stories : A snap of Aid for Trade on the ground*. Author.

OECD. (2017). *Promising Practices in Supporting Success for Indigenous Students*. OECD Publishing. https://read.oecd-ilibrary.org/education/promising-practices-in-supporting-success-for-indigenous-students_9789264279421-en

Oh, S. Y., Bailenson, J., Krämer, N., & Li, B. (2016). Let the avatar brighten your smile: Effects of enhancing facial expressions in virtual environments. *PLoS One*, *11*(9), e0161794. doi:10.1371/journal.pone.0161794 PMID:27603784

Oh, Y., Byon, Y., Song, J., Kwak, H., & Kang, S. (2020). Dwell Time Estimation Using Real-Time Train Operation and Smart Card-Based Passenger Data : A Case Study in Seoul, South Korea. *Applied Sciences (Basel, Switzerland)*, *10*(476), 12. doi:10.3390/app10020476

OMG. (2015). *Kernel and Language for Software Engineering Methods (Essence)-Version 1.1*. Object Management Group.

Open Education. (n.d.). Retrieved from https://hewlett.org/strategy/open-education/

Orcas, L., & Aris, N. (2019). Perceptions of secondary education teachers in educational robotics as a teaching resource in the STEM approach. *Opción*, *35*(90), 810–843.

Ortiz-Vivar, J., Segarra, J., Villazón-Terrazas, B., & Saquicela, V. (2020). REDI: Towards knowledge graph-powered scholarly information management and research networking. *Journal of Information Science*. Advance online publication. doi:10.1177/0165551520944351

Ortmann, C. (2015). Mujeres, ciencia y tecnología en las universidades: ¿la excepción a la regla? *Revista del IICE*, (38), 95-108.

Osuna, E., Rodríguez, L.-F., Gutierrez-Garcia, J. O., & Castro, L. A. (2020). Development of computational models of emotions: A software engineering perspective. *Cognitive Systems Research*, *60*, 1–19. doi:10.1016/j.cogsys.2019.11.001

Otón, S., Ingavélez-Guerra, P., Sanchez-Gordon, S., & Sánchez-Gordón, M. (2020). Evolution of Accessibility Metadata in Educational Resources. In R. Mendoza-González, H. Luna-García, & A. Mendoza-González (Eds.), *UXD and UCD Approaches for Accessible Education* (pp. 1–20). IGI Global. doi:10.4018/978-1-7998-2325-4.ch001

Oussous, A., Benjelloun, F.-Z., & Ait Lahcen, A. (2017). Big Data technologies: A survey. *Journal of King Saud University – Computer and Information Sciences, 30*(4), 431-448.

Palacin-Silva, M., Khakurel, J., Happonen, A., Hynninen, T., & Porras, J. (2017). Infusing Design Thinking into a Software Engineering Capstone Course. *Proceedings - 30th IEEE Conference on Software Engineering Education and Training*, 212–221. 10.1109/CSEET.2017.41

Palomino, M. del C. P. (2017). Teacher Training in the Use of ICT for Inclusion: Differences between Early Childhood and Primary Education. *Procedia: Social and Behavioral Sciences, 237*(June), 144–149. doi:10.1016/j.sbspro.2017.02.055

Pamučar, D., Atanasković, P., & Milicic, M. (2015). Modeling of fuzzy logic systems for investment management in the railway infraestructure. *Technical Gazette, 22*(5), 1185–1192. doi:10.17559/TV-20140626104653

Panamá Vieja Escuela. (2014). *La historia del ferrocarril de Chiriqui.* Panamá Vieja Escuela. https://www.panamaviejaescuela.com/historia-ferrocarril-chiriqui/

Pan, S. J., & Yang, Q. (2010). A survey on transfer learning. *Transactions on Knowledge and Data Engineering, 22*(10), 1345–1359. doi:10.1109/TKDE.2009.191

Paravizo, E., Chaim, O. C., Braatz, D., Muschard, B., & Rozenfeld, H. (2018). Exploring gamification to support manufacturing education on industry 4.0 as an enabler for innovation and sustainability. *Procedia Manufacturing, 21*, 438–445. doi:10.1016/j.promfg.2018.02.142

Patrício, R., Moreira, A. C., & Zurlo, F. (2018). Gamification approaches to the early stage of innovation. *Creativity and Innovation Management, 27*(4), 499–511. doi:10.1111/caim.12284

Pattanaik, L. N., & Yadav, G. (2015). Decision support model for automated railway level crossing system using fuzzy logic control. *Procedia Computer Science, 48*(C), 73–76. doi:10.1016/j.procs.2015.04.152

Patterson, M. L. (1982). A sequential functional model of nonverbal exchange. *Psychological Review, 89*(3), 231–249. doi:10.1037/0033-295X.89.3.231

Pavlou, P. (2018). Internet of Things – Will Humans be Replaced or Augmented? *GfK Marketing Intelligence, 10*(2), 43–48. doi:10.2478/gfkmir-2018-0017

Pavlov, D., & Yahontova, I. (2020). Formation of Effective Leading Project Teams: A Multi-Objective Approach. In *Proceedings of the 6th International Conference on Social, economic, and academic leadership* (pp. 84-90). Atlantis Press. 10.2991/assehr.k.200526.013

Pavlovich, K., & Krahnke, K. (2012). Empathy, Connectedness and Organisation. *Journal of Business Ethics, 105*(1), 131–137. doi:10.100710551-011-0961-3

Pech, F., Martinez, A., Estrada, H., & Hernandez, Y. (2017). Semantic Annotation of Unstructured Documents Using Concepts Similarity. *Scientific Programming.* Retrieved from https://www.hindawi.com/journals/sp/2017/7831897/

Pedreira, O., García, F., Brisaboa, N., & Piattini, M. (2015). Gamification in software engineering – A systematic mapping. *Information and Software Technology, 57*, 157–168.

Pellón, R. T., Miranda, D. R., Gonzalez, S. B., & Reyna, I. C. H. (2017). Las tecnologías de la información y la comunicación en la enseñanza de inglés en Ciencias Médicas. *Educación Médica Superior, 31*(2).

Peña, A., & de Antonio, A. (2009). Using Avatar's Nonverbal Communication to monitor Collaboration in a Task-oriented Learning Situation in a CVE. In *Workshop on Intelligent and Innovative Support for Collaborative Learning Activities* (p. 19). Academic Press.

Peña, A., Aguilar, R.A., & Casillas, L. A. (2012). The Users' Avatars Nonverbal Interaction in Collaborative Virtual Environments for Learning. *Virtual Reality and Environments*, 69-94.

Peña, A. (2010). Collaborative virtual environment for distance learning When to use 3D? *Innovación Educativa (México, D.F.)*, *10*(52), 25–33.

Peña, A. (2014). A Collaboration Facilitator Model for Learning Virtual Environments. *Computer Science and Information Technology*. *HRPUB*, *2*(2), 100–107. doi:10.13189/csit.2014.020207

Peña, A., & de Antonio, A. (2010a). Nonverbal communication as a means to support collaborative interaction assessment in 3D virtual environments for learning. In *Monitoring and assessment in online collaborative environments: Emergent computational technologies for E-learning support* (pp. 172–197). IGI Global. doi:10.4018/978-1-60566-786-7.ch010

Peña, A., & de Antonio, A. (2010b). Inferring interaction to support collaborative learning in 3D virtual environments through the user's avatar Non-Verbal Communication. *International Journal of Technology Enhanced Learning*, *2*(1-2), 75–90. doi:10.1504/IJTEL.2010.031261

Peña, A., & Jiménez, E. (2012). Virtual Environment for Effective Training. *Revista Colombiana de Computación*, *13*(1), 45–58.

Peña, A., Lara, G., & Estrada, E. (2020). Navigation in Virtual Environments. In *Virtual Reality Designs* (pp. 10–26). CRC Press.

Peña, A., Muñoz, E., & Lara, G. (2019). A model for nonverbal interaction cues in collaborative virtual environments. *Virtual Reality (Waltham Cross)*, 1–14.

Peña, A., Rangel, N. E., & Maciel, O. E. (2015). Comparison of the effects of oral and written communication on the performance of cooperative tasks, *International Review of Social Science. Academy of IRMBR*, *3*(11), 487–499.

Peña, A., Rangel, N. E., Muñoz, M., Mejia, J., & Lara, G. (2016). Affective Behavior and Nonverbal Interaction in Collaborative Virtual Environments. *Journal of Educational Technology & Society*, *19*(2), 29–41.

Peña, A., Rangel, N., & Lara, G. (2015). Nonverbal interaction contextualized in collaborative virtual environments. *Journal on Multimodal User Interfaces*, *9*(3), 253–260. doi:10.100712193-015-0193-4

Pereira, C. K., Siqueira, S. W. M., Nunes, B. P., & Dietze, S. (2018). Linked Data in Education: A Survey and a Synthesis of Actual Research and Future Challenges. *IEEE Transactions on Learning Technologies*, *11*, 400–412. doi:10.1109/TLT.2017.2787659

Pérez Medina, J. L., González Rodríguez, M. S., Pilco, H., Jimenes, K., Acosta-Vargas, P., Sanchez-Gordon, S., Calle-Jimenez, T., Esparza, W., & Rybarczyk, Y. (2019). Usability study of a web-based platform for home motor rehabilitation. *IEEE Access Journal*, *7*, 7932–7947. doi:10.1109/ACCESS.2018.2889257

Perry, D. E., Staudenmayer, N. A., & Votta, L. G. (1994). People, organizations, and process improvement. *IEEE Software*, *11*(4), 36–45. doi:10.1109/52.300082

Perry, D. E., & Wolf, A. L. (1992). Foundations for the study of software architecture. *SIGSOFT Software Engineering Notes*, *17*(4), 40–52. doi:10.1145/141874.141884

Petrie, H., & Bevan, N. (2009). The evaluation of accessibility, usability and user experience. *The Universal Access Handbook*, 299–315.

Petrie, H., & Kheir, O. (2007). The Relationship between Accessibility and Usability of Websites. In *Proceedings of the SIGCHI Conference on Human Factors in Computing Systems* (pp. 397–406). 10.1145/1240624.1240688

Pfeifer, R., Lungarella, M., & Iida, F. (2007). Self-organization, embodiment, and biologically inspired robotics. *American Association for the Advancement of Science*, *318*(5853), 1088–1093. doi:10.1126cience.1145803 PMID:18006736

Picard, R. W. (Ed.). (1997). *Affective computing*. MIT Press.

Picard, R. W., & Daily, S. B. (2005). Evaluating affective interactions: Alternatives to asking what users feel. In *CHI Workshop on Evaluating Affective Interfaces: Innovative Approaches* (pp. 2219-2122). New York, NY: ACM.

Piedra, N., Chicaiza, J., Lopez, J., Tovar-Caro, E., & Bonastre, O. M. (2011). Finding OERs with Social-Semantic Search. In *Proceedings of IEEE EDUCON Education Engineering 2011* (pp. 1–6). Amman: IEEE.

Piedra, N., Chicaiza, J., Lopez, J., Martinez, O., & Tovar-Caro, E. (2010). An approach for description of Open Educational Resources based on Semantic Technologies. In *Proceedings of IEEE EDUCON 2010 Conference*, (pp. 1111–1119). 10.1109/EDUCON.2010.5492453

Piedra, N., Chicaiza, J., Lopez, J., & Tovar-Caro, E. (2014). Supporting openness of MOOCs contents through of an OER and OCW Framework based on Linked Data Technologies. *Proceedings of IEEE Global Engineering Education Conference, EDUCON*. 10.1109/EDUCON.2014.6826249

Piedra, N., Chicaiza, J., Lopez, J., & Tovar-Caro, E. (2015). Seeking Open Educational Resources to Compose Massive Open Online Courses in Engineering Education an Approach based on Linked Open Data. *Journal of Universal Computer Science*, *21*, 679–711.

Piedra, N., Chicaiza, J., Lopez, J., & Tovar-Caro, E. T. (2016). Integrating OER in the design of educational material: Blended Learning and Linked Open Educational Resources Data Approach. *Proceedings of IEEE EDUCON Conference*. 10.1109/EDUCON.2016.7474706

Piedra, N., Chicaiza, J., Lopez, J., Tovar-Caro, E., & Martínez, O. (2012). Combining Linked Data and Mobiles to Improve Access to OCW. In *Proceedings of Global Engineering Education Conference (EDUCON)*, 2012 (pp. 1–7). doi:10.1109/EDUCON.2012.6201202

Piedra, N., Chicaiza, J., Quichimbo, P., Saquicela, V., Cadme, E., Lopez, J., & Tovar-Caro, E. (2015). *Framework for the Integration of Digital Resources based-on a Semantic Web Approach*. Revista Iberica de Sistemas e Tecnologias de Informacao. Associacao Iberica de Sistemas e Tecnologias de Informacao. doi:10.17013/risti.e3.55-70

Piedra, N., Tovar-Caro, E., Colomo-Palacios, R., Lopez, J., & Chicaiza, J. A. (2014). *Consuming and Producing Linked Open Data: The case of OpenCourseWare*. Program. doi:10.1108/PROG-07-2012-0045

Pilco, H., Sanchez-Gordon, S., Calle-Jimenez, T., Rybczyk, Y., Jadán, J., Villarreal, S., Esparza, W., Acosta-Vargas, P., Guevara, C., & Nunes, I. L. (2019a). Analysis and improvement of the usability of a tele-rehabilitation platform for hip surgery patients. In Advances in Human Factors and Systems Interaction. Advances in Intelligent Systems and Computing (pp. 197-209). Cham, Switzerland: Springer. doi:10.1007/978-3-319-94334-3_21

Pilco, H., Sanchez-Gordon, S., Calle-Jimenez, T., Pérez-Medina, J. L., Rybczyk, Y., Jadán, J., Guevara, C., & Nunes, I. L. (2019b). An agile approach to improve the usability of a physical tele rehabilitation platform. *Journal of Applied Sciences (Faisalabad)*, *9*(3), 480.

Pino, J. F., García, F., & Piattini, M. (2008). Software process improvement in small and medium software enterprises: A systematic review. *SQJournal, 16*, 237–261.

Pirzadeh, L. (2010). *Human Factors in Software Development: A Systematic Literature Review*. Chalmers University of Technology. https://odr.chalmers.se/handle/20.500.12380/126748

PMI. (2017). *A Guide to the Project Management Body of Knowledge (PMBOK Guide)* (6th ed.). Project Management Institute.

Pons, O., Calvet, M. D., Tura, M., & Muñoz, C. (2013). Análisis de la igualdad de oportunidades de género en la ciencia y la tecnología: Las carreras profesionales de las mujeres científicas y tecnóloga. *Intangible capital, 9*(1), 65-90.

Portela, C., Vasconcelos, A., Oliveira, S., & Souza, M. (2017). The Use of Industry Training Strategies in a Software Engineering Course: An Experience Report. Proceedings - 30th IEEE Conference on Software Engineering Education and Training, 29–36. 10.1109/CSEET.2017.16

Potter, N., & Sakry, M. (2006). *Making Process Improvement Work: A Concise Action Guide for Software Managers and Practitioners* (pp. 2–5). Addison-Wesley.

Prabhat, N., & Kumar-Vishwakarma, D. (2020). Comparative Analysis of Deep Convolutional Generative Adversarial Network and Conditional Generative Adversarial Network using Hand Written Digits. In *Proceedings of International Conference on Intelligent Computing and Control Systems* (pp. 1072-1075). IEEE Press.

Pranoto, H., & Panggabean, F. M. (2019). Increase the interest in learning by implementing augmented reality: Case studies studying rail transportation. *Procedia Computer Science, 157*, 506–513. doi:10.1016/j.procs.2019.09.007

Prasetya, I. S. W. B., Leek, C. Q. H. D., Melkonian, O., Tusscher, J. t., Bergen, J. v., Everink, J. M., . . . Zon, W. M. v. (2019). Having fun in learning formal specifications Proceedings of the 41st International Conference on Software Engineering: Software Engineering Education and Training. 10.1109/ICSE-SEET.2019.00028

Presidencia de la República de Panamá. (2017). *Memoria de la presidencia*. Memoria.

Pressman, R. (2009). *Software Engineering: A Practitioner's Approach* (7th ed.). McGraw-Hill Science.

Pressman, R. S. (2002). *Ingeniería de Software: Un enfoque práctico. 5a edición*. McGraw-Hill.

Pribeanu, C., Fogarassy-Neszly, P., & Patru, A. (2014). Municipal web sites accessibility and usability for blind users : Preliminary results from a pilot study. *Universal Access in the Information Society, 13*(3), 339–349. doi:10.100710209-013-0315-2

Prokofyev, K. G., Dmitrieva, O. V., Zmyzgova, T. R., & Polyakova, E. N. (2019). Modern Engineering Education as a Key Element of Russian Technological Modernization in the Context of Digital Economy. doi:10.2991/iscfec-18.2019.160

Prokofyev, K. G., Polyakova, E. N., Dmitrieva, O. V., & Zmyzgova, T. R. (2017). Digital economy of the Russian Federation as a directing factor for the development of professional personnel in the IT sphere. *Proceedings of the Regional scientific-practical conference The Concept of Development of the Productive Forces of the Kurgan Region*, 90-96.

Puerta, L. N. Z., & Alvarez, M. C. G. (2018). A methodological proposal to learn to program through the development of video games. *Iberian Conference on Information Systems and Technologies*, 1–6. 10.23919/CISTI.2018.8399326

Pyrgidis, C. N. (2016). Railway transportation systems. Design, construction and operation. Taylor and Francis Group. doi:10.1201/b19472

Qian, M., & Clark, K. R. (2016). Game-based Learning and 21st century skills: A review of recent research. *Computers in Human Behavior, 63*, 50–58. doi:10.1016/j.chb.2016.05.023

Quiñonez, Y., Maravall, D., & de Lope, J. (2012). Application of Self-Organizing Techniques for the Distribution of Heterogeneous Multi-Tasks in Multi-Robot Systems. In *Proceedings of Electronics, Robotics and Automotive Mechanics Conference* (pp. 66-71). IEEE Press 10.1109/CERMA.2012.19

Quiñonez, Y., Barrera, F., Bugueño, I., & Bekios-Calfa, J. (2018). Simulation and path planning for quadcopter obstacle avoidance in indoor environments using the ROS framework. In J. Mejia, M. Muñoz, Á. Rocha, Y. Quiñonez, & J. Calvo-Manzano (Eds.), *Trends and Applications in Software Engineering* (pp. 295–304). Springer. doi:10.1007/978-3-319-69341-5_27

Quiñonez, Y., de Lope, J., & Maravall, D. (2009). Cooperative and Competitive Behaviors in a Multi-robot System for Surveillance Tasks. In R. Moreno-Díaz, F. Pichler, & A. Quesada-Arencibia (Eds.), *EUROCAST* (pp. 437–444). Springer. doi:10.1007/978-3-642-04772-5_57

Quiñonez, Y., de Lope, J., & Maravall, D. (2011b). Bio-inspired Decentralized Self-coordination Algorithms for Multi-heterogeneous Specialized Tasks Distribution in Multi-Robot Systems. In J. M. Ferrández, J. R. Álvarez Sánchez, F. de la Paz, & F. J. Toledo (Eds.), *Foundations on Natural and Artificial Computation* (pp. 30–39). Springer. doi:10.1007/978-3-642-21344-1_4

Quiñonez, Y., Lizarraga, C., Peraza, J., & Zatarain, O. (2020b). Image recognition in UAV videos using convolutional neural networks. *IET Software*, *14*(2), 176–181. doi:10.1049/iet-sen.2019.0045

Quiñonez, Y., Maravall, D., & de Lope, J. (2011a). Stochastic Learning Automata for Self-coordination in Heterogeneous Multi-Tasks Selection in Multi-Robot Systems. In I. Batyrshin & G. Sidorov (Eds.), *Advances in Artificial Intelligence* (pp. 443–453). Springer. doi:10.1007/978-3-642-25324-9_38

Quiñonez, Y., Ramirez, M., Lizarraga, C., Tostado, I., & Bekios, J. (2015). Autonomous Robot Navigation Based on Pattern Recognition Techniques and Artificial Neural Networks. In J. Ferrández, J. Álvarez-Sánchez, F. de la Paz, F. Toledo-Moreo, & H. Adeli (Eds.), *Bioinspired Computation in Artificial Systems* (pp. 320–329). Springer. doi:10.1007/978-3-319-18833-1_34

Quiñonez, Y., Zatarain, O., Lizarraga, C., & Peraza, J. (2019). Using Convolutional Neural Networks to Recognition of Dolphin Images. In J. Mejia, M. Muñoz, Á. Rocha, A. Peña, & M. Pérez-Cisneros (Eds.), *Trends and Applications in Software Engineering* (pp. 236–245). Springer. doi:10.1007/978-3-030-01171-0_22

Quiñonez, Y., Zatarain, O., Lizarraga, C., Peraza, J., & Mejía, J. (2020a). Algorithm Proposal to Control a Robotic Arm for Physically Disable People Using the LCD Touch Screen. In J. Mejia, M. Muñoz, Á. Rocha, & J. Calvo-Manzano (Eds.), *Trends and Applications in Software Engineering* (pp. 187–207). Springer. doi:10.1007/978-3-030-33547-2_15

Rajkumar, R., Lee, I., Sha, L., & Stankovic, J. (2010). Cyber-physical systems: the next computing revolution. In *Proceedings of the design automation conference*, (pp 731–736). IEEE.

Ramírez, P. A., & Sosa, H. A. (2013). Aprendizaje con robótica, algunas experiencias. *Review of Education*, *37*(1), 43–63.

Rashed, H., Yogamani, S., El-Sallab, A., Das, A., & El-Helw, M. (2019). Depth Augmented Semantic Segmentation Networks for Automated Driving. In C. Arora & K. Mitra (Eds.), *Computer Vision Applications* (pp. 1–13). Springer. doi:10.1007/978-981-15-1387-9_1

Rathmann, L. (2020). Mujeres fuertes, valientes y comprometidas. Mujeres al fin…. In Matilda y las mujeres en ingeniería en américa latina II. Consejo Federal de Decanos de Ingeniería de Argentina CONFEDI. Latin American and Caribbean Consortium of Engineering Institutions.

Razo, M. L. (2008). La inserción de las mujeres en las carreras de ingeniería y tecnología. *Perfiles Educativos*, *30*(121), 63–96.

Real, B., Carlo, J., & Jaeger, P. T. (2014). Rural Public Libraries and Digital Inclusion : Issues and Challenges. *ITAL Information Technology and Libraries, 33*(March), 6–24. doi:10.6017/ital.v33i1.5141

Redacción de TVN noticias. (2017). *El Ferrocarril de Chiriquí en el Panamá de ayer.* Variedad. https://www.tvn-2.com/variedad/Ferrocarril-Chiriqui-Panama-ayer_0_4911258844.html

Regier, T., & Carlson, L. A. (2001). Grounding Spatial Language in Perception: An Empirical and Computational Investigation. *Journal of Experimental Psychology. General, 130*(2), 273–298. doi:10.1037/0096-3445.130.2.273 PMID:11409104

Rehman, I., Mirakhorli, M., Nagappan, M., Uulu, A. A., & Thornton, M. (2018). Roles and impacts of hands-on software architects in five industrial case studies. In *Proceedings of International Conference on Software Engineering*, (pp 117–127). Association for Computing Machinery. 10.1145/3180155.3180234

Rehmat, N., Zuo, J., Meng, W., Liu, Q., Xie, S. Q., & Liang, H. (2018). Upper limb rehabilitation using robotic exoskeleton systems: A systematic review. *International Journal of Intelligent Robotics and Applications, 2*(3), 283–295. doi:10.100741315-018-0064-8

Reis da Silva, T., Medeiros, T., & da Silva Aranha, E. (2015). The use of games on the teaching of programming: a systematic review. ESELAW 2015, Lima, Peru.

Republica de Panama & Consorcio linea 1. (2010). *Contrato-N°SMP-28-2010.* Secretaria del Metro de Panama.

Ribes, M.D. (2011). *El juego inf. y su metodología.* Eduforma, Ediciones.

Richards, R. (2016). *Nuevo Instituto Técnico Superior de Panamá Oeste capacitará sobre mantenimiento del Metro.* Nacionales.

Rich, E., & Knight, K. (1991). *Artificial Intelligence* (2nd ed.). McGraw-Hill Education.

Rieles multimedio. (2020). *Mexico: Parlacen respalda tren mesoamericano de Panamá a Chiapas.* REvista Rieles Multimedio.

Rivas & Revelo. (2017). *El proyecto integrador como proceso investigativo en el aula: Proyecto de Investigación. Fundación Academia de Dibujo Profesional.* Available: http://fido.palermo.edu/servicios_dyc/encuentro2007/02_auspicios_publicaciones/actas_diseno/articulos_pdf/A6029.pdf

Rivera, L. (2019). *Presidente Varela entrega la Línea 2 del Metro de Panamá, obra construida con "transparencia y eficiencia."* Metro de Panamá. https://www.elmetrodepanama.com/presidente-varela-entrega-la-linea-2-del-metro-de-panama-obra-construida-con-transparencia-y-eficiencia/

Robinson, G. (1992). Regulation of division of labor in insect societies. *Annual Review of Entomology, 37*(1), 637–665. doi:10.1146/annurev.en.37.010192.003225 PMID:1539941

Rohan, R. D., Patel, Z., Yadavannavar, S.C., Sujata, C., & Mudengudi, U. (2019). Image Segmentation and Geometric Feature Based Approach for Fast Video Summarization of Surveillance Videos. In Computer Vision Applications (pp. 79-88). Springer.

Rojas, D., Zambrano, C., Varas, M., & Urrutia, A. (2011). A multi-level thresholding-based method to learn fuzzy membership functions from data warehouse. In *Iberoamerican Congress on Pattern Recognition* (pp. 664–674). Springer. doi:10.1007/978-3-642-25085-9_79

Rojas, J. M., White, T. D., Clegg, B. S., & Fraser, G. (2017). Code defenders: crowdsourcing effective tests and subtle mutants with a mutation testing game. *Proceedings of the 39th International Conference on Software Engineering.* 10.1109/ICSE.2017.68

Romero, C., & Ventura, S. (2010). Educational data mining: A review of the state of the art. *IEEE Transactions on Systems, Man and Cybernetics. Part C, Applications and Reviews*, 40(6), 601–618. doi:10.1109/TSMCC.2010.2053532

Romero, O., & Abelló, A. (2009). A survey of multidimensional modeling methodologies. *International Journal of Data Warehousing and Mining*, 5(2), 1–23. doi:10.4018/jdwm.2009040101

Roy, D. K. (2002). Learning Visually-Grounded Words and Syntax for a Scene Description Task. *Computer Speech & Language*, 16(3-4), 1–39. doi:10.1016/S0885-2308(02)00024-4

Ruan, J., Jiang, H., Zhu, C., Hu, X., Shi, Y., Liu, T., Rao, W., & Chan, F. T. S. (2019). Agriculture IoT: Emerging Trends, Cooperation Networks, and Outlook. *IEEE Wireless Communications*, 26(6), 56–63. doi:10.1109/MWC.001.1900096

Rundensteiner, E. A., & Bic, L. (1989). Aggregates in possibilistic databases. *Proc. Conf. Very Large Databases*.

Runeson, P. (2001). Experiences from teaching PSP for freshmen. *Software Engineering Education Conference Proceedings*, 98–107. 10.1109/csee.2001.913826

Salatino, A., Thiviyan-Thanapalasingam, Andrea-Mannocci, A., Osborne, F., & Motta, E. (2018). The Computer Science Ontology: A Large-Scale Taxonomy of Research Areas. *Proceedings of International Semantic Web Conference 2018*. 10.1007/978-3-030-00668-6_12

Sampaio, A., Sampaio, I. B., & Gray, E. (2013). The need of a person oriented approach to software process assessment. *2013 6th International Workshop on Cooperative and Human Aspects of Software Engineering (CHASE)*, 145–148. 10.1109/CHASE.2013.6614752

Sanchez-Gordon, S., & Luján-Mora, S. (2013b). Accessibility considerations of Massive Online Open Courses as creditable courses in Engineering Programs. In *Proceedings of International Conference of Education, Research and Innovation* (pp. 5853-5862). Academic Press.

Sanchez-Gordon, S., & Luján-Mora, S. (2014). Web accessibility requirements for massive open online courses. In *Proceedings of the V International Conference on Quality and Accessibility of Virtual Learning* (pp. 530-535). Academic Press.

Sanchez-Gordon, S., & Luján-Mora, S. (2015a). Adaptive content presentation extension for open edX. Enhancing MOOCs accessibility for users with disabilities. In *Proceedings of the 8th International Conference on Advances in Computer-Human Interaction* (pp.181-183). Academic Press.

Sanchez-Gordon, S., & Luján-Mora, S. (2016a). How could MOOCs become accessible? The case of edX and the future of inclusive online learning. *Journal of Universal Computer Science (J.UCS)*, 22(1), 55-81.

Sanchez-Gordon, S., Calle-Jimenez, T., Villarroel-Ramos, J., Jadán-Guerrero, J., Guevara, C., Lara-Alvarez, P., Acosta-Vargas, P., & Salvador-Ullauri, L. (2020a). Implementation of controls for insertion of accessible images in open online editors based on WCAG guidelines. Case studies: TinyMCE and Summernote. In Advances in Human Factors and Systems Interaction. AHFE 2019. Advances in Intelligent Systems and Computing, 959 (pp. 315-326). Cham, Switzerland: Springer.

Sanchez-Gordon, S., Luján-Mora, S., & Sánchez-Gordón, M. (2020c). E-government accessibility in Ecuador: A preliminary evaluation. In *Proceeding of the Seventh International Conference on eDemocracy & eGovernment* (pp. 50-57). Academic Press.

Sánchez-Gordón, M., & Colomo-Palacios, R. (2018). Characterizing DevOps Culture: A Systematic Literature Review. In I. Stamelos, R. V. O'Connor, T. Rout, & A. Dorling (Eds.), *Software Process Improvement and Capability Determination* (pp. 3–15). Springer International Publishing. doi:10.1007/978-3-030-00623-5_1

Sánchez-Gordón, M., & Colomo-Palacios, R. (2019a). Taking the emotional pulse of software engineering—A systematic literature review of empirical studies. *Information and Software Technology*, 115, 23–43. doi:10.1016/j.infsof.2019.08.002

Sánchez-Gordón, M., & Colomo-Palacios, R. (2019b). Developing SPI Culture in the SME Arena: An Exploratory Study. In A. Walker, R. V. O'Connor, & R. Messnarz (Eds.), *Systems, Software and Services Process Improvement* (pp. 222–234). Springer International Publishing. doi:10.1007/978-3-030-28005-5_17

Sánchez-Gordón, M., & Colomo-Palacios, R. (2020a). Factors influencing Software Engineering Career Choice of Andean Indigenous. *Proceedings of the ACM/IEEE 42nd International Conference on Software Engineering: Companion Proceedings*, 264–265. 10.1145/3377812.3390899

Sánchez-Gordón, M., & Colomo-Palacios, R. (2020b). Security as Culture: A Systematic Literature Review of DevSecOps. *Proceedings of the IEEE/ACM 42nd International Conference on Software Engineering Workshops*, 266–269. 10.1145/3387940.3392233

Sánchez-Gordón, M.-L. (2017). Getting the Best out of People in Small Software Companies: ISO/IEC 29110 and ISO 10018 Standards. *International Journal of Information Technologies and Systems Approach*, *10*(1), 45–60. doi:10.4018/IJITSA.2017010103

Sánchez-Gordón, M.-L., Colomo-Palacios, R., & Herranz, E. (2016). Gamification and Human Factors in Quality Management Systems: Mapping from Octalysis Framework to ISO 10018. *EuroSPI*, *2016*, 234–241. doi:10.1007/978-3-319-44817-6_19

Sánchez-Gordón, M.-L., de Amescua, A., O'Connor, R. V., & Larrucea, X. (2017). A standard-based framework to integrate software work in small settings. *Computer Standards & Interfaces*, *54*(3), 162–175. doi:10.1016/j.csi.2016.11.009

Sánchez-Gordón, M.-L., & O'Connor, R. V. (2016). Understanding the Gap Between Software Process Practices and Actual Practice in Very Small Companies. *Software Quality Journal*, *24*(3), 549–570. doi:10.100711219-015-9282-6

Sánchez-Gordón, M.-L., O'Connor, R. V., Colomo-Palacios, R., & Herranz, E. (2016). Bridging the Gap Between SPI and SMEs in Educational Settings: A Learning Tool Supporting ISO/IEC 29110. *Proceedings of the IEEE/ACM 42nd International Conference on Software Engineering Workshops*, 3–14. 10.1007/978-3-319-44817-6_1

Sánchez-Gordón, M.-L., O'Connor, R. V., Colomo-Palacios, R., & Sánchez-Gordón, S. (2016). A Learning Tool for the ISO/IEC 29110 Standard: Understanding the Project Management of Basic Profile. *Proceedings 16th International Conference on Software Process Improvement and Capability DEtermination (SPICE 2016)*, *609*, 270–283. 10.1007/978-3-319-38980-6_20

Sánchez-Gordón, M., Rijal, L., & Colomo-Palacios, R. (2020). Beyond Technical Skills in Software Testing: Automated versus Manual Testing. *Proceedings of the IEEE/ACM 42nd International Conference on Software Engineering Workshops*, 161–164. 10.1145/3387940.3392238

Sanchez-Gordon, S., Estevez, J., & Luján-Mora, S. (2016c) Editor for accessible images in e-learning platforms. In *Proceedings of the 13th Web for All Conference* (pp. 1-2). 10.1145/2899475.2899513

Sanchez-Gordon, S., Jadán-Guerrero, J., Arias-Flores, H., & Nunes, I. L. (2020b). Model for Generation of Profiles for Persons with Disabilities in e-Learning Environments. In I. L. Nunes (Ed.), *Advances in Human Factors and Systems Interaction. AHFE 2020. Advances in Intelligent Systems and Computing, 1207* (pp. 242–249). Springer.

Sanchez-Gordon, S., & Luján-Mora, S. (2013a). Web accessibility of MOOCs for elderly students. In *Proceedings of the 11th International Conference on Information Technology Based Higher Education and Training* (pp.1-6). 10.1109/ITHET.2013.6671024

Sanchez-Gordon, S., & Luján-Mora, S. (2015b). An ecosystem for corporate training with accessible MOOCs and OERs. In *Proceedings of the IEEE International Conference on MOOCs, Innovation and Technology in Education* (pp. 123-128). 10.1109/MITE.2015.7375301

Sanchez-Gordon, S., & Luján-Mora, S. (2015c). Accessible blended learning for non-native speakers using MOOCs. In *Proceedings of the IEEE International Conference on Interactive Collaborative and Blended Learning* (pp. 19-24). 10.1109/ICBL.2015.7387645

Sanchez-Gordon, S., & Luján-Mora, S. (2016b). Design, implementation and evaluation of MOOCs to improve inclusion of diverse learners. In R. Mendoza-Gonzalez (Ed.), *User-Centered Design Strategies for Massive Open Online Courses* (pp. 115–141). IGI Global. doi:10.4018/978-1-4666-9743-0.ch008

Sanchez-Gordon, S., & Luján-Mora, S. (2016d). Barriers and strategies for using MOOCs in the context of Higher Education in Ibero-America. In P. Gómez Hernández, A. García Barrera, & C. Monge López (Eds.), *The culture of MOOCs* (pp. 141–160). Editorial Síntesis.

Sanchez-Gordon, S., & Luján-Mora, S. (2018a). Research challenges in accessible MOOCs: A systematic literature review 2008-2016. *Universal Access in the Information Society, 17*(4), 775–789. doi:10.100710209-017-0531-2

Sanchez-Gordon, S., & Luján-Mora, S. (2018b). Lifecycle for MOOC development and management. In R. Queirós (Ed.), *Emerging Trends, Techniques, and Tools for Massive Open Online Course (MOOC) Management* (pp. 24–48). IGI Global. doi:10.4018/978-1-5225-5011-2.ch002

Sanchez-Gordon, S., & Luján-Mora, S. (2018c). Technological Innovations in Large-Scale Teaching: Five Roots of MOOCS. *Journal of Educational Computing Research, 56*(5), 623–644. doi:10.1177/0735633117727597

Sanchez-Gordon, S., & Luján-Mora, S. (2019). Implementing Accessibility in Massive Open Online Courses' Platforms for Teaching, Learning and Collaborating at Large Scale. In A. Meier & C. Terán (Eds.), *eDemocracy & eGoverment. Stages of a Democratic Knowledge Society* (pp. 151–160). Springer.

Sandler, M., Howard, A., Zhu, M., Zhmoginov, A., & Chen, L. (2018). MobileNet V2: inverted residuals and linear bottlenecks. In *Proceedings of Conference on Computer Vision and Pattern Recognition* (pp. 4510-4520). IEEE Press.

Sangwan, R. S. (2014). *Software and Systems Architecture in Action*. Auerbach Publications. doi:10.1201/b17575

San, P. P., Ling, S. H., & Nguyen, H. T. (2016). Deep learning framework for detection of hypoglycemic episodes in children with type 1 diabetes. In *Proceedings of Conference on Engineering in Medicine Biology Society* (pp. 3503-3506). IEEE Press. 10.1109/EMBC.2016.7591483

Sanz-Bobi, J., Vazquez-Brunel, J., & Berbey-Álvarez, A. (2010). Sistemas y Tecnologías de Transporte Urbano Ferroviario. Universidad Tecnologica de Panamá. Patrocinado por la Aecid(España) y la Secretaria del Metro de Panamá(Panamá).

Sanz-Bobi, J., Berbey-Álvarez, A., Caballero, R., & Alvarez, H. (2009). *C/025994/09 - Cooperación interuniversitaria para la ejecución de acciones dirigidas a la ejecución y desarrollo otorgada según la publicación de BOE de enero del 2009 dentro del Programa de Convocatoria de ayudas para programas de cooperación interuniver*. Aecid.

Sapir, L., Shmilovici, A., & Rokach, L. (2008). A methodology for the design of a fuzzy data warehouse. In *4th International IEEE Conference Intelligent Systems* (Vol. 1, pp. 2-14). IEEE. 10.1109/IS.2008.4670400

Sasidharan, M., Burrow, M. P. N., Ghataora, G. S., & Torbaghan, M. E. (2017). *A Review of Risk Management Applications for Railways*. Railway Engineering., doi:10.25084/raileng.2017.0065

Scarpato, N., Pieron, A., Di Nunzio, L., & Fallucchi, F. (2017). E-health-IoT Universe: A Review. *International Journal on Advanced Science. Engineering and Information Technology, 7*(6), 2328–2336.

Schefer-Wenzl, S., & Miladinovic, I. (2018). Teaching Software Engineering with Gamification Elements. *International Journal of Advanced Corporate Learning, 11*(1).

Schroeder, R. (2010). *Being There Together: Social interaction in shared virtual environments*. Oxford University Press. doi:10.1093/acprof:oso/9780195371284.001.0001

Secretaría del Metro de Panamá. (2010a). Ingeniería conceptual. Especificaciones funcionales, técnicas y contractuales. Tomo II. Equipamientos. II. Sistemas de vías. II.1.2. Ingeniería conceptual diseño geométrico. *Línea, 1*, 1–60.

Secretaría del Metro de Panamá. (2010b). *Ingeniería conceptual. Especificaciones funcionales, técnicas y contractuales Tomo II Equipamientos. II. O. Normas generales. II.0.1. Ingeniería conceptual de la operación. Línea 1*. Secretaría del Metro de Panamá.

Secretaria del Metro de Panamá. (2010c). *Ingenieria Conceptual, Especificaciones funcionales, tecnicas y contractuales. Tomo I Obras civiles I.6. Secretaria del Metro de Panamá Arquitectura de estaciones. 1.6.1. memoria descriptiva, N°1, 17/03/2010.*

Secretaria del Metro de Panama. (2010d). *Nota Tecnica*.

Seeliger, K., Güçlü, U., Ambrogioni, L., Güçlütürk, Y., & van Gerven, M. A. J. (2018). Generative adversarial networks for reconstructing natural images from brain activity. *NeuroImage, 181*, 775–785. doi:10.1016/j.neuroimage.2018.07.043 PMID:30031932

Seffah, A., Donyaee, M., Kline, R. B., & Padda, H. K. (2006). Usability measurement and metrics : A consolidated model. *Software Quality Journal, 14*(2), 159–178. doi:10.100711219-006-7600-8

Serin, O., Serin, N. B., & Saygili, G. (2009). The effect of educational technologies and material supported science and technology teaching on the problem solving skills of 5 th grade primary school student. *Procedia: Social and Behavioral Sciences, 1*(1), 665–670. doi:10.1016/j.sbspro.2009.01.116

Serracin, E. (2014). *La historia olvidada del ferrocarril de Bugaba*. http://www.soydebugaba.com/blog/la-historica-y-olvidada-estacion-del-ferrocarril-de-bugaba

Shackelford, R., Lunt, B., McGettrick, A., Sloan, R., Topi, H., Davies, G., . . . Lunt, B. (2006). Computing Curricula 2005: The Overview Report. Proceedings of the 37th SIGCSE Technical Symposium on Computer Science Education - SIGCSE '06, 38(1), 456. 10.1145/1121341.1121482

Shah, D. (2019). *By the numbers: MOOCs in 2019*. Retrieved from https://www.classcentral.com/report/mooc-stats-2019

Shahbazian, A., Lee, Y. K., Brun, Y., & Medvidovic, N. (2018). Making well-informed software design decisions. In *Proceedings of the 40th International Conference on Software Engineering*, (pp. 262–263). Association for Computing Machinery. 10.1145/3183440.3194961

Shahrour, G. J., & Russell, M. J. (2015). Recognizing an individual, their topic of conversation, and cultural background from 3D body movement. *World Acad Sci Eng Technol Int J Comput Electr Autom Control Inf Eng, 9*(1), 311–316.

Shailaja, K., Seetharamulu, B., & Jabbar, M. A. (2018). Machine Learning in Healthcare: A Review. In *Proceedings of International Conference on Electronics, Communication and Aerospace Technology* (pp. 910-914). IEEE Press.

Sharma, V., Vineeta, Som, S., & Khatri, S. K. (2019). Future of Wearable Devices Using IoT Synergy in AI. In *Proceedings of International conference on Electronics, Communication and Aerospace Technology* (pp. 138-142). IEEE Press. 10.1109/ICECA.2019.8821915

Shaw, M., & Garlan, D. (1996). *Software Architecture: Perspectives on an Emerging Discipline*. Prentice Hall.

Silva, S., & Leite, L. (2015). Technology Acceptance Evaluation by Deaf Students Considering the Inclusive Education Context. In *Human-Computer Interaction* (pp. 20–37). INTERACT.

Silveira, K. K., & Prikladnicki, R. (2019). A Systematic Mapping Study of Diversity in Software Engineering: A Perspective from the Agile Methodologies. *Proceedings of the 12th International Workshop on Cooperative and Human Aspects of Software Engineering*, 7–10. 10.1109/CHASE.2019.00010

Simpson, R., & Storer, T. (2017). Experimenting with Realism in Software Engineering Team Projects: An Experience Report. Proceedings - 30th IEEE Conference on Software Engineering Education and Training, 87–96. 10.1109/CSEET.2017.23

Singer, L., & Schneider, K. (2012). It was a bit of a race: Gamification of version control. In *2012 Second International Workshop on Games and Software Engineering: Realizing User Engagement with Game Engineering Techniques*, 5–8. 10.1109/GAS.2012.6225927

Singh, A. S., & Segatto, A. P. (2020). When relational capabilities walk in education for sustainability scenario. *Journal of Cleaner Production*, *263*, 121478. Advance online publication. doi:10.1016/j.jclepro.2020.121478

Singholi, A. K. S., & Agarwal, D. (2018). Review of Expert System and Its Application in Robotics. In Intelligent Communication, Control and Devices (pp. 1253-1265). Springer. doi:10.1007/978-981-10-5903-2_131

Skouby, K., & Lynggaard, P. (2014). Smart home and smart city solutions enabled by 5G, IoT, AAI and CoT services. In *2014 International Conference on Contemporary Computing and Informatics (IC3I)*. Mysore, India: IEEE. 10.1109/IC3I.2014.7019822

Slomanson, W. R. (2014). Blended Learning: A Flipped Classroom Experiment. *Journal of Legal Education*, *64*, 93–102. doi:10.2307/24716075

Smart, K. L., & Csapo, N. (2007). Learning by doing: Engaging students through learner-centered activities. *Business Communication Quarterly*, *70*(4), 451–457. doi:10.1177/10805699070700040302

Smith, C. (2020). *Coursera Statistics and Facts*. Retrieved from https://expandedramblings.com/index.php/coursera-facts-statistics/

Smith, H. J., & Neff, M. (2018, April). Communication behavior in embodied virtual reality. In *Proceedings of the 2018 CHI Conference on Human Factors in Computing Systems* (pp. 1-12). Academic Press.

SMP. Secretaria del Metro de Panamá. (2010). *II.7 Material rodante. Pliego de cargos. Diseño y construcción de la línea 1 del metro de Panamá. 2010.* Secretaria del Metro de Panama.

Sobrevilla, G., Hernández, J., Velasco-Elizondo, P., & Soriano, S. (2017). Aplicando Scrum y Prácticas de Ingeniería de Software para la Mejora Continua del Desarrollo de un Sistema Ciber-Físico. *ReCIBE*, *6*(1), 1–15.

Sodhro, A. H., Obaidat, M. S., Abbasi, Q. H., Pace, P., Pirbhulal, S., Yasar, A. U. H., Fortino, G., Imran, M. A., & Qaraqe, M. (2019). Quality of Service Optimization in an IoT-Driven Intelligent Transportation System. *IEEE Wireless Communications*, *26*(6), 10–17. doi:10.1109/MWC.001.1900085

Software Engineering Institute. (2007). *CMMI Performance Results. TATA Consultancy Services.* Software Engineering Institute (SEI), Carnegie Mellon University. Available at: http://www.sei.cmu.edu/cmmi/results/org29.html#BC2

Sommerville, I. (2010). *Software Engineering* (9th ed.). Addison-Wesley.

Sommerville, I. (2011). *Software engineering*. Pearson.

Song, I.-Y., & Zhu, Y. (2016). Big data and data science: What should we teach? *Expert Systems: International Journal of Knowledge Engineering and Neural Networks*, *33*(4), 364–373. doi:10.1111/exsy.12130

Sousa, V. E. C., & Lopez, K. D. (2017). Towards usable e-health. A systematic review of usability questionnaires. *Applied Clinical Informatics*, *8*(2), 470–490. doi:10.4338/ACI-2016-10-R-0170 PMID:28487932

Spante, M., Heldal, I., Steed, A., Axelsson, A., & Schroeder, R. (2003). Strangers and friends in networked immersive environments: Virtual spaces for future living. In *Proceeding of Home Oriented Informatics and Telematics*. HOIT.

SPU. (2020). *Estadísticas Universitarias, Secretaría de Políticas Universitarias, Ministerio de Educación, Argentina*. Recuperado de http://estadisticasuniversitarias.me.gov.ar/#/home

Sriganesh, R., & Ramjee, P. (2018). Impact of 5G Technologies on Smart City Implementation. *Wireless Personal Communications*, *100*(1), 161–176. doi:10.100711277-018-5618-4

Sternberg, R. (1997). *Inteligencia exitosa*. Paidós.

Stezano, F. (2017). The Role of Technology Center as Intermediary Organizations Facilitating Links for Innovation: Four Cases of Deferal Technology Centers in Mexico. *The Review of Policy Research*, *1*, 45–67.

Stoia, L. (2007). *Noun phrase generation for situated dialogs* (PhD thesis). Ohio State University.

Streitzig, C., Schön, S., Griese, S., & Oetting, A. (2013). Practical education of young academics for railway operation and research. *EURO – ZEL 2013 21st International Symposium*, 240–245.

Su, C. H. (2016). The effects of students' motivation, cognitive load and learning anxiety in gamification software engineering education: A structural equation modeling study. *Multimedia Tools and Applications*, *75*(16), 10013–10036. doi:10.100711042-015-2799-7

Sun, Y., Shaikh, O., & Won, A. S. (2019). Nonverbal synchrony in virtual reality. *PLoS One*, *14*(9), e0221803. doi:10.1371/journal.pone.0221803 PMID:31525220

Sustika, R., Yuliani, A. R., Zaenudin, E., & Pardede, H. F. (2017). On comparison of deep learning architectures for distant speech recognition. In *Proceedings of International conferences on Information Technology, Information Systems and Electrical Engineering* (pp. 17-21). IEEE Press. 10.1109/ICITISEE.2017.8285488

Su, X., Giancarlo, S., Moscato, V., Picariello, A., & Esposito, C. (2019). An Edge Intelligence Empowered Recommender System Enabling Cultural Heritage Applications. *IEEE Transactions on Industrial Informatics*, *15*(7), 4266–4275. doi:10.1109/TII.2019.2908056

Swamidason, I. T. J. (2019). Survey of data mining algorithm's for intelligent computing system. *Journal of Trends in Computer Science and Smart Technology*, *1*(1), 14-23.

Szegedy, C., Vanhoucke, V., Ioffe, S., Shlens, J., & Wojna, Z. (2016). Rethinking the inception architecture for computer vision. In *Proceedings of Conference on Computer Vision and Pattern Recognition* (pp. 2818-2826). IEEE Press. 10.1109/CVPR.2016.308

Taborda, H., & Medina, D. (2012). *Programación de Computadores y Desarrollo de Habilidades de Pensamiento En Niños Escolares: Fase Exploratoria. Cali*. Universidad ICESI. Obtenido de http://eduteka.icesi.edu.co/pdfdir/Icesi_Investigacion_Scratch_FaseI.pdf

Taibi, D., Fulantelli, G., Dietze, S., & Fetahu, B. (2016). Educational Linked Data on the Web - Exploring and Analysing the Scope and Coverage. In D. Mouromtsev & M. d'Aquin (Eds.), Lecture Notes in Computer Science: Vol. 9500. *Open Data for Education* (pp. 16–39). Springer. doi:10.1007/978-3-319-30493-9_2

Tandon, A. (2019). Reconciling Your Data and the World with Knowledge Graphs. *Towards Data Science*. https://towardsdatascience.com/reconciling-your-data-and-the-world-with-knowledge-graphs-bce66b377b14

Tang, A., Tran, M. H., Han, J., & Vliet, H. V. (2008). Design Reasoning Improves Software Design Quality. In S. Becker, F. Plasil, & R. Reussner (Eds.), Lecture Notes in Computer Science: Vol. 5281. *Quality of Software Architectures, Models and Architectures* (pp. 28–42). Springer. doi:10.1007/978-3-540-87879-7_2

Tang, B., Chen, Z., Hefferman, G., Pei, S., Wei, T., He, H., & Yang, Q. (2017). Incorporating Intelligence in Fog Computing for Big Data Analysis in Smart Cities. *IEEE Transactions on Industrial Informatics*, *13*(5), 2140–2150. doi:10.1109/TII.2017.2679740

Tan, M., Chen, B., Pang, R., Vasudevan, V., Sandler, M., Howard, A., & Le, Q. V. (2019). MnasNet: Platform-Aware Neural Architecture Search for Mobile. In *Proceedings of Conference on Computer Vision and Pattern Recognition* (pp. 2815-2823). IEEE Press. 10.1109/CVPR.2019.00293

Tapia-Leon, M., Aveiga, C. A., Chicaiza, J., & Suárez-Figueroa, M. C. (2019). Ontological Model for the Semantic Description of Syllabuses. In *Proceedings of 9th International Conference on Information Communication and Management* (pp. 175–180). 10.1145/3357419.3357442

Taran, G. (2007). Using games in software engineering education to teach risk management. *Software Engineering Education Conference Proceedings*, 211–218. 10.1109/CSEET.2007.54

Telecommunication standardization sector of ITU. (2016). *Recommendation ITU-T Y.4900/L.1600.* http://handle.itu.int/11.1002/1000/12627-en?locatt=format:pdf&auth

TensorFlow. (2020). *TensorFlow Documentation.* Retrieved June 1, 2020, from https://www.tensorflow.org/api_docs

Teo, T. F., Hayati, A. A., Lee, G., Billinghurst, M., & Adcock, M. (2019, November). A technique for mixed reality remote collaboration using 360 panoramas in 3d reconstructed scenes. In *25th ACM Symposium on Virtual Reality Software and Technology* (pp. 1-11). 10.1145/3359996.3364238

Thathachar, M. A. L., & Sastry, P. S. (2002). Varieties of learning automata: An overview. *Transactions on Systems, Man, and Cybernetics*, *32*(6), 711–722. doi:10.1109/TSMCB.2002.1049606 PMID:18244878

The Panama Railroad. (2008). *The Panama Rail road.* The Panama Railroad. http://www.panamarailroad.org/

Thompson, E. M. (2016). What makes a city 'smart'? *International Journal of Architectural Computing*, *14*(4), 358–371. doi:10.1177/1478077116670744

Tian, Y., Wang, H., & Wang, X. (2017). Object localization via evaluation multi-task learning. *Neurocomputing*, *253*, 34–41. doi:10.1016/j.neucom.2017.01.098

Togneri, R., Kamienski, C., Dantas, R., Prati, R., Toscano, A., Soininen, J. P., & Cinotti, T. S. (2019). Advancing IoT-Based Smart Irrigation. *IEEE Internet of Things Magazine*, *2*(4), 20–25. doi:10.1109/IOTM.0001.1900046

Torre-Bastida, A. I., Del Ser, J., Laña, I., Ilardia, M., Bilbao, M. N., & Campos-Cordobés, S. (2018). Big Data for transportation and mobility: Recent advances, trends and challenges. *IET Intelligent Transport Systems*, *12*(8), 742–755. doi:10.1049/iet-its.2018.5188

Towey, D., & Ng, Y.-k., R., & Wang, T. (2016). Open Educational Resources (OERs) and Technology Enhanced Learning (TEL) in Vocational and Professional Education and Training (VPET). *Proceedings of the IEEE International Conference on Teaching, Assessment, and Learning for Engineering*, 301–305. 10.1109/TALE.2016.7851808

Towey, D., Chen, T. Y., Kuo, F. C., Liu, H., & Zhou, Z. Q. (2017). Metamorphic testing: A new student engagement approach for a new software testing paradigm. *Proceedings of 2016 IEEE International Conference on Teaching, Assessment and Learning for Engineering*, 218–225. 10.1109/TALE.2016.7851797

Towey, D., & Walker, J. (2018). Traditional Higher Education Engineering versus Vocational and Professional Education and Training: What can we Learn from Each Other? *International Conference on Open and Innovative Education (ICOIE 2018)*.

Trauth, E. M., Cain, C. C., Joshi, K. D., Kvasny, L., & Booth, K. (2012). Embracing Intersectionality in Gender and IT Career Choice Research. *Proceedings of the 50th Annual Conference on Computers and People Research*, 199–212. 10.1145/2214091.2214141

UNCTAD. (2012). *Information economy report 2012: The software industry and developing countries*. United Nations Publications.

UNESCO. (2017). *E2030: educación y habilidades para el siglo XXI. Informe, Naciones Unidas para la Educación, Oficina Nacional de Educación en América Latina y el Caribe. Santiago*. Recuperado de https://unesdoc.unesco.org/

UNICEF. (2009). *It's about ability. Learning guide on the convention on the rights of persons with disabilities*. Retrieved from http://www.unicef.org/publications/files/Its_About_Ability_Learning_Guide_EN.pdf

United Nations. (1948). *Universal declaration of human rights*. Retrieved from http://wwda.org.au/wp-content/uploads/2013/12/undechr1.pdf

United Nations. (2006). *Convention on the rights of persons with disabilities*. Retrieved from https://www.un.org/disabilities/documents/convention/convention_accessible_pdf.pdf

United Nations. (2008). *Convention on the rights of persons with disabilities and optional protocol*. Retrieved from https://www.un.org/development/desa/disabilities/convention-on-the-rights-of-persons-with-disabilities.html

United Nations. (2012). *Clasificación Industrial Internacional Uniforme, CIIU Rev.4*. United Nations Statistics Division. Recuperado de http://unstats.un.org/unsd/cr/registry/isic-4.asp

United Nations. (2017). *World population ageing*. Retrieved from https://www.un.org/en/development/desa/population/publications/pdf/ageing/WPA2017_Highlights.pdf

UNLaM. (2019). *Indice de TICs, Universidad Nacional de La Matanza*. Disponible en https://indicetics.unlam.edu.ar/it/

Upegui, O. (2009). *The Golden Era of Streetcars in Panama*. Lingua Franca. https://epiac1216.wordpress.com/2009/03/05/the-golden-era-of-streetcars-in-panama/

Uriarte, L. M., & Acevedo, M. (2018). Sociedad Red y transformación digital: Hacia una evolución de la consciencia de las organizaciones. *Revue d'Economie Industrielle*, *407*(1), 35–49.

Urrutia, A., Galindo, J., Jimenéz, L., & Piattini, M. (2006). Data Modeling Dealing with Uncertainty in Fuzzy Logic. *IFIP World Computer Congress*, *8*, 201-217. 10.1007/978-0-387-34732-5_19

US Department of Justice. (2015). *Justice Department reaches settlement with edX Inc*. Retrieved from http://www.justice.gov/usao-ma/pr/united-states-reaches-settlement-provider-massiveopen-online-courses-make-its-content

van der Aalst, W., Adriansyah, A., & van Dongen, B.WIREs Data Mining Knowledge Discovery. (2012). Replaying history on process models for conformance checking and performance analysis. *WIREs Data Mining and Knowledge Discovery*, *2*(2), 182–192. doi:10.1002/widm.1045

van Veenendaal, E. (2020). Next-Generation Software Testers: Broaden or Specialize! In S. Goericke (Ed.), *The Future of Software Quality Assurance* (pp. 229–243). Springer International Publishing., doi:10.1007/978-3-030-29509-7_18

VanBreusegem, V., Campion, G., & Bastin, G. (1991). Traffic Modeling and State Feedback control for Metro lines. *IEEE Transactions on Automatic Control*, *36*(7).

VandenBos, G., Knapp, S., & Doe, J. (2001). *Role of reference elements in the selection of resources by psychology undergraduates*. Retrieved from http://jbr.org/articles.html

Van-Ma, L., Park, J., Nam, J., Ryu, H., & Kim, J. (2017). A Fuzzy-Based Adaptive Streaming Algorithm for Reducing Entropy Rate of DASH Bitrate Fluctuation to Improve Mobile Quality of Service. *Entropy (Basel, Switzerland), 19*(477), 1–18. doi:10.3390/e19090477

Vargas-Enríquez, J., García-Mundo, L., Genero, M., & Piattini, M. (2015). Análisis de uso de la gamificación en la enseñanza de la informática. *Actas de las XXI Jornadas de la Enseñanza Universitaria de la Informática (JENUI 2015)*.

Vashi, S., Ram, J., Modi, J., Verma, S., & Prakash, C. (2017). Internet of Things (IoT): A vision, architectural elements, and security issues. In *Proceedings of International Conference on IoT in Social, Mobile, Analytics and Cloud* (pp. 492-496). IEEE Press. 10.1109/I-SMAC.2017.8058399

Vasiliev, V., Kozlov, F., Mouromtsev, D., Stafeev, S., & Parkhimovich, O. (2016). ECOLE: An ontology-based open online course platform. In D. Mouromtsev & M. d'Aquin (Eds.), Lecture Notes in Computer Science: Vol. 9500. *Open Data for Education* (pp. 41–66). doi:10.1007/978-3-319-30493-9_3

Vázquez-Castañeda, C., & Estrada-Guzman, E. (2015, August 20). *Towards the preparation of the Guadalajara's SmartCity Metrics Structure*. IEEE-GDL CCD Smart Cities White Paper. https://smartcities.ieee.org/images/files/pdf/whitepapermtx_v8.pdf

Vega-Gorgojo, G., Asensio-Pérez, J. I., Gómez-Sánchez, E., Bote-Lorenzo, M. L., Munoz-Cristobal, J. A., & Ruiz-Calleja, A. (2015). A Review of Linked Data Proposals in the Learning Domain. *Journal of Universal Computer Science, 21*, 326–364.

Velasco, J., & Fernandez, J. (2010a). Diseño Conceptual Geometrico-Via Argentina. Secretaria del Metro de Panama.

Velasco, J., & Fernandez, J. (2010b). Diseño Conceptual Geometrico Linea 1-Iglesia del Carmen. Secretaria del Metro de Panama.

Velasco, J., & Fernandez, J. (2010c). Diseño conceptual geometrico Linea 1-San Miguelito. Secretaria del Metro de Panama.

Velasco, J., & Fernandez, J. (2010d). Diseño conceptual geometrico-5 de mayo. Secretaria del Metro de Panama.

Velasco-Elizondo, P., & Lau, K. (2010). A catalogue of component connectors to support development with reuse. *Journal of Systems and Software, 83*(7), 1165–1178. doi:10.1016/j.jss.2010.01.008

Verdict media. (2022). *Bogota Metro*. Railway Tecnology.

Vergara, Y. (2015). *Estación del Metro en San Isidro abre sus puertas a los usuarios*. Transporte. TVN 2. https://www.tvn-2.com/nacionales/transporte/Estacion-Metro-San-Isidro-usuarios_0_4278322129.html

Vicerrectoría académica. (2020). *Evaluacion del desempeño docente. Resultado Individual por Profesor*. Universidad Tecnologica de Panamá.

Vizcaíno Recio, P. (2011). *Sistemas inteligentes para mundos virtuales*. Academic Press.

Vos, T. E. J., Prasetya, I., Fraser, G., Martinez-Ortiz, I., Perez-Colado, I., Prada, R., ... Silva, A. R. (2019). IMPRESS: Improving Engagement in Software Engineering Courses Through Gamification. *Proceedings of the 20th International Conference on Product-Focused Software Process Improvement (PROFES)*.

Waidyasekara, K. G. A. S., Gamlath, M., & Pandithawatta, S. (2020). Application of Robotic Technology for the Advancement of Construction Industry in Sri Lanka: A Review. In *Proceeding of International Conference on Engineering, Project, and Production Management* (pp. 43-54). Springer. 10.1007/978-981-15-1910-9_4

Warnicke, C. (2019). Equal Access to Make Emergency Calls : A Case for Equal Rights for Deaf Citizens in Norway and Sweden. *Social Inclusion*, 7(1), 173–179. doi:10.17645i.v7i1.1594

Weinberg, G. M. (1971). *The psychology of computer programming* (Vol. 932633420). Van Nostrand Reinhold.

Weiss, K., Khoshgoftaar, T. M., & Wang, D. J. (2016). A survey on transfer learning. *Journal of Big Data*, 3(9), 1–40.

Williams, T. (2008). How do organizations learn lessons from projects and do they? *IEEE Transactions on Engineering Management*, 55(2), 248–266. doi:10.1109/TEM.2007.912920

Winter, R., & Strauch, B. (2003). A method for demand-driven information requirements analysis in data warehousing projects. *36th Annual Hawaii International Conference on System Sciences, Proceedings of the IEEE.*

Wolpert, D. H., & Macready, W. G. (1997). No free lunch theorems for optimization. *IEEE Transactions on Evolutionary Computation*, 1(1), 67–82. doi:10.1109/4235.585893

World Health Organization. (2011). *World Report on Disability.* Retrieved from https://www.who.int/disabilities/world_report/2011/en/

World Wide Web Consortium. (1997). *World Wide Web Consortium launches international program office for Web Accessibility Initiative.* Retrieved from https:// www.w3.org/Press/IPO-announce

World Wide Web Consortium. (2008). *Web content accessibility guidelines (WCAG) 2.0.* Retrieved from https://www.w3.org/TR/WCAG20/

World Wide Web Consortium. (2018). *Web content accessibility guidelines (WCAG) 2.2.* Retrieved from https://www.w3.org/TR/WCAG21/

World Wide Web Consortium. (2019). *Introduction to Web Accessibility.* Retrieved from https://www.w3.org/WAI/fundamentals/accessibility-intro/

World Wide Web Consortium. (2020). *Web content accessibility guidelines (WCAG) 2.2.* Retrieved from https://www.w3.org/TR/WCAG22/

Wu, Q., Liu, Y., Li, Q., Jin, S., & Li, F. (2017). The application of deep learning in computer vision. In *Proceedings of Chinese Automation Congress* (pp. 6522-6527). IEEE Press. 10.1109/CAC.2017.8243952

Xie, S. X. (2018). *Smart classroom and university classroom teaching innovation. DEStech Transactions on Computer Science and Engineering.* IECE.

Yager, R. R. (1994). Aggregation operators and fuzzy systems modeling. *Fuzzy Sets and Systems*, 67(2), 129–145. doi:10.1016/0165-0114(94)90082-5

Yamashita, R., Nishio, M., Do, R. K. G., & Togashi, K. (2018). Convolutional neural networks: An overview and application in radiology. *Insights Into Imaging*, 9(4), 611–629. doi:10.100713244-018-0639-9 PMID:29934920

Yañez-Pagans, P., Martinez, D., Mitnik, O. A., Scholl, L., & Vazquez, A. (2019). Urban transport systems in Latin America and the Caribbean: Lessons and challenges. *Latin American Economic Review*, 28(1), 15. Advance online publication. doi:10.118640503-019-0079-z

Yang, J., & Chung, K. (2019). Newly-Coined Words and Emoticon Polarity for Social Emotional Opinion Decision. In 2019 IEEE 2nd International Conference on Information and Computer Technologies. Kahului, HI: IEEE. 10.1109/INFOCT.2019.8711413

Yang, J., Shiwakoti, N., & Tay, R. (2019). Train dwell time models – development in the past forty years. *Australasian Transport Research Forum 2019 Proceedings*, 1–12.

Yang, B., Sun, X., Cao, E., Hu, W., & Chen, X. (2018). Convolutional neural network for smooth filtering detection. *IET Image Processing*, *12*(8), 1432–1438. doi:10.1049/iet-ipr.2017.0683

Yazdani, M., & Jolai, F. (2016). Lion Optimization Algorithm (LOA): A nature-inspired metaheuristic algorithm. *Journal of Computational Design and Engineering*, *3*(1), 24–36. doi:10.1016/j.jcde.2015.06.003

Yenorkar, R., & Chaskar, U. M. (2018). GUI based pick and place robotic arm for multipurpose industrial applications. In *Proceeding of International Conference on Intelligent Computing and Control Systems* (pp. 200-203). IEEE Press. 10.1109/ICCONS.2018.8663079

Yonaitis, R. B. (2002). *Understanding accessibility: A guide to achieving compliance on web sites and intranets.* HiSoftware.

Yousaf, M., & Wolter, D. (2017, November). Spatial Information Extraction from Natural language Place Description for Incorporating Contextual Variables. In *Proceedings of the 11th Workshop on Geographic Information Retrieval* (pp. 1-2). 10.1145/3155902.3155910

Yu, H., & Zhang, X. (2017). Research on the Application of IoT in E-Commerce. In *Proceedings of International Conference on Computational Science and Engineering and International Conference on Embedded and Ubiquitous Computing* (pp. 434-436). IEEE Press. 10.1109/CSE-EUC.2017.269

Yu, Z., Macbeth, S., Modi, K., & Pujol, J. (2016). Tracking the Trackers. In *Proceedings of the 25th International Conference on World Wide*. Web Conferences Steering Committee. 10.1145/2872427.2883028

Zadeh, L. A. (1965). Fuzzy sets. *Information and Control*, *8*(3), 338–353. doi:10.1016/S0019-9958(65)90241-X

Zakarian, A., & Kusiak, A. (1999). Forming teams: An analytical approach. *IEEE Transactions*, *31*(1), 85–97. doi:10.1080/07408179908969808

Zamazal, O. (2020). A Survey of Ontology Benchmarks for Semantic Web Ontology Tools. *International Journal on Semantic Web and Information Systems*, *16*, 47–68. doi:10.4018/IJSWIS.2020010103

Zambrano, C., Rojas, D., Carvajal, K., & Acuña, G. (2011). Análisis de rendimiento académico estudiantil usando data warehouse y redes neuronales. *Ingeniare. Revista Chilena de Ingeniería*, *19*(3), 369–381. doi:10.4067/S0718-33052011000300007

Zambrano, C., Rojas, D., & Salcedo, P. (2018). Un método para analizar datos de pruebas educacionales estandarizadas usando almacén de datos y triangulación. *Formación Universitaria*, *11*(4), 3–14. doi:10.4067/S0718-50062018000400003

Zambrano, C., Urrutia, A., & Varas, M. (2017). Análisis de rendimiento académico estudiantil usando Data Warehouse Difuso. *Ingeniare. Revista Chilena de Ingeniería*, *25*(2), 242–254. doi:10.4067/S0718-33052017000200242

Zambrano, C., Varas, M., & Urrutia, A. (2012). Enfoque MDA para el diseño de un data warehouse difuso. *Ingeniare. Revista Chilena de Ingeniería*, *20*(1), 99–113. doi:10.4067/S0718-33052012000100010

Zapata, C. M. (2007). *Requirements game: teaching software project management.* Academia.Edu. Retrieved February 18, 2020, from https://www.academia.edu/download/32419252/v10i1p3.pdf

Zapata, C. M., & Duarte, M. I. (2008). Consistency game: a didactic strategy for software engineering. *Revista Universidad de Zulia*, *31*(1). http://tjfeonline.com/admin/archive/117.09.20141410966981.pdf

Zeadally, S., Siddiqui, F., Baig, Z., & Ibrahim, A. (2019). Smart healthcare: Challenges and potential solutions using the internet of things (IoT) and big data analytics. *PSU Research Review*, ahead-of-print.

Zeballos, E. (2016). *Capacitarán en mantenimiento del Metro*. Periodico El Siglo.

Zeng, C., Yang, C., & Chen, Z. (2020). Bio-inspired robotic impedance adaptation for human-robot collaborative tasks. *Science China. Information Sciences, 63*(7), 170–201. doi:10.100711432-019-2748-x

Zhang, D. (2017). High-speed train control system big data analysis based on the fuzzy RDF model and uncertain reasoning. *International Journal of Computers, Communications & Control, 12*(4), 577–591. doi:10.15837/ijccc.2017.4.2914

Zhao, H., & Liu, H. (2020). Multiple classifiers fusion and CNN feature extraction for handwritten digits recognition. *Granular Computing, 5*, 411-418.

Zhao, J., Qi, Z., & de Pablos, P. O. (2014). Enhancing enterprise training performance: Perspectives from knowledge transfer and integration. *Computers in Human Behavior, 30*, 567–573. doi:10.1016/j.chb.2013.06.041

Zhu, H., Wu, C. K., Koo, C. H., Tsang, Y. T., Liu, Y., Chi, H. R., & Tsang, K. F. (2019). Smart Healthcare in the Era of Internet-of-Things. *IEEE Consumer Electronics Magazine, 8*(5), 26-30.

Zhu, R., Hardy, D., & Myers, T. (2019). Co-designing with adolescents with autism spectrum disorder: From ideation to implementation. In *Proceedings of the 31st Australian Conference on Human-Computer-Interaction* (pp. 106-116). 10.1145/3369457.3370914

Zmyzgova, T. R., Polyakova, E. N., & Karpov, E. K. (2020). Digital Transformation of Education and Artificial Intelligence. In *2nd International Scientific and Practical Conference "Modern Management Trends and the Digital Economy: from Regional Development to Global Economic Growth" (MTDE 2020)* (pp. 824-829). Atlantis Press.

Zoph, B., Vasudevan, V., Shlens, J., & Le, Q. V. (2018). Learning transferable architectures for scalable image recognition. In *Proceedings of Conference on Computer Vision and Pattern Recognition* (pp. 8697-8710). IEEE Press. 10.1109/CVPR.2018.00907

About the Contributors

Adriana Peña Pérez Negrón received her Ph.D. in Computer Science in 2009 from the Universidad Politécnica de Madrid, Spain. Her main research interest is on the user's avatar display of nonverbal communication in Collaborative Virtual Environments. She is a research professor at the Computer Science Department at the CUCEI of the Universidad de Guadalajara, Mexico

* * *

Margarita André Ampuero, Full Professor at the Software Engineering and Management Department of the Universidad Tecnológica de La Habana, Cuba. Her research interests include applied research in software project management, people in software projects, algorithms and methods for optimization troubleshooting and software quality. She received her PhD in Technical Sciences from the Universidad Tecnológica de La Habana (2009). She also holds a Master in Computer Science from the Universidad Tecnológica de La Habana (1999).

Aranzazu Berbey Alvarez, PhD in Automation and Robotics from the Polytechnic University of Madrid (2008). Her doctoral thesis entitled "Real-time rail traffic planning" obtained the rating of Outstanding. Additionally, at the request of the Secretary of the Panama Metro, Dr. Berbey did an professional training at the Alstom company in Paris, France by the Panama Metro line 1 Project(2011). Dr. Aranzazu completed a postdoctoral stay at the University of Granada (Feb-March 2014); through a joint scholarship from the Carolina Foundation of Spain and the Technological University of Panama. Additionally, she has a Master's degree in Plant Engineering (2004) from the Faculty of Mechanical Engineering of the Technological University of Panama. Postgraduate in Higher Teaching from the Universidad Especializada de las Americas (2004). Degree in Industrial Engineering from the Technological University of Panama (1998). Graduated within the Honorary Chapter of the Instituto Justo Arosemena (1992). Dr. Berbey was the leader researcher of the project "Methodologies and performance indices for rail transport systems" its project received a recognition by SENACYT(2015). In this project, Dr. Aranzazu is in charge of the mechanical simulations of the trains on the metro line and analysis of parameters related to travel times, stop times, speeds, train time diagram. In the last stage, electrical simulations of the Panama metro line 1 are being carried out. These simulations corresponded to the determination of variables such as active power in traction substations, number of traction substations, current intensity per substation for both track 1 and track 2. She has published articles in international conferences in reference to the railway engineering field. She has been a consultant in the area of ISO 9000 standards, quality management systems since 2000.

Janneth Chicaiza is a full-time professor in the Computer Science Department at the Universidad Técnica Particular de Loja (UTPL), Ecuador. In 2016, she received a Ph.D. in Software and Systems from the Universidad Politécnica de Madrid. Her research interests include Open Access, Semantic Web, Data Science, Information Retrieval, and Knowledge Representation.

Elsa Estrada Guzmán is a research professor at the University of Guadalajara in the department of Computational Sciences, participates in the degree program for Computer Engineering, and for Computer Engineering, as well as for the Master's Degree in Applied Computing in the Internet research line of Things and Cloud Computing, which covers the topic of Smart Cities. She obtained the degree of Doctor in Information Technology from the same University in 2018, with the dissertation on the Framework for the evaluation of the Smart City: case study of Education analysis for the development of Smart People. She directs student projects that involve the development of applications and computer systems for decision-making that provide solutions to city problems.

Gloria Piedad Gasca-Hurtado is associated professor-researcher in the Engineering Faculty of Universidad de Medellín. She is an undergraduate Software Engineering and Systems Auditory Specialist. Her Ph.D. was taken in Universidad Politécnica de Madrid, Spain in Languages, Informatics Systems and Software Engineering Department in Informatics Faculty. Her research areas include Information technology and communications (TIC) software process improvement and optimization, multi-model environment for software development, software development and agile methodologies applied to small enterprises (SME's), security informatics, among others. Her teaching interests are Software Engineering, Software Management Project, Project Planning, Software Risk Management, Software Development Methodologies, and Software Process Improvement. She serves as Director of Software Engineering Academic Program.

María Clara Gómez-Álvarez is associated professor-researcher in the Engineering Faculty of Universidad de Medellín. She is Systems Engineer and Engineering Magister for Universidad Nacional de Colombia Sede Medellín. Her Engineering Ph.D. was taken at the same university. Her research areas include software engineering education, software process improvement, gamification and requirements engineering. Her teaching interests are Software Engineering, Information Systems, Business Process Modelling and Management, and Software Development Methodologies.

Jessica Guevara-Cedeño, PhD in electrical engineering by the University of Chile (2012). Bachelor in Electrical-electronics engineering by the Technological University of Panama (2005). Dr. Guevara-Cedeño is full professor at the Faculty of Electrical engineering in the Tecnological University of Panamá from 2012. Her engineering course like full professor are: Electric Power Production, Circuits I, Fundamentals of Electrical Engineering, Electrical and Electronic Schemes, Electric systems, Industrial electronics, Microwave oven, Optoelectronics, Control Theory, Communications Laboratory II, Electronics Laboratory III, Industrial Electronics Laboratory, Electronics Laboratory IV, Control theory II and Discreet Time control system. In addition, Dr. Guevara-Cedeño is extension activities´s Coordinator at the Faculty of Electrical Engineering.

Ana Lilian Infante Abreu graduated in Computer Engineering in 2008 and Master in Applied Computing in 2012. Professor of software engineering and software management. Researching in the area of artificial intelligence and software management, specifically in the field of optimization and management of software projects.

Graciela Lara López received her Ph.D. in Computer Science (Software and Systems) in 2016 from the Universidad Politécnica de Madrid, Spain. a Master in Information Systems (2001-2003) and Degree in computer science (1996-2000) from the Universidad de Guadalajara. She received a Ph. D. in Teaching Methodology from the Instituto Mexicano de Estudios Pedagógicos in 2012. Her areas of interest are in virtual reality, mainly on its application for training, 3D object modeling, and spatial mental models. She is an associate professor at the Computer Science Department at the CUCEI of the Universidad de Guadalajara, Mexico. Likewise she is member of the Researchers National System (México).

Bell Manrique Losada received her M.Sc. and Ph.D. in Engineering from the University Nacional de Colombia-Medellín in 2006 and 2015, respectively. She is a Titular Professor at The University of Medellín-Medellín, researcher from ARKADIUS Research Group, and professor of Software Engineering and Research Methodology in graduate and undergraduate programs. She writes and researches on issues of Computational Linguistics, Acquiring and Representing Knowledge, Software Engineering, and Engineering Education.

Beatriz Marín is Associate Professor at Diego Portales University, Santiago, Chile. She received her PhD in Computer Science at Polytechnic University of Valencia, Spain, in 2011. She has published more than 40 papers at top conferences (CAISE, ESEM, QSIC, MENSURA, ER, RCIS, SEKE, etc.) and journals (such as Data & Knowledge Engineering (DKE), ACM Transactions on Software Engineering and Methodologies (TOSEM), Software Quality Journal (SQJ), Information Systems (IS), IEEE Transactions on software engineering (TSE) and Information and Software Technology (IST). Her research focuses on software engineering, with special interest in quality, testing, functional size measurement, model-driven development, empirical software engineering, gamification and serious games.

Martha Patricia Martínez Vargas obtained her PhD in Information Technology in 2015 from the University of Guadalajara. Currently, he is a full-time lecturer in the Systems Department and a member of the UDG-CA-931 Academic team of the University Center for Economic-Administrative Sciences. His area of research interest is data analysis. She has directed various theses of the Master in Information Technology and the Bachelor of Information Technology. As well as, participating as co-author of various publications in the area of Technologies.

Alicia Mon has a PhD in Languages and Computer Systems from the Rey Juan Carlos University of Madrid, Masters Degree in Software Engineering from the Polytechnic University of Madrid, a diploma in Advanced Studies in Anthropology doctorate from the Complutense University of Madrid and a Bachelors Degree in Sociology from the University of Buenos Aires. She received the National Research Award "José Antonio Balseiro" in the category of Young Researcher in 2001 and is a Class 1 researcher at the Ministry of Education of Argentina. She currently works as a professor of Software Engineering at the National University of La Matanza and at the Technological Institute of Buenos Aires, as well as Project Director of Scientific and Technological Researches by the Science and Technology Ministry of Argentina. She gives classes in various postgraduate studies such as a specialization in Data Sciences at the Technological Institute of Buenos Aires, a Masters degree in Computer developments for Space Applications at the National Commission of Space Activities and at the National University of La Matanza and a Doctorate in Engineering from the National University of Lomas de Zamora. She has also been a Visiting Professor for the Masters degree in Software Engineering at the Polytechnic University of Madrid and has held management positions such as Director of the Systems Department at the CAECE University, Director of the Masters degree in Computing at the National University of La Matanza, Director of the Masters degree in Software Engineering at the Technological Institute of Buenos Aires and Research Secretary for the Department of Humanities and Social Sciences at the National University of La Matanza. She has directed numerous masters and doctoral thesis and has been part of several examining boards for postgraduate studies and competitive selection for professors in various universities. She is a Member of the Academic Committee at several national and international Congresses, a reviewer for scientific journals and an examiner for research projects. She has written numerous specialized articles and is the author of several books in the area of software engineering for different international publishing companies. Her research focuses on software engineering, Human-Computer Interaction and the development of ICT for Industry 4.0.

Itza Morales is systems and computer engineer, Panama. Actually, she is a student of the scientific master's degree in Information Technology and Communication from the University of Technology University of Panama. His research interests include software engineering, human-computer interaction, artificial intelligence and decision support systems.

Lilia Muñoz is a regular Professor at the Faculty of Computer Systems Engineering of the Technological University of Panama. She obtained her Doctorate in Computer Applications from the University of Alicante within the Lucentia Research group. Master in Computing with an emphasis on Information Systems at the Technological Institute of Costa Rica. Computer Systems Engineer from the Technological University of Panama. He has published several research articles on data warehouses, data warehouse quality, metrics, robotics applied to education, Computer science applied to business environments in national and international conferences (DOLAP, ADI, MiproBIS, JISBD, CISTI and CLEI) and in magazines such as Sensors, Information & Software Technology, Ingeniería Solidaria, Revista I + D Tecnológico, Iberoamerican Scientific Magazine of Educational Technology, Journal of Information Systems Engineering & Management and IEEE. Her areas of interest are Educational Informatics, Internet of Things, Electronic Health, Open Data. She has 26 years of experience as a Full Time Professor at the Technological University of Panama and at the Universidad del Istmo, Universidad Latina de Panamá, Universidad Autónoma de Chiriquí teaching Postgraduate, Master's and Doctorate courses.

Yadira Quiñonez is from Mexico, she is PhD in Computer Engineering in the official program of doctorate in Artificial Intelligence, in the Department of Artificial Intelligence in the Faculty of Informatics of the Polytechnic University of Madrid in Spain, where she received mention of Cum Laude. She is currently a full-time Professor and Researcher at the Faculty of Informatics in Mazatlan of the Autonomous University of Sinaloa, she is leader of the academic group: Trends and Technological Innovation in Robotics and Education. Her current interest in research focuses on autonomous robotics, educational robotics and the study of multi-robot systems.

Sandra Sanchez holds a PdD in Applications of Informatics by University of Alicante, Spain. Sandra is researcher and professor of the Department of Informatics and Computer Sciences of National Polytechnic School of Ecuador. Her main research interests include HCI, e-Health, e-Education, MOOCs, web accessibility, software requirements engineering, software testing engineering, software quality assurance, and IT governance. She has twenty eight years of experience in teaching at graduate and undergraduate level. She has published several research papers in scientific journals and conferences. She has twenty nine years of experience in development and implementation of software solutions in Ecuador, Panama and USA. She practices Yoga, Tai-Chi Zazen and Reiki. She is a Kichwa learner.

Mary Sánchez-Gordón is an Associate Professor at the Computer Science Department of the Østfold University College. Formerly she worked at Universidad Central del Ecuador. Her research interests are software process, software process improvement, knowledge management and human factors. She holds a Ph.D. and Master's degree in Information Science and Technology from Universidad Carlos III de Madrid.She also holds a Master's in Education and a bachelor's degree in Informatics from Universidad Central del Ecuador. She has been working as Software Engineer, Project Manager and Software Engineering Consultant in several companies.

Angélica Urrutia is a specialist in fuzzy logic, fuzzy database modeling and data analysis using data mining techniques.

Vianca Vega has a Ph.D. in Computer Science from the Polytechnic University of Madrid. Computer Engineer from the Universidad Católica del Norte. She is an academic of the Department of Systems and Computing Engineering of the Universidad Católica del Norte (Chile). Her area of work is Software Engineering. Member of the Program Committee of the Master in Computer Engineering of the Universidad Católica del Norte. She is part of the Software Process Improvement Network made up of institutions from Colombia, Chile, and Mexico. She has participated as a lecturer in various international events and has published scientific articles in international journals. She is part of the official translation team of the CMMI process improvement models of the Software Engineering Institute. Head of the Computer and Informatics Engineering Degree at the Universidad Católica del Norte from 2012 to 2018 and 2019 to 2020. Currently, in addition to his academic activity, he is part of the coordinating team of the GirlByte Association, whose mission is to be a benchmark for collaboration networks between women who carry out work in the technological area and to encourage the entry of more women to the careers of Computing and Informatics. Her core research areas are Software Process Improvement and Quality Assurance in Software Development. She also works in applied research in the area of Technological Development for the Inclusion of People with Disabilities.

Carolina Zambrano-Matamala is Master of Computer Science and Doctor of Education. She has developed research in the areas of: Data Warehouse in the field of education, Fuzzy Data warehouse in the field of education, Technology in education, Learning and Educational Innovation.

Index

U

V

W

Purchase Print, E-Book, or Print + E-Book

IGI Global's reference books are available in three unique pricing formats:
Print Only, E-Book Only, or Print + E-Book.

Shipping fees may apply.

www.igi-global.com

Recommended Reference Books

ISBN: 978-1-5225-5912-2
© 2019; 349 pp.
List Price: $215

ISBN: 978-1-5225-8176-5
© 2019; 2,218 pp.
List Price: $2,950

ISBN: 978-1-5225-7811-6
© 2019; 317 pp.
List Price: $225

ISBN: 978-1-5225-7268-8
© 2019; 316 pp.
List Price: $215

ISBN: 978-1-5225-7455-2
© 2019; 288 pp.
List Price: $205

ISBN: 978-1-5225-8973-0
© 2019; 200 pp.
List Price: $195

Do you want to stay current on the latest research trends, product announcements, news and special offers?
Join IGI Global's mailing list today and start enjoying exclusive perks sent only to IGI Global members.
Add your name to the list at **www.igi-global.com/newsletters.**

Publisher of Peer-Reviewed, Timely, and Innovative Academic Research

www.igi-global.com   ✉ Sign up at www.igi-global.com/newsletters   f facebook.com/igiglobal   t twitter.com/igiglobal   in linkedin.com/igiglobal

Ensure Quality Research is Introduced to the Academic Community

Become an IGI Global Reviewer for Authored Book Projects

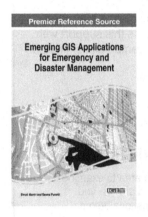

Premier Reference Source

Emerging GIS Applications for Emergency and Disaster Management

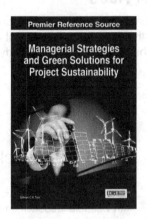

Premier Reference Source

Managerial Strategies and Green Solutions for Project Sustainability

Premier Reference Source

Comparative Approaches to Using R and Python for Statistical Data Analysis

Premier Reference Source

Solutions for High-Touch Communications in a High-Tech World

The overall success of an authored book project is dependent on quality and timely reviews.

In this competitive age of scholarly publishing, constructive and timely feedback significantly expedites the turnaround time of manuscripts from submission to acceptance, allowing the publication and discovery of forward-thinking research at a much more expeditious rate. Several IGI Global authored book projects are currently seeking highly-qualified experts in the field to fill vacancies on their respective editorial review boards:

Applications and Inquiries may be sent to:
development@igi-global.com

Applicants must have a doctorate (or an equivalent degree) as well as publishing and reviewing experience. Reviewers are asked to complete the open-ended evaluation questions with as much detail as possible in a timely, collegial, and constructive manner. All reviewers' tenures run for one-year terms on the editorial review boards and are expected to complete at least three reviews per term. Upon successful completion of this term, reviewers can be considered for an additional term.

If you have a colleague that may be interested in this opportunity, we encourage you to share this information with them.

IGI Global Proudly Partners With eContent Pro International

Receive a 25% Discount on all Editorial Services

Editorial Services

IGI Global expects all final manuscripts submitted for publication to be in their final form. This means they must be reviewed, revised, and professionally copy edited prior to their final submission. Not only does this support with accelerating the publication process, but it also ensures that the highest quality scholarly work can be disseminated.

English Language Copy Editing

Let eContent Pro International's expert copy editors perform edits on your manuscript to resolve spelling, punctuaion, grammar, syntax, flow, formatting issues and more.

Scientific and Scholarly Editing

Allow colleagues in your research area to examine the content of your manuscript and provide you with valuable feedback and suggestions before submission.

Figure, Table, Chart & Equation Conversions

Do you have poor quality figures? Do you need visual elements in your manuscript created or converted? A design expert can help!

Translation

Need your documjent translated into English? eContent Pro International's expert translators are fluent in English and more than 40 different languages.

Hear What Your Colleagues are Saying About Editorial Services Supported by IGI Global

"The service was very fast, very thorough, and very helpful in ensuring our chapter meets the criteria and requirements of the book's editors. I was quite impressed and happy with your service."

– Prof. Tom Brinthaupt,
Middle Tennessee State University, USA

"I found the work actually spectacular. The editing, formatting, and other checks were very thorough. The turnaround time was great as well. I will definitely use eContent Pro in the future."

– Nickanor Amwata, Lecturer,
University of Kurdistan Hawler, Iraq

"I was impressed that it was done timely, and wherever the content was not clear for the reader, the paper was improved with better readability for the audience."

– Prof. James Chilembwe,
Mzuzu University, Malawi

Email: customerservice@econtentpro.com   **www.igi-global.com/editorial-service-partners**

www.igi-global.com

Celebrating Over 30 Years of Scholarly
Knowledge Creation & Dissemination

InfoSci®-Books

A Database of Over 5,300+ Reference Books Containing Over
100,000+ Chapters Focusing on Emerging Research

GAIN ACCESS TO **THOUSANDS** OF
REFERENCE BOOKS AT **A FRACTION**
OF THEIR INDIVIDUAL LIST **PRICE**.

InfoSci®-Books Database

The **InfoSci®-Books** database is a collection of
over 5,300+ IGI Global single and multi-volume
reference books, handbooks of research, and
encyclopedias, encompassing groundbreaking
research from prominent experts worldwide that
span over 350+ topics in 11 core subject areas
including business, computer science, education,
science and engineering, social sciences and more.

Open Access Fee Waiver (Offset Model) Initiative

For any library that invests in IGI Global's InfoSci-Journals and/
or InfoSci-Books databases, IGI Global will match the library's
investment with a fund of equal value to go toward **subsidizing
the OA article processing charges (APCs) for their students,
faculty, and staff** at that institution when their work is submitted
and accepted under OA into an IGI Global journal.*

INFOSCI® PLATFORM FEATURES

- No DRM
- No Set-Up or Maintenance Fees
- A Guarantee of No More Than a
  5% Annual Increase
- Full-Text HTML and PDF
  Viewing Options
- Downloadable MARC Records
- Unlimited Simultaneous Access
- COUNTER 5 Compliant Reports
- Formatted Citations With Ability to
  Export to RefWorks and EasyBib
- No Embargo of Content (Research
  is Available Months in Advance of
  the Print Release)

*The fund will be offered on an annual basis and expire at the end of
the subscription period. The fund would renew as the subscription is
renewed for each year thereafter. The open access fees will be waived
after the student, faculty, or staff's paper has been vetted and accepted
into an IGI Global journal and the fund can only be used toward
publishing OA in an IGI Global journal. Libraries in developing countries
will have the match on their investment doubled.

To Learn More or To Purchase This Database:
www.igi-global.com/infosci-books

eresources@igi-global.com • Toll Free: 1-866-342-6657 ext. 100 • Phone: 717-533-8845 x100

www.igi-global.com

www.igi-global.com

Publisher of Peer-Reviewed, Timely, and
Innovative Academic Research Since 1988

IGI Global's Transformative Open Access (OA) Model:
How to Turn Your University Library's Database Acquisitions Into a Source of OA Funding

In response to the OA movement and well in advance of Plan S, IGI Global, early last year, unveiled their OA Fee Waiver (Read & Publish) Initiative.

Under this initiative, librarians who invest in IGI Global's InfoSci-Books (5,300+ reference books) and/or InfoSci-Journals (185+ scholarly journals) databases will be able to subsidize their patron's OA article processing charges (APC) when their work is submitted and accepted (after the peer review process) into an IGI Global journal. *See website for details.

How Does it Work?

1. When a library subscribes or perpetually purchases IGI Global's InfoSci-Databases and/or their discipline/subject-focused subsets, IGI Global will match the library's investment with a fund of equal value to go toward subsidizing the OA article processing charges (APCs) for their patrons.

   Researchers: **Be sure to recommend the InfoSci-Books and InfoSci-Journals to take advantage of this initiative.**

2. When a student, faculty, or staff member submits a paper and it is accepted (following the peer review) into one of IGI Global's 185+ scholarly journals, the author will have the option to have their paper published under a traditional publishing model or as OA.

3. When the author chooses to have their paper published under OA, IGI Global will notify them of the OA Fee Waiver (Read and Publish) Initiative. If the author decides they would like to take advantage of this initiative, IGI Global will deduct the US$ 2,000 APC from the created fund.

4. This fund will be offered on an annual basis and will renew as the subscription is renewed for each year thereafter. IGI Global will manage the fund and award the APC waivers unless the librarian has a preference as to how the funds should be managed.

Hear From the Experts on This Initiative:

"I'm very happy to have been able to make one of my recent research contributions, "Visualizing the Social Media Conversations of a National Information Technology Professional Association" featured in the *International Journal of Human Capital and Information Technology Professionals*, freely available along with having access to the valuable resources found within IGI Global's InfoSci-Journals database."

– **Prof. Stuart Palmer**,
Deakin University, Australia

For More Information, Visit: www.igi-global.com/publish/contributor-resources/open-access/read-publish-model
or contact IGI Global's Database Team at eresources@igi-global.com.

Are You Ready to Publish Your Research?

IGI Global offers book authorship and editorship opportunities across 11 subject areas, including business, computer science, education, science and engineering, social sciences, and more!

Benefits of Publishing with IGI Global:

- Free one-on-one editorial and promotional support.

- Expedited publishing timelines that can take your book from start to finish in less than one (1) year.

- Choose from a variety of formats including: Edited and Authored References, Handbooks of Research, Encyclopedias, and Research Insights.

- Utilize IGI Global's eEditorial Discovery® submission system in support of conducting the submission and blind review process.

- IGI Global maintains a strict adherence to ethical practices due in part to our full membership with the Committee on Publication Ethics (COPE).

- Indexing potential in prestigious indices such as Scopus®, Web of Science™, PsycINFO®, and ERIC – Education Resources Information Center.

- Ability to connect your ORCID iD to your IGI Global publications.

- Earn royalties on your publication as well as receive complimentary copies and exclusive discounts.

Get Started Today by Contacting the Acquisitions Department at:

acquisition@igi-global.com